# The Destruction of the Imperial Army

*Volume 2:*
*The Battles Around Metz*

Grenville Bird

Helion & Company

**To Chris, Peter, Jeff and Dennis**
**Thanks for all the encouragement and support**

Helion & Company Limited
Unit 8 Amherst Business Centre
Budbrooke Road
Warwick
CV34 5WE
England
Tel. 01926 499 619
Email: info@helion.co.uk
Website: www.helion.co.uk
Twitter: @helionbooks
Visit our blog at blog.helion.co.uk

Published by Helion & Company 2023
Designed and typeset by Mary Woolley (www.battlefield-design.co.uk)
Cover designed by Paul Hewitt, Battlefield Design (www.battlefield-design.co.uk)

Text © Grenville Bird 2023
Images © as individually credited

Cover: Heinrich XVIII, Prince Reuß, at the head of the 5th Squadron 1st Guard Dragoon
Regiment at Mars la Tour by Emil Hünten (Open Source)

ISBN 978-1-804511-85-5

British Library Cataloguing-in-Publication Data.
A catalogue record for this book is available from the British Library.

For details of other military history titles published by Helion & Company Limited contact the
above address or visit our website: http://www.helion.co.uk.

We always welcome receiving book proposals from prospective authors.

# Contents

# List of Illustrations

## Key to Sources

(A) Photographs taken by, or material from, the author's collection.

(D) Dayot, *Le Second Empire 1851–1870* (Paris: Ernest Flammarion, 1900)

(EK) Krügers, *Landschafts – album vom kriegsschauplatz*, (Hamburg: 1871)

(IGK) Anon, *Illustrirte Geschichte des Krieges* 1870/71 (Stuttgart: Union,1875)

(LH) Lüders & Helmuth, *Das Schlachtfeld von Gravelotte-Saint Privat* (Berlin: G. Pfeiffer, 1874)

(M) Maurice, *The Franco German War 1870–71* (London: 1900)

(O) Open Source; every reasonable effort has been made to identify copyright holders and the author and publisher apologise for any errors in misattribution or omissions in this work and would be grateful if notified of any necessary corrections that should be incorporated in future reprints or editions of this book.

(PH) Pflugk Hartung, *Krieg und Sieg* 1870–71 (Berlin: Schall & Grund 1895)

(R) Rousset, *Histoire Générale de la Guerre Franco-Allemande* (1870–1871) (Paris: 1910)

(RT) Rousset, *Les Combatants* (Paris: Libraire Illustrée, 1891)

# List of Maps

many of his men and all his artillery have pulled back to Marengo to replenish their ammunition and, understandably, are reluctant to enter the maelstrom again. (G)    N

15    The final assault. The Prussian Guard and Saxons close in on Saint Privat; to the north 4th Foot Guards and 45th Brigade; from the west 1st and 2nd Foot Guards, from the south, 4th Guards Brigade with the 4th Grenadiers making for Jérusalem so as to cut off any retreat by the French still defending Saint Privat. Those defenders who can escape the inferno head for Marengo. (G)    O

16    The situation in front of Amanvillers towards the close of the battle; the Hessians from 25th Division attacking to the north of the railway line. To the south the Gardeschützen, 1st and 3rd Guard Grenadiers are stalled in front of Amanvillers. Further south IX Corps artillery maintain the pressure against the defenders of Montigny la Grange. Despite repeated attempts Manstein is unable to make any progress into the Bois de la Charmoise, with both 3 and 4 corps putting up a determined defence. (R)    P

17    The situation in the Mance ravine around 7:45 p.m. After launching a counter attack the French troops return to their start positions without seeking to exploit their success. Fransecky's II Corps are committed to the fighting, serving little purpose other than add to the confusion and already high casualty list. What the plan fails to convey is the utter confusion which existed in the rear areas of I Army at this time as the advancing troops attempted to force their way through the exhausted and demoralised masses that had fallen back in disarray. (G)    Q

## Key to Map Sources

(B) Bonnal, General H, *L'Espirit de la Guerre Moderne, La Manoeuvre de Saint Privat Atlas* (Paris: Libraire Militaire R Chapelot et Cie. 1904)

(G) Großen Generalstabe *Studien zur Kriegesgeschichte und Taktik V Der 18 August 1870 Karten* (Berlin: Ernst Siegfried Mittler und Sohn, 1906)

(R) Captaine Roy *Études sur le 18 Aout 1870* (Paris: Libraire Militaire Bergier Levrault 1911)

(SH) Section Historique de l'État-Major de l'Armée, *La Guerre de 1870–71 Les Opérations Autour De Metz Atlas* (Paris: Librairie Militaire, R Chapelot et Cie, 1903–05)

# Introduction

This volume continues the story of the Destruction of the Imperial Army and resumes from where the first concluded; early afternoon on Sunday 14 August 1870. It recounts the events of three critical battles fought around Metz over the course of five days which did much to shape, if not seal, the fate of Napoleon's Imperial Army. Whilst the fighting is chiefly remembered for Moltke's victory at Gravelotte-Saint Privat, had the French taken advantage of the many opportunities presented to them by the mistakes and dissention within the Prussian command during these three battles, then the outcome of the campaign could have been very different.

This is something overlooked or disregarded in many of the pro-German works published in the years following the war. These studies, both official and semi-official, successfully masked or downplayed the shortcomings and discord within the victorious armies and in the main, presented a one-sided narrative emphasising a Prussian superiority in command, organisation and tactics somewhat divorced from reality. As with the previous volume, this book draws heavily on the works of Palat and the French Section Historique as well as memoirs left by participants on both sides which provide a useful counterbalance to the somewhat 'Prussian-centric' viewpoint reflected in the German official and semi-official accounts. Again, where the respective official histories give contradictory or conflicting accounts of the same incident, I have adopted that which seemed most rational in the circumstances. I appreciate this approach is no guarantor of accuracy and would apologise in advance for any errors as well as any mistakes made in my translation of these somewhat obscure works but hopefully, this volume will provide the reader with a better understanding and appreciation of the events around Metz in the summer of 1870.

# 1

# The Battle of Borny[1] 14 August 1870

## French Plans Disrupted

The morning of Sunday August 14th passed peacefully enough as the Imperial Army began its withdrawal to the far bank of the Moselle in accordance with Napoleon's plan to concentrate his forces around Châlons. Since daybreak, there had been a desultory exchange of small arms fire between outposts but for the most part, Bazaine's troops stood to arms idly waiting for the 5,000 baggage wagons to work their way through the congested streets of Metz – the early morning fog concealing their retreat from the ever-watchful Prussian patrols.

Frossard's 2 Corps held the south of the French line, covering the main road leading to Strasbourg around the village of Peltre. Vergé's and Bataille's divisions were on the heights between Peltre and Magny sur Seille with Laveaucoupet's division having been selected to furnish the garrisons for the outlying forts surrounding Metz following the French withdrawal. Lapasset's brigade[2] was at Château Mercy. 3 Corps, now led by General Decaen following Bazaine's appointment as commander in chief, covered the centre of the French line; Montaudon's division occupied Grigny, Metman the area around Colomby, Castagny at Montoy and Aymard around Nouilly. 4 Corps covered Decaen's open left wing; Greniers division occupied Mey, Cissey and de Lorencez's divisions secured the roads leading to Bouzanville and Kédange. 6 Corps were in Metz and Woippy on the left bank of the Moselle, with the Guard to the rear of Decaen between Fort Queuleu and Fort Les Bordes.

Bazaine's plan was for the corps on either wing to fold back onto the centre, covered by 3 Corps who would then withdraw into the city under the protection of the guns of Fort Bellecroix, before making their way to safety across the Moselle. Predictably, the enemy could not fail to notice the movement of so many men. At 12:15 p.m., Major General von Pritzelwitz[3] reported from Château Gras that the French camps at Borny had been broken but their infantry still occupied the villages of Vremy, Poix, Servigny, Noisseville and Montoy.

---

1    Also known as the battle of Colombey-Nouilly.
2    Originally part of 5 Corps but now under Frossard's command.
3    Commander, 2nd Infantry Division, I Corps, I Army.

A little later at 3:00 p.m. Captain von Jarotzki, a staff officer with 2nd Division, discovered that Vremy had been evacuated and the line north of the road from the village to the fort at St Julian was now devoid of their troops. At 3:30 p.m., a patrol from 3rd Cavalry confirmed that Chieulles and a French camp near Grimont Wood were deserted. It was a similar story on the left wing of the Prussian line; around 12:30 p.m. General Hartmann, on the heights north of Mécleuves, sent news that strong detachments were withdrawing from the camps between Mercy and Metz. On receiving this intelligence, General Manteuffel[4] rode forward to his outposts to conduct his own assessment. In his appreciation of the situation, the movement in the French lines could either presage an attack against I Army or, more likely, a move against II Army, as it was strung out on its flanking move to the south of Metz.

Either way, he was determined not to allow the initiative to pass to the enemy and despatched the following report to Steinmetz at Varize: 'A reconnaissance made by my orders proves that the enemy is leaving his camp at Metz; at the same moment the fire of artillery is heard and detachments of the VII are already engaged. I order I Corps to move to the front.'[5] As the retort of canon from the direction of Metz reverberated around Steinmetz's headquarters in Varize, he despatched two staff officers to investigate. When they returned with the news that his corps were engaged with the French, a furious Steinmetz exclaimed 'What, a battle? There will be no battle, I have forbidden it!'[6] before ordering Zastroff and Manteuffel to break off the action. It was already too late, 'the engagement was too general to be stopped by anything short of a victory or the coming of night.'[7]

The fighting that Sunday afternoon took place along a front of about seven miles, the battlefield stretching from the village of Mey in the north, to Ars Laquenexy in the south and across to Peltre in the west. The ground was generally undulating and hilly, cut by ravines and valleys, with the little villages dotting the landscape contained solidly constructed stone houses, surrounded by walled gardens and orchards. Numerous small woods, copses and vineyards covered the hillside which generally limited the movement of cavalry and artillery to the roads and as far as the guns were concerned, served to restrict their field of fire. As Major Hale's study notes:

> Of exceeding importance is the generally steep valley which at first tends northwards by Colombey and afterwards bends away as the bed of the Vallières brook, in a westerly direction towards the Moselle. The entire plateau is divided by it into smaller south-western and a larger north-eastern half, which may be designated briefly from their main features, as that of Borny and St Barbe. Of the brooks which flow from the east and north-east into the Colombey and Vallières valley, that coming from St Barbe and flowing between Servigny and Noisseville past Nouilly is of special importance. The

4     Commander, I Corps.
5     A von Schell, *The Operations of the First Army under General Steinmetz to the capitulation of Metz*, (London: Henry S King & Co. 1873) p.77. Manteuffel's orders were: 'To act attack the enemy with energy and drive him back, but to avoid being drawn under the guns of the fortress.'
6     Pierre Lehautcourt, *Histoire de la Guerre 1870–71 Tome IV La Retraite sur la Moselle. Borny* (Paris: Berger-Leverault & Cie. 1904) p.301. Still sulking following his reprimand after the battle of Spicheren, Steinmetz reacted by slavishly following his orders to the letter; if this resulted in Moltke's plans going astray, as far as he was concerned, so much the better.
7     Michael Howard, *The Franco Prussian War* (London: Rupert Hart Davis 1962) p.143.

vine clad slopes of this watercourse are contiguous to the northern bank of the Vallières brook as far as the Moselle. The deep bottom of the brook coming from St Barbe separates the plateau of that name into a west and east position.[8]

As Manteuffel prepared to launch his spoiling attack, Bazaine still had four corps on the east bank,[9] although Frossard's men had already begun their retreat into Metz, with Lapasset's brigade being the last to leave its position around 3:00 p.m.[10] As a consequence, the bulk of the fighting in the ensuing battle fell to Decaen and Ladmirault, with support from the Guard and the guns of the outlying fortresses.

## The Westphalian Attack

As mentioned in Manteuffel's despatch to Steinmetz, it was actually elements from VII Corps who initiated the attack on the French position around 3:30 p.m. From his position at Laquenexy General von der Goltz[11] had also observed movement in the enemy lines, but unlike Manteuffel who was still unsure as to French intentions, it was clear to him that Bazaine was retiring into Metz. Despite Moltke's directive to avoid getting drawn into a fight under the walls of Metz, he considered the strategic position would be best served by disrupting his retreat and decided upon an immediate attack. After informing I Corps of his intentions and calling upon support from 13th and 14th divisions and 1st Cavalry, he led his advance guard[12] forward towards Colombey, his action subsequently drawing elements of three German corps and two cavalry divisions[13] into a bloody and confused struggle under the walls of Metz.

Goltz's initial objective was Colomby and to this end, Colonel von Barby's force[14] advanced on Marsilly, his left screened by 7th Rifles moving up from Ars Laquenexy, his right by three squadrons of hussars who covered the ground between Marsilly and Ogy. The troopers soon made contact with French dragoons, so both batteries of artillery deployed to give covering fire but as the Rifles pushed onto Ars Laquenexy, the enemy horse withdrew leaving the guns without any target.

Led by Major Bergius, the musketeer battalions of the 15th, supported by the 6th Light, seized Château Aubigny and then pushed on to a small pine wood[15] north-west of Colombey, but their advance was brought to a halt by superior forces concealed in shelter trenches hidden in the copse. As the main force approached Coincy, they came under artillery fire so their batteries were brought forward to provide support; Schreiber's 5th taking up a new position south-west of the village, Gasch's 6th moving north of the Château d'Aubigny. After first engaging the

---

8    Major Lonsdale A Hale, *Tactical Studies of the Battles of Colonelumbey–Nouilly and Vionville* (London: W Clowes & Sons, 1877) p.9

9    Bourbaki's Imperial Guard, Frossard's 2 Corps, Decaen's 3 Corps and Ladmirault's 4 Corps.

10   The only formation from 2 Corps involved in the days fighting was de Laveaucoupet's divisional artillery.

11   Commander 26th Brigade, 13th Division, VII Corps.

12   The advance guard comprised 1st and II/15th, 6th Light battery, one squadron 8th Hussars under Colonel von Delitz. It was reinforced by the 5th Light battery.

13   I and VII corps, part of 18th Division from IX Corps and 1st and 3rd Cavalry Divisions.

14   Fusilier battalion 15th, the 55th and 5th Light battery.

15   This wood has no name but is shown as the 'Tannen Wäldchen' on some plans of the battlefield.

enemy infantry lining the edge of a wood 1,400 paces away, they shifted their attention to their artillery located some 1,800–2,000 paces to their front. This provoked a prompt response from the French who brought forward additional batteries that rapidly found their range, forcing Gasch to retreat and redeploy on the left of Schreiber's battery.

Goltz, left with no illusion that he was confronted by superior forces who showed no inclination of breaking off the fight, ordered forward the II/55th to counter the tirailleurs from the 1st and the 2/90th moving against la Planchette. Deploying into company columns at open intervals, the battalion assaulted the hamlet from the south and east, the rapidity of the fusilier's advance resulting in the French abandoning their positions in the vineyard to the west of the village.

The fusilier battalion of the 15th moved from the wooded valley south of la Planchette towards the château park at Colombey, whilst the regiment's musketeer battalions directed their attack against the village itself. In this sector, the fighting had been underway for almost an hour and although Colombey had fallen to the Westphalian attack, the French were strongly ensconced in the Tannen Wäldchen with their main line, which ran between the Colombey and Borny roads, being further strengthened as fresh troops were fed into the line.

## French Reaction

The attack caught Decaen's 3 Corps just as it was beginning its withdrawal into Metz. After hours of delays, towards 4:00 p.m. Montaudon's 1st Division, deployed to the north of the road running from Grigy to la Grange aux Bois, finally began to move; his artillery led the way, followed by 1st Brigade leaving Clinchant's 2nd Brigade to cover their retreat from Borny wood. From Castigny's 2nd Division, Duplessis had assembled his brigade[16] around the junction of the Saarbrücken and Saarelouis roads and was patiently awaiting the order to move off. In Nayral's 1st Brigade, the 19th Line were forming up prior to withdrawing into Metz; the 41st had just evacuated their positions in front of Colombey, leaving four companies in the château as rearguard, whilst 15th Chasseurs abandoned their defensive works along a tree lined lane known as Poplar avenue[17]

The long suffering men from Amyard's 4th Division, located between Bellecroix and Vantoux, having stood to arms at 4:30 a.m. were still waiting for their turn to file into Metz. Meanwhile, to the west of Colombey, where 3rd Division were located, Metman had just begun to pull in his outposts when a sharp outbreak of rifle fire accompanied by several cannon shots, heralded Manteuffel's attack. To the west of Colombey château, Lieutenant d'Origny's patrol[18] caught sight of strong columns of enemy troops advancing silently along the Strasbourg and Saarelouis roads and galloping back to raise the alarm, alerted the 41st of the impending danger with the cry: 'Aux armes! Les Prussiens!'[19]

16   69th and 90th Infantry.
17   This feature was later renamed 'Todten Allée', or 'Death Alley' by the Germans and comprised a flat sunken way lined on both sides with closely planted lines of poplar and fir trees
18   From 5th Squadron, 2nd Chasseurs à Cheval
19   Dick de Lonlay, *Francais & Allemandes Histoire Anecdotique de la Geurre de 1870–1871 Tome II*, (Paris: Garnier Frères, 1888) p.490.

The outlying screen of troops covering Metman's withdrawal[20] alerted General Poitier[21] of the imminent assault, reporting that large numbers of infantry accompanied by artillery, were marching towards the château at Aubigny.[22] Confronted by superior numbers, his rearguard fell back offering little resistance, abandoning their shelter trenches, with Jupin's company of 7th Chasseurs being left isolated in the château. Fearful of being surrounded, the chasseurs withdrew, coming under fire from the guns of the 5th Light battery deployed on the heights to the north of Marsilly. Following Jupin's example, the 59th, covering the right of the French line opposite Ars, similarly abandoned their shelter trenches and withdrew to Borny

Manteuffel's attack placed Decaen in a difficult position. It was clear from his position on the heights overlooking the city, that the withdrawal through Metz was not going to plan; wagons, caissons and limbered artillery were backed up for miles while men and horses stood idle, waiting for the roads to clear. If the enemy succeeded in penetrating the French rearguard, their retreat would be thrown into complete chaos. The general, accompanied by his aide sous Lieutenant Kergorre and an escort from 3rd Squadron 10th Chasseurs, immediately gave orders for 2nd and 3rd divisions to retrace their steps.

After sending one of his officiers d'ordonnance to appraise General Bourbaki of developments and request that he halt the withdrawal of the Guard into Metz, Metman ordered his division to reoccupy their defensive works. Unfortunately, Potier had already ordered his brigade to pull back so his men took up positions further to the rear; the 7th held a small wood just west of Colombey,[23] two battalions from the 29th were deployed to their left,[24] the line of battle being continued by three companies of the 7th Chasseurs.[25] The 41st occupied the southern sector of Poplar avenue, the 5th Chasseurs were to their rear, whilst the 19th continued the line as far as the Borny-Colombey road.

Quickly retracing his steps, Arnaudeau deployed his brigade; formed in two lines, the 59th were placed to the south of the road, with the 71st in a similar formation, to the north, along the crest of the plateau running from Colombey to Lauvallières. The divisional artillery were to the rear of the infantry, the 6th and 7th batteries in the centre of the line; the 5th (mitrailleuses), under Captain Mignot, were to the south from where he engaged 7th Rifles on the heights

20  4th Company 7th Chasseurs in the château d'Aubigny, the wood to the south-east was held by a company of the 59th, the heights near the château by a company from the 1/7th Infantry, the clearing by the road from Colombey to Ars Laquenexy by a company from the 7th Infantry and two outposts within the wood at Ars Laquenexy by another two companies from the 7th.

21  General of Brigade, 1st Brigade, 3rd Division.

22  The attack was not unexpected; in his post combat report Metman noted 'All the information sent in by the outposts indicated a concentration of the enemy forces during the night and the likelihood they would attack when we retreated' See Section Historique de l'État-Major de l'Armée, *La Guerre de 1870–71 Les Opérations Autour De Metz Du 13 au 18 Août I Journées des 13 et 14 Août Bataille de Borny* (Paris: Librairie Militaire, R Chapelot et Cie, 1903) pp.114–115.

23  Eight companies of the 2nd and 3rd battalions manned a line of trenches constructed along the edge of the wood, the 1st Battalion being held in reserve.

24  The 1/29th were held in reserve

25  2nd, 3rd and 4th companies, the 5th Company deployed alongside two companies from the 29th who occupied a line of shelter trenches covering the right rear of the small wood, the 1st Company was held in reserve and the 6th Company acted as escort to the divisional artillery.

opposite at a range of 1,600 metres.[26] George Boyland was with the Red Cross in Metz and witnessed the effects of the mitrailleuse at first hand:

> It was 2 o'clock in the afternoon when a few shots reached our ears. The pickets were engaging. These were followed by a sharp musketry fire and volley after volley now rolled out. The Prussians, coming briskly out of the wood which lies just beyond the village of Borny, commenced a lively attack upon our lines …The fighting done by the French could not have been better. This was their first battle and their spirit and vim were admirable. One regiment in particular, the 6th of the line, marched into fire singing 'Mourir pour la patrie'… I happened to be at the Porte Serpenoise when the firing began; and I at once mounted the bastion above the gate, from which a tolerable view of what was passing might be obtained. I could see the bombs rising in quick succession and bursting over our soldiers, who now poured a murderous fire into the enemy's ranks. The rattle of the musketry was interspersed with the booming of field guns and the whirr-r-r-r of mitrailleuse. The latter cannon is about the size of an ordinary six pounder and contains twenty-five small barrels … There is a crank behind to move the mitrailleuse from side to side as the discharge is made, in order to mow the men down, as the French thought 2,000 metres is a good range …The mitrailleuse made a terrible noise, but that was about all. In conversation afterwards with Prussian officers upon this subject, they have more than once informed me that the gun does not scatter and that men had been found among their dead with twenty-five balls in them.[27]

Decaen's instructions to his subordinate commanders were simply to reoccupy the positions they had abandoned earlier that day. He echoed the orders issued by Bazaine who, attracted by the sound of cannon fire, galloped onto the heights and alarmed that his plans for an orderly withdrawal were going astray, told every general he met: 'I gave orders that no-one should accept battle today. I absolutely forbid anyone to advance a foot.'[28] Consequently, for the remainder of the day, his subordinates conducted a strictly passive defence, denied the opportunity of utilising their numerical advantage to punish Manteuffel for his impetuosity.

## I Corps Fully Engaged

With Glümers 13th Division hurrying to the support of 26th Brigade at Colombey, I Corps began to deploy on their right. As the fighting intensified, Manteuffel ordered his subordinates to support his advance guard from their positions at Silly and Les Etangs. Bentheim's 1st Division's pushed forward from Silly along the Saarbrücken road towards Coincy – the guns of

---

26    Mignot reported that he found an excellent map of the area which enabled him to calculate the range with great precision; he claimed his fire was so effective that the first few salvos stopped the German advance in its tracks.

27    George Halstead Boyland, *Six Months Under the Red Cross with the French Army* (Cincinnati: Robert Clarke & Co. 1873) pp.36–38. His timing seems a little out; the attack began around 4.00 p.m.

28    Howard, *Franco Prussian War*, p.142.

his advance guard[29] being the first into action, opening fire about 4:45p.m. against the French infantry on the heights north of Colombey.

Further to the right at Les Etangs, Pritzelwitz's advance guard[30] moved towards Noisseville, General von Memerty leading the artillery and dragoons forward at the trot, the infantry following in their wake. His guns deployed either side of the road, with the cavalry in their rear as the infantry shook out into formation, the I/44th formed in company columns being the first to arrive. 4th Company was ordered to occupy the brewery at L'Amitié, as the remainder of the battalion, under Major Zeigler advanced towards Nouilly, just to the north of Noisseville.

After driving in the French outposts, 1st Company's progress was thwarted by troops embedded within the shelter trenches on the wooded heights to the east of Mey. As 2nd and 3rd companies struggled to make headway through the barricaded streets of Noisseville, reinforcements were provided to the hard-pressed 1st, by 6th and 7th companies from Noisseville; the other half battalion, the 5th and 8th companies, being held in reserve. Despite their support they struggled to sustain the combat against the superior French forces dug in along Mey heights, where in places the opposing sides were within 2–300 paces of one another.

Although the withdrawal of 4 Corps was well underway when the fighting erupted,[31] Ladmirault was quick to respond to the attack and immediately issued orders to Cissey to turn about and march to the assistance of Grenier whose men, acting as the corps rearguard, occupied the crest of the heights running from Mey to Villers l'Orme. Similar instructions were given to Lorencez whose division was still winding its way down into Metz.

The earlier withdrawal of these divisions had left Grenier's flanks dangerously exposed to being turned by the Prussian advance and awaiting the arrival of reinforcements, he countered this threat by deploying 5th Chasseurs, 13th and 43rd Infantry on the high ground running north-east from Mey north to the Bouzonville: 1st and 2/98th were in the second line north of the road, with the 3rd out front towards Varny as advance guard. The 64th with a battery[32] from the divisional artillery were around Villers l'Orme,[33] the 43rd being held in reserve near Fort Saint Julien, supported by the remaining divisional batteries.[34]

Meanwhile Bentheim recalled his outposts[35] prior to launching a divisional attack in support of Goltz's brigade to the south. Two companies from 1st Rifles assaulted the heights north of Montoy, as Colonel von Busse and the fusiliers of the 43rd advanced to the high ground to the east of the village. In response to the deployment of Duplessis' 2nd Brigade in front of Lauvallières, which to the Prussian generals seemed to presage a French counter attack, Busse's fusiliers moved to occupy the heights to the west of Montoy. The II/43rd marched into line on their right and were then reinforced by I Battalion.

29   Hoffbauer's 1st Light Field battery, escorted by a squadron from the 1st Dragoons.
30   2nd Division: 4th and 44th Regiments, 10th Dragoons, 5th and 6th Light batteries.
31   1st Division had already made its way to the I'lle Chambière.
32   6/1st Field Artillery Regiment.
33   1st Battalion at Failly, 2nd at Villers l'Orme 3rd in reserve.
34   5th and 7th batteries 1st Field Artillery Regiment.
35   III/43rd, 1st and 2nd companies 1st Rifles.

The French advance against Lauvallières and la Planchette forced the enemy skirmishers back onto their main line[36] as the 2nd and 3rd battalions of the 90th reoccupied a line of shelter trenches they had previously abandoned, from where their heavy fire deterred any further Prussian advance in this area. As this fire fight ensued, the remainder of Memerty's 3rd Brigade[37] moved into position at the rear of Noisseville; this freed up the 4th Company who now advanced to support the struggle around Mey. Towards 6:00 p.m. Aymard's 4th Division deployed to the north of the road running from Bellecroix to Lauvallières; in the front line 11th Chasseurs and the 44th took position along the crest of the heights,[38] with the 60th, 80th and 85th being held a few hundred yards in reserve.

The 1/41st continued the firing line north, towards the mill at Latour, with one company deployed as skirmishers. The 3/44th, with two companies from the 1st Battalion, moved closer to the mill and deploying at an angle to cover any attack from the direction of Nouilly, formed the extreme left of the French line. In turn, to counter this apparent threat against his right wing, Memerty, alongside 3rd Brigade's reserve to the rear of Noisseville,[39] told the fusiliers of the 4th to hold themselves ready to reinforce his flank, whilst the other battalions were ordered to Bellecroix, where Manteuffel's 1 Corps were coming under increasing pressure.

The subsequent assault by the 1st and 4th companies of the 4th, the III/43rd and the 1st and 2nd companies' 1st Rifles against the heights to the west of Lauvallières, was easily repulsed; the concentrated fire of the 11th Chasseurs, 1/44th, 69th and the 90th regiments stopped Memerty's advance in its tracks, his men falling back in disorder to the shelter of the valley in front of la Planchette.

An attempt by the 2nd and 3rd companies of the 4th, against the heights north of the village, similarly failed to make any progress. With their attack stalled, the East Prussian's firing line was extended to the right by the 5th and 8th companies who pushed forward in a north westerly direction to outflank la Planchette to assist the hard-pressed 4th Regiment, whilst to the left, three half battalions from the 43rd moved up to provide much needed support.

The attack by the 4th and 43rd fell on the 69th and the 2/90th; at such close range the Dreyse was at no disadvantage to the chassepot and they suffered heavy losses. This renewed assault pushed the 90th Ligne from the crest of the heights and they fell back, seeking shelter further to the rear. Poor fire control meant the French soon exhausted their 90 rounds and with many officers falling to the enemy fire, 1st and 3/69th fell back to replenish ammunition, seeking cover behind the 1/19th who were in reserve some distance to the rear.

The remaining commanders managed to restore some order, after which the battalions retreated to the north of Borny and the protection of Bourbaki's 3rd Guard Grenadiers. To fill the resultant gap in the line, 1/19th and 2/69th were sent forward and closing to within 250 yards of the advancing East Prussians, their concentrated fire succeeded in driving them down into the valley. Meanwhile Decaen had been struck on the left knee about 5:00 p.m.

---

36   The German line was formed as follows: -

| 1st and 2nd Co's | 9th and 12th | 10th and 11th | 6th and 8th | 5th and 8th |
|---|---|---|---|---|
| **1st Rifles** | 2nd and 3rd | **43rd Regt** | 1st and 4th | |

37   III/44th and 4th Regiment.
38   The 11th Chasseurs deployed four companies in a skirmish line a few hundred yards in front of the main position.
39   4th Regiment and 5th and 8th companies and III/44th Regiment.

and although he attempted to conceal the wound, his ADC Commandant Murier noticed the growing blood stain on his uniform and urged him to leave the field to have the injury tended. Decaen refused and it was only around 6:00 p.m. after his horse was shot from under him, the fall exacerbating the wound, that he finally allowed himself to be carried to the rear.

Command of 3 Corps passed to General Metman who was firmly reminded of Bazaine's instructions to 'hold all points and conduct an energetic defence before falling back slowly in the direction of Borny.'[40] Although exhibiting his customary bravery – he remained under fire for much of the day despite receiving a blow from a shell fragment which struck his left shoulder – Bazaine left the individual corps commanders to their own devices and failed to exercise any strategic control.[41]

## The Fighting Intensifies

With the Westphalian infantry struggling to make progress and unable to press home their attack, their Reserve artillery was rushed forward to lend support. Three batteries[42] from 1st Field Division were deployed to the south of the Saarbrücken road near Montoy a few hundred paces in front of Hoffbauer's battery. Under cover of their fire, a few companies from Goltz's brigade[43] crossed the stream at Colombey and advanced towards the French positions. Two heavy batteries from 13th Division [44] pushed ahead of their infantry; the 5th moving into the firing line to provide close range support where it came under fire from the French infantry who were less than 900 yards away.

Hostile artillery and mitrailleuses also found their range and after firing just 28 rounds, the battery was withdrawn to the shelter of Colombey farm, one gun lacking its limber being hauled to safety by a single horse. After repairing his guns, Schnackenberg resumed his place in the firing line alongside the 5th and 6th Light batteries of Goltz's advance guard, the latter having taken up position at the southwest corner of Montoy from where they supported the efforts of 1st Division's artillery who were shelling the far bank of Colombey brook. In the face of 3 Corps determined resistance, Goltz had barely secured a toe hold on the far bank of the Colombey brook at Lauvallèrie and la Planchette and even this scant success seemed under threat as French reinforcements continued to deploy on the heights opposite.

## The French Reinforce Their Positions

To counter the pressure against this sector, de Castagny's and Aymard's divisions were recalled and sent to reinforce Metman, the former pushing two companies[45] of the 2/41st into a small copse of fir trees[46] north-west of Colombey. The remainder of the 2nd and the 1/41st were

---

40    Lehautcourt, *Borny*, p.259.
41    Typical of the behaviour he exhibited throughout his tenure as commander, he spent most of his time busying himself with minor tactics and directing the movement of individual battalions and batteries.
42    1st and 2nd Heavy, 2nd Light.
43    From the 15th and 55th Regiments.
44    5th, Schnackenberg and 6th, von Gostkowski.
45    5th and 6th.
46    The 'Tannen Wäldchen'.

deployed in a thick skirmish line along the southern section of Poplar avenue but failed to reoccupy the château as it had already been seized by the enemy. The 3/41st were held in reserve on the road running from Colombey to Borny; the 15th Chasseurs to their left, two companies being sent forward as skirmishers along the ridge line east of the copse of fir trees. Further north, 2nd and 3/19th were deployed along the crest of the hill, the 1st held in reserve. The divisional artillery unlimbered to the left of the 19th, the battery of mitrailleuse a little to the rear by Bellecroix whilst two batteries from the reserve were to their right to counter any advance from Lauvallières, with Duplessis' 2nd Brigade held in reserve near Bellecroix.

Under heavy enemy fire, Castagny was calmly supervising the deployment of his division when Bazaine approached, inquiring: 'Everything alright Castagny?' 'It's all going well Monsieur Maréchal,' he replied 'I've been wounded in my side, but it's nothing.'[47] Castagny thought Bazaine seemed a little irritable as he pointed at his men, scolding him: 'It's crazy that they're firing like this. You couldn't care less, wasting all these cartridges!' before once again reminding him not to advance 'one step.'[48]

Aymard moved 4th Division into position between Bellecroix and Vantoux, 11th Chasseurs in front, the 44th deployed to their left and rear about 500 metres east of Vantoux near the mill. The 60th formed a second line along the Bellecroix heights with 2nd Brigade,[49] 2,000 metres to the rear, acting as divisional reserve. All three batteries of divisional artillery took position either side of the road near to the mill at Latour to cover the valley in front of Nouilly. Clérembault then brought his cavalry forward, his intention being to charge the enemy if they broke through the French lines; De Juniac's brigade[50] were held in reserve near Bellecroix, with de Maubranches' dragoons[51] a little in front and Bruchard's chasseurs[52] to the right between Borny and Colombey.

Further north, Greniers' division[53] moved into position along the crest of the hill that ran from the small wood[54] north of Mey to the tavern situated on the Bouzonville road, south of the village of Villers l'Orme. Through his field glasses, Grenier observed enemy detachments deploying on the heights to the east between the villages of Poixe and Failly. To counter this move, Ladmirault instructed him to establish a skirmish line with 'the right at Mey, the centre pushed up against the Bois de Grimont and the left east of the road to Kédange.'[55]

Grenier ordered 5th Chasseurs to occupy the eastern edge of the little wood by Mey and to push three companies 300 metres forward to cover the small ravine that ran south towards Nouilly[56] with the 4th being held in reserve to the rear of the wood. The remainder of 1st Brigade[57] continued the line to the north; 1/13th was immediately north of the wood, three companies in the first line, three in reserve, 2/13th was to their left, with one company forward

47    de Lonlay, *Tome II*, p.518.
48    Lehautcourt, *Borny* pp.253–254,
49    The 80th and 85th.
50    5th and 8th Dragoons.
51    2nd and 4th Dragoons.
52    2nd and 3rd Chasseurs and 1st Squadron 10th Chasseurs.
53    From 4 Corps.
54    Shown as the Wäldchen von Mey on German maps of the battlefield.
55    Lehautcourt, *Borny*, p.263.
56    The 1st, 5th and 6th.
57    13th and 43rd.

on the crest of the slope overlooking the valley that ran to Nouilly. The 3/13th were held in reserve at the rear of the wood, although two companies, the 2nd and 5th, were detached to cover the ground to the south of the wood. The 43rd extended the firing line to the north and sent out a thin screen of skirmishers behind a lane that ran from Mey towards Villers l'Orme. Their divisional artillery took position along the same track; 7/1st was in front and to the left of a small wood, 5/1st (mitrailleuses) in the centre of the line, with 6/1st on the extreme left wing of the line, about 10 metres from the inn on the Bouzonville road.

Initially held in reserve a little to the east of the château de Grimont, Grenier's 2nd Brigade[58] were ordered forward and took position about 600 metres to the rear of the firing line. The 64th, deployed in column of battalions at half distance, was north of Mey; the 2/98th to the left of the Bouzonville road near Villers l'Orme. The 1st Battalion stood guard over the division's bivouac, with one company being detached to act as escort for the 6/1st artillery

As Grenier completed his deployment, Pritzelwitz's division moved to the attack, their advance screened by the fire of the 5th and 6th Light batteries who, escorted by 10th Dragoons, unlimbered a little to the west of the Amitié tavern. I/44th were the first into action and after dropping a company off at the inn, moved through Noisseville into Nouilly, where they came under heavy fire from the infantry deployed across the valley. Struggling to make headway, they were subsequently reinforced by the 6th and 7th companies of the II/44th, the 5th and 8th being left to secure Noisseville. As these five companies became embroiled in a fire fight, the remainder of Memerty's 3rd Brigade[59] arrived on the heights at Noisseville providing them with much needed and timely support.

## 14th Division are Committed to the Battle

Around 4:00 p.m., VII Corps' commander, von Zastrow, had been informed that 13th Division's advance guard were shadowing the French as they fell back into Metz. Fifteen minutes later, news reached him that heavy fighting had broken out; he then received Glümer's request to commit 25th Brigade in support of the 26th. Understandably concerned about incurring Steinmetz's wrath by disobeying his explicit orders which forbad any action under the guns of Metz, he reluctantly gave orders to 14th Division and the corps artillery, to advance to the heights between Laquenexy and Colligny.

Again, in this encounter battle, the German tactic of placing the bulk of their artillery in the van of their marching columns paid dividends, affording their generals the time and space to bring forward and deploy their infantry under the protective fire provided by the guns. By 6:00 p.m., 60 guns[60] were in action and the support they provided allowed the van guard to sustain the fight against a more numerous opposition, although reinforcements from VII Corps soon began to make their presence felt.

Zastrow rode forward to where Goltz's men were engaged to assess the situation and on reaching the high ground overlooking Colombey, found 25th Brigade had already been

58    64th and 98th.
59    III/44th and the 4th Grenadiers.
60    On the left wing, south of Coincy three batteries from VII Corps, between the brook and Montoy, four batteries from I Corps and one from VII: on the right wing by the brewery two further batteries from I Corps.

committed at Coincy, I/13th leading their attack, supported by Major General von Osten Sacken and the remainder of his command.[61] It was obvious that this was no mere skirmish between outposts; matters had gone too far to be easily broken off and assuming command over the left flank, he approved Osten Sacken's introduction of his brigade into the line at Colombey; the 28th were ordered to support Goltz's left wing with the 27th moving up to Marsilly to act as general reserve.

I/13th advanced from Coincy into the valley and then across the brook to the north of Colombey. The losses incurred during this short advance, including its commanding officer and all four company commanders was evidence of the intensity of the fighting. Deployed in half battalions and with the I/73rd and 15th lending their weight to the assault, they slowly pressed the French line back to Poplar avenue. With Osten Sacken at their head, they charged forward seeking to seize control of the 'Tannen Wäldchen' from the 15th Chasseurs. I/13th then gained the open ground north of the wood and succeeded in pushing back the skirmish line of the 19th as more companies from 15th and 55th, emerging from Colombey, directed their attack against the 15th Chasseurs and 41st Ligne. The opposing sides closed to within 40 metres of one another and driven back in front and with their flanks threatened, the chasseurs withdrew from the wood onto their second line supports. Here they were rallied by their chef de battalion and with officers out in front, swords in hand, they launched a desperate counter attack which drove Osten Sacken's men out of the wood and back down the valley.

Mindful of Bazaine's explicit instructions 'not to advance one foot,' they refrained from pursuing the retreating enemy despite their local superiority in numbers and 25th Brigade were able to rally under the protection afforded by their artillery.[62]

## The Seizure of Todten Allee

Despite this setback, Osten Sacken launched a fresh assault with II/73rd and III/13th now leading the advance.[63] The II were directed against the sector of Poplar avenue to the north of 'Tannen Wäldchen', the fusiliers against the wood itself, with the II/13th in support. Having run low on ammunition, the troops to the north of the 'Tannen Wäldchen' – 2nd and 3/19th – were unable to counter this advance and withdrew to the shelter of Poplar avenue to replenish their supply.

Their retreat had a domino effect on the adjoining French battalions; it uncovered the flank of 1/19th to their north, so they fell back into line with the remainder of the regiment. In turn, this left the chasseurs defending the wood, feeling decidedly exposed and they withdrew to the rear of the 3/71st who alone stood firm against the Westphalian advance.[64] In an attempt to regain

---

61  Two battalions of the 13th and two battalions of the 73rd, III Battalion having been left at Pange.
62  In the sector between Lauvallière and Colombey the French could muster 33 battalions against 11 available to the Germans.
63  The attack was also supported by 1st and 2nd companies, 1st Rifles and parts of 2nd Brigade.
64  During this fight the 3rd Battalion suffered losses of 12 officers and 307 men, almost 50 percent of its effective strength. It held on until between 7:30 and 8:00 p.m. when it fell slowly back and its position in the firing line was taken by the 2/29th.

the lost positions, Colonel Launay led the 19th Ligne forward again but hit by the fire of five enemy battalions,[65] they were forced back a second time.

Their withdrawal left the 41st, on the edge of Colombey, in danger of being outflanked and abandoning their position, they fell back 4–500 metres to the west where a new defensive line was established. Following close on their heels the Westphalians were at last able to secure Poplar avenue but after this limited success, there was stalemate in this area; every subsequent attack they attempted was driven off, whilst the French, content that any danger they posed had been contained, prepared to resume their retreat into Metz.

## The Struggle Around Mey

As Osten Sacken's men consolidated their position along Poplar avenue, further north, 2nd Division's attack had stirred up a hornet's nest. Although the 44th initially made some progress against Grenier's men in Mey, he received timely reinforcements from Cissey's 1st Division, the general recalling how after being ordered to advance, his men dropped their packs and set off to their old positions at the double with cries of 'Vive l'Empereur!' Lieutenant Patry, whose regiment formed part of Cissey's division, observed the battle from near Fort Saint Julien:

> I saw the column about face and within a few strides I'd re-joined my company. We were all very excited, officers and soldiers alike; we sensed battle close at hand and we accepted it with pleasure …The regiment having faced about, that is to say facing the enemy, we marched towards the sound of the guns. Everything was fine now! Who said our generals understood nothing! And we marched briskly. We left the roads and entered the fields. There the regiment was formed in company columns at full distance. We were halted in this formation for some time. But the cannonade was growing; it was now in front of us. We see our artillery going at a gallop up the road which passed in front of the fort. In the midst of a cloud of dust it passed like a whirlwind; the horses going flat out, the drivers giving the teams the spur and whipping them on with all their strength. The sun darting obliquely on the bronze cannon makes them sparkle like gold, the wheels turning so fast they look like solid discs. Seated on the caissons the gunners are shaken like leaves in the wind, hanging on for grim death. All this appeared like some magical spectacle. It was truly superb and filled us with joy. At that moment war seemed a wonderful thing and I felt my heart swell with an indescribable fervour. 'Come on, brave lads, we're here to support you and we'll show you how we go about clearing the ground in front of you.'[66]

1st Division's artillery had reached the l'île Chambière when the firing broke out, but the gunners immediately wheeled their teams about and followed their infantry back to the heights overlooking Metz. When they reached the battlefield, the enemy offensive was already underway

65   I, II and III/13th and I and II/73rd.
66   Patry, *La Guerre*, pp.71–72.

and so the guns[67] unlimbered to the right of Grenier's 6th battery, facing Servigny, Poixe and Noisseville.[68]

On their arrival on the plateau, Brayers 1st Brigade was initially held on the heights near Château Grimont but he was then ordered forward to occupy the village of Mey with the 1st Ligne and 20th Chasseurs. Given the strength of the French line, another Westphalian attack by five companies of the 44th was easily driven off and Osten Sacken's men retreated to Nouilly. However, as the French official history relates: 'The enemy then attempted a vigorous attack. They advanced at the pas de charge, cheering and made two attempts to seize the wood. The fire of our tirailleurs stopped them dead and decimated their ranks.'[69]

Although the 44th inflicted heavy losses on the 5th Chasseurs in this latest fire fight, a counter attack by the 1/13th on the left of the wood caught them in a deadly cross fire and with mounting casualties,[70] they fell back once more to the shelter of the valley. Following this setback, III/4th withdrew to Servigny to secure Memerty's open right flank whilst the fusiliers from the 44th were ordered to support the 5th and 8th companies at Noisseville. Despite this reorganisation, Manteuffel's right wing was still dangerously exposed; Gayl's 1st Brigade[71] had yet to reach Montoy and Zglinitzki's 4th Brigade[72] was some way to the rear. Dohna's 3rd Cavalry Division,[73] marching to the sound of the guns had, at the request of General von Pritzelwitz,[74] taken up position to the rear of Retonfay with a squadron from the 7th Lancers being despatched to cover the right flank.

As these troops hurried forward, Cissey provided further support for the French line deploying Goldberg's brigade[75] in reserve a little to the north of the road to Bouzonville near Mey. Brayer's brigade was held further to the rear at Grimont, as described by Patry:

> We marched. In passing into the park of a château, no doubt Grimont, we witnessed preparations which had nothing very cheering about them; medical orderlies assisted by musicians were spreading straw on the lawn and making beds from it for the wounded. But here came the shells again. They passed over our heads with an infernal noise and went on to burst behind us. Then a few rounds, at the limit of their range fell around us, at our feet, embedding themselves in the ground with a muffled sigh, as if regretting not having met some bones to break along the way. Now we passed many stretchers bearing wounded to the field hospitals; then the cacolets, to which the pace of the mules imparted a rocking motion which drew cries of pain from the poor devils they carried. The firing increased in volume. The battalion was deployed in line and we

67    5th, 9th and 12th batteries, 15th Field Artillery Regiment.
68    The French batteries were deployed to the right of the road as follows: -

‖ □ Tavern

| ↔ | ↔ | ↔ | ↔ | ↔ |
|------|------|------|------|-------|
| 6/1 | 5/15 | 9/15 | m5/1 | m12/15 |

69    L'État-Major *Borny*, p.151.
70    The companies involved in this attack lost 10 officers and 242 men in an hour and a half.
71    1st Grenadiers and 41st.
72    5th Grenadiers and 45th Regiment.
73    8th Cuirassiers, 5th, 7th and 14th Lancers with 1st HA, 7th Field Artillery Regiment
74    Commander of 2nd Infantry Division.
75    From Cissey's 1st Division.

crossed a large open space in perfect order. Because of its number (the third out of six) my company was in the middle of the battalion. Our commanding officer on his big light bay horse rode in front of the centre of the battalion, turning round every moment to keep it in good order...The ground fell away in a gentle slope. We reached an orchard planted with fruit trees; the battalion was formed en colonne double serrée en masse; and in this order the 3rd (mine) and 4th companies were at the head. We halted and the commandant gave us the order to have the men kneel down. We remained in this position for a long while. The bullets were flying thick and fast, almost shaving our heads. It sounded like the buzzing of bees. In passing through the trees the bullets cut up the leaves and broke the small branches, the debris of which rained down on us. The canon thundered steadily all around. It was all go.[76]

The French positions were further reinforced by 2nd Division as General Pradier led the 1/98th into line to the left of the 64th, 300 metres north of Mey. As they moved into position towards 6:00 p.m., Lorencez assembled his 4th Division around Fort Saint Julien to guard against any attempt to outflank the French positions through Servigny. 2nd Brigade formed up a little to the east of the fort, 1st Brigade deployed in two lines to the south with the divisional artillery to the rear, where they were reinforced by four batteries of artillerie montée from the corps' Reserve. From his position on the heights at Noisseville, Manteuffel noted the French extension of their left wing, which looked to him as though they were making preparations to outflank his position. Unaware that Bazaine had forbidden any attack, he issued instructions to counter this perceived threat:

> Major General Memerty will hold, under all circumstances the positions of Noisseville and the Nouilly Valley. To co-operate in this, the corps artillery will be brought up closer to Noisseville. The 1st Infantry Brigade, now advancing along the Saarbrücken road will on arrival, be posted near the brewery as general reserve. The 4th Infantry Brigade will pass around the north of Noisseville and after leaving two battalions there as reserve, will meet the outflanking movements of the enemy by a counterstroke on his left flank. [77]

General Bergman[78] instructed 1st Field Division[79] to remain on the left flank; the corps artillery[80] were to occupy the line between Noisseville and Lauvallier, whilst 3rd Field Division[81] deployed opposite the left flank of the French line between Poix and Servigny. The 5th Light was the first in action to the north-east of Noisseville with 1st Horse Artillery, 5th and 6th Heavy batteries lending their support. To counter the French artillery deployed on the left of their line

---

76   Patry, *La Guerre*, p.74.
77   FCH Clarke, *The Franco-German War 1870–71 Vol. 1* (London, Topographical and Statistical Department of the War Office, 1874, p.320.
78   Corps artillery commander.
79   1st and 2nd Light, 1st and 2nd Heavy deployed to the south of Lauvallier.
80   The 2nd Horse artillery, 3rd Horse artillery, 6th Light, 3rd Heavy, 4th Heavy, 4th Light and 3rd Light between Noisseville and Lauvallier.
81   5th and 6th Heavy, 5th and 6th Light.

on the high ground around Villers l'Orme, the batteries positioned around Noisseville were moved into more advantageous positions around Servigny. They were given additional backing from I Corps' artillery reserve; including the horse artillery from 3rd Cavalry, 15 batteries were committed to the gun line, although the undulating terrain prevented them all from deploying and a number had to relocate to find new firing positions from where they could better engage the French lines.

## The Fighting Around Colombey

As Manteuffel supervised the deployment of his corps, to his left, 14th Division from VII Corps made its way into the line from Domangeville, with 27th Brigade taking up position between Marsilly and Colombey to serve as general reserve. When the 28th appeared on the battlefield to the south-west of Colombey around 7:00 p.m., Woyna only had four battalions at hand[82] so was offered additional support in the shape of 1st Light battery and four squadrons of the 15th Hussars, the cavalry being sent towards Grigy to cover his left flank.

Colonel von Gerstein deployed the II/53rd into company columns on the left of 7th Rifles whose progress was blocked by seven companies of the 7th Ligne who occupied a line of shelter trenches dug along the edge of the Colombey wood north of Grange aux Bois. To the right, three companies of the 15th were pinned down in the château at Colombey by the heavy fire from the 29th Ligne and three companies of 7th Chasseurs who held the ground between the wood and the crossroads. The Westphalians were unable to make any progress in this sector until the sudden retreat of the 41st exposed the left flank of the Potier's line running south from Colombey through the wood.

Taking advantage of this opportunity, the 53rd began their attack; II Battalion led the way, the I formed into half battalions in their rear with 1st and 4th companies extending the line to the left of the II. The 2nd and 3rd companies moved further to the south-west through Grange aux Bois in an attempt to outflank the French line at Grigy, as Conrad's 77th extended the firing line further to the left. With five companies advancing along the poplar lined avenue leading towards Grigy, another two were directed against Borny wood where they engaged the defenders in a stand up fire fight. As the 77th assailed the copse from the south, the II/53rd and 7th Rifles launched a simultaneous assault against the north-east corner with fire support provided by 1st Light battery deployed by Ars Laquenexy wood.

With this struggle underway, Wrangel's 18th Division,[83] marching to the sound of the guns from their bivouac at Buchy, arrived at the front, whereupon their advance guard[84] pushed up to the high ground at Mercy le Haut, from where their artillery opened fire on the infantry occupying Grigy. Wrangel was supported by elements of 1st Cavalry which had been tasked with screening the right wing of II Army as it bypassed Metz to the south. Although Lüderitz's

---

82    III/53rd occupied the station at Courcellres sur Nied and the fusilier battalion and 8th Company of the 77th Regiment were acting as escort to the corps and divisional artillery.

83    Part of Manstein's IX Corps from II Army.

84    Two squadrons of the 6th Dragoons supported by the 2nd and 3rd battalions 36th and 2nd Light artillery battery. They were commanded by Colonel Brandenstein.

cuirassier brigade was of limited use, their attached artillery[85] took position on the ridge north of Peltre.

As these guns opened fire on Grigy, Major General von Blumenthal, who had assumed command of the advance guard, occupied Peltre with the 6th and 7th companies of the 36th, moving the remainder of the regiment into Mercy le Haut where they supported the advance of Woyna's men from Grange aux Bois.

Confronted by this concentric attack, with his left exposed and his right in danger of being outflanked, Potier gave orders to withdraw from the Bois de Colombey, his men falling back in good order to form a new defensive line a few hundred metres to the rear, anchored on a line of shelter trenches defended by the 2/81st. His retreat was covered by the mitrailleuse of the 5th whose fire kept the enemy bottled up in Colombey wood and as the brigade consolidated their new position to the east of Sebastopol farm, they unmasked the divisional batteries[86] who then opened fire.

A little later, Metman called on two batteries[87] from the 1st Division near Grigy, for additional support and towards 7:00 p.m., Potier was ordered to move his brigade a little to their left to assist the 41st and 59th. His new position ran along the crest of the hill south of the Borny-Colombey road, through Borny wood into Grigy. To the north, the 59th and 41st continued the defensive line towards Bellecroix and their defence was further strengthened when the 71st eventually gave up their struggle to hold onto Poplar avenue and withdrew to Borny.

Bruchard's Light Cavalry Brigade[88] was placed some way behind the firing line but with no obvious target and lacking any opportunity to charge, wheeled about and made their way back into Metz after, on Bazaine's orders, detaching 2nd Chasseurs as escort to the 5th mitrailleuses. Metman, who had both his brigades close to hand, considered that the enemy no longer presented any threat and resumed his retreat into Metz.

## Stalemate in the South

Brandenstein's men pressed close on the heels of the retreating French; Grange aux Bois was immediately seized by the II/77th and to the north, Colombey wood was occupied by the 53rd and 7th Rifles. Further west, the 84th moved up in support, occupying Peltre which in turn, freed up the 6th and 7th companies of the 36th who advanced along the main road into Grigy. In the face of this vigorous pursuit, Montaudon was inclined to launch a counter attack, but around 5:00 p.m. Bazaine galloped up and ordered him to resume his withdrawal into Metz.

At this time, the 51st was covering the division's retreat from Grigy; 1st Battalion occupied the shelter trenches south-east of the village, the 2nd and 3rd were a little to the west by the road running from Metz to Strasbourg supported by the guns of the 5/4th. The remainder of 1st Brigade were held back to the north of Grigy; the 18th Chasseurs in the quarries, the 62nd by the side of the main road; Clichant's 2nd Brigade being positioned around Borny wood. As Montaudon resumed his retreat, the 95th left a battalion in the wood to cover their withdrawal,

---

85    1st Horse artillery battery, 1st Artillery Regiment.
86    The 6th and 5/11th.
87    6th and 8/4th.
88    2nd Chasseurs, 3rd Chasseurs and 1st Squadron 10th Chasseurs.

with three companies being deployed as skirmishers to forestall any advance from Mercy le Haut.

When the fighting between Borny and Vantoux flared up again, Clichant thought it prudent to send forward the 2nd and 3/95th to reinforce the 1/95th; at the same time, 2/81st extended three companies along the ridge line overlooking the northern edge of Grigy, as 1st and 3/81st deployed to the north of Borny wood. A little after 6:00 p.m., the 1/62nd was sent to support the 95th, the 3rd Battalion being sent to the small wood between Borny and Colombey to cover the flank of the 7th. The 2/65th remained to the south-east of Borny until, in response to the appearance of enemy troops to the south around Peltre, it was moved closer to Grigy.[89]

The division's remaining artillery[90] unlimbered some way to the rear on the heights by Fort Queuleu and as Montaudon's men took up position, they were supported by Deligny's Voltigeurs from the Imperial Guard with Bricourt's brigade[91] together with the divisional artillery[92] assembling to the west of the Strasbourg road between the fort and village of Queuleu. Around 6:00 p.m., the Guard mitrailleuses, together with a section of guns from the 2nd battery, unlimbered on the sloping glacis in front of the fortress to counter the threat posed by enemy troops on the heights to the north of Mercy le Haut.

Meanwhile, 1st Voltigeurs deployed in echelon by battalions between the guns and the road running to Strasbourg. Leaving two companies to cover the approaches from Grigy, the Guard Chasseurs, 2nd Voltigeurs and remaining batteries withdrew to the outskirts of Queuleu village. Further north, Picard's Grenadier Division moved to Borny, with two battalions from the 3rd Grenadiers occupying the gardens surrounding the village, whilst 1st Brigade took post further to the north, facing Bellecroix with the divisional artillery deployed on the glacis in front of Fort Bordes. The Guard Reserve artillery and cavalry division stood ready to intervene, bridles in hands, in their camp to the west of the fortress.

Alfred Chapelle had accepted an invitation to lunch with officers of the Imperial Guard that afternoon and recorded his impressions of the battle:

> The cannons and mitrailleuses began their deadly work on each side. I was standing close to a fourgon of ammunition; all soon became confusion; men falling around me, bullets whizzing past my ears and plunging into the midst of the battalions. It is awful to be cool and inactive in in the middle of such a bloody holocaust; the cries of the wounded, the rage of their friends, their thirst for revenge, all seemed fantastic and demoniacal as in a bad dream; but no, it was not a nightmare; some of my friends, amongst them the Baron de Vatry, commanding one of the battalions of the Garde, passed me and reminded me of the danger I was incurring without reason; but their words sounded as a murmur only in the roars of a contest. They soon disappeared in the smoke; and I continued to look at the scenes of carnage before me with a strong feeling of uncertainty of returning to tell my sad tale. A battery of artillery with a mitrailleuse made a fearful havoc in the Prussian ranks. I heard frantic bravos announcing its new

---

89    The 2nd maintained this position until 11.00 p.m. until it was joined by the other two battalions and the regiment.

90    6th and 8/4th.

91    Guard Chasseur battalion, 1st Guard Voltigeurs, 2nd Guard Voltigeurs.

92    1st, 2nd and 5th (m) Field Artillery Regiment of the Guard.

exploits; the aiming was so well directed, the precision so great that each fire was positively mowing down the Prussian ranks. Their columns fought desperately, their artillery replying with great effect and destroying French battalions left and right ... The Imperial Garde, commanded by Bourbaki had been kept in reserve; their artillery from a strong position began the defensive, the Grenadiers advanced and from that moment until a quarter to nine you might have thought you were in the middle of the eruption of Mount Vesuvius; Fort de Queuleu sweeping with its powerful batteries the flank of the advancing columns, regiments charging on the wings; at a quarter to nine precisely the Prussians were retreating.[93]

On the receiving end of this fire, 2nd Heavy battery unlimbered alongside the guns of Preinitzer's horse artillery in front of Peltre sometime after 8:00 p.m. and although their fire added to Montaudon's discomfort, it did little to threaten his position. He had deployed the 51st in battle formation to the south-east of Grigy, four battalions[94] were in support to the rear of the village and four more in Borny wood.[95] Confronted by this show of force, the Prussians made no attempt to attack Grigy, being content to engage in a long-range bombardment of the French positions.

In response, the 12-pdr guns of Fort Queuleu opened fire against their positions at a range of 2,320 metres. A little later, a battery of mitrailleuses, two more from the divisional artillery[96] and two Guard artillery batteries[97] added their support. Preinitzer maintained a desultory fire as long as the flashes of the enemy's guns provided a target, until darkness descended across the field of battle and his guns fell silent. The troops of 18th Division then withdrew to their bivouacs behind a screen of vedettes sent out by 4th Lancers. On the French side of the lines, the 51st remained in position in Grigy until 11:30 p.m.; the 95th withdrew from Borny wood about 10:30 p.m. the same time as the 1/62nd made their way back to Metz.

## Renewed Fighting in the Centre and North

In the centre, the struggle continued to rage around Lauvallières where Falkenstein's 2nd Brigade[98] supported by Osten Sacken, were reluctant to break off the engagement. On Falkenstein's right flank, six companies of the 44th from Memerty's 3rd Brigade were embroiled in struggle around Nouilly and Mey, two battalions of the 4th Grenadiers were fighting for possession of the Bellcroix heights whilst the fusilier battalion was sent north to Servigny to counter what Manteuffel believed to be the French outflanking manoeuvre from Villers l'Orme.

Unsurprisingly, given these competing priorities, the East Prussians offensive stalled, so Memerty ordered Major Dallmer to deploy 3/44th around Nouilly and the heights to the north.

---

93    Count Alfred de la Chapelle, *The War of 1870. Events and Incidents of the Battlefields* (London: Chapman & Hall 1870) pp.46–48.
94    18th Chasseurs, 2/62nd and 1st and 3/81st.
95    1/62nd and 1st, 2nd and 3/95th.
96    These guns were from de Laveaucoupet's 3rd Division, 2 Corps. The three batteries, the 7th, 8th and 11/15th, fired just 60 rounds.
97    5th and 2nd batteries which between them fired 25 rounds.
98    43rd Regiment and two companies' 1st Rifles.

The 5th and 8th companies of the 44th were directed to recapture the heights south-west of the village whilst the remaining six companies[99] were to reinforce the men being driven back from Nouilly.

Reinvigorated by the introduction of these reinforcements, the Prussians again went over to the attack, crashing up against Amyard's division to the south-east of Vantoux where he had placed de Brauer's brigade out in front, with the 1/44th Ligne positioned alongside the divisional artillery, the 3rd Battalion and two companies of the 2nd around Latour mill. The 2nd and 3/60th were in support guarding against any attack out of the valley that ran east to west from Nouilly to Vantoux along the northern flank of the French line with 11th Chasseurs to the right, by the Metz-Saarelouis highway.

Sanglé-Ferrière's brigade were held in reserve, to the rear of the crest along which the divisional artillery deployed. The left of the second line was anchored by the 85th, the 1st Battalion facing north-east, the 2nd and 3rd covering the valley which ran to the south of Vantoux. The 80th continued the line to the south of the main road; the 1st Battalion being tasked with defending Bellecroix, the 2nd and 3rd were a little in front of the lane running north from the farmstead to Vantoux. The 2/69th, from Castagny's 2nd Division, formed a third line a few yards to the rear of the 1/80th.

Mindful of the need to avoid getting drawn into a protracted struggle for no good reason, the 60th fell back to Bellecroix and seeing this retrograde movement, Castagny also withdrew the 69th, calling upon Colonel Cornat's 4th Dragoons to charge the enemy line to cover their retreat. The dragoons advanced, one squadron along the Saarelouis road, a second down the route to Sarrebrücken. However, Cornat quickly grasped that the difficult terrain and strong opposition offered little prospect for success, so sensibly wheeled his troopers about and withdrew to the rear of Bellecroix.

Covered by the cavalry, Amyard's division took up a new defensive position; the north of his line being anchored on the heights overlooking Vantoux, the south just in front of Bellecroix. The 69th fell back along the main road leading to Metz, the 1st Battalion deploying just to the rear of Bellecroix,[100] the 2nd and 3rd withdrawing several hundred metres to the shelter of the glacis of Fort Bordes.

After securing Nouilly, Dallmer led the 44th up the vine clad slopes towards Mey, the fusilier's eight divisions[101] being deployed in a thick skirmish line supported by another four in close order formation in rear; two companies from II Battalion were in support on their left flank. As the battalions formed up, the French defences were reinforced by the arrival of the remainder of Lorencez's division; Ladmirault had seen the Prussian move towards Servigny and Poixe and directed Pajol's 1st Brigade to extend the French line to the north-west, the 15th occupying the farm at Grimont, as the 33rd took position a few yards south of the road running to Bouzanville.

---

99   5th, 8th, 9th, 10th, 11th and 12th.

100  One company occupied the farm itself; the battalion only relinquished this position at 10:30 p.m. During the day, even though they saw only limited fighting, the 69th lost two officers killed, 11 wounded, 21 men killed, 152 wounded and 15 missing. Of 85 recorded wounds, 74 were caused by rifle shots and only 11 from the German artillery.

101  There were two Divisions or Züge in each company.

Pending the arrival of these reinforcements, Grenier utilised the resources he had to hand to counter any attack from Servigny. The 3/64th was ordered to occupy Mey, where they rapidly barricaded the streets leading towards the enemy with 1/64th being placed in reserve behind the small wood to the north of the village, the 13th deploying additional companies to strengthen their already dense skirmish line.

As the firefight continued, Pradier led the 1/98th down the Bouzonville road before striking out across the fields to take up a defensive position along the lane running between Mey and Villers l'Orme. The 2/64th moved into the small wood to relieve the 5th Chasseurs who had fallen back to replenish their ammunition and pushing through the trees, deployed three companies as skirmishers amongst the vineyards covering the slopes running down to Nouilly, just as Major Dallmer's men were beginning their advance on Mey. The tirailleurs greeted his men with a 'violente fusillade' which stopped the 44th's attack in its tracks sending the men recoiling down the hillside to the shelter of Nouilly.

Across the valley at Lauvallières, 1st Infantry Brigade's commander[102] was directing the attack against Bellecroix and ordered 3rd Grenadiers to Nouilly intending to establish a link between 1st Division at Mey and Pritzelwitz's 2nd Infantry Division around Nouilly and Lauvallières. At the head of the Grenadiers, Colonel von Legat directed I Battalion to advance from Flanville, through Montoy towards Nouilly and having deployed two flank companies as skirmishers, formed two lines before advancing towards the fighting. From the heights east of Montoy, they could see heavy fighting to their front; the French had just recaptured the vineyards around Nouilly and seemed intent on outflanking their left wing.

To counter this threat, Legat ordered I Battalion towards Lauvallières deploying the II on its right flank, with the fusiliers in reserve. In the confusion, only the 3rd and 4th companies received the order to move on Lauvallières, the 1st and 2nd continued towards Nouilly. The II Battalion moved towards the south-western corner of the village, with the fusiliers covering their left wing as they advanced on the mill at Goupillon. As this attack gained momentum, away to the south the fusiliers of the 43rd, two companies of the 1st Rifles and 1st and 4th companies' 4th Grenadiers were reorganising themselves following their failed attack on the Bellecroix heights.

Reinforcements in the shape of six companies of the 43rd arrived[103] and with these fresh troops leading the way, they once again resumed the offensive, gradually driving the French back and creating space on the western side of Vallières brook where 1st Field Division could deploy their guns. 3rd Company 3rd Grenadiers assisted in this attack and between seven and eight o'clock in the evening they at last succeeded in occupying the ground where Poplar avenue met the Saarebrücken road, so bringing Falkenstein's Brigade into line with 13th Infantry Division to their south. To the north, 3rd Brigade failed to make any headway against Vantoux, so Colonel Tietzen brought up the II/4th Grenadiers to relieve the hard-pressed defenders clinging onto Latour mill[104] before attempting to push onto Vantoux.

Despite valiant efforts, the grenadiers failed to make any inroads against the heavily defended village and to compound their difficulties, Tietzen's right wing became dangerously exposed when the 44th on their flank fell back from the Nouilly heights to avoid being encircled by the

---

102  Lieutenant General von Bentheim.
103  2nd, 3rd,5th,6th,7th and 8th.
104  I/4th and I and II/43rd.

French. Rather than retreat, he renewed his attack, the colonel leading the advance of an ad hoc force comprising elements of four regiments.[105] The difficult undulating terrain hampered his progress and the 44th suffered heavy losses without making any noticeable headway against the strongly defended position until Colonel von Legat arrived from Flanville at the head of his two battalions of 3rd Grenadiers.

These fresh troops gave new impetus to the attack and Legat's battalions charged forward onto the Mey heights, supported by 6th and 7th companies, 4th Grenadiers and detachments of the 44th. In the face of this determined assault, the commander of the 2/64th Ligne fed another company into his skirmish line as 1/64th and 1/13th moved around the north-east, east of the Bois de Mey to confront this new threat, which by now had closed to within 150 metres. After a short lived and destructive stand up fire fight, the French withdrew into the cover of the trees.

Meanwhile, the Prussians brought forward additional supports who attempted to encircle the wood and during the ensuing heavy fighting, the 64th came close to losing their eagle. Seeking to avoid being surrounded, Captain Desmos ordered the retreat, with the 2/64th and the 1st and 2nd battalions of the 13th falling back and rallying to the rear of three companies of the 5th Chasseurs, who having replenished their ammunition, had taken up a blocking position along the edge of the wood.

Assailed from the front, the 5th were caught in a sudden cross fire as the grenadiers swept around the wood with their right flank being pushed back onto the centre and after losing most of their officers, the chasseurs fell back. II/3rd Grenadiers pushed on through the trees; to the north, 12th Company 3rd Grenadiers and 6th and 7th companies' 4th Grenadiers added their weight to the attack. Faced with this fresh assault, 2/64th and 1st and 2/13th also withdrew to the rear of Mey, taking with them the guns of the 7/1st.

Without affording the French time to rally, Major von Arnim advanced towards Vantoux as out on his right flank, three companies of his grenadiers[106] took up covered firing positions amongst the gardens on the outskirts of Mey. The 3/64th holding the village succeeded in stabilising the French line, their position being supported by the 20th Chasseurs whilst the 1/98th secured the road that ran north to Viller l'Orme. These reserves were supported by additional artillery from 4 Corps, with this fresh display of force halting the enemy's progress.

The guns of the 10/1st were the first to deploy north of Mey wood, alongside the mitrailleuses of the 12/15th but they soon came under close range fire from the Prussians sheltering in the wood and forced to retire,[107] gave up its place to the 9/1st which pushed its way to the front through successive lines of infantry.

During this engagement, the mitrailleuses fired off 27 rounds, their concentrated fire serving to keep the enemy infantry penned up in Mey wood.[108] A little later, additional batteries from

---

105  I/4th Grenadiers and parts of the II/4th were in the first line; the 1st and 4th companies of the 43rd and the 4th Company of the 3rd Grenadiers followed in the second line.
106  12th Company 3rd Grenadiers and 6th and 7th companies' 4th Grenadiers.
107  During the short time it was engaged, the battery fired 98 shells and 13 rounds of shrapnel.
108  By way of comparison the 9th fired off 30 shells, 17 rounds of shrapnel and 27 of canister indicative of the close quarters' nature of the struggle.

the corps' Reserve were moved up in support[109] and to counter this weight of fire, Major Coeste ordered VII Corps horse artillery[110] into the gun line running south of Noisseville.

Unfortunately, the advance of his infantry on Mey masked their targets, so Coester moved all four batteries of horse artillery from I and VII corps forward to the edge of the valley north of Nouilly, from where, seeking to prepare the way for the attack of the III/4th Grenadiers, they opened a counter battery fire against the French guns deployed north of Mey. As Lieutenant Colonel von Pallmenstein deployed his fusiliers, with the 12th Company out front and the 9th covering its right flank, the French were still busily reorganising their forces in the village following their recent retreat from Mey wood.[111]Facing an imminent attack, Colonel Lion of the 13th took control of the situation recalling: 'There wasn't the time to place each unit in its correct position; the companies were thrown into line anyhow and ordered to open fire on the wood.'[112]

### The French Reinforce Their Fighting Line

As fighting continued to rage around Mey, Cissey deployed his division in support of Grenier. De Goldberg's brigade[113] moved along the Bouzonville road to the north of Mey whilst from Brayer's brigade, the 20th Chasseurs occupied the village itself, with the 3/1st deploying between the hamlet and the wood.[114] The 1st and 3/6th were also pushed up in support with the 3rd Battalion being ordered to occupy Grimont château. George Boyland recalled how this regiment marched into battle singing 'Mourir pour la Patrie' whilst Lieutenant Patry, in the 1st Battalion, left this account of his experiences:

> Evening had come but the din increased all the time. At last, the commandant ordered us to stand up and the battalion deployed. Then we saw a long line of troops to the right and left. After a terrible fire fight lasting some minutes, this entire mass was launched in a charge charging towards a wood in front of them from which came thousands of tiny lights sparkling like stars. This was Mey Wood, taken and retaken several times in the course of the battle. We ran across and took possession of it. Night began to envelop friends and enemies with its protective shadows; we went no further.[115]

Seeing their comrades driven from the woods, the 20th Chasseurs moved forward at the double and after a brief fight, threw the Prussians out at bayonet point, pursuing them across the open plateau until they came into line alongside the 3/1st and the ad hoc formation[116] thrown together by Colonel Lion where, formed in a semi-circle running around the western edge of

---

109 There were 60 guns deployed in defence of Mey; from left to right: 11/1st, 6/1st, 5/15th, 9/15th, 12/1st, 5/1st, 9/1st, 9/8th, 6/8th and 8th/1st. Three batteries, the 7/1st, 10/1st and 12/15th had already withdrawn from the fight.
110 The 2nd and 3rd horse artillery of the 7th Field Artillery Regiment.
111 1st and 2/13th, the 64th, the 5th Chasseurs and the 1/98th.
112 L'État-Major, *Borny*, p.249.
113 57th and 63rd.
114 The 1st and 2nd battalions were held in reserve behind Greniers left flank.
115 Patry, *La Guerre*, p.75.
116 2th Chasseurs, 3/1st, 1st, 2nd and 3/13th, 1st, 2nd and 3/64th 1/98th and 5th Chasseurs.

Mey wood, they blazed away at the grenadiers sheltering in its interior. Shortly after, with Lion at the head of the 1st and 2/13th, they charged into the wood, pursuing the II/3rd Grenadiers back down the valley towards Nouilly.

Bentheim, sword in hand, had difficulty in rallying the disorganised mass[117] but assembling them into two groups, led them forward again to the eastern edge of the valley, their advance being supported by a heavy fire laid down by their artillery. However, with night falling fast they were in no shape to resume their attack and they halted well short of the French lines at the end of the valley. It was now about 8:30 p.m. and as the fighting along this section of the front died away, the sound of cheering and beating drums could be heard away to the north around Mey.

Throughout the continuing struggle around Mey, both sides continued to reinforce their positions. Cissey's 2nd Brigade pushed forward along the Bouzonville road on the French left flank with 2/98th taking up a position on the outskirts of Villers l'Orme to cover Grenier's open left wing. To their right, the 43rd deployed along the edge of the lane running south to Mey with the 3/73rd in support to their rear.

On the Prussian side, the I/41st reinforced the centre of their line near the Latour mill south-west of Nouilly. The fusiliers of the 41st took position north of Noisseville to safeguard against any French outflanking manoeuvre, whilst II Battalion moved up to the Amitié brewery in the rear of Lauvallières to act as reserve. As further security against any attack from the direction of Villers l'Orme, General von Zglinitzki[118] ordered forward the 45th; the musketeer battalions took up position in the rear of Pallmenstein's 4th Grenadiers, whilst the fusiliers were held back to the north-west of Noisseville, alongside III/5th Grenadiers.

With night falling this movement was misinterpreted by the French as yet another attempt to outflank their line and in the twilight, they allowed the 45th to close within a few yards of their lines before opening a devastating fire. Calling on the 73rd for support, Grenier ordered the 43rd to charge. In the face of this attack, the Prussians gave way and disappeared into the gloom. After recalling his men, Grenier resumed his withdrawal into Metz unimpeded by the actions of an enemy who were too exhausted and too few in number to interfere.

## The End of the Engagement

By 9:00 p.m. firing had ceased all along the line and Patry took the opportunity to explore Mey wood, the scene of his first combat:

> The fight must have been desperate, for there were many corpses. In a corner, behind a little rise of ground which formed an enclosure, six or seven Germans lay entwined in a pitiful jumble; they all must have been dead because nothing moved. I was heading in another direction when, in moving around a large tree, I found myself face to face with a great devil of a German standing bolt upright leaning against the trunk with his left arm up in the air. A moonbeam struck full on his pallid face. I stopped, terrified … On the plain starkly illuminated by the moon lay many cadavers of both armies. Many

---

117  It consisted of parts of the 3rd and 4th Grenadiers and 43rd and 44th Regiments.
118  4th Brigade's commander.

of our men bore the numeral '64'. Among the Germans, a very young man with blond hair with immaculate white gloves and sword in hand caught my attention. A typical detail; he was already without his boots. No doubt they were already being worn by some smart chap on our side who had found a good opportunity to trade his hobnailed shoes in for a fine pair of boots. This was moreover a general practice; each time the battlefield remained in our possession all the dead were stripped of their footwear in the blink of an eye and the operation was carried out with such skill and speed that I was never able to catch anybody in the act.[119]

## Steinmetz Intervenes

Although I Army's commander had ordered his subordinates to disengage, throughout the late afternoon the fighting had increased in intensity and by early evening, showed little sign of subsiding. Enraged that his orders had been ignored, Steinmetz rode towards the front pausing at Petit-Marais to despatch another orderly to Zastrow instructing him to break off the engagement and withdraw VII Corps 'behind the Nied'[120] Continuing towards Metz, he arrived at the Amitié brewery around 8:00 p.m. where, encountering Manteuffel and his staff, the incandescent septuagenarian delivered a furious dressing down, accusing the corps commander of insubordination, yelling at him 'You've lost the battle' and that he alone would bear responsibility for the consequences.[121]

Somewhat ironically, just as he finished delivering this diatribe, the regimental bands started playing their traditional victory anthem 'Heil dir im Siegerkrantz.' Steinmetz ignored Manteuffel's protestations that breaking off the battle would have handed the French a material and moral victory and still furious, instructed I and VII corps to retreat, although by then, the fighting had generally ceased with the exhausted troops falling back towards their start lines, their withdrawal being covered by a screen of cavalry and pioneers.

In a further sign of his displeasure, Steinmetz ordered both corps to retire beyond the Nied so depriving the men the honour of bivouacking on the field of battle, the time-honoured way by which an army demonstrated victory in combat, with Manteuffel being given only an hour to implement the order. Understandably piqued at this reprimand, he refused to implement the instruction until the following day, advising Steinmetz that 'I shall keep possession of the field unless ordered, in order to bring off those that were wounded in the storming of the enemy's positions and to clench the victory.'[122]

Given the late hour, Zastrow simply ignored the instruction, telling his subordinates that his corps should bivouac on the contested ground, firelock in hand: 'In order not to allow any wounded to fall into the enemy hands and to maintain the honour of having held the battlefield.'[123] To add to Steinmetz's displeasure, the actions of his subordinates were then given

119 Patry, *La Guerre*, pp.76–77.
120 Lehautcourt, *Borny*, p.214.
121 General H. Bonnal, *L'Espirit de la Guerre Moderne, La Manoeuvre de St Privat I* (Paris, Libraire Militaire R Chapelot et Cie. 1904) p.593.
122 Clarke, *Franco German War Vol I*, p.334.
123 *Ibid.*

the seal of Royal approval, as Moltke ordered the troops to remain where they stood.[124] Rubbing salt into his already inflamed wounds, the following day as troops were still clearing away the dead and wounded, the Royal entourage toured the battlefield and upon meeting with von der Goltz, the king personally congratulated him on his initiative.[125]

## Honours Even

Unsurprisingly, both sides claimed victory; Napoleon sent a despatch from his quarters at Longeville at 10:10 p.m. to the Empress: 'The army began to cross to the left bank of the Moselle this morning. Our advance guard had no knowledge of the presence of any force of the enemy. When half of our army had crossed over, the Prussians suddenly attacked in great force. After a fight of four hours, they were repulsed, with great loss to them.'[126]

King Wilhelm's message to Queen Augusta the following day was similarly upbeat: 'A victorious combat near Metz ... The troops are reported to have, all of them, fought with a wonderful energy and gayety not to be expected. I have seen many of them and have thanked them from my heart. The joy was overpowering. I spoke with generals Steinmetz, Zastrow, Manteuffel and Goeben.'[127]

Both sides had some merit to their claims. The strategic importance of the days fighting only became apparent later, but as night fell, the French who had deployed elements of three corps[128] during the afternoons fighting could take some comfort from the fact they had never been seriously endangered. If their generals had not been hindered by Bazaine's strident instructions to maintain their positions, their outnumbered opponents[129] could have been seriously embarrassed. As it was, the French suffered losses of 3,644[130] whilst inflicting losses of about 4,900[131] on the enemy. Indicative of the key role played by the French artillery in the battle, 3 Corps guns alone fired off over 3,600 rounds[132] compared with the 2,800 fired by the three enemy corps.

---

124  It read: 'His Majesty directs the I Army to keep possession of the ground won in yesterday's battle, so far as it is not under the guns of the fortress. The VII Corps will move forward at once to support the I and VII.' See Schell, *Operations*, p.90.

125  The praise heaped on his corps commanders by the king and Moltke only served to increase Steinmetz's resentment as he was left to ponder why his subordinate's disobedience received such commendation, when his unauthorised attack against Frossard at Forbach resulted in censure and a dressing down from Moltke.

126  See Section Historique de l'État-Major de l'Armée, *La Guerre de 1870–71 Les Opérations Autour De Metz Du 13 au 18 Août I Journeés des 13 et 14 Août Bataille de Borny Documents Annexes* (Paris: Librairie Militaire, R Chapelot et Cie, 1903) p.127.

127  Melville de Lancey Landon, *The Franco Prussian war in a nutshell* (New York: G. W. Carleton & Co. 1871) p.155.

128  See French Order of Battle, Appendix I.

129  See German Order of Battle, Appendix II.

130  See French casualties, Appendix III.

131  See German casualties, Appendix IV.

132  2,600 rounds fired by the canon de 4, 340 rounds by the canon de 12 and 700 rounds by the mitrailleuses. By comparison I Corps and I Cavalry Division fired off 2,032 rounds of shell and six of case, VII Corps and 3rd Cavalry Division 678 rounds and the artillery of IX Corps 102 rounds.

On the Prussian side, their impetuous attacks served to disrupt the French withdrawal and by accident rather than design, they held the field of battle at the close of the days fighting. Given the manner in which both sides received reinforcements throughout the afternoon, it is difficult to establish accurately how many men on either side were actually involved in the fighting, but the Prussians fielded around 50,000 infantry and 7,000 cavalry.

The French forces on the east bank of the Moselle, including Brincourt's division of Guard Voltigeurs, numbered over 105,000,[133] but far fewer were engaged in the fighting and of those that were, their actions were severely constrained by Bazaine's directive 'not to advance one foot.' In retrospect, it is clear he missed an opportunity to inflict a humiliating defeat on Manteuffel's and Zastrow's outnumbered corps; instead, anxious to avoid getting caught in Metz[134] he failed to take advantage of his superior numbers[135] to brush aside I Army and then threaten II Army's exposed flank as they marched towards the Moselle. However, such initiative and aggressive manoeuvring was seemingly beyond the competence of Bazaine, or indeed, any French commander in 1870.

## The Aftermath of Battle

Although the fighting had subsided, there was no shortage of work for the medical staff of both armies as described by George Boyland:

> In the silence that ensued shortly after the battle we could distinctly hear the hurrahs of the victorious enemy, who were lighting their camp fires and bivouacking. All along the lines the Prussian national hymn is sung and an accompaniment played by the bands of the different regiments. Above the stars are brightly shining ... As we enter the flower adorned gates of the cosy villa a strange sight presents itself to our view. On either side of the road that winds up to the villa is a large grass plat. On this the wounded were lying in rows. Some were on stretchers, some on the ground; others less severely wounded sitting on the steps of the porter's lodge; others again leaning against the parapet of the villa balcony. Those leaning against the parapet and sitting on the woodpile had come off the best. These we dressed first as being the most urgent. Their

133  *Heft 11* of the *Kriegsgeschlichtliche Einzelschriften* published in 1899 states that the French had 76,000 infantry, 7,300 cavalry, 288 guns and 60 mitrailleuses on the field of battle compared with 50,000 Prussian infantry, 7,250 cavalry and 240 guns. Of those actually engaged in the fighting the French numbered 50,700 infantry, 690 cavalry, 206 guns and 48 mitrailleuses. On the Prussian side there were 30,000 infantry with 130 cavalry and 150 guns engaged. Unsurprisingly, Bonnal, Lehautcourt and Von Der Siehe all give differing numbers and as ever it is difficult to state with any certainty an accurate figure both for the overall numbers present or in the vicinity of the battlefield and those who participated in the fighting.

134  When one of Montaudon's ADC's asked for permission to go over to the attack Bazaine told him: 'Make clear to your general I do not want a battle. I am not going to play the enemies game whose sole purpose is to delay our retreat across the Moselle.' See l'État-Major, *Borny*, p.235.

135  If all of 4 Corps had been recalled, the French would have fielded twice the number of men available to the Germans.

wounds were mostly about the arms and shoulders … We had a very active night of it, making incisions, extracting balls, washing, binding etc. [136]

A little later, his field ambulance was ordered to join the columns of troops still making their way towards Metz:

The sound of soldiers marching at this moment reached our ears; going out to the door I saw the infantry of the Third Corps, to which our ambulance belonged, filing past; they marched in silence; the bright scabbards of their officers, who wore the hoods of their overcoats over their heads and the smooth bayonets of the men, glittered in the moonlight. The retreat had already commenced and all the troops that remained were on their way to re-join the rest of the army. Soon the artillery came rattling along, while the cavalry brought up the rear. General Bourbaki, then in command of the Imperial Guard, had ordered the movement to be made without further delay. Our eight army fourgons, which were nothing more than the wagon in use in the American and Prussian armies (box like and oblong in shape with a top) could contain but 96 of the more slightly wounded; those who were able to sit up; and we had altogether 210 on our hands. We had no time to spare and we were rather put to it to know what we should do. We were not long deciding, however and resolved to bring a sufficient number of horses and hayracks belonging to the inhabitants into requisition … The wagons, ten in number, each drawn by two horses, we filled with straw. We placed the wounded carefully upon the straw, folded the stretchers and joined the retreat … Our ambulance fell into the line of retreat behind the artillery. The fires that had a few hours before lighted the country far and wide, were deserted and smouldering; and as we rode back towards Metz, we were pushed and hustled about by the cavalry, who had come up and wished to pass us. The clock on the tower of the château at Borny struck three as we left the village. On the road we were often blocked and at these times I had the opportunity of glancing about; the cavalry were still pressing us hard but we would not make room for them and they were obliged to remain behind, which it was their place to do. The men were all very tired; and I could see the weary artillerymen every now and then drop their heads and lean down on their horse's necks, to catch a few minutes sleep. We found troops breaking up camp all about that district. Soon all were gone and only the dead remained behind in the village and on the field. Many of our wounded complained, but we could do nothing for them then, as we could not stop the column. The French wounded are generally conveyed from the field on 'cacolets'. These 'cacolets' are very badly arranged; viz a mule is harnessed with a large wooden saddle, on either side of which is a wooden chair. Unfortunately, these chairs move and if two wounded men who are to occupy them are not put up at exactly the same moment, the chair sinks on the side of the one that reaches it first; if on the contrary, they are not taken down together, the one that is left receives a jerk and a shock that would be sufficient to throw a weak man to the ground. Moreover, ever step the mule takes, jolts

136  Boyland, *Six Months*, pp.42–43.

the wounded and gives them pain. A wounded captain, who was borne on one of these, exclaimed to us 'For the love of God, gentlemen, take me down and let me die.[137]

The following day, Boyland related how the Prussians sent an emissary to request 24 hours armistice so as to afford both sides the opportunity to bury the dead and clear the field of any remaining wounded; he volunteered for this task and described the desolate scene which greeted him:

[the battlefield] presents the appearance of a field of blood (the red on the dead giving that idea) whilst the entrails of sheep, horses, cows etc are scattered about. Knapsacks, guns, muskets, sabres, bayonets, everywhere. We make a halt, observing the Prussians moving about their portion of the field; above them floats the white flag with the red cross. On perceiving our train, one of their officers with two men advance. We likewise send an officer and two men from our number forward, to meet them. Observing what is passing, I gallop out into the field to see the genie, who are hollowing out long ditches within which to put the dead. They are unarmed, in accordance with the stipulations of the armistice. As soon as the ditches are ready, the dead are picked up, each body by two men and laid not over cautiously into their final resting place. This done, a Catholic priest walks the length of the grave, sprinkling it with blessed water and all is over. One squad of dead in particular attract my attention; they all lie in a row in exactly the same position as when the fatal bullet arrived, showing that death must have been instantaneous. One is on his knee; another lying full length behind his knapsack ... a third was in the act of throwing up his hands, as if just struck, while a piece of skull was broken in and the protruding brain showed the cause of death; a fourth was still loading his chassepot ... I saw that our ambulance had turned the angle and were now hurrying down the Courcelles road ... It seems to have been the dividing line of the two columns attack; for on the right were our dead, on the left, those of the enemy. They lay in pools of gore. I noticed one without a head; another cut in two in the middle; this had evidently been done by a shell, for the wound was ragged and not like that made by a sabre. The upper part of the body was some twenty feet distant from the lower part, to which it was connected by the intestines, which were thus making almost a straight line from the duodenum to the sigmoid flexor. As we rode along the route, I noticed a dead soldier, who was lying upon his face at the foot of a rude stone crucifix, to which he had evidently been able to drag himself after being wounded, for I could follow the tracks of fresh blood for some hundred yards back. Fresh graves were everywhere to be seen on the Prussian side, the only tombstone of some, being a sabre driven into the ground; others had small crosses made from the branches of trees.[138]

Although Boyland believed the Prussians had been victorious in the battle, Napoleon was more than satisfied with the outcome. On the evening of the battle, Bazaine moved his headquarters

---

137  Boyland, *Six Months*, pp.45–46.
138  *Ibid* 49–53.

to the west bank of the Moselle at Moulins les Metz and later made a courtesy call to the emperor at nearby Longeville to update him on developments:

> The Emperor greeted me with his usual kindness and when I explained my fears lest the Germans should cut in on my line of retreat and referring to my wound asked to be relieved of my command, the Emperor, touching my bruised shoulder and the broken epaulette, gracefully said 'It will be nothing, a matter of a few days and you have broken the spell. I await an answer at any moment from the Emperor of Austria and the King of Italy. Compromise nothing by too much haste and, above all things, no more reverses, I rely on you.'[139]

As for Moltke, he was still unclear as to the intentions and whereabouts of the French army. It was only during the evening of the 14th as his headquarters set up office in the Maire at Herny that reports trickled in of the fighting in front of Metz. Still unsure of the strategic position, he issued the following update to his army commanders: 'Observations by the First Army have not resulted in any definite clearing up of the situation. Still, we may assume that the greatest part of the hostile army is this side of Metz.'[140]

Instructions were given for I Army to continue to observe and screen Metz, II Army were ordered to hold their corps in the positions they occupied whilst the cavalry divisions were to cross the Moselle in order to scout the roads leading from Metz to Verdun. Following the engagement at Borny, VIII and IX Corps were to move closer to Metz in the event there was a resumption of fighting. However, as recalled by Verny du Vernois, even as the king toured the battlefield on the 15th, the strategic situation became clearer:

> The battlefield was already cleared to a remarkable extent, although comparatively few hours had passed since the end of the struggle. Only in one small copse we still found some hundred wounded Frenchmen; a large number of dead, however were still unburied. The King conversed with Generals von Steinmetz and von Manteuffel, then he rode on in the direction of Metz, we others following ... On this side of Metz nothing was to be seen of any French troops outside the fortifications; only on the glacis there seemed to be some movement going on. But we noticed quite distinctly strong columns ascending the heights on the left bank of the Moselle, to which our attention was drawn in the first instance by clouds of dust and the flash of arms.[141]

139  Marshal F A Bazaine, *Épisodes de la Guerre de 1870 et le Blocus De Metz* (Madrid, Gaspar, Éditeurs, 1833) pp.70–71.
140  Conrad H Lanza, *Franco-German War of 1870 Source Book* (Fort Leavenworth: General Service Schools Press 1922) p.256.
141  General Julius von Verdy du Vernois, *With The Royal Headquarters In 1870–71* (London: Kegan Paul, Trench, Trübner & Co, 1897) pp.68–69.

## German and French Plans

Following this reconnaissance, Moltke despatched a telegram at 11:00 a.m. to III Army: 'French completely thrown back into Metz and probably by this time in full retreat to Verdun. All three corps of the right wing (III, IX and XII) are now placed at the free disposal of the army commander in chief. The XII is already on the march to Nomény.'[142] Later that afternoon, concerned that the French were slipping out of his grasp, further orders were issued to the two army commanders: Steinmetz was told to leave I Corps at Courcelles sur Nied, so as to screen Metz, whilst VII and VIII corps were ordered to reconnoitre crossing points over the Moselle.

The Red Prince was urged to push forward in an effort to catch the retreating French army as it made its way to Verdun: 'The fruits of victory can only be obtained by a strong offensive by the Second Army against the roads from Metz as well as via Fresnes and Etain towards Verdun. It is left to Headquarters Second Army to conduct such an offensive with all available means at hand.'[143] In Pont à Mousson, Frederick Charles had pre-empted these instructions having issued the following order to his forward corps commanders:

> X Corps will march tomorrow in a straight-line westward from Pont à Mousson towards Verdun on the supposition that the enemy's advanced troops on his retreat may already be approaching that town. The troops will complete more than half the distance during the day and their advance guards will push on as far as St Hilaire. Not before reaching that place is it thought possible that they will come across the enemy. III Corps will move on Gorze and it is likely to make some contact with some of the enemy tomorrow evening.[144]

In turn, X Corps commander, Voights Rhetz, instructed Rheinbaben's 5th Cavalry Division to push westwards in an attempt to intercept the retreating French: 'I send you here with a report, the contents of which agree with the other intelligence received, that the enemy's forces leaving Metz are on their retreat to Verdun. I request you to start at once for Fresnes en Woëvre in strength and to try to bring the enemy to a halt.'[145]

By the evening of 15 August, Moltke, working on the assumption that Bazaine had made good his escape, directed all his available forces westward; if he had lost the opportunity to encircle the Imperial Army in Metz, there was at least the prospect that he could intercept their rearguard as they made their way to Verdun. As the authors of one of the many post war histories remarked: 'Great stress was laid on the paramount importance of their ascertaining whether the bulk of the hostile army had already left Metz, or whether it was still in the act of departing. It is significant that the third possible case, that the enemy might simply be remaining stationary before Metz was not even taken into consideration.'[146]

142  Lanza, *Franco-German War*, p.258.
143  *Ibid.*
144  David Ascoli, *A Day of Battle, Mars la Tour 16 August 1870*, (London: Harrap Ltd. 1987) p.108.
145  General von Pelet-Narbonne, *Cavalry on Service* (London: Hugh Rees, Ltd, 1906) p.301.
146  Maurice, Major General J. F. (trans), *The Franco-German War 1870–71 by Generals and Other Officers who took part in the campaign* (London: Swan Sonnenschein and Co Ltd, 1900) p.135.

What of the French? In stark contrast to the activity exhibited by the Prussian staff, after concluding his interview with Napoleon at Longeville on the evening of the 14 August, Bazaine retired to his villa in Ban St Martin, to the west of Metz. Exhausted and nursing his injured shoulder, he only reached his quarters at 1:00 a.m. and went to bed without issuing any orders.[147] After being woken at 10.00 a.m. the following morning, he issued brief instructions for the army to continue its retreat. Consequently, in obedience to the marshal's ill-conceived orders, the entire French Army struggled along the single steep, narrow road that ran from Metz, by way of the Rozerieulles heights, to the crossroads at Gravelotte.[148] As Canrobert was to comment at Bazaine's Courts Martial after the war, the organisation of the retreat was no simple matter: 'Not everyone can command an army a hundred and forty thousand strong; it is difficult to manage when one isn't used to it.'[149]

The contrast with the Prussian forces, who advanced on a broad front along multiple routes, is harder to imagine and matters soon went from bad to worse as the marching columns were encumbered by the immense number of wagons which accompanied the army. Robinson described the scene:

> Never was any army accompanied by anything like such a collection of impedimenta. Impedimenta they truly were; they blocked up the roads in all directions. Artillery could not get forward. Troops had to leave the highways and flounder through the fields and by-ways, cavalry took to steeple chasing and everybody swore at everybody, especially at the immovable, stolid, stupid, hindering body of Auxiliaries. These men, picked up anyhow, anywhere, under no known direction, were always clubbing themselves and their carts at a corner, or getting into hopelessly extricable confusion. Forced to make long journeys at all hours, some of them had not had their clothes off for three weeks; the consequences of this overwork was that their natural stupidity was enhanced by perpetual sleepiness and the only way to make them understand an order was, literally and physically, to beat it into them. So long as the pain of the blow remained, they would recollect the order, but after that, it passed into the Lethe of their brain and was immediately forgotten.[150]

Poor march discipline and bad organisation exacerbated an already complex operation and through a misunderstanding over orders, 2 Corps halted at Rezonville, several miles short of its intended destination at Mars la Tour; this resulted in additional delays for 6 Corps and the Guard. Further confusion arose following the enterprise shown by an enemy patrol[151] who were monitoring the retreat from high ground near Montigny on the east bank of the Moselle. As their commander recalled:

---

147  When questioned about this omission at his Courts Martial after the war Bazaine replied: 'I was tired; I had spent three or four days in the saddle and my wound was giving me pain.' See Anon, *Affaire de la Capitulation de Metz, Procés Bazaine* (Paris: Libraire du Moniteur Universal, 1873) p.163.
148  It numbered around 170,000 men with 4,000 wagons.
149  Howard, *Franco Prussian War* p.146.
150  G.T. Robinson, *The Fall of Metz*, (London: Bradbury, Evans & co. 1871), pp.60–61.
151  Commanded by Colonel Count von Gröben the force comprised two squadrons of 3rd Lancers, a squadron of the 6th Cuirassiers and a section of two guns under First Lieutenant von Gizycki of the 2nd Horse Artillery battery of the 3rd Brandenburg Field Artillery regiment.

I observed a large camp of the enemy on the left bank between Longville and Moulins les Metz, where absolute silence still reigned. According to all the inhabitants, all the camps on the right bank had been abandoned in the night and the troops were said to have marched away for the most part towards Verdun. Though the reconnaissance on the right bank had gained its object, I could not resist the pleasure of disturbing the peacefulness of the camp at Longville. The two guns came into action west of Brandin's Farm and opened fire on the camp. The effect was most amusing. Shouts and confusion everywhere. The section of two horse guns fired 48 rounds at ranges of 2,200 and 2,800 paces.[152]

The surprise was complete. The first shells dropped amongst a group of French officers from the 10th Ligne, killing one and wounding several others.[153] The shelling fell close enough to the emperors' lodgings to cause the Royal suite to rapidly relocate to Gravelotte.[154] In the alarm that followed, Bazaine fearing yet another spoiling attack by the Prussians, ordered the destruction of the main railway bridge across the Moselle. Another observer to the surprise bombardment reported that:

Balls and shells which whizzed at six this morning over my head, killed the commandant of a line regiment and severely wounded other officers of the same regiment. Six or seven soldiers were also struck and were borne past me to the ambulance. The fort which commands Longueville, where the enemy surprised us, discharges some twelve pounders and dislodges the enemy who retire … It is half past seven. The Emperor mounts his horse, with the Prince Imperial and Prince Napoleon. Marshal Le Boeuf comes up. General Chargarnier speaking of the cannon fire that had broken out says smiling to those who surround him 'Those are the Prussians, who wished to compliment the Emperor on his féte.' A bouquet for a sovereign it may be, but a dangerous bouquet and one which would have been kept far from the Imperial Quarters if a better look out had been kept. But it is always the same story. We keep no watch and allow ourselves to be surprised by an enemy whose vigilance is extraordinary. [155]

As a result of Bazaine's poor planning and the inevitable resultant confusion, the army fell well short of its intended destination on the 15th; Barail's cavalry division only reached Jarny on the northern road out of Gravelotte and Forton's division set up camp at Vionville with outposts facing Trouville and Mars la Tour. 2 Corps left Sainte-Rufine at 4:00 a.m. and was still several miles from Mars la Tour when it bivouacked at 10:00 a.m. in front of Rezonville to the left of the Metz-Verdun road. General Henry, 6 Corps' chief of staff, noted in his diary:

152  Pelet-Narbonne, *Cavalry*, pp.292–293.
153  Captain Reboulet. One of the injured was the celebrated military author Colonel Ardant du Picq who later died from his wounds.
154  The emperor's first thought was for the safety of his son; he rushed to the bed of the sleeping Prince shouting: 'Up Louis! Up and dress! The Prussians are shelling the villa.' See Theo Aronson, *The Fall of the Third Napoleon* (London: History Book Club,1970) p.124.
155  De Lancey Landon, *The Franco Prussian*, pp.161–162.

About 11:00 p.m. on the 14th an officer from headquarters arrived with verbal orders for the 6 Corps to move out at daybreak on the 15th. Tixier's division to cross the Moselle by the railway bridge. This movement was completed by 5:00 a.m.; several minutes after the engineers blew up on arch of this bridge; but the destruction of the bridge at Jouy and at Novéant was entirely forgotten and the enemy crossed over them at once. The division halted on the Longeville-Moulins road where it received some shells from a Prussian battery which had followed and which fired from across the river. Marshal Canrobert took post at daybreak at the Porte de France; there was no officer from headquarters to inform him of the direction to take; he directed his own staff to supervise the march.[156]

As related by Henry, Tixier's division arrived at Longville les Metz by 5:00 a.m. and were then thrown into confusion by Gröben's bombardment. They only resumed their march two hours later, finally setting up camp at St Marcel at 11:00 a.m. The 9th Line arrived at Rezonville at 5:00 p.m.[157] and La Font's division halted 4,000 metres west of Gravelotte; Levassor's division bivouacked at 4:30 p.m. in front of Gravelotte, facing the Bois des Ognons.

In the confusion surrounding the retreat, 3 Corps, which needed to replenish ammunition expended during the previous days fighting,[158] bivouacked far short of their planned destination and somehow ended up in front of 4 Corps, rather than behind it as intended. The delay meant that Montuadon camped between Montigny la Grange and the farmstead at Chantrenne, facing north-west to guard against a possible attack from that direction. Castigny arrived later during the evening and bivouacked in the vicinity of Vernéville. Amyard's division began its march at 5:00 p.m. and only just cleared the heights above Ban St Martin before it halted again and set up camp. Metman reached Plappeville at 7:00 a.m. after a long night march with the divisional cavalry bivouacking close to the Moselle.

4 Corps also needed to replenish stocks of food and ammunition and made similarly slow progress; Ladmirault's request that he be allowed to take the northern route by way of Woippy was rejected by Bazaine who was concerned about reports that Steinmetz was attempting to encircle Metz from the north. As a result, Lorencez's division only reached Lorry with Cissey, Grenier and the corps cavalry camping at Woippy. Patry recalled the confusion in Metz as the army retreated through the city:

> It was full daylight when we crossed the Moselle by a pontoon bridge but the column was completely clogged up. Everybody was pushing to get to the other side and as there were neither generals nor staff personnel present in adequate numbers the confusion within the units increased with every passing minute. Finally, we reached the island and there a little order could be restored in the regiment. At about ten o'clock in the

156 Section Historique de l'État-Major de l'Armée, *La Guerre de 1870–71 Les Opérations Autour De Metz Du 13 au 18 Août II Journées des 15 et 16 Août Documents Annexes* (Paris: Librairie Militaire, R Chapelot et Cie, 1904) pp.47–48.

157 This was the only regiment from Bisson's 2nd Division to reach MacMahon's corps.

158 3 Corps was resupplied with 272,767 cartouches for the Modèle 1866, 21,062 for the Modèle 1863, 2,343 shells for the 4-pdrs, 102 for the 12-pdrs.

morning we arrived at Longeville, where we were told to make camp. We had taken nine hours to travel just two leagues.[159]

From the Imperial Guard, Deligny's Voltigeurs reached their bivouac between Saint Hubert and Pont du Jour at 2:00 p.m. The Guard cavalry left Ban St Martin at the same time, reaching Gravelotte around 5:00 p.m. where they set up camp alongside Piccard's Grenadiers.

## The Road to Verdun

On the afternoon of 15 August, Napoleon was to be found sat outside an auberge in Gravelotte, watching his weary, sullen, army trudge past. Later, Bazaine approached, handing him a bunch of flowers to mark the Fête Napoleon. Here, they agreed that the emperor would leave the army and make his way back to Châlons where MacMahon was assembling his forces following the defeat at Woerth. The escort of Guard Dragoons only arrived late in the day and when Napoleon asked Bazaine if it was safe to set off for Verdun, the marshal counselled caution, advising him to make the journey the following day as he was unable to guarantee his security. Demonstrating remarkable complacency, Bazaine then took his leave, returning to his quarters in the Maison de Poste at Moulins les Metz, leaving Jarras and the remainder of the general staff in complete ignorance as to his intentions notwithstanding the perilous strategic position of his army, when every minute lost to the enemy increased the chances of it being encircled.

As the Imperial Army wasted precious time in clearing Metz, the Prussians forged ahead; Brandenburg's brigade of Guard Dragoons were instructed to push forward on a broad front from Ménil in the south, to Thiaucourt in the north. 5th Cavalry were to advance to Fresnes en Woëvre, 18 kilometres east of Verdun where it was hoped they would be able to intercept stragglers from Bazaine's army. At the same time, it was to send detachments north to establish a link with Steinmetz's cavalry patrols and east, towards Metz to observe the French.

Rheinbaben ordered Redern's Brigade[160] to Lachaussée where it would be well placed to intercept and harass any movement along the Metz-Verdun high road. The 4th Cuirassiers were ordered from Thiaucourt to Dommartin to cover Redern's flank guard, whilst Bredow's brigade was order forward to Thiaucourt. Redern led off his force, six squadrons[161] and a battery of horse artillery, at 4:00 a.m. although the thick fog restricted visibility to around 200 yards.

At Lachaussé a squadron of the 17th under Captain Brauns were sent off in the direction of Latour en Woëvre. Another patrol from the 11th, commanded by Captain von Knobelsdorf, headed towards Mars la Tour. At 8:30 a.m., just as both patrols were reporting that there was nothing to be seen, the French opened fire on the cavalry. Redern galloped forward with four squadrons to Xonville and peering through the fog, made out two regiments of French dragoons. Captain Schmirer's battery of horse artillery[162] unlimbered and after firing six rounds, the enemy retreated.

---

159  Patry, *La Guerre*, pp.78–79. A league is just over three miles.
160  10th, 11th and 17th Hussars.
161  He left three squadrons of the 10th Hussars at Beney.
162  2nd Horse Artillery of the 10th Hanoverian Field Artillery Regiment.

Escorted by a squadron of hussars, Schmirer moved to a new position about 1,800 paces south of Mars la Tour and again opened fire on Forton's cavalry[163] who were around Mars la Tour. 1st Dragoons, who were leading the French retreat, sighted the Prussian scouts and supported by 2nd Dragoons, pursued the enemy patrol beyond Puxieux when they came across Redern's brigade coming up at the gallop. As they fell back in the face of this superior force, Forton ordered up the 7th and 10th Cuirassiers supported by two batteries[164] of horse artillery which opened fire on the Prussian cavalry.

After about an hour, during which the French fired off between 30 and 40 rounds per gun, Redern ordered his men to retreat about 1,500 paces to the shelter of some rising ground.[165] Forton, satisfied with this minor success and with no apparent desire to establish the strength or identity of the enemy force, fell back and spent the next three hours watering his horses in Mars la Tour.

Attracted by the sound of the cannon fire, the remainder of Rheinbaben's division[166] assembled in the area south of Mars la Tour, anxious to renew the contest. However, by this time, Forton, concerned at the gap that had opened up between his cavalry and the corps following in his wake, had withdrawn closer to Vionville. Likewise, the ever-cautious Rheinbaben, rather than seeking to exploit his numerical advantage,[167] also thought it prudent to withdraw and went into bivouac, later justifying his decision by claiming his trooper's mounts were 'tired.'[168] Following their commander's lead, Redern's brigade made camp at Xonville, Barby at Puxieux and Bredow at Suzemont, to the west of Mars la Tour. As a consequence, neither Rheinbaben nor Frossard had any clear understanding of the whereabouts and strength of the opposition confronting them.

For the remainder of the afternoon, there was intermittent skirmishing between the mounted outposts and Barby's brigade, unable to counter the long-range rifle fire of the French dragoons relocated further to the rear. Bredow sent a squadron[169] from 16th Lancers northwards with the mission: 'To advance by Mars la Tour to Jarny and from there to seek for the cavalry of the First army by means of patrols'[170] but due to the inexperience of their commander, they blundered into Barail's outposts at Jarny. Hotly pursued by the Chasseurs d'Afrique. the lancers hurriedly withdrew, losing four men killed, nine men and 18 horses missing in the ensuing skirmish. 2nd Squadron, who had been sent to support Wulffen, captured an itinerant German cobbler

---

163  From 3rd Reserve Cavalry Division.

164  7th and 8th batteries 20th régiment d'artillerie à cheval.

165  Schirmer had three men wounded and 11 horses killed.

166  At 2:00 p.m. Rheinbaben had 34 squadrons and two horse artillery batteries to hand. One squadron from the10th had been sent to Nancy and a squadron of the 13th Dragoons was away keeping open communications with the Guard cavalry division to the south.

167  Rheinbaben had about 4,250 sabres compared to Fortons' 15 squadrons which amounted to about 1,680 sabres. At 1:00 p.m. he sent the following message to X Corps HQ: 'Arrived with five regiments and one battery at 12 noon at Tronville; encountered hostile cavalry and superior artillery which at present moment are falling back on Metz. The light cavalry is now going closer to Metz. Bredow's brigade will soon follow. I intend to remain in Tronville or nearer Metz. Communication with I Army not yet established.' See Pelet-Narbonne, *Cavalry*, pp.311–312.

168  *Ibid*, p.312.

169  1st Squadron under Captain von Wulffen.

170  Pelet-Narbonne, *Cavalry*, p.312.

from Metz who was making his way to Vedun and as later related by their commander, von Porembsky, he explained that:

> … as the whole French army was going to Verdun the next day, he would find no more work in Metz and wanted to look for opportunities in Verdun. He was a German. The whole French army, under Marshal Bazaine, were encamped between Metz and Vionville. Napoleon had been in Metz till early in the morning but the artisan had heard that he had left Metz that morning to go to Verdun.[171]

Porembsky sent the cobbler, escorted by an NCO, to his regiment for further interrogation, although it seems that he gave his guard the slip somewhere along the way, as the divisional headquarters remained in ignorance of this vital intelligence. Elsewhere during the afternoon, a squadron from the 11th Hussars, under Captain von Kotze, passed to the south of Rezonville and noted the camp fires of a force which he estimated at 20,000 men. This information was confirmed by a personal inspection undertaken by Captain von Heister of the divisional general staff; a note was sent to Voights Rhetz at X Corps advising: 'A reconnaissance has shown that the enemy's vedettes are at Vionville and that a large camp of all arms is somewhere near Rezonville.'[172]

Additional intelligence regarding the French Army was obtained by a party from 3rd Squadron 9th Dragoons, under Captain von Blumenthal, who were patrolling on the west bank of the Moselle between Metz and Pont à Mousson; he reported: 'A schoolmaster, just met with on the road from Metz, states that the French army, 50,000 strong, marched out of Metz at 6.00pm last night via Longeville, Moulins, St Ruffine, the Route Impériale, Gravelotte, Rezonville, Vionville, Mars la Tour. He has been arrested and is handed over herewith.'[173]

From the intelligence garnered by these patrols, the realisation was starting to dawn at Rheinbaben's headquarters that they were confronted by something more substantial than a rearguard, although these concerns were dismissed by Voights Rhetz at X Corps who believed that the bulk of Bazaine's army had long made good its escape. As night fell on 15 August, Moltke was equally in the dark as to the positions occupied by the French and sharing Voights Rhetz's appreciation of the strategic situation, made his plans accordingly. As such, the following day's events were to come as an equal surprise to both French and German commanders and for the fourth time in succession, the opposing forces would be engaged in yet another bruising and bloody encounter battle.

171  *Ibid*, p.320.
172  *Ibid*, p.321.
173  *Ibid*, p.322.

**2**

# The Battle of Rezonville[1] 16 August 1870

---

## Napoleon's Departure for Châlons

Bazaine was informed of Forton's skirmish at Mars la Tour during the afternoon of the 15th and later that evening, Frossard and Canrobert[2] both reported the presence of large numbers of enemy troops. Despite this worrying news, which seemed to confirm other reports that the Prussians had crossed the Moselle both north and south of Metz intending to encircle the French Army,[3] Bazaine failed to react; he merely issued a bland warning to his corps: 'At 4:00 a.m. tomorrow morning soup will be served. At 4:30 a.m. troops will be ready to march, horses saddled and tents rolled. General Frossard and Marshal Canrobert inform me, from intelligence they have received, that the 2 and 6 Corps will probably have a hostile force of about 30,000 men in their front and should expect an attack tomorrow.' He requested his commanders to notify him of their precise location so that he could forward any orders, 'if I have any to give you,'[4] with the minimum of delay and, content with this, retired to his bed.

Given even the limited intelligence available at that time, Bazaine's vacillation is hard to understand and reflected poorly on his capabilities as a commander in chief. It reinforced the picture painted by his critics of an officer who although personally brave, was simply out of his depth when faced with such a rapidly changing situation, lacking any clear idea as to what he should do.

When Intendant Wolff asked for instructions early on the 16th he was told: 'If I have all my forces to hand, I might be inclined to throw them against the enemy at Pont à Mousson. If not, we'll go to Verdun which will be our new base of operations, leaving behind a force to safeguard

---

1    This was known to the Germans as the Battle of Vionville-Mars la Tour.
2    In bivouac around Rezonville.
3    French observers posted in the Cathedral in Metz sent repeated messages to Bazaine throughout the 15th warning of the movement of large numbers of German troops south of the city towards the Moselle.
4    L'État-Major, *16 Août Documents*, p.69.

Metz.'[5] He was still pondering his options when Alvesleben took the initiative; this indecision was to cost France and the Imperial Army dear.

The morning of Tuesday, 16 August found Bazaine's forces strung out along the roads between Metz and Mars la Tour; Forton's 3rd Cavalry Division were around Vionville; Murat's dragoons and the divisional horse artillery, to the north of the main Verdun-Metz road and Gramont's brigade of cuirassiers, to their rear. At the head of 2 Corps, Valabrègue's cavalry division were camped along both sides of the road west of Vionville. Frossard's infantry were to the south of the highway; Bataille's division was bivouacked 1,600 yards west of Rezonville whilst Vergé's troops were deployed in two lines on a spur running south to Côte Mousa.

Lapassat's brigade, from 5 Corps, was on Vergé's left, facing Bois de St Arnould. Canrobert's 6 Corps were to the north of the main road; Le Vassor-Sorval was east of Rezonville close to the highway, the left of La Font de Villier's division rested on Valabrègue's cavalry, its right on the small hamlet of Saint Marcel, which in turn, was occupied by Bisson's division.[6] Tixier's division was camped between St Marcel and the Jarny Road.

The Imperial Guard were west of Gravelotte, parallel to the road running from Malmaison to Mogador; the cavalry along both sides of the road, Deligny's Voltigeur's on the right extending as far as Malmaison, Picard's Grenadier's on the left. Two divisions from 3 Corps[7] were bivouacked between St Marcel and Vernéville, facing north-west; Clérembault's cavalry were in front of Nayral, with Aymard's division to the rear. Their artillery reserve were to the west of Rezonville and a little way to the north, Margeuritte's Brigade of Chasseurs d'Afrique were at Conflans awaiting the arrival of the emperor's cortege. Legrand's cavalry bivouacked around Saint Privat whilst the remainder of Ladmirault's corps[8] and Metman's division[9] had still to make their way up to the plateau from the Moselle valley.

At 2.:00 a.m., 'à cheval' sounded in the Guard cavalry division's bivouac. At 4:00 a.m., de France's brigade of dragoons and lancers were ordered to mount and followed by their baggage train, made their way to the inn at Gravelotte where Napoleon spent the night. When Bazaine dutifully arrived to bid the emperor farewell, he found him seated in his carriage accompanied by his son, Louis; the Prince Napoleon and an aide-de-camp sat opposite. Looking tired and worn out the emperor told the marshal: 'I have decided to leave for Châlons. To your charge I commit the last army of France. Think of the Prince Imperial.' His final instructions were clear and unambiguous: 'Put yourself on the road to Verdun as soon as you can.'[10] At 5:00 a.m. the

5    Section Historique de l'État-Major de l'Armée, *La Guerre de 1870–71 Les Opérations Autour De Metz Du 13 au 18 Août II Journées des 15 et 16 Août Bataille de Rezonville* (Paris: Librairie Militaire, R Chapelot et Cie, 1904) p.143.

6    This consisted of just three battalions of the 9th Ligne.

7    Montaudon's and Nayral's.

8    1st and 2nd Division and Reserve artillery, 4 Corps.

9    From Le Boeuf's 3 Corps.

10   Aronson, *The Fall* p.125 and Ascoli, *A Day of Battle*, p.117 When questioned on this exchange at his Courts Martial after the war, Bazaine said that Napoleon had left it to him, as the commander in chief, to decide when to commence the retreat. By this time, the emperor was dead, unable to refute the claim. See l'État-Major, *Rezonville* p.136.

trumpeters sounded 'au trot' and in columns of four, the Empress Dragoons led the Imperial cortege out of Gravelotte.[11] Lieutenant Pomeyrac of the Guard Lancers recalled:

> Accompanying the emperor's carriage, I rode with my platoon to the left of the column. The pace was very fast and in no time at all we left a number of lancers struggling at the side of the road. We lost about thirty troopers who stopped to secure their equipment or adjust their belongings. I mentioned this to my commanding officer who was trotting at my side and he warned the emperor about the problems this would cause to the lancers if we sustained this pace. This is how we continued to Doncourt, where we met with Margueritte who relieved de France's brigade.[12]

Fortunately, the cortege took the northern route to Verdun, away from the probing Prussian patrols along the Mars la Tour road but even so, approaching Conflans, the column was halted after a local priest warned of the nearby presence of a large body of enemy cavalry; scouts were sent forward to reconnoitre but found nothing.

Resuming their march, the Imperial party breakfasted at Etain,[13] where fresh troopers from Margueritte's brigade of Chasseurs d'Afrique took over escort duties. The emperor, looking fatigued with a blotchy and bloated appearance, arrived at Verdun at 2:00 p.m.[14] where he assured the mayor: 'Bazaine's following me. He'll be here tomorrow.'[15] After lunching at a hotel, he left for the station, where he requested a train to take him to Châlons:

> 'Sire' said the station master 'I have nothing to offer you but a third-class carriage' 'I will content myself with that.' replied the Emperor, who took his seat on the hard board, refusing a cushion from his carriage. He asked for a glass of wine and the station master washed out the glass he had just used at breakfast and gave the Emperor a drink. The Prince Imperial, who was greatly fatigued, demanded to wash his hands and face

---

11   The Imperial baggage train, the cause of much resentment to the regular formations, which followed on behind the emperor was escorted by a detachment of Cent-Gardes, a squadron of guides and the 3/3rd Grenadiers. In the War Diary of the 2 Corps Quarter Master Bouteiller recorded the confusion and delay occasioned by its passage: 'When Headquarters train was about to start its march, Army General Staff officers came down the road and caused all wagons to get off to the right and left in order to leave space for the emperor's baggage train. All our wagons had to take to the fields, our convoy, which we had so much trouble to get in order, was cut in several places and the head of the convoy had to wait hours at Maison Neuve before being able to resume the march.' See l'État-Major, *16 Août Documents*, pp.19–20.

12   Jean-Francois Lecaillon, *Été 1870 La guerre racontéé par les soldats*, (Paris: Bernard Giovanangeli, 2020) p.111.

13   George Boyland recalled in his memoirs that the emperor 'arrived at Etain at 11 o'clock and was taking his ease at the Hôtel du Cygne while the noise of the battle at Rezonville could be distinctly heard in the distance. These circumstances were afterward told me by the proprietor of the Swan while I was dining in the very chair which Napoleon had occupied.' See Boyland, *Six Months*, p.58.

14   This according to the *Journal de marche* of the 1st Chasseurs d'Afrique. The war diary of the 3rd Chasseurs d'Afrique gives the time as 3:00 p.m.

15   Geoffrey Wawro, *The Franco-Prussian War, The German Conquest of France in 1870–71*, (Cambridge, New York, Cambridge University Press) p.149. In fact, the next time the two would meet would be 10 weeks later, when both were prisoners of the Prussian king in Wilhelmshöhe.

and performed ablutions in the station-masters glass, using his pocket handkerchief for a towel.[16]

The emperor was anxious to get underway and by the time a breathless staff officer galloped into Verdun with news that fighting had broken out at Rezonville, his train had already departed for Châlons.

## Bazaine Assumes Command

Meanwhile at Gravelotte, finally free of the emperor's presence, 'Marshal Bazaine found himself alone, master of his own destiny, freed from annoying interference' and 'could not refrain from expressing his delight in the most unequivocal terms.'[17] He had been informed the previous evening that it would probably be midday before 3 and 4 corps cleared Metz and despite reports of enemy activity on his flanks, almost as if to demonstrate his new found independence from the emperor, countermanded his earlier order for an early departure, informing Le Boeuf at 5.15 a.m. 'After giving consideration to your letter, I've decided to suspend the march of the army until after midday,' cautioning that: 'the danger for you is from the direction of Gorze, on the left of 2 and 6 corps.'[18] Evidently under the impression that the enemy did not present any immediate danger and despite Napoleon's explicit instruction that he should resume the retreat without delay, Bazaine issued a new directive to his corps commanders:

> Instructions for the morning of the 16th; Distribute any supplies you are sent by the Intendent General.[19] All civilian wagons employed by the auxiliary train will be sent to Gravelotte. The opportunity should be taken to send to Metz the sick who are to be placed in hospital. Make sure that all the men have their full complement of cartridges. If not, then have them distributed immediately and replenish supplies from the divisionary parks. Since our reconnaissance patrols have reported that the enemy

---

16  Rich, Elihu, *Germany and France a popular history of the Franco-German War Vol. I* (London: James Hagger, 1884) p.258.

17  Baron d'Andlau, Metz: *Campagne et Négotiations par un Officier Supérieur de l'Armée du Rhin* (Paris, Libraire Militaire de J. Dumaine, 1871) p.66.

18  L'État-Major, *16 Août Documents*, p.275. This warning reflected the contents of a note Frossard sent him at midnight on the 15th advising that a strong force of Germans had passed through Gorze at 9:00 p.m. making their way towards Verdun.

19  The immense supply column which left Metz late on August 15 carried the following: Bread: 6,000 rations each of 750g; Hard Tack: 94,633k or 172,050 rations of 550g, Flour: 76,006 k or 136,800 rations of 750g; Salt: 10,000 k or 600,000 rations of 16.05g; Coffee: 12,000k or 650,000 rations of 16g; Sugar: 13,000k or 619,000 rations of 21g; Wine: 50,851 or 20,340 rations of 25cl; Eau de Vie:19,879l or 318,004 rations of 6cl; Hay: 5,000k or 1,000 rations of 5k, Oats: 132,450k or 26,490 rations of 5k. During the morning of the 16th, the Intendance made a distribution of hard tack to 6 Corps, but following the battle most of these supplies were simply abandoned at the side of the road and set on fire as the wagons were commandeered to evacuate the wounded into Metz.

is not in force in the neighbourhood,[20] the men can pitch their tents[21] but should not go for water except in groups. Prevent anyone from leaving camp. The cavalry posts should be adjoined to the advance guards for the purpose of placing vedettes (by twos) as far as possible, in order to be warned in time of the approach of the enemy. The roads should remain free. All the baggage for the administration service should be placed in rear of that front by which is expected the enemy will attack. We shall probably leave in the afternoon as soon as I ascertain that the 3 and 4 corps have entirely arrived upon the heights (that is to say as far west on the northern road to Verdun as the 2 corps had advanced on the middle road). Further orders will be issued in due course. [22]

Bazaine's sudden change of mind and failure to issue timely directions coupled with poor French staff work, resulted in thousands of men standing around waiting for orders that never arrived. Within 2 Corps, the men had been roused at 2.00 a.m. for their breakfast soupe and were ready to march off at 4.30 a.m. Canrobert's men had been roused at the same time in accordance with Bazaine's previous warning order; at 8:00 a.m. he was just about to send a staff officer to find out the reason for the hold-up when news of the delayed departure arrived. Along with the other corps commanders he then received fresh instructions from Bazaine;

> It's imperative that you send me any intelligence about the strength of the enemy in your location and their precise position as quickly as possible … You should send out small patrols of cavalry … You should seek intelligence from local mayors and forestry officials … You should send out civilian spies and use locals to gather intelligence … All information gathered should be passed to me with the minimum of delay so that I can take the necessary measures which circumstances dictate.[23]

Such a directive to experienced corps commanders was unlikely to quash the growing concerns about his suitability as commander in chief and simply reinforces the picture of a man at a loss at what to do. Apparently resigned to relinquishing the strategic initiative to the enemy, he did not have long to wait for them to show their hand; around 6:00 a.m., Fauvart Bastoul's advance guard noted the presence of cavalry along the edge of the Bois de Vionville [24]

---

20  It is difficult to understand how Bazaine can have made such a statement given all the intelligence concerning the large numbers of Germans around Metz, the activity on his flanks and the warnings given to his corps commanders the previous evening about an anticipated attack by 30,000 men.

21  After the war, Bazaine wrote to Marshal Baraguey d'Hilliers concerning his order for the men to pitch their tents, giving the improbable explanation: 'It was a ruse to suggest to the enemy that it was not our intention to go to Verdun, but to manoeuvre around Metz. In a word, I didn't want to show him the direction of our retreat.' See l'État-Major *Rezonville*, p.141.

22  *Ibid*, p.136.

23  L'État-Major, *Rezonville*, pp.139–140. Having encouraged his corps commanders to seek information from local civilians, they typically ignored any intelligence provided; for example, when the Mayor of Gorze visited Frossard to inform him that the country to the south-west of Metz was awash with enemy troops, he dismissed him with the words: 'I know all that you have to tell me and you know nothing about the enemy forces.' See Robinson *Fall of Metz*, pp.62.

24  The advance guard was formed by the 66th Regiment; part of Bataille's 2nd division from Frossard's 2 Corps who bivouacked to the south of Rezonville. The previous evening Lieutenant Devaureix of the 66th obtained permission to conduct a reconnaissance towards the southwest with a handpicked

## The French Surprised

Captain Schirmer unlimbered his guns on hill 901 to the north-east of Tronville[40] and shortly after 9:00 a.m., opened fire on the unsuspecting men of Prince Murat's dragoon brigade as they fed and watered their horses. The surprise was complete: 'In the blink of an eye, the main road and the surrounding fields are swamped by a horde of fugitives, their numbers growing with each bivouac they come across. Civilian drivers, Prince Murat's dragoon, Forton's gunners, a frightened mob flees towards Metz, dragging with them their teams, limbers or even whole batteries.'[41] Camp fires were swiftly extinguished and cooking pots emptied as the troopers hurriedly saddled their horses and galloped off to the rear, the precipitous flight uncovering one of their batteries that had taken up position to the west of Vionville.

Körber moved his remaining artillery[42] into position on the left of Schirmer and engaged the enemy guns at a range of 1,500 paces. A squadron of French cuirassiers and another battery attempted to deploy north of Vionville, but coming under fire, they quickly withdrew which only added to the sense of panic. Körber leapfrogged his guns forward to the hillock south of Vionville alongside the cemetery, from where he continued to shell the enemy as they fell back on Rezonville. Shortly after Schirmer began firing on Murat's dragoons, the artillery attached to 6th Division's advance guard[43] unlimbered alongside his battery at Tronville. After sending a few rounds in the direction of the French camp, they moved up alongside Körber's battery, despite coming under heavy fire from the enemy infantry who had hurriedly taken up positions in Vionville.

As Rheinbaben cautiously manoeuvred 5th Division into position to the west of the French bivouac, from the south, 6th Cavalry made their way up the steep valley leading from Gorze onto the plateau overlooking Vionville. As Rauch's brigade advanced toward Flavigny, they were met with a fierce fire from Vergé's outpost line in the Bois de Vionville which forced them to retire and seek cover behind the Bois de Gaumont to the west of Auconville. Meanwhile, Diepenbroick-Grüters brigade, accompanied by the divisional horse artillery,[44] headed towards St Apolline Farm, a little to the east of Buxières and as the skirmishing intensified, were ordered to swing to the north.

After a difficult march during which one of his guns was left behind, Wittstock's battery came into action on the right wing of Grüters brigade, targeting a cavalry encampment to the west of Vionville. By chance rather than design, the guns opened fire shortly after Schirmer's battery started shelling Forton's cavalry; this only added to the confusion within the French command, giving them the misleading impression that they were under coordinated attacks from both south and west.[45]

---

40    Shown as hill 286 on French maps.
41    Pierre Lehautcourt, *Histoire de la Guerre de 1870–1871 Tome von Rezonville et Saint Privat* (Paris: Berger-Leverault et Cie, 1905) p.110.
42    1st, Frisch and 3rd Saalmüller, Horse Artillery, 10th Regiment and 1st, Bode, Horse Artillery, 4th Regiment.
43    Müllers 5th and Schlict's 6th Light batteries.
44    2nd Horse Artillery battery (Wittstock) 3rd Field Artillery Regiment.
45    In his account of the battle Frossard stated: 'Two simultaneous and clearly defined attacks were made against 2 Corps; one on its left flank through the Bois de Vionville and de St Arnould; the other on its right flank in front of Vionville.' See M.A. *The War of 1870–71* (London: Edward Bumpus, 1873) p.303.

Forton had originally intended to begin his day's march at 5:00 a.m. but after Bazaine postponed their departure, instructed his division to unsaddle and water their horses. Shortly before the Prussian guns opened fire, a dragoon officer in command of the division's piquet line, twice sent in warnings of approaching cavalry and artillery; a staff officer was despatched to investigate but returned after a cursory inspection saying it was of no significance. With no apparent threat, the order went out around 9:00 a.m. to take the horses to the drinking hole east of Vionville; one squadron per regiment was to remain at the ready whilst the other three were being watered.

The dragoons of Murat's brigade had barely commenced this task when a hail of shot exploded amongst their bivouacs. There was total panic; officers were unable to maintain order as troopers forced their way through a maze of abandoned baggage wagons and caissons that encumbered the main road. Frossard, surveying the scene from the height to the west of Vionville, ordered his horse artillery to join him; one section of the 7th battery 'mounted the hill at full gallop, cutting a passage through the middle of the horsemen who were falling back along the road in complete disorder.'[46] As Murat attempted to rally his dragoons, Bazaine arrived and ordered Forton to pull back and take up a new position to the north of Rezonville in the shelter of the Bois de Villers.

Gramont's cuirassiers were stationed to the rear of the dragoons and escaped the worst effects of the fire; after saddling their mounts, the brigade withdrew a few hundred yards seeking cover from the enemy guns, but concerned that his flank was open to attack by Bredow's cavalry and deprived of support following Murat's precipitous retreat, fell back again, this time rallying his squadrons a little to the rear of the dragoons. De Valabrègue's troopers,[47] who served as 2 Corps advance guard, saddled up and with commendable calm, withdrew in good order through the lines of de Villiers infantry taking up position north of Rezonville to the rear of Forton.

## French Reaction

With shells raining down on the French encampment, their artillery were the first to react: 'Most of our guns began firing with just two or three gunners. Little by little, their numbers grew as men who let themselves be drawn into the debacle, resumed their posts.'[48] The first battery into action was from Bataille's division who within five minutes, had deployed on hill 296 about 300 metres from their overnight parc.[49] Shortly after, they were joined by the 7th whose guns were positioned slightly to their front and left. The divisional mitrailleuses were watering their horses at Tronville when the shelling began, so Captain Dupré ordered his guns to be manhandled into position in front of their bivouac from where they engaged the enemy artillery on the heights behind Vionville; although given the range, some 2,800 metres, their fire had little effect.

As soon as his teams were harnessed, the battery moved alongside the others with the divisional ammunition and baggage train being sent to the rear, midway between Rezonville

---

46   L'État-Major, *Rezonville* pp.163–164.
47   De Valabrègue's brigade, 4th and 5th Chasseurs and Bachelier's brigade: 7th and 12th Dragoons.
48   Lehautcourt, *Rezonville*, p.110.
49   8/5th Artillery Regiment 2nd Division, 2 Corps.

and Gravelotte. Simultaneously, Colonel Baudoin sent 2 Corps' Reserve artillery[50] to the south of the main road, a few hundred metres west of Rezonville 'to be ready to act as required.'[51] To the north of the road, de Villiers batteries[52] also made ready; within 10 minutes his guns deployed in the intervals between their infantry, Grimaud in the centre, Heintz on the left, Delabrousse on the right. Whilst the teams from Tixier's divisional artillery[53] were being hooked in, Lieutenant Colonel de Montluisant[54] undertook a swift reconnaissance of the ground in front of Tronville where he intended to deploy the guns:

> I mounted my horse and galloped to the highest point of the plateau. The artillery fire increases on our left and the Prussians debouch from the woods near Vionville to our front. It is a double attack. I am almost in the centre and certainly on a decisive point which must be held at all costs. I order Captain Abord to occupy the left of the ridge, to hold it to the last extremity. I then place Blondel's battery alongside the other, with the same orders, all guns in echelon and at 30 metres from each other. I despatch Major Vignotti to post Ostler's battery someway to our right to clear the ground, search out the ravines and to do everything in its power to assure our position.[55]

The appearance of mysterious horsemen on the horizon had also aroused General Bataille's[56] curiosity and around 9:00 a.m., ordered Lieutenant Colonel Cools to 'investigate the identity of the troops advancing on Mars la Tour'[57] but almost immediately, shells started exploding in the French camp. With the flight of Forton's cavalry, 2 Corps unexpectedly found themselves in the front line, so Bataille ordered Beaulieu's 12th Chasseurs into Vionville whilst the remainder of Mangin's brigade made ready for action; the 1/8th occupied Flavigny, the 2nd and 3rd battalions taking position to their left. 1/23rd were to the rear of the chasseurs, the 3rd deployed to their right whilst part of the 2nd Battalion went to the support of the 8th.

As Mangin secured these key villages, Bataille accompanied Fauvart Bastoul's 2nd Brigade as they moved to the east of Flavigny to confront Mecklenburg's 6th Cavalry. Colonel Ameller led the 66th off to the left, despatching an advance guard down the track running to Chambley where, from the crest of the heights, they could monitor the woods to the south. Colonel Thibaudin followed with the 67th and took position to their rear. 1st Division's piquet line[58] opened fire on Rauch's troopers as they approached Flavigny and as Vergé's men stood to, a squadron of cavalry[59] was despatched to investigate this disturbance. Jolivet's 2nd Brigade[60]

---

50  10th and 11/5th, 6th and10/15th and 8/17th.
51  L'État-Major, *Rezonville* p.170.
52  5/14th, Grimaud, 6/14th, Heintz and 7/14th, Delabrousse, 3rd Division, 6 Corps.
53  5/8th, Abord, 12/8th, Blondel and 7/8th, Oster, 1st Division, 6 Corps who were bivouacked a little to the south near the Roman road.
54  Commander of Artillery 1st Division 6 Corps.
55  M.A. *The War*, pp.308–309.
56  Commander 2nd Division, 2 Corps.
57  L'État-Major, *16 Août Documents*, p.156. Cools was Valabrègue's chief of staff.
58  From the 55th Regiment.
59  3rd Squadron, 7th Dragoons.
60  76th and 77th regiments.

faced the northern edge of the Bois de Vionville, whilst Valazé deployed 1st Brigade[61] further to the right, between the wood and the track running from Rezonville to Chambley, facing southwest.

Colonel Février formed the 2nd and 3/77th in line of battle; the 1st Battalion was placed in reserve, a little to the rear of the crest of hill 311–312 where it was supported by the divisional artillery; the 76th being to the rear. On Valazé's right wing, the 1st and 2/55th were deployed in echelon of divisions, their left being pushed forward towards the Bois de Vionville and the 317 heights. The positions occupied were about 1,000 yards from the northern fringes of the wood, well within effective chassepot range but beyond the reach of the Dreyse.

The 3/55th was held back by Maison Blanche farm together with the 32nd which stood in line of battle as support. The brigade's battalion of chasseurs had been thrown into disarray by the flight of the civilian contractors and rallied a little to the rear, in a fold of ground that provided them with some cover from the shelling as they reformed their ranks. Picard, a second lieutenant in the 3rd Chasseurs described events:

> Towards eight we received the news that the cavalry reconnaissance had returned without finding anything and we were told to brew up. Fires were lit, pans were put on to cook and as for my part, I made my way towards Rezonville to oversee the distribution of supplies. Weapons were cleaned, rifles stripped. The batteries had unlimbered their teams and taken them to water. Such was the scene when towards 9:30 the artillery opened up which signalled the start of the battle. The distribution of supplies was quickly abandoned; I jogged back with my men to find the camp of the 3rd Battalion; it was under heavy fire. The men had left, leaving everything behind and were moving towards the main road where the commander and other officers were trying to rally the men; that's where I found them. There was a scene of indescribable confusion, the habitants of Vionville who fled shrieking, the cavalry who'd left for Rezonville at top speed, the conscripted wagon drivers who'd driven off at high-speed leaving their goods all over the road despite the efforts of the administrative officers to restore order. Shells swept the road and the surrounding ground to the south. A battery of the 5th artillery from Bataille's division whose teams were being watered turned up, deploying their guns about 1500 metres west of Rezonville, to the south of the main road, the artillerymen pushing the guns into place with their bare hands, without having time to don their jackets.[62]

## French Counter Attack

After deploying his infantry, Vergé ordered the divisional artillery into position along the crest of hill 311; Maréchal's 5th was first into line, followed soon after by Dupuy's 12th and the mitrailleuses of Besançon's 6th. Around 9:45 a.m., they opened fire on Stülpnagel guns as they unlimbered on the bare plateau to the west of the Bois de Vionville. As this artillery duel began,

---

61    3rd Chasseurs, 32nd and 55th regiments.
62    Lecaillon, *Été 1870*, pp.112–113.

the 1st and 2/55th Ligne engaged the Prussians, pushing their way forwards from Gorze, at a range of 400 metres. The 3/76th then moved up into the space between the 55th and the wood and began skirmishing with the enemy infantry.

To Vergé's left, following earlier sightings of the mysterious horsemen, Lapassat had gathered his generals together and briefed them on the defensive positions they were to occupy should they come under attack. When the shelling erupted, his brigade[63] quickly deployed around the farm at Maison Blanche, facing east towards the Bois des Ognons and south to cover the Bois St Arnould. On his right, the 1/84th were sent forward to screen the eastern slope of the Gorze ravine, the other battalions keeping watch over the valley running down to St Catherine. The 97th formed the second line[64] whilst the 3rd Lancers were despatched to the left wing to observe the trails that led into the Bois des Ognons as Dulon's battery[65] unlimbered on the crest of hill 308 facing south. Following this initial hasty deployment, Frossard's defensive line formed an arc that ran for some 3,000 metres from Vionville and Flavigny in the west to the woods of St Arnould in the south.

To the rear of 2 Corps' bivouac, the gunfire was clearly audible at Canrobert's headquarters in the Marie at Rezonville and although he was unable to see what was happening around Vionville, the sight of Forton's dragoons streaming to the rear, alerted him to the fact that all was not well. Again, reflective of the ingrained mindset of the French commanders, rather than despatching patrols to investigate and establish the facts for himself, he simply ordered his under strength corps into a defensive posture.

La Font de Villier's division[66] were bivouacked to the right rear of Bataille between the main road and the woods skirting the Roman road. When the shelling began, he ordered his artillery to engage the enemy as his infantry stood to arms and calmly dressed their ranks before moving to the high ground north-east of Rezonville. Becquet de Sonnay's 1st Brigade[67] deployed about 150 metres to the rear of the artillery, his regiments in echelon with the centre battalions forward, the 91st on the left covering the highway to Verdun, the 75th on the right parallel to the Roman road. From Colin's brigade, the 94th took position alongside the 91st, with the 93rd in the second line guarding their bivouac. Bisson's single regiment deployed along the lane running north from Rezonville at the junction with the old Roman road to the rear of de Villiers. Further north, Tixier's division stood to at their overnight bivouac between Villers aux Bois and Saint Marcel.

Further to the east around Gravelotte, General Bourbaki called the Imperial Guard to arms, his infantry fronting the valley that led south to Ars sur Moselle, so as to cover the army's open flank. Deligny's division of Voltigeurs were on the left wing, the bulk of his troops, formed in bataillons en masse, being arrayed in a double line to the south of the main road with 2nd Voltigeurs placing two battalions along the northern edge of the bois de Jurée. Picard's division

63  14th Chasseurs, 84th and 97th Line Regiments.
64  Assorted detachments from other regiments of 5 Corps formations including the 11th, 46th, 49th, 68th and 88th, were mixed in with the 97th.
65  7/2nd escorted by the 2nd Company of Chasseurs.
66  3rd Division, 6 Corps.
67  The 75th and 91st.

of Grenadiers was placed south of the highway; 1st Brigade[68] rested on the road, 2nd Brigade[69] was to the left, its wing refused, to watch over the bois des Ognons and the route that led down to Ars sur Moselle through the Mance Ravine. Two batteries[70] took position to the rear of Jeanningros, another[71] escorted by a squadron of Guides, unlimbered on Poittevin's left wing; a company of the 2/2nd Grenadiers and the 1/3rd Grenadiers were pushed a little way into the bois des Ognons to provide additional security against any attack from this direction. 1st Guard Cavalry Brigade were parcelled out to support the infantry divisions with the 3rd being retained by General Desvaux as reserve.

## German Reaction

As General Bülow urged forward the divisional and corps artillery reserve to support Rheinbaben's attack, the guns already in action found it increasingly hard to maintain their positions in the face of heavy chassepot fire, having to resort to case shot to repel the enemy skirmishers threatening to overrun their position. Montluisant's three batteries engaged Körber's horse artillery shortly after they appeared on the heights south of Vionville. A little later, de Villiers and Bataille's divisional artillery added their support, the combined firepower of these nine batteries inflicting considerable damage on his isolated guns. Having secured Vionville and Flavigny, Mangin now ordered the 1/8th to send two companies in skirmish formation to the crest of the heights between the two villages from where they could bring Körber's guns under fire at a range of less than 900 metres. With the enemy batteries seemingly unsupported, he ordered the charge to be sounded and as the 8th and 23rd surged forward 'the position of the batteries at Vionville already became critical.'[72]

The French infantry continued to close on the enemy, with Müller's team losing a number of horses to their fire as he attempted to pull his guns back from their exposed position. Becke ordered his artillery to withdraw to the reverse slope of the heights and the batteries,[73] unable to withstand the heavy chassepot, mitrailleuse and cannon fire, began a general retreat. One team, belonging to Schlicht's battery was cut down; its gun was abandoned and only recovered with some difficulty by a detachment led by Lieutenant Maas.

Bredow's cavalry, seeking cover from the hail of fire,[74] withdrew to make room for the artillery and took up a new position in the rear of Barby's brigade whilst the 10th Hussars sought shelter behind du Sauley farm. To the east, the chassepot fire had driven Diepenbroick-Grüters cavalry off the plateau and deprived of their support, Wittstock's battery also fell back from their exposed position along the northern edge of the Bois de Gaumont, finding shelter in the ravine by Auconville.

---

68    General Jeanningros, Guard Zouaves and 1st Grenadier Guard.
69    General Le Poittevin de la Croix, 2nd and 3rd Grenadier Guard.
70    4th and 6th (m) batteries of the Field Artillery Regiment of the Guard.
71    3rd battery Field Artillery Regiment of the Guard.
72    E Hoffbauer, *The German Artillery in the battles Near Metz* (London, Henry S. King & Co, 1874) p.80.
73    Bode's battery, which enjoyed the shelter of the poplars lining the main road, escaped the worst of the fire and were able to remain in action throughout.
74    Not all French cannon fire was so deadly; German observers commented that their fire, although brisk, was not very effective at first; the shells either exploded well short of their intended target or exploded mid-air, generally at a height of 100 feet, with the balls flying over their heads.

Following close on the heels of the retreating guns, Mangin's infantry were on the point of overrunning Körber's batteries when III Corps artillery fortuitously arrived on the plateau. Beck brought forward 6th Division's heavies[75] from du Sauley farm to a slight rise to the south-west of Flavigny, the guns coming into action around 10:00 a.m. Thirty minutes later, as Mangin's battalions occupied the crest recently vacated by Körber's artillery, Major Lentz galloped forward with the corps horse artillery division[76] and taking station on hill 271 south of Flavigny, raked the flank of the advancing troops, forcing them to withdraw to the shelter of Vionville and Flavigny. Schlicht then resumed his position in the firing line, unlimbering his guns alongside those of Lenz, before Wittstock galloped forward, deploying on their right flank. Bülow instructed Colonel von Dresky[77] to assume command of these batteries, who related:

I received no orders at Tronville and therefore moved on Vionville. I had just commanded two horse artillery batteries to unlimber, when General von Bülow told me to go and occupy, with the corps artillery, the hill which runs east to west to the south of Flavigny and hold my ground there. General von Alvesleben warned me that the corps artillery was intended to form the centre of his position and that he counted fully on me to hold my ground. I gave orders to limber up again and, while the Horse Artillery Brigade were doing so, pushed on quickly to the front to search for a point where we might cross the deep and marshy ditch which extends to the west from Flavigny. I found a bridge at Tantelainville, on the other side of which the hill on which I was to take position rises immediately from the stream in a steep slope. Before leaving the bridge, I examined its situation in order to make sure that it could not be commanded by the enemy's fire. The nearest place occupied by the enemy was Flavigny. I could see only infantry there, the distance between us being, as I judged, about 1,600 paces; for this reason, I did not consider that there was any danger to be anticipated in passing the bridge. But at the moment when the head of the brigade was about to cross it, we suddenly received from Flavigny such a hail of chassepot bullets that one officer, the trumpet-major, three men and six horses were hit. I sounded the 'Gallop!' upon which the guns and wagons which had not been hit quickly crossed the bridge and found an immediate shelter behind the hill, which here has a very steep slope. The troops re-formed and we gained our first position without any further loss. The gun which we had been obliged to leave behind was quickly repaired; it re-joined the battery after a short time, without suffering any other damage, though the infantry fire continued from Flavigny. After the Horse Artillery Brigade had taken up its position on the hill near the bridge, I opened fire against Flavigny. Our shells soon set the farm in flames. When the French abandoned it, I advanced in echelon and pursued the enemy with a fairly effective fire.[78]

75    5th Heavy, Eunicke, 6th Heavy, Meinecke Field batteries, 3rd Field Artillery Regiment.
76    1st, Scheringer and 3rd Rödenbeck, Horse artillery batteries 3rd Field Artillery Regiment.
77    Commander of 3rd Field Artillery Regiment which provided the 3 Corps artillery reserve.
78    Prince Karl August Eduard Friedrich Kraft zu Hohenlohe Ingelfingen, *Letters on Artillery* (London: Edward Stanford, 1890) pp.96–97.

Half an hour later, after an approach march of four miles along poorly made roads, the guns of 2nd Field Division[79] from the corps' Reserve, under Captain Stumpf, reached the outskirts of Tronville and were immediately ordered into the gun line by Bülow. 3rd Heavy was the first to deploy on the left of Dresky who was still under heavy French fire and soon after, around 11:45 a.m., the remainder of the corps artillery reserve went into action. Dresky recalled:

> At this moment the Field batteries arrived and when the enemy had evacuated Vionville and Flavigny and had retired to Rezonville, I advanced the whole of the corps artillery in echelons and arranged my troops in such a manner that the two batteries under Captain Stumpf stood together to the north of Flavigny, while the whole of the remainder were on the south of the place. The horse artillery was on the right and its flank rested on the slope of the hill marked 311/998. The left wing of 5th Division was at this point; and here, on account of the excellent view to be obtained from it, I remained with Generals von Stülpnagel and von Schwerin during the greater part of the battle. I occupied this position at 2 p.m. and I remained there until 7 p.m.[80]

## Germans March to the Sound of the Guns

As 5th and 6th Cavalry Divisions probed the French positions, Stülpnagel's infantry began their advance from Gorze along the road leading to Rezonville. Major General von Döring[81] ordered two companies of the II/8th Lieb Guard Grenadiers into St Thiebault farm, another two occupied the hamlet of Côte Musa whilst 1st and 2nd Squadron's 12th Dragoons pushed out of the valley onto the plateau in front of the Bois de Vionville. The cavalry were met with the same welcome from the skirmishers lining the wood that previously greeted Rauch's brigade and seeking cover from their chassepot fire, galloped away to the south-west to the rear of Anconville farm. Following their repulse, Colonel von Garrelts sent two battalions from the 48th, with orders to clear the wood and move onto Flavigny; the 1st was to the left of the sunken road from Gorze to Flavigny, II on the right, each battalion forming two lines.

Pushing forward the 48th was opposed by tirailleurs deployed by the 1st and 2/55th[82] who in turn, were supported by skirmishers from the 3/66th.[83] To their left, Colonel Février led the 2nd and 3/77th Ligne[84] into the northwest corner of the Bois de Vionville. The 76th were initially held back in reserve but Jolivet committed the 1st and part of the 2/77th on the right of the 55th, who then engaged the II/48th in the woodland on the eastern slopes of the valley leading down to Gorze.

Noting the positions taken up by 2 Corps and illustrative of the aggressive mindset of the Prussian officer, Döring briefed Stülpnagel: 'The French are deploying; they're stronger than

---

79    3rd Heavy Field battery, Vosz, 4th Heavy Field battery, Fromme, 3rd Light Field battery, Pressentin, 4th Light Field battery, Müller.
80    Ingelfingen, *Letters on Artillery*, p.98.
81    Commander of the advance guard.
82    From Valazé's 1st Brigade, 1st Division, 2 Corps.
83    From Fauvart Bastoul's 1st Brigade, 2nd Division, 2 Corps.
84    From Jolivet's 2nd Brigade, 1st Division, 2 Corps.

us but don't have any depth. If 10th Brigade advance on my left wing and get behind them, then we'll push them back. Tell the General to send me the artillery.'[85] Lieutenant Colonel Kit Pemberton, another English journalist attached to the Second Army, accompanied the infantry as they made their way to the battlefield noting:

> Long before we reached the plain the unpleasant whistling sensation overhead told us that the enemy were making but average practice at the troops in front, but admirable for those in rear of them. So, we quickly found that 'distance leant no enchantment to the view' and, practically, that the nearer you were the safer you were. Soon we came upon the 'Krankenträger', carrying back their ghastly loads and each of the various little wisps of blue, which were coiled up in every describable shape and form, represented what a few minutes previously had been one of God's creatures, but which was now '6,436, Hans Schultz, tod am schlacht des 16'. One poor boy struck me; he was about seventeen and what is called a 'Fähnrich' or ensign. He was lying with his sword in his right hand, pointing towards the enemy, haven fallen on his right side and must have died instantly, as the left hand, grasping his left side, told too plainly where the fatal bullet had struck him. He had his gloves on, which first attracted my attention; and his face, which was turned upwards, betrayed none of the emotions that it must have exhibited as the bullet struck him, for he looked wrapped in the softest slumber.[86]

Towards 10:00 a.m. 1st Light battery under Captain Stöphasius deployed on the open ground to the left of the 48th, but under fire from the 55th and the 3/66th, suffered heavy losses coming into action, with three of his guns being temporarily disabled. Undeterred, he opened a rapid fire at a range of 800 paces against the hostile skirmishers, eventually driving them back, which created space for two more batteries[87] to unlimber on his right, although this aggressive handling of the artillery, deployed in the van of the division's advance, inevitably resulted in heavy casualties.

Knobbe's 2nd Heavy battery was initially ordered to remain in reserve as the restricted ground meant that it would have blocked the road but given the desperate situation, he nonetheless moved forward and went into action on the left of the gun line. Döring then called up the remainder of his brigade, leaving just a single battalion, III/8th Lieb Guard Grenadiers in Gorze. The two grenadier battalions advanced towards Rezonville whilst the fusiliers of the 48th formed up in two lines at Auconville farm and moved into the firing line on the left of the Stöphasius's guns, their axis of attack being the track running north-east from Chambley towards Rezonville. 3rd Rifles moved through the woods in support of the 48th, leaving behind a single company to occupy the farm. Stülpnagel quickly reacted to the sound of fighting in the woods to his right; instead of marching towards Flavigny as originally ordered, he directed the remainder of his division to support Garrelts and the advance guard.

As two companies[88] of the 8th Lieb Guard struggled through the Bois de St Arnould against the stubborn resistance of Lapassat's brigade, both I and II Battalions were drawn into the fight.

---

85   L'État-Major, *Rezonville*, p.197.
86   Rich, *Germany and France*, p.359.
87   1st Heavy, Nöldecke and 2nd Light, Vollbrecht, commanded by Major Gallus.
88   5th and 8th under Major von Verschner.

Finally, after calling up the fusilier battalion from Gorze, the 8th slowly pushed the skirmishers back, although on 9th Brigade's left wing, the attack by the III/48th ended in disaster. Major Selle led forward one company in a frontal assault on the French line whilst Lieutenant Colonel von Estocq attempted to manoeuvre the others around their wing. The colonel's men were then hit in the flank by a counter attack from the 3/66th, the 48th flooding back in complete disorder to the shelter of the Bois de Gaumont, losing most of their officers and some 600 men.

By now, Frossard had eight and half battalions deployed along the crest of the plateau between the Rezonville-Chambley road and the Bois de Vionville and after driving back the infantry escorting Stülpnagel's batteries, Fauvart Bastoul urged his brigade forward in an attempt to roll up the Prussian gunline. The 1st and 2/66th were echeloned along the crest of the plateau to the right of the 3rd Battalion whilst Colonel Thibaudin deployed the 2nd and 3/67th around hill 314.[89] This placed Stülpnagel in a precarious situation; outnumbered, his guns were under fire from the tirailleurs of the 55th and the 76th as well as being targeted by Vergés divisional artillery, some 1,800 metres away on hill 311.

In response to his urgent calls for assistance, the leading battalion[90] from General von Schwerin's 10th Brigade,[91] advanced at the double from Gorze. Without waiting for his troops to deploy, Major Count Schlippenbach launched his company columns against the 66th and 67th Ligne on the crest of height 312, their counter attack thwarting the French attempt to flank the gun line. As they engaged Fauvert Bastoul's men in a fierce fire fight, the I/52nd were in turn, hit in the flank as Colonel Thibaudin suddenly appeared on their left at the head of the 1/67th. After giving the Prussians a volley, the 67th charged with the bayonet and with their officers all wounded, Schlippenbach's men were pushed back into the woods.

It was now approaching 11:00 a.m. and as the fighting intensified, von Döring fell mortally wounded. Reinforcements in the shape of Colonel von Wulffen at the head of the 52nd ascended the heights; with II Battalion on the left, the fusiliers to the right, he charged forward crashing into the French. Attacked in front and with the II/12th threatening his flank, Thibaudin's men were thrown back at point of bayonet towards Flavigny.

Meanwhile on the right of Stülpnagel's position, the struggle continued unabated in the woods; by 11:00 a.m., I and II/48th, despite losing many officers, inched forward to the edge of the Bois de Vionville in the direction of Flavigny as the Lieb Guard struggled to force their way through the Bois St Arnould. With the outcome of this contest still in the balance, unexpected reinforcements arrived in the shape of Colonel Lyncker's detachment who had been sent to support Lehman's 37th Brigade at Chamley.

After crossing the Moselle at Nouvéant, they had made their way to Gorze when the noise of gunfire was heard from the plateau. Lyncker immediately placed his attached battery at Stülpnagel's disposal, deploying II and III/78th to protect his gunline. Reinforced, Stülpnagel's artillery[92] slowly edged forward and by noon, the left of the gun line lay close to the intersection

---

89    The 1/67th were held back in reserve, covering the breach that had opened up in the French line between the Bataille's two brigades.
90    I/52nd.
91    II and Fusilier battalion, 52nd and II and Fusilier battalion 12th regiments.
92    With Knaur's battery this now had a strength of 30 guns.

of the Gorze–Flavigny and Buxières–Rezonville roads,[93] its right resting on the corner of the Bois de Vionville.[94]

Vergé's artillery struggled to hold their own when confronted by these reinforcements; at a range of 1,800 metres his mitrailleuses had little effect so were pulled out of the line, which left just two batteries to oppose the massed firepower of the Prussian artillery which now turned its attention to the French infantry. Exposed to the combined force of Dresky's and Stülpnagel's guns, Fauvert Bastoul's and Valazé's men suffered heavy losses[95] and by 11:30 a.m., both brigades were falling back towards the shelter of Rezonville.

To their left, Jolivet's men were engaged in a bloody close quarter combat in the Bois de St Arnould; Vergé's retreat had exposed his right flank, so he ordered his brigade to withdraw to the crest of the ridge overlooking the northern edge of the Bois de Vionville, whilst to his left 1/84th, 3/55th and 2/84th formed a new defensive line watching over the northern edge of the Bois de St Arnould. Further east, around Maison Blanche farm, the remainder of La Passat's brigade continued to fend off the Lieb Guard's attempts to force a passage through the woods towards Rezonville.

With the fusiliers of the 12th and the II/52nd pressing forward onto Flavigny, Schwerin gathered the remainder of his brigade around the still uncommitted II/12th, assembling his troops on both sides of the track that led from Rezonville to Buxières. Reinforcements arrived in the shape of 6th Company 64th Regiment; assigned to escort III Corps Headquarters they were unable to re-join their division and instead made their way to the scene of the fighting and although few in number, the hard-pressed Stülpnagel was grateful for every man he could lay his hands on.

From the heights south of Tronville, the Prussian command watched the developing action with a growing sense of unease about just how few troops they had at their disposal to counter the forces opposed to them. It was dawning on Caprivi that this was no mere rearguard action and conceding it was probable that they were confronted by the bulk of the Bazaine's army, sent an urgent despatch to Voights Rhetz at Thiacourt, asking him to bring X Corps forward without delay.

Although Alvesleben still refused to believe they faced the whole of Bazaine's army, even he acknowledged that they were confronted by superior forces; with Rheinbaben's cavalry and Stülpnagel's infantry struggling to maintain their positions, he took the view that only forceful action could convince the French that they were opposed by a sizeable force and prevent them from brushing aside his men and continuing their way to Verdun. His aggressive deployment of the divisional and Reserve artillery characterised the Prussian officer corps talent for improvisation and audacity, as with all his available assets committed, Alvesleben had to buy time pending the arrival of 6th Division.

---

93   The cross roads were held by the advance guard of Schwerin's 10th Brigade.
94   The wood was occupied by the 48th and 3rd Rifles.
95   The 67th lost 8 officers killed, 18 wounded, 54 men killed, 126 wounded and 296 missing. A subsequent analysis revealed just how effective the guns were; out of 411 casualties, 315 were caused by artillery, 96 by rifle fire.

## 6th Division Enter the Battle

In accordance with Alvesleben's orders, Buddenbrock resumed his march to Jarny, seeking to intercept the French as they made their way to Verdun and by 11:00 a.m., was approaching the outskirts of Tronville. Here, he received fresh instructions to wheel right and advance on Vionville without delay: 'The enemy appears to be attacking General von Stülpnagel, in great force. General von Buddenbrock will advance with all of his forces in line.'[96] Halting his men, who had already been on the march under the hot August sun for six hours, he galloped off to reconnoitre and noting the strength of the forces defending Vionville, gave orders for his division to deploy.

To the left, 12th Brigade advanced along both sides of the main highway; the 64th launching a two-pronged attack on the village from the west and north, whilst the 24th formed a refused echelon, covering their left flank against any attack out of Tronville Copse. On the right, 11th Brigade moved forward parallel to the track running from Tronville to Vionville, the 35th Fusiliers leading the way, the 20th in the rear. As noted by their regimental history:

> From time-to-time small clouds of smoke could be seen dancing high in the air. French shrapnel exploded with a crackling noise and struck the ground, but without reaching the flat heights behind which the brigade was situated. As yet the impressions were not sufficiently serious to stop the mouths of the jokers; 'Levi, cheer up' said a private of the 2nd company to his front rank man; 'We are going to the fair; they are tearing up the calico.' There was soon enough to be an end to the merriment and wanton wit. The mouth that made the above remark was closed for ever before an hour had passed. 'Packs off!' ordered the battalion commanders. A few minutes later, on the order of the brigade commander, Fusilier Regiment No 35, which was in the 1st line, was deployed into fighting formation. The 20th Regiment followed at 2nd line distance, having the fusilier battalion on the right flank.[97]

The fusiliers deployed all three battalions in line; I directed on Vionville, II towards the cemetery to the south of the village, with III on Flavigny. In concert with Buddenbrock's attack, Becke again ordered forward 5th Cavalry's horse artillery to provide fire support to the assault; 1st Battery deployed alongside Bode's guns which had remained in action throughout, whilst the 2nd and 3rd reoccupied their former positions on cemetery hill, the guns escorted by a squadron from 2nd Dragoon Guards.

To meet this impending attack, Mangin occupied the villages with the 12th Chasseurs, 23rd and 93rd Ligne,[98] whilst the 8th took up position around the watering hole to the north of Flavigny. With Bülow's artillery providing support from the cemetery heights to the south, Buddenbrock's men commenced their assault; III/35th were on the right wing of 11th Brigade's advance, one company fronting towards Vionville, the other three approaching to within

96    Lanza, *Franco-German War*, p.460.
97    Colonel H. T. Hildyard A. A. G, 'Précis of the Regimental History of the 3rd Brandenburg Infantry Regiment (No 20) During the Campaign of 1870–71', *Royal United Services Institution. Journal*. 35:163, 972–1027, DOI: 10.1080/ 03071849109416687 p.977.
98    From Colin's 2nd Brigade, 3rd Division, 6 Corps.

400 paces of Flavigny. The II/35th deployed in two lines and attacked the watering hole; the companies leading the assault divided, with the 6th veering to the south against Flavigny, the 7th to the north, where they stumbled into men from 1st Battalion assaulting Vionville.

As the two rear companies descended from the heights, they were hit with a hail of fire from the defenders and fell back to reform, seeking cover within the cemetery south of the village. The 20th followed the fusiliers and received a similar warm welcome: 'Shells plunged into the ground in front and between the battalions, shrapnel burst high over the men's heads; it appeared almost to be a miracle that the regiment did not suffer heavy losses.'[99] In view of the heavy fire, two battalions were ordered to remain in reserve in the shelter of the small valley east of Tronville, whilst III Battalion supported the attack against the two strong points. The 64th advanced along the highway with orders to seize Vionville; the fusilier battalion, originally in the second line, swung out to the flank with the aim of attacking the village from the north and in concert with the 11th and 12th companies, pushed through the southern part of Tronville Copse without meeting any opposition.

As they moved into position, Colonel von Wunsch wheeled the 9th and 10th companies to the right and followed by the 11th, launched an assault on the village. Simultaneously at the head of II/64th, Major von Görschen led his men against the west of Vionville, whilst to his left, I Battalion, deployed in skirmish formation, laid down a heavy suppressive fire onto the defenders. Attacked from three sides and running low on ammunition, the 1/23rd and 12th Chasseurs had little option other than to pull back.[100]

Although Vionville finally fell to 6th Division's attack around 11:30 a.m.,[101] Mangin's brigade stubbornly held onto their positions on the high ground overlooking the village which prevented any further advance by the Brandenburgers. As the struggle continued, Buddenbrock's last uncommitted regiment, the 24th, pushed one battalion into Tronville Copse, the others taking position in the corner of the wood nearest Vionville. After dropping off the 8th Company as reserve, Major von Rechtern led II Battalion out of the wood, along a shallow valley running north towards the Roman road.

General Péchot[102] defended this sector of the French line and positioned one of his regiments[103] at the southern edge of the Bois de Saint Marcel to cover the batteries[104] engaging the Prussian guns west of Vionville. To oppose Rechtern's advance, Péchot placed two battalions along the edge of the wood, whilst a third was pushed forward on his left at an angle so as to enfilade the Prussian attack; as a precaution he also called up the 4th Ligne from Saint Marcel as support.

---

99  Hildyard, '*Précis*', p.977.
100 The after action report of the 12th Chasseurs drafted by Commandant Jouanne Beaulieu is short and to the point: 'Taking position between the villages of Rezonville and Vionville, the battalion received the first blows of the Prussian army; forced to abandon the village, the chasseurs fell back step by step. Losses, five officers killed, 6 wounded; 266 chasseurs killed, wounded or missing.' See l'État-Major, *16 Août Documents* pp.163–164.
101 Some accounts claim that it was after midday when the village fell to the Prussian attack; other sources state the village changed hands a number of times in the fierce fighting before the French eventually fell back.
102 Commander 1st Brigade, 1st Division 6 Corps.
103 10th Ligne.
104 9th and 10/11th and 8/8th (m) from Aymard's 4th Division.

In danger of being overwhelmed, Rechtern ordered forward his reserves from Tronville Copse and subsequently deployed all three battalions in line.[105]

Although Vionville had been secured, Buddenbrock's men were under constant fire from the French divisional batteries located on the high ground overlooking the village and suffered heavy casualties. To make matters worse, his artillery was running low on ammunition, with some guns having to cease fire so as to conserve their limited supply.[106] Alert to the threat, Péchot posed to his left wing, he sent the 2/20th forward from the east of Tronville and then ordered the divisional artillery[107] to relocate to a new position closer to Vionville from where it could provide more effective fire support to the beleaguered 24th.

By this time, all Alvesleben's infantry and artillery had been committed and lacking any other reserves, he called forward the cavalry to help sustain his overstretched fighting line; Bredow and Barby's brigades took up position[108] to the rear of 6th Division; Mecklenburg's cavalry formed up on the right wing of Schwerin's 10th Brigade. The pressure on 6th Division was becoming unbearable; unwilling to retreat and abandon his hard-won gains, Alvesleben therefore gambled on renewing his attack so as to drive the French from their commanding positions overlooking Vionville. As related in the Brandenburger's regimental histories;

> Already fresh troops were drawn into the fighting line, which covered the ground about the poplar copse with renewed showers of lead. It was not possible to remain here. Already some of the troops began to waver. A retrograde movement must inevitably lead to destruction, unless a line of cover could be reached. 'Forward,' was therefore the cry on all sides, 'up to the road.' A new lusty hurrah! And the road is also in the hands of the Brandenburg Regiments. It was just noon …This success had certainly been purchased by the regiment with heavy sacrifice. On their way to the road the six companies had been lost in killed and wounded, 19 officers and about 300 men.[109]

Major Stockern brought up his last reserves[110] massing them in sheltered ground between the village and the cemetery before, in concert with the 35th, they edged towards the heights; at the

---

105  From right to left, 5th Company, 6th, 7th, 3rd, 1st, 2nd, 4th, 11th, 12th, 9th, 10th. The 8th, in reserve, was also subsequently fed into the line.
106  Meinecke's battery expended all the ammunition in its limbers, in the first line wagons and an ammunition wagon belonging to another battery. After reserving five common shells per gun for emergencies, it held fire for an hour until the second line wagons to arrive, although the guns remained in the firing line throughout.
107  5th Light battery at first followed by Beck's two Heavy batteries.
108  On the western slopes of hill 901 between Vionville and Mars la Tour.
109  Hildyard, 'Précis', p.981. A footnote records that during the attack 'Suddenly Lieutenant Wegener fell and struggled convulsively. 'Shot through the heart' remarked the major to Colonel von Flatow. After a few minutes Wegener made signs to have his neck loosened. This was done and a few minutes later he was standing up fresh and unhurt. It appeared that when standing with lips parted to take breath on the summit, a chassepot bullet had passed between them, literally taking away his wind. A few days later a thick scar showed itself on each lip.' A lucky escape.
110  The I/20th. During the regiments advance, their commander 'passed along the firing line, he found the Colour bearer of the 1st Battalion, with Colours, alone 30 paces behind. If he had been hit and the battalion had moved on, the Colours would have remained there. He was therefore, ordered up with the Colours into the line'. See Hildyard, 'Précis', p.982.

same time, the 64th charged forward from Vionville, advancing on his left.[111] Buddenbrock's men pushed forward 1,000 paces and after a 'long and embittered struggle'[112] during which the copse changed hands several times, his men advanced 1,000 paces, finally dislodging the French from their stronghold and driving them from their positions on the heights. The 64th claimed to have seized a gun abandoned by the French horse artillery in their precipitous retreat[113] and at the suggestion of Colonel von Voights Rhetz,[114] two squadrons of cavalry[115] were launched against Pouget and Colin's brigades as they withdrew, but their presumptuous charge was driven off with heavy losses.

## 2 Corps Fall Back In Disorder

Following the fall of Vionville, Bataille ordered Mangin to fall back on Rezonville, but under constant shelling from the artillery to his front and flank, the withdrawal quickly degenerated into a rout and he only succeeded in rallying his men around Gravelotte. With 1st Brigade no longer capable of offering effective resistance, de Villiers[116] moved two of 6 Corps regiments forward to help stabilise the line. The 91st deployed between the watering hole and the small copse 300 metres to the north of the main road but as their 1st Battalion advanced towards Vionville, it was hit at close range by heavy rifle fire and withdrew in disarray to the northeast. The 2nd, shaken by their retreat also fell back to the east.

The 94th were formed in line of battle facing south-west along the crest of 312 and after executing a sharp change of front to face south, advanced at the double under heavy enemy shellfire to support the beleaguered 1/8th defending Flavigny; 1/94th targeted the guns around Vionville cemetery, the 3rd engaged the batteries to the south around the crossroads at Sainte Marie. As this French redeployment was underway two battalions from 10th Brigade[117] who pushed across the plateau from Gorze, added their weight to the assault against Flavigny, their efforts being supported by 3/35th who moved up from Tronville. With covering fire being given by the guns on cemetery hill, they edged closer to the hamlet although at first, only the skirmishing divisions of the 10th and 11th Fusilier companies were able to secure a toehold in the buildings on the outskirts, the remainder being driven off by the heavy chassepot fire. Flavigny, obscured by clouds of smoke and with terrified cattle stampeding through the streets, presented a dreadful sight;

> This small village, bombarded by nine or ten batteries, nearly 60 guns, was soon in flames and no longer offered its defenders shelter against the Prussian shells which fell there en masse in an incessant torrent. After most of the buildings had been set

---

111  4th 3rd 2nd 1st 9th 10th 11th 5th 7th 8th 12th      1st 2nd 4th      1st 2nd 4th 7th 11th
  64th                20th        35th
112  Clarke, *The Franco-German War*, appendices, p.373.
113  No such loss was recorded in the French accounts.
114  III Corps' chief of staff.
115  From 17th Brunswick Hussars and 2nd Dragoon Guards; the latter squadron lost 70 horses in the attack indicating that the French infantry initially withdrew in good order.
116  Commander, 3rd Division, 6 Corps.
117  The III/12th and II/52nd from Schwerin's Brigade.

ablaze by the artillery, Schwerin's infantry charged forward again, three companies enveloping the defenders from the west.[118]

Surprised by the sudden appearance of enemy infantry moving up from the south, the 94th broke and fled to the rear. With their flank suddenly exposed by this collapse, the 1/8th abandoned Flavigny, forsaking their wounded who were captured by the Brandenburger's as they finally stormed the village. To fill this sudden gap in his defence, de Villiers pushed forward the 75th who deployed in line of battle along the crest of height 312 north-west of Rezonville. For half an hour, the regiment held its ground under intense rifle and cannon fire before it too, gave way, the survivors seeking shelter on the reverse slope of the ridge. 6 Corps artillery similarly struggled to maintain their position on the exposed plateau in the face of superior numbers; their commander, Lieutenant Colonel de Montluisant recalling how the Prussians:

> Attempted to crush us by a formidable battery of more than 40 guns at 2,200 metres from us. Our twelve little 4 pounders hold their own well. The ground about us is soft, their shells sink into it, then explode and cover us with showers of splinters, which for the most part are harmless. My horse is struck ten times but not once seriously. Had the ground been hard we should have been annihilated. At noon more than 40 men are already killed or wounded, 50 horses on the ground. I send Major Vignotti to inform the Marshal and to demand reinforcements.[119]

Another French gunner left this description of the effectiveness of the enemy artillery:

> We arrived under a hail of grapeshot; fourteen horses were killed. We lost a limber and a caisson was destroyed. The 'conducteurs' were unable to bring the teams forward. The Colonel and the Commandant were laid up in the village. We were utterly pummelled, only the Captain and Lieutenant remained with the battery and by their example they kept the men at their guns. The Lieutenant and his adjutant aimed the pieces without the help of the gunners. The adjutant loaded; a shell bursts at his feet and shrapnel punctures his kidneys; two maréchaux de logis were killed and four wounded; six men dead and eight wounded. The 4th battery fell back on our left with five gunners. An hour later we limbered up the guns. The Lieutenant and his men dragged the guns back to the village in the midst of a hailstorm of shrapnel.[120]

It was now around 12:15 a.m. and with his division falling back around him, de Villiers committed his last reserve, the 93rd, in an attempt to stabilise the line. Keeping three companies to hand, he deployed nine[121] as tirailleurs who engaged the left wing of the Prussian line at a range of less than 400 metres. Villers then placed another six[122] to the north of the main road, forming a dense skirmish line which advanced to within 700 metres of the enemy line. In addition, two

118  L'État-Major, *Rezonville*, p.268.
119  M.A. *The War*, p.309.
120  Lecaillon, *Été 1870*, pp.116–116.
121  2nd Battalion and three from the 1st.
122  Three from both the 1st and 3rd battalions.

battalions[123] were sent to reinforce Péchot's position with Tixier deploying the remainder of le Roy de Dais' 2nd Brigade[124] in a line running north-west from the left rear of Vincendon's 4th Ligne, to the edge of the Bois de Saint Marcel.

## Le Boeuf and Ladmirault's Inactivity

Meanwhile, at his headquarters in le Bagneux farm Marshal Le Boeuf was growing increasingly impatient; his aide-de-camp, Colonel d'Ornant, was sent to Gravelotte for orders only to be told by Bazaine: 'Hold your position until I issue new instructions.'[125] When cannon fire erupted around Vionville, he was still without instructions and merely drew his forces together around Saint Marcel. Aymard arrived on the outskirts of the village about 10:00 a.m. and his divisional artillery were sent forward to shield the corps deployment; one battery[126] was sited to cover the valley that ran from Saint Marcel to the Bois de Tronville, the others[127] positioned to the west of the Bois Saint Marcel.

At 11:30 a.m., some two hours after the opening salvo's crashed into Forton's camp, Bazaine finally galloped up to Le Boeuf and ordered Aymard to deploy along the Rezonville-Mars la Tour highway; Brauer's brigade[128] were brought forward and the 11th Chasseurs and 3/60th occupied the gardens and hedgerows around Rezonville. The 3/44th was held in reserve whilst the remaining battalions[129] formed line of battle along the slight ridge running south-east from Saint Marcel wood.

At the same time, General Sanglé-Ferrière placed his brigade[130] in line of battalions 'en colonne de division' to the rear of Tixier's reserves[131] after first positioning four companies in the small clearing between the Saint Marcel and Bois Pierrot woods. 3 Corps' Reserve artillery were brought forward at the same time; Lécrivan and Margot's batteries[132] deployed in front of the clearing and shortly after, finally engaged the Prussian infantry to the east and west of Vionville, their presence soon attracting the attention of the enemy guns.[133] Le Boeuf sent two batteries of horse artillery[134] from his reserve to the plateau north-east of Saint Marcel so as to cover the open ground towards Mars la Tour; the remainder[135] took position west of the village along the track running to Greyère Farm. Their nearest target was about 3,000 metres away and

---

123  3/12th and 3/100th.
124  1st and 2/12th and 1st and 2/100th.
125  L'État-Major, *Rezonville*, p.269. Again, this demonstrates the lack of initiative amongst senior French commanders; a German corps commander would have simply marched to the sound of the guns, deploying his troops as seemed most appropriate.
126  Vivenot's 8/11th.
127  9th and 10/11th.
128  1st Brigade 4th Division 3 Corps.
129  1st and 2/44th and 1st and 2/60th.
130  80th and 85th Ligne.
131  The 4th, 12th and 100th Ligne formed the second line of Tixier's 1st Division.
132  7th and 10/4th.
133  The 7th lost one officer killed seven wounded, the 10th, one killed, five wounded. Each battery fired off about 900 rounds during the day.
134  1st and 2/17th.
135  3rd and 4/17th and 11th and 12/11th.

although a few shots were fired off around midday, the range was too great for the guns to have any effect.

Meanwhile Nayral and Clérambault made their way to Saint Marcel; the infantry division took up position to the west of the village, the cavalry, deployed en colonne serrée, to their right on the crest of the hill overlooking d'Urcourt farm, from where they could observe Tronville Copse. Meanwhile, out on the right flank of the French line, awaiting the arrival his 4 Corps, Ladmirault watched developments from a vantage point on the outskirts of Bruville. Noting Prussian cavalry[136] on the heights to the northeast of the Bois de Tronville, he called forward two batteries of horse artillery[137] and after each gun fired off three rounds, the enemy squadrons retreated from view below the crest. Soon after, the remainder of Legrand's cavalry division and General Veron de Bellecourt's brigade arrived at Doncourt as the forward elements of 4 Corps finally reached the battlefield.

## A Brief Respite

The seizure of Vionville and Flavigny provided Alvesleben with a secure base from where he could develop his attack against Bazaine's positions, although Buddenbrock's men were in no shape to continue their assault, needing time to reorganise their depleted ranks after the prolonged and costly struggle to capture the villages. With 2 Corps also seeking to reorganise, the fighting in this area subsided, as did the struggle on Alvesleben's left flank around the Bois St Arnould. L'Estocq had taken command of II and III Lieb Guard battalions and after a determined struggle, gained the northern edge of the wood but his exhausted men were simply unable to make any further progress across the open ground towards the French positions.

The troops[138] on his right cleared the enemy out of the Bois de Vionville but with the exception of Schwerin's battalions from 10th Brigade who participated in the capture of Flavigny, their advance also ground to a halt. To his left, the open ground between the north-east corner of the wood and the track running from Rezonville to Buxières was occupied by three half battalions from X Corps and the troops[139] hastily assembled by Schwerin. Shaken and outnumbered, the infantry were unable to reply to the long-range chassepot fire and only held onto their exposed positions due to the selfless support provided by III Corps artillery. Stülpnagel's men were exhausted after several hours of combat and lacking the strength to make any further advance, he sent his chief of staff Major von Lewinski to Alvesleben for instructions, who told him: 'I have seen everything; Tell General von Stülpnagel to hold what he has gained but not to advance further under any consideration.'[140]

On the right wing, Stülpnagel's guns, now commanded by Captain Stöphasius,[141] continued to pound Vergé's positions on the plateau heights. To their left and slightly to the rear, around

---

136  From 13th Dragoons.
137  5th and 6/17th batteries à cheval.
138  I and II/48th; 4th Company 3rd Rifles and 5th and 8th companies, 78th.
139  6th 7th and III/ 78th, II/12th, I and III/ 52nd, III/ 48th, 6th Company, 64th.
140  Lanza, *Franco-German War*, p.463.
141  Stöphasius had assumed command of the battery after Major Gallus had been wounded for the third time.

the Sainte Marie heights, Dresky's artillery[142] added their support. Further west, 11 batteries provided covering fire for Buddenbrock's men around Vionville; five under Colonel de Becke were deployed on the cemetery ridge,[143] another six under the command of Major Körber on the heights to the north-west.[144] When the reinforcements from 37th Brigade finally arrived,[145] with the exception of the II/91st, they were all sent to the left of the line where the 24th and the II/20th struggled to hold their positions against increasing numbers of French infantry.

For the time being, until X Corps could march to their aid, it was down to the artillery to sustain the struggle, with Alvesleben determined to hang onto his hard-won positions at all costs, observing: 'Bazaine might beat me, but he would not be rid of me for a long time.'[146]

## Bazaine's Fears

Despite the Emperor's clear instructions to hasten to Verdun with all speed, in the confusion following the initial attack the French commander seemingly failed to appreciate the strategic significance of the capture of Vionville which effectively cut his escape route. Rather than use his superiority in numbers to force open the road, Bazaines preoccupation with the threat to his left wing led him to focus his efforts on securing communications with Metz and notwithstanding the worsening situation around Flavigny, he refused to release any of the troops massed around Rezonville[147] and in fact took additional steps to reinforce his left wing by ordering Marguenat's brigade[148] to move up to the crest overlooking the ravines that led to Gorze, even though Bourbaki's corps secured the routes running south to Ars sur Moselle.

A little later, towards 11:00 a.m. as Chanaleilles' brigade[149] approached Rezonville, it was also ordered into position to the south of the village along with the divisional artillery;[150] this, together with the subsequent deployment of eight batteries[151] of horse artillery from the army Reserve, further evidencing Bazaine's concern to secure his communications with Metz.

142  6th Light, Meinecke,, 3rd Heavy, Vosz, 1st Horse artillery, Scheringer, 2nd Horse artillery, Wittstock and 3rd Horse artillery, Rödenbeck.
143  3rd Light, von Pressentin, 4th Light, Fromme, 4th Heavy, Müller II, III Corps; 2nd Horse artillery, Schirmer, 3rd Horse artillery, Saalmüller, X Corps.
144  5th Heavy, Eunicke, 6th Heavy, Meinecke, 5th Light, Müller II, III Corps, 1st Horse artillery, Bode, IV Corps; From 5th Cavalry Division, 1st Heavy, Kleine and 1st Horse artillery, Frisch, X Corps.
145  Part under Lyncker had already made its way on to the battlefield to assist 5th Division but around 11:45 a.m. Colonel Lehman made his way on to the field from Chambley with the remainder; 91st Regt (less 1st and 2nd companies) and I/78th.
146  Ascoli, *A Day of Battle*, p.150.
147  Bazaine had 13 battalions (1st and 2/97th, 2nd and 3/25th, 1st, 2nd and 3/ 26th, 1st, 2nd and 3/28th, 1st, 2nd and 3/70th) and 8 regiments of cavalry (Four regiments from Valabrègue's division, 2nd Chasseurs, 3rd Lancers and the Carabiniers and Cuirassiers of the Guard).
148  25th and 26th Ligne 1st Brigade 4th Division 6 Corps.
149  28th and 70th Ligne 2nd Brigade 4th Division, 6 Corps
150  7th and 8/18th.
151  11th and 12/13th and 1st, 2nd, 3rd, 4th, 5th and 6/18th

## The French Line Comes Under Increasing Pressure

A little after midday, following the withdrawal of Becquet de Sonnay's brigade and Bataille's retreat, the troops opposing any advance from Vionville held a line which ran from the eastern edge of the Bois de Saint Marcel for some 2,000 metres south to the main Verdun road.[152] The 93rd were out in the front, with their right resting on Péchot's brigade; behind the infantry 13 batteries[153] were arrayed in a line along the crest of the plateau 312, another two occupying the clearing between the Bois Pierrot and Bois de Saint Marcel.[154] Further to the rear, Tixier's division[155] was deployed along the crest of the plateau 266–255; although his infantry had yet to see action, the artillery[156] deployed in their support, engaged the Prussian batteries around Vionville.

In the sector east of the highway running south towards the Bois des Ognons, Alvesleben's guns had forced Fauvart Bastoul and Vergé to withdraw, but they improvised a new defensive line which ran from the track leading to Buxières, across to the Gorze ravine. On the left wing, the 77th were engaged in a struggle with Major von Jena's 3rd Rifles who were attempting to push through the northern edge of the Bois de Vionville. Further east, three battalions of the 84th were deployed on the slopes watching the road which ran down from Vionville to Gorze; their chassepots keeping the II and Fusilier battalions of the 8th Lieb Guards bottled up in the Bois de Saint Arnould. The remainder of Lappasset's men occupied a clearing overlooking the Bois des Ognons and the ravine running down to Saint Catherine, but had yet to see action. The 3/97th supported by two batteries, formed a second line, the remaining battalions of the 97th having been sent by Bazaine to help defend Rezonville.

Although the guns[157] located east of the lane leading to Buxières outnumbered Alvesleben's artillery, they were unable to suppress the accurate enemy fire which continued to pound away at their positions, forcing the French batteries to withdraw out of the line so as to undertake repairs and replenish their ammunition.

The gap created by the retreat of Mangin's brigade in the sector running from the track to Buxières and the main highway, was of increasing concern to Canrobert and to fill this breech, he ordered Bisson to deploy the 9th in line of battle; its left, being about 600 metres from Rezonville, its right, a similar distance from where the track from Saint Marcel to Flavigny

---

152  From north to south the French line consisted of the 1st, 2nd, 3rd companies 2/10th; 3/10th; 4th, 5th, 6th companies 2/10th; 1/10th; 1st, 2nd, 3rd companies 1/93rd; 2/93rd; 4th, 5th, 6th companies 1/93rd; 4th, 5th, 6th companies 3/93rd. Lieutenant Colonel de Linière was rallying three companies of the 23rd companies along the highway.

153  From right to left; one grande batterie under the command of Colonel de Montluisant consisted of the 10/4th, 7/4th, 7/8th, 7/11th, 12/8th, 5/8th. A further grande batterie under Lieutenant Colonel Jamet consisted of the 6/14th, 7/5th, 5/14th, 1st, 2nd, 3rd and 4/18th, 9/13th, 9th and 10/13th. Although the 5/14th deployed on the heights towards 11:00 a.m., during the course of the day it only fired off about 14 rounds.

154  7/4th and 10/5th.

155  From right to left, the 1st, 2nd and 3rd battalions 4th Ligne, 1st, 2nd and 5th companies 9th Chasseurs. To the rear of his fighting line Tixier had deployed the 1st and 2/12th; 1/100th; 3/100th and 2/12th. The 2nd/100th was en-route for Rezonville.

156  8/8th, 9th and 10/11th; 10/4th, 7/4th, 7/8th, 7/14th, 8/12th and 5/8th.

157  From right to left: 5/5th, 6/5th, 6/18th, 6/15th, 7/2nd, 11/5th and 5/18th (the last two batteries were on the left flank and as such were not engaged in the counter battery fire.

crossed the main highway. The infantry soon attracted the attention of the Prussian artillery, being forced to seek cover in the ditches and hedges either side of the road; even so, they were unable to hold this exposed position and were forced to withdraw.

When Bazaine returned to Rezonville after conferring with Le Boeuf, he was equally alarmed at the apparent collapse of his right wing and called forward the 25th from Marguenat's brigade to help bolster Canrobert's defence. One battalion deployed along the crest of the hill to the west of Rezonville, the others in a more sheltered position within a shallow valley a little to the south. Five batteries[158] were placed to the south of the main highway to provide fire support and a little later, another eight moved into position to the north of the route,[159] although lacking any adequate infantry escort,[160] their exposed position left them open to a flanking attack which only added to the general air of insecurity pervading the French command at that time.

Meanwhile, the relentless pounding of the 'artillerie massen' assembled to the south-west of Rezonville, had thrown the French defences along Verdun-Metz road into confusion. As enemy guns raked their positions, Valazé's brigade was pushed out of the Bois St Arnould and fell back onto the highway, adding to the disorder caused by the earlier retreat of de Villiers and Mangin from Vionville.

In an attempt to stabilise a rapidly deteriorating situation, Bataille led Fauvert Bastoul's brigade forward in a counter attack but enfiladed by artillery fire, he made little progress. Bataille fell mortally wounded, then Valazé was hit and with Merle's 32nd covering the retreat, both brigades withdrew. Picard, who was with the 3rd Chasseurs, described how the enemy fire wreaked havoc in the French ranks:

> Our march was executed under a violent artillery and infantry fire; we were fired on from the front and fired on from the flank as we approached the crest of the heights south of Flavigny. The battalion of chasseurs followed in the tracks of the 32nd, their progress marked by the wounded or men that had fallen out of the ranks. The battalion suffered heavy losses, shells blowing away entire ranks. The officers tried to maintain formation and continuously called out 'Close up! Close up!' to prevent the battalion spreading out, which of course presented the enemy with an excellent target. On reaching the crest between Flavigny and Gorze we took up position, crouching down. To our front there was a battalion of enemy soldiers who'd occupied a fold in the ground so we could only see their heads. After commencing fire, the 3rd advanced and moved to within a hundred metres of the enemy formation. We opened up again, the battalion laying down such a heavy fire that we expended most of our ammunition. The situation was very trying; we were getting fired on from all directions. The infantry deployed on the left of the 3rd Chasseurs became disordered and ran back through our lines and disappeared in the direction of Rezonville. All the efforts of the officers couldn't halt them. In an instant our officers and NCO's found themselves alone. Commandant Petit gave orders to the officers to catch up with the men; this meant chasing back after

---

158  From right to left 8/5th, 9/5th, 10/15th, 10/5th and 8/17th batteries à cheval.

159  6/14th,7/5th,1st, 2nd, 3rd and 4/18th, 9th and 10/13th.

160  Following the retreat of the 94th from Flavigny only three battalions (1/25th near the road, the 1/77th on the track to Buxières and the 3rd Chasseurs who were deployed to the rear of the others) were available for close escort duty for the guns

them for about 500 metres under an extremely heavy fire from the enemy infantry and artillery.[161]

This sudden rout left Vergé's artillery exposed to the full weight of the enemy fire; one battery[162] had already pulled out of the gun line and as with the others, [163] was only able to maintain their fire by constantly shifting position, Bazaine ordered Colonel Toussaint[164] to support them with two horse batteries, the guns unlimbering alongside Lapasset's brigade.

Things were similarly tense on the Prussian side; with most of 6th Division still reorganising after the earlier struggle for Vionville, the only force available to pursue the French driven out of Flavigny were Schwerin's troops[165] whose surprise appearance resulted in the rout of the 94th. Given their heavy casualties, command of these two battalions had devolved to Captain Hildebrand and formed in line of company columns, he pressed hard on the heels of the 32nd as they fell back on Rezonville. The III/12th was to the left and slightly in advance and initially had one company out in front but, some 600 metres north of Flavigny and nearing the Metz-Verdun highway, deployed a second in skirmish formation. The II/52nd was to its right and having pushed two of its companies out to cover their open flank, Hildebrand's attention was drawn to the French cavalry at Rezonville, apparently forming up for a charge.

### Charge of the Guard Cuirassiers

As the debris of the 94th made its way to the east covered by the dogged withdrawal of the 32nd, the 9th and 1/25th, deployed to the west of Rezonville, also seemed on the verge of collapse. To the north of the highway Bequet de Sonnay's brigade, unable to withstand the fierce shelling and seeking some respite from the fire of the Prussian guns, had also given way. Concerned by the apparent disintegration of his defence Bazaine belatedly called up two battalions of the 97th to help stabilise the line but as these would take time to deploy and with no other reserves to hand, as at Froeschwiller, the French looked to their cavalry to buy them time. Frossard galloped over to Bazaine and suggested:

> 'Order a cavalry charge to halt the enemy infantry.' The Marshal responded 'I think you are right. What cavalry do we have to hand?' 'The 3rd Lancers [166]but they are only light.' and then I added 'They will need support; the Guard cuirassier regiment is close at hand.' 'Yes,' said the Marshal, 'Give General Preuil orders to support you with a regiment of the Guard cavalry.'[167]

The Guard's 3rd Cavalry Brigade were positioned around Rezonville. Their commander, General du Preuil had initially ordered them to saddle up when Forton's troopers streamed back

---

161  Lecaillon, *Été 1870*, p.117–118.
162  The 12th /5th.
163  5th and 6th(m)/5th.
164  Commander of the 18th Artillery Regiment.
165  III/12th Grenadiers and II/52nd.
166  From Lapasset's Brigade.
167  L'État-Major, *Rezonville*, p.294.

through their following their rude surprise at Vionville. As Colonel Sainte-Chapelle of the Guard Cuirassiers recalled:

> We mounted and as the carabiniers assembled we followed in their rear in colonne de peletons. When the whole brigade had completed forming up, we set off at the trot, crossing the fields north and parallel to the highway. We halted in this formation to the north-east of Rezonville. A few moments later General Preuil formed the carabiniers in line of battle to the north of Rezonville and then told the cuirassiers 'Head of column to the left and form line of battle by platoons to the right' and ordered us to deploy parallel to the road running from Rezonville to Gorze, between Rezonville and hill 308. We'd formed in line, our five squadrons facing east in the usual order, when we were greeted with a few shells, fired from a great distance, which didn't bother us. Our view was obscured by the plateau of hill 314, but we soon noted 2 Corps infantry regiments coming towards us, retreating but in good order nonetheless and every now and then alternative sections stopped to turn and fire at the enemy.[168]

Two batteries of Guard horse artillery accompanied the cavalry and when the brigade halted, the 1st deployed in front of the Carabiniers, the 2nd moved to the south of the highway alongside the cuirassiers, the 3rd Lancers then moved from their position south east of Rezonville and deployed in front of the Guard Cuirassiers.

Frossard rode over to Preuil and ordered: 'General, take command of the lancers and cuirassiers and charge the batteries and their supporting train.' At the same time, according to the brigadier's post combat report, Bazaine also drew near and called out: 'Charge Preuil, it's urgent, don't waste a moment!'[169]

It seems that a heated discussion took place between the three commanders with Frossard insisting that the cavalry be committed at once to save his men. Unsurprisingly as the only cavalry officer amongst them, Preuil wanted to wait until the Prussian infantry crested the nearby hill so that his charge would take them by surprise, but Frossard would not countenance delay, so reluctantly he made his way forward to reconnoitre the terrain where his cavalry would attack. He noticed 3rd Lancers were moving forward and as they worked their mounts into a gallop, rode over to their colonel, furious that they had charged without his instructions. In fact,

---

168  *Ibid*, p.269.
169  Unsurprisingly in view of the outcome of their attack there are differing accounts of just what happened; according to the Guard Cuirassier's history, published in 1889, Frossard spoke directly to Colonel Dupressoir and demanded that he charge; he refused, saying that he needed orders from his divisional commander. A staff officer was sent to speak to Desvaux, who then rode over to speak with Bazaine. Frossard continued to press the officer: 'It's critical that they're stopped. You have to sacrifice a regiment.' Frossard then sent another staff officer over to the 3rd Lancer's, ordering them to charge the advancing enemy, before turning to address Dupressoir again: 'The Guard Cuirassiers will support the 3rd Lancer's charge.' He then despatched another officer to brief Desvaux and Bazaine. According to another version, it was Frossard alone who was pressing for the cavalry to charge, with both Desvaux and du Preuil complaining that it was wrong time to launch such an attack as Bazaine stood by, refusing to issue an order and 'making evasive replies, as was his custom.' Bourbaki stated that Frossard gave the order to charge and this was confirmed by Bazaine. See l'État-Major, *Rezonville*, pp.294–296 and *16 Août Documents* p.406.

their commander Colonel Thorel had been given a direct order by a staff officer from 2 Corps and so without further ado, had launched his men directly at the Prussian guns.

Sous Lieutenant Bergasse related how: 'The ground was cut up with hedgerows and as we gathered speed our ranks were thrown into disorder by the uneven ground, with Squadrons and peletons thrown into general confusion. Fortunately for us, an officer of the general staff galloped up and halted the advance.'[170] After rallying his troopers to the rear of the cuirassiers, Thorel was again ordered to charge the Prussian guns but as the French official history comments, the confusion resulting from this succession of order and counter order, undoubtedly made a difficult task even more challenging. With Thorel and his lieutenant colonel at their head, the lancers set off once again; 1st and 2nd squadrons in front, the 3rd and 5th followed a short distance to their rear under the command of chef d'escadron Doridant.

As a result of this delay, Hildebrand was given a few minutes valuable notice of the impending attack; within the 12th Grenadiers, the 9th and 12th companies, formed in line, wheeled to their right to confront the threat. To the south, the 10th Company formed square and to their right, the 11th Company deployed from column into line, again fronting towards the enemy cavalry. Although Thorel's charge was carried out with great precision, the troopers couched lances presenting an 'alignement magnifique', the hurried manner in which it was undertaken, with no opportunity to reconnoitre the ground and the imprecise nature of their orders[171] meant that as they crested the rise to their front, they were surprised to find a solid square of Prussian infantry blocking the way less than 400 metres to their front. Bergasse recalled:

> Despite the pace of our advance the lancers maintained great order, the horses leaping over all obstacles in their way and I'm convinced that nothing could have stood in the way of this hurricane. Unfortunately, the call then went up from the 1st Squadron[172] 'To the right, to the right' and as a consequence of this change of direction the 3rd and 4th peletons of the 2nd Squadron swept past the left corner of the square, where we received a volley at a range of 60 metres; this had a murderous effect on both the 4th and 3rd, which I commanded, which lost 17 horses and 12 men killed or wounded.[173]

Thorel, whose horse had been shot from beneath him, rallied the first two squadrons by the side of the highway; the second wave sensibly chose not press home their attack and wheeled off to the right about 700 metres from the Prussian line, outside the effective range of the Dreyse.

After ordering the lancers to charge, Pommeraye galloped over to Dupressior instructing him to support their attack. The colonel had already briefed his men and immediately ordered 'Escadrons en avant; escadron de droite, escadron de direction.'[174] According to some accounts, the cuirassiers followed so closely on the heels of the lancers that they were on top of the infantry even as Thorel rallied his shaken troopers. Sainte-Chapelle related how when the cuirassiers

---

170  L'État-Major, *Rezonville*, pp.297–298.
171  They were simply told to charge 'the Prussian batteries.' See l'État-Major, *Rezonville*, p.299.
172  On the right of the line
173  L'État-Major, *Rezonville*, p.300. The 3rd Lancers lost a total of three officers, 34 men and 46 horses during the battle; Thorel blamed the lack of success on the fact that 'no definite object of attack had been pointed out to them.'
174  L'État-Major, *Rezonville*, p.301.

moved off, a number of troopers threw away the heavy sacks of oats they carried on their saddles; others undid the straps that held their ration packs so as to lighten their loads.

Dupressior issued his curt command: 'Sabre main' and 'Au gallop, marche!'[175] and despite the mutterings of the chefs de peletons who protested that they should be charging with drawn pistols rather than swords, the five squadrons – some 698 officers and men – advanced in line abreast towards the Prussian infantry. They had only gone 150–200 yards when they stumbled into the same hedges and enclosures that disrupted the lancers attack.

After a moment's hesitation, Dupressior led his men to the left and in colonne de peletons, moved a short distance to the south to clear the obstacle; the pelotons then wheeled to the right before rushing towards the waiting infantry. As a result of this manoeuvring, as the cuirassiers worked their mounts into a charge, there were only two squadrons in the front line, the 6th on the left, 4th on the right.[176] The 3rd and 2nd were behind, whilst the 1st formed a third, with 100 metres between successive waves.

Whereas the attack by the lancers had fallen mainly on three companies[177] of the Grenadiers, the cuirassiers charge struck the II/52nd and as the 'growing rumble of the hurricane' threatened their right and rear, skirmishers from the 6th and 7th companies fell back into the ranks, forming a solid wall of rifles. The 5th and 8th deployed from company column into line on their right, echeloned to the rear to cover any flank attack whilst to the north, 11/12th took position alongside the 6/52nd, as Saint Chappelle recalled:

> The sight of the Prussian skirmishers deploying gave a dynamic stimulus to the cuirassiers. Cries of 'Charge!' and Vive l'Empereur!' erupted spontaneously from their ranks as, at the same time, their sabres were raised above their helmets. The ground was excellent, the stubble cut low and the ground sloping gently towards the enemy. The horses lengthen their gallop whilst maintaining a superb alignment. Even on Grand Revue days, cavalry will never perform a more perfect attack.[178]

The 6th and 7th companies were directly in the path of the 4th Squadron;[179] Hildebrand, at the centre of the line called out to the 52nd to hold their fire until the cuirassiers were within 250 yards and then gave the order 'Shoulder arms! Fire!'[180] At the head of the cuirassiers Colonel Sainte-Chapelle noted:

> We clearly saw the main group to the right forming up; then loading their weapons and taking aim, with the commands being heard distinctly; in a very clear and high note, as is customary in Prussia. The command 'Fire!', which was awaited with some

175  *Ibid.*
176  Each having a frontage of about 75 metres, with 50 metres between them.
177  9th, 12th and 10th.
178  Lehautcourt, *Rezonville*, p.190.
179  The 6th Squadron to their left had no enemy to their front; their charge took them along the right bank of Flavigny stream.
180  Hildebrand was killed sometime during the ensuing struggle.

trepidation, was followed by a salvo and immediately after, by a very rapid fire. By then, we were within 100 metres of them.[181]

Three volleys rang out, the infantry then opened a rapid independent fire which drove back the centre of the attacking squadron. As the shaken troopers reined in their horses, the rear rank of the infantry faced about and continued to pour fire into the men and horses[182] as the remnants of the first wave passed to either side of the Prussian line. Captain Benoît Prosper Casadavant of the Guard Cuirassiers described the attack:

The moment the charge was sounded we were eight hundred metres from the Prussians. They were formed into three squares, some way apart, with a number of guns deployed in the intervals; in addition, they had a number of skirmishers thrown out on either flank. When we set off, they began to fire, but at three hundred, at two hundred metres it was like hail. At a little over a hundred metres, when my squadron approached their line there was such a wall of bodies, of horses, of men, that it was difficult to get over. However, the front rank made its way forward, whilst those in the rear just crashed into it, swelling the heap. I was one of those who fell, not knowing if my horse was dead. It didn't move and I couldn't reach my sabre which was underneath it.[183]

Another Guard lieutenant described how it felt to be on the receiving end of this fire:

We formed up as if on a parade ground surrounded by a hail of bullets. There were so many shots whistling past our ears that it sounded like a howling wind. Everything was dropping around me. All of a sudden, my poor mount staggers, I keep her up, she's still going forward but a heap of corpses blocks her path; she wants to cross it and I jump across the pile. A squadron is behind me and they only serve to add to the piles of dead and dying … I go down, the horse falling on me but am saved by my cuirass; another horse is on my legs, with my head up against the body of another, my left hand trapped under my saddle. I am only able to move my right arm, which I use to pound the back of my poor beast which I can still feel moving. Throughout this time, I could hear the crack of bullets which pierced the flesh of the pile of men and horses which covered me, the Prussians were shooting at everything that stirred. After a superhuman effort I managed to move my mount, free my arm and stand up. This had taken about quarter of an hour and struggling out of the pile of bodies I hurriedly made my way on foot towards Rezonville, without any weapons, as I had lost everything in my fall. My trumpeter who'd had also fallen was on my left, a corporal of my squad had crashed to the ground to my right; we were making our way to the rear when all of a sudden, the firing started up behind us; the trumpeter was hit; telling me 'I'm dead'.

---

181 L'État-Major, *Rezonville*, p.306. Some accounts state that the Prussians held their fire until the cavalry were less than 100 metres from their line, possibly as close as 50 metres.
182 An officer of the cuirassiers described that the bullets rained which rained down on them sounded like 'flac' when they hit something soft, such as a saddle or a horse and a harder sound, 'tac', when striking a trooper's helmet or cuirass.
183 Lecaillon, *Été 1870*, pp.118.

The corporal had a broken arm and I continued to make my way back with no end of bullets whizzing around my head. I then saw that five or six Prussians who'd taken shelter in a ditch from the fire had seen me. I continued to hurry back when I noticed to my right a dozen troopers who were charging to my rescue; they wore the uniform of the Guides; I was saved; I then heard their famed war cry 'Hourra!' I threw myself into a ditch; there was a dead body besides me. I prised a sword from his stiff hand and waved it above my head. The cavalry passed me like an avalanche and I didn't see them again; their attention was fixed on a battery which was deployed to my right. The shells began to fall again and I was relieved to find a hollow where I could shelter from the fire as one of the projectiles, which would have certainly cut me to pieces, fell no more than nine paces away from me. When I got my breath back, I jumped on a poor wounded horse which I found nearby; I gave it a few blows with my sword and the poor animal managed to break into a gallop and I made my way back to my regiment, where I arrived covered in bruises and unable to move.[184]

The cuirassiers who cleared the enemy line to their front were fired on by the fusilier companies of the 12th to the north and the infantry from 6th Division moving up from Flavigny; 4th Squadron only mustered some 20 troopers as they rallied; their officers all dead or wounded, as were most of the NCO's. The 6th suffered fewer casualties but were thrown into disarray as the left wing of the 4th, veered to the south to avoid the Prussian fire. Two captains were dismounted in the confusion and as the squadron attempted to rally to the south of Flavigny brook, they were struck by fire from the 5th and 8th companies who had turned to face the troopers.

Meanwhile, the second wave, with Commandant de Vergés and General du Preuil at their head, closed on the 52nd's line. Finding their way blocked by a wall of dead and wounded men and horses, the squadrons veered off to the right where they were struck at a range of 60 metres by a volley that 'threw the two ranks into indescribable confusion.'[185] Nine officers were killed, wounded or dismounted including de Vergés with few, if any, troopers closing with the infantry.[186]

1st Squadron's attack, led by their colonel, fared no better; hit by a volley fired at close range and their ranks disordered by the debris of the preceding squadrons, it also failed to charge home. Wounded, Dupressoir fell from his horse but assisted by his aide Lieutenant Davignon, remounted and led the remnants of his shattered regiment to the rear to rally around Gravelotte.[187]

184 Lecaillon, *Été 1870*, pp.118–119.
185 L'État-Major, *Rezonville*, p.308.
186 It was reported that one of the cuirassiers, the gigantic Quartermaster-Sergeant Fuchs, having lost his sword, was seen in the midst of the 52nd swinging his helmet by its chin strap at the enemy.
187 Dupressoir's report, drafted immediately after the battle recorded losses of seven officers killed/died of wounds and missing (including the lieutenant colonel), 12 officers wounded (including the Colonel), 133 troopers killed/missing/captured, 55 men wounded and 208 missing horses. The French official history lists six officers killed, 12 wounded, 140 troopers killed/missing and 30 wounded. Lieutenant Colonel Bonie, in the *Tactical Results of Cavalry* gives the losses as 22 officers, 208 rank and file and 243 horses.

## Bazaine Narrowly Avoids Capture

Following the failure of the cuirassiers attack, Bazaine instructed Donop's 2nd Guard horse artillery to move forward to provide cover for their retreat. Attended by just a few close aides,[188] the marshal galloped over to one of the battery's section commanders, Lieutenant Comte d'Esparbès de Lussan, telling him where he wanted the guns to be sited. As d'Andlau noted, such actions were characteristic of the French commander in chief: 'He was everywhere, not sparing himself for a moment, but entirely confusing his responsibility as a commander in chief with the more modest duties of a general or even an ordinary colonel.'[189] Intent on overseeing their deployment, he then accompanied d'Esparbès to the designated location, a few hundred yards west of Rezonville, when the battery was suddenly overrun by enemy cavalry, Bazaine coming within a whisker of being killed or captured.

From his position near Flavigny, Caprivi had observed the French cavalry manoeuvring to charge and ordered Redern's brigade to launch a counter attack. Lieutenant Colonel von Rauch advanced at the head of a mixed force of hussars and dragoons[190] and after passing through the intervals of their own infantry in colonne de pelotons, the troopers formed line before charging towards the broken cuirassiers. To Rauch's right rear, the 11th Hussars advance was halted by the marshy ground to the south of Flavigny so Lieutenant Colonel von Eberstein wheeled his squadrons off to the left, towards the main highway, from where he then launched his attack against Frossard's infantry who were still falling back on Rezonville.

Despite coming under fire from the 3rd Chasseurs and the guns of the 3/18th to the north of the highway, Redern's brigade pursued the retreating Guard Cuirassiers towards Rezonville where Rauch, at the head of 20 troopers from the 1st Squadron of Brunswickers, overran d'Esparbès section at the very moment his guns were unlimbering, his troopers swinging in from the flank as Captain von Vaerst's 11th Hussars hit their front. Donop managed to deploy three guns and fired off a few rounds of grape before being swept away. In the ensuing mêlée, d'Esparbès was killed, another six men and 10 horses cut down, with the supporting artillery[191] being thrown into confusion as the remnants of the Guard battery galloped through their lines, closely pursued by the hussars.

Bazaine and his staff were carried away by this torrent of men and horses and in imminent danger of being captured or cut down, were forced to draw swords as the enemy hussars swarmed around them. Although he attracted much criticism regarding his leadership qualities, no-one could doubt his courage; with the enemy cavalry swirling around him, the marshal found himself alongside a young, excited subaltern; 'Come on young man, calm down' he remarked, 'See, you are no longer a young child. It's nothing.'[192]

---

188  The majority of the general staff were to the rear around Hill 299. The duty squadrons, the 5/5th Hussars and the 1/2nd Chasseurs were about 300 yards away, the 5th near the guns of the 10/15th; the 1st with the General Staff.
189  Ascoli, *A Day of Battle*, p.143. As the author noted 'That he was thus exposed tells us much about his personal bravery. That he was there at all tells us even more about his inadequacy as a commander in chief.'
190  1st, 2nd and 4th Squadrons 17th Brunswick Hussars and part 2nd Squadron 2nd Dragoon Guards.
191  10/15th and 10/5th.
192  Philip Guedalla, *The Two Marshals, Bazaine Pétain* (London, Hodder and Stoughton, 1943) p.184.

Swept away in the rout, Donop galloped over to one of the nearby duty squadrons and led them in a desperate charge against Rauch's men calling out 'En avant, les hussards!'[193] The second duty squadron[194] also launched themselves into the mêlée and as the outnumbered troopers fought their way to the marshal's side, Frossard's personal escort, the 3/4th Chasseurs, charged into the fray. Threatened by the advance of Murat's dragoons and hit with three successive attacks from different directions, Redern's brigade fell back; the Brunswicker's[195] rallying in the valley south-west of Flavigny, the 11th Hussars[196] on the cemetery hill by Vionville.

Although Bazaine escaped unharmed, in the ensuing confusion, he became separated from his staff; Jarras recalled that it took over an hour for the état-major to reassemble to west of Rezonville, during which time the army was without orders. According to the testimony of one of Bazaine's officiers d'ordonnance, Capitaine de Mornay Soult, who gave evidence to the post war Inquiry into his commander's competence, this delay may have been more to do with the mutual antagonism between Jarras and his commander, than the confusion caused by the enemy attack:

At this time, when the charge of the Brunswick hussars separated the marshal from both the état-major général and his état-major particulier, I began to search for him, as I'd been tasked with bringing back the escort squadron of the 5th Hussars, who after having charged, made their way back in very good order, but had retreated too far into our lines. When I returned there was no sign of the marshal, so I went over to the right side of the battle field, as far as I could go, but it took me ages before I found the marshal. In the meantime, I came across an officer from the escort squadron, who told me that the marshal was alive, as he'd just left him, having been sent to deliver a despatch. This officer pointed out to me at the same time that my horse was slightly wounded in the thigh. I paused for a moment, then I returned to the village of Rezonville, where I met General Jarras at the head of the état-major general and made my way to him, somewhat emotional because of the good news I'd just received and announced to him that the marshal was alive and that I even knew where he was. After having spent a few moments talking with Colonel d'Andlau, commandant Samuel and the other officers, I asked General Jarras if he would join the marshal. He answered me with these words, which I recall perfectly: 'It's all about you, monsieur l'officier d'ordonnace!' This reply stung me, so I then turned to the other officers of the état-major general and asked if they wanted to come with me; they replied that they couldn't as General Jarras wasn't going. I saluted the general and made my way back to the marshal. It was only half an hour later, that is about towards four or four thirty, that the officers of the état-major general re-joined the marshal.[197]

193  The 5th Squadron 5th Hussars had a strength of about 70 troopers, 30 men having been detached on other duties. In the ensuing struggle the squadron's commander, Captain des Courtis was captured and two officers and several troopers were killed.

194  1/2nd Chasseurs.

195  The 17th lost dead; eight men, 74 horses; wounded two officers, 68 men; missing 14 men.

196  The 11th lost; dead; one man, eight horses; wounded, one officer, 18 men, five horses; missing two men, 17 horses.

197  Anon, *Procés Bazaine* pp.359–360. de Mornay Soult's timing seems suspect; the charge of the cuirassiers took place around 12:30 p.m.

It seems such feelings were mutual; when the aide reported this exchange to Bazaine, he replied 'Ah, these buggers are looking to hang me out to dry.'[198]

At the same time Caprivi launched Redern's brigade against the Guard Cuirassiers, Alvesleben called up 6th Cavalry Division[199] with the intention of launching them against the shaken infantry, but they struggled to clear their own gun line and by the time they were in position, the opportunity had passed. Deployed in line of squadron columns between Flavigny and the track from Buxières to the main road so as not to mask the fire of their batteries, this mass of immobile horsemen soon attracted the attention of the French artillery. Suffering heavy losses for no good reason, Colonel Schmidt[200] wheeled the 15th about and led them to the rear. Ignoring the enemy fire, Grüter's brigade continued their advance towards Flavigny where the 15th Hussars briefly clashed with the 9th and 12th Dragoons sent forward by Murat to support the outnumbered duty squadrons.

Lynar's 6th Cuirassiers attempted to force their way to the main highway but under increasingly effective cannon and chassepot fire, both regiments wheeled about and made their way to the rear, their retreat being covered by Gröben's 3rd Lancers.

Although Caprivi's cavalry failed to trouble Frossard's retreat, the diversion they created enabled Stülpnagel's artillery to move to more advantageous firing positions; on his southern flank the gun line wheeled slightly to the right, so as to cover the ground in front of the Bois St Arnould to deter any advance by the French from their position on the heights overlooking the woods. On his left, Dresky placed three batteries of horse artillery to the north of the track running from Gorze to Flavigny. To the west Shirmer moved 2nd Horse Artillery into the line and he was followed soon after by 6th Light and 3rd Heavy batteries from III Corps. Colonel von de Becke relocated his guns[201] to the north of Flavigny and General Rothmaler brought forward the 3rd Light Battery from Vionville to a better position north of the main road from where they could provide 6th Division with more effective fire support.

Although Stülpnagel's infantry[202] were relatively secure in their positions along the northern edge of the wood, they were low on ammunition and exhausted after several hours of combat and in no shape to renew their attack. As a result, the fighting in this sector of the battlefield subsided into a desultory exchange of rifle fire with neither side having the strength or inclination to close with one another.

## The Fighting Around Vionville

In the lull following the cavalry action, the III/12th and II/52nd attempted to continue their advance towards the highway to the west of Rezonville. However, under a hail of rifle fire from

---

198  Guedalla, *Two Marshals*, p.185.
199  Rauch's 15th Brigade (16th Hussars and 3rd Hussars) was to the right, Diepenbroick-Grüters 14th Brigade (15th Lancers, 6th Cuirassiers and 3rd Lancers – only two squadrons strong) was on the left and a little to the rear.
200  Schmidt assumed command of 15th Brigade when Major General von Rauch was wounded. Other casualties included Colonel von Zeiten of the 3rd 'Zieten' Hussars whose regiment lost had lost 80 men and 100 horses.
201  3rd Horse artillery X Corps, 4th Light, 4th Heavy from III Corps.
202  I and II/48th, 3rd Rifles, 5th and 8th companies 78th and III/8th

the heights to the north and running low on ammunition, they withdrew through Flavigny to Vionville. Buddenbrock also took advantage of the pause to reorganise his division, where following the capture of Vionville and Flavigny, elements of the 35th,[203] under Lieutenant Colonel von Alten, attempted to push along the main highway towards Rezonville.

Coming under increasingly heavy fire from Canrobert's men lining the edge of the Bois de St Marcel, Alten wheeled his troops to confront this threat, his men sheltering in the ditch on the northern side of the road, receiving support from 2nd and 3rd Horse artillery who took position alongside them. As this action was ongoing, the remainder of the 35th[204] occupied Flavigny, with three companies from the 64th[205] assembling to the east of the watering hole, facing Rezonville. Another 12 companies[206] were deployed along the slopes of the plateau to the north-east of Vionville, their line running between a fold of ground overlooking the valley that ran down to Vionville and the Roman road.

In the valley itself, Rechtern's men[207] were fighting a losing battle against Péchot; although he had four companies[208] covering his left flank and I/20th was in support to the rear, his men were low on ammunition and having lost a number of senior officers, struggled to hold their ground in the face of superior French firepower.[209]

With their line in danger of collapse, Alvesleben committed his last reserves, Colonel Lehman's demi brigade[210] from Tronville. The II/91st led their advance and on reaching the highway, Major von Kienitz deployed the 6th and 7th companies to prop up the 64th, as the 5th and 8th, under Captain Goldschmidt, traversed the Tronville Copse to support the firing line of the II/24th.

A little later the remainder of the Oldenburg Regiment were sent into the copse; the 3rd and 4th companies on the right, the fusilier battalion on the left and after struggling through the dense undergrowth, they emerged at the north-eastern edge, alongside the I/78th. Their appearance immediately attracted the attention of Péchot's infantry whose chassepot fire proved deadly; Major von Runckel of the 78th fell wounded, Colonel von Kameke, the Oldenburg's commander was killed.

Major von Napolski then endeavoured to deploy his two musketeer companies in the open ground beyond the copse in an effort to bring Péchot's men within effective range of his needle guns, but outflanked and confronted by superior forces, Napolski fell back into the shelter of the wood.

---

203  1st, 2nd, 4th, 7th and 11/35th. The 5th and 8th companies of the 35th were in reserve in support of this advance.
204  3rd, 6th, 9th, 10th and 12/35th.
205  9th, 10th and 12/64th.
206  9th, 10th, 11th and 12/20th; 5th, 7th, 8th, 1st, 2nd, 3rd, 4th and 11/64th. They were subsequently reinforced by the 7th and 6/91st.
207  10th, 9th, 11th and 12/24th, 1st, 2nd, 3rd and 4/24th, 5th, 6th, 7th and 8/20th. They were subsequently reinforced by the 8th and 5/91st.
208  7th, 6th, 5th and 8/24th.
209  From the 20th Colonel von Flatow and majors Blum and von Steuben were wounded; from the 64th Lieutenant Colonel von Winterfield and Major von Görschen wounded. From the 24th majors von Sellin and von Rechtern were killed, von Lüderitz badly wounded.
210  3rd, 4th, 5th, 6th, 7th, 8th, 9th, 10th, 11th and 12/91st 1st, 2nd, 3rd and 4/78th.

## The French Reorganise

Seemingly content that the threat from Vionville had been dealt with, Bazaine reorganised his already strong defences around Rezonville. Deligny's division were sent south from Malmaison to cover the Bois des Ognons, the battalion of Guard Chasseurs being deployed in the wood itself, whilst the Voltigeurs kept watch over the roads leading from Gorze and Novéant. The 1/25th was moved to the crest of the hill a few hundred metres west of Rezonville with the remainder of Chanaleilles' brigade[211] being held in reserve alongside Marguenat to the rear of the village.

Following the repulse of Redern's attack, Bazaine also committed the 70th, two battalions deploying to the north of the highway, the 3rd to the south in support of the 9th. Their deployment attracted the attention of the Prussian artillery and coming under heavy fire, the regiment was unable to hold its position, falling back to its bivouac to the north of Rezonville.[212] To fill the breach, Bazaine called up Picard's division of grenadiers and the Guard artillery; General Jeanningros posted the 1/1st Grenadiers along the crest of hill 299 where it took up position to the left of the 1/25th, the 2nd Battalion deployed along the western edge of the village, whilst the 3rd occupied Gravelotte itself.

Accompanied by the divisional batteries[213] two battalions of the Guard Zouaves were then deployed on the plateau to east of Rezonville, alongside Levassor-Sorval's division. The 3/2nd Grenadiers were held in the village whilst the 1st and 2/3rd Grenadiers assembled on the open ground to the south east.[214] Another gap opened up in the line when Jolivet withdrew from his exposed positions to the south of Rezonville, his brigade unable to withstand the fire of Stülpnagel's guns. At Frossard's suggestion, General le Poittevin de la Croix[215] posted 1st and 2/2nd Grenadiers in line of battle on the ground recently vacated by the 77th, their skirmishers being hit with a hailstorm of shot from the enemy batteries located to the south-east of Flavigny[216] as they took up position. The grenadiers attempted to respond but the range was too great even for the chassepot and with their fire having negligible effect, they fell back, seeking shelter on the rear slope of the crest.

As Bazaine strengthened his defence around Rezonville, the other corps commanders took the opportunity to reorganise their artillery; Le Boeuf assembled six batteries[217] on his right flank around Saint Marcel whilst a seventh[218] took position near the Bois de Saint Marcel. To the south of the Roman road, 6 Corps established two 'grande batteries' on the plateau

211  28th and 70th Ligne from le Vassor-Sorval's 4th Division, 6 Corps.
212  The regiment lost all its superior officers; its war diary records 13 officers killed, 14 wounded. 79 men killed, 138 wounded.
213  4th and 6th (m).
214  Following this latest redistribution – further evidence of his fixation with Metz–Bazaine had eleven battalions – 1st, 2nd and 3/70th, 1/25th, 1/1st Gren, 1st and 2/2nd Gren, 2nd and 3/25th 1st and 2/3rd Gren – deployed around Rezonville, with thirteen – 1st, 2nd and 3/26th, 1st, 2nd and 3/28th, 1st and 2/97th, 2nd and 3/1st Gren, 3/2nd Gren and 1st and 2nd Zouaves – in reserve.
215  Commander 2nd Brigade, 2nd Division
216  1st Horse artillery, Scheringer and 3rd Horse artillery, Rödenbeck.
217  3/17th à cheval, 4/17th à cheval, 11/11th, 12/11th, 8/11th, 9/4th.
218  The 8/8th.

running south-east from towards the Metz-Verdun highway; the first[219] commanded by Colonel de Montluisant, the second, larger battery[220] by Lieutenant Colonel Jamet. Nine[221] batteries were placed on the high ground between the main road and the track leading from Rezonville to Buxières and further to the east, another 'grande batterie' stood ready to guard against any thrust from Gorze.[222]

## 6 Corps Deploy Along the Roman Road

On learning that 3 Corps were finally moving into position on his right flank, Canrobert took the opportunity to reposition his men, establishing a new defensive line on the plateau, running south-east from the Roman road to Rezonville.[223] Anxious to avoid any repetition of the rout which followed 2 Corps withdraw, Bazaine released Marguenat's brigade from Rezonville to help reinforce 6 Corps position. Canrobert was later to claim in his post combat, *Journaux de marche* that this limited reorganisation of his defensive line was in fact, the precursor to an all-out assault against the Prussian positions, stating 'There was a vigorous cannonade between the two armies. Towards 2:00 p.m. the fire from the enemy between Rezonville and Flavigny subsided; it seemed to us that the enemy attack had come to a halt. Our troops went over to the offensive.'[224]

As the French official history acknowledges, this was something of an exaggeration; contrary to Canrobert's claim, excepting a minor advance by Péchot's brigade[225] there is simply no evidence that 6 Corps made any advance beyond the protection afforded by Montluisant and Jamet's grande batteries and even these guns struggled even to suppress the fire of the Prussian artillery arrayed around Vionville.

Regardless of Canrobert's intentions, with Stülpnagel's division incapable of further offensive action and Buddenbrock thrown back on the defensive, Alvesleben became increasingly concerned about his precarious position. III Corps had been engaged without respite for over three hours and with 'the fire from the enemy artillery becoming ever more unbearable'[226] his guns were low on ammunition and his outnumbered men were close to exhaustion. With no reserves to hand and X Corps still two hours march away, the growing dust clouds to the north of the Bois Saint Marcel led Alvesleben to conclude that Bazaine intended to envelop his left flank. Of more immediate concern, he interpreted the reorganisation of Canrobert's line as preparations for a counter attack against Vionville and with no ready reserves, desperate measures were called for. As noted in one regimental history:

---

219  10/4th, 7/4th, 7/8th, 7/14th, 12/8th, 5/8th.
220  6/14th, 7/5th, 5/14th, 3/18th à cheval, 9/13th, 10/13th.
221  8/5th, 9/5th,11/5th, 10/5th, 5/5th, 3rd batt montée de la garde, 8/17th à cheval, 2/18th à cheval, 4/18th à cheval.
222  6/18th à cheval, 6/15th, 7/2nd, 7/18th à cheval, 8/18th à cheval, 5/18th à cheval, 1st à cheval de la garde, 2nd à cheval de la garde, 3rd à cheval de la garde, 4th à cheval de la garde.
223  At this time, Canrobert had still to receive any orders from Bazaine.
224  L'État-Major, *16 Août Documents*, p.354.
225  Supported by elements of Tixier's division, Péchot edged forward a few hundred yards through the woods bordering the Roman road on the right of Canrobert's position.
226  Lehautcourt, *Rezonville*, p.210.

The situation began to be critical. The troops had become extremely exhausted after the hour's fight in the hot August sun. And it was still little past two o'clock! Not a gun or a battalion remained in reserve and fresh masses of enemy continued to assemble against our position. In this situation it became necessary for the cavalry to sacrifice itself.[227]

Alvesleben hurriedly conferred with Rheinbaben as to how they could stave off defeat; with the majority of his forces deployed it seemed that the numerically superior French would overwhelm his exhausted men before X Corps arrived on the battlefield. Barby's and Redern's brigades had been sent to bolster III Corps left wing, so the only troops at his disposal were from General von Bredow's 12th Brigade; the 7th Magdeburg Cuirassiers and 16th Altmark Lancers.[228]

Alvesleben believed Canrobert presented the most immediate threat and decided to disrupt his attack; as he was later to comment: 'I had to take the battle area for better or for worse as I found it and make the most of it. This meant that I had to match the physical inferiority of my numbers by the moral superiority of my offensive action.'[229] He related how:

> The ascendancy which III Corps had hitherto established over the enemy seemed threatened …it was not yet two o'clock … a retrograde movement had therefore been expected and envisaged but the thought of abandoning our wounded and the field of battle was unbearable. I took the decision to hit the enemy with a new attack by cavalry as 6th Division was no longer capable of such action owing to its losses and fatigue.[230]

## Von Bredow's Charge

The situation called for extreme measures and although a cavalry charge against unshaken infantry and artillery would most likely result in disaster, given the limited resources available, it was his only option. He despatched his chief of staff, Colonel von Voights Rhetz, to explain to the cavalry commander why he was being asked to sacrifice his men:

> I went to the west of Vionville, a little to the south of the Bois de Tronville where I found the brigade of cavalry and I recognised General Bredow who was stood there with two officers, in a fold in the ground, where they couldn't be seen by the French batteries. When I had explained the mission to him the general pointed out that the wood in front of us was held by the French. I told him that the wood was still held by our infantry, so I didn't believe it presented any danger and if he skirted the wood and went alongside it towards the left, he would find himself on the flank of the enemy batteries (a fold in the ground led up towards the batteries). I told him that at the express wish

---

227   Hildyard, 'Précis', p.987.
228   13th Dragoons having already been despatched to the west of the Tronville Copse to observe 3 Corps advance
229   See Lanza, *Franco-German War*, pp.457–458.
230   Lehautcourt, *Rezonville*, p.211.

of General Alvesleben he was to attack and given the crisis of the situation, it required immediate action.[231]

Still uncertain if the enemy occupied the wood flanking his advance, Bredow first detached two squadrons[232] to screen Tronville Copse as a precaution against a possible French ambush; this reduced his already weakened brigade to just six squadrons. Despite Alvesleben's demand for urgent action, Bredow spent more time carefully reconnoitring the ground before an insistent Voights Rhetz again urged him to charge.[233] Grudgingly, he led his men from the north-west of Tronville forward over the main highway in closed line of squadrons, by platoon columns, the cuirassiers leading the way.

Skirting the copse on his left, he wheeled to the north, advancing along a gentle depression in the ground to the north of Vionville. On reaching the shallow valley leading up to Canrobert's position, he could just make out the French gun line deployed along the crest; wheeling his brigade to the right by divisions, his 805 troopers[234] took intervals as they trotted forward and then finally deployed into line of battle. Bredow's skilful use of the ground and the dust and smoke of battle effectively concealed his brigade's advance,[235] and just before 2:00 p.m. he ordered the charge, his final observation reportedly being 'It will cost what it will.'[236]

The cautious approach march and the undulating terrain meant their attack went almost unseen by the defenders and although French post combat reports mention that the brigade was glimpsed as they moved into position, for the most part their attack went unnoticed, especially by the artillery whose attention was fully engaged by the Prussian gun line 1,500 metres away around Vionville. Lieutenant Colonel Jamet, commander of one of the grande batteries deployed

231  L'État-Major, *Rezonville*, p.348.
232  Believing the woods to be held by enemy troops, one squadron from each regiment, the 3rd from the Cuirassiers, the 1st from the Lancers, was tasked with screening the main attack. As this mission was regarded as tantamount to 'certain death' these squadrons were chosen by lot. See Bonnal, *St Privat II*, p.270.
233  Voights Rhetz said to Bredow, 'The general commanding and General von Rheinbarben, commanding the cavalry division are agreed that it is your business to charge along the wood and still you remain here.' Bredow replied: 'Do you mean to say that I ought to overthrow that infantry along the wood?' 'Certainly' was the answer; 'we have already taken the village and, as we were not able to advance against the wood, the fate of the battle depends on this, that you sweep away everything along the wood and that you must attack with the greatest vigour.' See Arthur L Wagner, *Cavalry Studies from Two Great Wars* (Kansas City: Hudson Kimberly Publishing Company, 1896) p.52.
234  This figure is taken from the last preceding return of 5th Cavalry Division dated August 11th; on that day the regiments averaged about 560 horses, which gives 35 horses per platoon, or 385 cuirassiers, 420 lancers.
235  Major von der Dollen commander of the 16th Lancers later remarked that 'Throughout, I never caught any sight the enemy before we charged.' See l'État-Major, *Rezonville* pp.353–354.
236  Wawro, *The Franco-Prussian War* p.156. According to Lehautcourt, at the moment Bredow crossed the Mars la Tour road, General von Buddenbrock, whose troops were most endangered by any French counter attack, shouted out 'Ah, I believe that we can do without them' and ordered Lieutenant v Kalckreuth to go and tell Bredow that if he was charging on his behalf, he need not do so. Kalckreuth passed on the message to Bredow but he responded at once 'I have got the order to charge from General v Rheinbarben; I'm off.' See P. Lehautcourt (1908) *Studies in Applied Tactics. Cavalry in Battle (15th and 16th August, 1870)*, Royal United Services Institution. Journal, 52:365, 948-946, DOI 10.1080/03071840809418836 p.951

along the heights, recalled that he had seen enemy cavalry but believed they were going to charge the right of the French position and so directed the 6/14th and a section of the 7/14th to cover this sector.

At the same time as Bredow's men began their attack, de Montluisant, commander of the adjoining grande batterie was looking to pull two of the batteries that had suffered most from enemy fire out of the line.[237] Forton had agreed to release his divisional horse artillery[238] to replace these guns and as the fresh batteries moved into position, the charge struck home. Major Count von Schmettow's cuirassiers were deployed on the left of Bredow's line; nine platoons in front with two in rear;[239] Major von der Dollen's lancers were slightly to the rear of the cuirassiers on his right with all three squadrons, 12 platoons, deployed in line.[240] A French officer whose men had been ordered to send out tirailleurs to screen the enemy batteries at Vionville described the moments preceding the attack:

> At last the order was given to deploy skirmishers, one company from each battalion and my company was one of those designated. What luck! We will be able to get into action. We can take up our weapons and exchange shot for shot. The deployment wasn't undertaken without difficulty, the problem was to get the men to stand; the shrapnel passing over them made them reluctant to straighten up. Thanks to the energy and example set by Lieutenant R****** and several other brave men, the manoeuvre was finally completed and we took position about five hundred metres in front of the battalion. There, hidden amongst the furrows and sheltering behind small piles of stones we opened fire on the batteries that were doing us so much harm. Despite our small numbers and the unfavourable position we occupied, we didn't retreat a single step and the fire of our excellent chassepot kept our adversaries at a respectable distance. Then all of a sudden I heard a cry 'Cavalry on the right! They're ours! They're not ours!' And before any of us had time to realise what we were dealing with we were ridden through by a charge of cavalry, 'en fourrageurs'.[241]

As Bredow's troopers closed on the French positions, Major von Körber directed the fire of his four horse batteries against Montluisant's artillery, seeking to draw their fire against his guns and divert their attention away from the cavalry. Screened by swirling clouds of smoke and dust, the brigade covered the 1,500 paces to Canrobert's line with surprisingly few casualties. In the French gunline, the 8/20th had just unlimbered three of its guns when it was hit by right of the cuirassiers' line and the left of the lancers; they managed to fire off a few rounds before they were ridden over as the remainder of the battery and the 7/20th wheeled about and galloped to the rear.[242]

237  5/8th and 12/8th.
238  The 7th and 8/20th horse artillery from Forton's cavalry division.
239  The first platoon of the 1st Squadron had been detached on relay service and only re-joined the regiment later in the day.
240  The cuirassiers had been given the order to charge just before the lancers had completed their deployment into line, as a result they were about 100–150 yards to the rear.
241  Lecaillon, *Été 1870*, pp.127–128.
242  The two batteries lost six officers, 51 men and 69 horses. Of the 49 wounded casualties, 17 had sword wounds, 11 lance wounds, six rifle wounds. Lieutenant Marquet of the 7th was killed, Sous Lieutenant

Bredow's cavalry crashed through the gun line, horses and gunners being put to the sword and careered forward into the supporting infantry, cutting down or dispersing all that stood in their path. The commander of the cuirassiers, Major Count von Schmettow, later recalled:

We formed two divisions, the cuirassier regiment on the left wing along the edge of the wood, the lancer regiment on the right wing and one hundred paces further back. Our brave General, with his staff of four officers, three of whom were killed, was nearly on a line with the cuirassiers. Before the French battery had discharged its third gun, we were masters of it. The honour of challenging the French commander I could not leave to another, and I rather think I found him. It was clear to me that in this death ride the object was not to bring home trophies, but to strike down everything between the wood and the road. At the battery all were put to the sword, and then we went in a tearing course at the infantry column, which was ridden over, and cut down. Its remnants sent a good many shots after us. At this time the lancers were close on our heels. A second battery was attacked, and all who did not run, put to the sword.[243]

In command of the lancers, Major von Dollen recalled:

After all, I don't see the enemy at all, whom we ought to attack. All at once there jumped up from the ground, a short way off, thick lines of infantry, who prepared to fire. The Prussian troopers reached them amid volleys and rapid fire, which left them almost intact. Some neighbouring batteries fired case shot rapidly, with the same results. An eyewitness writes that he had the impression that it was a charge in time of peace. The same officer states that when the Prussian troopers went through the lines of our infantry, the latter threw down their arms and fled wholesale. Some men were struck by the Uhlans, who finally became ashamed to kill their unarmed adversaries. Kalckreuth himself shouted out, 'Let them live, they won't do us any more harm.'[244]

Three companies from the 9th Chasseurs[245] escorting the artillery, opened a rapid fire before they too were ridden over. General Henry, 6 Corps' Chief of Staff was in the French gun line as the charge struck home and related:

On taking position with my battery nothing was to be seen of the Prussian cavalry. Where in the world had these cuirassiers come from? All of a sudden they were upon my guns like a whirlwind, and rode or cut down all my men save only one. And this one was saved by Schmettow. The gunner ran towards the Cuirassiers, crying 'Je me rends! Je me rends!' But the Prussians, not understanding this were for despatching him, and were only prevented from doing so by their colonel, Count von Schmettow. It was only by the skin of my teeth that I myself escaped as the mass of furious horsemen swept

Tocanier suffered six sabre cuts and a rifle wound. nine men received between three and seven wounds, one unfortunate individual suffering seven lance wounds.
243  Rich, *Germany and France*, p.359.
244  Lehautcourt, *Studies*, p.952.
245  The 3rd, 4th and 6th.

past me, trampling down or sabreing the gunners. But it was a magnificent military spectacle, and I could not help exclaiming to my adjutant as we rode away 'Ah! Quelle attaque magnifique.'[246]

The 93rd were still reorganising their ranks following the earlier losses caused by the Prussian shelling when the charge hit them; the 2nd Battalion had been thrown into disorder by the rout of the artillery train and in the ensuing struggle, the staff of the regimental colours was broken; although the flag fell into enemy hands, they managed to retain the precious eagle.[247]

Thrown into confusion by the attack, their colonel rallied part of the regiment on a small hillock (306), as the remainder fell back to the shelter of the woods lining the Roman road. Swept away in the elation of the moment 'the enemy cavalry carried their memorable charge even further, with an energy to which we must pay respect.'[248] The troopers pursued the terrified gunners down the valley towards Rezonville where, after a charge of some 3,000 metres, Bredow attempted to rein in his maddened troopers and rally his exhausted squadrons.

## Forton's Cavalry Responds

Although Canrobert's gun line had been taken by surprise by the charge, the French cavalry deployed to the north of Rezonville were well placed to take advantage of the situation presented to them and eager to take revenge for their earlier humiliation, as Forton related:

> All in front was in complete disorder and from a distance presented the appearance of disorganised mob. Then through this mass the enemy cavalry appeared from the heights to the right of my division, their left flank around 400–500 metres away, as they passed before my regiments formed in line of battle. Without delay I gave the order for Murat's brigade to attack.[249]

A little later, with the terse command 'Allons le 7e!' Forton unleashed part of Gramont's cuirassier brigade[250] against the flank of Bredow's cavalry whilst the 2nd Chasseurs à Cheval from Valabrègue's division charged them head on. Alexander Farinet, a junior officer in one of the French cuirassier regiments that took part in the counter attack recalled his feelings as his regiment was ordered to charge:

> Off we go! I thought that I'd ignore the troopers and instead try to engage one of the officers; that was my intention, when suddenly I received a violent blow which struck the rim of my cuirass and cut the underside of my shoulder. This cut from behind was

---

246  L'État-Major, *Rezonville*, p.359.
247  The standard was subsequently recovered by Trooper Mangin of the 5th Chasseurs à Cheval.
248  L'État-Major, *Rezonville*, p.359.
249  *Ibid*, 359–360. According to the post battle reports a large part of Forton's brigade never heard the orders given by the general – 'sabre au main' and 'Au gallop!' and simply followed the units to either side of them.
250  The 1st Squadron 10th Cuirassiers supported this attack, the remaining three squadrons being held in reserve.

no doubt aimed at my head but it hit too low with little effect. At the same instant I saw the lancer officer who'd struck the blow gallop past me. I followed him. He turned to face me, about three or four metres ahead, as the ground opened up. I caught up with the German and plunged the blade of my sabre into the side of his magnificent mount. Before he responded, I withdrew my sword and without waiting a second struck the man. My blade penetrated his body, man and horse spraying blood. It's hard to describe my feelings; it was my first time in combat; I went into a cold sweat and shivered as the drops of blood fell from my blade onto my face. The eyes of the dying officer were fixed on me; I still shudder still when I think about it.[251]

Bredow's exhausted troopers were swept aside as the French cavalry shepherded them back to Vionville and as Bonie related:

> After the hostile horsemen had traversed our batteries General de Forton charged them with his dragoons and part of his cuirassiers. They advanced with deployed regiments and threw themselves on the approaching lines. At the collision the 9th Dragoons broke through the Prussian cuirassiers, who readily opened their ranks and turned to the right and left in order to retreat to the position of our artillery and re-join the uhlans which had already passed them in retreat. At the end of their charge, the latter had turned about in order to retreat, but were even then assailed by the remaining squadrons of our cuirassiers at the mere call 'Attention, les cuirassiers! Partez!' As this order failed to designate any formation, the advance was made in disorderly crowds; the officers had to put their horses to their best speed so as to remain at the head of their men who were going at full tilt. A terrible confusion resulted; the 16th Uhlans, taken in flank and overthrown, were cut down and briskly pursued until the white column of the cuirassiers approached and rescued them. In consequence of the long distance covered at a gallop the horses were completely blown and at the end of their strength. At this moment the horsemen of De Valqabrègue's Division, joining those of General de Forton, threw themselves upon the enemy; everything became intermixed as in a tornado and both sides fought with frenzy.[252]

Bachlier's brigade of dragoons charged the flank of the enemy troopers and succeeded in capturing a number of prisoners, although the few casualties they suffered would indicate only a limited involvement in the engagement.[253]

As Bredow's shattered troopers made their way back to Vionville, Redern brought the 11th Hussars forward to cover their retreat, but as Forton's troopers seemed unwilling to press home their pursuit, he chose not to commit them. Given the uncoordinated nature of the French counter attacks, with some 25 squadrons being committed within a confined area, many of Bredow's men were able to make their way back to their own lines, shepherded by just a few

251  Lecaillon, *Été* 1870, pp.124–125.
252  General T. Bonie, *La Cavalerie Française* (Paris, Amyot,18710) pp.67–68.
253  Bachliers' brigade of dragoons formed part of 2 Corps' cavalry division; the 7th lost three officers and eight men wounded, the 12th one officer and three men wounded.

flankers. The French pursuit was, as their official history concedes, 'très moll'[254] with Forton's cavalry seemingly preferring to make prisoners of the wounded rather than close with the enemy. However, if the regimental history of Flatow's 3rd Brandenburgers is to be believed, Bredow himself had a narrow escape:

> Now come a scattered crowd of Cuirassiers past our position, then we see in their rear a senior officer, soon recognised as General von Bredow, who is pursued closely by the French Cuirassiers. The French are every moment gaining on the General, whose horse is exhausted; they must soon overtake him, when a soldier of the 11th Company, running forward, shoots the leading French officer as he raises his sword to cut the General down. Our men cheer and the French retire.[255]

As was anticipated, Bredow's 'Death Ride' (as the attack was later known), incurred considerable losses; when the cuirassiers rallied near Vionville they formed two squadrons[256] of four platoons, 220 men of all ranks; their casualties totalled 205 men and 261 horses.[257] Six officers and 80 men of the 16th Lancers rallied at Flavigny; when the 1st Squadron re-joined the regiment along with other stragglers, they mustered 12 officers and 210 men, many of whom were slightly wounded. The lancers recorded losses of 192 men and 200 horses;[258] it could have been worse for, as one Prussian battery commander explained, the charge came just in time: 'We'd been routed by the blinding French fire; all of our battery horses were dead and we were about to be overrun when Bredow's cavalry flashed by; they saved the day.'[259] As far as Alvesleben was concerned, any sacrifice which bought him a little time and allowed reinforcements to support his hard-pressed and outnumbered corps, was justified; around 3:00 p.m. he was heard to mutter: 'Like Wellington at Waterloo, give me night or give me X Corps.'[260]

Given the respite afforded by Bredow's charge and with no immediate threat from 6 Corps, Buddenbrock took the opportunity of the ensuing lull in the fighting to undertake another reorganisation of his depleted forces. The I and III/20th took up position to the north of the highway facing the Roman road;[261] part of the 64th were to their left, the 6th and 7th companies of the 91st to their right. Four companies[262] deployed to the south of the road, again fronting to the north-east.

254  'Very feeble.'
255  George Heinrich Kirchof, *Das 3 Brandenburgische Infanterie Regiment Nr 20 in den Feldzug 1866 und 1870–71*(Berlin, Mittler und Sohn, 1881) p.267.
256  This included the 3rd Squadron that had been sent to screen Tronville Copse and the first platoon from 1st Squadron that had been away on relay services.
257  Dead; one officer, 43 men, 33 horses; Wounded; six officers, 72 men, 25 horses; Missing; 83 men, 203 horses
258  Dead; two officers, 28 men, 172 horses; Wounded; five officers,101 men 28 horses; Missing two officers, 54 men. Their losses included their commander von der Dollen and Second Lieutenant Vogt. Both were wounded and lying helpless under dead horses, were captured by the French.
259  Wawro, *The Franco-Prussian War* p.156.
260  Bonnal, *St Privat II*, p.277.
261  The right of this new line was about 1,100 paces east of Vionville and rested on the road; the left was 400 paces east of Vionville about 300 paces north of the road.
262  1st, 2nd, 4th, 7th and 11/35th.

The 6th and 7th companies of the 35th took up position along the Flavigny road; the 5th and 8th in Vionville; whilst the 9th, 10th and 12th, along with the remnants of the II/52nd and the III/12th occupied Flavigny. The remainder of the 64th were withdrawn to the rear of Vionville to create a new reserve.

On the French side, Forton's cavalry suffered only minor losses[263] in the mêlée although their artillery and infantry on the ridge were left completely disorganised by Bredow's attack; on the right of the line, 12 companies[264] of the 93rd and several companies of the 9th Chasseurs withdrew into the woods by the side of the Roman road alongside the 73rd to rally and reform. Of the 12 batteries that had been ridden through, only two[265] remained in the gun line; the others fell back to reorganise and resupply. Following the charge, a 1,000-metre-wide gap had opened up between the right of the 70th and six[266] companies of the 93rd, leaving the centre of Canrobert's line almost devoid of troops. The Guard Zouaves were sent forward to fill the breach and 'aligned as though they were on parade'[267] both battalions advanced across the crest of the plateau, the 2nd pushing out two companies as tirailleurs.

A little later around 3:00 p.m., two batteries[268] of Guard artillery moved to their support but after firing off six or eight rounds, they were ordered to withdraw 1,500 metres to the rear. Shortly after, the Zouaves were also recalled to Rezonville with General Picard, the divisional commander excusing his action by stating that his guns 'came under a flanking fire from the enemy artillery' and that he thought 'another French corps was moving up from the right.'[269] Whatever the reason for their sudden withdrawal, the centre of the French line was again denuded of troops and more importantly as far as Canrobert was concerned, any plans, real or imaginary he may have had for assaulting Vionville, were hastily abandoned; his efforts were now all given over to rebuilding his defensive line, although initially, the only support he received was a battery sent forward by General Canu, commander of the artillery reserve.[270] In the hiatus following the cavalry action, Montluisant took advantage of the pause:

> ... to rapidly reorganise Blondel and Ostler's batteries with the debris of the 5th and with carriages that have been abandoned on the field. I have the wounded taken up and at half past three proceed towards the crest of the plateau, whence I perceive the

263  18 officers wounded, 7 men killed, 51 wounded and 38 missing. An analysis of their injuries showed that 20 suffered sabre wounds, 12 lance wounds, 18 suffered rifle wounds and 21 were struck by shells.

264  1st, 2nd and 3rd, I/93rd; II/93rd; 1st, 2nd and 3rd III/93rd.

265  7th and 12/8th; the batteries withdrawn from the firing line comprised the 5/8th, 5th, 6th and 7/14th, 7th and 8/20th, 7/5th, 3/18th, 9th and 10/13th. The batteries reported casualties of 195 men and 194 horses. The 11 batteries for which records exist show they fired off a total of 5,935 rounds, an average of some 540 rounds per battery or 90 per gun. The highest expenditure was recorded by the 6/14th, which fired off 1,100 rounds, an average of 183 per gun. This battery, from de Villiers division, had been one of the first to deploy around 9:30 a.m. and even assuming it was continuous action for the preceding 5 hours, it still equates to one round being discharged per gun every 100 seconds, a truly impressive rate of fire.

266  4th, 5th and 6th I/93rd; 4th, 5th and 6th III/93rd.

267  L'État-Major, *Rezonville* p.369.

268  4th and 6th (m).

269  L'État-Major, *Rezonville* p.370. Presumably the men Picard saw were from Le Boeuf's 3 Corps or possibly Ladmirault's 4 Corps.

270  The 5/18th.

Prussian artillery proceeding anew towards the centre of the action. I am alone, not a single company on this immense plateau. Everyone is fighting on my right and my left. Forton's cavalry is in our rear at the bottom of the valley near the bog of Villers aux Bois. One battery, that of Blondel is close at hand. I lead it to the crest to open fire on the advancing enemy. Major Vignotti again rides off to procure us support. Colonel Défaudais sends us a battery. Colonel Lewal who has noticed the enemy's movement sends us another.[271]

To the south of the main road, Bazaine's defensive line was in a similar precarious position; after being subjected to constant shell fire for over an hour, the gunline located between the highway and the track leading from Rezonville to Buxières had been reduced to just three batteries. Further to the east, the artillery deployed alongside the Maison Blanche suffered from the attention of Stülpnagel's guns, the effectiveness of which, as the French Official History observed, resulted in a 'véritable debacle.' The few batteries that remained in action had to constantly shift position to escape the destructive fire whilst the majority were pulled out of the line due to the casualties suffered or to replenish ammunition and repair damaged guns and limbers.

On the left of the French line where Deligny's Voltigeur division watched over the Bois des Ognons, Bazaine ordered Picard's division of the Imperial Guard to the crest of the heights south of Rezonville, so as to provide a bulwark behind which Frossard's shattered 2 Corps could rally. The Zouaves took station to the right of the village, the 1st Grenadiers on their left. To their left, two battalions of the 2nd Grenadiers under General Lacroix extended the line further to the east and although their deployment was carried out under the cover of six batteries,[272] they could do little to shield Picard's men from the incessant fire, with 1st Brigade attracting the attention of Stülpnagel's artillery, 2nd Brigade being targeted by skirmishers pushing forward through the Bois des Ognons.

## Alvesleben Under Continued Pressure

It was now a little after 3:00 p.m. and as the fighting between the exhausted infantry again subsided, it was left to the equally fatigued artillery to continue the struggle.[273] Whilst the danger posed by Canrobert's 'offensive' against Vionville had passed, Alvesleben's left wing was still threatened by the presence of 3 and 4 corps who, as evidenced by the huge dust cloud that broadcast their progress, were assembling between St Marcel and Bruville. Although they were shadowed by Rheinbaben's cavalry, they were too few in number to delay their advance and as his troopers fell back on Mars la Tour, the Prussian commander became increasingly concerned

---

271  M.A. *The War of 1870–71* p.309.
272  3rd and 4th Batteries of the Field Artillery Regiment of the Guard and the 3rd, 4th, 5th and 6th Batteries of the Horse Artillery Regiment.
273  Alvesleben in particular was dependent upon his gunners to sustain the battle: 'The artillery is, for the moment, our only support; the infantry can hardly be counted on. If the artillery withdraws, the infantry will not be able to hold on and the battle will be lost. If the artillery remains, the outcome will be at least indecisive'. L'État-Major, *Rezonville* p.377.

about this new threat, given that promised reinforcements from X Corps had still to arrive on the battlefield.

Meanwhile, Bazaine finally stirred himself from his indecision and 'suggested' to Le Boeuf that he bring the remainder of his corps into line on the right of Canrobert, between Bois St Marcel and Mars la Tour where Tixier's 1st Division were slowly gaining ascendancy over Lehman's demi brigade in their protracted struggle for possession of the northeast edge of Tronville Copse. Tixier's firing line[274] was less than 400 metres from the wood; the 4th Ligne having deployed one company per battalion as tirailleurs to engage the enemy, the 12th Ligne, two.

Supported by six batteries from 3 Corps positioned to the south-east of Saint Marcel, these seven companies poured a hail of fire into the copse and by 2:30 p.m., it was evident that the enemy resistance was weakening. The deployment of 4 Corps artillery and Bellecourt's infantry on the plateau to the north of Tronville Copse provided Tixier with timely support and he ordered Péchot to drive Lehman's men out of the wood. The 4th and 12th Ligne advanced to the attack but the weight of the defender's fire brought their skirmish line to a halt 150 yards from the copse; Colonel Vincedon then called up the 4th and with their support, forced Lehman's men back into the heart of the wood. To their left, the 12th, under Colonel Lebrun, pushed forward and slowly fought their way through the dense undergrowth. As Péchot's men entered the copse from the northeast, the northwest corner was assaulted by part of Bellecourt's division[275] and after an hour's fierce struggle, this pincer movement finally drove the enemy out of the eastern half of the copse, the survivors seeking shelter in Tronville and the western part of the wood.

The tirailleurs deployed along the southern edge of the treeline and at a range of about 1,000 metres opened fire on Körber's artillery to the west of Vionville. As the attack against the western part of the copse got underway, Tixier's second line went over to the offensive as three companies from the 9th Chasseurs and the 3/80th advanced along the shallow valley running south to Vionville.[276] Although their attack was halted after a few hundred yards, the Brandenburgers[277] withdrew into the southernmost part of the copse and following more hard fighting,[278] were finally expelled from the wood, the units left exposed by this retreat also being compelled to fall back to avoid being outflanked.[279]

As Tixier's attack steadily made ground, Le Boeuf's corps continued their leisurely deployment; Aymard division was by now to the north of the Bois de Tronville and the head of Nayral's division, which had been tasked with supporting Tixier, had reached St Marcel.[280] However, before these troops could deploy, Nayral was told by Bazaine to return to Villers aux Bois, with

274  The front line comprised three battalions of the 4th and two battalions of the 12th; the second line was formed by one battalion of the 100th and from Le Boeuf's corps, three battalions of the 80th and one battalion of the 85th.
275  3/43rd.
276  The 80th was one of the few regiments from Le Boeuf's Corps that actually took part in the days fighting.
277  1st and 3/24th, 2/20th and 5th and 8th companies of the 91st.
278  The 20th suffered over 1,000 casualties, killed wounded and missing; the 24th over 750.
279  6th and 7th companies, 91st, 3/20th, 1/64th and 7th, 8th and 11th companies, 64th.
280  Le Boeuf's 3rd Division, under Metman was still making their way to the front, their commander subsequently blaming the delay on a staff officer sent to guide them, for taking the wrong way.

Aymard being ordered to send additional troops[281] to bolster the defences around Rezonville. Only then could Aymard deploy what remained of his division in support of Montuadon; the 80th was sent to the north of the Tronville Copse, with two battalions of the 60th and the 44th occupying the clearing between Bois de Saint Marcel and Bois de Pierrot. However, other than this inconsequential deployment, 3 Corps took no further part in the day's action.

In his post combat report, Le Boeuf used Bazaine's depletion of his combat strength to excuse his corps lack of activity, but with the exception of Montaudon's division and the 3/80th that supported Tixier's attack, hardly any of his infantry fired a shot in anger. As Bonnal observed in his commentary,[282] between 1:00 p.m. and 3:30 p.m. the former Chief of the Staff had some 24 battalions and 10 batteries to hand which, if employed more aggressively could easily have swept away Alvesleben's defence around Vionville. It is difficult to imagine that any Prussian officer would have acted in such a passive manner if confronted by such a situation and again, this episode serves to highlight the differing tactical ethos of the opposing corps commanders.

## 4 Corps Enter the Fray

Earlier that morning, Ladmirault had ridden forward with his staff from Sainte Marie aux Chênes to investigate the firing that had broken out a way to his left. He was informed by one of Lorencez's officers that Bazaine was battling against superior forces and awaiting the arrival of his corps, endeavoured to obtain a better picture of the situation: 'At this moment I knew that 2 Corps was already engaged and was supported by the Guard and that 6 Corps, to its right, was equally engaged; to the rear, part of 3 Corps under the command of Marshal Le Boeuf had just arrived.'[283]

From the heights east of Bruville, he observed Le Boeuf's infantry marching into position between le Caule Farmhouse and the Roman road, their open flank covered by Clérembault's cavalry, whilst enemy patrols were visible to the north of the Tronville Copse. Around 11:30 a.m., General Veron dit Bellecourt's brigade[284] arrived at Doncourt and despite the noise of battle raging to his front, Ladmirault ordered his men to unhorse their wagons, erect tents and in typical French fashion, 'prescrivit de faire le café.'[285] As the remainder of Grenier's division completed their leisurely assembly around Doncourt, he made his way to the south of Saint Marcel and although still without orders and in complete ignorance of Bazaine intentions, his vantage point at least allowed him to form a reasonable appreciation of the situation.[286]

Whilst Prussian cavalry patrols were visible around Mars la Tour and heavy cannon fire continued to be heard coming from the direction of Rezonville, the only enemy infantry in evidence on this sector of the battlefield, were Lehman's demi brigade lining the northern edge

---

281  The 85th, the 11th Chasseurs and a battalion of the 60th.
282  *La Manoeuvre de Saint Privat.*
283  L'État-Major, *Rezonville* p.397.
284  1st Brigade, Grenier's 2nd Division; 5th Chasseur battalion, 13th and 43rd Ligne.
285  L'État-Major, *Rezonville* p.398.
286  At the post war Court of Inquiry, Ladmirault declared that he had never once seen an officer of the general staff and during the engagement he received no information about the neighbouring 2 and 3 Corps. See l'État-Major, *Rezonville* p.409.

of Tronville Copse. He therefore ordered Veron dit Bellecourt[287] to drive off the enemy scouts and following a few bursts from his mitrailleuses,[288] the Prussian cavalry fell back to the south and south-east of the village.

The 5th Chasseurs then took up a covering position in a small copse to the north of Mars la Tour whilst the 98th moved to Greyère Farm. Hot on the heels of the retreating cavalry, Grenier's divisional artillery and the guns of the corps' Reserve, made their way to the heights overlooking the Tronville Copse and, supported by the 13th and 43rd Ligne, opened fire on Lehman's men along the edge of the copse.

By accident rather than design, Ladmirault found himself ideally placed to roll up the enemy position; with his open flank secured by a large body of cavalry,[289] it was evident that on the left of the Prussian line there was little or no opposition to be found and as noted within his post combat report: 'At this time our right wing completely outflanked the left of the enemy and we conceived the idea of throwing them out of Vionville.'[290]

Bellecourt ordered the 13th and 43rd to send a battalion against Tronville Copse and in concert with Tixier's attack, the two battalions succeeded (following a hard struggle), in driving the Prussians out of the northern part of the wood. It was about 3:45 p.m. and the way now lay open for 4 Corps to fall on the flank of Alvesleben's over committed forces.

As 1st Brigade pushed forward to consolidate their hold on the wood, Ladmirault was scanning the countryside to the south when:

> All of a sudden, like something you see at the theatre, the horizon, until then so calm was suddenly crowned with hordes of men who seemed to spring out the ground. From one side of Tronville there was a sudden movement and compact battalions emerged from the clouds of dust, the heads of the columns heading towards the woods. To the rear of Mars la Tour, towards Suzemont and Puxieux, we saw rising clouds of dust, a clear sign of impending reinforcements and finally, their artillery which took up a threating posture.[291]

287 Veron dit Bellecourt commanded 1st Brigade, 2nd Division 4 Corps; 5th Chasseurs, 13th and 43rd Line. According to Lehautcourt's account, as Ladmirault was surveying the ground from a position alongside a battery of guns deployed near St Marcel, an elderly man on horseback rode up; this was General Chargarnier, one of Bazaine's confidants who had been recalled from the reserve list at the outbreak of the war. Motioning towards the Prussians, in a loud voice he chided Ladmirault: 'Ah, well General; are we not going to present our carte de visite?' Shortly after, a battery opened fire on the Prussians in the Bois de Tronville, the enemy responding with rifle fire. Chargarnier continued: 'They're close. Aren't we going advance?' It was only then that Ladmirault issued his orders to attack. See *Rezonville et Saint Privat*, p.242.

288 5th Battery, 1st Artillery Regiment.

289 The cavalry on Ladmirault's flank consisted of Clérembault's division from 3 Corps, Barail's 2nd Chasseurs d'Afrique with the 5th and 6th batteries of the 19th à Cheval and de France's Lancers and Dragoons of the Guard who were deployed around Jarny. After escorting the emperor to Etain, the Guard cavalry had set up camp when the noise of firing was heard away to the south. In a show of initiative rare amongst French officers, de France broke camp and marched to the sound of the guns.

290 L'État-Major, *Rezonville*, p.410.

291 Lieutenant Colonel Rousset, *Le 4 Corps de L'Armée de Metz* (Paris, Henri Charles-Lavauzelle. 1900) pp.126–127.

From his vantage point, Ladmirault discerned 'a strong enemy column between Mars la Tour and Vionville'[292] and despite the presence of Le Boeuf's corps to his left and the Guard cavalry on his right, it seems his nerve simply failed him at this critical juncture with Bellecourt being ordered to fall back into the copse, taking with him the prisoners captured in the fighting.

In his post combat report he claimed 'Just then, Grenier's division was the only part of 4 Corps on the battlefield; it was evident that the enemy, understanding the threat to his left wing, had brought forward strong reserves; it would have been too dangerous for us to continue with the attack.'[293] When pressed at the post war Commission of Inquiry on why he failed to pursue this offensive, he fell back on the excuse used by so many senior French officers during this short campaign: 'Pas d'ordres.'[294]

## X Corps to Alvesleben's Rescue

The 'army of infantry' that caused Ladmirault so much consternation were in fact the advance guard of the long-awaited reinforcements from X Corps whose hard marching columns had reached the battlefield just in time to deter 4 Corps' offensive. In accordance with the prince's orders, Voights Rhetz had directed his corps to march on Verdun by way of St Hilaire en Woëvre; Schwartzkoppen's 19th Infantry Division and the brigade of Guard Dragoons led the way, followed by Kraatz Koschlau's 20th Infantry Division. During the morning, cannon fire was heard away to the right and Voights Rhetz initially took this to be an action between Rheinbaben's cavalry and the French rearguard. As the firing persisted, he made his way to Jonville seeking to clarify the situation, accompanied by the 3rd Squadron 2nd Guard Dragoons, where he was handed Caprivi's despatch calling for X Corps urgent support. He rode across to high ground near Tronville and appreciating the true extent of the engagement, immediately issued orders for his corps to make their way to the battlefield with all possible speed.

Kraatz left Pont à Mousson at 7:00 a.m. and after some hard marching, by 11:30 a.m., his division reached its intended destination at Thiaucourt, where they were to bivouac. After his men fell out to set up camp, officer patrols were despatched to investigate the source of the cannon fire that could be heard away to the north. Kraatz had just resolved to march to the sound of the guns when Caprivi's messenger arrived requesting assistance and he at once set off by way of Charey and St Julien, the 16th Dragoons leading the way. The two leading battalions of 39th Brigade[295] reached Chambley around 2:30 p.m. and accompanied by General von Woyna continued to Tronville.

II Army headquarters at Pont à Mousson first heard news of the engagement around Vionville at 10:30 a.m. but initially, it was believed to be a merely an action between rear-guards. Only when Kraatz's despatch arrived at 2:00 p.m. did the full extent of the fighting became apparent. Prince Frederick Charles left at once for the action, arriving at the northwest corner of the

292  Lehautcourt, *Rezonville*, p.249.
293  L'État-Major, *16 Août Documents*, p.410.
294  Fritz Hoenig, *Inquiries Concerning Tactics of the Future* (London, Longmans, Green and Co. 1899) p.92. Ladmirault told the post war Enquiry, this 'army of infantry appeared to be heading towards Mars la Tour which would have threatened Bellecourt's brigade if he had waited for this movement to develop.' See Lehautcourt, *Rezonville*, p.249.
295  I and II/79th.

Bois de Vionville in the rear of 5th Division, having covered the 14 miles in just two hours.[296] Their exhausted troops were in no position to renew their attack but assured by Stülpnagel that he would hold his position to the last man, the prince rode over to Flavigny to confer with Alvesleben and Voights Rhetz, where the imminent arrival of X Corps seemed to offer better prospects of renewing the offensive against the French right flank.

Approaching the battlefield, Kraatz rode forward to Tronville and noting how Buddenbrock's troops were stretched to breaking point, directed Woyna to send a regiment[297] and four of his leading batteries[298] to support 6th Division around Flavigny. As the infantry made their way towards the fighting, the commander of the corps artillery[299] requested and received permission to take his two light batteries[300] on ahead of the marching column. They subsequently took position to the west of Tronville from where they opened fire on Bellecourt's men in Tronville Copse.

These guns were engaged by three of Grenier's batteries, but as the French infantry withdrew from the copse, Goltz advanced his batteries to the main road and before long, their concentrated fire forced Grenier's artillery to pull out of the firing line. Supported by two squadrons from the 4th Cuirassiers, Goltz attempted to leapfrog the guns forward, but his efforts came to nothing in the face of concentrated chassepot fire. His small force then received welcome support from the 4th Heavy and 4th Light and after they unlimbered to the south of Bruville, the four batteries concentrated their fire on Ladmirault's artillery although Körbers attempts to bring his guns forward to support Goltz were thwarted by swarms of tirailleurs advancing out of Tronville Copse.

At this critical time, 2nd Horse Artillery moved into the gunline,[301] the support they provided helping to drive the skirmishers back into the depths of the wood. As the batteries continued to pound the French positions, the leading infantry formations from 20th Division at last reached the battlefield; around 3:30 p.m. I and II/79th formed up to the south of Tronville and after deploying in company columns at open intervals, advanced to support Lehman's struggle for control of Tronville Copse.

Whilst I Battalion secured the village and provided cover for Körber's guns, the II, passing to the east, moved into the copse and after a fierce struggle, expelled the tirailleurs of the 4th Ligne from the southern part of the wood. As the remainder of his division arrived, Kraatz moved the 17th to the west of Tronville, each battalion pushing its flank companies into the first line, the remainder following in line of half battalions at deploying intervals. Edging their way forward under heavy fire, the 2nd and 3rd companies I/79th forced their way into the southernmost part of the copse as II/79th attempted to drive the French out the northern section. As this struggle intensified, Kraatz deployed his remaining battalions[302] along the main road, which afforded them some cover from the chassepot and artillery fire.

---

296 According to Hoffbauer's account, quoting Major von Scherff, the prince arrived at 3:45 p.m. covering the 14 miles in just 1¼ hours.
297 In fact, the I and II/56th and III/79th.
298 3rd Light, 3rd, 5th and 6th Heavy batteries.
299 Colonel Baron von der Goltz.
300 5th and 6th.
301 1st Horse artillery IV Corps, 3rd Light III Corps, 1st Heavy, 1st and 2nd Horse artillery X Corps.
302 I and III/92nd and 10th Rifles; they were subsequently reinforced by the III/56th.

With 20th Division advancing from the south, Schwartzkoppen approached the battlefield from the west. 19th Division had left Thiaucourt at 5:30 a.m. that morning, its destination being the small hamlet of St Hilaire midway between Mars la Tour and Verdun. 3rd Brigade Dragoon Guards and Planitz's battery of horse artillery, marched in the van followed by von Wedell's 38th Brigade. Following, or so he believed, in the wake of the retreating French Army, Schwartzkoppen expected to stumble across their rearguard at any moment. Fritz Hoenig, a lieutenant in the 57th recalled the air of expectancy:

> It was an oppressively hot August day but the infantry, nevertheless, marched so well that it reached St Hilaire soon after 11:00 a.m. One halt and that of ten minutes only, had been made at Woël. The enemy was supposed to be in retreat on Verdun and indeed, partly upon the road on which we ourselves now were. The consequence of this opinion was that during the march to St Hilaire a certain tension prevailed in the minds of the Staffs. Great then was our surprise to find ourselves on one of his lines of retreat and see nothing of him. The five battalions, both batteries and the two Pioneer companies moved to an encampment south-east of St Hilaire. The II Battalion, 57th and Trotka's squadron of the 2nd Dragoon Guards furnished the outposts for its security. In the meantime, the bells of the churches in the neighbouring villages were ringing violently, to announce our arrival to the enemy.[303]

Intermittent cannon fire had been heard away to the east for much of the morning so the cavalry commander, Count Brandenburg, rode off to investigate, taking with him the 1st Dragoon Guards and the artillery. Almost alone amongst the Prussian commanders, on the 16th, Schwartzkoppen chose not to march to the sound of the guns and after reaching St Hilaire, ordered his men to cook dinner, a decision which attracted understandable criticism from his subordinates who were anxious to get into action. It was not long however before the order came through calling for the Brigade to make its way forward to the fighting:

> While the fires were blazing some single horsemen came at full speed from the east, which roused everybody's attention. On the right wing of the 57th Regiment, from whence we had a clear survey to the right, the feeling was that an advance was imminent. So certain was this among the rank and file, that they had already poured out the bubbling soup, before orders for that were given; but the alarm did not ensue till an officer arrived on a horse covered with foam. There was now a general emptying of the cooking kettles and the troops entered on the march. It was 12 o'clock[304] and the objective was Chambley. We did not trust our eyes, as we had found it on the map.[305]

The direct route to Chambley led through Jonville and Xonville but en-route, Schwartzkoppen received fresh intelligence and took the main road leading to Mars la Tour from where he intended to march on Ville sur Yron, which would place his division on the flank of the French

---

303  Hoenig, *Tactics*, pp.74–75.
304  12:30 p.m. according to the German official history and shortly after 12.30 p.m. according to the history of the 16th Regiment.
305  Hoenig, *Tactics*, p.77.

position. Reaching Suzemont around 3:30 p.m., all that could be discerned 'were long lines of fire and thick clouds of dust'[306] but the reports Schwartzkoppen received left him under no illusion about Alvesleben's precarious position and he resolved to march to the support of III Corps left wing at Vionville. The streams of injured and wounded men encountered along the way only added to the sense of urgency, Hoenig recounting:

> Among the wounded I recognised a Lieutenant Dreising, adjutant in the 52nd Regiment. Horse and rider were bathed in sweat and dust; and it seemed to me as if the rider had had a fall. He had also a shot-wound through the leg. His features were scarcely recognisable. As we had been cadets together, I rode up to him, held out my hand and said something; but he rode on showing absolutely no interest. The servant being asked how the fighting was going, answered 'Badly!' Soon after I was met by another officer, of the 20th Regiment who had been shot through the chest. Before I got a word out, he said: 'Well, I hope you will have better luck than we had. You will be astonished. It is no cat-shooting, like in 1866.' This was not exactly cheering, but there was in the officer's tone a touch of soldier like humour.[307]

## 38th Brigade Deploy for the Attack

At 3:30 p.m., some 1,000 metres south-west of Mars la Tour, the brigade halted and as the men readied for action, they were addressed by the field chaplains. As Hoenig recalled, the first sermon did not go down well:

> The Evangelical preacher Aebert, who was the first to speak, showed by his manner so much emotion, chose his words so awkwardly and used such a whimpering tone, that people could not be exactly edified by this 'spiritual consolation'. While the preacher was speaking, we saw a single rider galloping towards us at top speed straight from Tronville, his stole fluttering in the wind. As he came closer, I recognised in him Stuckmann, the Catholic chaplain and a dear acquaintance from 1866. He stopped his horse like a perfect Cavalryman before Colonel Cranach, so that this picture of resolution had by itself a reanimating effect. After exchanging a few words with the Colonel, he rose in his stirrups and spoke thus, with his sharp Westphalian accent 'Comrades, the III Army Corps is heavily engaged. To you falls the task of rescuing it. Attack the enemy, then, defying death; then God will be with you. Amen!' That was to the point and worked like a spell. Immediately after this the regiment had orders to uncase the colours and load; and Colonel von Cranach addressed to the men some words like these 'You have shown on the march what brave fellows you are. Show it now in the fight and, whatever may happen, hold your colours high and let no Frenchman's hand touch them. Nun mit Gott.'[308]

306  *Ibid*, p.84.
307  *Ibid*, p.91.
308  *Ibid*, pp.92–94.

In typical bull-headed Prussian style, Schwartzkoppen made no attempt to reconnoitre the ground over which von Wedell's brigade was to advance and decided upon an immediate attack. As the men formed up,[309] he met with his corps commander who approved this course of action, both men taking the view that III Corps precarious position justified such precipitous action, although their impetuosity was to cost the brigade dear.[310] As Hoenig related, not everyone shared this view and the orders caused consternation amongst the officers who were to undertake the assault:

> General von Schwartzkoppen had communicated his intentions to General von Wedell but in all ranks subordinate to them a complete uncertainty prevailed: and even to Colonels von Cranach[311] and von Bixen[312] only the general direction was indicated. At any rate, no timely and exhaustive mutual understanding ensued as at Popowitz; but the whole matter from the first was characterised by precipitation and confusion. I know for certain that, for instance, the battalion commanders did not know what they had to do. For Lieutenant Colonel von Roell Hoenig, who fell, made the sarcastic remark 'If Stuckmann had not been there I should have known nothing at all. The little I do know, I learnt from his speech. Today, it seems, Stuckmann has the whole business.'[313]

With his left covered by cavalry[314] and without waiting for his artillery to soften up the enemy lines, Wedell launched his attack. As Hoenig observed, given the haste with which the attack was launched, the formations on the left of the brigade closed with the French positions before those on the right had even begun to deploy:

> The last companies had to execute a wheel, extending to some 2,500 metres, the result was a movement of scattered character from start to finish … But despite greater speed, no proper unity was attainable in the movement; the battalions, rather, were drawn off individually from the left to the right wing; and the right wing only reached the enemy line in a state of complete exhaustion, at a moment when the battalions of the left wing were already repulsed … It is comprehensible how that wing, despite the acceleration of its march, came into the fighting line certainly half an hour later than the left.[315]

---

309 The formation was as follows:

| I/57th | F/57th | 2 Pioneer Co's. |
|---|---|---|
| 2nd Heavy Batt | 1st Light Batt | |
| II/16th | I/16th | |

310 Schwartzkoppen was evidently ignorant about the strength of the opposition he faced, later telling an officer who was present at the battle 'And who could suppose there was such a force against us?' See Hoenig *Tactics*, p.136.
311 CO 57th.
312 CO 16th.
313 Hoenig, *Tactics*, pp.94–95.
314 Barby's brigade, together with the 13th and 16th Dragoons near Tronville; 10th Hussars to the north of Puxieux, two squadrons of 4th Cuirassiers and 1st Dragoon Guards south-east of Mars la Tour.
315 Hoenig, *Tactics*, pp.97–107.

Reacting to Ladmirault's order to hold position following the sighting of the mysterious enemy column between Mars la Tour and Vionville, Grenier's division withdrew to a line running along the heights between Tronville Copse in the east and Ville sur Yron in the west. This already formidable defensive position overlooked a deep ravine, known as the fond de la cuve[316] and presented a serious obstacle to any attacking force. The 1/98th and a company of engineers held Greyère Farm on the extreme right of his position; two batteries of horse artillery[317] from Barails' division, had unlimbered on the high ground to their rear, whilst the lancers and dragoons of the Guard along with the 2nd Chasseurs d'Afrique, were in support some 800 metres south-west of Saint Catherine's farm.

The 2nd and 3/64th from Pradier's brigade held the line on the right of Grenier's positions, overlooking the ravine between Greyère Farm and the road running from Mars la Tour to Bruville; 1/64th were in the second line, the 2nd and 3/98th in reserve. Three batteries[318] from Cissey's division unlimbered either side of the road running from Bruville to Mars la Tour, the 2/13th and a company of the 3/16th formed up in their rear. To their left, nine batteries[319] were positioned across the crest of the heights, with a company from the 5th Chasseurs forming a screen along their front. To the rear of the gun line stood the 1/43rd, four companies from the 2nd, a company of the 5th Chasseurs and two from the 2/43rd.

The northwest corner of the Tronville Copse was held by three companies of chasseurs and two companies of the 3/13th occupied the left front of the gun line; the 1/13th and three companies of the 3/13th were held in reserve to the left rear of the artillery. Three regiments from Legrand's cavalry division, supported by the 11th Dragoons, were deployed along the rear of this formidable position.

Further north, the remainder of Cissey's division slowly made its way from Doncourt with Lieutenant Patry recording his regiment's approach march:

> After numerous stops and hitches, around ten or eleven, we emerged onto a vast plateau which afforded a great view out to the horizon. For some time we had heard the sound of canon to our left; once on the plateau we see small puffs of white smoke which suddenly appear in the sky, dissipate, only to be replaced by others. It's German shrapnel which bursts in the air and scatter amongst our men a veritable hail of iron which tears everything in its path, causing atrocious wounds. We continue our march along field tracks, heading west. We pass through the hamlet of Habonville, the village of Jouaville where we veer towards the south which brought us closer to the fighting if the noise of the cannon and gun fire, which is getting louder and louder, is anything to go by … As soon as we pass Bruville and reach high ground we get a general view of the battle. Two almost parallel lines of thick greyish smoke, forming veritable clouds, which were lit up at every instant by powerful red flashes, show where the opposing batteries are engaged in a terrific duel between themselves. Roughly midway between these two lines, there were persistent clouds of white smoke which extended along the whole fighting front, sometimes gathering in hollows, sometimes rolling along the

316  'Bottom of the Tub'.
317  5th and 6/19th.
318  3rd, 9th and 12/15th.
319  11/1st; 6/17th; 7/1st, 6th and 9/8th; 5/17th; 5th, 6th and 12/1st.

crest of the hills; this was the firefight between the two lines of infantry which in places were within a few hundred metres of one another. The brigade was deployed on the plateau; it seems that things are getting hot for orders were given to drop our packs and the battalions, formed in line, advance at the pas gymnastique. My battalion, which was to the rear of the column was preparing to deploy into battle formation when our commander received the order to hold our ground so as to guard the convoy which had halted to our rear. This was really bad luck![320]

Hoenig, writing some years after the battle, described Grenier's position as it appeared to the attackers:

One surveyed from horseback, the French array, which stretched from height 846 as far as the Greyère Farm. Indeed, one made out from the body on the height 846 a considerable ·group of horsemen. It was General Ladmirault with his staff. To it were joined long lines right and left that could be followed west to Greyère Farm. Between the infantry, lines of artillery were observable, which already at this time were directing a lively fire on Mars la Tour and the 4th Cuirassiers. An adequate estimate of the hostile strength was not possible, but it was beyond all doubt that we had a division straight before us. Besides, the sun was shining upon the whole length of the French array, which was still clear of gunpowder and dust ... The watch showed 4 o'clock when the 38th Brigade set forward.[321]

The 16th deployed on the left, the 57th to the right, with each regiment arrayed in two lines 150 yards apart; Colonel Brixen of the 16th was keen to get his attack underway and shortly before the arrival of the 57th, gave the command 'Forward!' designating the 2nd Company as the 'compagnie de direction' with the regiment fronting towards the north-west as ordered.[322] With flags flying and drums beating, they 'advanced in the then favourite rapid step, without any pause at all'[323] and as the 16th moved forward, Hoenig noted:

General von Schwartzkoppen and his Chief of the General staff, major von Scherff were on horseback in the midst of a heavy artillery bombardment. The troops were rapidly advancing were getting over the ground as fast as they could and when the skirmishers of the I/57th, with which Lieutenant Colonel von Roell was riding, passed Schwartzkoppen, the brave General joined him, addressing some cheering words to the men. At that time, the liveliness of the mitrailleuse, artillery and infantry fire from

---

320  Patry, *La Guerre*, pp.83–85.
321  Hoenig, *Tactics*, p.133.
322  L'État-Major, *Rezonville*, p.485. The brigade was deployed as follows: Left Wing; First line: 5/16th, 7/16th, 3/16th, 2/16th, 11/16th, two subdivisions 2/57th, 10/57th, one subdivision 2/57th distance 165 yards. Second line: 8th and 6/16th, 4th and 1/16th, 12th and 9/16th and 4th and 3/57th. Right Wing: First line: Three subdivisions I/57th extended as skirmishers to the Bois de Tronville a distance of 165 yards. Second line 11th and 9/57th, 12th and 10/57th and two engineer companies.
323  Hoenig, *Tactics*, p.112. The German official history states that the advance was made by the companies making alternative rushes of 100–150 paces and then lying down; See Clarke, *The Franco-German War*, p.407. Hoenig dismisses this as nonsense.

the left front astounded everybody; Schwartzkoppen, said to Roell 'Just extend thick swarms of skirmishers and we will soon settle them' and afterwards 'bring your left shoulder up a little, there, on the corner of the wood' pointing at the same time to the northwest angle of the Bois de Tronville. Meanwhile, the 1/57th had extended two Züge as skirmishers and taken this direction, so that a gap appeared inevitable between the 16th and the 57th. Schwartzkoppen then said 'Roell, put a whole company in there' and the 2nd company 57th was pushed in. Soon after, the horse of the captain of that company was killed; the captain, being very short sighted and pinned to the ground for a little while, lost control over his company, which then brought its right shoulder too far forward.[324]

Given the hasty and uncoordinated manner in which the attack was launched, it seems that two companies[325] on the brigade's left wing advanced due north, to the west of the Mars la Tour–Bruville road where the terrain provided good protection from the French fire. The bulk of the brigade continued towards the north-east, its progress hampered by the numerous wire fences strung across the hillside which had to be cut, allowing the second line to push up to fill the gaps torn in the first.

Although under heavy artillery fire, they suffered few losses until they had crossed the brow of the hill running down to the fond de la cuve, where the exposed ground provided little cover. Struck by a murderous hail of chassepot and mitrailleuse fire, the attackers 'with no word of command'[326] instinctively turned to confront this threat but on approaching to within 100–150 yards of the ravine, threw themselves to the ground seeking shelter from the chassepot fire, unable to continue their advance.

I and II/57th deployed to the rear of a hedge that ran across the plateau and attempted to engage the 43rd Ligne on the opposite side of the ravine, although given the range, about 1,000 metres, their fire had little effect unlike their opponents, whose chassepot proved deadly.[327] Exhausted by the rapidity of their advance, Wedell's men found it difficult to respond and faced with a murderous hail of shot and shell, the shaken infantry refused to follow their officers as they tried to get them to close with the enemy; Hoenig described how:

At this moment Vicefeldwebel Thiel, leader of one Zug of the II/57th came from the left to Lieutenant Colonel von Roell and made the following report 'I most respectfully report that my Zug no longer follows me. It is lying down. I have repeatedly rushed forward. It has been no good.' Lieutenant Colonel von Roell, a very brisk nature, turned to me with the words 'These fellows!' and gave the order shortly 'Ride back with the Zug leader.' ... I came to the Zug and the brave Zug leader, a hero in the finest sense of the word, waving his sword and crying out 'Forward,' succeeded by his exertions

324  Hoenig, *Tactics*, p.98.
325  5th and 6th companies' 16th Regiment.
326  L'État-Major, *Rezonville*, p.492.
327  Hoenig noted 'Needle and Chassepot opposed to each other did not both work devastation. The devastation affected us alone.' See *Tactics*, p.110.

in getting some non-commissioned officers and men from the ground. Most of the remaining men lay on the earth dead or wounded, as in the ranks where they stood.[328]

Even when the officers managed to get their men to return fire, in the confusion those in the front line were often shot at by their supports as the second line pushed forward:

> Just then 11th and 9/57th formed up and fired two or three volleys. Lieutenant Colonel von Roell remarked 'Well, Warendorff will be pleased!' Riding straightforward he turned to me, asking and 'Is that Lieutenant Colonel Sannow?' I answered 'Yes.' Von Roell said 'I am glad. Some order must come into this business. F/57th is shooting my first Company in the back. My second is quite rent asunder by the 16th. If only Bernewitz (commander of the 3/57th) keeps a good look out with the colour. It is indeed an infernal fire' [329]

In the turmoil, some officers tried to encourage their men by personal example:

> Sannow had caused Ohly's Half Battalion to lie down behind the hedge ... On the flank lay his adjutant, severely wounded and both their horses shot. In the centre of the 12th and 9/16th was, halted Captain Ohly on horseback, the colour beside him. He had a rifle in his hand, encouraged the men and repeatedly fired from horseback. Skirmishers lay in front and on both flanks of this Half battalion; to the left those of the 10/16th and II/57th; to the right, those of the I/57th. The Half battalion itself was in close order. From the front of the column few shots were fired; but the half battalion did not keep up a regular firefight. I have never seen an officer so calm and brave as Captain Ohly ... His keen voice sounded through the fearful roll of the hostile infantry fire; 'At them lads!' 'There they come; look alive!' then again; 'The colour up!' In the end he dashed forward, to carry all with him. In vain. There were too many dead and wounded.[330]

## The Battle Within the Fond de la Cuve

With momentum lost, there was little the attackers could do except bide their time. Roell had just dismounted alongside Sannow when his horse was shot dead, the colonel telling him 'Here we have the only cover. As long as the fire is as fierce as this we cannot get forward. We must wait until they run out of ammunition.'[331]

On the northern side of the ravine, Grenier's division were quick to react to this attack; on the extreme right, the 1/93rd holding Greyère Farm engaged Wedell's brigade as it crossed the brow of the hill. The 2nd and 3/64th easily countered an attempt by two companies of the 16th to outflank the French position as they moved forward to the west of the Mars la Tour–Bruville

---

328  *Ibid*, p.137.
329  *Ibid*, p.138.
330  *Ibid*, pp.138–139.
331  *Ibid* p.139.

road. To their left, the 13th and 48th deployed along the northern slopes of the fond de la cuve, prepared to engage the main attack. Swarms of skirmishers were pushed forward to line the hedges along the edge of the ravine whilst the main body of infantry, supported by the divisional artillery and mitrailleuse were arrayed further to the rear along the crest of the heights.

On the opposite side of the ravine, Hoenig watched the French advance with some trepidation, recounting later how he:

> Clearly observed, advancing southwards, a portion of Grenier's division. Lieutenant Colonel von Roell reckoned it at 6 battalions. It moved with great speed, doubling down the slope and before we arrived 80–100 metres south of the ravine, it gained the northern edge. Facing the hostile infantry stood the greatest part of F/16th, I/57th, F/57th and 2 companies of Pioneers. However, II/16th and I/16th found the far side of the ravine unoccupied, for Cissey's division was only then in the act of advancing between Greyère Farm and the great road from Bruville to Mars la Tour. I could clearly perceive its advance from horseback. The right wing and the centre of the Brigade were subjected to a heavy fire in tiers (I from the north edge of the ravine and the II from height 846 to the road Bruville-Mars la Tour) The losses increased and soon we, who had thought to outflank the enemy, were ourselves outflanked from Greyère Farm (Cissey's Division). Three hostile brigades in deployed lines moved against us at 5 o'clock; and there came, in addition, a half brigade (of Cissey's Division) and one chasseur battalion (of Grenier's division) The adversary, who till then was lying flat on the ground and of whom nothing was visible but the peaks of the kepis pointing upwards, overwhelmed our detachments on the coverless surface with a devastating fire.[332]

Despite the hail of shot and shell which tore through their ranks, a number of companies forced their way across the ravine, seeking to close with the French formations. In the 16th, Lieutenant Pilger recalled: 'Around our ears there was an incessant buzzing and whistling. We were crammed together on the ground. All of a sudden came the cry "Stand up! Forward!" We got up and once more, "Forward!" '[333]

The German official history claims all five battalions participated in the assault and closed to 'within 150, 100, yea, even within 30 paces from the French line.'[334] Hoenig, who by this time had been hit and lay wounded on the south side of the ravine, is adamant that only part of the brigade succeeded in crossing the western section of la cuve; 'The five battalions did not spring up as doughty stormers on the far side of the Mars la Tour ravine; but of 20 companies only eight reached its northern edge.'[335] The remainder of the brigade were pinned in position on the southern side of the ravine, unable to move: 'During our advance the French, as I have shown, had thrown forward a strong line against F/16th, 1/57th, F/57th and 2 companies of Pioneers as far as the northern edge of the ravine. On its southern edge, at 80–100 metres distance from it,

332 *Ibid*, p.109.
333 Bonnal, *St Privat II*, p.388.
334 Clarke, *Franco-German War Vol. I*, p.407.
335 The 1st, 2nd, 3rd, 4th,7th, 8th and 11/16th and 11/57th. See *Tactics*, p.110.

those 3½ battalions halted and came not a step further forward.'[336] Within one of the foolhardy units attempting to push their way across the ravine, Pilger described how:

> Both sides opened the most destructive fire, at a distance of one hundred and fifty paces, forming four to six ranks deep, much like in the old days of linear tactics. The firing line of the 16th soon exhausts their cartridges, the rear ranks passing spare rounds to the front rank. Over our heads there's a constant incessant hissing and buzzing and we lie flat on the ground... One attempts to get them to advance, but there is so much noise that you can't be heard by your neighbour. A few men stand up and advance a few steps. Colonel Brixen of the 57th then attempts to renew the attack. His horse is shot from beneath him and although bruised by his fall, he descends into the ravine and climbed the opposite bank, leaning on his sword. He orders the commander of the 3rd company to sound the charge but the buglers were already out of action. He repeats his order again and the men move forward a short distance from us, but then halt to open fire.[337]

On the left of the brigade, 8th Company led off the attack, supported by the 7th in echelon to its left. After crossing the valley, they came up against the 1st and 2/43rd deployed in line along a front of around 600 metres in a small depression which helped shield them from the view of the attacking force. According to one French account, the Germans were surprised to find the enemy so close; suddenly 'the alarm is given by two or three German soldiers who, surprised, can't stop themselves from firing their weapons from the hip as the mass of 38th Brigade advances without firing, in line of company columns, bayonets fixed, in admirable order such that one can clearly make out the regular intervals of six or eight paces between the companies.'[338]

Another French eyewitness related how the Westphalians 'remained silent and quickened their pace; they're only 100 metres away. Immediately and with remarkable coolness our soldiers open a formidable volley fire on the enemy who are now only 30 metres away; we can see the points of their bayonets clearly. Our two battalions are fully deployed, their fire converging on the enemy columns.'[339]

Lieutenant Pilger, on the receiving end of these volleys, recalled 'the men were shooting as fast as they can; our shots struck home because at this distance it was difficult to miss the target even though the smoke rendered them invisible.'[340] Given the volume of fire that greeted their advance it is surprising anyone succeeded in crossing the ravine,[341] but to the right of the 7th, the 3rd and 2nd companies, later reinforced by the 4th and 1st, struggled into the firing line, with the 11th and the 2nd Company 57th taking position on their open flank.

336  Hoenig *Tactics*, pp.136–137.
337  Lehautcourt, *Rezonville*, p.284.
338  *Ibid*, p.279.
339  L'État-Major, *Rezonville*, p.501.
340  *Ibid*, p.505.
341  Hoenig estimated that during the battle for the ravine Grenier's men fired about 954,000 rounds. See *Tactics*, p.167.

their sacrifice disrupting the enemy charge sufficiently enough to allow Planitz to withdraw his battery to the safety of Mars la Tour. [380]

Noting the dragoon's predicament, their commanding officer, Colonel Count Finckenstein galloped across to Rheinbarben's 5th Cavalry Division requesting support from Colonel von Brauchitsch's 13th Schleswig Holstein Dragoon which had been ordered forward from the south-west of Tronville to deter any attempt by the French to outflank the Prussian line. As the 13th moved to assist Hindenburg, the remainder of the division took ground to the west of Mars la Tour; 19th Oldenburg Dragoons on the right of the front line, two squadrons from the 4th Westphalian Cuirassiers in the centre, three squadrons 13th Hanoverian Lancers[381] on the left.

In the second line, three squadrons 10th Magdeburg Hussars took position on the right, 16th Hanoverian Dragoons on the left. The brigade was formed in part open, part closed line of squadrons in platoon columns and numbered around 3,000 horsemen.[382] With Hindenburg's troopers being pushed back towards Mars la Tour, Finkenstein placed himself at the head of the 13th Dragoons and charged the chasseurs disordered ranks, pushing them back towards Greyère Farm.

Satisfied with having driven away the enemy cavalry, Brauchitsch's trumpeter sounded the recall and rallied his squadrons. Martièrie, unwilling to break off the skirmish, then ordered his chasseurs to engage the Schleswig Holsteiners from a distance with their chassepot carbines. Following this brief clash, the stage was now set for the last great cavalry engagement on European soil as, in a scene reminiscent of the battles of the Napoleonic Wars, almost 6,000 horsemen manoeuvred into position on the open ground to the east of Ville sur Yron.

Given his previous timidity, it is no surprise to learn that Ladmirault interpreted the minor redeployment of Rheinbarben's cavalry[383] to the west of Mars la Tour as an attempt by the Prussian's to envelop his right wing and immediately despatched an aide-de-camp with orders for Legrand and de France to 'clear the threat on the flank.'[384] In response, Legrand led the Guard cavalry division forward from their position west of Bruville to support the Chasseurs d'Afrique and after crossing over a ravine by the road, took position to the south of Greyère wood in preparation for a charge against the enemy horse.[385] 3 Corps' cavalry division, which was also to hand, made no move to support the action as, typically, Clérambualt was reluctant to act without express orders from Le Boeuf.

---

380  Casualties for the battery: three horses dead; three men and four horses wounded; all the casualties being caused by the fire of French infantry skirmishers.

381  The 3rd Squadron under Captain Schlick had been sent to help cover Wedell's brigade as it rallied its men.

382  Ignoring previous losses, the cavalry, based on the average strength given in the returns for the 11th August were as follows: 19th Dragoons 560, 13th Lancers (3 squadrons) 420, 4th Cuirassiers (2 squadrons) 280, 13th Dragoons 560, 10th Hussars (3 squadrons) 16th Dragoons 560, 2nd Dragoon Guards (2 squadrons) 280; in total 3,080 horses.

383  In his post combat report he described it as a 'grosse masse de cavalerie.' See l'État-Major, *16 Août Documents*, p.282.

384  Bonnal, *St Privat II*, p.417.

385  De Montaigu's brigade; 2nd and 7th Hussars were in the front line, 3rd Dragoons were in the second 100 metres to the rear, slightly overlapping the hussars' right wing. The Lancers of the Guard were echeloned to the right rear of the dragoons and the Guard Dragoons were in the fourth line, echeloned to the right rear of the lancers.

Du Barail,[386] noting that Brauchitsch had already rallied his dragoons, rode up and somewhat excitedly told Legrand: 'It's too late; the opportunity has passed, the enemy has already had plenty of time to take up its positions.' Legrand snapped, somewhat irritably: 'When I've ordered a charge, I charge!'[387] 'In that case,' du Barail replied, 'I want the support of the Guard brigade' and rode across to General de France telling him to 'Charge!' 'But we're the Guard, we're not under your command.' 'Oh! There's no "We are the Guard" here. Couch your lances and charge! That's a direct order.'[388]

Colonel Carrelet of the 2nd Hussars then suggested that his men should first engage the enemy with their carbines, so as to disrupt their ranks but Legrand, his blood up replied 'Non, non, au sabre!'[389] and ordered Montaigu to charge. Carrelet repeated his suggestion to General Montaigu who responded 'No, a direct order has been issued' and drawing his sword cried: 'A l'arme blanche, Lets go gentlemen!'[390] Similar curt instructions were issued to the hussar brigade: 'Escadrons, garde à vous! Pour charger! Sabre à la main! Au galop, marche!'[391]

The horsemen moved off, some still in column at half distance, before charging uphill for some considerable distance, with the predictable result that their mounts were more or less blown by the time they closed with the enemy.[392] Colonel Chaussée of the 7th Hussars recorded in his post combat report that as his men closed to within 100–150 metres of the enemy line, there was a hesitation in their ranks as the call went up 'It's the Guard!'[393] It seems that the hussars were misled by the calm demeanour of the Schleswig Holsteiners as they closed with them, causing them to mistake the troopers for their own Empress Dragoons, an error which was to cost them dear.

Brauchitsch noted how Montaigu's charge was looking to outflank his line and so trotted a short distance to the right with his platoons before wheeling left into line and after giving the hussars a volley, ordered his men to charge. This last-minute manoeuvring opened up a gap between his squadrons so Montaigu's hussars managed to penetrate their line whereupon Finkenstein ordered his squadron of Dragoon Guards to charge, whilst to the rear, Colonel von Wiese brought up the Magdeburg Hussars as reserve. Chaussée's charge at the head of the 7th, pushed through the Schleswig Holsteiners ranks and enveloped 2nd Dragoon Guards left flank; then, in turn, they were hit in the flank by a charge of the 3rd and 4th squadrons, Magdeburg Hussars. After a short struggle, the French were driven off and retreated towards Greyère wood pursued by Wiese's hussars who, as they approached the ravine, were greeted with a heavy fire from the Chasseurs d'Afrique.

386  Commander 1st Cavalry Division.
387  Bonnal, *St Privat II*, p.421.
388  Lehautcourt, *Rezonville et Saint Privat*, p.302.
389  de Lonlay, *Tome II*, p.315
390  *Ibid.*
391  *Ibid*, p.316.
392  According to Montaigu's account, Carrelet's 2nd Hussars were on the right, the Chaussée's 7th on the left. Lieutenant Niel, Ladmirault's ADC, who carried the order for the attack stated in his account that the 2nd were on the left, the 7th on the right. In the words of Colonel Carrelet of the 2nd Hussars, the charge was undertaken over a 'distance énorme.' See l'État-Major, *Rezonville*, p.526. Accounts differ as to what distance the charge was launched; the history of the 7th Hussars says 600 metres, that of the 2nd, 900–1,000 metres.
393  See l'État-Major, *Rezonville*, p.527.

Legrand watched the enemy cavalry manoeuvring against Montaigu's brigade and placing himself at the head of the 3rd Dragoons, ordered them to attack. The charge had scarcely begun when the squadrons on the left of his line were carried away by the retreat of the hussar brigade and in the ensuing confusion, Legrand was felled by a sword thrust from a trooper of the 10th Hussars.[394]

Meanwhile, the Oldenburg Dragoons advanced at the trot, following on the heels of the Schleswig Holstein Dragoons and Magdeburg Hussars. As the Holsteiner's came abreast of Ville sur Yvron, the Oldenburger's moved to counter a charge by Latheulade's Lanciers de la Garde who, after wheeling into line to the rear of Legrand's division, were slowly advancing towards the swirling mêlée. However, even before they completed their manoeuvring, the Oldenburger's were hit in the right flank by the two squadrons of the 3rd Dragoons untouched by the hussar brigade's retreat.

This charge was seen just in time by one squadron commander[395] who wheeled his men half right and galloped towards them, his vigorous attack bursting through the French lines. This enabled the three remaining squadrons to resume their advance against Latheulade's lancers whose charge, launched in haste by General de France, had also been thrown into disarray by the 3rd Dragoons as they manoeuvred prior to their attack against the Oldenburgers right flank.

To add to the confusion, Colonel von Schack's Hanoverian lancers who were following on the heels of the Oldenburgers, skirted around to their left and then charged the right wing of the Guard Lancers. Marcel de Baillehache, a maréchal de logis in the lanciers de la Garde, recalled how, just before his regiment charged:

> There was a moment of uncertainty, as to whether or not we were confronted by the enemy; they were a considerable distance away; the day was wearing on and all this time we were wondering who they were. Then, all doubt vanished and colonel Latheulade, sword in hand, called out 'They're the ones! Charge!' This order was repeated by all the officers and led by our valiant chief; the regiment galloped off with couched lances. The Prussians advanced at the trot, with sabres held high, calling out "Hourra! Hourra!" No-one who has never seen such a spectacle can have any idea of how you feel at such a time. At twenty yards they broke onto a gallop and the two lines crashed into one another. The shock was terrible and their front line was almost completely broken. My lance was violently torn from my hand as we passed through their line; either I left it in a body of a German trooper or it was torn from my hand. I think it was the former, because I felt such a shock that I would have been thrown out of the saddle had I not acted instinctively and dropped my lance. In any case I hardly had time to draw my sabre, as whilst I was engaged in this movement a German dragoon made a

---

394  Struck through the chest, the sixty-year-old Legrand fell at the feet of his charger; here he received another slashing blow across his left ear, blood spurting over his epaulettes and the cross of the Légion d'honneur. Another wounded officer carried him away to the shelter of a ditch, where he fell, almost inanimate. The wound to his breast caused considerable pain; the blood, not being able to flow out of the wound, slowly suffocated him, as Legrand repeated over and over 'My God, how it hurts.' He was taken to Bruville where he died and was buried the following day in the cemetery at Doncourt en Jarnisy (now Doncourt les Conflans).

395  First Lieutenant Haake of 1st Squadron, Oldenburg Dragoons.

vigorous blow with his sword against my head which fortunately struck my schapska. I saw a second and then a third line of enemy cavalry who galloped to the aid of their compatriots and from that moment I have no clear recollection of what happened, but what is certain is that the mêlée became general; there were exchanges of sword blows and pistol shots; horse and men crashed into one another, cries of all descriptions, of rage and pain; in a word a terrible chaos.[396]

As the 19th Dragoons ripped open Latheulade's line, his lancers were hit with a simultaneous flank attack by Captain von Trezbinski at the head of 1st Squadron Hanoverian Lancers. The remaining squadrons, von Durant's 2nd and von Rosenberg's 4th, skirted this clash and their charge struck Colonel Sautereau-Duparts régiment de dragons de la Garde, the 2nd hitting them in front, the 4th their right.[397]

The Hanoverians were supported on their left by 5th Squadron Dragoon Guards under Captain von Trotha who, taking a metre high hedge in their stride, galloped forward in platoon columns before wheeling right into line and crashing into the rear of the Empress Dragoons. 4th Cuirassiers then charged into the desperate mêlée between Trezbinski's lancers and the Guard cavalry and to add to the growing confusion, an attack by Lieutenant Colonel von Wuldo at the head of the 16th Hanoverian Dragoons struck the enemy line at the point where Legrand's division and de France's brigade had collided with one another. Meanwhile, the Chasseurs d'Afrique having rallied, once again launched themselves into the fray and charged into the swirling mêlée.

As Bonie was to comment: 'It was no longer a mere attack, a mere conflict; it was a dizzy, whirling throng of battle, a furious tornado, in which 6,000 horsemen of all colours and all arms slaughtered one another, some with the point, others with the full weight of the sword.'[398]

Within the Imperial Guard Dragoon's post combat report, Colonel Sautereau-Dupar detailed how: 'A mêlée of ten minutes ensued, during which struggle man fought man with the sword, whilst those who'd been dismounted used their chassepot. The officers and trumpeters, who stood out because of their braided epaulettes, were singled out for attention.'[399] To add to the confusion some French troopers mistook the lanciers de la Garde for Prussian dragoons, Bonie relating how:

> Our unfortunate lancers were taken, on account of their blue revers, for Prussian dragoons and were accordingly slain without mercy. In the midst of pistol shots and the swords clashing one against another, one could hear cries of 'Don't attack us; we are French' 'No quarter!' was the only answer from our dragoons, who went on killing, thinking it was ruse on the part of the enemy.[400]

---

396 Marcel de Baillehache, *Souvenirs Intimes d'un Lancier de la Garde Impériale* (Paris, 1894) pp.185–187.
397 According to Lehautcourt's account, the Empress Dragoons engaged the enemy lancers with their chassepot carbines, 'having fired more than 100 rounds which had considerable effect.' See *Rezonville et Saint Privat*, p.306.
398 General T. Bonie, *La Cavalerie Française* (Paris: Amyot,1871) p.58.
399 L'État-Major, *16 Août Documents*, p.478. The dragoons lost five officers killed, five wounded, 27 men killed, 33 wounded and lost 40 horses killed or missing.
400 Wagner, *Cavalry Studies*, p.203.

Perhaps unsurprisingly, Colonel Bilhau made no reference to this misunderstanding in 3rd Dragoons' post combat report, although Colonel Chausée of the 7th Hussars acknowledged:

> The presence, generally unknown, of the brigade of Guard cavalry gave rise to an unfortunate misunderstanding. Their blue uniforms were mistaken for those of the Prussian dragoons and in the swirling flood of friend and foe, it was hard to distinguish the French uniforms and they were attacked like the enemy. This disastrous error caused great disorder. The lancers and dragoons of the guard fled to the rear, the speed of their retreat infecting the other regiments. Very fortunately a similar disorder struck the Prussians and they abandoned the battlefield, fleeing hell for leather to the rear.[401]

De France ordered the recall to be sounded and as the Guard regiments withdrew, they were followed by the remainder of the French cavalry who, in complete disarray, flooded back to the north of Greyère Farm. The Prussians attempted to pursue but were hit by fire from the Chasseurs d'Afrique, two companies of the 5th Chasseurs posted alongside the road leading to Jarny and the 98th who occupied the wood between the road and Greyère Farm.

Initially, 3 Corps' cavalry division made no attempt to support Legrand and de France's attack, but de Clérambault could not help but notice the huge dust cloud raised by the thousands of horsemen and took his troopers forward from their position south-east of Bruville to investigate. As he descended into the ravine, his chasseur regiments were swept away by the retreat of de Mortaigu's hussars, so Clérambault ordered forward the 4th Dragoons, their commanding officer, Colonel Cornat recalling:

> We soon found out how difficult it was to cross the deep ravine that lay between our position and the Prussians. When I reached the scene of the combat, I'd only rallied two squadrons. I immediately launched the squadron on the right against the Prussians 'en fourrageurs' which hit them in the flank, whilst the left squadron acted as a base around which the regiment could rally.[402]

On the call of 'À moi dragons!' Cornat led his 1st Squadron against the enemy horsemen, cutting them down and shepherding the survivors back towards Mars la Tour. Rheinbarben sounded the recall and as his exhausted cavalry rallied, they came under fire from the 12-pdr battery sent forward by de Ladmirault, so withdrew to the south of the village. Cornat recalled his dragoons and following their withdrawal 'the most important cavalry engagement of the war'[403] drew to a close. Colonel de Latheulade, who was wounded during the clash, gave some idea as to the intensity of the struggle as he listed some of the injuries sustained by the Guard Lancers:

> Chef d'escadron de Villeneuve-Bargemont, sabre cut to the head, another to the hand; lance wound to the arm; Captain Castel, seven sabre cuts, lance wound, several contusions; Captain Poinfier, sword cut to the front, two sabre cuts to the right hand

---

401 L'État-Major, *16 Août Documents*, p.337.
402 *Ibid*, p.265.
403 So described by the German official history. See Clarke, *The Franco-German War Vol. I*, p.412.

and several bruises; Captain Moyret, gunshot; Captain Boisdofré, seven sabre cuts to the head, another to his right arm, three lance wounds to his back; Captain adjutant major Le Roy, sabre cut to the right forearm; Lieutenant Marceron, sword cut to the forehead; Lieutenant Decormon, sword blow to the head, another to the left hand; Second Lieutenant Lamy, three sabre wounds, one of which was a sharp cut to the neck and a second to the jaw; four other wounds to his ribs and chest. Second Lieutenant Perrot de Chazelle, gunshot wound to his left arm, a sabre wound in the same place, sabre cut to the head. Second Lieutenants Dubéarnés and Boquet were wounded on the left shoulder. Twenty officers and lancers killed, fifty wounded and forty missing[404]

The mêlée lasted barely half an hour from start to finish; Prussian casualties amounted to 42 officers, 443 men and 391 horses. The dead included Colonel Count Finckenstein of the 2nd Dragoon Guards, Major von Hertell of the 10th Hussars and Colonel von Schack of the 13th Lancers.[405] French casualties amounted to 97 officers and 388 men,[406] the Lancers of the Guard suffering heavily with 19 officers and 108 men listed amongst their losses.

Legrand was mortally wounded leading the charge and Montaigu was captured in the ensuing mêlée by Lieutenant von Wedell of the 10th Hussars after he had fallen, severely wounded, from his horse; de Clérambault's division escaped with minor casualties following their brief involvement in the struggle. Away to the east, Patry had heard, if not witnessed, the great cavalry clash:

> Soon our attention was drawn towards the right by the strangest of noises. The ground trembled, as if shaken by a volcano and on the plateau two or three kilometres to the west, rose an immense cloud of dust from which came cries, blows and the clink of weapons. It was the great cavalry clash where more than eighty squadrons[407] engaged in violent hand to hand combat. We didn't see any more at that time but distinctly recall seeing several hours later the return of solitary individuals, lost on this immense battlefield and looking to re-join their units. Even throughout the night more of them continued to turn up at our picket line. There were both French and German, but common to all and quite typical was the way they were all on foot and leading their horses by the bridle, at least those I saw coming in.[408]

---

404 De Lonlay, *Tome II*, p.332.
405 The casualty ratio of officers to men killed was 1:3; the organisation of the regiment provided for a ratio of one officer to 26 men. In his post combat report General Barby wrote, 'The charges were ridden by the regiments with great gallantry and determination and it is to be regretted that the horses no longer possessed the requisite strength to ride the charges with greater vehemence. The efforts of the day in riding to and fro on the battlefield in deep soil and hilly terrain and the fatigues of the preceding days, coupled with bivouacs, had considerably impaired the strength of the horses.' See Wagner, *Cavalry Studies*, pp.206–207.
406 Figures collated from the various regimental after action reports.
407 The French initially had 29 squadrons engaged, the Germans 32. Clérambault brought forward another 20 squadrons but these took little part in the engagement.
408 Patry, *La Guerre*, p.87.

Following the great cavalry mêlée, the survivors of Wedell's brigade assembled to the south-west of Tronville and Ladmirault withdrew his men to the north of the fond de la cuve. Fighting in this sector of the battlefield petered out around 7:00 p.m. and although any further French offensive seemed unlikely, Voights Rhetz took the precaution of withdrawing his six batteries to the south of the Metz-Verdun highway.

Rheinbaben's cavalry took position on the left of this new defensive line, von Kraatz's 20th Infantry Division on the right, around Tronville. The I/92nd held the village whilst the III/56th occupied the western part of the Tronville Copse, the 10th Jäger Battalion the eastern sector. As the firing died away, Ladmirault was still without orders and having no idea of his commander's intentions, consolidated 4 Corps positions along the northern edge of the fond de la cuve.

On his extreme left, two battalions[409] of the 13th engaged in a desultory skirmish around Tronville Copse; a few companies of the 5th Chasseurs were scattered over the slopes of the ravine and five battalions deployed along its edge[410] and on the right three and a half battalions, who had still to fire a shot, assembled to the west of the road running to Bruville.[411]

## Alvesleben's Dogged Resistance

As the fighting around the fond de la cuve reached a crescendo, to the east, more batteries were brought into the firing line to support Stülpnagel's increasingly hard-pressed division, his infantry and cavalry having long given up any attempt to close with the French. The gun lines established by Dresky and Gallus had been under fire for several hours and many of the batteries were low on ammunition. The first reinforcements to join the fight were the guns sent forward by 20th Division; two batteries commanded by Major Krause[412] deployed alongside Dresky's horse artillery; two more under Major Cotta[413] unlimbered to the left of 5th Division's gun line shortly after Gallus had been mortally wounded.

Under the overall command of General von Bülow they maintained a dogged, steady fire against the enemy positions and with their superior accuracy and more effective munitions, succeeded in negating the impact of the more numerous French artillery, although at no small cost in men horses and equipment.[414]

As Alvesleben struggled to sustain his position, reinforcements continued to march to his assistance.

Despite the lateness of the hour, on receipt of instructions around 3:00 p.m., he directed 18th Division with the corps artillery to Arry, the 25th Grand Ducal Hessian Division to Corny; Seton accompanied one of his formations, 32nd Brigade,[415] during their approach march recalling:

---

409  1st and 3rd.
410  2/13th, 1st and 2/43rd, 2nd and 3/6th. Two battalions of the 6th were virtually unscathed.
411  1/64th, 1/98th, half the 2/98th and the 3/98th.
412  3rd Light and 3rd Heavy, X Corps.
413  5th and 6th Heavy, X Corps.
414  Bülow stated that from the time Flavigny was captured up to the posting of outposts at the end of the days fighting, there was not a single friendly infantry soldier supporting the artillery in the centre; Flavigny itself being occupied by two companies. Throughout the day the artillery had to defend itself against enemy skirmishers.
415  From Goeben's VIII Corps.

I was riding with a detachment of hussars, one of whose officers was predicting a grand shout from the men on again seeing their beloved Moselle, when, topping the ridge which shuts in the valley on the east, we could see Artillery smoke on the opposite side; so far however, as yet no sound of fire was to be heard. A halt and form up took place just then and it was generally supposed that we should be too late for anything; certainly, from what I could judge of the course of the fight was taking, it appeared to be gradually drawing northwards.[416]

Previously, Lieutenant General von Wrangel[417] had been informed by Geoben that he intended moving VIII Corps across the Moselle at Corny to join the struggle and so despatched the 11th Grenadiers to secure the bridge, with the regiment being placed under Goeben's orders. On reaching Arry at 1:00 p.m., Barnekow's 16th Division from VIII Corps set off at once for Corny and after crossing the river, his advance guard, accompanied by Colonel von Schöning's Grenadiers, arrived at Gorze around 3:30 p.m.

In response to the urgent calls for support, Barnekow sent his artillery ahead, escorted by three squadrons of hussars, as the bulk of his infantry were not expected at Gorze for another half hour, his intention being to swing through the Bois des Chevaux and the Bois des Ognons around the French left flank. However, the hard-pressed Stülpnagel was in need of more direct support so II/72nd were tasked with this flanking manoeuvre, whilst Barnekow led his remaining five battalions[418] along with the 11th, directly to the front by way of Côte Mousa and the Bois de St Arnould. Seton accompanied their advance and described how as they made their way towards the fighting:

A squadron of the 9th Hussars rode up and the captain took me on with him. Going up the valley at first along the road to Mars la Tour and then turning somewhat to the right, towards Flavigny, we came on General von Alvesleben, on a high plateau not far from the edge of the wood called by some Bois de Vionville. The captain of Hussars reported himself as sent by General von Barkenow to announce that he would work up through the woods on the right of the III Army Corps and then rode off with his squadron. It was about 3:00 p.m. and what I could see of matters was this: the Staff was fronting east towards the ravine which runs nearly N and S from near Rezonville towards Gorze. A short way half left stood some batteries maintaining a steady duel with those of the French standing east of the ravine and on ground, which I find by one map, to have a command of 124 feet over that, whereon the Prussians stood. The distance was, I should say, within 1,500 yards. Echeloned about were some company columns of the 8th Body Grenadier Regiment, lying down as much as possible under cover. I have at present no recollection of having seen more troops to our left, or of having been able to make out any distinct bodies of French … All looked very anxious and it seemed to be a matter of patient waiting, giving and receiving fire, rather than of manoeuvring or even then gaining ground. The artillery with whom I passed a little

416  J. L. Seton, *Notes on the Operations of the North German Troops in Lorraine and Picardy, etc.* (London: W Mitchell and Co, 1872) p.130.

417  Commander of the 18th Division.

418  I and III/72nd, I, II and III/40th.

while, were firing with their usual steadiness and attention. French shells came fast enough, but wildly, many exploding in the air. Several men and horses were, however lying about and fortunately, notwithstanding my losses, I had a bottle of wine left to distribute among such of the former as still lived; also, I was able to cover some of them with horse cloths … Chassepot bullets also came by, but I don't quite remember whether very plentifully. By one, or by the splinter of a shell, I saw General Alvesleben's horse struck and he told me it was the third he had hit under him that day. Presently Colonel Hildebrand arrived with his three batteries, which Barkenow had sent up at once to the open ground, while he started what infantry he had into the wood on the flank.[419]

25th Division started for the battlefield around 4:30 p.m. After learning of the engagement at Rezonville, Prince Louis of Hesse ordered his men over the Moselle by the suspension bridge at Corny; General Wittich and the 49th Brigade led the division's advance with 2nd Squadron 1st Cavalry scouting the way ahead. As noted earlier by Seton, in response to the desperate calls for assistance, the brigade's artillery[420] was sent to bolster 5th Divisions defence:

> Just before it got dark, while the French fire slackened, Captain Cardinal of Barnekow's Staff brought up two Batteries of the Hesse Darmstadt Division under a Field Officer, which I accompanied as they galloped down towards the ravine. They could not do more than fire a few rounds, for it instantly became too dark to distinguish at any great distance friend from foe.[421]

Meanwhile, the remainder of the division hurried their way through the woods along the narrow paths towards the fighting. An officer from VIII Corps staff was sent to guide them, but even so, it was after 7:30 p.m. before the six leading companies of the 1st Regiment came up against the Guard Chasseurs in the Bois des Ognons, but after driving them out of the wood, their advance was halted by the main French line. Unable to make any further advance, desultory fighting continued in this area until 10:00 p.m. when General Manstein ordered them to break off the fight and the brigade camped in the position it held, in a clearing in the wood.

## The Continuing Struggle Between Vionville and Rezonville

As the struggle in the west subsided, throughout the late afternoon, small units of reinforcements continued to make their way to the centre and east of the battlefield; never in sufficient numbers to seriously threaten the French position but enough to enable Buddenbrock and Stülpnagel to cling onto their hard-won ground and to keep Bazaine guessing where the next attack would fall. Around 4:00 p.m., I Battalion Lieb Guard regiment made its way forward from the Moselle

---

419  Seton, *Notes*, p.132.
420  5th Light, 5th and 6th Heavy, VIII Corps under Lieutenant Colonel Hildebrand.
421  Seton, *Notes*, p.133.

valley to the rear of the Bois de Vionville and took over escort duty of 5th Division's artillery which in turn, freed up two battalions of the 78th East Friesland Regiment.[422]

Lyncker then ordered a fresh advance against the French position on hill 989 to the south of Rezonville; the fusiliers deployed to the left, the half battalion on the right, but only managed to struggle forward a few hundred yards in the face of the defender's overwhelming fire before their advance ground to a halt, the colonel and every company commander being wounded in the attempt. At the same time, to their left, Lieutenant Colonel von Kalinowski advanced to the attack at the head of the I and II/12th Grenadiers but again confronted by a hail of fire, all they achieved was to push their skirmish line a few hundred yards closer to the French positions.

A little later, around 4:30 p.m., Colonel von Block arrived in their rear at the head of three battalions he brought forward from Chambley.[423] After struggling through the Bois de Gaumont, they deployed into line, the 56th to the left, the 79th on the right and advancing past the Prussian gun line, launched yet assault against the heights occupied by the French. Hit on their left flank by the 3/2nd Grenadiers, 3/3rd Voltigeurs and skirmishers deployed along the main Metz-Verdun highway, this attack similarly ground to a halt. Block's hard-pressed battalions held onto their exposed positions for some time but were unable to make any further progress, with both battalion commanders of the 56th being killed in this unsuccessful attack.[424]

Although costly and having little to show for their casualties, these constant probes against the French left wing were successful in diverting Bazaine's attention from the west where the Prussian forces were at their weakest. In the centre of their line, Buddenbrock and 6th Division retained their hold on Vionville but again, lacked the strength to make any further advance; the 64th occupied the village whilst the remnants of the 20th and 24th were on the heights to the north-east. Körber's guns maintained their desultory fire against the enemy artillery deployed along the Roman road. However, with both sides exhausted and running low on ammunition, after eight hours of almost incessant struggle, the firing gradually subsided, with Bazaine lacking the inclination and the Prussians – the strength – to continue the fight.

Fixated with the threat to his left wing, around Rezonville Bazaine assembled, in the words of the French official history, 'forces très considerable'.[425] Frossard had by now, rallied 2 Corps and along with part of the Guard and Montaudon's division,[426] was detailed to watch over the routes leading south to Ars, the Bois des Ognons and the Bois de Bagneux where they subsequently clashed with Colonel von Helldorf at the head of the I and III/72nd as he attempted to push towards Rezonville.[427]

---

422 5th and 6th companies were in the Bois de Vionville, 6th, 7th companies and 3rd Battalion were with the gun line.
423 I and II/56th and the fusilier battalion of the 79th.
424 Majors von Zielberg and von Hennings.
425 L'État-Major, *Rezonville*, p.548. They included Lapassat's brigade, Levassor-Sorvals division, Picards division of Guard Grenadiers, supported by 2nd and 3rd Guard Voltigeurs and the 51st and 1st and 2/62nd from Montuadon's division. To the north of Rezonville were five battalions from Aymards division, the 11th Chasseurs, 3/60th and 83rd and a battalion from Tixier's division, the 2/100th, as well as the remnants of the 9th and elements of La Font de Villiers division. Fortons and Valabrègue's cavalry were to their rear, south of the Bois Leprince and Pierrot.
426 These included 1st and 4th Guard Voltigeurs, the Guard Cuirassiers and Carabiniers, 2nd Company Guard Chasseurs battalion and 81st and 95th Line.
427 The regiment was part of Colonel Rex's 32nd Brigade.

During his approach march to the front, Helldorf had stumbled across two battalions of the Lieb Guard recuperating in the depths of the Bois de Prêtres; they were in poor shape; the men had been in action for over six hours, their senior officers[428] were all wounded and the men low on ammunition. Nonetheless, they agreed to support his attack as Helldorf deployed his battalions either side of the Rezonville road and charged towards the heights in the face of a hailstorm of fire.

The first line of this formidable position comprised the 1st and 3/84th from Lapassat's brigade who occupied Maison Blanche farm. The 1/3rd Grenadiers and 1/2nd Voltigeurs were held in reserve with the second line being formed by the 3/97th and 2/2nd Voltigeurs and a third by the 2/3rd Grenadiers and the 3/2nd Voltigeurs. They received fire support from two batteries montée of the Guard, two batteries of Levassor-Sorval's divisional reserve and two batteries of horse artillery from the Guard cavalry division.

The impetuosity of Helldorf's attack drove the 84th out of the farm buildings, but they were rallied a short distance to the rear and with Lapassat at their head and reinforced by the 1/3rd Grenadiers and 1/2nd Voltigeurs, launched a counter attack which drove the 72nd back into woods. Helldorf's men were shelled by the 7/2nd as they attempted to rally, although opposition gun fire forced two other batteries sent to assist Lapassat to withdraw.[429] During this fighting, both Helldorf and Major von Oertzen were killed and as the 72nd fell back, they encountered Colonel von Eberstein bringing up the 40th.[430] The welcome sight of these reinforcements stayed the retreat of the 72nd and they advanced once more in support of Eberstein's assault which this time sought to outflank Lapassat's line by swinging through the woods against his open left wing. This attack, launched around 5:30 p.m., succeeded in driving the French out of Maison Blanche for a second time and forced the 7/2nd to withdraw.

Unwilling to give ground, Lapassat ordered forward the 3/97th and 2/2nd Voltigeurs from his reserve, their weight of numbers once more putting the Prussians to flight. To secure against future attack, he distributed them along a new defensive line having a frontage of about 800 metres facing the Bois St Arnould. Determined to maintain the pressure on the French, Colonel Rex called on the 11th Grenadiers for assistance;[431] Schöning lead his three battalions forward, their renewed attack being supported by elements of the 56th under Captain von Mobart and the II/72nd who, pushing their way through the dense woods, struck the left wing of the French line.

The impetus these fresh troops brought to the attack, drove Lapassat back for a third time and to counter this, Bourbaki committed the 1st Battalion Guard Zouaves and the Guard Chasseurs.[432] Commandant Bessol deployed his chasseurs in a line across the crest of hill 307, their rapid salvo fire halting the Prussian advance in its tracks.[433] Taking advantage of this

---

428  Lieutenant Colonel von l'Estocq, Majors von Seydlitz, von Verschuer and von Schlegell

429  7/18th which lost five men, eight horses and fired off 120 rounds and the 8/18th which lost nine men, 16 horses and fired off 300 rounds. The batteries abandoned two caissons in their retreat.

430  II/40th were deployed across the road, the I Battalion along the ravine on his right, with the fusiliers by the gully on his left.

431  From 18th Brigade who had been placed under VIII Corps orders.

432  The chasseurs had dropped off two companies in the Bois des Ognons and so entered the fight just six companies strong.

433  During the fighting, the commander of the chasseurs, Chef du Bataillon du Bessol, reported that some of the Prussians made as if to surrender by raising the butts of their rifles in the air and taken in by

respite, Lapassat rallied his men again and reinforced by the introduction of 3/2nd Voltigeurs and 2/1st Grenadiers, the men put down a murderous fire against Rex's firing line. With the enemy pinned, Lapassat sent the 3/51st and the 2/62nd from his reserve to outflank their left wing and around 7:15 p.m., with his command having suffered heavy losses, Rex reluctantly withdrew.[434]

Determined, nonetheless, to maintain the pressure against the French positions, he then deployed his men in a skirmish line along the northern edge of the Bois St Arnould wood from where they maintained a desultory fire against the French lines but lacking the strength to cross the open ground, the fighting gradually subsided as darkness descended. Seton who by now had made his way to the front alongside the 72nd witnessed the struggle:

> Colonel von Eberstein … instantly ordered a line of skirmishers to be thrown out by the II Battalion and the rising ground to be seized. This was done at the double, the left coming as I understand it, to the edge of a ravine, the supports occupying the border of the wood on either side of the Rezonville road, while reserve consisting of the 8th Company remained under cover until an opportunity offered for this last to take ground top the right and show a front from a projecting bit of the wood, about as far forward as the skirmisher of the battalion. Between these two stood now a previously formed line of the 8th Regiment, also extended with supports and the detached company held the extreme right of the Prussian force until nightfall and the contemporaneous arrival of the Hessian Infantry put a stop to the fight. It was able to pour a flanking fire into at least one of the enemy's columns of attack, which advanced to within 900 paces, but instead of pushing on, halted and opened fire on the wood and one of its Zügen took up a position within 250 paces of the French skirmishers, whence its fire frustrated more than one attempt of these to gain the edge of the wood … The 6th Company, all its officers having been hit, was brought out of action by the Feldwebel … The movements of the III Battalion I have not been able to make out as accurately as those of the II. However, two of its companies took up a position in a ravine, on the French side of the wood, while the other two occupied the edge of the same, all holding their positions till dark and exchanging a constant fire with the enemy: the between 600 and 700 strong battalion expending 4,550 rounds during the two hours and a half it was engaged.[435]

These sanguinary engagements cost the three regiments involved almost 2,100 men,[436] similar losses to those incurred by Wedell in his equally bloody assault across the fond de la cuve against

---

this deception, the chasseurs, approached the enemy, whereupon they opened a heavy fire against them at close range. The Brigade commander, Deligny, subsequently requested Bourbaki to bring this act to the attention of Bazaine, commenting: 'This way of acting is unspeakable. The rules of War, which authorises tricks of all kinds, do not allow acts of such treachery. Such tricks, as used by the Prussian army must be brought to light and made known to public opinion in Europe, which can only serve to stigmatise them.' See l'État-Major *16 Août Documents*, p.424.

434 The 1st Company of the I/72nd lost 113 men, the II 176 men. Colonel von Schöning was amongst the dead.

435 Seton, *Notes*, p.135. The limited number of rounds fired is probably more indicative of the short range of the Dreyse rifle rather than a reflection on the intensity of the fighting.

436 40th;17 officers, 94 men; 72nd; 36 officers, 852 men, 11th; 41 officers, 1,119 men.

the French right. Although only receiving scant mention in the German official history, these repeated attacks, which gained little if any ground, served to reinforce Bazaine's fears that the enemy intended to sever his links with Metz and succeeded in diverting his attention from his right where Alvesleben's hard-pressed corps was in danger of being overwhelmed.

To the south and west of Rezonville, it was left to the 108 guns deployed by the Prussians between the Bois de Vionville and Flavigny to sustain the fight, as Stülpnagel's infantry were simply too weak and exhausted to resume any offensive action. Although Colonel Block's earlier thrust had been easily repelled by the 3/2nd Grenadiers and 3/3rd Voltigeurs, the French infantry deployed along the 321–311 heights, suffered considerably from the Prussian artillery despite efforts to suppress their fire with their chassepots.

A little before 5:00 p.m., General Marguenat brought forward the 26th from 6 Corps' Reserve to reinforce Bazaine's defence around Rezonville and despite coming under 'une pluie de projectiles'[437] from the enemy guns, moved calmly into position along the crest of hill 312, the 1st and 2nd battalions taking position between the Guard regiments and the 25th Line, with the 3rd being placed a little to the rear. His infantry were supported by the 1st and 2nd Batteries de 4 from the Voltigeur division, but around 5:30 p.m., these guns came under a sustained bombardment and hurriedly withdrew from the line. Their precipitous retreat coincided with the death of Marguenat and this unfortunate combination of events precipitated a panic amongst the 26th and 25th Ligne, both of whom suffered heavy losses to the enemy shelling.[438]

This sudden rout created a breach almost a kilometre in length between the heights and Maison Blanche, leaving just the 3/26th, sheltering from the artillery fire below the crest of the plateau, to hold the line. Believing his line to be in danger of collapse, Bazaine ordered forward Montaudon's 1st Brigade; the 51st deploying three battalions between points 308 and 311 and the valley running down to Gorze, whilst two battalions from the 62nd took position facing south by Maison Blanche. The 3/51st and the 1/62nd supported by the 3/2nd Guard Grenadiers and the 3/3rd Guard Voltigeurs then advanced to within a few hundred yards of the Prussian line which triggered a rout by the remnants of 12th and 56th who fled in panic to the rear of their gun line. The French chose not to press home their advantage and with the Prussians close to exhaustion, the fighting in this sector subsided, neither side willing or able to take the offensive.

## The Red Prince Assumes Command

Believing the battle to be at an end and with the firing dying away, General Bülow[439] gave explicit orders to his men that under no circumstances should they make any further advance and then rode over to confer with Alvesleben. As the two officers discussed how best to disengage the artillery in view of the fast-fading light, Prince Frederick Charles and his staff were observing the battle from the heights above Flavigny.

Unlike Bülow, he considered the day's business to be far from concluded and no doubt wishing to enhance his reputation as a dashing military commander, ordered a renewed assault against

---

437 L'État-Major, *16 Août Documents*, p.399.
438 The 25th lost 22 officers, 429 men, the 26th, 19 officers and 340 men.
439 III Corps artillery commander.

Rezonville. Given the lateness of the hour – it was now around 7.00 p.m. – and the limited resources available, this decision came in for much criticism after the war, being dismissed as the actions of a glory seeker, looking to steal the plaudits due to Alvesleben. The German official history, unwilling to criticise such a distinguished member of the Royal family, offered this excuse for his action:

> The staking of the last strength of man and horse after hours upon hours of sanguinary fighting was to show that the enemy that the Prussians had both the ability and firm will to triumph in the yet undecided struggle. The moral impression of such an advance, enhanced by the consternation to be expected from a sudden attack in the twilight, appeared to guarantee a favourable result.[440]

Such a gamble was, after all, little different to the actions taken by Alvesleben during the day to convince Bazaine that he faced far stronger forces. Whatever the motive, despite the gathering gloom, III and X corps were ordered to assemble all available forces for an assault against Rezonville, the strongest point in the French line. Voights Rhetz's exhausted troops were simply incapable of any such action, as were the majority of Alvesleben's men and so it fell to a few detachments from 6th Division to assault the village.

Buddenbrock's divisional artillery, low on ammunition and with their teams and limbers shot away, were incapable of any further advance and could only offer limited fire support for the attack from the positions they had occupied throughout much of the afternoon. It was therefore, left to Lieutenant Colonel Stumpff at the head of three batteries[441] who had just arrived from Gorze, to lead his guns forward from the Bois de Vionville. Concealed by the gathering gloom, he succeeded in occupying the 312 heights overlooking Rezonville, before he was engaged by 2/51st and 1/62nd at close range which forced him to withdraw.

In the centre, Colonel von Dresky ordered those batteries that were still capable of movement, to advance[442] and although his guns were short of ammunition, they made their way forward at a slow walk, given that in the evening twilight it was impossible to distinguish anything more than 100 paces distant.

Bülow, in complete ignorance of the prince's intentions, was amazed to see his batteries limbering up and advancing towards the French positions in apparent contradiction of his

---

440  Clarke, *Franco-German War Vol. I*, p.418. Moltke was less reticent in his criticism of the prince and in his account of the war wrote: 'It was clearly most unadvisable to challenge by renewed attacks an enemy who still outnumbered the Germans; which action, since on further reinforcements could be hoped for, could not but jeopardise the success so dearly bought. The troops were exhausted, most of their ammunition was spent, the horses had been under the saddle for fifteen hours without fodder; some of the batteries could only move at a walk and the nearest Army corps on the left bank of the Moselle, the XII was distant more than a day's march. Notwithstanding all these considerations an order from Prince Frederick Charles headquarter issued at seven o'clock, commanded a renewed and general attack on the enemy's positions. The X Corps was quite incapable of answering this demand; and only part of the artillery went forward on the right followed by some infantry.' See Helmuth von Moltke, *The Franco – German War of 1870–71*, (London, Harper and Brothers, 1907) p.45.

441  Frank's 1st Light and Hoffman's 2nd Heavy batteries from the Hesse Darmstadt division and 1st Light battery of X Corps who had just replenished their ammunition.

442  Scheringer's 1st, Wittstock's 2nd and Frank's 3rd Horse artillery (previously commanded by Rödenbeck and Schlicht's 6th Light, from III Corps and Heyn's 3rd Heavy and Burbach's 3rd Light from X Corps.

orders. Straining to make out what was happening in the fading light and with the battlefield enveloped in thick layers of smoke, he galloped over to Dresky and demanded to know why he had launched this attack, which he considered complete folly, whereupon he was informed of the Frederick orders.

Cautiously making his way through the semi-darkness, Dresky edged forward, observing some infantry on hill 308 whom he took to be Prussians. Frank's battery, which was on the right of the line, had just faced left to engage a skirmish line deployed in front of Rezonville, when both his and Scheringer's batteries came under fire from the 'Prussians' on hill 308. Wheeling about, the batteries responded with shell and were promptly withdrawn a few hundred yards by Major Lenz, the guns being loaded with case to repel any infantry attack. On the left flank, as Burbach's and Heyn's batteries opened fire on Rezonville, they were subjected to several heavy volleys from troops lining the ditches alongside the main highway so Major Krause ordered them to withdraw 100 paces to the rear.

In the centre of the line Captain von Schlicht sought to identify a suitable position where he could deploy his batteries[443] and was mistakenly informed that the heights to the south of the highway near Rezonville were held by Prussian troops. As he approached to within 150 paces, he discovered it was in fact, occupied by the Imperial Guard. They immediately opened fire and although his mount was shot from under him, Schlicht managed to struggle back to his battery which had meanwhile deployed for action; seven rounds of case followed by a dozen shells sufficed to keep the guardsmen at a respectable distance. With darkness descending across the battlefield, the batteries were then limbered up and retired at a walk, the gunners on foot, some 600 paces to the rear before deploying to cover the retreat of Wittstock's battery.

To the north of the main Metz-Verdun highway, elements of Rothmaler's 11th Brigade[444] began to advance towards Rezonville supported by two batteries[445] from III Corps but coming under heavy fire from the skirmishers lining the highway, their attack petered out without making any ground. The regimental history of the 20th described the confused fighting as the commander of I Battalion led around 200 exhausted men forward into the gloom:

> The 9th and 10th companies formed the first line with the rifle züge extended; the 11th and 12th companies followed behind, the 1st Battalion was on the left flank. The din of the day had been replaced by stillness; only here and there was it broken by the dull boom of artillery, or the sharp report of a volley far on the eastern horizon. The crest of the heights had now been approached within about 500 paces. Suddenly masses of cavalry were seen to emerge from the enemy's position. 'Lie down!' was shouted by the officers, in the expectation of being attacked at once. Instead, the next moment the cavalry wheeled outwards and unmasked the enemy's infantry position. At 100 points the musketry fire broke out at the same moment and a shower of bullets whizzed through the air, happily too high to cause us serious loss ... The fire was taken up on our side and a brief fire action ensued. It had already become dusky. A dark

443 6th Light and 2nd Horse artillery.
444 Detachments of the 35th under Lieutenant Colonel von Alten and the I and fusilier battalions of the 20th under majors Stocken and von Pirch.
445 The 4th Light and 4th Heavy attempted to support the advance but were also targeted by the French infantry lining these ditches.

mass approached on our left flank. Everyone observed it with breathless expectation. Suddenly the cry arose 'Hostile cavalry!' The 11th and 12th companies wheeled up and together with the 1st Battalion, opened a rapid fire that forced the cavalry to turn about quickly. At this moment our Zieten Hussar Regiment came up from the rear.[446]

To support the infantry and artillery, Friedrick summoned 6th Cavalry Division from their position to the south west of Flavigny, instructing: 'Grüters Brigade to attack Rezonville in two lines in a fan shaped formation; Rauch's Brigade to accompany the right of the attack to be made along the chaussée by the 6th Infantry Division.'[447]

Just prior to receiving the Prince's orders, 15th Cavalry Brigade had responded to an urgent call for support from Buddenbrock who noted movement amongst the French cavalry and suspected they intended to charge his guns. Colonel Schmidt[448] moved forward with the 3rd Hussars, his advance being supported by three squadrons from the 9th Dragoons.[449]

By the time he was in position the threat had evaporated so turning his troops around, Schmidt was making his way back to the rear of Flavigny when he was intercepted by the Prince's orderly carrying orders for the brigade to support 6th Division's attack. Wheeling his troopers about once again, he called up the 16th Hussars who took position on the right with the 3rd Hussars on the left, both formed in line of squadrons in platoon columns at deploying intervals. The three squadrons of dragoons, in similar formation, formed a second line. Passing Flavigny on their right, the brigade advanced and crossed the main highway; by now the 3rd Hussars were in the lead followed by the two left squadrons of the 16th. Some 300 yards north of the highway they came across dense blocks of infantry who were firing in all directions, some of their rounds striking his cavalry.

In the dark it was impossible to tell if they were friend or foe so Schmidt rode forward to investigate, on the way meeting an adjutant who told him that the men were from 6th Division who were being threatened by French cavalry. He immediately called forward the remainder of the brigade to the north of the highway, passed through the ranks of Buddenbrock's infantry and galloped forward into the gloom against another dark mass which he assumed to be hostile cavalry.

This mysterious body moved off to the right and immediately after, his men came under fierce close range rifle fire. Schmidt's troopers rode down the lines of enemy skirmishers and he claimed to have dispersed several large bodies of formed men, although given the limited visibility and confused situation, this seems unlikely. During this brief engagement the mount carrying the hussar's guidon bearer, an NCO named Grotte, was hit twice and stumbled. Two soldiers attempted to capture the standard, but Grotte heaved the horse to its feet and galloped off to the rear. French accounts record that element of the 70th, 91st, 93rd and 94th regiments

---

446  Hildyard, *Précis*, DOI:10.1080/03071849109416687_p.989
447  Wagner, *Cavalry Studies*, p.211.
448  He assumed command of the brigade when Rauch was wounded.
449  The 16th Hussars were left at Flavigny.

## Following the Battle

As the French retreat got underway, the unenviable task of clearing the wounded from the battlefield was still ongoing. George Robinson accompanied a group of medical staff from Metz who volunteered to help evacuate the casualties and described the gruesome scenes which greeted him and his colleagues:

It was not before midnight that we felt assured we should have no more cavalry raids made on us. And it was even then with some trepidation that we started forth. At midnight we leave the quarter general, laden with hospital bandages, with lint, wine, brandy, water and other stores and started on our errand of mercy. The ambulance flag borne aloft in front of us, is a point to rally to, when we find ourselves separated, an event of very frequent occurrence, for we have to thread our way through a confused mass of carts, men and horses and to tread carefully wherever we go. Those things which look like sacks of potatoes strewn on the ground are men tired with their day's hard work, who have gone to sleep covering themselves with their tent cloth; so, we tread gently ... Six kilometres more along the fine Route Impérial, with its double row of tall poplars standing like funeral cypresses in the light of the rising moon, past many a camp fire, out into the silent night, we reach the avant post of the French army at Vionville. All is still, scarcely a sound is to be heard and we see as it were the innumerable lights of the two cities; that behind us is the French camp – in front the invaders. And now begins our work. Lighting our lantern at the last camp fire we descend cautiously into the valley, for our banner does not show very plainly and that wood in front is said to be occupied by Prussian sharpshooters, whose aim is certain death. Here at every turn we found all our aid was wanted. Thousands of dead and wounded were all around us and we, a few strangers, were all that were present to help them. In spite of all the elaborate ambulance arrangements existing at Metz, not a single thing was obtainable here ... It was evident that we could do but little. Plugging and bandaging such wounds as were hopeful of cure and giving a lifesaving drink here and there, moving a broken limb into a more easy position and speaking a word of encouragement where the heart was beginning to fail. This was all we could do; but all that night each worked his utmost and when our water failed, two of us walked back again to Gravelotte and brought a bucketful. There was a brook, it is true, at the bottom of the hill and a wood fringed it. We shouted 'Ambulance' and descended, but alas! So many poor fellows had crawled down to it, in the despairing agonies of thirst, that the nearly dried up puddles, which contained all the water the hot sun had left, were more filled with blood than water; many a man had staggered there in pain, but to fall forward on his face and die, without that one last cooling drop he risked his life for; so, four miles back for water we had to send ... Here we would come upon a piled-up heap of dead, yet a low moan would issue somewhere from it and then came the horror of finding where. Stiff, stark and heavy, the dead fell with an awesome thud, as we turned over their ghastly rigid forms in the clear cold moonlight, until we reached some wounded, but still living man, half crushed beneath the weight of his dead comrades. Him we bind up and do the best we can for and leave till daylight. We can dress, but not remove the wounded now. Here and there we find a ghastly pile of dismembered men and horses, whose fragments lie in extricable confusion, as shattered and mingled by a shell they are torn from the living bodies. It is horrible, but far more horrible is it to come upon some poor soldier half cut away, but yet living. Nothing we can do for him, poor fellow! He must lie and wait for that death which seems so long in coming … Daylight begins to dawn and we seek carriage, that is jolting unhung carts and mule cacolets, to convey our wounded. Now as we raise them up and torture their poor wounds by moving them, for the first time we hear a cry. The groans of the dying, the shrieks of the wounded, do not exist on the battlefield. There is a low quivering moan that floats over it – nothing more … With the smallest streak of daylight, we commenced loading our convoy of suffering and selecting some sixty or seventy of those whose wounds were sufficiently serious to make instant removal necessary, but not too serious to bear the journey safely.[487]

To assist with casualty evacuation, hundreds of supply wagons that were backed up around Gravelotte, were emptied of their contents and commandeered to transport the injured to Metz; even so, many of the wounded and their doctors were left behind and taken prisoner by the Prussians. As troops retreated to take up new positions, they were invited to help themselves from the huge piles of supplies that had been dumped at the side of the road, but in the prevailing disorder most of the abandoned stores were simply torched to prevent them falling into the hands of the enemy.[488]

There were similar sights in the Prussian rear areas; as Randall Roberts made his way to Gorze he noted, 'What a scene! Every house a hospital, the streets lined with wounded, the gutters positively running with blood.'[489] Allanson Winn also spent the night on the battlefield recalling, 'This night we were not lulled by the strains of Prussian music; but on all sides through the black darkness came the sounds of groans from the dying.'[490] Little had changed the following morning when he made his way into Gorze:

The scene along the road was beyond all description; every two or three yards you came to either a Prussian who had died of his wounds in the night, or some poor wretch waiting for the stretcher and surgeon's knife. Blood was literally running downhill to the town. Now and then you would pass six or seven wounded lying side by side, attended by the doctors and nuns – improvised out door hospitals, for every house in Gorze was full.[491]

487  Robinson, *Fall of Metz*, pp.77–82.
488  Sous Intendent de Boisbrunet reported that the roads were blocked with abandoned vehicles and troops and so proposed to Bazaine that the supplies be distributed to the men. The formations who benefitted most from this were 2nd Division 6 Corps, the 9th Line from Bisson's Division, Metman's division and a few batteries of artillery. Cases of hard tack were left by the side of the road in Gravelotte with soldiers told to help themselves.
489  Randal H. Roberts, *Modern War, or The Campaigns of the First Prussian Army, 1870–71* (London: Chapman and Hall, 1871) p.55.
490  C. Allanson Winn, *What I saw of the War at the battles of Speichem, Gorze & Gravelotte* (Edinburgh, William Blackwood, 1870) p.58.
491  *Ibid*, pp.59–60.

The Prussian Royal Headquarters relocated from Henry to Pont à Mousson during the 16th, Verdy du Vernois recording in his diary:

> On our arrival at Pont à Mousson in the afternoon we immediately received news of a fierce combat which was raging about Vionville and Mars la Tour. Wounded men, staff officers with reports and orders for bodies of corps further to the rear, came in continuous succession; ammunition columns and ambulances went rumbling, at full speed, in the direction of the battlefield, while compact masses of troops arrived from the right bank and had to seek rest towards the evening, after a forced march, here and further on.[492]

## Moltke Seizes the Advantage

Even before the days fighting died away, Moltke, ever alert to the bigger picture, was seeking to exploit the situation to his strategic advantage. At 5:00 p.m. from his new quarters in Pont à Mouson, he instructed Steinmetz:

> The enemy retreating from Metz has been attacked today at Rezonville by III Corps coming from Gorze. X Corps is being brought up from the west. In order to force the enemy in a northerly direction away from Châlons and Paris, His Majesty orders that the two disposable corps of the I Army cross the Mosel immediately after the troops of IX Corps. The subsequent direction of VIII and VII will be regulated by Army Headquarters with due regard to bringing these in touch with the enemy as soon as possible.[493]

To assist the passage of his troops across the Moselle, the pioneer trains of VII and VIII corps erected three pontoon and trestle crossings near the suspension bridge at Corny, whilst General Goeben constructed an additional bridge at Arry alongside one built previously by III Corps. Given the late hour, there was little that Moltke could do to actually influence the outcome of the fighting around Rezonville, for as Vernois related, 'It had become too late for us to put in an appearance on the battlefield; we should have only reached it after nightfall. Any dispositions to be made there fell moreover within the provenance of Prince Frederick Charles, who was on the spot.'[494]

Moltke issued this brief to Frederick regarding his intentions:

> Headquarters First Army has received orders to cross the troops of the VIII and VII Army Corps over the Mosel immediately behind the troops of the IX Army Corps tomorrow and send them by the shortest direction against the enemy. Proper formation

---

492  Vernois, *Royal Headquarters*, p.71.
493  Lanza, *Franco-German War*, p.259. By placing VII and VIII under his direct control, it seems that Moltke was seeking to prevent Steinmetz from disrupting his carefully laid plans as the wayward general had succeeding in doing at Spicheren. He was to fail.
494  Vernois, *Royal Headquarters*, p.71.

of the First and Second Army, in the sense of a subsequent advance westward, can be attended to later; at present the most important point is to force as large a part of the hostile army away from Châlons and Paris in a northerly direction and to pursue it to and into Luxemburg territory.[495]

Subsequently, Moltke explained his thinking to Major General von Stiehle, II Army's chief of staff: 'According to our views the success of the campaign rests in driving northwards the main hostile forces retreating from Metz. The more the III Corps has in front of it, the greater the victory will be tomorrow when the X, III, IX, VIII, VIII and finally the XII Corps will be available against the hostile force.'[496] Later that evening the Crown Prince issued his orders:

> The enemy appears to draw back in part north-westward and in part toward Metz. The II Army and the VIII and VII Corps will look tomorrow in a northerly direction for the retreating enemy and beat him … The corps furnishing outposts will have officers reconnoitre the terrain in their front to ascertain suitable roads for further advance, in so far as the enemy permits.[497]

III Corps were to remain in camp between Vionville and Flavigny; IX Corps were to occupy the right wing and the heights above Gorze. XII (Royal Saxon) Corps left their quarters at Pont à Mousson between 2:00 and 3:00 a.m., with orders to head for Mars la Tour by way of Thiaucourt, where they were to assemble in the rear of X Corps who were around Tronville. The Guard Corps were to move without delay, to Puxieux in the rear of Mars la Tour by way of Chambley and take post on the left of the Saxons. II Corps were to leave Pont à Mousson at 4:00 a.m. and make for Buxières, where II Army established their headquarters.

By 4:30 a.m. on 17 August, the Crown Prince was again on the heights overlooking Flavigny, apprehensive that Bazaine would seek to brush his weakened forces aside before reinforcements arrived. Bugles were heard in the French camps as their troops stirred and when morning broke, lines of skirmishers could be seen on the heights between Bruville and Rezonville. It looked as though Frederick's worst fears were about to be realised, although unknown to him, the movement in the enemy camp in fact presaged a withdrawal to new defensive positions in front of Metz.

As the French retreat got underway, covered by Metman's division, Robinson was still tending to the wounded:

> The bugles sound the reveille, hill answers hill, muffled by the woods the Prussian bugle call comes up the valley and there is a lark singing high up in the air to greet the coming sun … in the sky. Bang! Right in our very faces spits out a cannon, spits out again. Good heaven! They are surely never going to begin this devil's work again already. Down in the valley there are thousands of men wanting, nay dying for want of aid. They will be ridden over by cavalry, ground to pieces beneath artillery wheels. We rush wildly about, seeking some information as to whether this can be prevented; but

495  Lanza, *Franco-German War*, pp.259–260.
496  *Ibid*, p.261.
497  *Ibid*, pp.397–398.

by the time we get an answer, we too are pushed aside, a battery of our artillery moves off to the crest of the hill and opens fire. Shot after shot rings out ... Now we hear come rattling down the road at rapid pace a huge body of cavalry. Is it French or Prussian? The dust hides it; but our artillery ceases fire and up rides Marshal Canrobert and the 6 Corps. Why, we don't know yet and they can't tell us. There is something said about turning the enemy's flank by another road, something about drawing him under the fire of our guns ... The cavalry passes on in brilliant array. The Chasseurs d'Afrique canter past as though coming from a review. Regiment after regiment moves by. The Zouaves march straight over the country – straight in a line they go – nor wood nor wall, nor steep hill-side, nor deep ravine stops them. It is their boast that they take a bee line from point to point and they would sooner risk half a dozen lives than deviate a yard.[498]

As Verdy du Vernois recorded, Moltke was also up and about anxious for news about Bazaine's intentions:

Very early in the morning of the 17th the Headquarters started for the battlefield, we officers of the General Staff, as early as half past two. The road ... was covered with vehicles bringing back the wounded, with prisoners under escort and troops marching to the front, as well as ammunition and supply columns ... On the height to the south of Flavigny the whole Headquarters assembled and here we practically remained during the greater part of the day, as it afforded a good view of the country ... The air was boiling hot, the ground hard and everywhere the traces were seen of yesterday's bloody fight. The village nearest to us had only been evacuated by the French during the night. Beyond it, on one of the ranges of hills running parallel with Metz, were distinctly visible the white lines of small tentes-d'abri which marked the presence of considerable French forces.[499]

As skirmishing continued around Gravelotte, conflicting intelligence was received about the movements of the Imperial Army. A patrol from the 11th Hussars reported an enemy camp at Bruville, from where men could be seen moving in the direction of Verdun. Movements of troops 'in a westerly direction towards Jarny'[500] were observed. Another patrol sent to Jarny noted clouds of dust between Doncourt and Jouville and drew the conclusion that the enemy were withdrawing towards Metz. A third report stated 'According to all appearances no attack by the enemy is to be expected. He has taken up a rearguard position at Gravelotte. To judge by the smoke, he is cooking. A few trains are departing for Metz just now.'[501] As Moltke himself noted:

At sunrise the French outposts were still occupying the sweep of front from Bruville to Rezonville. Behind them were noticed a stir and much noise of signalling, which

---

498  Robinson, *Fall of Metz*, p.84.
499  Vernois, *Royal Headquarters*, p.73.
500  Clarke, *Franco-German War Vol. I*, p.443.
501  *Ibid.*

might be indications equally of an attack or of a retirement ... The reports sent in to headquarters were somewhat contradictory; they left it uncertain whether the French were concentrating towards Metz or were pursuing their retreat by the two still open roads through Etain and Briey.[502]

He was still concerned that Bazaine, as military logic dictated, would seek to make good his escape and as von der Goltz observed:

> The possibility that the enemy would take a position with his rear towards Metz and the steep wooded ravines on the left bank of the Moselle and there accept a second battle was not entertained at the headquarters of the Second Army. Such a decision had to be considered as fatal to the enemy considering the German numerical superiority. That superiority in numbers the enemy was doubtlessly aware of and they also knew that the German troops were in the immediate vicinity.[503]

## The French Withdrawal

On the extreme right of the Prussian line, Steinmetz accompanied VII Corps as their advance guard[504] moved forward from Novéant towards Ars and Gravelotte where they clashed with the French in the Bois de Vaux. The 77th and the 55th shadowed Metman's division – acting as Bazaine's rearguard – as he withdrew through Gravelotte into 3 Corps' bivouac on the Pont du Jour plateau.[505] Colonel Fay described the French withdrawal in his Journal:

> The retreat began on the 17th at daybreak. The troops on the right[506] moved to their new positions through Vernéville; those on the left[507] by the road from Gravelotte. Metman's division[508] took position between Malmaison and the Bois des Ognons and covered the retreat, which took most of the day, in bad spirits and some anxiety. Our never-ending column followed the only road which ran through Gravelotte, down towards the Mance stream and then up to the Rozerieulles plateau; regimental baggage; munition caissons, administrative wagons, transport for the wounded, artillery and troops all pressing along this road, without break, from right to left, all in the middle of an indescribable confusion.[509]

---

502  Moltke, *The Franco – German War*, p.47.
503  Lanza, *Franco-German War*, p.394.
504  28th Infantry Brigade (less the fusilier battalion of the 77th which had been detached as escort to the corps artillery), 2nd Squadron 15th Hussars and 1st Light battery.
505  During the skirmish the 7th Chasseurs lost two men wounded, the 71st one dead, two wounded.
506  3 and 6 Corps.
507  2 Corps and the Guard.
508  From 3 Corps
509  Charles Fay, *Journal d'un Officier de l'Armée du Rhin* (Paris: J. Dumaine, 1871) p.99.

Boyland was in the rear of the French Army during their move and witnessed the chaotic scenes as his ambulance train moved to a new position:

> We pursued the road I had just taken and we were soon on the plateau of Gravelotte. From where we now were the Ferme de la Moscowa was about three hundred yards to our right. We had come up a by-way and the main road lay between us and the Ferme. This was filled with infantry. It was impossible to pass at that moment ... The retreating column was now blocking the route entirely and moving slowly on ... The 13th Lancers were coming up, not in the regular column, but through the field in which we were waiting for an opportunity to proceed. Troops were to be seen in all directions, still moving. They seemed to bear to the north, in the direction of Saint Privat ... Frossard's division cross the plain, not far off; and their buttons and the barrels of their muskets shine in the sunlight. The reserves are filing down the hill behind us and only their bayonets are still visible, making a hedge on the border of the plain. We are completely surrounded by troops ... We have been waiting three hours for an opportunity to cross the road and proceed to the farm, which is within a stone's throw. Here again the French showed bad organisation in not allowing the ambulance train to cross the road. The halt would have lasted but a minute. The wounded were suffering, perhaps dying; and we were losing time, when every minute was valuable. At 3:00 o'clock we could see the end of the column. At 3:30 we were able to cross the road and draw up before the Ferme de la Moscowa.[510]

A little later, Boyland reached Maison Rouge where he left this description of the French bivouacs:

> Three regiments were encamped there ... The arms were stacked here and there, without any particular attention to order. I have generally seen them stacked in order. The soldiers were dirty and undersized. As usual, they were trying to amuse themselves; and some were cooking chickens that they have evidently stolen from the neighbouring farms. Their tents were also pitched here and there ... The trumpets summon the men to roll call. These trumpets were used upon every occasion. Drums were also beaten constantly and such a din and clatter kept up, that had the enemy been deaf they must have heard them. This is the case throughout the whole French army. The Prussians are seldom heard until they are upon us like a whirlwind. From this position I could command the plain of Gravelotte and see the enemy still behind the village. A train of the enemy is coming up to Gravelotte. Upon this a battery just in front of the camp opens a brisk fire. I see some of their horses hit and the men fall from the boxes. The Prussians do not reply. The train soon disappears. To the left of the battery are two lines of infantry, firing in open order into the wood, into which I can see the Prussians running at the other end. The first line of this company is firing on their knees. This skirmishing lasted until dark.[511]

---

510 Boyland, *Six Months*, pp.59–60.
511 *Ibid*, pp.62–63.

Boyland and his colleagues continued their search for casualties, observing, 'amongst these warriors, as they lay broadcast on the earth, many signals of distress made in various ways; here was a ramrod stuck in the ground with a piece of white paper on it to catch the eye of the krankanträger … there a bayonet with a piece of red cloth on it.'[512] He approached one badly wounded French soldier who 'gazing wistfully at the revolver' his companion carried on his belt 'breathed the words, 'Que votre ami donne un coup de pistolet, voilà tout ce que je demande.'[513] A few yards away lay another casualty:

> A lieutenant colonel of the Grenadiers of the Imperial Guard. On his left breast, amongst many other decorations, I recognised our own Crimean medal … I attempted to talk cheerfully to him … and when he attempted to answer … I heard a gurgling sound from the hole in his chest as he bled internally … I placed his head again on my knee; and I suppose some sudden attack of internal bleeding set in … and with it I am sure his last breath. I laid him down and took the medals off his breast. I then slit the lining of his tunic and place them inside and sewed up the cut with a needle and thread, which I took from the bobbin that almost every soldier of France carries in his knapsack.[514]

Later as Boyland made his way back to Gorze, he turned off the road:

> To examine the effect of the Prussian shells on a little cow-house which we saw at about the middle and to the rear of the French position. We looked through the iron bars of the window and there we saw the corpse of a French soldier thrown back, but still in an erect position, leaning against the wall. The head was almost destroyed and the sides of the room, which was not more than eight or nine feet square, were plastered with bits of flesh from a comrade, who must have been literally blown to pieces. Going round to the door, we entered the stalls. Here was a sight; some twenty or thirty dead bodies. It must be understood that the entire house was not more than 25 feet by 20.[515]

Allanson Winn was also exploring the battlefield and emerging from the Bois des Ognons noted:

> In our immediate neighbourhood lay nothing but corpses of the 11th, 35th and 72nd Regiments of the Prussian line … To the right of the road which we were on lay chiefly bodies of the French 73rd Voltigeurs of the Line and foremost amongst these, about forty yards from the nearest German body, lay a sergeant. The disposition of the corpses of the two armies was very remarkable; and it was quite clear that whatever

---

512  *Ibid*, p.73.
513  *Ibid*.
514  *Ibid*, pp.74–75. If correct in his identification of the rank of this wounded officer it would appear to be Lieutenant Colonel Bigault de Maisonneuve of the 2nd Grenadiers who was injured on the 16th and died from his wounds on the 17th. See, A Martinien, *État Nominatiff par affaires et par corps des officiers tués ou blesses*, (Paris, Libraire Militaire R Chapelot et Cie, 1902) p.38.
515  Boyland, *Six Months*, pp.80–81.

happened at another part of the field, nothing like crossing bayonets had been arrived at here.[516]

## Moltke Bides His Time

28th Brigade made no attempt to follow up Metman's retreat although Steinmetz, Kameke and Zastrow, accompanied by their staffs, rode forward towards Gravelotte to reconnoitre the French positions. Their presence drew some well-aimed mitrailleuse fire, but nonetheless, the assembled generals could discern an extensive encampment around Moscou and Point du Jour; it was evident that the enemy occupied the heights in some force and by early afternoon, it was clear that Bazaine had not yet commenced his breakout to Verdun. Moltke originally intended to resume the battle on the 17th, although as Vernois related from their vantage point on the heights overlooking Flavigny:

> It was already afternoon and yet not all the forces the forces assembled which were near enough to be brought up for battle. But it soon became evident, on the other hand, that the French would not do anything more that day ... There was, therefore, no need to hurry the execution of our plans. The southern and most direct line of retreat of the enemy, towards the interior of France was now blocked and he certainly had not yet set his columns in motion on the roads towards the north which still remained open.[517]

Comforted by the inactivity of the enemy, Moltke allowed his weary troops to disperse to cook food, replenish their stocks of ammunition and tend their battered formations. Prussian cavalry patrols again lost contact with the French as they drew off to the north and east, but as far as Moltke was concerned, as long as they moved away from Verdun, he had no concerns; it would allow him to concentrate his armies for the decisive battle he intended to fight the following day.

Throughout the remainder of the day, his reinforcements trudged into position along the line of the Metz-Verdun highway, which still bore the bloody evidence of the previous days fighting, with General Prince August of Württemburg's Guard Corps arriving at 3:00 p.m. after undertaking an exhausting 12-hour march. By the evening of the 17th, the bulk of Moltke forces were arraigned along a line running from Ary in the east to Hannonville in the west; the Saxon cavalry division were at Parfondrupt out in front of the main body, with II Corps at Pont à Mousson and 1st Cavalry Division at Corny if needed.

## Uncertainty in the French Command

As Moltke pondered his options, the emperor was still uncertain as to just what had transpired on the 16th; it would seem that Bazaine's initial despatch informing him of the battle failed to reach Napoleon, for just after 2:00 p.m. on the 17th, one of his aides sent a telegram to General Coffinières in Metz: 'By order of the Emperor; Have you any news of Marshal Bazaine's army?

516  Allanson Winn, *What I saw*, pp.70–73.
517  Vernois, *Royal Headquarters*, p.73.

Send an immediate response to His Majesty at the camp of Châlons.'[518] Shortly after, the following reply was despatched: 'Yesterday, the 16th, there was a very serious engagement near Gravelotte; we came out best in the fighting, although suffered heavy losses. The Marshal has regrouped around Metz and has camped on the high ground at Plappeville. We need food and ammunition. Metz is virtually blockaded.'[519]

This last observation understandably set alarm bells ringing at Imperial Headquarters; shortly after, Bazaine received the following missive: 'By order of the Emperor; Received your despatch. Give us all the details. What have you received, what do you need?'[520] His typically obstruse response[521] prompted a direct rejoinder from the emperor: 'Tell me the truth about your situation, so that I can plan accordingly. Send your reply in code.'[522] Bazaine simply ignored this demand, with another evasive response: 'Immediately I received your request, I have written to your Majesty. Commandant Mangin has been sent with a letter which will provide your Majesty with all the necessary information you requested; I am still awaiting reports from the corps commanders.'[523]

After travelling through the night, Mangin arrived at Châlons a little after 9:00am on 18 August where he was immediately sent to see the emperor. As the French official history commented, Bazaine's report on the battle[524] was filled with inaccuracies and half-truths and serves better to illustrate the fanciful ideas he had about enemy intentions and the bizarre conclusions he drew from an insignificant cannonade against Fort Queuleu, than it did to furnish the emperor with a detailed analysis of his situation. In any event, it was too late for Napoleon to do anything.

As well as delivering this despatch, Mangin was ordered, in the name of Bazaine, to request the emperor's consent to replace Frossard and Jarras. After some discussion between the emperor, MacMahon and Prince Napoleon, it was agreed that Frossard would be recalled to Paris to help organise the city's defences, being replaced by General Deligny. General Cissey would assume the role of chief of staff in place of Jarras.

However, Napoleon was in no position to offer Bazaine any practical assistance or support and Moltke was not going to let this opportunity pass. By the time Mangin arrived at Gravelotte with his response, his forces were already on the march and with the positions of the two armies reversed, it was clear that the outcome of the next battle would be decisive.[525]

518  L'État-Major, *18 Août*, *Documents*, p.10.

519  *Ibid*, The message was headed 'Le Maréchal, commandant supérieur, à l'Empereur.' Bazaine never used such nomenclature and Coffinières was a general, not a marshal. It was never discovered who actually drafted this telegram.

520  *Ibid*, p.11.

521  'I had the honour to inform your Majesty yesterday of the battle lasting from 9:00 a.m. to 8:00 p.m. with the Prussians which attacked our positions between Doncourt and Vionville. The enemy was repulsed and we spent the night in our conquered positions. Shortages of supplies and ammunition have obliged me to retire on Metz to replenish stocks as soon as possible. I have deployed the army of the Rhine on the line Saint Privat – Rozerieulles. I hope to be able to resume our march the day after tomorrow by the more northerly route.' See L'État-Major, *18 Août*, *Documents*, p.11.

522  L'État-Major, *18 Août*, *Documents*, p.11.

523  *Ibid*.

524  See Appendix V.

525  Bazaine's forces faced west, whilst Moltke's armies fronted east with their backs to Paris.

# 3

# The Battle of Gravelotte,[1] 18 August 1870 – Stalemate

## Moltke's Battle Plan

By the evening of 17 August, Moltke had assembled seven army corps and three cavalry divisions along a front that ran for 11½ miles between Ars in the east to Hannonville in the west, in anticipation of the first set piece battle of the campaign. From II Army, IX Corps were camped to the west of the Bois de Vionville, III Corps along with 6th Cavalry Division were deployed around Flavigny, Vionville, with one division at Buxières-Chambley.[2] X Corps were at Tronville, with 5th Cavalry to their rear. The XII (Royal Saxon) Corps were at Puxieux to the south of Mars la Tour, the Guard infantry and cavalry at Hannonville au Passage with II Corps to the rear between Pont à Mousson and Buxières.[3] From I Army, VII Corps were in bivouac at Ars with VIII Corps camped further to the south around Gorze.

Although Moltke had a considerable force of cavalry to hand, once again they had failed to maintain contact with the French, so at 1:45 a.m. on the morning of 18 August when orders[4] were issued from his field headquarters south of Flavigny, he was still uncertain as to their whereabouts or intentions. Did Bazaine intend to force his way to Verdun as any competent commander would do, or was he going to fall back on Metz? In response to this conundrum, Moltke's plan was masterly in its simplicity; Frederick Charles' II Army would begin their advance from the left and move in echelon towards the north. If the French were caught strung out in line of march retreating along the central or northern routes to Verdun, his corps would fall on them in succession. If Bazaine had taken up a defensive position with his back to the city, Frederick would simply pivot to the right, outflank their line and crush them before the walls of Metz.

---

1   This battle was also known to the French as the Defence of the Amanvillers Line and to the Germans, as the Battle of Saint Privat.
2   5th Infantry Division, as there was insufficient water on the plateau.
3   IV Corps were at Boucq.
4   'The 2nd Army will form up at 5:00 a.m. tomorrow, the 18th August and will advance in echelon from the left between the Yron and the Gorze brooks, or generally speaking between Ville sur Yron and Rezonville.' See Lanza *Franco-German War*, p.261.

From the outset of hostilities, Moltke's intention had been to confront the Imperial Army with an overwhelming force and he regarded the forthcoming engagement as the culmination of this strategy. No doubt concerned by the prospect of Steinmetz upsetting his carefully made plans yet again, he took particular care to keep the headstrong general on a tight rein, making clear he should not engage his forces without direct orders from the king.[5]

Satisfied with developments, the chief of staff returned to Pont à Mousson to seek suitable quarters in which he and the elderly monarch could find a few hours rest before the expected battle. Frederick Charles, who spent the night with the Saxon Corps at Mars la Tour, digested Moltke's orders and directed:

> The II Army will continue the march this forenoon with the same task: to drive the enemy away from his line of retreat on Verdun–Châlons and to defeat him wherever found. For that purpose, the XII Corps will start as left wing echelon promptly at 5.00am; the Guard Corps in its right rear; on the right rear of the latter the IX Corps, starting at 6:00 a.m. The XII will take direction on Jarny, the Guard on Doncourt. After it has passed between Vionville and Rezonville the IX will march past the immediate left of St Marcel. VIII Corps advances in the right rear of the IX, the VII farther towards Metz. The III will follow the IX and insert itself between that corps and the Guard. 6th Cavalry Division will receive instructions from General Alvesleben. X Corps to which the 5th Cavalry Division is attached, will follow the XII in such a manner as to advance in the march direction between the XII and Guard. It is difficult to state where the enemy may be found. He is supposed to have been marching off toward evening on both roads in front of and toward Conflans. A bivouac of three divisions, observed yesterday at Gravelotte, probably has also marched off. If that is not the case, General von Steinmetz will attack there. It is possible that the IX Corps can interfere first. If all of this demands a turn by II Army, either to the right or the left, cannot be said. The corps artillery of III Corps will remain at my disposition as army artillery reserve. III Corps[6] may find employment possibly only in demonstration.[7]

Given the expectation that II Army could stumble across French forces at any time, the prince directed that 'The advance will be made not in long thin march columns, but in divisions massed, the two infantry brigades behind each other, the corps artillery between the divisions

---

5    'The 8th Corps will conform to this movement and close in on the right flank of 2nd Army. The 7th Corps will at the beginning have the duty of covering the movements of the 2nd Army against any attempts of the enemy from Metz. Further orders from his Majesty will depend upon the actions of the enemy.' The practical consequence of such an order was to leave only VIII Corps under Steinmetz's direct command as I Corps remained on the far side of the Moselle to screen Metz. In his headquarters at Ars, Steinmetz, as expected, was enraged at this slight, considering Moltke's instructions to be 'wanting in consideration and that if it was proposed to thus pass over the army commander and address orders to the corps, an army command would become useless.' See Lanza *Franco-German War*, pp.261–262.

6    No doubt in consideration of the losses it suffered on the 16th.

7    F. C. H. Clarke, *The Franco-German War 1870–71 Vol. II* (London: Topographical and Statistical Department of the War Office,1876) pp.9–10.

of each corps. For the present the question is merely one of a short march of less than four miles to occupy the northern road to Verdun. A rest will take place at noon.'[8]

## The Civilian Perspective

On the east bank of the Moselle, the correspondent of the *Daily News* left this description of the activity within the Moltke's forces as they prepared for action:

> At midnight, or a little after, all the trumpets for miles around began to sound. This was the first time we had been startled at that hour by such wild music. Trumpet answered trumpet through all the bivouacs around the little city. For several days previous there had been troops almost perpetually marching through; but now the tramp through every street and by-way made between midnight and dawn a perpetual roar. I ran out into the darkness and managed to get a seat on a wagon that was going in the direction of the front. The way was so blocked with wagons that I finally concluded that I could go the six or seven miles remaining better on foot. At Novéant aux Pres, on the Moselle, about half way to Metz, I found vast bodies of cavalry, Uhlans and Hussars, crossing the river by a pontoon bridge and hurrying at the top of their speed towards Gorze.[9]

Another civilian out and about early on the 18th was George Boyland; roused from his slumbers in Metz around 2:00 a.m. he was ordered to recover some of the French wounded:

> Following M Liégeois to the large place in front of the cathedral, I found four fourgons and ten men, some of whom carried lights all ready to start. I felt quite important, placed in charge of this train, which I ordered forward at once. Our destination was the village of Gravelotte ... I pressed the men on, as the Prussians had sent us word that all must be over by daylight. I had no difficulty in passing our lines and still less entering those of the enemy, who were on the lookout for us. As we galloped up to Gravelotte (we had four horses to each fourgon) I could see nothing but the dark outline of the houses. At the entrance of the village a Prussian officer of the medical staff rode up and after saluting, said 'The French ambulance, I presume?' I replied 'Yes; this is a detachment of the first French ambulance; Third Army Corps, under my orders.' He then told me that there were thirty-eight French wounded in his ambulance, where they had been placed temporarily. He explained that they were from the battle of the 16th and the skirmishing of the 17th. I requested him to conduct me thither. It was in the village school-house. I was struck at once with the neatness of everything and with the completeness of the arrangements ... 'These are your men' he said leading me to one part of the room; 'take them at once. Our forces are behind the village, which they must occupy at daylight. I too, must evacuate. To-morrow we expect a great battle.' He then called a dozen of his men to aid us. We soon transferred the wounded to our

---

8    Harry Bell, *St Privat, German Sources*, (Kansas: Staff College Press, Fort Leavenworth, 1914) pp.49–50.
9    Anon, *The War Correspondence of the Daily News 1870*, (London, Macmillan And Co, 1871) pp.61–62.

fourgons. The first streaks of the approaching day had already marked the east when we rode away from the old school-house. We bade the Prussian officer farewell and hurried forward. We were a few hundred yards from Gravelotte and had reached the last German pickets. They halted us. I told them my name and pointed to the flag. I saw that they were not the same ones that were there as we came. They saluted and allowed me to pass on. It was getting lighter every minute. Casting a glance behind me I could see the main body of the Prussian army marching quietly up behind the village. There must have been at least 100,000 in that army. I could clearly make out the dark blocks of troops and the dull steel of their muskets ... The road here bends and we were now half way between the French and Prussian lines. Knowing the eccentric habit of the French, their base organisation and, moreover, that their pickets had been changed, I could not guarantee for our safety until we were so near that they could recognise us as their men. As I rode into their outposts I turned again and now saw the Uhlans riding about in Gravelotte, while a Prussian battery was getting into position. Our pickets would not wait until our train was at a distance, although I requested them to do so, but cried out, 'There they are!' and opened fire. The Prussians, be it said to their credit, waited until we had disappeared under the brow of the plateau. I then heard a sharp skirmish commence.[10]

## Advance to Contact

18 August 1870 dawned cloudless, with bright blue skies and by noon the temperature was to reach 86° Fahrenheit. With little idea as to when or where they would encounter the enemy, Prince Albert's Saxon Corps began their advance; Lieutenant Colonel Gustav von Schubert, 23rd Division's chief of staff recalled:

At 5:00 a.m. 18 August our headquarters were called to the bivouac of our army corps, whose two divisions were camped close together and here verbally received orders from Prince Frederick Charles for the movements of the day ... The enemy was to be attacked wherever found. Thus, a decisive battle could be counted on with certainty. We rejoiced at this, although we wondered why we Saxons were drawn from the centre to the extreme left wing, which necessitated crossing with the Guard Corps on our left.[11] We felt that we were to be cheated of our chance to participate in the impending

---

10  Boyland, *Six Months*, pp.63–65.
11  This relocation caused great inconvenience to both the Saxon and Guard Corps, but Friedrick clearly wanted the Guard in the centre of his battle line, rather than the Saxons whose reliability he questioned. Major General Schubert commented 'The valiant and ambitious Prince was not without prejudices and one of them was that only the Guard Corps and possibly the II and III Corps of the entire army deserved complete trust in regard to their efficiency. What could be expected of the little Saxons, when a heavy and decisive battle threatened?' The commander of the Prussian artillery Prince Kraft von Hohelohe was opposed to this change in dispositions and 'implored General Stiehle, Prince Frederick Charles's chief of staff, to avoid such a crossing of the two army corps, which would spread disorder and uncertainty among everything coming up in our rear, because Columns, trains, ammunition reserve and field hospital, who knew that the Saxons were on our left, would lose their way or, in the most

battle and that the Guards were given the preference ... The army corps massed itself in battle formation south of Mars la Tour in two parallel columns and crossing the village started with its advance guard at 6:45 a.m. ... It was a glorious summer morning, followed by a clear day and not too hot. After we had passed Mars la Tour and the mass of the Guard Corps, which waited for our passing, we halted; the rifles were loaded and the colours unfurled amidst cheers. For the first time we saw the entire army corps, with the exception of the cavalry division, assembled at full strength and when the bands commenced playing their inspiring marches confidence and lust of battle filled everyone's heart. The military spirit of our advance was increased when we passed the battlefield where the bloody cavalry charges had taken place on the 16th. The corpses of riders and horses were still lying unburied and had to be stepped over by our battalions, which must have shaken the nerves of many of our young soldiers who had never seen such a sight. We saw the brave riders lying as death had overtaken them, most of them with their sabre in their right hand, many with gaping wounds on the head and upper part of the body.[12]

The prince's orders caused some unforeseen difficulties amongst the Saxon staff; due to the difficult terrain, XII Corps were unable to adopt the prescribed march formation until they had cleared the ravine outside Mars la Tour. Major Haase, who served as an ensign in the 12th Field Artillery Regiment, complained:

The advance was materially delayed by complying with the orders to march in mass of brigades. In the first place we had not practised such march formations in peacetime and besides it could not be done in that terrain. The troops in several instances encountered obstacles which could be overcome or avoided by the infantry without having to break the formation but which compelled the divisional artillery, which had orders to march with contracted battery fronts between the infantry brigades, to take up column formation, subsequently again deploying at the trot to gain their prescribed formation. The corps artillery also, marching between the two divisions, was in in many instances, forced to assume column formation, deploying again subsequently.[13]

There were further hold ups as their route took them across Guard Corps line of march and given there was little love lost between the two former enemies, having fought on opposite sides just four years previously, the Guards assumed that they had deliberately adopted this formation so as to obstruct their advance; their artillery commander Prince Hohenlohe later remarked:

Instead of in mass of brigades the Saxons passed us in march columns. Thus, we lost three and a half valuable hours in waiting. At that time, we were very indignant over

favourable case, cross and delay each other. His protests were in vain. Stiehle said that the prince has duly considered these matters but still insisted on having the Guard Corps fight in the centre; that the prince was not acquainted with the XII Corps; that he knew what he could expect of the Guard Corps; that the best troops were invariably placed in the centre.' See Bell, *St Privat*, pp.428–429.

12    *Ibid*, pp.406–407.
13    *Ibid*, pp.468–469.

Shortly after the chief of staff's despatch, timed at 10:00 a.m., arrived at I Army headquarters, news came in from Manstein that local inhabitants had reported bodies of troops north of Jouaville and cavalry and artillery northeast of Vernéville. Another message from First Lieutenant Scholl advised: 'Report from hill near Batilly: Hostile patrols opposite St Marie–Amanvillers; troops marching on main road; camp at Saint Privat la Montagne; hostile patrols advancing at a trot.10:25 a.m.'[34] In response to these developments, around 11:30 a.m. the prince issued the following orders:

To the Royal Saxon Corps:

The XII Corps receives orders to march on St Marie aux Chênes, to secure by cavalry towards Briey and beyond Conflans and to send as much cavalry as practicable into the valley of the Mosel to interrupt railroad and telegraph to Thionville. The VII, VIII, IX and Guard corps will, within two hours, attack the enemy, who is in position on the heights from Leipzig to the Bois de Vaux, rear towards Metz.

To Guard Corps:

The enemy appears to stand in battle position on the ridge from the Bois de vaux through Leipzig. The Guard Corps will hasten its march through Vernéville, extend it to Amanvillers and from there advance envelopingly for a serious attack against the hostile right wing. The IX Corps will at the same time advance to the attack on la Folie. The Guard Corps may also take the road through Habonville. The XII Corps goes towards St Marie.

To IX Corps:

The Guard Corps now receives orders to advance through Vernéville to Amanvillers and from there eventually to make an enveloping attack on the hostile right wing. A serious engagement by the IX Corps, in case the hostile front before it extends still farther to the north, must be delayed until the Guard Corps attacks from Amanvillers. The troops probably will still have time enough to boil coffee.

Half an hour later his reserves were issued with their orders;

To X Corps:

The enemy is in position from Leipzic to the Bois de Vaux. He will be attacked there today – by the Guard from Amanvillers; by IX Corps from la Folie; by the VII and VIII corps in front. In the second line follow in support: the XII Corps on Sainte Marie, the X Corps on St Ail, the III Corps on Vernéville, the II Corps on Rezonville.

34  Bell, *St Privat*, p.229.

II Corps were informed:

> The II Army Corps will march from Buxières on Rezonville, as reserve for the right wing. The First and Second Army will today attack the enemy in his positions this side of Metz. There will be time to cook meals, special haste to reach Rezonville is not necessary. The Saxon cavalry covers towards Verdun.[35]

## The French Army on the Morning of the 18th

In contrast to the disciplined activity displayed by Moltke's well drilled corps, Bazaine's disorderly retreat on the 17th found the French bivouacked at right angles to the enemy forces, facing west, their position running north from Rozerieulles along the heights to Roncourt, a distance of about seven miles. Frossard's 2 Corps was deployed to the south of the line along the Metz-Mars la Tour highway along a frontage of about 2,000 metres. Vergé's 1st Division occupied a very confined space, in column of brigades, along and to the south of, the old Roman road, its left resting on the bend in the road by Point du Jour. Vergé placed seven battalions in the front line, one occupying the trench[36] linking the buildings at Point du Jour, with the 3rd Chasseurs garrisoning the farmhouse itself. Five battalions were positioned in the hedges lining the main road, six being held in reserve with four companies sent out front to serve as advance guard. Two divisional batteries de 4[37] were positioned behind earthworks thrown up alongside the farm from where they could cover Gravelotte, about 2,000 metres away on the opposite side of the ravine.

From Bataille's 2nd Division, the regiments from 1st Brigade[38] were divided between the area to the north of the Roman road and a small mound along the edge of the Bois de Vaux next to the sharp bend in the main Metz-Verdun highway. A little to the rear, 2nd Brigade,[39] under the command of Colonel Ameller, took position along the edge of the bois de Châtel, facing south-west. The 12th Chasseurs and the corps artillery deployed in the space between them.

Lapassat's brigade formed in line of battle on the ridge overlooking Rozerieulles[40] as did 3rd Lancers; they were supported by the guns of the 7/2nd posted to cover the sector between Rozerieulles and Sainte Ruffine. Illustrative of the poor organisation within 2 Corps – in common with the remainder of the army – no orders had been issued as to which formation was to furnish the advance guard; as a consequence, each regiment had to provide their own outposts.

---

35    Clarke, *Franco-German War Vol. II*, Appendix XXIII.
36    The *Journal de marche* for 2 Corps engineers records that during August 17, they constructed a number of tranchée-arbris at Bellevue and Saint Hubert for the infantry and a number of arbris for four batteries. These simple earthworks had a significant impact on the fighting that followed.
37    5th and 6/5th.
38    8th and 23rd.
39    66th and 67th.
40    Later, during the evening of 17 August the 84th withdrew a short distance to a valley behind the Roman road.

Lapassat occupied Sainte Raffine with one company whilst three others kept watch over Jussy; the 3/77th deployed a company in the quarries at the Point du Jour, placing two more along the main road. From 2nd Division, outposts furnished by the 23rd were placed along on the ridge overlooking highway.

Within 3 Corps, Montaudon's division was bivouacked in two lines between the farmsteads of la Folie and Leipzig[41] overlooking the ridge as it fell away towards the Bois de Charmoise, a few hundred metres to its front. The 2/95th furnished the outpost line and deployed along the northern edge of the wood keeping watch over the slope running down to Chantrenne. 3 Corps staff was located between Leipzig farmstead and l'Arbre mort alongside 2nd Division who were again deployed in two lines.[42] 4th Division occupied the ground between Moscou farmstead and the bend in the main highway, near Point du Jour. De Brauer's 1st Brigade[43] was grouped around the main road in three lines[44] with the 2/80th sent to occupy Saint Hubert farmhouse about 600 metres in front of the main position. The 6th Company from the 3/80th was pushed forward to watch over the cutting which crossed the Mance ravine.

2nd Brigade was held in reserve,[45] to the right of the heights some 300 metres east of Moscou farm; the 60th deployed its 3rd Battalion along the tree line on the edge of the ravine. The divisional artillery parked by the edge of the bois de Châtel. Clérambault's cavalry division and corps artillery reserve were bivouacked near Nayral's 2nd Division on the rear slope of the ridge.

Finally, around 2:00 p.m. on the 17th, Metman's 3rd Division moved onto the plateau by Moscou farm; given the lack of space between the 2nd and 4th, he deployed his troops north of the farm in column of regiments.[46] Following this deployment, 3 Corps held a front of about 3,500 metres and to render this highly defensible position even more secure, Le Boeuf gave instructions for the farmhouses to be loop holed and placed into a state of defence with earthworks and rifle pits[47] being constructed along the ridge.

From Ladmirault's 4 Corps, Lorencez's 3rd Division arrived on the plateau of Saint Vincent late in the day and formed two lines facing Plappeville and the heights of the Saint Maurice farm. As Rousset recorded in his history:

> Because 6 Corps had to march from Vernéville to Saint Privat and 4 Corps from Doncourt to Amanvillers, crossings and stoppages in the march resulted and the troops reached their bivouac places only late at night. When thereafter Cissey's division arrived at the Jérusalem farm it had to be drawn back to Amanvillers because troops of the 6

---

41  From right to left, in the front line the 95th and 81st, second line 18th Chasseurs, 51st and 62nd. One battery was at la Folie, two more at Leipzig.

42  In the front line 19th, 15th Chasseurs and 41st; in the second line 60th and 80th. The divisional artillery was camped close to l'Arbre mort.

43  80th and 85th.

44  First line,1/85th and 1/80th, second line 2/85th, 73/80th, third line 3/85th.

45  From right to left 11th Chasseurs, 60th and 44th.

46  From right to left, 7th Chasseurs, 7th, 29th, 59th; in the second line 1st and 2/71st (the 3/71st were at Moscou) and the divisional artillery.

47  Archibald Forbes described these as 'a small half-moon excavation, the convexity toward the enemy – the earth from the hole breasted up in front, over which the marksmen fired in a kneeling position. The maximum garrison of one of these rifle pits must have been about twelve men, half of them firing while the other half rested behind the shelter.' See *My Experiences*, p.168.

Corps arrived at Saint Privat. A new position was taken up in the dark and outposts placed out on the east while a few cavalry regiments went into a bivouac facing Metz and thus offered their rear to the enemy. Those very important points for the defence, like St Marie aux Chênes, St Ail and the woods de la Cusse and Champenois situated in front of the position had not been occupied and not a single picket was posted west of the bivouacs. Thus, it happened that stragglers from the 6 Corps wandering around the field during the night entered the bivouac of 4 Corps and made such a noise that everyone was called to arms and that alarm spread throughout the entire army.[48]

Cissey's 1st Division bivouacked in two lines near Amanvillers, along the road leading to Saint Privat, besides Levassor-Sorel's division from 6 Corps. The 73rd were sent to occupy Saint Privat[49] with the divisional artillery setting up camp near the railway cutting. The cavalry division took station to the north of Amanvillers. The four regiments of Grenier's 2nd Division bivouacked in line of battle;[50] their right almost at Amanvillers, their left, touching Montigny farm, being refused so that the flanking regiment, the 98th, faced south. The divisional batteries were to the rear, on the reverse slope, a short distance from Amanvillers, close to the corps artillery reserve. Picquets were sent out in the direction of Vernéville, the 13th providing men for one outpost at Champenois farm,[51] and another a little to the north.

A company of the 64th was hidden in a clump of trees lining the road about 500 metres in front of the division's bivouac; the 98th sent one company to the rear of its left flank alongside the road from Amanvillers to Châtel, another to a small rise facing Montaudon's division. Although orders had been issued to dig defensive rifle pits, due to their late arrival, none were constructed. A request from the 2nd Division's artillery commander for earthworks to be constructed for his guns was similarly ignored.

In accordance with his orders, Canrobert initially established 6 Corps' bivouac on 17 August at Vernéville, his divisions formed in a semi-circle around the village. He met with Colonel Lamy of the General Staff around midday and protested that Bazaine's order had left his corps 'très en l'air,' with the proximity of the adjoining woods only adding to the difficulty of defending the position. At 3:00 p.m., Bazaine responded to Canrobert's request to abandon this exposed position and authorised his withdrawal to the ridge line of Saint Privat, alongside and to the north of Ladmirault.

Canrobert called his divisional commanders together and his corps moved off at 4:30 p.m. with General Barail and the 3/100th acting as rearguard. Font de Villiers division was the first to arrive at their new destination and deployed in two lines[52] between Saint Privat and Roncourt, along the edge of the plateau which dominated the glacis-like slope running down to Sainte Marie aux Chênes.

Later that evening, around 9:00 p.m., Bisson's 9th Ligne moved into position about 300 metres to the south of Roncourt. Levassor-Sorval's men deployed to the south of Saint Privat, again in

---

48    Rousset, *4 Corps*, pp.200–201.
49    It was later withdrawn when Canrobert's corps moved into the village.
50    From right to left, 5th Chasseurs, 13th, 43rd, 64th and 98th.
51    2/13th.
52    Front line; 75th and 91st; second line: 93rd and 94th. The artillery was positioned between the two brigades.

two lines,[53] the first by the hamlet of Jérusalem, the second along the road running to Châtel. Tixier's division only reached its destination after nightfall and it was with some difficulty that three of his regiments[54] moved into their assigned position east of the village, where Canrobert established his headquarters. The 9th Chasseurs camped just short of Jérusalem; the 100th, which was at the tail of the column, spent the night in the midst of 4 Corps bivouacs and as recorded by Rousset, their late arrival caused much confusion and alarm.

Montluissant's four batteries, following on the heels of the infantry, halted near Saint Privat. Barail's cavalry division[55] also arrived late in the evening and camped on western edge of the village, in front of La Font de Villiers division; his two batteries of horse artillery bivouacked to the north of Saint Privat. Canrobert told his divisional generals to assemble at Jérusalem at 8:00 p.m. for orders, with the wagons of the parc being despatched to look for supplies on Plappeville plateau.

## French Indecision

During the 17th, Bazaine moved his headquarters from Gravelotte to Plappeville, which was connected by telegraph to an observation post stationed in the tower of Metz cathedral. Unfortunately, this resulted in a constant stream of messages reporting the passage of hostile troops across the Moselle being sent through to Army Headquarters which did little to allay his concerns about the threat to his left wing and he ordered the Imperial Guard to establish their bivouac between the fortress at Plappeville and the col de Lessy. The general Army Reserve and Guard artillery were on the plateau by St Quentin, alongside Brincourt's Voltigeur division and the 2nd Brigade of Grenadiers; the remainder of Picard's division being at Fort Pappeville. General Desvaux's cavalry division reached the plateau around 4:00 p.m. on the 17th and set up camp alongside Forton and Valabrègue's troopers.

The positions occupied by the Imperial Army ran along a generally open and broad ridge, the western slope of which fell away in a gentle decline with little cover which lent itself well to the defensive capabilities of both their artillery and chassepot. The left of the line, between Leipzig farm and Rozerieulles was afforded additional strength by fort St Quentin and the deep gorge of the Mance stream that presented a formidable barrier to any attacker.

The weakness of the position lay on the right; although Saint Privat occupied a commanding position overlooking Sainte Marie and the ground to the west, it was open to being outflanked from the north, by way of Montois and Roncourt. Bazaine issued instructions that the corps should fortify their naturally strong positions with additional rifle pits and gun shelters and whilst some earthworks were constructed by Frossard and Le Boeuf, the late arrival of Ladmirault and Canrobert meant that little was done in the sectors which would have benefitted most from the defensive works.[56]

From the contents of a staff report, replete with errors, prepared on the 17th, it is evident that Bazaine was still uncertain as to which enemy formations confronted him on the 16th and more importantly, the forces now opposing him. He had little knowledge of the whereabouts

---

53   First line 25th and 26th, second: 93rd and 94th, again the divisional artillery camped between the lines.
54   4th, 10th and 12th.
55   2nd Chasseurs and 2nd Chasseurs d'Afrique
56   6 Corps was missing most of its engineering train and so was short of tools to undertake the work.

or intentions of the enemy and even less idea as to what he should do. In addition to worrying intelligence about enemy movements from the War Ministry and Le Boeuf, he was briefed by Canrobert on reports from an inhabitant of Gorze that 10,000 troops had left Pont à Mousson and could be expected on the battlefield within five hours.

The situation called for decisive action but despite his earlier undertakings to the emperor, as Howard noted, 'there can be little doubt that he was morally if not physically exhausted; that the weight of responsibility had paralysed him, annihilating all power of action and independence of will.'[57] Giving evidence to the post war Commission of Enquiry, Bazaine sought to excuse his inaction by stating that: 'it seemed to me that by fighting one or perhaps two defensive battles, in positions which I considered impregnable, I would wear down the strength of my adversary, forcing him to sustain heavy losses, which repeated several times, would weaken him enough to oblige him to let me pass without being able to offer serious opposition.'[58]

Even before battle commenced, it would seem he had abandoned any idea of reaching Verdun,[59] and at his later Courts Martial, he perhaps came closer to the truth when he declared that he 'believed and the Emperor believed as well, that by giving time to the army of Châlons to form, it would reach a considerable size which would allow it come and relieve us'.[60] The French official history compared his conduct 'to that of a simple soldier who abandons his post in the face of the enemy,'[61] whilst his chief of staff, Jarras, with whom it must be said he did not enjoy the most harmonious relationship, left this scathing assessment of his superior:

> The Marshal was absolutely devoid of character; his words and deeds did not coincide; what he would praise today he would blame tomorrow and vice versa; and these contradictory actions were quite natural with him. He was unscrupulous. The Marshal was incapacitated by his ignorance, faulty military education and weakness of character from saving the Army of the Rhine in the perilous position it found itself in when he assumed supreme command. He was mainly deficient in one characteristic, indispensable in difficult situations and that is the energy to order things; he could not say I WILL and to give a clear and precise order was an impossible thing on his part … he felt in his heart that the situation and the events were beyond his strength. He succumbed under the weight of this overwhelming truth. For want of anything better, he has abandoned himself to chance, the last resort of those who no longer rely on themselves.[62]

Clearly out of his depth and faced with a rapidly changing situation he did not comprehend, the supplies stockpiled within Metz and the safety afforded by its outlying fortresses, simply proved too much of a draw for the risk averse marshal. Late on the 17th August, he instructed General Lewal of the General Staff to find suitable sites for the army closer to the city in anticipation of

57    Howard, *Franco Prussian War* p.175.
58    Ascoli, *A Day of Battle*, p.213.
59    At the post war Inquiry, a staff officer, Captain Yung, stated that Bazaine had made the decision to retreat to Metz as early as 3:30 p.m. on the 17th; See l'État-Major, *St Privat*, p179.
60    Ascoli, *A Day of Battle*, pp.213–4
61    L'État-Major, *18 Août, Documents*, p.84.
62    Lanza, *Franco-German War*, p.680.

a further withdrawal. Satisfied with this, he reverted to type, devoting his time and efforts in dealing with the minutia of army administration, no doubt to convince himself, at least, that he was doing something productive with his time.

## Warning signs ignored

Early the following morning, as the Prussians began their perpendicular march across the front of the French position, Le Boeuf informed Army Headquarters that masses of enemy troops were marching in battle formation on Doncourt. Bazaine simply ignored the warning, sending his officier d'ordonnance to instruct 'that he should hold himself in his strong position.'[63] A little later, towards 9:00 a.m., as hostile formations were strung out across his front and highly vulnerable to counter attack, Bazaine was in conference with Jarras his chief of staff, reviewing commendations for promotions and medals.

As further reports arrived warning of larger bodies of troops marching on St Marcel and of the appearance of strong columns emerging from the woods of St Arnould, he again seemed indifferent, remarking to his staff that 'the defensive position occupied by his army completely secured against attack, that no serious attack was to be feared and that such an attack could not succeed in any case.'[64] This lack of concern was evidenced in the order issued to Canrobert:

> Marshal Le Boeuf reports to me that strong hostile forces are marching against his position … However this may be, you should arrange yourself firmly in your position and maintain good connection with the right wing of 4th Corps. The troops should camp in two lines and on a narrow front as possible. You would also do well to have the roads which lead from Marange upon your extreme right reconnoitred and I am ordering General Ladmirault to do the same with respect to the village of Norroy le Veneur. If the enemy appears to be deploying in your front and appears to make a more serious attack on Saint Privat, you should take all necessary security measures so as to hold your position until the entire right wing of the army can execute, if necessary, a change of front to occupy the positions situated further to the rear, which are at present being inspected. I do not like to be forced by the enemy to take that step; but if the movement is going to be made it will be done for the purpose of facilitating resupply, to get more water for the horses and to give the troops an opportunity to wash themselves. Utilise this momentary pause to bring up everything you still need. I am told that the meat was rejected yesterday because it smelled; however, this is no time to be stingy and the supply department undoubtedly could procure fresh meat by butchering. I sent you Bruchard's brigade which will remain with you until another cavalry division can be formed.[65]

As the French official history remarked:

63   L'État-Major, *St Privat*, p.154.
64   *Ibid*, p.180.
65   *Ibid*, pp.181–182.

These orders, if nothing else, show clearly why the battle had to be lost. The carelessness of the Marshal, his indifference to the reports coming in, the inexplicable task he set his right wing corps and the already expressed intention of falling back with the entire army, sufficiently explain the conduct of the commander in chief on this unfortunate day.[66]

Bazaine seemed reluctant to admit that the enemy forces posed any threat; when cannon fire broke out along the front, his chief of staff Jarras recalled:

> I gave the order to saddle and prepare the horses and I went to see the Marshall, convinced that he'd be ready to leave. Instead, he told me to be patient and deal with the staff promotions which were awaited by the army, the work on which had been interrupted by the goings on of recent days. At the same time, he repeated his view that he didn't think anything serious was going on.[67]

In view of this indifference, it is perhaps not surprising that when the commander in chief finally took to horse, sometime after 2:00 p.m., he did not go to where the battle was raging but, preoccupied with the imaginary threat to his left, made his way to fort Saint Quentin which overlooked the Moselle valley. This at a time when several hundred guns were already in action and there could no longer be any doubt as to the scale of the action unfolding to his front. It is to the credit of the French troops that despite Bazaine's evident indifference, they came within a hair's breadth of inflicting a major defeat on Moltke's forces, in this, the first set piece action of the campaign.

## Manstein's Attack Against Amanvillers

In accordance with Frederick Charles' orders, Manstein's IX Corps halted at la Caulre so as to afford time for the Guards to complete their encircling manoeuvre. Communications were established with VIII Corps at Villers aux Bois whilst his cavalry patrols made contact with a squadron of Hussars of the Guard at Batilly. As the troops lit fires to prepare a meal, the advance guard[68] of Wrangel's division, commanded by General Blumenthal, pushed forward through the Bois Doseuillons. Here, they came across a few horsemen and some stragglers were discovered in Vernéville; formed bodies of infantry and cavalry were seen to east but there was no contact with the enemy. Towards 10:00 a.m., Blumenthal's outposts occupied Vernéville and took up positions between Bois Doseuillons and Bois des Génivaux, awaiting instructions.

---

66    *Ibid.*, p.182. E. Von Schmid, in his commentary on the battle is even more scathing: 'If we do not consider at all the incorrect or faulty composition of these orders, it still appears to us inexplicable for the marshal to order the retreat of a part of his army of 150,000 men on the flimsy pretext of giving the soldiers an opportunity to wash themselves. Such a reason for retreating was probably never before stated in military history.' See Lanza, *Franco-German War*, p.669.

67    General Jarras, *Souvenirs du Général Jarras*, (Paris, Librarie Plon, 1892) pp.122–123. As the French Official History comments 'Thus expressing at the outset of the battle an opinion which he obstinately clung to for the rest of the day.'

68    6th Dragoons, 36th Regiment, 9th Rifles and 1st Heavy Battery.

Shortly after, Manstein received Moltke's earlier order directing IX Corps to assault the French positions between Bois des Geniveaux and Vernéville; unfortunately, this arrived before Prince Frederick's subsequent despatch, which ordered him to wait for the Guard and Saxon corps to commence their attack before beginning his offensive. Any hopes that Moltke may have held for a synchronised attack against the front and flank of the French line evaporated as Manstein ordered his men into action.

At 10:30 a.m., IX Corps moved off in two parallel columns through the forest clearings towards Vernéville. The 25th Grand Ducal Hesse Infantry Division was to the left, supported by von Schlotheim's 25th Cavalry Brigade which, after initially scouting ahead of their supporting infantry, headed off to the west by the Bois Doseuillons and Arnoux la Grange towards Habonville so as to secure their open flank. On the right, Blumenthal passed to the east of the wood and then on towards Vernéville; he was followed by the corps artillery under Colonel von Yagemann. Blumenthal was ordered 'to la Folie to occupy the wood and the farm in front, but not to pass beyond that point for the present.'[69]

Just after 11:00 a.m., he advanced on Chantrenne farm with two battalions of the 36th and three companies of the 9th Rifles[70] but encountered stiff resistance from the garrison[71] who greeted their approach with a fusillade of shots at a range of 800 metres as soon as they quit the shelter of the churchyard at Vernéville. One of the companies moved out of the cover of Génivaux wood, intending to engage the Prussians but their commanding officer, Colonel de Tourneur considered such an unsupported advance across the open ground to be impracticable and ordered them to fall back. Subsequently, all four companies withdrew towards Leipzig farm alongside 3rd and 4th companies' 1st Ligne and 2/69th.

Their withdrawal cleared the way for the Prussians to seize Chantrenne as two companies from the 36th moved up at the double and occupied the farm without firing a shot. The remaining fusilier companies pushed into the edge of the wood recently vacated by the 69th as the 2/36th and three rifle companies advanced on their right. Later, around 12:30 p.m. the advance guard of the Hessian division,[72] under Colonel von Lyncker, was ordered towards Arnoux la Grange.

Meanwhile, accompanied by his staff, Manstein rode forward to a hill outside Vernéville from where his scouts identified a large French camp between Amanvillers and Montigny la Grange. The enemy troops appeared to be cooking and off their guard. Surveying the scene through his glasses, Manstein exclaimed 'All are not yet gone; the road is not yet open for them; they are cooking.'[73] As his view to the north was obstructed by the Bois de la Cusse,[74] Manstein understandably assumed, although mistakenly as it turned out, that he had located the right flank of the French Army; it was after all, where the chief of staff had suggested it would be found in his earlier despatch to the Crown Prince. With Moltke's instruction to attack 'if the enemy's right wing was at la Folie' fresh in his mind and with the enemy apparently caught off guard, Manstein was not going to let this opportunity pass.

69    Clarke, *Franco-German War Vol. II*, p.23.
70    The remainder of the advance guard had been held back at Vernéville.
71    Four companies (the 1st, 2nd, 5th and 6th) of the 1/69th.
72    2nd Rifles, 4th Regiment, 1st Heavy and 1st Light batteries.
73    Bell, *St Privat*, p.231.
74    This 'wood' was in fact a number of scattered copses providing little cover but did serve to screen the view to the north.

Since the crossing of the Rhine, he had marched in the rear and supported other corps; at last, he was in the van of the advance and was anxious for his men to win glory before the French withdrew. As far as Manstein was concerned, his task was to 'attack, hold and annihilate as quickly as possible the enemy who had fallen into his clutches'[75] and instructed his corps to prepare for action. Mindful of Frederick's instructions to limit his attack to a 'strong deployment of artillery' around 11:30 a.m., Major General Freiherr von Puttkammer was ordered to bring the guns from 18th Division and the corps' Reserve forward at the trot.

Escorted by two squadrons of the 6th Dragoons, the batteries took position on a flat ridge which extended north-east from Vernéville to Amanvillers hill which seemed to offer some shelter from enemy fire. As they came within effective range of the French position, they unlimbered and opened their bombardment. Major von Gayl, in charge of the deployment, placed one battery from the advance guard[76] on the west of the valley so as to add to the confusion amongst the French; the first shot being fired at 11:45 a.m.

A little later, the remaining divisional batteries[77] were brought up and after experiencing considerable difficulty traversing a deep ditch, moved 1,000 paces in advance of 1st Heavy and deployed along a ridge overlooking the French lines from where they engaged the enemy artillery to the west and south of Montigny la Grange.[78] Werner II then leapfrogged his battery forward into the divisional gun line. To provide protection for the artillery, General Wrangel deployed two companies to screen the Bois de la Cusse,[79] another two were sent to screen l'Envie farmstead[80] although, as Ladmirault failed to garrison the farm, it was captured without a shot being fired. After a short delay,[81] the corps artillery then moved into position at a fast trot, somewhat to the left of the divisional guns before opening fire around 12:30 p.m.[82]

## The French Response

Even with their dismal record of inept scouting and intelligence gathering skills, the French could not but help notice the dust clouds produced by several enemy corps marching perpendicular across their front.[83] On the left of their line, Frossard's 2 Corps enjoyed a generally quiet night, but as daylight broke, firing increased as his outposts clashed with enemy skirmishers along the

75  Bell, *St Privat*, p.231.
76  1st Heavy battery, von Werner II.
77  2nd Light, von Eynatten; 1st Light, Koch; 2nd Heavy, Kindler.
78  As remarked upon by Bonnal, in response to the criticism directed against the late deployment of the artillery in the war against Austria in 1866, the Prussian commanders seem to have gone out of their way to ensure that their guns were employed at the first opportunity, often to their disadvantage.
79  2nd and 3/36th.
80  1st and 4/36th.
81  When the corps artillery halted prior to moving into the gun line, most of the batteries sent their horses to be watered whilst the men dispersed to collect wood and water. As a consequence, when the order came to advance, men from the reserves were pressed into service which delayed their deployment.
82  From right to left 3rd Heavy, Roerdansz; 3rd Light, von Bastineller; 4th Light, Mente; 1st Horse artillery, König, 4th Heavy, Werner I.
83  For example, Frossard had three cavalry divisions, some 13 regiments, available at Longeau, but they did little except send out a few ineffective patrols in the direction of Jussy and St Ruffine.

edge of the Bois de Vaux. Informed of the proximity of large numbers of enemy troops, Frossard ordered his men into position around 9:00 a.m.

The previous evening, General Vergé observed hostile infantry and artillery moving into Gravelotte and the valley that led down toward Ars sur Moselle; he therefore assumed the outbreak of fighting foretold a renewed attack and ordered his men to stand to. His divisional batteries[84] took ground on the main highway on both sides of the farm at Point du Jour; the buildings being occupied by the 3rd Chasseurs. 2nd Division's artillery[85] were deployed behind the high banks of the old Roman road on hill 346 from where they enjoyed a clear field of fire over the Bois de Vaux, Rozerieulles and Jussy.

A little later, two batteries de 12 from the corps' Reserve moved into position; the 11/5th to the left of Vergé's artillery, the 10/5th on the Rozerieulles heights. As the guns prepared for action, the 1/32nd manned a trench by the bend in the highway north of the Point du Jour;[86] the 2nd and 3rd battalions were held a little to the rear. The 1st and 2/55th, 1/76th and 1st and 2/77th occupied trenches and ditches alongside the road between the quarry at Point du Jour and Saint Hubert farm; the remaining battalions from these units were to the rear, forming a second, reserve line. On the extreme left of 2 Corps, five battalions[87] from Lapassat's brigade occupied the crest of the hill overlooking Rozerieulles, with the 3/97th being sent to Sainte Ruffine. At 11:30 a.m., Frossard left his quartier general at Châtel Saint Germain and around noon, took up position on the heights of the Point du Jour, just as the sound of cannon fire was heard from the direction of Vernéville,

Within 3 Corps, Le Boeuf's divisional cavalry struck their tents at 5:00 a.m. and the men stood to. Scouting parties were despatched and before long, reports of Prussian columns moving through the bois de Génivaux began to reach corps headquarters at l'Arbre mort. One noted 'The approach of numerous enemy columns towards Vernéville and along the road from Gravelotte towards Malmaison' whilst another stated, 'Prussians are marching in battle formation across the plateau behind Gravelotte in the direction of the heights of Doncourt. The troops are heading obliquely across our front and seem to be undertaking a grand encircling manoeuvre, pivoting about our position. We can clearly see the Prussian officers in front of their men.'[88]

Le Boeuf immediately sent an officer to Army Headquarters to brief them on developments and request instructions; Bazaine, apparently unconcerned by this news, simply replied, 'hold onto the positions which you have already been assigned.'[89] By the time the aide returned, Le Boeuf had already taken matters into his own hands; after sending a messenger to warn Frossard of developments, he belatedly ordered General Vialla[90] to prepare the buildings at Moscou, Leipzig and la Folie for defence. Earthworks were constructed along the crest of his position for the artillery and infantry which enjoyed excellent fields of fire over the Mance

---

84   5th, 6th and 12/5th.

85   7th, 8th and 9/5th.

86   Two companies were sent forward into the scrub bordering the Mance stream.

87   84th, 1st and 2/97th.

88   L'État-Major, *St Privat*, pp.153–154.

89   L'État-Major, *St Privat*, p.154. On his return, the officer tasked with delivering the message met General Bourbaki and briefed him as to the situation. Bourbaki then asked what Bazaine had said; 'Oh' the aide replied 'Marshal Bazaine doesn't think the fight is serious. In any case, our positions are excellent.'

90   Commander of 3 Corps engineers.

ravine The commanders of the first three divisions were ordered to push troops into the bois de Génivaux,[91] and empty caissons and carts were sent to the rear, with orders to bring forward provisions and additional ammunition.[92] Patrols continued to feed news to Le Boeuf at his command post at l'Arbre mort and at 8:25 a.m., it was reported that the Prussian columns had:

> … changed front, diagonally to the left. The main force seems to be directed against Saint Marcel and the south of Saint Marcel. New columns can be seen emerging from the Bois St Arnould and directed against the heights west of Rezonville which are already strongly held.[93]

Scouts from the cavalry squadron attached to 1st Division pushed out to the western edge of the bois de Génivaux and around 7:00 a.m., discovered enemy columns marching towards Saint Marcel and Rezonville. A little later, the same patrols sent news that 'several columns' were marching towards Vernéville and along the road running from Gravelotte to Malmaison. Even General Metman, on the heights between Leipzig and Mousou, discerned 'the movement of considerable bodies of men to the rear of Gravelotte.'[94]

Le Boeuf was no longer in any doubt as to the Prussian's intentions and around 8:30 a.m., despatched another warning to Bazaine: 'Large numbers of enemy troops (infantry and cavalry) are advancing towards Gravelotte on quite an extended and parallel front in battle formation. It seems to me that we should prepare for an engagement today.'[95] Convinced that an attack was imminent, he issued instructions to his men to occupy the fortified buildings, defensive works and emplacements constructed by the corps engineers.

Aymard's 4th Division were bivouacked between 2 Corps and Moscou farm. He had already deployed seven companies[96] amongst the undergrowth lining the edge of the ravine and during the morning, constructed a series of shelter trenches between the farm building and the large bend in the highway. Towards 10:00 a.m., Sanglé-Ferrière[97] occupied the works on the right with the 1/85th whilst four companies of the 1/80th manned those to the left.[98] One officer belonging to 4th Company, Captain Tissonnière, later recalled the events of that fateful morning:

> The sun rose, shining brightly. The 'diane' sounded cheerfully over the French camp. There was movement everywhere; the working parties departed; the horses were taken to the watering holes. I could see, from our mess set up on the side of the road, the makings of a fine meal when I was distracted by the shouts of the soldiers: 'It's a hedge!

---

91    The 1st five battalions, the 2nd, six and the 3rd, one and a half.
92    These wagons were noted by Prussian scouts who reported that the French appeared to be retreating; this may have been one of the factors that encouraged Manstein to launch his attack against la Folie.
93    L'État-Major, *St Privat*, p.155. The enemy troops noted were from IX Corps. Again, Le Boeuf forwarded this information to Bazaine.
94    *Ibid.*
95    *Ibid*, p.156.
96    6th Company 3/80th and the 3rd Battalion 60th.
97    Commander 2nd Brigade, 4th Division
98    3rd, 4th, 5th and 6th. The 1st and 2nd companies occupied the ground between the two main buildings of the Point du Jour.

1    This photograph purports to depict the departure of Napoleon from the Préfecture in Metz on the afternoon of August 14. The crowds were far more subdued compared with the jubilant scenes that greeted his arrival. Bottom; the same view today. (A)

2    A post war photograph showing Poplar avenue, or 'Todten Allée' and below, the view today. (A)

3    A view looking north along the 'Todten Allée', now somewhat overgrown. The memorial to the 2nd Westphalian Infantry Regiment No 15 is on the left and insert, an old postcard depicting the same scene. The original memorial to 6th Westphalian Infantry Regiment can be discerned in the background amongst the trees on the left. (A)

Blick in das Gelände westlich des Weges Colombey—Belle-Croix, Stellung der 3. Division Welchau des 3. französischen Korps, von dem Denkmal des J. R. 55 in der Totenallee aus.

(Plan 4 des Generalstabswerks. — Gruppenheft 00. II. 12/4.)

4    This photograph from a collection of battlefield studies shot shortly after the war is taken from the monument to the 6th Westphalian Infantry Regiment, looking north-west. The line of trees in the background marks the track that ran south from Belle Croix–Limite (visible on the right hand side) towards Borny. It shows the ground where 3rd Division were positioned following the loss of the 'Todten Allée'. Note the grave markers in the foreground and left rear. Inset, left, the original monument was a column surmounted by an eagle. It had fallen into disrepair by the end of the century and was demolished. Inset right, the replacement memorial was inaugurated on the 14th August 1903. Originally surmounted by an eagle and a plaque, both disappeared after the First World War. (A)

5    Another photograph taken shortly after the war depicts the view from the junction of 'Todten Allée' with the D4, facing east. The 2nd Westphalian Infantry advanced across the open fields towards the photographer, who took the picture from the right flank of position held by the 3/41st and inset, the same view today. The woods and gardens of the Château de Colombey and the Westphalian Jäger memorial are off to the right, out of shot. (A)

6          Although the vast majority of field graves around Mey were cleared away under the various 'regroupements' there were two notable exceptions; when this photograph was taken, this small plot had remained undisturbed for almost 150 years, set on the side of a peaceful valley to the north of amidst grazing cattle, unfortunately, residential development has now encroached on the setting. It contains the graves of five officers from I Corps who fell in the fighting around Mey; Captain von Puttkammer and lieutenants; Küntzel and Schneider of the 7th East Prussian Regiment No 44 and Captain von Horn and Lieutenant von Bühl of the 6th East Prussian Regiment No 43. (A)

7          Residential development has also intruded on the setting of this small cemetery, on the northern outskirts of Nouilly which contains the remains of 20 men from the fusilier battalion of the 2nd East Prussian Grenadier Regiment No 4 who fell in the fighting around Mey. (A)

8    I Corps' memorial near L'Amitié brewery was inaugurated on 19th January 1873 to honour those men who were killed in the battles around Metz on the 14th, 18th and 31st August 1870. Lions have featured on the coats of arms of Hessian rulers since the 12th Century and recumbent lions are often featured on their memorials. (A)

9    The 73rd launch their attack across open ground towards 'Todten Allée' and below, the memorial to the Hanoverian Fusilier Regiment No 73 with 'Todten Allée' in the background. Originally surmounted by an eagle, it was unveiled on 5 October 1890 on the site of a mass grave. (R/A)

10       One of the most recognisable memorials of the war, that belonging to the 1st Westphalian Regiment No 13. The female figure, symbolising Westphalia, stands alongside a wounded soldier, wearing campaign dress, his helmet by his side. Located alongside the D4 at Colombey, it was erected by the veterans of the regiment being unveiled on the 25th anniversary of the battle, 14 August 1895. Although it suffered some vandalism after the First World War, it is one of the best-preserved memorials from the war. (A)

11     The Porte des Allemands; a photograph taken after the war. The fortified gate served as a bridge over the river Seille into the city and was a vestige of the medieval ramparts which once enclosed Metz. Although the road layout in front of the gates has undergone considerable alteration and the outer works demolished, the fortifications remain unchanged. (A)

12 The house in Longville where Napoleon III spent the night of 14th /15th August 1870. (A)

13 An etching of the house in Gravelotte where Napoleon III spent the night of the 15th/16th August. The property today is little changed although the plaque bearing the Prussian coat of arms has been removed. (A)

14    Centre; this sketch from Eugen Krügers '*Landschafts album vom kriegsscbauplatz*' depicts the village of Vionville from where the French horse were being watered; the high ground where Schirmer initially deployed his artillery is to the rear left of the church tower, with the tower of Tronville church visible to the rear. Note the numerous grave markers in the foreground; a number of officers from the Brandenburg Fusilier Regiment No 35 were buried here. Top; the same view today, the red star making the high ground where the guns were deployed and bottom, the same area as viewed from the high ground above Flavigny. The red star marks the high ground where Schirmer deployed his guns, the blue, Vionville church and the green, the area where the French horses were being watered. (EK/A/A)

15    A German grave just outside Vionville, the scene of bitter fighting during 16 August and inset, the same view today. The majority of such field graves were cleared away during the 'regroupements' undertaken post the First World War, with the remains being reburied in the cemetery at Gravelotte. (A)

16    Top; the village of Rezonville from the south, as depicted by Krügers. The road to the right runs towards Gorze with the Bois Pierrot to the rear and below; the village today. (EK/A)

Tot: 4 Offiziere, 199 Mann
Verwundet: 28 Offiziere, 394 Mann
Vermißt: 32 Mann

17      Left; the memorial to the East Frisian Infantry Regiment No 78 located at a junction in the
farm track running across the plateau between Gorze and the Metz-Verdun road; the track to the left
originally led to Vionville, that on the right, to Flavigny. Right, the author and Ben. (A)

18      Top; this photograph depicts the view from the track running north across the plateau looking
down on Flavigny. The line of poplar's in the background delineates the Metz-Verdun highway with
Vionville to the left rear. Note the number of field graves. Below; the view today. (A)

19      The 52nd at Vionville; the Guard Cuirassiers are felled by the deadly close range fire of the Dreyse; inset, Captain Hildebrand, commander of the 52nd, was killed during attack and was buried on the battlefield. His grave was cleared away during the 'regroupements' with his remains interred at Gravelotte cemetery. (M/A)

20      Some of the survivors of the Guards charge, depicted during the siege of Metz and left, a casque and cuirass as worn by the cuirassiers. (A)

21 Left; 2nd Westphalian Hussar Regiment No 11 catch Donlop's Guard Horse artillery as the battery deploys. Right; Lieutenant Emmanuel d'Esparbès de Lussan (1842–1870) commanded a section of guns and was buried where he fell but after the war his remains were transferred to the family plot at Bardigues. The monument erected in his honour fell into disrepair over time; the name plate disappeared and the original cross was broken. When the farm land was cleared during 2003, the monument was dismantled and put into storage before it eventually found its way to its present location, 500m to the north, alongside the Metz-Verdun highway. (R/A)

22    Top; Bredow's under strength brigade – the general can be seen between the two regiments – crashes into the French gun line just as Montluisant was pulling two batteries out to replenish their ammunition. The 16th Altmark Lancers are to the left, the 7th Magdeburg Cuirassiers to the right. Bottom; the same view today; the Bois St Marcel off to the right. (D/A)

23    The memorial to 12th Cavalry Brigade was inaugurated on the 7 October 1872. It stands a short
distance to the north of Rezonville. (A)

24    Top; the postcard depicts the view looking west along the fond de la cuve; just below the tree to the left, the memorial belonging to Lieutenant Colonel von Roell and Lieutenant Ernst Weinhagen of the 8th Westphalian Infantry Regiment No. 57 which today is in the cemetery at Gravelotte. At the base of the slope, can be seen the monument to the Arnim brothers and their fellow officers which, although in poor condition, remains in its original position. The inscription refers to Rudolph Adolph von Arnim, his brother Oswald, as well as August Scholton; the panel on the reverse records the names of Friedrich Heidsiek and Oswald Schwartz. Bottom, a present-day view looking east along the valley. (A)

25      Top; another postcard depicting the view looking east along the fond de la cuve with inset, the memorial on the northern side of the valley to Julius Mebes. Bottom, the memorials to the 3rd Westphalian Regiment No 16 and on the left, the replacement memorial to the 1st Dragoon Guards inaugurated on 19 August, 1909. (A)

26    The view from the northern side of the valley, looking south to the German positions. The memorial to Julius Mebes is to the right and across the valley, just discernible, the Westphalian memorials in the centre and to the left, the memorial to Sous Lieutenant Chabal of the 57th Line. (A)

*Drapeau du 2ᵉ ba- taillon du 3ᵉ régi- ment d'infanterie pris à Rezonville par le lieutenant Chabal.*

481. - MARS-la-TOUR
Le Commandant Chabal et sa famille au Monument, le 16 Août 1909

27    Sous Lieutenant Francois Hector Chabal (1842–1920) pictured with his family and below, the memorial commemorating the capture of the standard. (R/A)

28    Heinrich XVII, Prince Reuß of Köstritz was killed at the head of the 5th Squadron 1st Guard Dragoons. His body was only recovered later that evening when the men searching for him recognised his horse; he is buried alongside the dragoons' memorial in Mars la Tour. (O/IGK/A)

29    The mortally wounded General Legrand is dragged from beneath his stricken mount by men of the
3rd Dragoons. Legrand was taken to this house in Bruville. To the right, this photograph of a dragoon
captain was taken during the siege of Metz and depicts the appearance of these troops on campaign.
(RT/A)

30    Fréderic Legrand (1810–1870) commanded 4 Corps cavalry at Rezonville and is buried in the cemetery at Doncourt les Conflans. (O/A)

31    The construction of the French memorial at Mars la Tour so close to the new border with Germany was beset with political problems given the challenging relations between the two countries in post war years. The female figure, symbolising France, is looking towards the border as she cradles the body of a dying soldier. At his feet, two children; one of them holds out his hand to retrieve the rifle, the other, an anchor, symbolising hope. The base was designed as a crypt to hold those remains collected during the frequent 'regroupements.' (A)

36　The terrain to the north of Amanvillers; the level crossing box is to the left with the church at Saint Privat to the rear and Amanvillers to the extreme right. Inset left, the signal box and right, the French cemetery at Amanvillers where some 550 soldiers are buried. (A)

37　Saint Hubert farm; the German cemetery can be seen to the right. Inset, left; on this photograph the loopholes made by the French defenders are clearly visible; inset right; the farm was destroyed during the fighting for Metz in WW2, this photograph showing the same scene today. (A)

38      Saint Hubert farm today; the road to the right of the farm did not exist in 1870 and as the
photograph, lower right, shows, there was far less cover for the French defenders. Again, note the
loopholed walls. To the left, a depiction of the assault against Saint Hubert; elements of the 8th Jägers
and 28th, 33rd, 60th and 67th regiments took part in the attack. (PH/A)

39    One of the many field cemeteries established after this battle; this by the side of a house just to the
west of Gravelotte and inset; the same scene today. (A)

40　The 9th Jäger Battalion at Gravelotte; the battalion is shown deployed to the north of the lane that runs from Vernéville towards Leipzig farm, advancing in line in an easterly direction towards Amanvillers. Chantrenne farm can be seen to the rear and in the background, the church spire at Vernéville. Inset; the same view today with the Jäger memorial in the foreground. (O/A)

41　The imposing memorial to the 25th Hessian Division as it appeared in 2013. In 2015 the 300kg bronze Lion was stolen, presumably for its scrap value and unfortunately, at the time of writing, there appear to be no plans to reinstate the monument to its former glory. Several smaller memorials around the base of the memorial were damaged or destroyed after the First World War and today just two remain. (A)

42    Left; Major von Hadeln leads a charge by the 1st Company 7th Rhenish Infantry Regiment No. 69
against the French positions to the east of Saint Hubert farm. The commanding officer, Colonel Beyer
von Karger, who was carrying the regiment's colours, was wounded by shrapnel and Hadeln seized the
flag in his right hand only to fall a few moments later, fatally wounded by a shot through the heart.
Centre; a photo of the same stretch of road taken shortly after the war and, bottom, the same scene
today. (O/A)

43    The 12th Jäger Battalion lead the assault into Sainte Marie aux Chênes, pushing towards the Catholic church at the centre of the village; little has changed during the last 150 years. (A)

44    The killing fields of Saint Privat, 1. The photo to the left depicts the lane running south from Saint Privat. 4th Guards Brigade advanced across this bare slope from left to right towards this lane which was held by de Chanelles brigade. To the right, the memorial to the 4th (Queen Augusta) Guards Grenadiers in the cemetery which was established on the summit of the slope captured at such cost. It held the remains of both the attackers and French defenders and later was used to bury soldiers who died from their wounds in the various aid stations established in Saint Privat and Jérusalem. (A)

45    This picture from after the battle is taken further down the slope and depicts one of the many graves for the 2nd Grenadiers. This one was located about 100 yards east of Sainte Marie aux Chênes, alongside the highway leading to Saint Privat where many of the grenadiers had sought cover in the roadside ditches from the French fire. Note the absence of cover. Inset; today the cemetery has been swallowed up by the growth of the village and the simple wooden crosses replaced by more substantial memorials. (A)

46    Top; this photograph shows the mass grave in close up; amongst the officer's names visible on the rough wooden crosses are Second Lieutenants von Hatton, von Stuckradt, Baron von Patow, von Kehler and Ensign Mirus. Another smaller grave is visible to the rear left of the burial mound. Bottom, some of the present-day memorials; on the left, Reserve Unteroffizier Linau; to the right two of the officers whose names were visible on the wooden crosses, 26-year-old Reserve Lieutenant Adalbert von Kehler and 18-year-old Ensign Richard von Mirus who, if the inscription is to be believed, died of his wounds on the 19th. (A)

47   The killing fields of Saint Privat, 2. This photograph was taken shortly after the war with several buildings still showing signs of battle damage. It was taken from the southern side of the road where the 2nd Foot Guards were deployed and again, provides a graphic illustration of just how little cover the terrain afforded. The tower of the old church is visible on the left and on the extreme right, the ruined Auberge du Mont Cernis. The present-day comparison was taken from alongside the main road. (A)

48     Top, Another view of Saint Privat, the ruined Auberge du Mont Cernis to the right. This was the location chosen for the memorial to the 3rd Foot Guards which was inaugurated with great ceremony on 25 September 1900. Today only the base remains, the Lion being blown upon the night of 8 March 1919 by members of the Souvenir français. (EK/A)

49    The killing fields of Saint Privat 3. Top; this photograph depicts the open ground where 2 Foot Guards were pinned down under French fire; Roncourt is to the left (A); Saint Privat centre, (B) and the position defended by de Chanelles brigade off to the right, (C). Bottom, the same view from the French positions within Saint Privat. Inset, right, this memorial, erected by l'Association pour l'ornementation des tombs, originally stood in the fields out alongside the north side of Saint Privat. Inset, left, it was relocated from the battlefield to the new cemetery alongside the road which runs between Sainte Marie and Saint Privat which holds the remains of 1,238 soldiers.

50    Many casualties from 1st Guards Brigade were treated at this aid station in Sainte Marie aux Chênes; note the shell damage to the buildings on the left. (A)

51    Sainte Marie aux Chênes and 1st Guards Brigade cemetery. The buildings featured in the earlier photograph are visible on the left with the cemetery to the right, a large wooden cross having been erected amongst the smaller grave markers. Inset left, pretty much the same scene was captured in this photograph of this improvised field service being held for German troops on their way to Verdun in the First World War. Inset, right, the same scene today. (A)

52 More then and now comparisons for the 1st Guards Brigade cemetery with the simple wooden crosses being replaced by substantial stone memorials. (EK/A)

53    Another Guards aid station was established in the sheltered, western, side of Sainte Marie where two mass graves were prepared for the many dead. A little later, a cemetery was established where the remains were gathered together, including a large number of men from the 2nd Foot Guards although men from other German and French units were also interred here. This photograph depicts the cemetery shortly after the battle. Pickelhaubes, ammunition pouches, a saddle and other detritus litter the foreground; to the rear, a medical orderly wearing a red cross brassard surveys the scene; to his right a pickelhaube atop a stick can be seen marking the spot of another burial and inset, the same view today. (A)

Das Regiment
verlor in der Schlacht von St. Privat
39 Offiziere, 1076 Mann

DEM OFFIZIERKORPS
DES 2. GARDE REGIMENTS ZU FUSS
SEINEN IN DER SCHLACHT BEI
GRAVELOTTE AM 18TEN AUG. 1870
GEFALLENEN KAMERADEN

54    The author stood beside the large stone memorial cross to the 2nd Foot Guards which was erected sometime before 1875. A number of the original memorials disappeared following the First World War and several more were brought into the cemetery for safekeeping following the various 'regroupements.' (A)

55    The road running south from Roncourt to Saint Privat, the Saxon memorial visible in the two
upper views. ((LH/A)

56    The memorial to General Ernst Adolph von Craushaar who was mortally wounded during the Saxon attack on Saint Privat. He was initially buried in Sainte Marie before his family brought his remains back to Dresden. His son in law, Eduard von Pape, a captain in the 107th also died in the attack. (A)

57    Left; Then and now depictions of the memorial to the 4th Foot Guards erected on the northern
      edge of Saint Privat in 1874. The Saxon memorial is visible further along the road and in the
background, across the open fields, Roncourt. Right: the Saxon memorial today. It was inaugurated on
      31 July 1873 in the presence of the Saxon Crown Prince. (A)

58    The most iconic painting of the battle, perhaps the war; Alphonse de Neuville's Le Cimetière de
      Saint Privat and inset, the same scene photographed today. (O/A)

59    Top, the Guard assault the gateway to the church. Bottom, the same scene today. The square has since been renamed Place Canrobert in honour of the French commander who led the defence of Saint Privat. (RT /A)

60   Several views of the ruined church which was demolished in 1875, with most of the civilian graves being transferred to the new church in 1876. Further changes took place when the adjoining street was widened, resulting in the reduction in size of the present-day cemetery. The importance of this gateway as a memorial to the battle was recognised when it was listed as an historic monument in August 1924. (LH/A)

61    The killing fields at Amanvillers; Top, the scene of 3rd Guard's Brigade attack. Saint Privat is to the extreme left, Amanvillers, centre right. The French line ran along the hedge row. Bottom, the view from what was the hedgerow looking west; the French position ran along the dirt track in the foreground, looking towards the attackers. Vernéville is to the rear of the trees, left of centre, the Bois de la Cusse, centre right. To the right, top and centre the Emperor Alexander Guards Grenadier Regiment No 1 memorial; bottom, that of the 3rd Queen Elisabeth Guards Grenadier Regiment. (A)

62    The Gardeschützen in action at Amanwillers; the battalion lost almost 45 percent of their strength, killed or wounded. The memorial was inaugurated on 18 August 1899; the bronze eagle and furnishings were removed following the First World War and it suffered further damage during the fighting around Metz in the First World War. (PH/A)

63    In 1924 the remains of 106 French graves in the area were gathered together and buried in this new cemetery at Amanvillers. Inset; This grave records the last resting place of two unknown lieutenants from the 45th. This regiment formed part of MacMahon's 1 Corps and whilst it is not impossible that men from that regiment were interred at Amanvillers, it seems likely that the men were from either the 41st or 44th. Such mistakes in reading old illegible or damaged grave markers were not uncommon. (A)

64 The site of the cemetery at Gravelotte was chosen shortly after the battle to receive the bodies of those killed in the fighting around the Mance ravine. Left; a couple of veterans and a serving officer pose in front of the memorials and right; the same scene today. (O/A)

## Key to Sources

(A) Photographs taken by, or material from, the author's collection.

(D) Dayot, *Le Second Empire 1851–1870* (Paris: Ernest Flammarion, 1900)

(EK) Krügers, *Landschafts – album vom kriegsschauplatz*, (Hamburg: 1871)

(IGK) Anon, *Illustrirte Geschichte des Krieges* 1870/71 (Stuttgart: Union,1875)

(LH) Lüders & Helmuth, *Das Schlachtfeld von Gravelotte-Saint Privat* (Berlin: G. Pfeiffer, 1874)

(M) Maurice, *The Franco German War 1870–71* (London: 1900)

(O) Open Source; every reasonable effort has been made to identify copyright holders and the author and publisher apologise for any errors in misattribution or omissions in this work and would be grateful if notified of any necessary corrections that should be incorporated in future reprints or editions of this book.

(PH) Pflugk Hartung, *Krieg und Sieg* 1870–71 (Berlin: Schall & Grund 1895)

(R) Rousset, *Histoire Générale de la Guerre Franco-Allemande* (1870–1871) (Paris: 1910)

(RT) Rousset, *Les Combatants* (Paris: Libraire Illustrée, 1891)

No, it's a line of battle!' Low down, in the distance, on the other side of Gravelotte, a long black line spread out across the terrain; it looked motionless, but shortly one noticed it began to move and then you could see the glint of bayonets. In our camp, everything was calm; it couldn't be the enemy. I went to the colonel's tent to show him; he took up his glasses but couldn't see anything but the hedgerows and fields. The long black line had disappeared. I didn't think any more about it until about an hour later, I noticed a lot of movement within the camp and officers calling out. You could see heavy columns marching towards Gravelotte; you could make out cavalry and artillery. We wondered what it could be but no-one could admit it was the enemy; we'd beaten them on the 16th! Towards nine o'clock generals Aymard and Sanglé-Ferrière arrived; on horseback. With great composure and few words Aymard told our colonel where to deploy. As a consequence of these orders a rifle pit was constructed along the firing line of the 1st and 3rd battalions from where they could cover the ground in front of Saint Hubert farm. Three companies (3rd, 5th and 6th) were deployed in the trench. One company (the 4th, mine) was sent out front, to the right along the side of the road, its left towards the Point du Jour. Two companies (1st and 2nd) were held in reserve, in some sand pits about 300 metres behind the firing line. The 3rd battalion, in column, was held in reserve behind the ridge line. I went out front, proud of the mission I'd been given. The first section had found good cover, behind the road embankment, by the bend in the road, but the second lacked any shelter, so they tried to improve their position with their sword bayonets. Behind us, on the other side of the road a battery took up position. The gunners quickly went about building earthworks for their pieces. In front of me stretched an open glacis of some 500 to 600 metres of cultivated ground behind which we could see the tops of the trees which covered the banks of the Mance ravine. The road from Gravelotte bent right towards the ravine and then wound its way up between our camp and the farm at Saint Hubert. In this farm, about 400 metres distant, the 2nd Battalion had set to work. They formed loopholes in the farmhouse and walls surrounding the courtyard. The commandant was talking to some peasants who'd gathered on the road outside the main gate; I could see lots of gesticulating. Old man Vincins[99] was striding across the ground with his long legs, hands behind his back, nose in the air. What a racket! A good-looking young peasant had stopped to chat with our men to tell them about the swarms of Prussians around Gravelotte.[100]

As related by Tissonnière the 2/80th garrisoned the farm at Saint Hubert; the remainder of 2nd Brigade formed a second line on the reverse slope of the crest.[101] To the right of Sanglé-Ferrière, Brauer[102] placed four companies from the 1/44th into the trenches with two held back in support. Two battalions[103] occupied the courtyard, buildings and trenches at Moscou farm

---

99  A Captain in the 2nd Battalion.
100 General H. Bonnal, *L'Espirit de la Guerre Moderne, La Manoeuvre de St Privat III* (Paris: Libraire Militaire R. Chapelot et Cie. 1912) pp.70–72
101 3/80th and 2nd and 3/85th.
102 Commander 1st Brigade.
103 3/44th and 2/60th.

whilst the remainder of 1st Brigade[104] were massed in reserve on the rear slope of the ridge near the bois de Châtel Saint German.

Aymard deployed his batteries along the front of the division, overlooking the ravine at Saint Hubert. On the far right, the 9/11th were to the south of Moscou farm,[105] their ammunition caissons concealed behind the walls of the outbuildings. On the extreme left, 10/11th deployed behind earthworks to the rear of the 1/80th; the mitrailleuse's of the 8/11th to the north of Moscou farm from where they enjoyed a good field of fire across the ravine to Gravelotte.

By 8:00 a.m., 3rd Division had struck their tents and despatched their wagons to the rear. Le Boeuf ordered Metman to throw up earthworks for his artillery and dig rifle pits for the infantry. The 59th occupied the trenches either side of Moscou farm, the buildings being held by 4th Division. To their right, the 29th placed 1st Battalion into the trenches, the 3rd being retained on the reverse slope of the plateau. Further to the north, the 7th deployed in three lines; 1st Battalion in a trench facing west, the 2nd and 3rd held in support on the rear slope of the crest.

The 7th Chasseurs, 2/29th and three companies of the 71st occupied the Bois de Vaux; the remainder of the 71st was held in reserve near l'Arbre mort.

Nayral's 2nd Division had cleared their tents away by 9:00 a.m. to take their assigned positions; from 1st Brigade, 1st and 2/19th manned the rifle pits either side of the knoll running down toward Génivaux, 700 metres south of Leipzig farm which had also been fortified by the divisional engineers. Five companies[106] occupied the farm; the remainder of the 3rd Battalion was deployed along Chantrenne brook where, with some difficulty, they penetrated the dense scrub on the opposite bank and pushed forward so as to line the edge of the copse opposite Vernéville.

The trenches constructed along the south-west edge of the orchard at Leipzig farm were held by the 2/69th; the 3rd Battalion was kept in reserve in the clearing south of the Bois de Charmoise. The 90th was also pushed into the area of Génivaux wood lining the left bank of the watercourse; its battalions echeloned to the rear from right to left; the 1st linking up with the 3/69th in the clearing. The 15th Chasseurs and the 41st formed the divisional reserve and were placed on the reverse slope, north of l'Arbre mort and the artillery parc.

Montaudon's company of divisional engineers had been at work since first light on the plateau of la Folie, constructing pits for the artillery on height 343 some 500 metres north-west of la Folie farm and loopholing the buildings. At 10:00 a.m., his infantry stood to arms; towards 11:30 a.m., two batteries[107] of the divisional artillery took position behind earthworks towards the north-west of la Folie farm, the third[108] on the left wing north-east of Leipzig. 1st Brigade held the main battle line between Leipzig and la Folie.

The divisional sappers and three companies of the 2/51st occupied la Folie, another three were in reserve along with the 1st Battalion a few hundred metres to the south-east; the 62nd were to their left and to their right the 18th Chasseurs. The 3/51st was to the south of la Folie; two companies were sent to occupy the crest of hill 313 which ran down towards the Bois de

---

104  11th Chasseurs, 1/60th and 2/44th.
105  Behind earthworks thrown up by the men of the 1/44th.
106  Three from the 3/19th; two from 1/69th.
107  6th and 8/4th.
108  5/4th.

Charmoise, the remainder held back to provide a link with Clinchant's 2nd Brigade who had been tasked with securing the wood and the road running to Chantrenne. Clinchant placed the 2/81st in the north-west sector of the wood with three companies lining its edge, the others being retained in reserve in the interior. The 1st Battalion was held in support to east of the Bois de Charmoise whilst the 3rd was in the clearing between Charmoise and Génivaux woods alongside the 3/69th, so as to establish a connection with Nayral's division.

The 95th was stationed between la Folie and Charmoise wood; three companies from the 1st Battalion were sent forward to hill 343.[109] The 3rd Battalion occupied the section of Génivaux wood which extended south-west towards the Bois de Charmoise facing Chantrenne farm.

Shortly after moving into the wood, Colonel de Courcy of the 90th met with Commandant Rigaud of the 7th Chasseurs to discuss tactics; it was agreed that the chasseurs would push two companies towards Malmaison, with two from the 90th supporting their right. The remainder of the battalion were withdrawn to a clearing at the rear alongside the 2/29th. Three companies of the 2/71st under Captain Schmedter covered the section of road from Malmaison to Saint Hubert where it crossed the Chantrenne brook.

Following this deployment, 3 Corps position ran for about 3,500 metres with the majority of Le Boeuf's men being placed in the firing line, between 500 and 1,000 metres back from the ravine, with relatively few battalions held in reserve.

Although Bazaine was apparently unconcerned about the reports of enemy troops marching across his front towards Saint Privat, he remained apprehensive about the threat to his left flank. He advised the commander of the Imperial Guard that an attack against 2 and 3 corps was expected and asked him to place a brigade on hill 313 overlooking Saint Germain to support them if their positions were compromised. Bourbaki protested that this was not the time to commit the reserve in small units. Bazaine's response was typical of his style, or rather lack, of leadership: 'You may either recall it or leave it there, as suits you best.'[110]

Bourbaki sent 2nd and 3rd Voltigeurs forward about 11:00 a.m. with instructions that they should take orders from no-one except him and the divisional general, Devigny. This deployment meant that by noon on the south of the French line between la Folie and Point du Jour, along a naturally strong position reinforced by extensive earthworks and rifle pits, seven infantry divisions, four cavalry divisions and thirty-four batteries were in place to meet the impending offensive. Unfortunately for the Imperial Army, the Prussians assault was launched against 4 Corps who were completely unprepared to meet such an attack.

## 4 Corps Under Attack

Ladmirault's men were late in arriving at their bivouac on the 17th; as a consequence, no outposts had been set although a few patrols were sent towards Vernéville. A squadron from the 7th Hussars was sent to Gravelotte, but for the large part, his cavalry division remained inactive at Amanvillers. At 7:00 a.m., he ordered all his troop vehicles and ammunition caissons back to Metz to replenish supplies. Around 9:00 a.m., reports began to trickle in from his scouts advising of the movement of large numbers of Prussian troops from left to right across

109 This position was also defended by skirmishers from the 81st and the 2/51st.
110 L'État-Major, *St Privat*, p.183.

his front. In addition to this intelligence, Ladmirault received copies of Le Boeuf's despatches to Bazaine: men out foraging for supplies in Vernéville similarly warned of the approach of hostile detachments,[111] a piquet near Montigny farm[112] noted enemy troops near Vernéville and Lorencez's division reported swirling clouds of dust between the farm at Saint Vincent and Malmaison.

Despite these worrying signs, Ladmirault decided against ordering his men to stand to; instead he sent staff officers to warn the divisional commanders to prepare for an attack, at the same time cautioning them against alerting their troops as he 'didn't want to interfere with their rest.'[113] Between 10:00 and 11:00 a.m., he received Bazaine's despatch updating him on Le Boeuf's report, together with instructions to reconnoitre the forest roads in the rear of his positions leading to Norroy.[114] Despite all these warnings, he still failed to recognise the seriousness of the situation; his artillery were ordered to harness their teams, but the only infantry to receive instructions were the 3/15th who were sent to the rear to watch over the tracks leading through the forest to Metz.

Instead, like Bazaine, Ladmirault seems to have spent his time dealing with mundane administrative matters, although as the French official history notes, he did make the 'vague recommendation that defensive works be constructed and the forest roads cleared.'[115] As a result, it came as a surprise to both him and his men when, shortly before noon, enemy artillery opened fire on his bivouac.

Lieutenant Patry recalled the bucolic scene within 4 Corps bivouac that morning and how, after writing a letter to his parents describing 'our two victories,' he had enjoyed a leisurely lunch. Then,

> After the meal we held an inspection of the men, who had put the morning to good use to tidy themselves up and get their arms and all their equipment in order. They looked good; one would never have said on seeing them so well turned out and polished that they had been marching without respite for three weeks and that they had just gone through two great battles in three days. I thought to post my letter and was heading towards the paymaster's wagon when on passing the majors tent, I noticed him shaving himself. I hailed him and said 'How handsome you look major. Are you planning on going to make some conquest in Metz?' 'Good Lord, no' he replied 'but since by chance I've been able to get hold on my trunk, I've changed completely. This way, if I'm killed today, I shall go into the other world properly dressed.' 'Do you think anything will happen today? It seems to me that things are dead quiet.' ... In front of the post wagon, I found the divisional paymaster finishing lunch with his two aides. I joined in conversation with them and we discoursed for a long time about the confusion which had prevailed in our marches, particularly in these last two few days ... I was about

---

111  Probably from IX Corps.
112  From the 3/64th.
113  L'État-Major, *St Privat*, pp.166–167. As the French official history comments, Ladmirault's apparent lack of concern probably resulted from his not unreasonable assumption that Bazaine would have issued orders had he been worried about an impending attack.
114  Again, this would seem to indicate that Bazaine had already decide upon on a further retreat into Metz.
115  L'État-Major, *St Privat*, p.168.

they too withdrew to replenish their munitions from the reserve parc alongside the Bois du Saulay.

## Manstein Bides His Time

On the right of IX Corps at Chantrenne, 18th Division, confronted by a more numerous opposition, had little to show for their efforts; seven companies[209] of the 36th supported by two from 9th Rifles[210] struggled to make any progress against the deadly flanking fire of the French infantry lining the edge of Charmoise wood. Blumenthal ordered the 85th, who were sheltering at Chantrenne farmhouse, to push through bois de Génivaux so as to fall on the flank of the French defenders.

I Battalion, under Lieutenant Colonel Koeppen, moved with difficulty through the thick undergrowth to the eastern edge of the wood, sheltering in a ditch prior to launching their attack across the 400 yards of open ground that separated them from the French. 1st Company led the charge, supported on their right by the 4th but had scarcely left the cover of the wood, when their advance was brought to a halt by the murderous chassepot fire.[211] Meanwhile, II Battalion, advancing in the rear of the I, endeavoured to drive the enemy from the eastern corner of bois de Génivaux but again, this attack ground to a halt in the face of the superior French firepower.

Colonel von Falkenhausen[212] recognised he was not going clear the objective with the limited force available to him, so withdrew both battalions to the northern corner of the wood, leaving the enemy in control of the remainder. It was a similar story to the east of Chantrenne where the French infantry[213] defending Charmoise wood, were given fire support by their artillery on hill 343; Brandenstein was killed and Blumenthal slightly wounded and with III/36th running low on ammunition and suffering increasing losses,[214] they were pulled back, so by 4:00 p.m., the line was held by just three companies from II/36th and a company of 9th Rifles. However, by this time, the fire from the French artillery on hill 343 had begun to decline and some of their batteries had already pulled out of the line.[215]

Montaudon, who was observing the combat from these heights, called up three companies of the 2/54th from reserve to fill the gap between the 1/54th and the 33rd; a little later, towards 4:00 p.m., elements of the 2/62nd were ordered to support the 69th occupying Leipzig farm, whilst three companies of the 1/62nd, along with the 18th Chasseurs, manned the shelter pits along the crest of the hill which covered the exits out of the woods. The remaining companies of 1st Battalion together with three from the 3/62nd, were held in reserve to the north-east of Charmoise wood at the disposal of General Clinchant.

209  5th, 7th, 8th, 9th, 12th, 11th and 10th.
210  1st and 2nd.
211  Both company commander's, 1st Lieutenant Faust and Captain Schuster, were killed at the head of their men.
212  The commanding officer of the 85th.
213  Elements of the 62nd, 81st and 95th in Charnoise, the 69th and 95th in Génivaux.
214  3rd Battalion lost 10 officers and 180 men.
215  6th, 7th and 10/4th although the 10th came back into action later, a little to the north.

As 18th Division's offensive ground to a halt, Manstein and his staff took up position by the Bois de la Cusse in order to monitor Prince August's progress. Although the planned simultaneous attack by IX and Guard corps against the French right wing was clearly no longer practicable, he was still anxious to coordinate his moves with those of August. He was informed that von Pape's 1st Guard Division had reached Habonville and August offered to send them to support his attack on Amanvillers. Manstein demurred; he felt the Guards could achieve more by taking Saint Privat and instead suggested that he retain just a brigade at Anoux la Grange which he could call upon if events took a turn for the worse. In line with this thinking, he had created a reserve from Prince Louis' Hessians [216] looking to commit them only when the Guards launched their attack.

Meanwhile, the bulk of the fighting in this sector was being sustained by five batteries of divisional artillery[217] that had been introduced into the firing line to the east of Habonville. Struggling against a well sheltered adversary they suffered heavy casualties but, supported by the infantry[218] lining the railway embankment whose fire kept the tirailleurs at bay, they gradually gained ascendancy over the French guns.

In view of the losses incurred by III Corps on the 16th, Alvesleben's role was to act as reserve for Manstein and so it was past 1:00 p.m. before he moved from Vionville and made his way to the south-west of Vernéville. 6th Infantry Division led his advance followed by the 5th and Corps artillery[219] with 6th Cavalry Division acting as escort. After first checking how the battle in front was faring, Frederick Charles ordered Alvesleben to despatch Putkammer's[220] four field batteries[221] to support Manstein at Vernéville. When the order reached the commander of the reserve, Bülow, in St Marcel, at 2:45 p.m. he immediately sent them forward together along with two additional horse batteries.

Forty-five minutes later, the field guns under Colonel Strumpf took position to the south-east of Vernéville along the ridge running towards the Bois des Génivaux, whilst the horse artillery were held in reserve at Vernéville alongside Alvesleben's infantry and 6th Cavalry. Strumpf's guns engaged the French artillery along the ridge to his north, before targeting the infantry posted further to the rear. To support Putkammer's barrage against Champenois, the two heavy batteries from III Corps moved to close the distance between themselves and the enemy, the 4th even accompanying the infantry in their attack, although finding no suitable position in which to unlimber, Captain Fromme returned to the main gun line.

Alvesleben meanwhile ordered forward the horse artillery, no easy task given the difficult terrain. Their commander, Major Lentz was seriously wounded and on taking position on the north of the gun line, their left flank was enfiladed by the French infantry and a battery of mitrailleuse battery at Amanvillers and so directed his guns fire in this direction. By this time,

216  From 49th Brigade; 1st Regiment, II/2nd Regiment and 4th Regiment less the 3rd Company.
217  3rd Heavy, Roerdansz; 3rd Light, von Bastineller; 4th Light, Mente; 1st Horse Artillery, König, 4th Heavy, Werner I.
218  2nd Hessian Rifles, part of the 36th, the fusilier battalion of the 84th and 3rd Company, 4th Hessian Regiment.
219  The corps artillery were supposed to follow on the heels of 6th Infantry but when the order to move off was given, their batteries were in the middle of harnessing 171 horses they had received to replace some of those lost on the 16th and their departure was delayed.
220  Commander of III Corps artillery, Major General Baron von Puttkammer.
221  3rd and 4th Light, 3rd and 4th Heavy.

around 4:00 p.m., there were 58 guns[222] in action to the south of the Bois de la Cusse. Soon afterwards, they were joined by the guns from IX Corps that had been withdrawn to repair and refit[223] so that a quarter of an hour later, that number had increased to 69.

## IX Corps' Artillery Renew the Struggle

At the outset of the engagement, Manstein found himself outgunned and outnumbered, but Ladmirault's reluctance to exploit his initial superiority allowed IX Corps artillery time to re-equip. By late afternoon, through their dogged determination and sacrifice, together with the additional firepower provided by III Corps, they succeeded in first subduing and then silencing the opposing guns. In face of this resurgent counter battery fire, Crassous's 6/4th were forced from hill 343 and attempted to find cover behind earthworks, alongside the mitrailleuses of the 8/4th. After coming under renewed fire from Alvesleben's guns, the 6th were pulled back to la Folie around 4:00 p.m. with the 10/1st quitting the line at the same time to replenish their ammunition.[224] They were replaced by Mason's 9/8th which within 30 minutes, had fired off all its shells against the enemy guns[225] deployed along the north-eastern edge of the bois de Génivaux 2,500 metres away, before they too, fell back to the railway station at Amanvillers. Barbe's mitrailleuses continued the uneven struggle for another hour despite being targeted by a number of enemy batteries and only withdrew to a new position alongside the 6th after fouling their fragile breech blocks.[226]

A little to the north, two batteries de 4[227] from 3 Corps' Reserve had already been driven from their exposed position and half an hour after Alvesleben's guns resumed their bombardment, were again forced to withdraw to the cover of the woods to reorganise. Margot then redeployed his battery near Montigny and engaged the guns around Champenois, although a number of French batteries in the same area were subsequently forced to pull out of the line due to the accuracy of the enemy fire. Wrangel concentrated his efforts on Cahous' horse artillery causing heavy losses[228] which forced it out of the line around 4:30 p.m.

Albenque's battery[229] suffered fewer casualties as the poplar trees lining the road to la Folie screened him and the adjoining battery, the 10/1st, from the enemy guns 1,000 metres to their front. However, the introduction of fresh artillery from III Corps into the Prussian gunline, finally drove Le Boeuf's remaining batteries off hill 343, leaving just Albenque's batterie à cheval to counter their fire. With mounting losses[230] and down to their last 50 rounds, they

---

222  Six batteries from III Corps, three batteries from the 18th Division and four guns from the Hessian horse artillery battery.

223  2nd Horse Battery and five guns from 4th Light.

224  Typical of the poor control exercised by the French artillery commanders this battery had deployed behind a row of poplars which obscured its view. Rather than relocate to a better position, it simply fired off all its ammunition in the general direction of the enemy without any noticeable effect and then withdrew to the rear.

225  3rd and 4th Light, 3rd and 4th Heavy.

226  The battery lost 11 men, 13 horses lost and fired off 650 rounds.

227  7/4th, Lécrivain and 10/4th, Margot from 3 Corps.

228  5/17th: 48 men and 78 horses lost; 719 shells expended.

229  6e batterie à cheval du 17e.

230  11 men and five horses lost; 1,036 shells expended.

finally withdrew to the château grounds at Montigny, their place being taken by Margot's guns after they had again replenished their ammunition.

As described by the French official history, the position on 4 Corps right wing at this time was 'disastrous'[231] although as Patry recalled, amidst the death and destruction, there were still moments of black humour:

> At this time the battle was at its height. Along the whole line as far as the eye could see there was nothing but smoke and detonations. My battalion changed positions, pressing right for a few hundred paces. As this move was undertaken, we came across an infantry ammunition caisson near the unfinished railway line. Several men per company went over to it and carried back in the tails of their coat's large numbers of cartridges packets which were shared out among all those present. Just as the first three companies reached the height – the only ones to push that far, the other three having been left on the railway line – they were greeted by intense artillery fire. The men were made to lie flat on their stomachs and, with their elbows resting on the ground, they engaged in a fierce firefight with the troops coming at us from the Habonville road. The captain, Rousset and I were stretched out in a furrow behind the centre of the company, swapping remarks, which were entirely lacking in jollity, when a frightful noise was heard to our rear and very close to us, at the same time the ground being was violently shaken. The caisson had exploded. A mass of debris of every sort was thrown in the air and fell back down around us, like some weird hail. The captain was stretched out at full length on his stomach, his nose against a clod of earth. Rousset and I saw him indulge in a violent pantomime which seemed demonstrate his profound disgust and with his right eye, always festooned with his eternal and unbreakable monocle, he examined with extreme repugnance an object which had fallen from the sky right beside his face. We took a look at what it was; Rousset turned something over and over with the end of his baton that had the appearance of a sausage. It was the thumb of an artilleryman that the exploding caisson had detached from its owner and which had rolled onto the august nose of our captain. He was so indignant that, had he dared, he would have stood up and had this impudent gunner, or at least the largest lump of the unfortunate fellow that could have been found, banged up in a cell for eight days. Despite the gravity of the situation, we rolled about laughing. Suddenly, our artillery disappeared and we saw it no more, at least on this part of the battlefield.[232]

After the Hessian artillery had seen off Cissey's guns, they switched their attention to six batteries positioned between hills 331 to 327. One of these, Guérin's mitrailleuses,[233] had been employed to good effect all day and attempted to engage Alvenleben's reserve batteries as they deployed, although the range, some 2,500 metres, reduced their effectiveness.

Around 4:00 p.m., Laffaille ordered Guérin to conserve ammunition and he withdrew to the south of Amanvillers. The 9/1st unlimbered on the road from Amanvillers to Habonville between the divisions of Cissey and Grenier, where exposed to the fire of the Hessian batteries

231  L'État-Major *St Privat*, p.244.
232  Patry, *La Guerre*, pp.102–104.
233  8th/1st. They fired off 344 'boites à balles'

around the Bois de la Cusse, they were soon driven out of the line[234] and around 4:30 p.m., fell back alongside Guérin's mitrailleuses; the 6/8th, from 4 Corps' Reserve, were also pulled out of the line at the same time having fired off all their ammunition.

It was the same story for Grenier's divisional batteries[235] who simply could not compete with the weight and accuracy of fire from the Hessian guns sited to the north of the railway and having fired off most of their ammunition,[236] they also withdrew to the rear of Amanvillers. Around 4:30 p.m., only four[237] of the 12 batteries originally deployed by the French on the heights of Montigny, remained in action. Half an hour later, 3 Corps had just one battery in action and 4 Corps two.[238]

By 5:00 p.m. most of Ladmirault's artillery had pulled out and he was forced to feed his infantry reserves into the firing line as cover for the guns and replace those troops who had run low on ammunition. Grenier deployed a dozen battalions in lines two or three deep to the west of Amanvillers, along a front of only 1,200 metres, with just the 2/54th and 3/65th in reserve and after the divisional guns withdrew to the rear of the 64th and 65th, only Ladrange's 12-pdrs remained in position. When first introduced into the firing line they had, initially, targeted IX Corps' artillery but after they were withdrawn, the 11/1st shifted its fire against his infantry in the Bois de la Cusse. Later, both batteries engaged III Corps guns but with the terrain obscuring their view, ceased firing after 15 minutes.

The guns had been in action since noon but with their losses increasing, General de Brigade Laffaille[239] instructed Ladrange simply to maintain position and hold fire so as to conserve his limited supply of ammunition.[240] When the last of Le Boeuf's guns in this sector pulled out of the line around 5:00 p.m., Montaudon's infantry held a line running for some 2,000 metres between the Mance valley and the plateau south of Montigny. There were seven battalions up front[241] with support being provided by a battalion of the 81st south of Charmoise; two companies[242] from the 62nd were deployed inside the wood; five[243] more to the north-east. Three battalions[244] occupied the shelter trenches running along the crest between Charmoise and Montigny with a single battery, the 10/4th, on the extreme right of the line. The few reserves available were deployed on the rear slope which afforded some cover from the Prussian guns; three companies of the 2/54th were in la Folie farm; five from the 2/62nd were in the wood to the rear of Leipzig farm with the remainder[245] occupying the rifle pits between these two points.

234 With 30 minutes, it lost 24 men and 18 horses; a caisson exploded and most of the limbers were damaged.
235 5th, 6th and 7/1st.
236 5th, 1,020 boites à balles', 6th, 647 rounds, 7th, 727 rounds.
237 8/4th, 10/4th, 11/1st and 12/1st.
238 3 Corps, the 10/4th. 4 Corps, Ladrange's 12-pdrs from the reserve; 11th and 12/1st.
239 4 Corps' Artillery Commander.
240 Losses for the day 11th: 22 men, 10 horses, 440 shells expended; 12th: 18 men, eight horses, 548 shells fired.
241 1st, 2nd and 3/95th; 1st, 2nd and 3/81st, 3rd, 4th, 5th and 6th companies' 3/62nd and half the 1/62nd.
242 3rd and 4th, 3/62nd.
243 5th and 6th, 3/62nd and 3rd 1/62nd.
244 Half the 3/51st, 1/51st, 3/51st and 1st and 2nd companies 3/62nd.
245 18th Chasseurs and 3rd Company 1/62nd.

By way of contrast, following the arrival of the 5th Light from the Guards artillery, Manstein now had 13 batteries with 75 guns positioned along the spur running from the Bois de la Cusse to the north-east of Vernéville; to the north of the wood, the Hessian field artillery and a battery from the corps' Reserve held the line. Although several batteries had run out of ammunition and others lacked their full complement of guns,[246] they were forbidden to pull out of the line to refit even though the French fire counter battery fire had subsided, due to the negative impact this would have on the morale of their infantry.

As far as his infantry were concerned, both 18th and 25th divisions were still embroiled in combat around the Bois de la Cusse; the 3rd Hessian Regiment held the eastern edge of the wood; three companies of the 2nd Hessian Rifles and a company of the 4th Regiment were deployed along the railway embankment and the northern copse. Within the depths of the wood stood two battalions of the 4th, two companies of the 36th and the remnants of the fusilier battalion of the 85th. Along the ridge south-west of Amanvillers, 1st Hessian Rifles covered the flank of the main gun line.

To the north of the railway embankment, six companies from the 49th Brigade and part of the 2nd Hessian rifles were screening the divisional artillery, with six companies from the brigade and three from 4th Regiment held as a general reserve to the rear of the railway embankment. A battalion of the 2nd Hessian's occupied Champenois, two companies from the 36th l'Envoie farm, whilst around Chantrenne, there were four battalions from the 36th and 85th, alongside three Prussian rifle companies. Vernéville was held by another rifle company and the II/84th with two battalions of the 11th in support.

Due to the unsuitable ground, the cavalry were held in reserve; 6th Dragoons on the right wing to the rear of the bois de Génivaux; the Hessian cavalry brigade on the left wing to the rear of the Bois de la Cusse. III Corps infantry were still to the south-west of Vernéville, with 6th Cavalry Division on their left. Although the dogged determination displayed by Manstein's men was undeniable, they had suffered heavy losses and there was no disguising the fact that his attack had stalled; with no immediate support to hand, the fighting in this sector of the field died away, the opposing sides having effectively fought one another to a bloody standstill.

## The Red Prince Takes Command

When firing erupted around Amanvillers a little before noon, Frederick Charles rode forward to Vernéville to investigate, but finding his view obscured by woods, continued to the west of Habonville from where he could get a better understanding of the fighting. It was here he received Moltke's despatch[247] who, at that time, was still under the impression that the French right wing was anchored on Amanvillers. However, the prince was already in receipt of intelligence from the Guard Corps which indicated that Bazaine's army actually extended as far as Saint Privat, one such message read:

---

246  For example, at the end of the day the Hessian Horse artillery was reduced to just two serviceable guns.
247  'The IX Corps is now engaged in an artillery battle in front of the Bois Doseuillons. The actual general attack along the entire line will not be made until considerable forces are ready to advance upon Amanvillers.' See Lanza, *Franco-German War*, p.263.

Doncourt 11:30 a.m. according to a report from the cavalry sent ahead, from the hill at Batilly, 10:50 a.m., people just coming from Sainte Marie bring information that French troops are at Saint Privat la Montagne. Consequently, the Guard Corps will, according to orders received, start immediately for Doncourt, but the corps commander believes, under these conditions, it is best to march not to Vernéville but Habonville.[248]

Similarly, XII Corps reported: 'Jarny 11:45 a.m. The enemy is said to be at Moineville and Sainte Marie aux Chênes. Therefore, XII Corps will proceed towards both points. Flank guard towards Valleroy.' From Doncourt, the Guard cavalry sent another update: 'One Saxon patrol encountered French cavalry – 10 troopers – at St Ail. Just now some shots were fired on the road from Amanvillers to Vernéville. It appears that cavalry is being sent forward from Saint Privat, about two squadrons and about 1½ companies of infantry in smaller detachments against Habonville and St Ail'[249] Another Guard Hussar officer described 'how everything between Saint Privat, Roncourt and Sainte Marie was full of the enemy.'[250] The prince's own observations from Habonville heights served to confirm the reports that the French positions extended to Saint Privat and in light of these developments, at 2:00 p.m. ordered the Guard Corps artillery forward to take position alongside IX Corps guns. Meanwhile, in the second line, Voights Rhetz's X Corps had arrived at Jouaville and was directed to Saint Privat with their corps artillery to the front. Frederick realised that Manstein's attack was too well advanced to be halted, but considering the fresh intelligence, issued new orders to X, XII and Guard's corps, calculated to bring about a coordinated attack against the right wing of the Bazaine's line. As a result, the Guards, who under Moltke's original scheme had been given the task of outflanking the French position, were now simply to extend the Prussian line with X Corps moving up from the second line to act as a hinge around which the Saxon XII Corps would then pivot and complete the envelopment of the enemy line.

In compliance with these revised instructions, 1st Guard Division were directed on Sainte Marie whilst 2nd Guard Division, after first making their way towards la Folie in accordance with the original plan of action, swung to the north, heading for Jouaville. The Royal Saxon's, with the head of their column just north of Batilly, marched towards the line Sainte Marie-Moineville. III Corps were at Vernéville whilst to the rear, II Corps had begun to advance on Rezonville with X Corps halted at Batilly. Meanwhile, IX Corps role was to maintain the pressure against the centre of the French line around Amanvillers.

## The Guards and Saxons Extend Their March to the North

Riding at the head of the Guards, Prince August of Württemburg reached the high ground at Habonville around 1:00 p.m. which afforded an uninterrupted view of the enemy positions to the north of Amanvillers. On receipt of Frederick's order – 'To conduct the fight only by artillery and to engage the infantry only when XII Corps could offer effective support.'[251] – he

248  Bell, *St Privat*, p.65.
249  *Ibid.*, pp.65–66.
250  Lanza, *Franco-German War*, p.242.
251  *Ibid.*

called forward his Reserve artillery, instructing them to engage the enemy positions around Saint Privat.

Meanwhile, General von Pape and his staff were on a hill[252] south of Habonville reconnoitring the ground where he intended to deploy his men. Informed by Guard Hussar scouts as to the presence of French troops at Sainte Marie,[253] from his vantage point he could discern 25th Division in the Bois de la Cusse, with other elements of Manstein's corps further to the southeast and the Hessian cavalry brigade at Arnoux la Grange. More alarmingly, he could also make out at least 20 French battalions and numerous batteries around Saint Privat. It was clear that their line extended much further to the north than Moltke anticipated and if the Guards were to fulfil their designated task of outflanking the enemy line, he would need to redirect his division towards the north rather than enter the line alongside IX Corps at Amanvillers.

In the knowledge that 2nd Guards Division and the Saxon's were in support, he ordered his men to change direction with the intention of outflanking the French position at Saint Privat. His projected route would bypass Habonville, St Ail and Sainte Marie and take him the north by way of Auboué, Montois and Melancourt.[254] To cover his exposed right flank and offer some support to the hard-pressed Hessian division, he deployed Lieutenant Colonel Bychelberg's divisional artillery, with the 1st Battalion Guard Fusiliers sent to Habonville to act as escort. The guns initially unlimbered in a line running from the ridge south-west of Habonville to just south of the railway cutting but finding the position unfavourable, repositioned to the north of the track, south-west of St Ail; their move being carried out under fire from the French batteries around Saint Privat. Their task was made harder by the challenging ground as related in the Great General Staff's account:

> The terrain offered great difficulties to the movement of the Guard batteries. The deep railroad cuts were enclosed with wire fences which had to be cut by the cannoneers with their sabres; the slopes were so steep that the other side of the cuts had to be taken at the gallop. The ravine northwest of Habonville, which also had to be crossed was steep and deep, the bottom marshy; the horses could get through only with the greatest of efforts. As the movements, especially that of the divisional artillery, offered the flank to the enemy, the hostile fire of which caused large losses. Three pieces and one caisson were left lying behind and were bought up only later on.[255]

---

252  Commander, 1st Guard Division. Hill 306, 700 metres south of Habonville offered a view to Sainte Marie and Saint Privat.

253  One report read 'After thorough examination through field glasses at least one French division bivouacs between Sainte Marie and Saint Privat', another, 'Troops from camp at Roncourt and Saint Privat march on Sainte Marie, also on Vernéville. I see two battalions in both directions, about 4 squadrons.' See Lanza, *Franco-German War*, p.240.

254  Although Moltke, Frederick Charles and Württemburg all shared the same appreciation and issued new instructions to reflect the changed situation, Pape's decision to alter the axis of his attack without reference to higher command provides another demonstration of the freedom of action given to Prussian generals and the initiative expected from subordinate commanders. It is hard to imagine any French officer of similar rank taking the same decision, that is to effectively rewrite the commander in chief's plans, in similar circumstances.

255  Lanza, *Franco-German War*, p.242.

Soon after, Colonel von Scherbening deployed the Guard Reserve artillery on their left; the gun line now consisting of nine batteries[256] although even this massed firepower failed to deter skirmishers from the 5th Company, 2/26th who, taking advantage of the undulating terrain, approached to within 80 metres of their position.

## The Hessians Attack

Shortly after 3:30 p.m., Prince Louis observed the Guard approaching Sainte Marie and assuming this movement heralded the start of their long-anticipated flanking attack against the French right wing, ordered his remaining reserves forward in support. General L. von Wittich, commander of the 49th Brigade recalled:

> These three battalions I moved close to the woods of la Cusse as far as the railroad cut, forming them in company columns one behind the other. On the left of the head of the column was the Hessian Battery Reh, which, with the few pieces still serviceable, was doing excellent work both on the thick firing line in the meadow south of Saint Privat and also on a sunken road in the direction of Amanvillers, from which hostile columns were trying to debouch, but each time prevented from doing so by some well-directed shells fired by the Battery Reh. The deep railroad cut, fenced in on each side by scarcely visible wires, ends about fifty paces from the right of the corner of the wood and the road and then continues towards Amanvillers on a fill about 15 feet high. The fill and cut were enfiladed by enemy fire. The edge of the wood was occupied by the 2nd Rifle battalion and the 3rd Infantry Regiment. Many men had flattened themselves against the sides of the fill and were mistakenly seeking shelter from the projectiles. Towards 4:00 p.m. when the Guard made its attack at our left, I gave orders to cross the railroad and take position beyond in rear of a little wood, front towards Amanvillers. The leading company of the 2nd Infantry Regiment was surprised by a heavy fire from the mitrailleuses in position near Amanvillers. The losses were insignificant, but it was necessary to offset the morale effect produced. Colonel Kraus, the regimental commander, himself quickly restored order in the company which had crossed the railroad. I had the detachments following stopped temporarily and then had them cross this dangerous point by platoons at a run. Thus was the crossing well executed, in spite of the depth of the cut and the steepness of the banks, by the 2/2nd Infantry and two companies of the 1st Infantry Regiment. I then received orders from the division commander orders to halt. Six companies were on the other side of the cut, six on the near side.[257]

On the far side of the railway, Major Hoffman wheeled the companies to the right, directing them towards a shallow depression where, unable to continue their advance against the heavy

---

256  From left to right: 4th Light, 2nd Horse, 3rd Light, 3rd Heavy, 4th Heavy, 3rd Heavy from the Corps' Reserve; 1st Heavy, 2nd Heavy, 1st Light, 2nd Light, from 1st Guard Division.
257  Bell, *St Privat*, pp.86–87.

French fire, they took up a defensive firing line.[258] Patry's 6th Ligne were amongst the regiments deployed to counter the Hessian attack, the lieutenant recalling:

> The Germans, no doubt encouraged by the silence of our cannon, launched a major attack against our positions. Large masses left the woods, advancing resolutely. They didn't head directly for our heights but moved off to our left, in the direction of Amanvillers; we therefore took them in their flank. Three companies opened up, firing at will, which within a short time sowed murder and destruction within their ranks. They received a similar courteous welcome from their front and it wasn't long before they melted away, seeking the shelter of the woods.[259]

## The Guards and Saxons March on St Ail

Following Pape's change of plan, the Guard Hussars were recalled from their screening duties and the squadrons assembled under cover of the copse to the north-east of Batilly, as officer patrols were despatched in the direction of Sainte Marie to reconnoitre his intended route around the French right flank. With Scherbening's artillery covering his flank, Colonel von Erckert, the commander of Pape's advance guard,[260] led his men towards Sainte Marie. I/Guard Fusiliers were directed toward Habonville as II and III battalions, together with the Guard Rifles, branched off into a ravine running parallel to St Ail which provided excellent cover from the French fire. As the remainder of the division moved up from its assembly area by the small copse to the north of Anoux la Grange, Pape rode ahead to St Ail to undertake a personal reconnaissance of his intended route. Noting the enemy activity in Sainte Marie, he quickly realised that he would not be able to bypass the village as originally intended; it would have to be taken by force of arms.

Pape met with General von Dannenberg, the Guard Corps' chief of staff at St Ail who whilst sharing his appreciation of the situation and the need to seize Sainte Marie, ordered him to delay his attack until the Saxons arrived. Pape put his own spin on this, relating in his papers:

> Towards 2:45 p.m. I saw the Saxon divisional commander von Nehrhoff coming up. It at once occurred to me that it would be well from a military and from a political standpoint to engage in a serious and presumably favourable battle in conjunction with our allies, although I was certain that I could carry the fight to an end with the advance guard supported by a few battalions. I rode to General von Nehrhoff, who was well known to me, greeted him and disclosed my intention to which he at once acceded. We agreed that he was to attack northwest, I the southwest front of Sainte Marie.[261]

258  From left to right 5/2nd, 1st and 4/1st, 8/2nd, 6th and 7/2nd.
259  Patry, *La Guerre*, p.104.
260  Pape's advance guard comprised the Guard Fusiliers Regiment and the Guard Rifles Battalion.
261  Bell, *St Privat*, p.251.

## XII Corps Advance to Sainte Marie

The Saxons intended line of march took them from Jarny, via Sainte Marie to Moineville and approaching Batilly, Crown Prince Albert galloped ahead to survey the intended route. After crossing the railway line east of Giraumont, hard on the heels of 24th Division's advance guard, he was approached by Major von Meyerinck of the Guard Hussars, who briefed him on the positions occupied by Württemberg's corps and cautioned that his men would be exposed to French fire as soon as they were east of Batilly. Albert turned to address his staff: 'See, now, the artillery is just starting in; we have come just in time'[295] before ascending hill 265 to the north of Jouaville to survey the French batteries positioned around Saint Privat.

Shortly after midday, Captain Planitz reported that his reconnaissance had found Sainte Marie to be unoccupied but the plateau running from Saint Privat to Roncourt was strongly held by 6 Corps and immune to a frontal attack. After hearing this news, 'The Crown Prince, following the report with his eyes on the map, said: "In that case we shall not attack in front, but go around" and made a corresponding movement with his left arm.'[296]

The news that there was no sign of the enemy along the banks of the Orne and Briey rivers or at Auboué, only served to underpin his decision that the best way to implement the spirit of Moltke's orders was to swing his corps to the north and outflank the enemy line by way of Roncourt. At 2:00 p.m., Albert issued his orders, with copies being sent to the Guards and Army headquarters:

> 1) The 1st Division with which the 46th Brigade, is once more placed, will take the road past Coinville, through the copse to the east of Auboué, in the direction of the Roncourt position.
> 2) To the 46th Brigade at Giraumont. You will immediately march to the west corner of the Bois de Ponty.
> 3) The corps artillery will follow the 1st Division from Giraumont.
> 4) The 2nd Division will pass by the west of Batilly then proceed through the hollow in the rear of the copse and from that point endeavour to press forward directly on Sainte Marie aux Chênes. The 48th Brigade will remain at the disposal of the corps commander in the rear of Batilly copse.[297]

On receipt of these instructions, his brother Prince George of Saxony,[298] assembled his men at Coinville to brief them on the change in plan but illustrative of the initiative ingrained in the German officer corps, von Craushaar, commander of his advance guard, had already put his men on the road towards Sainte Marie; the II/108th from Moineville, the III Battalion from Valleroy via Serry whilst the I was to follow in their rear, accompanied by 1st Light battery from Beaumont; 1st Light Cavalry were tasked with screening the left flank of the advance and the thicket to the north of Sainte Marie.

---

295  Bell, *St Privat*, p.247.
296  *Ibid.*
297  *Ibid*, p.248.
298  Commander of the 23rd Division.

Not everything went so smoothly; due to a misunderstanding, the 46th Brigade went to Moineville instead of Coinville, some two kilometres from its intended assembly point. The 45th were also slow to respond[299] and when they finally got underway, took a circuitous route around the Bois de Ponty before descending into the shallow valley running to Auboué, north-west of Sainte Marie.

General Nehrhoff von Holdenberg[300] received orders to march on Sainte Marie around 2:15 p.m. just as 47th Brigade, at the head of the column, was to the east of Batilly. About half an hour later, the brigade veered to the left and marched north along the valley, seeking cover from the French fire and then deployed either side of the road running from Sainte Marie to the Bois de Ponty, a little to the north of 1st Guard Division. Holdenberg then moved his divisional artillery into position; the two heavy batteries[301] on the eastern slope of the valley, the 4th Light further to the right, close to the left flank of Pape's advance guard. 48th Brigade and 2nd Cavalry Regiment were held in reserve near Batilly alongside the Guards Hussar Regiment and 2nd Cavalry Regiment; the Guard and 3rd Cavalry regiment, together with the 1st Horse Battery were stationed to the west of the Bois de Ponty.

## The Assault on Sainte Marie

With the Guard Corps moving up from the south, the Saxons from the west, the preparatory barrage got underway. From the Guard artillery arrayed to the south of St Ail, von Mutius[302] and two divisions[303] of von Grävenitz's 2nd Horse Artillery repositioned to the west of the hamlet, opening fire at ranges of between 1,200–1,700 paces. They directed their attention against the men deployed in front of Saint Privat, looking to prevent them from reinforcing the troops in Sainte Marie, but could do little to deter Canrobert's batteries to the northwest of Saint Privat from targeting the Saxon infantry.

In turn, the Guard artillery found themselves threatened by French skirmishers who made full use of the undulating terrain to close with their guns, with I/4th Guard Grenadiers being deployed as close protection.[304] Holdenberg ordered Major Richter's 2nd Saxon Field Division into position to the south-west of the village. However, space could only be found for three batteries[305] as most of the open ground was occupied by the troops forming up for the assault and they commenced fire with shell against Sainte Marie at ranges of between 800–1,000 paces.

To the north-west of the village, the 1st and 2nd Light[306] opened up at roughly the same time with shell and shrapnel at slightly longer ranges of between 1,600 and 2,000 paces. Colonel Funcke's corps artillery took position to the west of the defile on the Sainte Marie-Hatrize

---

299  The 100th Grenadier's were distributed throughout the Bois de Ponty, the 101st Grenadier's and 1st Light and 2nd Heavy were in reserve to the south of the wood
300  Commander of 24th Division.
301  The 3rd Light remained in the valley as it was unable to find a suitable position in which to deploy.
302  4th Light.
303  4 guns.
304  Commanded by Major von Rosenberg the battalion formed company columns in the intervals between the guns, lying down to seek cover from the French fire.
305  Von der Pforte's 4th Light, Keysselitz's 3rd Heavy and Groh's 4th Heavy.
306  Commanded by Captains Lengnik and Westmann.

road; Hoch's 3rd Field Division[307] on the right, Oertel's 4th Field Division[308] together with Müller's 2nd Horse Artillery on the left. Leonardi's 2nd Heavy Battery unlimbered in the space between and in front of, both divisions. At ranges of between 2,000 to 2,400 paces, these guns targeted the skirmishers of the 25th and 93rd deployed between Sainte Marie, Roncourt and Saint Privat, seeking to suppress their harassing fire as, on the left of the line, 10 guns from the Guards[309] shelled the troops in Sainte Marie.

Observing the attack from a ridge north of Batilly Schubert described their objective:

> In our front, about 2,000 metres off, on the other side of the basin, was situated the village of Sainte Marie aux Chênes, large, solidly built, enclosed with walls and hedges; on the other side of it, about 15 minutes march from there, rose a gradually ascending, open, glacis-like slope, crowned on its top by the imposing fortress like village of Saint Privat. To its right and left the edge of the plateau continues evenly and entirely open and there we perceived the French in strong position with numerous artillery. On our left wing ran a rolling, partly wooded terrain down to the Orne valley from which we saw our Rifle Regiment marching against Sainte Marie aux Chênes.[310]

A church stood in the centre of the village, as did the large château like Marie, with open, corn stubble fields on either side of the roads leading to Auboué and St Ail which served as the axes for the combined Prussian and Saxon attack. Around 3:00 p.m., Pape and Nehrhoff, judging the bombardment had sufficiently softened up the defences, gave the order to advance; the Saxons from the west, the Guard from the south.

Accompanied by Holdenberg, Colonel von Leonhardi's 47th Brigade was the first to move off. Having assembled in a shallow valley about 1,000 metres west of Sainte Marie, Major Count Holtzendorff deployed the 12th Rifles in line of company columns with their skirmishing divisions out front and moving out of cover, charged towards the village without firing a shot. Colonels von Eterlein and von Tettau followed with the 104th and 105th in close support,[311] the regiments deployed side by side in three lines. In front, I battalions were formed in line of company columns; behind them the centre companies from II Battalions were combined with the wing companies detached and, to their rear, III Battalions in column of double companies.

The fire from the massed Guard and Saxon batteries quickly blew breaches in the enclosures and stone walls and a number of buildings were set ablaze, the guns only falling silent as the infantry assault masked their targets. Responding to the defender's ineffective fire with a cheer, the Saxons advanced at the double, forcing their way into the gardens on the south-western edge of the village. On the right wing, I Battalion, under Major Almer II, charged directly towards the village church, surrounding it before pushing one company down the road leading to Montois. II Battalion, under Major Bartcky, attacked the northwest corner of the village and suffered a number of casualties, including the colour bearer, Sergeant Böhm. Lieutenant von

---

307  Hammer's 5th Light, Verworrner's 5th Heavy and von Zeschau's 6th Heavy.
308  Fellmer's 6th Light, Bucher's 7th Heavy and Portius' 8th Heavy.
309  4th Light and 2nd Horse Artillery
310  Bell, *St Privat*, p.410
311  104th on the right, 105th on the left.

Egidy seized the fallen standard and placing himself at the head of the 7th Company, led them into the centre of the village. As noted by von Schimpff:

> Difficult situations were encountered within the village; The Saxons and Prussians who had charged shoulder to shoulder were crowded close together in the narrow village streets. The stone houses stood close together and on the side toward the enemy neither doors nor windows so that the men could find cover only by crowding through narrow gaps between houses to behind the low stone walls ... In front of the village the bullets whistled sharply; high in the air burst shells, the pieces of which travelled with a horrible noise through the air, striking the roofs and houses.[312]

On the right wing, the 1/105th, under Major von Kessinger, were directed along the south side of the Bois de Ponty-Sainte Marie road before pushing through to the eastern outskirts of the village, facing Saint Privat. The II/105th, with Major von Tettenborn leading the way, attacked the enclosures to the north-west, with Captain Scheffel at the head of 12 men, being killed as he forced his way into the western entrance. Most of the defenders lining the walls melted away as the lead elements of the Saxons pressed forward through the streets, their progress only being halted by the fierce fire from the French supports as they emerged onto the open ground to the east of the village. A few attempted to hold their ground, although the majority fell back, seeking cover behind the garden walls.

After dislodging the last of the obstinate defenders, the leading battalions, along with the 12th Rifles, pushed through the village, emerging at the north-west edge, where a small depression afforded some shelter from the French fire. The I/104th held itself in readiness in the centre as three companies from the I/105th took up position on the edge of Sainte Marie between 12th Rifles and the Guard, whilst 4th Company were to the north, facing Roncourt. Von Schubert witnessed the capture of the village and the steps taken to protect it against counter attack:

> Sainte Marie was very poorly adapted for defence; the houses, built closely together along the narrow village street, had neither windows nor doors on the side facing the enemy and the companies crowded together in the village could utilise but a very few gaps between the houses to get to some stone walls facing the enemy and to secure from there and from ditches on the left of the village the possibility of some sort of fire effect. The conduct of the men, standing in the streets and continually harassed by a hot artillery fire, was most excellent. Several times it appeared as if the enemy intended to charge; but the appearance and the fire of the Saxon corps artillery prevented this intention.[313]

The formations in the second wave formed an extended line which overlapped the village and as II/104th closed in on their objective, the 6th Company pushed its way into and through Sainte Marie, advancing as far as the road leading to Auboué. Meanwhile, 5th Company found itself to the south of the village, the 7th and 8th to the north. II/105th entered Sainte Marie to the

---

312  Bell, *St Privat*, p.184.
313  *Ibid*, p.442.

north of the track running to Hatrize and moving through the village to the ravine, took up position alongside the men from the first line so as to be ready support the struggle which had broken out between Roncourt and Sainte Marie.

Two companies[314] pushed out of the village towards Saint Privat but the heavy chassepot fire halted their advance in its tracks, the colour bearer 1st Lieutenant von Egidy being one of many casualties. Meanwhile, Captains Panse and von Bunau at the head of the 4th and 5th companies, 105th, were struggling to hold their ground in the small meadow northeast of Sainte Marie which provided scant cover against the intense enemy fire. Seeking to steady their nerves, their commander, Colonel von Tettau, stood out in front of his men; one of his shoulder straps was torn away by shrapnel, another fragment killed his horse but unperturbed, he remounted, his cool demeanour under fire serving as an example to his men.

Leonhardi, keen to maintain the momentum of the attack and looking to take Saint Privat on the bounce, directed two battalions from the third line of the assault force to swing around to the north of Sainte Marie to reinforce the troops that had already made their way through the village. III/104th took position on the right of the firing line, where they immediately came under heavy fire and rapidly deploying into skirmish formation, took shelter in the Hautmécourt cutting.

Meanwhile, III/105th swung out to the north where their advance, if left unchecked, threatened the right flank of the French line at Roncourt.

Although the Saxons encountered little opposition during their advance into Sainte Marie, the Guards were confronted by a more determined defence. As XII Corps jumped off in the east, to the south, Pape set his advance guard in motion; III Guard Fusiliers were sent out to the right near St Ail, the II pushing along a shallow valley which ran from the village, with two companies lining the edge of the defile to provide protection for their exposed flank. To their left, Guard Rifle battalion deployed three companies along the edge of a copse facing the objective where they traded volleys with the defenders holding the village.

Annoyed by this fire, Major von Schmelling led his skirmishers forward and gained a position to the rear of a hedge line a few hundred paces to their front. As the 6th and 7th companies were drawn into this fight, the remainder of the battalion were called into action. Three companies from III/Guard Fusiliers were ordered up from St Ail; on the right, the 10th advanced along both sides of the lane leading to the objective, the 12th acted as a link with the II Battalion whilst the 9th was held in reserve. Following this reinforcement, I Battalion were then ordered to join the attack. Pape brought forward the remainder of 1st Division from Habonville and as the fighting intensified, the Fusiliers of the 4th Guards deployed on the open flank of the rifle battalion;[315] the remaining 11 battalions being held in readiness to the rear of a wood to the south-west of Sainte Marie.

Closing to between 450–700 metres, the Guard opened a fierce but largely ineffective fire against the 94th sheltering behind the village's stout stone walls. To the south of the road running between Sainte Marie and Saint Privat, several companies of the 2/93rd Ligne[316] supported by their artillery on height 295, poured fire onto the flank of the Rifles as they

---

314 6th and 7th.

315 North to South III/4th Foot Guards, Guard Rifles Battalion, II and III/Guard Fusiliers.

316 Colonel Ganzin ordered the five companies deployed as skirmishers to wheel to the right so they could take the Guard Fusiliers in the flank as they advanced from St Ail against Sainte Marie.

stormed into the village. Leading from the front, Colonel von Erckert, the Guard Fusilier's commanding officer, gave encouragement to his men, instructing them to lie low and to only stand when firing, leaving just the dismounted officers and NCO's standing to supervise the evacuation of casualties to the rear.

Over the next quarter of an hour, he steadily augmented the strength of his firing line, ordering forward supports by successive rushes. Meanwhile, as the artillery bombardment continued and the Saxon's manoeuvred into position, Pape sent Colonel von Neuman[317] and two grenadier battalions to support the left wing of his advance guard. Around 3:00 p.m. as the Saxon's 47th Brigade completed their preparations, Pape gave the signal for the Guards to begin their final assault. I Battalion Guard Fusiliers moved up from Habonville taking position behind their right wing, both grenadier battalions from the 4th to the rear of their left. With these supports in place and after warning the artillery that he was about to commence his attack, Erckert closed his men up into the firing line.

Taking position in front of the left flank of III Battalion's skirmish line, he commanded: 'Rise! Double-time!'[318] The whole line scrambled to their feet and charged forward without firing a shot, the Guard Rifles being carried along in the rush, despite being ordered to remain in reserve.[319] III/4th Foot Guard Regiment and II Battalion Guard Fusiliers reached the edge of Sainte Marie with negligible losses, the outnumbered defenders having fled. The path taken by III Battalion along the St Ail road, led to a section of the village which had escaped the intense artillery bombardment and here they initially received a warm welcome, but again, the French melted away in the face of their determined attack.

Gaining cover in the gardens surrounding the village, the fusiliers paused to take breath before Pape, who accompanied the rifle battalion as they moved into Sainte Marie, urged them on again, directing them to clear the buildings of the remaining defenders. In the face of this concerted assault, Geslin pulled the 3/94th out of village; his men had been shaken by the heavy artillery bombardment and in danger of being encircled, he slowly fell back in a north-easterly direction towards Hautmécourt to avoid masking the fire of De Sonney's men.[320]

Meanwhile, having expended all their ammunition during the Guards' attack, the 2/93rd Ligne also made ready to withdraw from their position overlooking St Ail.[321] As the Saxon and Guard infantry poured into the village, Geslin ordered the supporting companies from the 94th to fall back along the Hautmécourt cutting, before taking up new positions to the rear of Becquet de Sonnay's brigade. However, in the confusion,[322] the greater part of the 3rd Battalion followed on the heels of the 2nd. When Geslin rallied his men in the cutting, there were only about 250 still under his command and they became embroiled in a fierce fire fight with the Guards pursuing them out of the village.[323] A few foolhardy men, especially to the south of

---

317 Commander 4th Guard Foot Regiment.
318 Bell, *St Privat*, p.254.
319 The Guard Rifle battalion had been ordered to hold its position, so as to serve as a rallying point in the event the attack was beaten back.
320 General Colin fell wounded just as the retreat got underway.
321 Unlike the Prussians, the French made no attempt to resupply their firing line, companies, battalions and regiments withdrew to the rear to resupply when they had fired off their available ammunition.
322 The 94th lost 11 officers and 317 men dead wounded and missing.
323 10th Company, Guard Fusiliers, 3rd Company Guard Rifle Battalion and 9th Company, 4th Foot Guard Regiment.

Sainte Marie continued firing until the last-minute but as the Saxons and Guards flooded into the crowded streets, the majority of defenders withdrew towards Saint Privat and safety.

Conferring with Erckert and his battalion commanders, Pape reorganised his men to secure the village against any counter-attack and a little later, sent a brief update to Prince August: 'Sainte Marie has been taken at 3:30 p.m. Losses few. 18.8.70' which elicited the response: 'For the present, possession of the village is to be secured; further action is to be taken only on receipt of subsequent orders.'[324] Pape took advantage of the pause in operations to draw the 1st Guard Division together; 2nd Foot Guards took ground to the right of the grenadier battalions of the 4th Foot Guards, so by 4:00 p.m. all three regiments of 2nd Brigade were in and about the village. 1st Brigade were then brought forward to a position some 600 paces south-east of Sainte Marie facing Saint Privat.

## The Saxon Advance Halted

As XII Corps closed in on Sainte Marie, General Colin sent a despatch to Lafont de Villiers requesting urgent support; initially no help was forthcoming and he only reacted after the Saxons appeared at the eastern exits of the village by ordering Becquet de Sonnay's brigade to counter attack. The 93rd was already deployed to the west of Saint Privat with skirmishers pushed forward in a wide arc towards Sainte Marie so the 91st took position on their left, the 75th to their right.

The 1/75th were placed to the front and west of Roncourt, covering the routes out of the Bois d'Auboué whilst the 2nd and 3rd battalions moved along the Montois–Sainte Marie road to a small rise, hill 827. Both battalions deployed skirmishers who opened a rapid and destructive fire on the flank of the 3/105th within the Hautmécourt cutting. The Saxon's commander, Major Günther, fell wounded and with several other officers already *hors de combat*, the 105th's advance on Roncourt ground to a halt. In concert with this counter attack by the 75th, the 2nd and 3/91st, supported by the 2/12th from Tixier's division, then made a counter attack along and north of the main Saint Privat-Sainte Marie road. This failed in its objective to recapture the village, but the aggression displayed by the French served to deter any further advance against Saint Privat.

As the Saxons fought their way into Sainte Marie, General Craushaar ordered up Prince George's advance guard[325] from Moineville to provide support and after brushing aside skirmishers from the 2/94th blocking their way, his front line battalions[326] continued their advanced along either side of the Coinville-Sainte Marie road.

The 7th Company, II Battalion had just opened fire against Sainte Marie's defenders when Craushaar received instructions from the prince to break off his attack and join the remainder of the division in their advance on Auboué. Initially only I and II battalions were able to respond, as Major Allmer's III Battalion had already entered the village along with 47th Brigade and he was unwilling to withdraw until the village had been secured. The III/108th then took position on the left of the Saxon line where they came under fire from the 2nd and 3/91st from Becquet

---

324  Bell, *St Privat*, pp.423 and 255.
325  From 23rd Division.
326  II and III/108th Rifle Regiment.

de Sonnay's brigade, the chassepots of the third battalion in particular having a 'plus meurtrier effet.' Commandant de Hay-Durand of the 1/91st dropped off his 3rd Company to cover Sainte Marie and wheeling the others half right, pushed two companies forward as tirailleurs to engage the Saxons along the Hautmécourt cutting.

Becquet de Sonnay's counter attack was given close support by a battery of Barail's horse artillery[327] which, following every move of the brigade, took up three successive positions each one closer to the enemy, the last being within 700 metres of their skirmish line. The III/105th within the cutting, were coming under serious pressure but fortuitously, Craushaar noted their precarious predicament and manoeuvred his men against Becquet de Sonnay's brigade as they sought to enfilade the 105th. Deploying at the run, his attack caught the 75th Ligne unawares and they were promptly driven back into the wooded ground between Roncourt and Auboué.

Major General von Nehrhoff initially thought his men would simply pursue the French back to Saint Privat, but soon realised the fight was going to be harder than anticipated and with little prospect of immediate success, sent orders to Elterlein[328] to break off the fight. Taking advantage of the respite to extricate his hard-pressed forces, around 5:00 p.m. he withdrew the Saxons[329] to the rear of their gun line, with 24th Division rallying to the north-west of Sainte Marie.

## The Guard and Saxons Consolidate Their Hold on Sainte Marie

Pape was equally alert to the danger posed by Becquet de Sonnay's counter attack and in particular the threat from the three battalions of the 91st who were doing serious damage to the Saxons in the Hautmécourt cutting. He could also see additional French reinforcements making their way forward and ordered up the two grenadier battalions of the 4th Guard Foot to support the fusiliers guarding the northern exit out of the village. Fearing that the battle for Sainte Marie was still in the balance, I Battalion were despatched at the double towards the Saint Privat road to secure the eastern entrance to the village and, as the roadway was under heavy fire, the battalion commander[330] ordered more openings to be made in the walls encircling the village, so as to speed the passage of his men. The 4th Company dashed forward, one platoon sprinting 200 yards beyond the walls to the shelter of a hedge from where it opened fire on the approaching infantry who by now had closed to within 500 metres. Neumann ordered II Battalion to support them and as they reached the road running to Auboué, two companies occupied the edge of the village facing Montois la Montagne where the fight was at its height. However, given the numbers of troops responding to this threat – the Saxons also sent reinforcements to this sector – by the time II Battalion forced their way through the crush, the danger had passed. Meanwhile the fusiliers deployed three companies in the open ground north of the village to confront Becquet de Sonnay's attack but returned to their previous position at the entrance to Sainte Marie when this threat subsided, enabling Pape to reorganise his forces within the village.[331]

---

327  6/19th.
328  He assumed command of 47th Brigade after von Leonhardi was wounded.
329  The III/108th remained in the Bois d'Auboué and served as a rallying point for the I and II Battalions.
330  Major von Sichart
331  There were seven Prussian Battalions (Fusiliers of the Guard, 4th Foot Guards, Guard Rifle Battalion) and eight Saxon battalions (104th and 105th Regiments, 12th Rifles and III/108th) in Sainte Marie.

Even as the Saxon infantry stormed into Sainte Marie, their artillery began displacing into new positions in anticipation of the forthcoming assault against Saint Privat. From reserve, Captain Bucher II placed his 3rd Light Battery to the left of Sainte Marie from where his guns could engage a troublesome French battery located in a copse to the north-east of the village, with the 2nd Reiter Regiment covering their exposed left flank. Bucher opened fire at a range of 2,200 paces and when Westmann's battery[332] engaged the same target, the enemy guns withdrew. Hoch's division[333] went to the left of Sainte Marie, Verworrner's battery deployed close to the road, Hammer's and von Zesgau's were further forward in advance of the road. Here they suffered heavy losses from skirmishers sent out by 2nd and 3/75th Ligne who had edged towards the Bois d'Auboué in an attempt to enfilade the Saxon line. In the face of their destructive fire, the guns promptly withdrew and took up a less exposed position beside 6th Heavy.[334] Bucher's battery moved alongside them and were joined shortly after by Groh's 4th Heavy. The remainder of Major Richter's 2nd Field Division[335] then deployed on the right of Hoch's division where the Saxon artillery – six batteries strong – combined their fire to drive off the repeated attacks of the French infantry. After completing this task, they engaged the enemy guns between Roncourt and Saint Privat, some 3,000–3,500 paces distant. As the artillery continued to trade shots, Oertel's 4th Field Division[336] moved into a sheltered position close by the main road, it being unable to deploy as the wooded ground east of Auboué was still held by the French. Subsequently, three batteries from Watzdorf's 1st Field Division[337] moved into the Orne valley, from where they could support the advance of the 23rd Division against the French right flank.

## The Saxons Flanking Attack

In anticipation of his flanking attack through the Bois d'Auboué towards Roncourt, Prince George ordered 23rd Division to assemble in the shelter of a ravine near Coinville. Unfortunately, von Moltke's 46th Brigade made a wrong turn and found itself at Moineville instead of its intended destination and from the 45th, initially only II and III/108th Rifle Regiment were present, after having been ordered to abort their attack against Sainte Marie.[338] Leonhardi's 47th Brigade, which had been caught up in the fighting, were rallied on the open ground to the north of the village, from where Prince George intended to launch his attack against Roncourt.

Prince Albert followed the progress of his corps from Hautmécourt ravine from where he could study the ground between Saint Privat and Roncourt and noting French infantry making their way towards the Bois d'Auboué, immediately gave orders for Prince George to seize the woods to prevent their occupation by the enemy. The lead battalion from 45th Brigade had just left Auboué on their way to Hautmécourt when the prince's adjutant arrived with the new instructions; the I/108th Rifle Regiment immediately wheeled to the right, their route to the

---

332  2nd Light.
333  Captain Hammer's 5th Heavy, Captain Verworrner's 6th Heavy and Captain von Zeschau's 5th Light.
334  Hoch and Hammer were wounded, two guns lost all their horses and most of their men.
335  Keysselitz's 3rd Heavy, von der Pforte's 4th Light.
336  Bucher I's 7th Heavy, Portius' 8th Heavy, Fellmer's 6th Light.
337  Legnik's 1st Light, Westmann's 2nd Light & Leonhardi's 2nd Heavy.
338  Subsequently the 108th were reinforced by 100th and 101st Grenadier Regiments.

southern part of the woods taking them across hill 247 some 800 metres east of Auboué. The brigade commander, Craushaar, despatched the II/108th in support and the remainder of the division were directed towards hill 407 where they could deploy in cover, screened by the two foremost battalions.

Meanwhile, two battalions[339] pushed their way into the Bois d'Auboué clashing with infantry from the 75th. As the fighting intensified, Craushaar committed 100th Body Guard Grenadier Regiment to the struggle; I Battalion reinforced the right wing of the 108th, deploying in the open ground to the south of the woods, III supporting the left with II being held in reserve. The Saxons pushed forward, driving the French out of the woods[340] but every time they attempted to pursue them across the open ground, they were hit with deadly chassepot fire from the troops sent to support the 75th. These included 1/9th – who deployed between Montois and Roncourt on their right – whilst 2/10th and part of the 91st extended the firing line in an arc to the southwest, effectively screening the eastern edge of the wood, the infantry receiving fire support from a battery[341] positioned south of Roncourt. The 108th Rifles suffered considerably from this fire so Craushaar sent them two companies forward in support.[342]

In view of the determined French resistance around the Bois d'Auboué, Prince George decided to call off his attack until such time as 48th Brigade had completed their outflanking manoeuvre, with Craushaar instructing 45th Brigade to close up their forces along the eastern edge of the wood with II and III/101st Grenadiers held back as reserve to the west. The artillery from 23rd Division[343] which had been drawn into the struggle, was ordered to pull out of the line and tasked with supporting 48th Brigade, who reached Auboué around 5:00 p.m. and from where, in accordance with George's orders, they began the long-awaited envelopment of Canrobert's line.[344]

The brigade's approach march was hidden from French view by the steep slopes of the Orne valley, their advance being screened by 2nd Cavalry Regiment, which until that time, had been employed in protecting the corps artillery. Subsequently, Prince Albert ordered the cavalry brigade[345] and the 1st Horse Battery covering the Saxon's left flank at the Bois de Ponty, to support the envelopment. Two other squadrons were sent into the Moselle valley around Maizières to destroy the railroad and telegraph lines.

339  I on the right, II/108th on the left.
340  The prisoners taken were from a number of French regiments including the 75th, 91st, 10th and 4th Regiments from 6 Corps and, surprisingly, the 51st from 3 Corps.
341  18/9th.
342  From the II/100th Body Regiment. In the general confusion, the Saxons mistakenly believed that the French had also occupied Montois la Montagne; the I/101st Grenadier Regiment were deployed on the open ground between the woods to screen this threat and fired several volleys into the village before realising their error.
343  2nd Heavy, 1st and 2nd Light Batteries; the 1st Heavy still being with the 46th Brigade.
344  The order read: 'Colonel von Schulz with the 48th Brigade reinforced by the 1st Cavalry Regiment and three batteries of the 1st Foot Battalion will take up the march in the valley of the Orne as far as the heights of Joeuf and Montois and will advance through the latter place to Roncourt. General von Craushaar with the 45th Brigade will drive the enemy completely out of the woods and advance from the west on Roncourt as soon as Colonel von Schulz's movement from the north becomes effective. The 46th Brigade will remain in reserve.' See Bell, St Privat, pp.190–191.
345  Guard Reiter Regiment and 3rd Reiter Regiment.

From the Prussian Guard, General Budritzki's 2nd Division reached the line Arnoux la Grange-Jouaville about 2:00 p.m. and, as directed, halted north of the wood at Jouaville so as to allow the Saxons time to develop their attack. He was then ordered to concentrate his forces at St Ail, whilst the guns of the 3rd Field Division came into action between the Sainte Marie and the cutting at St Ail, increasing the number of batteries already in action around Habonville. Meanwhile, the Guard's artillery commander, Prince Kraft zu Hohenlohe Ingelfingen, took the opportunity to straighten his gun line so as to better protect his extended position against the waves of French skirmishers attempting to outflank him. When I Battalion Guard Fusiliers moved off to Sainte Marie, I/4th Guard Grenadier Regiment were then tasked with their protection with 1st and 2nd companies taking post near St Ail to the left rear of the gun line. 3rd Company cleared away the enemy skirmishers within the valley north of Habonville whilst the 4th moved into the centre of the line, where the men were dispersed in front and between the Guard batteries.

## 6 Corps Artillery Responds

Confronted by a rapidly changing situation, Canrobert's 'batterie de position' constantly shifted their fire to meet each new threat as first IX Corps, the Guards and then the Saxons, entered the fray, although presented with such an abundance of targets and lacking any overall direction, their fire had limited impact. The 7/8th and 9/13th engaged Prince Louis's infantry between Habonville and the Bois de la Cusse before switching their attention to his artillery as they wheeled into position. The other batteries, including Kesner's horse artillery, which were positioned around hill 333,[346] directed their fire against the nine Guard batteries.

Canrobert had been unable to fully replenish his caissons following the battle on 16 August and given the gunners poor fire control, they soon exhausted their available ammunition which further limited their effectiveness.[347] Of the batteries deployed between Sainte Marie and Saint Privat, the horse artillery of the 5/19th let loose around 200 rounds before the superior weight of fire of the Saxon guns obliged them to retire. From their new location to the north of the road, they managed to get off a few more rounds before the four guns in the centre and right of the battery had to withdraw again, Canrobert ordering them to higher ground where they took up another less exposed position behind the garden walls at the entrance to Saint Privat.[348] Somewhat isolated on hill 312, Grimard's battery[349] quickly expended their ammunition and together with 6/14th, withdrew to the north to replenish. Kesner's batteries lost a number of men and horses to the Hessian artillery and both withdrew to a new position north of Saint Privat.[350]

---

346 The 5th and 6/14th, 5th and 6/19th, 8/8th and the 7th and 8/18th à cheval.
347 One such example being provided by the 8/8th who, in their excitement, fired off a dozen or so shells per gun against the enemy infantry before Canrobert, observing their shot falling well short, ordered them to cease fire.
348 The section on the left remained where they had originally unlimbered.
349 5/14th.
350 In just a few minutes the 7/18th lost 10 men and 18 horses and when the battery withdrew, two teams had just a single horse.

Towards 3:00 p.m. as the attack against Sainte Marie gained momentum, Canrobert's artillery was confronted with an increasingly difficult situation; on the left of his corps, three batteries under Montluisant's direct command had been forced to cease their bombardment fire of the Hessian guns so as to retain a few rounds per gun for emergency use. To the north of hill 333, only six batteries remained in position to counter any attack against Saint Privat;[351] even so, they were all running low on munitions and had been ordered to reduce their rate of fire so as to conserve their limited supplies. On the reverse slope, the 12-pdrs of the 9/13th maintained a slow steady fire against Habonville and a little later, following the withdrawal of Cissey's artillery to the south, enjoyed the distinction of being the only French battery in the sector between the railway line and Saint Privat still in action against the Hessians.

Canrobert had previously warned Bazaine that he was short of ammunition[352] and around 2:00 p.m., sent Captain Chalus to repeat his request for an infantry division 'as they would have munitions.'[353] Unfortunately, when Chalus returned accompanied by just four caissons de 4, it was already too late; as the French official history concedes, due to the lack of ammunition, a little after 3:00 p.m., the Saxon and Guard batteries had effectively established their dominance over 6 Corps' artillery. Unable to provide his outlying troops with fire support, Canrobert pulled his infantry closer into Saint Privat and as the firing subsided in this sector, Frederick and his corps commanders were left free to prepare for their next move, the envelopment of Bazaine's right flank.

## Steinmetz's Frustration

As dawn broke over the south of the battlefield, I Army's embittered commander was still seething at the subservient role allocated to his emasculated command. Nonetheless, Steinmetz dutifully ordered VII Corps to close up on Gravelotte from its bivouac near Gorze, whilst VIII Corps held position on their left. On his arrival at Royal headquarters, he briefed Moltke that during his earlier reconnaissance of the French positions, large encampments and defensive works were visible around Gravelotte; as far as he was concerned, this demonstrated that Bazaine had no intention of retreating and he sought to persuade Moltke that I Army should be given the task of carrying the fight to the enemy. The chief of staff had no intention of letting the firebrand general upset his plans again and, so as to leave him under no doubt as to the subordinate role he was to play, instructed 'VII Corps will at first maintain a defensive attitude. Its connection with the VIII can only be made to the front. Should it then appear that the enemy's army is retiring upon Metz, we shall carry out a change of front to the right. The I Army will be supported, if necessary, by the second line of II Army.'[354]

As this debate was taking place at headquarters, in accordance with the orders issued by Steinmetz the previous evening, Zastrow's VII Corps broke camp at first light; From Kamecke's

---

351  The 7/8th on hill 333, the 8/8th and 5/19th on the road to Briey; the 6/19th north-west of Saint Privat and the 7th and 8/18th north of the village.

352  When Bazaine was informed of 6 Corps predicament he merely suggested that Canrobert send his empty ammunition caissons to Metz to resupply, even though the caissons of the Reserve artillery park were a few hundred metres away at St Quentin.

353  L'État-Major, *St Privat*, p.296.

354  Clarke, *Franco-German War Vol. II*, p.5.

14th Division, 7th Rifles and I and II/53rd deployed along the northern edge of the Bois de Vaux facing the Rozerieulles quarries, with orders to hold their ground at all costs. The I and II/77th were stationed in the Bois des Ognons near Gravelotte,[355] with the III/53rd in reserve. The remainder of the division assembled in the Mance valley to the south of the mill, whilst the corps artillery and 13th Division were in the valley west of Ars. Steinmetz retained the 25th Brigade, one battery and a squadron under his direct control. The II and III/13th were hidden in the wood in support of Kamecke, with I Battalion stationed to the north of Mance mill.[356] The remainder of the brigade were divided; part in Ars, part lower down the Moselle.

Steinmetz was later to claim that these dispositions reflected his concerns that if Bazaine went over to the attack, VII Corps would be hard-pressed to provide an effective counter given that Zastrow's force was split between two narrow valleys. VIII Corps, its closest support, were some four and a half miles away near Gorze and no longer under his direct command. The knowledge that II Army were to swing to the north, potentially opening up a gap between his forces and those of Frederick, only increased his sense of isolation, so at 7:00 a.m., he ordered Manteuffel on the east bank of the Moselle, to push forward a brigade and some batteries to Vaux so as to cover the exposed right flank of VII Corps from the far side of the river. Around 8.00 a.m., as he rode forward to the south-west of Gravelotte, he received a despatch advising that Goeben had advanced towards Rezonville and was 'acting in conjunction with, in communication with IX Corps' with VIII Corps proposing take up 'position at Rezonville, in readiness to move either to the left or right'[357] This news only increased Steinmetz's resentment at how his command had been emasculated and served to reinforce his growing sense of isolation and resentment.

Later that morning, Steinmetz sent his chief of staff to Flavigny to receive the day's orders. No doubt in a further attempt to persuade Moltke to give Steinmetz a free hand in attacking the French positions, Sperling briefed headquarters on the latest reports from his patrols over on the east bank of the Moselle, seeking to portray that the French were making off to the north: 'On the road to Thionville, moving to the rear, enormous number of vehicle columns, field hospitals; appears to be a movement to Thionville and to Metz; stationary columns of troops head toward Thionville.'[358] Moltke was having none of it and when Sperling returned to Gravelotte around 11:30 a.m., it was with the firm instruction that I Army were to take no action until II Army came into action on its left.

Further evidence of Steinmetz's aggressive intent was provided by Allanson Winn; inspecting the French positions around Gravelotte early on the 18th he was approached by a Prussian staff officer who asked to borrow his glasses; he then confided that 'General Steinmetz had decided to attack the French in the strong positions that they now held, if they did not retire under the heavy guns of Fort Pappeville and Mont St Quentin, his object being to drive them completely into Metz and not to leave them alone where they now were to throw up rifle pits and redoubts.'[359]

355  The 1/77th sent a number of small detachments to occupy the village.
356  The 1st and 4th companies made their way through the wood in the direction of the quarries.
357  Clarke, *Franco-German War Vol. II*, p.9.
358  Bell, *St Privat*, p.236. This report was forwarded to HQ by Steinmetz despite the misgivings expressed by his Quartermaster General Count von Wartensleben as to the accuracy of the intelligence.
359  Allanson Winn, *What I saw*, p.89.

Still unwilling to accept a supporting role, the recalcitrant commander sent another despatch calculated to convince Moltke that the French were indeed in retreat:

> Though the French camp remained in the morning hours in its previous location and strength between the bois de Génivaux and Bois du Châtel and strong columns had started out from it, apparently to occupy the former woods, the situation has now materially changed. At first it continued doubtful whether the start of the troops from the camp was not for the purpose of taking up the position on the plateau between Point du Jour and Leipzig, since advanced guards and pickets still showed themselves. It can now be stated with evident positive certainty that the mass of hostile troops is retreating in the direction of Metz, a smaller part north and northwest. A rearguard still stands on the camping ground and the enemy is keeping up a weak but continuous skirmish fire on the Bois de Vaux. The I Cavalry Division has been ordered to the plateau of Rezonville.[360]

By the time this message reached Royal headquarters, firing had erupted to the north. With the firebrand general impatient to engage a retreating enemy and Manstein getting embroiled into a fight around Amanvillers, Moltke must have realised that his plan for a coordinated attack by several front line corps was looking problematic. Even so, he was still concerned to forestall any precipitous action by Steinmetz before II Army completed its envelopment of the French line which, at that time, was believed only extended as far north as Amanvillers. He therefore issued a warning order at noon advising: 'The isolated action which can now be heard going on in front of Vernéville does not call for a general attack by the I Army. There is no necessity on this account to show large masses of troops and if you must act, it should be only by using the artillery as a prelude to a later attack.'[361] Unfortunately, given the distance, about 6,600 yards, between his headquarters and I Army's command post south of Gravelotte, by the time the courier delivered this despatch, both VII and VIII corps were heavily engaged with the enemy.

Given that Steinmetz was clearly looking for a fight, it is unlikely that any restraining order would have influenced on his actions. Moltke's control was fast slipping away with the battle degenerating into a series of independent actions by his subordinate commanders. As a result, for the remainder of that bloody day, he was to remain a more or less interested observer, having little ability to shape the fast-moving events which were often taking place many miles distant from his command post overlooking Flavigny.[362]

## VIII Corps Move to Contact

When Goeben reached Villers aux Bois at 8:00 a.m., he ordered VIII Corps to front to the north-east so they could react to events on either flank. General von Weltzien's 15th Division

360  Bell, *St Privat*, p.236.
361  Lanza, *Franco-German War*, p.263.
362  Royal HQ was later to relocate to a hillock to the north-west of Gravelotte but even here Moltke could only observe the fighting around the Mance ravine, developments in the centre and north of the extensive battlefield remaining hidden from view.

were to the west, the corps artillery astride the main road at Rezonville and Barnekow's 16th Division were south of the village. Seton, who accompanied 32nd Brigade recalled:

> We crossed the scenes of the last struggle on the 16th and halted on the slope of the ravine just short of the high road. The six battalions formed mass, facing about east and piled arms. Nothing was to be seen from this cover, but by riding up the western slope and a little to the left rear I came on the Staff of the 8th Corps waiting on the road, on which also and further to the rear, stood the Reserve artillery ... A view was to be had of the French standing in apparently great force on as much of the Moscou-Leipzig slope as was not masked by woods on our right front and half left. There was no doubt that a pitched battle different from anything I had seen before, was coming off.[363]

The 7th Hussars were out front tasked with maintaining communications with Manstein on their left and Zastrow on the right and as they pushed into the Mance ravine, their patrols exchanged fire with French skirmishers from the 3/80th and the 3/60th. Across the ravine, along the edge of the bois de Génivaux, the enemy outpost line was manned by three companies[364] commanded by Captain Schmedter who held the causeway carrying the main road across the defile. Another two companies[365] lined the wood facing Mogador farm from where they engaged in intermittent skirmishing throughout the morning with patrols sent out by von Rosenzweig from the 28th. Although, as the French official history comments, the absence of effective local leadership and poor communication served to reduce the efficiency of their outpost line. Subsequently Lieutenant Colonel Isnard of the 29th assumed command of the troops[366] in this area but even then, Schmedter's forces watching over the causeway remained outside this structure, so there was little advance warning of the attack that was shortly to fall on their positions.

As cannon and musketry fire erupted to the north around Vernéville around 11:45 a.m., Goeben understandably took this to herald the commencement of the general attack against the French line which Moltke had mentioned in his earlier order Half an hour later, in preparation for a full blown attack against the French positions across the Mance ravine, he instructed the 15th Division 'To advance, with one infantry brigade on Gravelotte and from there and to the right of the road crossing the ravine, with the other brigade left of the village to the Mance forest.'[367] Allanson described the scene within VIII Corps as they expectantly waited for the battle to commence:

> About half a mile in front of us was Gravelotte and deployed immediately behind it in contiguous columns was the 40th Regiment. The scene was altogether striking; General von Goeben surveying the view before him, surrounded by a numerous staff of all the regiments; the 33rd, 60th and 69th regiments taking up ground in the Vernéville woods, to the left rear of Gravelotte; everything getting ready, as it were, for the horrid

363  Seton, *Notes*, p.148.
364  1st, 3rd and 5th, 2/71st.
365  6th Company, 1/7th and 6th Company from the 7th Chasseurs
366  This included the 7th Chasseurs, the advance guard of the 7th and the 2/29th who were in reserve in the wood.
367  Bell, *German Sources*, p.236.

carnage about to ensue. Presently a general of brigade and aide-de-camp rode up and delivered a despatch. Within five minutes the artillery of the Guard on our extreme left opened, at first feebly, on the right of the French position and then against the hamlet of Malmaison. The French returned the fire at once from Moscou.[368]

The distance between Rezonville and the defile, about 2,400 yards, took about 30 minutes to traverse and Weltzien directed 15th Division along the south-western edge of the Bois de la Jurée where, after crossing the old Roman road, the lead regiment, the 33rd, was detailed to occupy Gravelotte. Seton was again on hand to observe their advance:

> The formation, while still advancing over open ground was (for the right brigade at least) 1st Line (Treffen) 4 company columns at 80 pace intervals, covered by their marksmen's Zügen skirmishing with supports; in 2nd line followed the other two battalions of the regiment in 'attack columns' opposite the outer intervals of the 1st; the remaining regiment formed a reserve, detaching however a battalion to escort guns. Although Gravelotte was not defended, the rush through it by the skirmishers was very pretty. I followed near the staff and was presently accosted by an Officer, who rode up and asked, in French, what I was doing there. On my answering in German that I was an English officer, he gave me a sort of hug and introduced me soon afterwards to Major General von Wedell, commanding the 29th Brigade. Gravelotte having been cleared, General von Goeben rode through to the south-east corner, where dismounting and leaving the bulk of his staff and horses by the church, he walked with his chief of staff along the outside of a garden enclosure to a point whence he could get a good view of the ground and the enemy without drawing down fire.[369]

To the rear of the fighting formations, the medical staff also prepared for the forthcoming battle:

> Each regiment had a party of men told off, who wore the red cross upon the left arm as a distinguishing badge. They numbered about a hundred and were unarmed, except with the most useless–looking horse pistols. It was their duty to follow in the rear of the regiment and when the corps went into action stretchers were distributed to them, which were carried in the staff ambulance wagons belonging to the brigade. In addition to this corps there were six doctors to each regiment and a regimental medicine wagon upon two wheels to each battalion, which always followed in the rear of the column, containing medical comforts and surgical instruments. This regimental ambulance is more for the use of the troops on the march than for the succour in the battlefield, for which purpose the staff or brigade ambulances are used ... They consisted of a large wagon upon four wheels, drawn by four horses. On the top, under oilskins which form tents for the hospital corps, are packed the stretcher. The back part is opened by folding doors and a perfect apothecary's shop is exposed, commencing with drawers,

368  Allanson Winn, *What I saw*, p.91.
369  Seton, *Notes*, p.149.

containing surgical instruments, bandages and cordials of every description and ending with chloroform and medicines of every sort and kind that can be useful in the field.[370]

## Goeben's Artillery Engage 2 Corps

Weltzen's artillery[371] were ordered to take up position in the shelter of a gulley that ran to the north-west of the village pending deployment of the division. However, as the infantry moved forward, the guns came under fire from the French artillery and mitrailleuses deployed on the far side of the ravine. 1st Field Division's commander, Major Mertens, ordered the immediate deployment of his batteries so as to counter their fire with the II/67th being told off to act as escort. Captain Geiszler's 1st Light was first into action, to the west of the road running north from Gravelotte to Malmaison, followed shortly thereafter by Busses's 1st Heavy. Within a few minutes, the 2nd Light and 2nd Heavy[372] had moved into the gun line between them, each battery selecting the position which afforded them greatest advantage. 7th Hussars were ordered to screen the open left flank of the gun line as Weltzien was still unclear about the French dispositions and whether they held any ground to the east of the ravine. His guns could see little of the ground between them and the enemy positions which made it difficult to estimate their range and around 12:45 p.m., they opened a largely ineffective fire at ranges of between 1,880 and 3,800 paces.

Frossard's sappers[373] were still engaged in constructing shelters for 2 Corps guns as Merten's artillery opened fire but the French batteries around the Point du Jour were generally well positioned to engage the enemy, as the ground they occupied was about 30 metres higher than the western side of the plateau. Nonetheless, given the dearth of completed emplacements, Maréchal's battery,[374] sited to the north of the farm, soon attracted the attention of 15th Division's guns and quickly limbered up and withdrew to the rear of the buildings. A little later, together with the 6th and 11/5th, they began an 'action vigoureuse' against VII Corps gun line south of Gravelotte.

Further to the north, Amyard's three batteries[375] took up the fight and although some earthworks had been thrown up by the divisional sappers, the 10/5th positioned near the road and the mitrailleuses of the 8th in the centre of the division, had little in the way of cover. North of Moscou farm, Metman's batteries du 4[376] entered the struggle and soon after, received support from the 12-pdrs from the corps' Reserve[377] who took position behind the earthworks a little in front of Point du Jour farm. Nayral's artillery[378] and the remainder of the corps' Reserve

---

370  Roberts, *Modern War*, pp.67–68.
371  1st Field Division, 8th FA Regiment.
372  Captains Leo and von Uthmann.
373  From the 12th Company of 3rd Engineer Regiment.
374  The 5/5th.
375  8th, 9th and 10/11th.
376  6th and 7/11th.
377  11th and 12/11th. Due to the range, about 3,000 metres, the divisional mitrailleuses of 5/11th were initially held in reserve.
378  9th, 11th and 12/4th.

batteries, were stationed behind the crest of the hill running between the l'Arbre Mort and Leipzig and took no part in the early stages of the battle.

As acknowledged by the French official history, in line with their tactical doctrine, initially relatively few batteries from 2 and 3 Corps were committed with most being held in reserve or tasked to cover the routes leading out of the Bois de Vaux, where there was little sign of enemy activity and even fewer targets. On the opposite side of the ravine, Mertens soon recognised the drawbacks of the location chosen for his guns and moved his batteries forward in succession, to the east of the road, to the commanding heights north-east of Mogador farm so as to close the range with the French artillery.[379] As a consequence of this forward deployment, Geoben had to push his infantry into the Mance ravine to drive the French skirmishers out of the bois de Génivaux from where their fire could harass the gun crews.

Moltke's message warning against the premature engagement of VII and VIII corps reached Goeben around 1:00 p.m. as he was overseeing the deployment of 15th Division and the corps artillery around Gravelotte. However, as far as he was concerned, matters were now too far advanced to disengage – a decision unsurprisingly endorsed by Steinmetz – and so continued his preparations for the infantry attack against the French positions on the far side of the ravine with Weltzien being ordered to deploy his brigades on either side of the road. This decision to assault a strongly defended position, in direct contravention of his superiors' instructions, represented a formidable undertaking and signified a serious escalation of the fighting and further evidence of Moltke's limited control over events.

Meanwhile, as Busse's battery prepared to move to a new position by Malamaison, Broeckeri's corps artillery[380] arrived at the trot, advancing across the open fields to the north of the main road running from Gravelotte to Rezonville; the field guns in column of batteries on the left, the horse artillery in column of divisions on the right. The artillery deployed on both flanks and in the intervals between Merten's guns,[381] and immediately engaged the batteries around Moscou farm and Point du Jour. The range was between 3,500 to 3,800 paces and although these reinforcements attracted the unwelcome attention of the French cannon and miltrailleuses, the enemy fire was largely ineffective and Broeckeri's men suffered few losses. Then, as 15th Division were forming up for their attack, Lieutenant General von Hartmann brought forward 1st Cavalry Division to the west of Malmaison, their battery of horse artillery[382] reinforcing VIII Corps gun line although in their advanced position, the guns quickly drew the attention of the French outpost line.[383] Verdy du Vernois observed:

> Everywhere along the whole range, guns sent out flashes and belched forth dense volumes of smoke. A hail of shell and shrapnel, the latter traceable by the little white clouds, looking like balloons, which remained suspended in the air for some time after

379  His initial positions were about 3,300 yards from the French guns.
380  Lieutenant Colonel Borkenhagen's Horse Artillery Division, 8th Field Artillery Regiment and Major Zwinnemann's 2nd Field Artillery Division, 8th Field Artillery Regiment.
381  On the left of von Uthmann's 2nd Heavy: von Wissels 3rd Heavy, Sommers's 4th Heavy, von Teichmann-Logischen's 3rd Light, Gehtmann's 4th Light. To the right of Geiszler's 1st Light, the batteries of horse artillery of von Fuchsius, Protze and Schlieben.
382  1st Horse Artillery Battery 1st East Prussian Field Artillery Regiment, Captain Preinitzer escorted by a squadron of the 3rd Cuirassiers.
383  The outposts were furnished by 1st, 3rd and 5th companies' 2/71st.

their bursting, answered the warlike greeting from the other side. The grating noise of the mitrailleuses was heard above the tumult, drowning the whole roar of battle.[384]

Across the Mance, Sous Lieutenant Picard of the 3rd Chasseurs recalled:

Almost at once the two houses at Point du Jour came under attack. The shells hit the gables and the ground between the buildings was sprayed with stone splinters. A few men manned the loopholes on the ground floor of the southernmost house – they didn't stay there long; a shell burst in the interior of the building in the midst of a group of men producing inexpressible misery; the men fell out of the house screaming and groaning; everyone had been hit by the shrapnel or stone splinters. The fire of the artillery became more violent. The 4-pdrs placed behind the earthworks tried to respond to the enemy fire, but from the start they were targeted by the Prussian guns which rendered their position untenable. One of the first strikes on one of the guns to our left took off the arm of the one of the gunners who held the rammer and the cries of this unfortunate man added to those who had just stumbled out of the house. It was a moment of crisis in our position; the accurate and violent fire of the Prussian guns made a big impression on the men of the 3rd Chasseurs and a number left their positions to avoid the shell fire and ran back along the road to Rozerieulles or took shelter on the reverse slope of the plateau. The firm bearing of Commandant Petit soon put a halt to this behaviour.[385]

## VII Corps Artillery Ordered Forward

Steinmetz and his staff were to the south of Gravelotte when the firing erupted around Vernéville. Like von Goeben, he assumed this to be the signal to commence the attack and true to form, lost no time in ordering VII Corps into action, despite Moltke's specific orders to the contrary.[386] 14th Division's batteries were the first to deploy, taking position to the south of Gravelotte between the village and the Bois des Ognons. Screened from the French by a small rise, they advanced at the trot in column of divisions, wheeled to the right and unlimbered in positions selected the previous day by Major Baron von Eynatten,[387] the left wing of their gun line being about 200 yards south of Gravelotte. Three batteries[388] took up position a few hundred yards west of the highway running from Ars to Gravelotte, whilst Hübner's 1st Heavy was east of the road, from where they immediately engaged the enemy gun positions across the ravine.[389]

Although the French were quick to respond to this new threat, their shrapnel was generally fused too short and the miltrailleuse rounds fell in front of the gun line limiting the effect of

---

384  Vernois, *Royal Headquarters*, p.81.

385  Lecaillon, *Été 1870*, p.147.

386  Moltke sent a despatch to Steinmetz at 1:45 p.m. reading 'The IX Corps is now engaged in an artillery battle in front of Bois Doseuillons. The actual attack along the entire line will not be made before than sizeable fighting forces can advance from Amanvillers.' See Bell, *German Sources*, p.263. Even if Steinmetz had received this order before he gave instructions to attack, it is doubtful as to whether he would have heeded it as he had already made his mind up to go over to the offensive.

387  Artillery Commander 14th Division.

388  1st Light, Schweder, 2nd Light, Goetz and 2nd Heavy, Wolff.

389  A number of limbers and ammunition caissons around the Point du Jour were seen to explode.

their fire.[390] Three more batteries under Major Wilhelmi were then deployed between and on the flanks of Eynatten's position so by 1:15 p.m., I Army had 108 guns in action; 11 batteries from VIII Corps to the north of Gravelotte,[391] seven from Zastrow's corps to the south.[392] Initially under the direction of Colonel von Kamecke and then Lieutenant General Schwarz, the unified command of both gun corps enabled the Prussians to effectively engage the artillery confronting them across the Mance ravine; Goeben's guns concentrated their fire between Moscou farm and the highway; Zastrow, the area between the road and Rozerieulles. Initially they targeted the French batteries but as they pulled out of the line, switched their attention to the farmsteads of Saint Hubert and Point du Jour and their supporting infantry.

The highway from Metz to Verdun that was to form the axis along which Steinmetz and Goeben were to attack, ran through a deep valley around 1,500 yards wide; just after Saint Hubert farm, the road swept down into a deep ravine, crossing an open, flat water meadow[393] on a raised masonry embankment before rising again to Gravelotte. The valley sides were thickly wooded and on the eastern slopes there were a number of quarries which served to channel any attacks onto the ground in front and either side of the farm. Overlooking the causeway, Saint Hubert farmhouse comprised a substantial two storey building standing close to the main highway, with stables and a courtyard to the north, having just a single entrance. To the rear, or east, of the building was a roughly triangular shaped garden, 120m deep at its widest point and some 180m in length, The garden had a wall some 2m high to its southern and western sides and a shoulder height wall to the north. The farmhouse and walled garden had been loopholed and an opening made between the courtyard and walled garden to assist the easy movement of troops.[394] Shelter trenches had been dug by the French and the buildings loop holed so as to make a naturally strong position even more formidable.

## The Advance into the Mance Ravine

As 15th Division's attack got underway, the 33rd held Gravelotte with the II/67th, now relieved of its escort duties, occupying Malmaison farmhouse. The II/33rd pushed out of the village, to the south of the main road and with all four companies in line, advanced into the ravine and crossed the valley floor. As they struggled through the dense undergrowth on the eastern slopes and attempted to close on the French positions around Saint Hubert, in accordance with their orders their outnumbered opponents from the 32nd Ligne fell back on the main defensive line.[395] Immediately upon leaving the shelter of the wood, the 33rd were hit with a withering

---

390  The two Light batteries suffered most, Captain Schweder losing a hand to a shell splinter.
391  North to south: 4th Light, 3rd Light, 4th Heavy; 1st Heavy, 3rd Heavy, 2nd Heavy; 2nd Light,1st Light; 3rd Horse, 2nd Horse, 1st Light.
392  From north to south: 5th Heavy, 2nd Light, 1st Light, 2nd Heavy, 6th Heavy; to the east of the Ars Road; 1st Heavy, 6th Light.
393  The stream from which the ravine took its name was dry so presented little obstacle to infantry.
394  After the battle Allanson Winn inspected the farm and found that the defenders had 'piled knapsacks in the windows and knocked holes in the walls.' See *What I saw*, p.96.
395  The 2nd and 3/32nd were deployed by the bend in the road at Saint Hubert just to the rear of the crest. 1st Brigade, 2nd Division (8th and 23rd) were deployed in two lines, 100 metres apart so as to reduce the effect of the enemy artillery. The division's engineer company constructed a shelter trench on the crest of the slope to the rear of Point du Jour farm, which was then occupied by the 12th Chasseurs.

fire, resulting in numerous casualties including their commander Major von Reinhard, who fell, mortally wounded. A few men managed to make their way to the shelter of the quarries which lay either side of the highway but here, their advance ground to a halt in the face of the fierce opposition from the companies lying in ambush in a trench running between the farm buildings.[396]

Meanwhile, Wedell brought forward the 60th to occupy Gravelotte, with the second battalion being tasked to provide close protection for the gun line, which was still under fire from the French outposts.[397] Archibald Forbes described their advance:

> Dimly and vaguely only could the movements be discerned from where I stood, but large detachments must have burst out of the wood and pushing down into the dip where was the bed of the Mance, breasted the opposite slope and debouched against Moscou and Saint Hubert. Through the glass I could see the broken battalions as they clambered piecemeal out of the hollow and tumbling together into approximate formation strove to push on up the gentler slope. Then there came heavier smoke banks on their right flank above the batteries at Point du Jour; the batteries of miltrailleuses at Saint Hubert raged like wild cats right in their faces; the French infantry men in position between Saint Hubert and Moscow, fringed their ranks with spurting white smoke from their chassepots.[398]

Wedell then ordered the I and III/33rd under Lieutenant Colonel von Henning to clear the enemy from the Bois de Vaux to the south-east of the ravine.[399] Dashing across the meadow, they captured 15 skirmishers of the 55th Ligne and facing little opposition, ascended the eastern slopes of the gully where around 2:00 p.m., emerged from the woods opposite Point du Jour farmhouse. As with I Battalion, any attempt to cross the open ground that lay between their position and the farmhouse was greeted with a withering fire from the companies of the 76th and 77th Ligne lining the edge of the road, which forced them back into the shelter of the gully.

Meanwhile Weltzien, no doubt emboldened by the apparent lack of opposition to the south of the highway, ordered General von Strubberg[400] to push forward into the bois de Génivaux. After passing through Gravelotte in column so as to avoid masking the fire of the corps artillery and with their right linking up with the 33rd from 29th Brigade, the three fusilier companies from the 67th deployed across the road.[401] They were immediately engaged by the 3/60th who held the edge of the wood a few hundred yards to the north, as Aymard's divisional batteries[402] and the 12-pdrs[403] located near Moscou greeted them with 'un feu très vif et très meurtrier.'[404]

---

396  From the 32nd, 55th and the 3rd Chasseurs.

397  6th Company, 1/7th and 6th Company,7th Chasseurs.

398  Forbes, *My Experiences*, pp.177–178.

399  2nd Battalion in the centre, flanked on either side by two companies of the 1st, 4th and 3rd companies to the north, 1st and 2nd to the south.

400  Commander 30th Brigade.

401  9th in front, 10th and 11th behind.

402  8th and 10/11th. Initially these batteries targeted VIII Corps gun line but as the range was too great, directed their fire on the infantry in the ravine.

403  11th and12/12th.

404  L'État-Major, *St Privat*, p.337.

The 3rd and 4th companies followed the fusiliers in half section columns, with the 2nd and 1st forming a third line. The first two companies launched an attack against the corner of the bois de Génivaux closest to the road but the warm welcome they received from the skirmish line deployed along its western edge, evidenced the strength of the defenders, so Strubberg ordered a general advance by the remainder of the brigade. From the 8th Rifles, four companies were formed in a continuous line on the flank of the I/67th whilst to their left, all three battalions of the 28th, deployed in two lines with skirmishing divisions thrown out in front, added their support to the attack.[405]

Ignoring their losses[406] the brigade quickly expelled the defenders from their earthworks along the edge of the wood and after driving forward about 1,000 yards, wheeled to the right, pushing the skirmishers of the 60th Ligne before them into a small side ravine which led to the main valley. The track through the gully was blocked by two low walls behind which the French sought cover as they endeavoured to halt the Rhinelander's advance, but they were driven off after a short struggle. After detailing two companies[407] to secure the barrier against any counter attack, Major Lange paused to rally his men together at the base of the ravine where, even at this early stage of the engagement, due to the difficult terrain, they had become widely dispersed and disorganised.

Meanwhile, II/28th and 12th Company 67th pushed northwards through the undergrowth, their left forming a refused flank along a brook which ran from la Folie farm into the Mance; here they became engaged in a desultory, inconclusive fire fight with Metman's outpost line that lasted until nightfall.[408]

Further south, with the enemy advancing on either flank of his position, Captain Schmedter ordered the three companies guarding the causeway to retire.[409] Given the lack of any effective coordination between the French outpost commanders, this sudden withdrawal left de Courcy's advance guard[410] exposed so they too fell back on the main defensive position along the ridge. In turn, Rigaud's outposts from the 7th Chasseurs were panicked into a hasty retreat when enemy infantry[411] suddenly appeared from the woods on their left flank which they presumed were occupied by de Courcy. The 5th and 6th companies fell back on their supports and two companies[412] of the 90th who were in the clearing in the woods to their rear.

Following their failed assault against Pont du Jour, the 33rd had become dangerously extended[413] with one group comprising the fusilier battalion and 3rd and 4th companies seeking

---

405  The first line comprised the 10th, 11th, 6th, 7th, 3rd and 2nd companies in extended order, the 12th, 9th, 8th, 5th, 4th, 1st in half battalions in the second, with the 12th Company taking position on the extreme left of the line.

406  Several company commanders were hit and most of the senior officers had their horses shot from under them.

407  5/28th and 12/67th.

408  This included the 1st, 3rd and 5th companies 2/71st, 6th Company 1/7th and 5th and 6th companies' 7th Chasseurs.

409  1st, 3rd and 5th companies, 2/71st.

410  From the 90th.

411  From the 6th Company 67th.

412  3rd and 4th companies' 1/90th. The remaining seven companies were positioned in the middle of the bois de Génivaux.

413  Their frontage exceeded 1,100 yards.

shelter within the quarries either side of the road west of Saint Hubert; II Battalion and the 1st and 2nd companies were about 750 yards further south in the gravel pits to the west of the Point du Jour. Goeben was unable to see their predicament due to the terrain but the constant stream of casualties and malingerers making their way to the rear, told their own tale. Other units within the ravine suffered similar problems; companies were over extended, officers and NCO's lost control of their men within the difficult terrain and seemed powerless to prevent the depletion of the firing line as troops continually dropped out of the ranks in a desperate attempt to find some cover from the murderous chassepot fire.

## 2 Corps' Response

Although the fire of his front line battalions[414] had so far served to keep the Rhinelander's bottled up in the ravine, Weltzen's determined assault against Saint Hubert prompted Frossard to order Fauvert Bastoul[415] to strengthen his 'ligne principale de résistance' between Moscou and Leipzig farms. Around 2:00 p.m., the 1st and 2/23rd moved up from reserve to the crest of hill 349, just to the north of the old road. A little later, the 3rd Battalion took position along the main road by the Point du Jour. Vergé called on Dupré's battery[416] 'to hold in check the enemy and to prevent them from taking the plateau' and around 2:30 p.m., the mitrailleuses unlimbered near the farm with orders to engage the 'retreating enemy columns.'[417]

Although sheltered between the buildings, the guns were still exposed to heavy rifle and artillery fire and in the space of 10 minutes, 23 horses and two officers were killed; two caissons were blown up with the battery being 'threatened with complete destruction.'[418] Dupré's kepi was cleft in two by a shell splinter and Captain Cornet fell dead with a bullet to the head. In the face of this onslaught, chef d'escadron Collangettes ordered the battery out of the line, their disengagement being covered by the 3/23rd.

As the mitrailleuses retreated, their place was taken by the 12th Chasseurs who took shelter in a roadside ditch to the left of the farm. To counter the threat posed by the 33rd, who were still doggedly holding on to their hard-won positions in the quarries to the south of the main road, Fauvert Bastoul ordered the 8th into the second line to replace the battalions committed to the firing line. Across the ravine, the infantry deployed by Goeben along the edge of the Bois de Vaux to cover VIII Corps gun line had also been drawn into the action. On the right, a division from the 7th Rifles which had been sent to link up with von der Goltz's 26th Brigade as they advanced northwards along the Moselle from Ars, became embroiled in a fire fight with the French outpost line.

Shortly after, the 33rd renewed their attack from the quarries to the east of the Point du Jour, supported on their right by the 53rd who dashed forward from the shelter of the woods. As the outlying tirailleurs fell back on their main defensive line,[419] the attacking force attempted to

---

414  1/80th, 1/85th, 1/44th, 1st, 2nd and 3/59th from 3 Corps, 3rd and 4th divisions.
415  Commander 2nd Division.
416  9/5th.
417  L'État-Major, *St Privat*, p.354.
418  *Ibid*, pp.361–362.
419  Held by the 1st and 2/77th Ligne; in addition, Jolivet's brigade had ample artillery support provided by the 8/5th, 7/5th, 10/5th and 7/2nd.

close with the main enemy line but on leaving the cover of the trees, they were struck by a heavy fire and their advance ground to a halt. III/13th from Osten Sacken's 25th Brigade was sent forward to give new impetus to their stalled attack, II Battalion being held back in reserve in the wood. To counter this move, Jolivet again reinforced his defence by bringing up four companies from the 3/77th who took position alongside the 2nd. Following their introduction into the fighting in this sector, the attackers went to ground and the firing subsided for a short time as both sides paused to draw breath and reorganise their forces.

## The Artillery Battle Intensifies

Observing the battle within the Mance and showing a commendable disregard for the French shells bursting about them, Allanson Winn and his companion;

> ... sat down on a gun carriage to eat our lunch, watching the battle and looking to avoid, if possible, bits of shrapnel that came burring about in all directions. However, we were well to the rear here as we had determined not to go into action until we had had a good luncheon; so we finished our meal with some very good Moselle wine and were just going forward, when a sight passed before us that I suppose neither will ever see excelled and which few people could ever hope to see equalled. I allude to the 20,000 cavalry who rode by, literally with ten yards of us, across the Verdun road, as they went to take up ground in a valley to the Prussian left. Strange to say, we did not notice the approach of this fine body of men until they were close upon us. The effect was startling and grand. First passed in solid squadrons three regiments of Cuirassiers – red, green and blue; then three regiments of Hussars in the same order. We calculated these six regiments alone, of three battalions each, each a thousand horses strong, at about 18,000. Bringing up the rear in a column, came a battalion of Uhlans and one of Brandenburg Dragoons. In describing the cuirassier regiments as red, green and blue, it must not be supposed that I mean to signify that their respective uniforms are of those colours. Their tunics are made of warm white flannel, bound, according to the regiment they belong to, either with red, green or blue braid. Their breeches are also white flannel; and over these they have immensely long jack boots, that can be worn either doubled below the knee, or pulled up so as to cover the thigh. Large steel spurs are strapped on the instep, after the fashion of the seventeenth century. The helmet and cuirass are of polished steel and, but for the shape of the former, would add greatly to the fine appearance of the wearers. It always seems too big for the bearer and forces the idea upon one's mind that he has been bonneted by his rear rank man. The Hussar uniforms are much the same as our own, but they wear tight breeches and Hessian boots instead of trousers. There is one regiment, however, of Hussars, whose officers have peculiar trappings to their chargers; the bridle and martingale are completely embroidered with cowrie shells. These are the Black Hussars and carry a skull and crossbones on their busby.[420]

420 Allanson Winn, *What I saw*, pp.92–94. He seems to have been confused, possibly having drunk too much of his 'very good Moselle wine,' about the strength and composition of Prussian cavalry

Around 2:00 p.m. with 1st Cavalry deploying around Malmaison, Barnekow's 16th Division moved up to the western outskirts of Gravelotte as Weltzien's sappers busily fortified the village against counter attack.[421] Goeben had taken advantage of the space freed up by 15th Division's offensive to push his gun line forward about 1,100 yards; this despite the heavy losses to the fire of the mitrailleuses.[422] The Rhinelander's were quick to respond, Seton noting 'I don't think they had fired more than half a dozen rounds when I saw, near Moscou, two French tumbrils explode in quick succession.'[423]

By this time, Zastrow's gun line had been reinforced by the deployment of the artillery of his corps' Reserve; first to arrive were Major Matthiasz's heavies[424] of the 2nd Field Division and they were followed by Captain Hahn's 2nd Horse, although due to limited space in the firing line, the remaining batteries were held to the west of Gravelotte. VII Corps artillery commanders[425] following Goeben's example, moved their batteries to better firing positions closer to the ravine, so that the artillery of both corps formed an almost continuous line running north and south of the highway. There were now 132 guns in action, with a further 36 unable to find space to deploy, being held in reserve.[426] With the combined gun line maintaining a steady methodical fire, their steady ascendancy over Frossard's artillery was evidenced by a succession of exploding limbers, caissons and a gradual decline in the French rate of fire.

As a result, as early as 1:30 p.m., out of the 10 batteries engaged by 2 and 3 corps, Dupré's mitrailleuses had already been pulled out of the line; 5th and 11/5th positioned by the Point du Jour then ran out of ammunition and were withdrawn being replaced by the 12-pdrs of 12/5th and the 10/5th. Although the heavier guns had more impact[427] they were unable to withstand the counter battery fire from the enemy guns and before long, both were pulled out of the line, their place being taken by two batteries of horse artillery from the corps' Reserve.[428] Testament to the skill of the enemy gunners, they came under heavy fire as soon as they unlimbered and the 8th withdrew to a new sheltered location alongside the batteries of the reserve.[429] Lieutenant Colonel de Franchessin[430] and Captain Saget rode over to the 7th and quickly reached the conclusion that its position was similarly untenable and ordered the battery to retreat.

It was later claimed that Frossard ordered 1st Division's batteries to cease fire as he did not want the noise of the cannon fire to mislead Bazaine as to the true point of the enemy attack; as the French official history commented, it is difficult to give much credence to this assertion and more likely, reflecting Bazaine's concerns, Frossard endeavoured to reserve his firepower to

regiments; 1st Cavalry Division numbered about 3,300 troopers in total.

421  2nd Field Pioneer Company.
422  The batteries moved in echelon from the left so as to maintain their fire against the French positions.
423  Seton, *Notes*, p.150.
424  Bleckert's 3rd and Lemner's 4th.
425  Major Baron von Eynatten and Major Wilhelmi.
426  These comprised 3rd and 4th Light battery, 3rd Horse artillery, VII Corps and three batteries from 16th Division.
427  Frossard's commandant d'artillerie General Gagneur reported after the battle 'The fire of 1st Division's 4-pdrs didn't have much impact on the enemy batteries, although the batteries de 12 were much more effective.' See l'État-Major *18 Août, Documents*, p.129.
428  7th and 8/17th commanded by Captain Saget and Captain d'Esclaibes d'Hust.
429  6th and 10/15th.
430  Chef d'Etat-Major de l'artillerie du 2 Corps.

counter any flank attack from the direction of the Bois de Vaux.[431] Whatever the reason, the fact remains that of the 13 batteries at his disposal, after the initial opening engagement, three and then just two[432] divisional batteries were deployed to counter VII Corps gun line, albeit they received supported from three 12-pdrs batteries of the reserve and seven from 3 Corps.[433] Given these odds, there could be little doubt as to the outcome of the artillery engagement and Frossard's handling of his guns attracted much criticism in the French official history although, as it concedes, the position he occupied lacked the open ground where large numbers of batteries could be deployed.[434] What is beyond doubt is that in contrast to Ladmirault, Frossard was unwilling to slug it out with the enemy artillery across the Mance ravine and a little before 3:00 p.m., not a single battery from 2 Corps remained in action.

## The Situation Within 3 Corps

Matters were little better in the sector held by Le Boeuf; the 10/11th sought to engage VII Corps gunline but unable to compete with their volume of fire, withdrew 200 metres behind the crest of the heights, their teams and limbers suffering heavy losses. The 8th Mitrailleuses engaged the columns of infantry from 30th Brigade as they descended into the ravine from Gravelotte but around 2:30 p.m. as the enemy batteries targeted them, they were also driven from their positions. The 4-pdrs of the 9/11th shifted their attention to VIII Corps gun line but as recorded by Lieutenant Colonel Maucourant, they 'had to give up their effort because of the superior calibre of the enemy batteries and instead reserved their fire to counter any attack against Moscou.'[435] 3 Corps' Reserve 12-pdrs[436] were located a little in front of Moscou farm from where they initially engaged VIII Corps gun line before targeting the infantry during their advance through the woods. They soon attracted counter battery fire from Goeben's artillery and around 2:00 p.m., were withdrawn to the reverse slope despite relatively few casualties.[437]

Their place was taken by three batteries[438] from Nayral's division who were called forward to the north of Moscou farm; the 11th and 12th occupied the earthworks recently vacated by the 12-pdrs, leaving the 9/4th to unlimber on open ground[439] where subsequently, all three supported the guns already[440] engaging 30th Brigade. Of the artillery deployed by Metman to the north of the farm, the 7/11th was forced out of the line around 2:00 p.m. although the 6th

---

431  See l'État-Major, *St Privat*, pp.351–352.
432  5th and 11/5th after the 6/5th were withdrawn.
433  8th, 9th and 10/11th, 6th and 7/11th and 11th and 12/11th.
434  Unlike 4 Corps where most of the available artillery was deployed at the outset of the battle to confront Manstein's artillery, 2 and 3 Corps only engaged less than a third of their available firepower; just nine out of the 30 batteries that were available to confront I Army's artillery which, in the space of half an hour, grew from 48 to 108 guns.
435  Commandant d'Artillerie 4th Division. See l'État-Major, *18 Août, Documents*, p.202.
436  11th and 12/11th.
437  Total losses for both batteries, eight men wounded.
438  9th, 11th and 12/4th.
439  The battery again left large intervals between the guns to reduce the impact of the Prussian artillery although the regimental history records that the majority of enemy shells which fell in the recently ploughed ground, buried themselves in the soil and failed to explode.
440  12/11th and 6th and 7/11th. The 11/11th having been forced out of the line by the Prussian fire.

held its position for another two hours.[441] At the same time, two batteries of horse artillery[442] from the corps' reserve were ordered forward to the left of the line and placed at Aymard's disposal. Deploying in front of the bois de Châtel on the heights which ran to Moscou farm, the 1st unlimbered a little in advance of the crest, the 2nd being held back in reserve at the edge of the bois de Châtel.

From 20 batteries available to 3 Corps, seven[443] were engaged in the bitter contest around Amanvillers with a similar number being committed to the struggle against I Army's gun line. Between 1:30 and 3:00 p.m., four more batteries were fed into the fight, but five were withdrawn due to losses in men and equipment or lack of ammunition and by then, there were only two batteries in reserve that had yet to fire a shot.[444]

Together, Le Boeuf and Frossard had some 30 batteries[445] available to counter the 22 initially deployed by Steinmetz but in reality, they never engaged more than 10 at any one time. As the French official history notes, this was the principal reason why the enemy gained such rapid dominance over their guns and once again, serves to highlight the Imperial Army's deficient tactics. Having driven off or silenced the French guns and with both Moscou and Point du Jour ablaze, I Army's guns then turned their attention against Saint Hubert farm.

## Goeben Renews his Attack

To the south of the main highway, 29th Brigade launched another attack out of the Mance ravine attempting to close on the French positions around Saint Hubert, but again, made only limited headway against the fierce defensive fire. To the north, having reformed their ranks in the shelter afforded by the ravine, the 67th made a simultaneous push against the same objective but confronted by a hail shot and shell, deviated to the right seeking cover in the quarries alongside the road. Following this failure, 1st and 2nd Company I/67th were sheltering in the workings on either side of the highway in the ground about 250 yards from Saint Hubert; the 3rd and 4th companies being dispersed amongst them, with the 9th, 10th and 11th Fusilier companies to their left. To their front four companies of 8th Rifles and I and III/28th were echeloned towards the farm whilst the II/28th and 12th Company of the 67th covered the brigade's left flank. Small parties from the 1st and 2nd crept out of the shelter of the quarries and took up positions within 200 yards of the farm buildings.

The three fusilier companies moved out of the ravine and dashed towards the farm into a hail of shot;[446] their advance was short lived as the men dived for cover, their commanding officer Major von Wittich being one of many casualties. A subsequent attack by Major von Oppeln-Bronikowski's 8th Rifles enjoyed more success; with all four companies in line, they rushed forward despite the heavy fire from the French infantry around Moscou and drove

---

441  The divisional battery of mitrailleuses, the 5/11th, were held in reserve.
442  1st and 2/17th.
443  5th, 6th and 7/8th; 7th and 10/4th and 3rd and 4/17th.
444  5/11th and 2/17th.
445  Five mitrailleuses, 21 batteries de 4 and four batteries de 12.
446  Each company had one section extended and two closed up in rear.

off Lacombe's company[447] of the 80th, who fell back on Commandant Molière's battalion[448] in Saint Hubert. The 8th, who lost many of their company commanders during this attack, reached a hollow about 200 yards north-west of the farm where they took shelter and opened an effective fire against its defenders, the Rifles being assisted by the increasingly accurate shelling of their artillery.

Additional fire support was provided by the three fusilier companies of the 67th who had edged forward alongside them and formed an extended line which ran in an arc around the east flank of Saint Hubert; another three sections,[449] their officers having prised the men from the cover afforded by the quarries, were also pushed forward to support the rifles. A subsequent attack by the skirmishing division of the 3rd Company was driven off but in the midst of this fierce firefight, one section of the 4th and part of the 1st managed to close to within 100 yards of Saint Hubert and engaged the garrison with a 'vive fusilade'. The remnants of four companies[450] held the quarries to the right of the road from where they also endeavoured to engage the French defences.

Further to the south, Major von Knobelsdorff led elements[451] of the 33rd in pursuit of the 55th when they abandoned the gravel and sand works to the south of Point du Jour. It soon became apparent that this position consisted of several interconnecting pits divided by stone walls; the scrape seized by Knobelsdorf afforded little cover so he urged his men forward again but was wounded scaling the first wall and the attack petered out. Nonetheless, despite being assailed by heavy chassepot and mitrailleuse fire from the French positions along the main road, the 33rd clung onto their hard-won positions on VIII Corps right flank.[452]

Tissonnière left his impressions of this bloody struggle:

> A number of shells were bursting in the bottom of the ravine. The cannons to our right (at Vernéville) growled. Our guns were in position; I heard the captain in command: 'First piece; Fire!' A terrible noise followed this order. A hail of shot fell about us; the fire of our guns increased. A poplar tree along the road, hit by a shell, fell on my 5th squad, killing the corporal and two men and wounding others. A caisson exploded, the debris killing a number of my 2nd squad. I sent the wounded to the rear to the two buildings at Point du Jour. A number of enemy skirmishers appeared through the woods; my men fired; they continued to advance without firing; some seemed to make hand signs. A chasseur approached from my left and told me that our advance guard were falling back; I ordered a cease fire. What's going on? Lacombe's company were falling back; they'd run out of ammunition. The cannon fire continued, although we suffered little within our shelters. The so-called enemy skirmishers advanced cautiously across the ground. They often fell to the ground, no doubt because on their right some other 'Pickelhaubes' had pushed forward from the sand pits (by Point du Jour) and opened fire. Our battery collected its limbers together and disappeared over

---

447  The 6th of the 3/80th.
448  3/80th.
449  From the 3rd and 4th companies 67th.
450  3rd Company 67th and 3rd, 4th and 11th companies 33rd.
451  1st and 2nd companies, on the right, II/33rd to the left.
452  Major von Gilsa, commanding the II Battalion was badly wounded in this attack.

the horizon. I withdrew my 2nd Section into the earthworks abandoned by the guns. Here we are in a good position. I fired a few trial shots which was fatal for one Prussian. At 400 metres! I say! The 2nd Section, well hidden, opened a vigorous fire against the 'Pickelhaubes' who fell back into the sandpits. Their men kept on coming, making lots of noise and responded with a few shots; call themselves skirmishers! Huh! My men reply with anger. The Prussians are across the Mance ravine. Just then the mitrailleuses come to our rescue.[453] They'd only fired off a few rounds before one of the limbers was damaged. The battery withdrew, leaving behind a gun when, after a few minutes, an officer, under fierce fire, took a 'prolonge',[454] fixed it to his horses' saddle and dragged the gun away. Bravo![455]

With the struggle around Saint Hubert reaching a crescendo, Frossard was forced to commit two divisions[456] simply to maintain the 'combat de feux' along the highway running to Point du Jour, whilst Le Boeuf deployed Aymard's division to cover the area between the road and Saint Hubert. Seven battalions[457] held the firing line between the farms of Saint Hubert and Point du Jour, overlooking the valley, whilst a few hundred yards to the rear another 12[458] awaited the impending attack on the reverse slope, but the intense fire of the enemy guns pinned them in position, preventing them from reinforcing the defences around Saint Hubert.

## The Capture of Saint Hubert

The arrival of 16th Division at Gravelotte around 2:30 p.m., allowed Goeben to release his reserves[459] to support the overextended 33rd and lend fresh impetus to his stalled offensive. The fusilier battalion of the 60th led the advance from Gravelotte with their commanding officer Colonel von Dannenberg at their head and after crossing the ravine under a murderous chassepot fire, deployed into an extended skirmish line to the south of the road.[460] The 6th and 8th companies with Lieutenant Colonel von Kittlitz, formed up on their right, with Major Müller and the 2nd, 4th and 3rd companies extending the line further to the south. The remnants of the 33rd[461] were swept up in the advance of these fresh troops, lending their support to the attack.

This new thrust again stalled in the face of a hail of shot and shell and as Dannenberg attempted to spur them forward, he fell wounded, his loss adding to the general sense of confusion. Despite heavy casualties, the fusilier companies inched their way into the gap between the two wings of the 33rd and as they did so, encouraged by 30th Brigade's advance, the 3rd and 4th companies from the I/33rd, together with III Battalion, edged to the right and closed in on Saint Hubert, seeking to extend the firing line in an arc to the south and east of the farm.

---

453  Captain Dupré's 9/5th Battery from the 2nd Division. Dupré was wounded on the 16th and so Captain Cornet commanded on the 18th.
454  This was the name for a cable the gunners carried in their limbers.
455  Bonnal, *St Privat II*, pp.157–159.
456  1st and 2nd.
457  3rd Chasseurs, 3/23rd, 1st and 2/32nd, 1/80th,1/85th and 1/44th.
458  I, II and III/67th, III/85th, III/32nd, I and II/23rd, I, II and III/8th, III/80th and II/85th.
459  Ten companies from the 60th.
460  North to south; 11th, 10th and 9th companies; the 12th was left by the wood.
461  From the 3rd, 4th and 11th companies.

Around 3:00 p.m., the remaining companies of the 60th emerged out of the ravine and as they approached the strongpoint, firing erupted from the Westphalian positions between Point du Jour and Moscou. Taking spirit from the presence of these reinforcements, the troops that had gone to ground around Saint Hubert, spontaneously rose to their feet and charged towards the farm in a mad rush, the main assault being undertaken by 'nine weak and almost leaderless companies.'[462] The outnumbered garrison,[463] already demoralised by the Prussian artillery, were in no shape to withstand this fresh attack and Molière gave the order to withdraw, although this was no easy task as many of the farmhouse exits were barricaded. One of the defenders, Captain Bertin[464] described how:

> Suddenly, from a semi-circle some 2–300 metres away a swarm of Prussians charged towards the farm yelling; they soon covered the ground, there were a good 2–3,000. At first our men held their positions, despite the shelling and opened a rapid fire; it was a lost cause, we couldn't do anything; the flood moved rapidly forward and submerged everything. Everyone fled towards the exits so that the wounded or those on the upper floors didn't fall into the hands of the enemy and made their escape towards the east.[465]

Despite being wounded, Molière successfully guided the greater part of the 3/80th back across the plateau and through the trenches occupied by the 1/80th and 1/85th to the relative shelter of the reverse slope. Hot on their heels, the 8th Rifles, with Bronikowski at their head, were the first to reach Saint Hubert and surged into the courtyard capturing some 40 prisoners.[466] The assailants suffered heavy losses[467] but were quick to fortify the buildings against counter attack as some of the riflemen took position behind the garden walls from where they engaged the French lines a little over 250 yards away. Another witness to the fall of the stronghold, Tissonnière, recalled:

> The defenders of Saint Hubert opened up from the loopholes on the southern side of the farm. The firing was very fierce. One could see the wall crumble under the blows of the German artillery. The guns of the men manning the garden wall fell silent. All of a sudden the crest of the slope south-west of the garden wall was filled with 'Pickelhaubes'. A line of flame! A burst of fire! Our men reply but many made their way to the rear. The battalion[468] seemed to be forming up in the courtyard. Shells

---

462  Fritz Hoenig, *Twenty-Four Hours of Moltke's Strategy* (Woolwich: Royal Artillery Institution, 1895) p.96.
463  From the 2/80th and the 1st and 2nd companies' 1/85th.
464  He died of wounds received in the defence of the farm in 1880.
465  Bonnal, *St Privat II*, p.155.
466  According to the German Official History the following took part in the capture of the farm; from the south a division of the 4th Company 67th, from the west a division of the 1st Company 67th, from the north-west were skirmishers from the 8th Rifles, in their rear from the quarries were the II/67th and elements of the fusilier battalion of the 67th. From the south there were two divisions from the I/67th. These units launched their attacks from along the main highway; the left wing of the 8th Rifles and a detachment of the I/67th moved round the north of the courtyard into the farm gardens.
467  The 67th lost 16 officers killed or wounded, in the short distance between the quarries and the farm.
468  II/80th.

Leading their advance, the 29th had been forced to break into sections so as to afford space on the narrow road for the cavalry and artillery to pass; in the resulting confusion their column was cut in half with the 10 rear companies separated from those in front so that initially, only the 1st and 4th, which were to the right of the road, were able to force their way onto the plateau. The 1st then attempted a charge against Point du Jour but were driven off and veered towards Saint Hubert taking shelter behind the garden walls; the 4th was also driven away from the farm and deployed on open ground alongside Gnügge's battery.

It was around 4:00 p.m. before the road cleared sufficiently enough for the 3rd and 2nd companies to resume their advance, the former towards Saint Hubert, the latter to the west where they occupied the quarries.[527] As these two companies reached the plateau, Colonel Eskens brought up the I and II/39th from Kameke's 14th Division, who occupied the eastern edge of the wood and pushed onto the ground between the Saint Hubert quarries and the gravel pits south of the Point du Jour. Eskens sent the 8th and 3rd companies to Saint Hubert; the 4th and 7th towards the quarries at the side of the main road to support the hard-pressed 29th.

Noting the precarious position of the batteries who were still clinging on to their positions on the far side of the ravine, he called forward the fusilier battalion to provide them with additional support, the flank companies taking position alongside the 8th and 3rd. On either side of the 33rd, groups of men from the 39th were sheltering from the hail of fire in the Saint Hubert quarries and the gravel pits in front of Point du Jour.[528]

When the III/29th reached the eastern side of the Mance, the battalion initially deployed to the north of the main road and Lieutenant Colonel von Blumröder pushed out strong detachments[529] towards Moscou farm. Unable to close on their objective, they clung to their hard-won positions for some time on the open ground between Moscou and Saint Hubert until increasing losses forced them to withdraw to the shelter of the ravine. The remainder of the battalion attempted to provide covering fire from the edge of the wood before advancing in support of the attack, but again were forced back by the heavy fire from front and flank, their only achievement being to inflate the already horrendous casualty list.[530]

Blumröder brought up the 5th Company to screen their retreat, but they too were driven off and the bulk of the fusilier battalion was then withdrawn to the cover of the ravine, south-west of Leipzig, with part[531] seeking cover alongside the men sheltering under the garden walls at Saint Hubert. The II/69th at the tail of the column was the last to reach the plateau and immediately charged forwards in the same bull-headed fashion, their officers seemingly oblivious to the fact that such unsupported attacks across open ground would simply be cut to ribbons.

The 6th and 7th companies[532] advanced past Saint Hubert where Captain Stephan directed two divisions of the 6th across the highway towards the French positions at Point du Jour. Even though the attack was undertaken with great courage and determination, closing to within 150

---

527  31st Brigade took almost an hour and a half to cover the 1½ miles.
528  The remains of the 9th, 10th and 12th companies 33rd were in the Saint Hubert quarries south of the main road, in and near Saint Hubert were the 3rd, 4th and 11th companies; in the gravel pit west of Point du Jour the II/33rd and in the Bois de Vaux the 1st and 2nd companies 33rd.
529  Five divisions from the 9th, 10th and 11th companies.
530  The 29th lost 26 officers and 450 men.
531  Two sections of the 12th and one from each of the 9th and 11th companies.
532  The 8th Company and the skirmishing division of the 3rd Company 67th were tasked with escorting Hasse's battery as he withdrew to the west of the ravine.

yards of the French shelter trenches, they were greeted by a murderous rifle and cannon fire and in Hoenig's words, 'they fell to pieces.'[533]

Eventually, the remnants of II Battalion assembled around Saint Hubert where the 1st Company 69th under Major von Hadeln, had rallied after the repulse of yet another attack against Moscou. The remainder of I Battalion struggled their way up the wooded slopes of the ravine but after failing to make any headway against Moscou,[534] fell back to the quarries and Saint Hubert where shortly after, they were joined by two companies of the II/69th.[535] Meanwhile, to the north, Lieutenant Colonel Marschall von Sulicki assembled the remainder of the 69th[536] and attempted to penetrate into the northerly parts of the bois de Génivaux.

The attack by the 10th Company against Moscou was easily repulsed, with the probe by 7th and 8th companies towards Chantrenne being blocked by superior enemy forces. After regrouping, the remnants of the fusilier battalion retreated down into the valley where, unable to take any further offensive action, they served as reserve for the left wing of VIII Corps fighting line. Allanson Winn was near Gravelotte at the time and encountered some of the fortunate survivors of these failed attacks, recalling:

> We met a major, of the 60th or 69th; he was covered with dust and dirt from head to foot and positively trembling and near speechless with excitement. 'My friends' he said 'I have had three horses killed under me today and lost many dear friends before my eyes.' Immediately after came a young and handsome officer with his arm broken and temporarily bandaged 'I cannot help being glad, now I have done my duty, that I have escaped with a shattered arm, which will not prevent my wearing our medal.' Leaning back against the bank we met with a private of the 33rd Regiment who, being shot through the hand, was going to the rear. We greedily asked him for news about the officers and quickly heard sad tidings. Major Rheinhart had been shot dead, having first had two horses shot from under him; the major of the III battalion was severely wounded; and finally, Major Baron von Gilsa, our own brave, honest, rough major of II battalion, was lying in an old mill at the bottom of the valley, shot through the arm and ankle.[537]

Whilst the appearance of fresh troops in the Mance ravine may have persuaded Jolivet to break off his counter attack, for the German commanders the introduction of the 60th into the firing line only served to complicate matters, as troops from VII Corps now encroached on VIII Corps battle space. On Goeben's left wing, a huge mass of soldiery, chiefly from the 30th and 31st Brigade, had congregated in the densely wooded ground bordering the Mance ravine. Around Saint Hubert and the quarries, some 43 companies– between 6–7,000 men –belonging to six

533  Hoenig, *Twenty-Four Hours*, p.124.
534  Hoenig states that in pushing through the thick woods the battalion 'lost their direction and their coherence.' See, *Twenty-Four Hours*, p.124.
535  5th and 6th companies.
536  7th, 8th and fusilier battalion.
537  Allanson Winn, *What I saw*, p.103.

different regiments and a rifle battalion were jumbled together, lacking any operational control or direction.[538]

To the south of the highway, dispersed in small groups, were the remnants of Esken's 39th and the greater part of 29th Brigade. Immediately to their rear, between Gravelotte and the edge of the wood, the 74th stood in readiness to engage. The 25th and 28th Brigades remained within the Bois de Vaux, close to where Zastrow's batteries were deployed. VIII Corps artillery were still in action, the left flank of their gun line being covered by five companies of infantry and the King's Hussar Regiment. In reserve, Steinmetz had three hussar regiments,[539] 32nd Infantry Brigade and three batteries of VII Corps. Around Malmaison, I Cavalry Division were still reorganising themselves following their abortive attempt to cross the Mance ravine.

Effective command of this mass of men was impossible and given the chaotic situation within the ravine, neither Steinmetz, Geoben or Zastrow had any real understanding of the state of affairs around Saint Hubert, nor how to best utilise the ample reserves that were available. As Hoenig was to comment in his critique of the battle: 'What was tactically prudent and practicable was not recognised, attempted or ordered, while what was tactically foolish and impossible was striven for with an amount of energy which would have been both necessary and successful at another point.'[540]

Shortly after 5:00 p.m., a lull descended over the Mance ravine as Steinmetz finally suspended his attack, seeking to reorganise his mangled forces. Across the Mance, Le Boeuf and Frossard similarly took the opportunity to reorganise their lines, their infantry exhausted following several hours of fierce combat with their guns falling silent to conserve ammunition.[541] As was the case in front of Amanvillers, the opposing sides had effectively fought one another to a standstill.

## Moltke Loses Control of the Battle

At 4:00 a.m. on the morning of 18 August, the Prussian king, accompanied by Moltke and his Staff, departed their quarters at Pont à Mousson, reaching the heights south of Flavigny two hours later. Passing through Gorze, Verdy du Vernois observed:

> We saw during our drive our telegraphic detachment still occupied in establishing telegraphic communication with Gorze. A comical impression was produced by seeing a French peasant in a white nightcap and blue blouse sitting by each telegraph pole already erected. The villagers had been made responsible for the safety of the poles, etc and had hit upon this plan of watching them in order to keep themselves from being punished.[542]

The renowned American general P H Sheridan accompanied the Royal party and recalled:

---

538 Hoenig observed 'A hotchpotch of this kind is unmanageable and a terrible cause of waste of strength.' See *Twenty-Four Hours*, p.125.
539 8th, 15th and 19th Hussars.
540 Hoenig, *Twenty-Four Hours*, p.126.
541 At this time only five French batteries remained in position, 7th and 6/11th, 11/4th, 9/4th and 9/11th.
542 Vernois, *Royal Headquarters*, p.78.

We mounted and moved off to the position selected for the King to witness the opening of the battle. This place was on high ground overlooking the villages of Rezonville and Gravelotte, about the centre of the battlefield of Mars la Tour and from it most of the country to the east of Metz could also be seen. The point chosen was excellent for the purpose,[543] though in one respect disagreeable, since the dead bodies of many poor fellows killed there two days before were yet unburied. In a little while the Kings escort began to remove these dead, however, bearing them away on stretchers improvised with their rifles and the spot thus cleared was much more acceptable. Then, when such exploded shells as were lying around loose had been cautiously carried away, the King, his brother, Prince Frederick Charles Alexander, the chief of staff, General von Moltke, the Minister of War, General von Roon and Count von Bismarck assembled on the highest point and I being asked to join the group was there presented to General von Moltke. He spoke our language fluently, explaining the position of the different corps, the nature of their movements then taking place and so on.[544]

Throughout the morning a constant stream of officers galloped back and forth to the command post at Flavigny as Moltke struggled to keep abreast of developments, Sheridan noting:

These reports were always made to the King first and whenever anybody arrived with tidings of the fight, we clustered around to hear the news. General von Moltke unfolding a map meanwhile and explained the situation. This done, the chief of staff, whilst awaiting the next report, would either return to a seat that had been made for him with some knapsacks, or would occupy the time walking about, kicking clods of dirt or small stones here and there, his hands clasped behind his back, his face pale and thoughtful.[545]

Given the extent of the battlefield, the time it took to transmit and receive orders and the personality of certain corps commanders, it was not surprising that Moltke lost control of the battle. Manstein's unintentional clash around Amanvillers and the subsequent discovery that the French line extended to Saint Privat meant he was always going to struggle to keep abreast of the rapidly developing situation. Accordingly, when Steinmetz and Goeben, in direct contravention of his orders, went over to the offensive, he became little more than an interested observer with the outcome of the day's fighting being dependent upon the actions of the individual corps commanders.

---

543  In fact, the heights only allowed the southern sector of the battlefield, where I Army were engaged, to be observed. The fighting around Amanvillers and St Marie aux Chênes could not be seen from this position.

544  General P. H. Sheridan, *Personal Memoirs Volume II* (New York: Charles L. Webster & Co. 1888) pp.367–369.

545  Sheridan, *Memoirs*, p.371.

## Bazaine's Apparent Disinterest

If the realisation was dawning on Moltke that his carefully laid battle plans to envelop the French line were going astray, for much of the day, Bazaine was reluctant to admit his forces were even engaged in a fight. Still fixated with the threat to his right flank, 'the sole object of his preoccupations,' he sent several messengers to observe the goings on in the Moselle valley. Seemingly confirming his fears, around 1:00 p.m. one officer reported that 'large numbers of men were passing across the river and making their way up the Gorze valley.'[546] Shortly after receiving this news, Lieutenant de Bellegarde arrived at headquarters with Canrobert's request for reinforcements; Bazaine, reluctant to leave his bivouac at Plappeville, replied:

> You tell Canrobert that I've ordered General Bourbaki to send you a Division of the Guard in case you are attacked and things become more serious; I'll also get General Soleille to send you a battery of 12-pdrs.[547] You can also tell Canrobert to send his caissons here to the parc to replenish their ammunition.[548]

Bazaine then ordered Bourbaki, whose Imperial Guard were deployed around Plappeville, to send a brigade to the spur north-west of Châtel Saint Germain; consequently, around midday, General Brincourt left his bivouac at the head of the 1st and 2nd Voltigeurs and a company of divisional engineers. Towards 1:00 p.m., they reached their designated position on height 313 and the engineers, assisted by the 1st Voltigeurs, rapidly excavated a rifle pit 200 metres long, across the spur of the hill.

The 1st Battalion were placed out in front deploying three companies as skirmishers along the eastern edge of the wood facing l'Arbre Mort, the remainder sheltering in the quarries next to the road running to Leipzig farm. The 2nd and 3rd battalions were arrayed along the crest overlooking the ravine behind scrub and the ruined castle walls. The 2nd Voltigeurs deployed to the left of the 1st with the brigade occupying this position until nightfall.

Back at Plappeville, Bourbaki ordered his remaining troops to stand to arms and around 1:00 p.m., instructed General Deligny[549] to send his 2nd Brigade to relieve Brincourt at Châtel Saint Germain; the men being told 'to keep hold of their knap sacks and not to lose sight of them.'[550] However, due to some inexplicable delay in transmitting these orders, the 3rd Voltigeurs did not leave Saint Quentin until around 3:45 p.m. A little later, General Garnier[551] was preparing to leave camp at the head of the 4th Voltigeurs when in quick succession he was first ordered to send them to Saint Privat, then to hold position at Saint Quentin and finally to recall the 3rd to Plappeville, although by the time these instructions reached Colonel Liau, they had already passed Châtel Saint Germain.

At the same time, Brincourt, responding to Le Boeuf's request for support, took it upon himself to countermand this order and instructed Liau to march to the aid of Aymard's division.

---

546  L'État-Major, *St Privat*, p.898.
547  The guns only departed for Saint Privat between 3:00 and 4:00 p.m.
548  Anon, *Procés Bazaine* p.277
549  Commander 1st Division.
550  L'État-Major, *St. Privat*, p.405.
551  Commander 2nd Brigade, 1st Division.

The Voltigeurs therefore once more turned about and made their way onto the plateau by l'Arbre Mort and after forming line of battle, moved into position to the rear of 1st Division. The 4th Voltigeurs, along with Guard Chasseur battalion, 1st Division's artillery and the guns of the reserve remained inactive on the plateau at St Quentin.

Due to the intervening hills, the sound of the battle raging between Point du Jour and Amanvillers was inaudible to Bourbaki at his camp at Plappeville. He had been given some sketchy information by Bazaine about Canrobert's position at Saint Privat[552] and around 2:30 p.m., after instructing his men not to leave their bivouacs, set off to undertake a personal reconnaissance accompanied by a few staff and a troop of dragoons.

When he reached Gros-Chêne the swirling clouds of gun smoke visible on the far side of the bois de Châtel left Bourbaki in no doubt as to the magnitude of the struggle taking place. Still without orders and not wishing to anticipate Bazaine's instructions, he decided to bring the only force still under his command closer to the fighting. Having earlier ordered General Picard to deploy his 2nd Division to front Saint Vincent farm around 3:20 p.m., he then ordered Picard's division forward to Gros-Chêne, astride the road running from Plappeville to Saint Privat. Bourbaki informed Bazaine of the actions taken and at the same time, despatched an officer to the fort at Saint Quentin 'To see if the enemy were making any progress along the banks of the Moselle in the direction of Vaux and Sainte Ruffine.'[553]

Towards 4:00 p.m., the head of Picard's column arrived on the plateau a little in front of Gros-Chêne, by Saint Vincent farm, where they deployed in two lines. 1st Brigade was to the front, its right resting on Saint Maurice farm;[554] 300 metres to the rear, 2nd Brigade was deployed by bataillons à demi distance; the regiment of Guides was behind the second line, the divisional artillery taking station between the two brigades. The 6th Company, 2nd Grenadiers occupied the farm buildings which commanded the road running to Sauly alongside the wood.

From his vantage position on the Saint Vincent plateau, Bourbaki became increasingly troubled about the huge clouds of dust visible to the north, which seemed to be coming from the direction of the road that ran between Woippy and Saint Privat. Concerned as to the cause, he sent his ADC, accompanied by several dragoons, off in the direction of Saulny in order to ensure the enemy were not intending to envelope Bazaine's right wing by way of the roads leading to Briey and Thionville.[555] At the same time, he ordered the grenadier division to move a short distance towards Amanvillers so as to be able to provide Ladmirault with support, if needed. Leaving behind the 6th Company to garrison the farm, the Grenadiers advanced along the road to Amanvillers in the same formation as they had previously deployed. Bourbaki halted the division at the mouth of the defile between the Bois de Saulny and Bois des Rappes, with orders to 'Deploy as necessary to defend this critical position in the rear of those corps already engaged.'[556]

---

552  This message, timed at 1:15 p.m. stated 'The Commander in Chief understands that Marshal Canrobert has been attacked on his right. At this moment intelligence is sketchy; it will probably prove to be a misinterpretation of the report given by Lieutenant de Bellegarde; as he left Saint Privat the guns of IX Corps were in action against Vernéville.' See l'État-Major, *St Privat*, p.401.

553  *Ibid*, p.402.

554  1st Grenadiers in line of battle to the right; the Zouaves to the left by battalions at half distance.

555  It was in fact the reserve batteries and the administrative train of 6 Corps.

556  L'État-Major, *St Privat*, p.404.

The 1/2nd Grenadiers were thrown into the wood on the right of the road and took position along its north-western edge; the 1/1st dug in and occupied the part of the wood that lay between the road and railway. The remainder of the division were to the rear; its batteries remained limbered along the road covering the defile and edge of the wood. It was a little before 5:00 p.m. and as noted by the French official history, at this critical time in the battle when '6 Corps positions had yet to be attacked … a full division of infantry, along with its artillery stood ready and waiting less than four kilometres from Saint Privat.'[557]

Bazaine's studied indifference to events meant his corps commanders were left to fend for themselves and as the French official history scathingly remarks, 'up to that time we cannot find any trace of any plans being made by the commander in chief who seemed content to simply wait for events to take their course.'[558] Earlier in the day, around 3:00 p.m. he received a message from Le Boeuf advising that 'he was being attacked all along the line;' about the same time Bazaine was handed Canrobert's despatch 'pressing him to send the ammunition column and infantry division he previously requested.'[559] The officer who delivered this report recalled:

> I explained to him the reasons for Canrobert's request and showed him on a map produced by a staff officer how 6 Corps was being attacked. I told him that when I left the situation was becoming very worrying. Bazaine responded by stating that the ammunition column had already left[560] and that an infantry division was about to be despatched. Just then the marshal was handed a note by a general de division[561] which said that everything was alright on 6 Corps' left wing.[562]

It would seem that the unidentified staff officer unwittingly sealed 6 Corps fate; on being informed that 'everything was alright' Bazaine halted the march of the infantry division, authorising just the release of the ammunition caissons.

Whilst the battle was raging to the west, Bazaine continued to receive regular updates about the situation to the south, where columns of enemy troops were reported to be making their way towards Gorze. Sometime between 3:30 and 4:00 p.m.,[563] he finally ordered his staff to mount up but as the French official history remarks, 'Somewhat curiously, given the despatches he'd received from Canrobert and probably Le Boeuf, the commander in chief instead made his way towards Saint Quentin as though he was still influenced by the concerns which had preoccupied his thoughts throughout the 16th.'[564] On arriving at the heights by the fortress, Bazaine discussed developments with generals Soleille and Canu, who briefed him on the

557 *Ibid.*, pp.404–405.
558 *Ibid.*, pp.406–407.
559 *Ibid.*, pp.406–407.
560 In fact, it only left Plappeville around 5:00 p.m.
561 The identity of this officer was never established.
562 See l'État-Major, *St. Privat*, pp.407–408.
563 There is some confusion about what time Bazaine left Plappeville; a number of staff officers thought it was around 2:00 p.m. others around 4:00 p.m. M. Viansson, the Maire of Plappeville later made a sworn statement that it was 'not until 4:00 p.m. that Bazaine left M. Bouteillers maison and made his way to St Quentin.'
564 L'État-Major, *St Privat*, p.408.

enemy movements along the road to Ars.[565] Canu then ordered the commander of the forts artillery to run a section up to ramparts, which at a range of 2,800 metres, opened fire on the enemy troops. True to form, Bazaine then 'spent considerable time overseeing the aiming of the guns and directing their fire.'[566]

After observing the Prussians continuing their march towards Jussy and Sainte Ruffine, Bazaine ordered Garnier to recall the 3rd Voltigeurs and then ordered Forton's cavalry to investigate this possible threat to his left flank. The cavalry left their bivouac at Maison Neuve around 5:00 p.m. with the cuirassiers at their head accompanied by two batteries of horse artillery. Whilst trotting through the village of Moulins, they came under harassing fire from a Prussian battery posted 2,000 metres away in the Moselle valley.[567] Ignoring the shelling, the troopers continued on their way and subsequently went into bivouac at Ban Saint Martin having seen little sign of enemy activity; such being the extent of Forton's involvement in the days fighting.

## The Flanking Attack Against Vaux

At the same time as he launched 1st Cavalry Division on their ill-fated sortie across the Mance ravine, Steinmetz instructed 26th Brigade[568] to make an energetic advance against the enemy's left flank from Ars. Any expectation of a coordinated action faded fast as the brigade's commander, General Baron von de Goltz, only received the order between 3:00 and 4:00 p.m. by which time the main advance had already descended into chaos. In accordance with Steinmetz's earlier orders designed to secure his left flank, Goltz had pushed the I/15th forward to the south-east of Vaux, whilst II Battalion held the railway bridge, the fusiliers the railway station at Ars. The 55th, artillery and cavalry were concentrated around the ironworks on the northern outskirts of the town with one company[569] being sent to occupy the vineyards at the Bois de Vaux.

On receipt of Steinmetz's instruction, von der Goltz directed the musketeer battalions of the 15th through Vaux towards Jussy. The fusiliers of the 55th followed in their rear and after clearing the Vaux vineyards, veered off towards the west side of Jussy, the 10th and 11th companies in the front line were sent in the direction of the Rozerieulles heights, whilst the remaining battalions[570] deployed to the east of Jussy, fronting towards Moulins les Metz. The general direction of the brigade's advance led them towards the Rozerieulles heights, which was held by Lapasset's brigade[571] on the extreme left flank of Bazaine's defensive line.

Earlier that morning, Lapasset had set an outpost line that ran from the Bois du Peuplier north-east towards Sainte Ruffine[572] with the village being held by the 3/97th. When the

565 The Prussian 26th Brigade.

566 L'État-Major, *St Privat*, p.409.

567 5/7th from 26th Brigade.

568 15th and 55th Regiments, 4th Squadron 8th Hussars, 5th Light battery.

569 12/55th.

570 The 2/55th only had 2½ companies; the 6th was with the train and a division of the 5th was escorting the guns.

571 84th and 97th, a company of the 14th Chasseurs and a battery of guns.

572 Three companies from the 84th were deployed between Jussy and the wood, with guards posted in the vineyard between Vaux and Jussy; two companies from the 2/97th held the ground between Jussy

cannonade erupted around Gravelotte at 1:00 p.m., he immediately reinforced his picquet line; Captain Ermenge who commanded the 2/97th, was ordered to send two companies to support the company[573] holding the Bois du Peuplier.

A little later, the remainder of the battalion, led by Captain Cambard, were sent to strengthen the defences within the wood so as to forestall any attempt by VII Corps to outflank the French left wing. To meet the impending attack, Lapassat placed the 2/97th in the Bois du Peuplier north of Vaux; three companies from the 84th were echeloned between the wood and Jussy; the outpost line of skirmishers deployed by both regiments were deployed amongst the vineyard on hill 236 and along the southern edge of the Bois du Peuplier. The area between Jussy and Ste Ruffine was held by three companies from the 2/97th; their positions covered by three companies of Voltigeurs; Ste Ruffine itself was occupied by the 3/97th. The 3rd Lancers, who had left their bivouac at Rozerieulles on their way to join up with Valabrègue's division at Châtel, were to the rear of the infantry. The guns of the 7/2nd were positioned on the 332 heights overlooking the Bois de Vaux.

Shortly after 4.00 p.m., Lapassat's tirailleurs opened fire on the foremost companies of the 15th as they moved into the open ground in front of Vaux. In response, I/15th pushed on through Vaux with Captain von Forckenbeck leading the bulk of the battalion along a sunken road which ran towards the heights, with Cambard's skirmish line falling back onto their supports. Forckenbeck's men were greeted by a few rounds from the fortress guns at Mont St Quentin that Bazaine had run out and at the same time the 2e batterie à cheval de la Garde[574] took position near Chazelles. A section of guns from the 1st Battery escorted by two squadrons of dragoons, deployed on the heights overlooking Jussy and Ste Raffine, where they were supported by three companies from the 4th Voltigeurs.

As III/15th pushed west, two companies[575] from the 55th took up defensive positions in the park alongside Vaux, seeking to secure the village against counter attack. Their skirmishers then pushed through to the northern outskirts of the village where, at a range of about 200 metres, they opened fire on the batteries of Guard artillery, forcing these guns and their supporting squadrons of dragoons, to retire.

No attempt was made to storm the strongly held heights and when, around 6:00 p.m., III/55th moved up to west of Jussy, they simply relieved the 15th who had exhausted their ammunition in a futile, long-range exchange of fire with the French tirailleurs. By 6.30 p.m., their attack, such as it was, had run out of steam; the remainder of the 55th deployed between Jussy and Vaux with the accompanying battery opening a long-range and largely ineffective fire against the French line from the north of Vaux. As the German official history concedes, this attack was too weak to bring about any decision on this part of the field and for the remainder of the day 'retained its character of a stationary action.'[576] By 8.30p.m., the firing ceased altogether, Lapasset's small force[577] having successfully kept von der Goltz's brigade at bay.

---

and Ste Raffine. In addition, three companies from the 4th Voltigeurs were also deployed between Ste Ruffine and Jussy.

573  From the 84th.
574  The battery did not fire a shot all day
575  1st and 3rd·
576  Clarke, Franco-German War II, p.109.
577  12 companies, supported by another six at Sainte Ruffine.

Similarly, an advance by Manteuffel along the east bank of the Moselle from Courcelles sur Nied, had little impact on the outcome of the days fighting. Major General von Zglinitzki led 4th Infantry Brigade toward Augny and around 4:30 p.m., ordered the 5th Light battery to deploy near Orly Farm and engage the French at Ste Ruffine. When 26th Brigade became embroiled in their firefight Manteuffel ordered forward the 3/5th to the eastern bank of Moselle in support, where they attracted the attention of the fortress artillery at St Quentin. When night fell, Manteuffel withdrew them to Augny and whilst 4th Brigade's efforts had no material impact on the days fighting, their presence no doubt played on Bazaine's concerns about the threat to his left flank

## Bazaine's Indifference to the Battle in the West

Whilst at Saint Quentin, Bazaine received Bourbaki's report expressing his concern about a possible threat to the French right flank. Seemingly, he failed to give much credence to this news, but half an hour later remarked to his staff, 'Let's go and see what's happening on that side of the road to Thionville.' One of his staff officers then suggested they send the artillery reserve off in this direction to which he responded: 'Yes, I think one might well send several batteries but we'll see about this later.'[578] Arriving on the heights 2–300 metres north-west of Fort Plappeville, Bazaine could make out signs of disorder in the rear of 6 Corps around seven miles distant and ordered Colonel d'Andlau to despatch two batteries from the reserve to 'so as to cover the pass at Saulny if it proves necessary.'[579]

Sometime later as the guns had still to depart, Bazaine, seemingly impatient to get them moving, rode off in the direction of the artillerie parc on the col de Lessy. En-route he met Bourbaki's officier d'ordonnance, Captain de Beaumont, of the Empress Dragoons who was returning from his scouting mission to Saint Quentin, quizzing him about the fighting. Beaumont recalled that on being recognised, Bazaine asked him:

'Captain, where are you going?' I then gave him an account of the mission I'd been tasked with. 'Since you are returning to General Bourbaki,' he told me, 'Tell him to warn Marshal Canrobert, who's to his front, that he's going to withdraw all the Guard.' Very much concerned by the importance of the order I'd received, I asked the marshal to allow me to repeat the order he'd just given me, in order to be sure that I'd understood him: 'You are giving me the order for General Bourbaki to return with all the Guard and to inform Marshal Canrobert, who's to his front, of this news?' One of the staff officers accompanying the Marshal then added 'That's what he's said to General Bourbaki and as Marshal Canrobert is on the front line, the general must warn him that he can no longer support him' and the marshal then added 'The day's done. The Prussians wanted to have a go at us and it's over.' I saluted the marshal and left to deliver the order that I'd been given.[580]

578  L'État-Major, *St Privat*, pp.411–412.
579  *Ibid* p.412.
580  Anon, *Procès Bazaine*, p.278. This statement was disputed by Bazaine who claimed he had instructed Borbaki to remain in place (rester) rather than to retire (rentrer). When challenged on this, Bazaine told the Court 'All this, incidentally, happened very quickly; Commandant Beaumont's horse was

As the French official history freely concedes, it is difficult to establish just what passed between the marshal and Commandant Beaumont but whatever was said during their brief exchange, it marked one of the few occasions on 18 August that the French commander in chief evinced any interest in the battle raging between Point du Jour and Saint Privat.[581] His preoccupation about the threat to his flank and evident intention to withdraw his forces into Metz may explain his apparent disinterest in the fighting but it does not excuse his failure to issue timely orders or provide support to his embattled corps commanders who were, effectively, left to their own devices.

## A Royal Rebuke for Steinmetz

Shortly after noon, Moltke received Frederick Charles' despatch advising that he had extended his flanking manoeuvre further to the north around Sainte Marie aux Chênes. Two hours later, when the noise of firing around Gravelotte grew too loud to ignore, the Royal party moved up to the Rezonville Heights, passing on their way the advancing columns of Fransecky's II Corps, whose commander was told to assemble his men at Rezonville and await orders. Encouraged by the positive reports from I Army, around 4:00 p.m., the decision was taken to relocate headquarters to Gravelotte. Accompanied by a large staff, the king rode forward and half an hour later, as he neared the scene of the fighting, was handed Steinmetz's despatch which 'reported the success of the Prussian artillery against the batteries at Point du Jour, the

trotting; me, I was riding very slowly, I called after him and I remember the word, 'Stay'. Bazaine's version of events was supported by his former officier d'ordonnance Capitaine de Mornay Soult who said that when Bazaine met with de Beaumont, he said to him 'Since you're going to find General Bourbaki, tell him to inform Marshal Canrobert that he'll be staying where he is, but especially, that he's not even to get lightly engaged.' De Mornay Soult told the Court that he thought de Beaumont had failed to hear this, because of the noise of the cannon fire in the background and was just about to repeat what Bazaine had said when the marshal interrupted him and repeated the order, word for word. As de Beaumont still looked confused and, apparently, still failed to comprehend what the marshal had said, de Mornay Soult leant across to de Beaumont and said 'I beg your pardon for repeating them to you, but the Marshal expressed himself thus: 'Tell General Bourbaki to get in touch with Marshal Canrobert and, above all, not even to engage lightly.' De Beaumont denied this – 'I absolutely stand by what I just said.' The French official history has a slightly different version of events; it details how Bazaine told the post war Inquiry he instructed de Beaumont to inform Bourbaki to 'Keep in touch with Canrobert but avoid any rash engagement.' The aide steadfastly maintained that he was told to 'Go to Bourbaki and tell him to warn Canrobert that he's withdrawing the Guard.' Afraid he had misunderstood the marshal, de Beaumont asked 'Is it Marshal Canrobert who should withdraw after informing General Bourbaki, or is it Bourbaki who should retire after informing Canrobert?' One of Bazaine's staff officer interjected 'It's General Bourbaki who should inform Marshal Canrobert that he can no longer support him and is going into his cantonments.' Bazaine then added 'That's right! The Prussians wanted to have a go at us, but we're done for the day. Now I'm going to withdraw.' See l'État-Major, *St Privat*, pp.442–443. It is impossible to determine just what words were exchanged between de Beaumont and Bazaine but an officer from the Guards general staff, Capitain de Lacale, having met the marshal, affirmed that he said to him 'It's useless, The Guard will return to their bivouacs. Another officer, Captain de Saney, recalled Bazaine saying 'Everything is fine. Our positions have been assaulted with great ferocity, but we have held them. The day can be considered as completed' See *Procès Bazaine*, pp.279–280.

581  Even this limited intervention counted for little; by the time Beaumont passed to order to Deligny, elements from 6 Corps were already falling back in disorder.

victorious advance of the troops through the woods east of Gravelotte, the capture of Saint Hubert and the advance of his cavalry and artillery across the Mance valley.'[582]

Although this development was contrary to Moltke's plan –the envelopment of Bazaine's right flank before engaging with their left – the king took this news at face value and believed that the French had indeed, been thrown back on Metz; victory seemed imminent. As Verdy du Vernois recalled it came as some surprise therefore when the true position became evident:

> But we soon perceived that the actual state of affairs was far from being what we had imagined. We had taken our stand directly behind the deployed artillery of the VIII Corps and therefore in close proximity to the line of battle. Now it is not advisable for the supreme commanders to approach too near to the fighting, as then minor incidents of the combat in the immediate vicinity force themselves upon their attention and occupy it to such an extent that the supervision of the whole becomes impaired. But one thing became clear from the first, which was by no means agreeable, viz. that the heights which Steinmetz had reported as taken, were by no means in our possession and that Hartmann's cavalry division, which was reported to have started in pursuit, was on this side of the defile, instead of on the other, to our right front, on the sloping ground towards Gravelotte.[583]

As Moltke was to caustically record in his memoirs: 'Chassepot bullets even reached the position of the Royal Commander in Chief and his personal staff and Prince Adalbert's horse was shot under him.'[584] Steinmetz's subsequent despatch to headquarters reluctantly acknowledged the setback; it admitted that his men had failed to 'pursue' the enemy and grudgingly conceded that the battle in front of Gravelotte 'was still swaying backwards and forwards in an indecisive manner and that in order to make progress … a vigorous attack upon his right wing was necessary.'[585] Sheridan recalled: 'Just after getting there, we first learned fully of the disastrous result of the charge which had been entered upon with such spirit; and so much indignation was expressed against Steinmetz, who, it was claimed, had made an unnecessary sacrifice of his cavalry, that I thought he would be relieved on the spot, though this was not done.'[586] The errant general then came forward to brief the king in person; Sheridan noted:

> Followed by a large staff Steinmetz appeared in the village presently and approached the King. When near, he bowed with great respect. When the king spoke to him, I was not close enough to learn what was said; but his Majesty's manner was expressive of kindly feeling and the fact that in a few moments the veteran general returned to the command of his troops, indicated that, for the present at least, his fault had been overlooked.[587]

582  Clarke, *Franco-German War II*, p.103.
583  Vernois, *Royal Headquarters*, p.83.
584  Count Helmuth von Moltke, *The Franco-German War of 1870–71*(London, Harper Brothers, 1907)
585  Clarke, *Franco-German War II*, p.104.
586  Sheridan, *Memoirs*, p.373.
587  *Ibid.*

According to Hoenig, his reception was somewhat was frostier:

> The meeting of the king and general took place at too great a distance from their staffs for the latter to be able to know what the king said to the general; but the witnesses judged from the forcible gestures of the king and from the seriousness of his face when Steinmetz left him that the king had expressed to the general his disapprobation of the steps which he had taken up to that time, especially with regard to the prematurely engaged attack of the I Army – and this was the case. From this moment a yet more marked ill humour took possession of Steinmetz and it would seem that he no longer inclined to seek the presence of the king, or to express to him his opinions on this matter. From that moment the general simply carried out what he was ordered to do so.[588]

It is not surprising that the Royal reaction was so frosty; the chief of staff's carefully laid plans had clearly gone astray and the realisation that I Army's disobedience had achieved little other than incur large number of casualties no doubt accounted for his cool reception. Whilst Steinmetz deserved censure for the premature and haphazard way in which he committed his men to the fighting in the Mance, he was probably more at fault for failing to seek to envelop their left wing which would have caused Bazaine more serious problems.

Whilst the actions of Steinmetz, Goeben and Zastrow all attracted varying degrees of censure after the war, Moltke's conduct also came in for criticism although this was glossed over in the German official history. One of his fiercest critics, Fritz Hoenig, highlighted his failure to relocate the Royal headquarters to a position where he could more easily supervise II Army's vital outflanking manoeuvre. Given the time taken to send and receive despatches from Flavigny, Moltke exercised little influence on the day's events and even less control. Even when it became clear that Steimetz and Geoben had, contrary to his instructions, committed their forces, he did nothing to rein them in.

Steinmetz's attack across the Mance had ground to a halt. Around Amnavillers, Manstein's corps had been drawn into a bloody and costly attack which had similarly failed to make any impression against the centre of the French line whilst to the north, although the Saxons and Wurtemburg's Guard Corps had secured Sainte Marie aux Chênes, they had still to find Canrobert's flank. With little to show for the heavy losses incurred in front of Saint Hubert and Amanvillers, matters were going to take a serious turn for the worse as Prince August launched the Prussian Guard in an impetuous and ill-considered attack against Saint Privat.

---

588  Hoenig, *Twenty-Four Hours*, p.145.

# 4

# The Battle of Gravelotte, 18 August 1870 – Defeat

## The Saxon Plan

Following the capture of Sainte Marie, Prince Albert reflected on how best to implement the orders he had been given to outflank the French line. Originally, he intended to seize Roncourt first and then assault Saint Privat but from his position to the west of Sainte Marie, noticed the French were moving troops into the Bois d'Auboué which would need to be secured prior to any attack on Saint Privat. He could not afford to leave this important bulwark in enemy hands and therefore, instructed his brother to drive off the enemy troops so as to open the way for his push on Roncourt.

Prince George tasked the I/108th Rifle Regiment under Major Freiherr von Lindeman with this mission, with Major von Dziembowsky's II Battalion in support on his left. The Hautmécourt ravine cut through the heavily overgrown wood which slowed their progress but the ground to the west of the cutting was found to be unoccupied. However, as the Saxons edged their way into the eastern part of the thicket, they came up against a strong force of skirmishers[1] and although Lindeman's men were sheltered from the worst of their fire by the ravine, their stubborn resistance brought the battalions advance to a halt.

A little after 4:30 p.m., Colonel von Hausen sent the III/108th to clear another sector of the wood and meeting with little opposition, soon pushed the tirailleurs back towards Montois. Following this success, Craushaar, the brigade's commander, committed 1st Body Guard Regiment No. 100; I Battalion reinforced the right wing of the 108th, the III the left, whilst the II, formed in half battalions, served as support. As these fresh troops edged into the firing line, they encountered stiffening resistance from the French; the 1st Company became engaged in a firefight with the 1/75th who were sheltering in a depression to the rear of a ditch and struggled to make any headway but the 10th and 12th companies, on the left, had more success and drove off the opposing tirailleurs.

The 2nd Grenadiers were then sent to support the rifles and Body Guard; their I Battalion had already begun its advance on Montois when Albert, worried that his plan for a coordinated

---

1    From the 75th Ligne.

assault on Roncourt could be derailed by this growing fire fight, called off their attack so as to allow time for the outflanking force to get into position. It was around 5:00 p.m. before the fighting in the woods subsided but Craushaar took the opportunity afforded by this respite to rally his brigade around the eastern edge of the wood; in fact, by this time, firing along much of the front from Saint Hubert in the south to Saint Privat in the north practically ceased as both sides paused to reorganise their troops and replenish ammunition.

During this lull in the fighting, Guard Corps' Reserve artillery[2] together with the guns of the 1st Field Division, had assembled to the southwest of St Ail.[3] Their commander, Prince Ingelfingen, requested fresh orders and was instructed by Prince August to conserve his ammunition for the decisive engagement at Saint Privat. Ingelfingen was then briefed by Dannenberg[4] that the Guards would only launch their attack after the Saxons had completed their envelopment. He would be notified when they were in position so his artillery could help prepare the ground with a preliminary bombardment. In the meantime, until XII Corps reached Roncourt he was to maintain a harassing fire on the French troops in and around Saint Privat.

2nd Guard's divisional batteries were initially deployed fronting Sainte Marie, being somehow unaware that the village had been captured, but when appraised of the true situation, they relocated a few hundred metres to the south facing Saint Privat; 6th Light on the right, 5th Heavy in the centre and 6th Heavy on the left. As there were no enemy batteries visible, they were instructed to target Saint Privat but had to break off their bombardment so as deal with the enemy tirailleurs who by now had closed to within 600 metres of their position. In response, I Battalion 4th Grenadier Regiment were tasked to serve as close escort so as to protect the guns from the enemy skirmishers whose long-range fire had already caused Hohenlohe considerable irritation.[5]

Further north, following the capture of Sainte Marie, as 47th Brigade formed up to the northwest of the village, the Saxon artillery began their preparations for the assault on Saint Privat with the guns from the corps' Reserve, 24th Division and the 6th Heavy taking up positions along the road running to Hautmécourt, facing east; the left of this gun line was anchored on the Bois d'Auboué, the right, close to Sainte Marie. Having completed their redeployment around 6:00 p.m., 12 batteries opened up on the French infantry occupying the open ground between Roncourt and Saint Privat. However, shortly after commencing fire, Albert ordered them to relocate to new positions from where they could provide better support for his forthcoming attack against his primary target, Roncourt.

2    2nd Field Division.
3    The 4th Light battery was by itself about 300m southeast of the village.
4    Guard Corps' chief of staff.
5    He was later to relate: 'Three French battalions all extended in skirmish order lay in front at a range of from 900 to 1000 paces, all their men being covered by three fences between the fields. A similar line lay 100 yards in rear and a third further back still. The foremost of these three lines fired without ceasing at the batteries ... The General commanding the Guard Corps had sent six companies of infantry as an escort to my extended line of artillery; they could not injure the enemy's infantry on account of the short range of the needle gun, but were kept in little groups in the intervals of the batteries in order to prevent small bodies of the enemy from rushing in on the guns. When the fire of the enemy's rifles became too troublesome, I ordered ... that two batteries should fire on the line of skirmishers. This kept them quiet.' See *Letters on Artillery*, pp123–124.

With regard to the Saxon infantry, from 45th Brigade I/101st Grenadiers occupied the Bois d'Aboué, II and III battalions to the west, 108th in the eastern corner and split between the north and south, the 100th deployed along the edge of the treeline. 46th Brigade, together with the 1st Heavy battery had yet to clear Moinville whilst the enveloping force, 48th Brigade, accompanied by 1st Horse battery and six squadrons from the Guard and 3rd Reiter regiments, were still en-route for Montois having only just left Aboué.[6] 1st and 2nd Lancers were sent to observe the road between Etain and Briey, with 1st and 2nd Reiter regiments supporting the 46th.

## Prince August and the Prussian Guard

Whilst waiting for the assault against Saint Privat, Prince Frederick and his II Army staff positioned themselves on a hill southwest of Habonville, south of the Metz-Etain railroad. Given the losses incurred by Manstein he was concerned that any French counter attack against IX Corps could pierce his line, placing both the Guard and Saxon corps in a perilous position. He therefore instructed 3rd Guard Infantry Brigade[7] to move up from Batilly in support of Manstein's left flank and hold themselves at his disposal. The infantry[8] deployed to the rear of the 25th Infantry Division south of Habonville, whilst the brigade's artillery reinforced IX Corp's gun line at Champenois. Prince Albert was to be found to the west of Sainte Marie from where he could monitor the progress of the Saxon flanking attack, whilst Manstein remained at his vantage point at the northern edge of the Bois de la Cusse.

From his vantage point to the west of Habonville the Guard's commander was only too aware of the heavy losses suffered by IX Corps during their failed attempt to take Amanvillers and shared Frederick's concern that Bazaine would most likely launch a counter attack against this weak point in the Prussian line before seeking to slip away into Metz. As such, he was anxious to get his assault on Saint Privat underway as soon as possible in order to disrupt the French plans; frustratingly both Moltke and Frederick had instructed him to hold his ground until XII Corps were ready to launch their flank attack. However, Albert's decision to extend his flanking manoeuvre to include Roncourt, meant further time would elapse before the Saxons were in position. In August's view, this would only increase the likelihood that the enemy would break off the fight and again make their escape. Concerned that night would fall or the French would slip away before XII Corps completed their envelopment, he was impatient to get the Guard moving.

In addition to these purely military considerations, it would seem that his subsequent actions were also influenced by more selfish motives; his men had yet to see any serious action to date and if this were to be the decisive battle of the campaign, he was anxious to ensure that his Guard claimed the victory laurels. Besides, as had been shown earlier in the day when the high

---

6    1st Squadron Guard Cavalry under Captain von Klenck was sent to Richemont, 2nd Squadron 3rd Cavalry under Captain von Polenz were sent to Uckange.

7    1st Guard Grenadiers, Kaiser Alexander and 3rd Guard Grenadiers, Königin Elizabeth. Commanded by Colonel Knappe von Knappstaedt, it was accompanied by the Guard Rifle battalion, 5th Light Guard battery and the 2nd and 3rd Guard Pioneer companies.

8    The Rifle Battalion, II and III/1st Guard Grenadier's were in the first line; 3rd Guard Grenadiers in the second. 1/1st Guard Grenadiers were sent to occupy Habonville, in place of the Guard Fusiliers.

command swapped the positions of the Guard and XII Corps, the Saxon's were not entirely trusted; there still being lingering doubts as to their reliability amongst some of the Prussian High Command. Moreover, how would it look politically if the Guard stood idly by whilst their erstwhile enemies, the Saxons, were seen to be delivering the decisive blow against the French? As the evening drew on, August became increasingly troubled with this quandary, persuading himself that the success or failure of Moltke's plan lay in his and the Guards, hands.

From his elevated viewpoint, August could clearly see Saint Privat although the full extent of the enemy defences, as was Roncourt, were obscured by powder smoke from the fierce fighting around Sainte Marie and the Bois d'Auboué. Sometime after 4:30 p.m., as the French artillery fire diminished, he thought he could see troops moving from Roncourt towards Saint Privat which he believed indicated a weakening of their position.[9] As with Steinmetz's earlier misjudgement about the French withdrawal from Saint Hubert, August's lust for glory seems to have triumphed over common sense and seeking some pretext to justify an attack, jumped to the erroneous conclusion that 6 Corps were pulling out of Saint Privat.

In his view, Canrobert was either intending to withdraw into Metz or possibly, to support Ladmirault's counter attack against Manstein. As either option would give rise to undesirable consequences, August needed little persuading to commit his infantry. It seems that his decision may have been, in part, influenced by his belief that XII Corps would begin their flank attack around 5:00 p.m. If he did not act immediately, the Saxons would steal his and the Guards, glory. It is also possible that he mistook the brief bombardment of Saint Privat by the Saxon artillery before they relocated to new positions, heralded an assault by their infantry; even more reason to get his men into action as soon as possible.[10]

Anxious to seize the moment and with it the victor's laurels, he was about to issue his orders when X Corps artillery commander[11] galloped over from Batilly asking to be briefed on the current situation. After learning of his intention to attack Saint Privat, Becke asked if he proposed to make use of the Guard artillery to prepare the way for the infantry. On being told by August that they were already engaged in support of Manstein's gun line, he urged him to postpone his assault as he thought he could deploy 10 of his batteries against Saint Privat within 20 minutes. August retorted that any delay would prevent him from supporting the Saxons and would leave them open to defeat; in any event, as night was fast approaching, he felt it important to get his attack underway as soon as possible so that his corps would 'gather the fruits of success.'[12]

Clearly, as far as August was concerned, it seems that his principal objective was to ensure his men got into Saint Privat before the Saxons, regardless of the cost. Whatever his reasoning, the Guard Corps would pay dearly for this rash decision.

---

9    This was in fact the withdrawal of the 75th and 91st from the fighting around Sainte Marie and Auboué.

10   In fact, the Crown Prince's despatch stated that the Saxons would begin their enveloping march on Roncourt-Saint Privat at that hour; as a consequence, it was probable that actual assault from Montois would not commence until sometime after 6:15 p.m.

11   Colonel Baron von der Becke.

12   Bell, *St Privat*, p.276. August held that his orders from Prince Frederick 'to wait with his serious infantry attack until XII Corps would be able to effectively interfere' gave him sufficient freedom of action to decide when to launch his assault. See Bell, *St Privat*, p.275.

## The Defence of Saint Privat

Canrobert had quickly concluded that he could not hold Sainte Marie against clearly superior enemy forces and concentrated his efforts on reinforcing his position at Saint Privat. The 2/10th and the 1/91st were deployed in a dense skirmish line on the open ground running down towards Sainte Marie whilst to the north, the shortage of men meant that Roncourt was occupied by a single battalion, the 1/9th. 1/75th was positioned forward of the crest facing the Bois d'Auboué with the 2nd and 3rd battalions lining the road that crossed the ridge running towards Saint Privat; the 3/10th being pushed forward 100 metres on their left flank. Five batteries[13] were deployed along the rear of the crest with another three[14] further to the rear; Barail's Light cavalry[15] and two batteries of horse artillery[16] were in reserve.

The village itself was strongly held by several battalions[17] with the 1st and 2/100th taking up position in hamlet of Jérusalem. To the south of Saint Privat, the 3/93rd were deployed about 450 metres down the slope in a line across the highway running to Sainte Marie, the 1/70th covering their left flank whilst the 9th Chasseurs and 1/12th stood further to their rear. To the south of the road, several companies[18] of the 2nd and 3/93rd were pushed forward to within 300 yards of the Prussian positions, their incessant chassepot fire causing considerable inconvenience to both the Guard artillery and infantry.

To the right of this skirmish line, three battalions of the 25th, their left flank refused, were deployed along the track which ran from Sainte Marie to Amanvillers; the 26th extended the line to the south. There were two batteries[19] in support and further to their rear, three battalions from the 28th.

In reserve, south-east of Jérusalem were Gondrecourt's brigade of dragoons;[20] to their left, the guns of the 5/19th, to their right the batteries of the 5th and 7/8th although most of the artillery had already withdrawn from the fighting line to resupply and make good their losses. The artillery promised by Bazaine had still to arrive,[21] but to the south of Saint Privat, De Narp's three divisional batteries[22] afforded some support. Cissey also deployed five companies from the 20th Chasseurs as tirailleurs to the north of the Metz-Etain railroad on knoll 328.[23] The 57th were on the reverse slope, to the rear of the skirmish line and, just to the north of the railway, 1/73rd and 1/6th. The 2/73rd formed a second line whilst in reserve, 1st Ligne were positioned to the west of the Saint Privat-Amanvillers road with all three battalions deployed in line of battle.

13  9/13th, 3rd, 6th and 7/4th and 6/19th.
14  2/9th, 4th and 3/100th.
15  2nd and 3rd Chasseurs and 2nd Chasseurs d'Afrique.
16  7th and 8/18th.
17  3/9th, 1st and 3/10th, 2/12th, 3/13th, 1/93rd and 1/ 94th.
18  1st and 2nd companies,1/93rd and 4th, 5th and 6th companies 2/63rd.
19  12/8th and 10/13th.
20  2nd Brigade from Legrand's Division; 3rd and 11th Dragoons.
21  6th and 7/13th; these guns later took position on the spur running south from Saint Privat between the 3/28th and the 2/70th.
22  5/15th, 9/15th and 12/15th from Cissey's 1st Division 4 Corps.
23  1st, 2nd 3rd, 4th and 5th.

Patry, who belonged to the 1/6th, described the frustration felt by the infantry towards the artillery who had seemingly abandoned them to their fate:

> How long did we stay in this position, exchanging ineffective rifle fire with the enemy, all the while enduring his shellfire … From time to time, we chatted amongst ourselves in the rear of the soldiers … Ravel, an old colleague from St Cyr said 'None of us will get out of here and as for me I'm sure I won't make it'. I tried in vain to reassure, although I wasn't in high spirits myself; not that I had the slightest apprehension concerning my own fate, but because it seemed very clear to me that we were engaged in bad business and incompetently engaged at that. Understandably, we couldn't help but criticise the fact the fact that the mass of cavalry which stood behind us, pointlessly taking casualties, had not been launched against the German infantry at the point when, disorganised by our fire, it had been forced to retreat. And then the artillery! Could one conceive of such a thing? Batteries which cannot sustain the contest for more than a few minutes and which are then obliged to bring up their limbers straight away! The infantry always bore the brunt of things and for the whole duration of the combat at that. We were being needlessly sacrificed. Moreover, there was never any regular issue of rations. As ever, you always had to fight on empty stomach.[24]

## Prince August Decides to Attack

Clear in his own mind as to what was required to secure the glory due to his corps, August issued his instructions for the attack on Saint Privat; 4th Guard Infantry Brigade from St Ail, 1st Guard Infantry Division from Sainte Marie and despatched his chief of staff, Dannenberg to obtain Frederick's approval. August's request fell on receptive ears; the prince had grown increasingly concerned with the situation. Manstein's corps had been roughly handled by the French, there was still no sign of the expected Saxon envelopment and only a few hours of daylight remained to secure victory. From his position southwest of Habonville, he observed movements in the French positions around Roncourt as well as activity between Saint Privat and Amanvillers; could this foreshadow the anticipated counter attack against IX Corps? The non-appearance of the Saxons was put down to the fact that they must have encountered enemy forces attempting to break out to the north.

Logically, or so ran the argument at II Army Headquarters, to regain the initiative and disrupt any planned counter attack, the Guard Corps must seize Saint Privat and break Canrobert's defensive position. Given the absence of enemy fire, it was assumed their artillery in this sector had already been silenced by the Prussian guns and even though the Saxons had failed to put in an appearance, X Corps had arrived at Vernéville and could be called on to exploit the Guard's success. Therefore, when Dannenberg briefed him on August's proposals, he needed

24    Patry, *La Guerre*, pp.105–106.

little persuading and immediately sanctioned the attack[25] and ordered Voights Rhetz to move up to St Ail for support.[26]

Having secured Frederick's approval, August lost no time in implementing his plan. Dannenberg rode over to General von Budritzki[27] at St Ail with instructions for 4th Guard Infantry Brigade 'To advance now simultaneously with the 1st Guard Division, which has taken Sainte Marie, to attack against Saint Privat, directing on the southern portion of the village of Jérusalem.'[28] He then galloped off to 1st Division at Sainte Marie leaving Budritzki to brief the brigade commander, General von Berger. In turn, he assembled his field officers in the shelter afforded by a small depression north of St Ail and at 5:15 p.m., announced to the expectant group:

> The brigade will advance south of the road on Saint Privat and the hill to the south of it; the attack will be supported by the 1st Guard Infantry Division advancing north of the road. Each regiment, on the left the Franz Regiment, on the right the Königen regiment, will send one battalion ahead in column of companies; the remaining battalions to follow in half battalions and take up company column formation when entering the effective hostile fire zone.[29]

The ground over which 4th Brigade were to attack, rose in a gentle incline north-east from St Ail towards Saint Privat and the ridge of high ground running to the south of the village. As a consequence, only the church, some tall buildings and a few houses at its edge were visible from the Prussian positions. Their proposed route extended to some 2,600 metres, which for the most part, was entirely devoid of cover. The battlefield to the south was bounded by the ravine running north from Habonville, the road running from Sainte Marie to Saint Privat formed its northern boundary.

Von Berger's attack was directed at the junction between 6 and 4 corps, with Canrobert's troops facing southwest along the ridge running from knoll 328 to hill 321, whilst Ladmirault's men fronted west along the slightly lower ground to the south. As 4th Brigade made ready to advance, the tirailleurs[30] screening Ladmirault's position, made another surge against the Guard's divisional guns positioned to the north of the Bois de la Cusse. Their attack was driven

---

25   Following the battle, Frederick was anxious to distance himself from any blame and let it be known he had simply 'acquiesced' to August's request rather than issuing him with a direct order. Frederick was of course, only a few hundred yards from August's position and had he had any doubts or concerns about the attack, he could have easily ridden across to check the position for himself. He did in fact move up to a new position west of Habonville as soon as the Guard marched off but by then it was too late and, in any event, he took no action to call off the assault.

26   X Corps set off from Batilly around 5:30 p.m. escorted by 5th Cavalry Division.

27   Commander 2nd Guard Infantry Division.

28   Bell, *St Privat*, p.280. At that time III/4th Guard Grenadier Regiment were immediately north of St Ail, behind it stood II Battalion facing east; to its left the 2nd Grenadier Regiment had also deployed in two lines; II Battalion in front, the fusilier battalion to the rear with the I on the left. I/4th Guard Grenadier Regiment had been previously detached as escort to the Guards gun line.

29   Bell, *St Privat*, p.280.

30   Probably from the 20th Chasseurs.

off by the escorts[31] who chased the skirmishers in the direction of hill 320 to the southwest of Saint Privat, their pursuit being brought to a standstill on open ground about 1,400 metres south-east of St Ail by the chassepot fire from the main French positions, whereupon the guards dropped to the ground, seeking cover on the exposed hillside.

## The Guard Attacks

4th Brigade formed up for their assault under an annoying fire which, even at long range, inflicted casualties. 2nd Guard Grenadiers, the Kaiser Franz, were to the left; in the front line 7th and 6th companies; to their rear the 8th and 5th companies formed a half battalion, the same formation adopted by the two second line supports who were echeloned to either side of the lead battalion.[32] To the right of the Kaiser Franz, the fusilier battalion, 4th Guard Grenadiers.[33] The 12th and 9th companies were out front, followed the 11th and 10th as a half battalion, the foremost companies of both leading battalions deploying skirmishers. To the right of the fusilier battalion, II Battalion; 7th and 6th companies in front, 8th and 5th again as a half battalion to the rear. To their right, 2nd and 1st companies I Battalion took up position east of St Ail, with the 4th and 3th some considerable distance to their right.

Deployed for the attack, the frontage of the brigade extended from St Ail halfway towards Sainte Marie, the formation taking care as they advanced not to mask the fire of the batteries of 2nd Guard Division. Berger took position in the centre of the brigade, followed by the divisional commander, Budritzki. Colonel Count von Waldersee[34] positioned himself at the head of his 2nd Battalion whilst Lieutenant Colonel von Boehn of the 2nd Guard Grenadiers rode out front amongst his skirmish line. Their advance was directed towards a high building on the southwest corner of Saint Privat which Berger had mistaken for Jérusalem and at 5:30 p.m., with drill ground precision and spacing, colours flying and the regimental bands playing the attack march, the brigade stepped off.

As the Guards formed up for their assault, the skirmishers deployed on the outskirts of Sainte Marie[35] hurriedly fell back, taking cover in the ditches alongside the road before retiring towards Saint Privat. The companies belonging to the 2nd Battalion quickly expended their remaining ammunition before withdrawing in good order towards the village; the 1st Company, having being in action for a shorter period, continued firing for some time before forming up on the right of the 3rd Battalion so as, in the words of the brigade commander Colonel Ganzin, 'to contain the enemy columns which were advancing from St Ail under the cover of a formidable artillery fire.'[36]

---

31  3rd and 4th companies of the Königen regiment, supported by 2nd and 4th companies' 1/1st Guard Grenadier Regiment from 3rd Guard Infantry Brigade who had been stationed in Habonville to act as support for Manstein's IX Corps.

32  From north to south, 3rd, 2nd, 4th 1st, then 11th, 10th, 12th and 9th.

33  The Königen Augusta.

34  Commander 4th Guard Grenadier Regiment.

35  1st and 2nd 1/93rd and 4th, 5th and 6th companies' 2/93rd.

36  L'État-Major, *18 Août, Documents*, p.387. The remaining 10 companies from the 93rd redeployed to the west of Saint Privat.

The French fire grew to a crescendo, inflicting increasing numbers of casualties on the advancing formations. Two shallow valleys, no more than slight depressions, ran eastwards up the slope towards Saint Privat along the brigade's axis of attack and despite affording next to no cover, acted as a magnet to the men of the Königen Augusta, desperate for some shelter from the enemy fire. As their 1st and 2nd companies entered the southern depression, the fusilier battalion to their left made a swing to the north, seeking protection in the other hollow; this oblique movement caused the first line of the Kaiser regiment to veer to the left with the result that one of the half battalions in the second line,[37] found itself to the rear of the Königen's fusiliers.

After traversing the length of the basin, all six companies deployed into company columns before attempting to close on the enemy positions. As a result of this involuntary deviation, a large gap had opened up between the 1st and 2nd Königen companies on the right and their fusilier battalion on the left. At this critical juncture, their commanding officer[38] fell mortally wounded, his loss causing the battalion's attack to falter. In view of the heavy fire, Budritzki sought to stay the advance until Kessel's 1st Guard brigade assault got underway to the north of the highway and instructed his men to take cover. Unfortunately, most of his mounted orderlies were cut down by the ferocious fire, which only served to add to the confusion with some companies dropping to the ground, seeking shelter from the deadly shot and shell, as others, who failed to receive the order, struggled forward into the hailstorm of bullets.

## The French Response

The sector of Canrobert's line opposing 4th Brigades attack, was occupied by Levassor-Sorval's division who were deployed part way down the slope leading to St Ail. The skirmishers of 25th Ligne quickly expended their ammunition against such an inviting target and it would seem that their 1st Battalion, to the left of the track running across hill 321, were amongst the first to fall back into Saint Privat, fearing their right flank was exposed to attack by 4th Brigades advance. This prompted the 9th Chasseurs and 1/70th to follow suit and as they fell back, the 2nd and 3/70th were moved into position alongside the hedge lined track that ran south from Saint Privat, from where they could bring 4th Guards under effective heavy fire. The 26th were deployed on the eastern side of hill 326 and, as such, effectively shielded from the action unfolding to the west although their skirmishers were involved in a long-range exchange of fire with the Hessians in the Bois de la Cusse.

Although Levassor-Sorval's infantry were putting up a strong resistance, they initially lacked artillery support as the eight batteries previously deployed on knoll 333, had withdrawn to the quarries at la Croix but when the 70th moved up into the firing line, the guns of the 8/8th went into position at Jérusalem.

Sometime later, the batteries[39] sent by Bazaine, deployed on the left of the 8th, some 3–400 metres south of the road on knoll 333. Unfortunately, from this position, the 12-pdrs were partially masked by the 70th. Being unable to engage the infantry, they directed their fire on

37   9th and 12th companies commanded by Captain Siefart.
38   Major Prince Salm.
39   The 6th and 7/13th.

the Guards artillery, although outnumbered and with the rays of the setting sun making the fall of shot difficult, their fire had limited impact.

Seeking to regain momentum and bridge the gap which had opened up in his firing line, Waldersee ordered up the Augusta's II Battalion from the second line; three companies sought to close the breach whilst the 5th swung further out to the right behind the 1st and 2nd in an effort to outflank the French line. This thrust dissolved into three distinct groupings; those in the north[40] directed their attention against the hedgerow lining the road that ran south-west from Saint Privat to Amanvillers from knoll 333; those in the centre,[41] under Waldersee's command, were further to the southwest on hill 326. The southern group,[42] led by Major Rosenberg, closed up on the position held by the remnants of the artillery escort[43] who had gone to ground after their pursuit was halted by the enemy fire. As the French skirmishers withdrew to their main line these three groups closed to within 1,200 metres of the enemy positions before flinging themselves to the ground, striving to continue their advance against the deadly fire by a series of short rushes.

With battalions and companies losing discipline, the formations quickly dissolved into an irregular mass of skirmishers, the brigade having little in the way of formed reserves. After closing to within 500 metres of the French lines, they opened fire although at this distance, it had little discernible effect being outside the effective range of the Dreyse. After several short dashes and suffering further heavy losses, Rosenberg's group managed to shorten the distance and gain the shelter of the western slope of hill 320, their advance helped in no small way by the efforts of the Hessians who had pushed north out of the Bois de la Cusse.

In the face of this determined push, the units defending[44] the plateau between hill's 328 and 326 suffered increasing losses. Having expended much of their ammunition, they began to withdraw to the east through the low-lying meadows to the south of Saint Privat and within a short time, the whole line had dissolved as officers struggled to maintain discipline. Two companies from the 1st Guard Grenadiers attempted to seize the heights but coming under fire from the troops sent north by Cissey to fill this breach, were forced to fall back, leaving behind large numbers of dead and wounded guardsmen in their wake.

Unable to advance and unwilling to retreat, Rosenberg's small force took shelter on the southwest slopes of hill 320 and from there, attempted to engage the enemy in a long-range fire fight. Waldersee, one of the few senior officers still mounted, soon recognised that a frontal attack had no chance of success and despatched 1st and 2nd companies to the southwest slope of the ridge in an effort to turn the French line whilst he led the others in a direct assault against their positions. The tirailleurs again fell back in the face of this fresh onslaught and Waldersee pushed his men onto the heights a few hundred metres south of the ground seized by Rosenberg; from here they engaged Cissey's troops at a range of 3–400 metres as he put in another counter attack. Rosenberg and the commander of the Kaiser Alexander detachment, Major von Seeckt

---

40  III/4th Guard Grenadiers and Siefart's half battalion 9th and 12th companies' 2nd Guard Grenadiers.
41  1st, 2nd, 6th, 7th and 8th companies' 4th Guard Grenadiers Regiment.
42  3rd, 4th and 5th companies' 4th Guard Grenadiers Regiment, 2nd and 4th companies' 2nd Guard Grenadiers.
43  3rd and 4th companies' 4th Guard Grenadiers and 2nd and 4th companies' 1st Guard Grenadier Regiment.
44  3/28th, 2nd and 3/70th, 2/28th and the 12-pdrs of the 6th and 7/13th.

were both wounded in this latest struggle, with command devolving to Captain Vogel von Falckenstein.

## 2nd Guard Grenadiers

Out on the brigade's left flank 2nd Guard Grenadiers were directed against the southwest corner of Saint Privat. In a futile attempt to reduce the regiments exposure to the enemy fire, their commanding officer, Boehn, ordered the leading half battalion to form columns of companies behind their skirmishers, so as to decrease their frontage, with the second line told to deploy into half battalions, thus forming an arc with their left resting on the main road, their right on the northern most depression. Despite these measures, in the face of the fierce enemy fire their advance faltered with further progress, such as it was, being made by a series of short, uncoordinated rushes, with the open ground affording practically no cover to the guardsmen.

When the Konigen fusiliers veered off to the right seeking some respite from the hail of bullets, II/2nd Grenadiers – who were leading the Kaiser's attack – made a similar move to the left, subconsciously drawn to the cover afforded by the roadside ditches, their deviation opening up a large gap between the two regiments.[45] It seems that so many men took cover in the ditches that, as Colonel Ganzin stated in his post combat report, some of the defenders in Saint Privat believed the attack had 'been repulsed.'[46] The fire from his brigade certainly took a heavy toll on the attackers, especially amongst the mounted field officers with Boehn and the second line battalion commanders being amongst the early casualties[47] and as a result of this loss of control, I Battalion followed the lead of II, and veered to the left also seeking shelter in the road side ditches. Casualties were growing and with all order lost, small groups of men clustered around the few remaining officers. The shocked guardsmen were to cling to these positions for over an hour and as their ammunition ran low, resorted to stripping the dead and wounded in order to continue the struggle.

## Ingelfingen's Disbelief

Prince Kraft zu Hohenlohe Ingelfingen and Colonel von Scherbening[48] watched with satisfaction as the escorts from the Königen and Kaiser regiments cleared the enemy skirmishers from his immediate front, although he continued to lose men to their annoying fire. Given that Dannenberg had promised to warn him before the Guards commenced their attack, Ingelfingen was understandably shocked as heavy firing broke out around Saint Privat and the slopes south of the village, cloaking the area in dense clouds of smoke. Taken aback, he exclaimed to Scherbening: 'What does this mean? For God's sake! Our infantry is making a frontal attack

---

45    As mentioned previously, Siefert's half battalion from the second line formation continued their march without deviating and found themselves behind the Königen regiment.

46    Colonel Ganzin, as quoted in l'État-Major, *18 Août, Documents*, p.389.

47    Lieutenant Colonel von Bentivegni and Major von Wittich. The lead battalion's senior officer Major von Lingsen was struck and unable to continue, picked up a rifle and sheltering behind a pile of stones, opened fire on the French positions.

48    Commander, Guard Field Artillery Regiment.

before the Saxons have completed their enveloping manoeuvre.[49] Both officers quickly came to the same conclusion – the Guard artillery would need to redeploy at once so as to support the infantry attack. As one French account relates:

> It was about six o'clock; we saw then opposite 4 Corps a thick column of dust rising above the woods and advancing towards Saint Privat; this dust could only be produced by artillery at a gallop. Each of us understood that we were going to receive the shock of the last moment according to Prussian tactics. In fact, this artillery was not long in getting into battery opposite the right of the 4 Corps, resting on the left of 6 Corps. Formidable detonations.[50]

The French artillery were quick to react to this deployment with Ingelfingen's artillery being hit by counter battery fire from the guns south of Saint Privat on knoll 333[51] and those positioned to the east around knoll 327.[52] He therefore ordered his batteries to divide their fire between the enemy infantry in Saint Privat and their guns on the outskirts of the village. Lieutenant Colonel Bychelberg led 1st Field Division forward from the centre, as Scherbening brought up the corps artillery in echelon from the left.[53] Further to the north, Lieutenant Colonel Rheinhaben deployed 3rd Field Division which, in concert with the batteries of von Mutius and von Grävenitz,[54] engaged both the French infantry and the buildings within Saint Privat. However, as 4th Brigade's attack edged forward partially masking their fire, several batteries had to change position so as to avoid hitting their own troops.

On the right of the Guards gun line, just north of the Habonville ravine, von Sametzki's 1st Heavy battery engaged De Narp's divisional batteries which had moved forward from reserve to take position on knoll 322 north of the Metz-Etain railroad. On the left wing, Captain von Prittwitz's 2nd Heavy advanced 150 to 160 metres but were brought to a halt by the enemy fire, their difficulties being compounded by the rising ground to their front which served to mask their targets.

With the words 'Here we shall be all killed without a return shot, so forward',[55] Prittwitz led the battery to the half right where Rosenberg's group were struggling to maintain their hold on the southern spur of hill 320. However, his exhausted teams could scarcely raise a trot and initially, only three guns wheeled into position on their right amidst a thin skirmish line formed by 2nd Company Kaiser Alexanders. Prittwitz's guns came under renewed heavy fire which claimed Lieutenant von Winterfield as one of their first victims, but he received timely support from von Friederici-Steinmann's 3rd Light, who deployed further to the north, their strength being further augmented by Captain Seeger's 4th Heavy.

Subjected to this bombardment, increasing numbers of Levassor-Sorval's infantry began to drop out of line, many having run low on ammunition and it appeared to Waldersee that the

---

49   Bell, *St Privat*, p.285.
50   *Ibid*, p.76.
51   8/8th.
52   12/8th and 10/12th.
53   2nd Field Division and Horse Artillery Division.
54   4th Light and 2nd Horse artillery.
55   Bell, *St Privat*, p.285.

French defences were wavering. He despatched an orderly to the brigade commander requesting cavalry support to exploit this opening but before his message reached its destination, the French line stabilised. Given his losses, especially amongst the officers, Waldersee had no option but to inform Berger that he lacked the strength to continue his advance, although he promised to hold onto the ground his men had secured at such heavy cost.[56]

Observing the stalled attack from the rear, the divisional commander Budritzki, requested Scherbening support 4th Guard Grenadiers with Major von Krieger's 2nd Field Division[57] which had taken up position at the base of the western slope of hill 320, about 1,600 metres from Saint Privat. After moving up to support Behr's position, the batteries were shortly joined by the 2nd Horse which deployed on their left and then the 3rd Light. Before they could unlimber, Berger, who had just received Waldersee's despatch requesting support, galloped up to Krieger[58] and pointing over his shoulder, pleaded with him: 'My battalions can no longer hold out on that hill over there; the artillery must go up there.'[59]

Krieger immediately despatched the 3rd Light to assist the beleaguered infantry but no sooner had their commander[60] given the order to redeploy, he fell from his horse, mortally wounded, 2nd Lieutenant Schmalz taking his place.

The battery then advanced and under intense rifle fire, deployed five guns about 15 metres on the right, rear wing, of Waldersee's battle group and opened fire on the enemy tirailleurs with canister. Just then Schmalz noted large numbers of formed infantry [61] approaching from the direction of Amanvillers; this threat posed a far greater danger so he ordered the guns be reloaded with shell, engaging them at a range of 800 metres.

## Cissey's Counter-attack

The strong enemy columns marching on Schmalz's position from knoll 328, were from Cissey's 1st Division deployed along the ridge running north from knoll 315 to the south of Saint Privat. Ordered to support Becquet de Sonnay's brigade, he called forward two battalions from his reserves[62] who were directed against Rosenberg's detachment and the exposed flank of the 4th Guards Brigade. They were reinforced by 1/28th, with fire support being provided by the divisional batteries on knoll 328 and for a time, it looked as though this counter attack would succeed. Indeed, Cissey related how the advance was undertaken with 'the calmness of a parade ground manoeuvre that caused the enemy columns advance to stutter to a halt'[63] with one account recalling how from 'the heights, three batteries of guns and mitrailleuses laid down an unbroken fire against the attackers.'[64] As Cissey detailed in his post combat report, 'everyone

---

56    Shortly after making this report, Waldersee was stuck and carried off to the rear with Major von Behr, the brigade's sole surviving uninjured field officer, taking command.
57    3rd and 4th Heavy batteries.
58    2nd Field Division's commander.
59    Bell, *St Privat*, p.287.
60    Captain von Friederici-Steinmann.
61    These included the 57th, 20th Chasseurs, 1st and 2/73rd and three companies from 1/6th from Cissey's division.
62    From Goldberg's brigade; one from the 57th and the 2/73rd.
63    L'État-Major, *18 Août, Documents*, p.242.
64    L'État-Major, *St Privat*, pp.438–439.

batteries from the 3rd Field Division then advanced and took ground a few hundred metres to the rear of the Kaiser regiment; the 6th Heavy crossed the road and unlimbered with its right flank on the highway but the Guard infantry to their front, masked their fire. Loath to withdraw and unable to defend itself, the battery drew fire from the skirmishers and enemy batteries[80] deployed between Saint Privat and Roncourt.

The remaining batteries deployed to the south of the road from where 5th Heavy engaged the infantry defending Saint Privat; 6th Light targeting the artillery on knoll 333.[81] Meanwhile, 1st and 3rd Horse artillery were brought forward from St Ail and took position alongside the 2nd on the left wing of the Corps artillery. The 2nd and 4th Heavy then moved up on their right and began to lob shells into Saint Privat so by 7:00 p.m., the entire Guard artillery were in action between the main highway and the Metz-Etain railroad. Despite this welcome support, the shattered remains of 4th Guard Brigade remained pinned to the ground; unable to make any further progress and unwilling to retreat, they could do little but wait for nightfall or the Saxons.

## 1st Guard Brigade's Attack on Saint Privat

1st Guard Division marched non-stop for a day and a half before arriving at their bivouac at 5:00 p.m. on 17th August. Rations were in short supply and the nearest water was 2km away so when they stood to at 5:00 a.m. on the following day, most men had empty stomachs and canteens. During their 18km advance to Sainte Marie, water had been equally hard to come by and following the capture of the village, the division enjoyed a well-earned rest, Pape having been told to stand down until fresh orders arrived.

Although ignorant of his corps commander's intentions, he was aware of the plan to envelop the right wing of the French Army with the Saxon corps and as a seasoned professional, expected that any infantry assault against Saint Privat would be proceeded by a prolonged artillery bombardment; a necessary prelude to any attack across open ground devoid of any cover against such a well defended objective. Pape was only too aware of the effectiveness of the French chassepot. Following an earlier discussion with Prince Frederick Charles about the heavy losses suffered at the battle of Wörth, he had been cautioned against making the same mistake.[82] Given no preliminary bombardment had taken place, he assumed it would be some time before his men would be called upon, so it came as something of an unwelcome surprise when August galloped up and instructed: 'You will now attack Saint Privat with your division and capture it.' Pape protested and pointed out the difficulties he would face undertaking a frontal attack against such a well defended objective with no preliminary bombardment having taken place. August retorted that the village had been fired on by the Corps artillery for the last hour; Pape exclaimed: 'Excuse me, the Corps artillery has been silent for the past hour; Saint

---

80  7th, 5th and 6/14th.

81  8/8th, 6th and 7/13th.

82  Prince Kraft zu Hohenlohe Ingelfingen left a chilling description of the effectiveness of the French fire: 'You can form some idea of the terrible effect of the fire, when I tell you that a flock of frightened sheep which burst out from Sainte Marie and galloped across the front of the Prussian infantry and, which perhaps in the dust which they raised were mistaken by the enemy for cavalry, were killed down to the last animal.' See *Letters on Infantry*, (London, Edward Stanford, 1892) p.51.

Privat is entirely intact.' August insisted: 'The Crown Prince of Saxony has informed me that he would attack Roncourt at 5:00 p.m. It's now 5:30 p.m.; we'll be too late. All you have to do is to move forward.'

Pape again remonstrated that the bulk of XII Corps had yet to commence its march, adding: 'Your Royal Highness can see both this as well as the silence of the artillery, if you will ride a short distance out of the village.' The Prince cut him short: 'No, no, the Crown Prince has said it and over there' – pointing toward St Ail and the 4th Guards Brigade – 'the other division is now advancing; it will be isolated; hurry up, now; everything takes so long with you.'[83] Stung by unwarranted rebuke, Pape wheeled his horse about and galloped across to the 1st Guard Infantry Brigade where he met with Dannenberg who, pointing over his shoulder to Saint Privat, designated the tallest building in the village as the objective for his attack.

Following the earlier capture of Sainte Marie, 1st Guards Brigade were assembled to the south-west of the village where they had been ordered to lie on the grass to escape the chassepot fire. They were in this position for over an hour and their commander, General von Kessel, took advantage of the pause to reconnoitre the ground between Sainte Marie and Saint Privat. From reports he received, he thought any attack would be impossible given the disadvantageous ground and the strength of the enemy defences and was understandably taken aback to hear from a passing officer, that his men would soon receive orders to attack Saint Privat.

Confirmation of this unwelcome news came a few moments later when Dannenberg rode up and pointing in the direction of Saint Privat directed: 'The Brigade will advance on the other side of the road and attack together with the 4th Guard Infantry Brigade. That brigade is already engaged; 1st Brigade must hasten to get ahead.' Kessel protested: 'That will hardly be possible; the brigade has been halted here for the past hour and a half; we've seen several intact battalions of French infantry deploying on the heights of Saint Privat in line and then apparently lying down in skirmish trenches.' The chief of staff responded: 'Those are troops beaten by the IX Corps.' Again, Kessel dissented: 'No! They're intact and haven't been fired on by artillery.' Dannenberg cut short further any debate: 'We attack. If we do not take Saint Privat, the Saxons will get it ahead of us. The brigade will reap the harvest of today.' Kessel pointed in the direction of Auboué: 'There the Saxons are marching; they're still far off; I'm awaiting orders from the division.'[84]

One of Kessel's adjutants, Count Pfeil later recalled:

> We knew that the two generals weren't on the best of terms and that Danneberg did not look with any great favour on the 1st Guard Regiment. Some distance away from us both generals argued in evident excitement, during which argument General von Kessel several times pointed in the directions where the Saxons were. We now found out what Kessel had told the chief of staff in that heated discourse, namely that we ought to wait with the attack to give the Saxons time to come up[85]

Dannenberg then rode off towards Sainte Marie leaving Kessel, mystified as to what he meant by 'reaping the harvest of today' and could only conclude that corps headquarters were under

83    Bell, *St Privat*, p.299.
84    *Ibid*, p.300.
85    *Ibid*, p.460.

the mistaken impression that Saint Privat was held by shaken, defeated troops.[86] Pape then approached Kessel to confirm Dannenberg's orders, instructing him to 'start for the attack with the brigade, directing on the highest building in Saint Privat.' Kessel asked what support would be made available, only to be told by Pape: 'Only the 4th Brigade on your right flank. The 2nd Brigade and advance guard remain at Sainte Marie aux Chênes.'[87]

## 1st Guard Brigade's Attack

Despite his reservations, Kessel had been given a direct order by two superior officers and as he recalled:

> Shortly after 5:30 the divisional commander, von Pape rode up to me and gave me the order to advance and storm the village; which he pointed out to our right flank. I called up the regimental commanders and repeated it verbally as I had received it and then added immediately after sounding the advance, I should order a change of front, quarter left on the right battalion. On completion of this, the skirmishers of the first 'treffen' were to be thrown out and then as soon as the chausée had been crossed, I should order a second, quarter right, change of front.[88]

After warning 4th Brigade that he would be manoeuvring in their rear, Kessel formed his brigade in three lines with 3rd Foot Guards to the right, 1st Foot Guards on the left. Both regiments deployed their fusiliers[89] with advanced wing companies in the first line; II Battalion[90] in half companies behind them, with I Battalion in the third line;[91] 1st Guard Pioneer Company were to the rear of 1st Foot Guards. As described in the German official history:

> The conditions of the attack were extremely unfavourable; for at all points there appeared an open slope gradually rising towards Saint Privat and Roncourt upon which only potato haulms and isolated trees or shrubs rose above the ground. The upper part of the slope at Saint Privat falls rather more steeply than the gently sloping foot so that about 600 yards west of this village there is a sort of terrace. At a short distance in front of the west and north sides of Saint Privat there were several parallel walls of knee-high masonry whilst at some places the adversary had thrown up shelter trenches. These lines successively commanded one another and were filled with compact lines of skirmishers and in their rear, upon the commanding height lay a natural like bastion

---

86  A study of the battle carried out by the general staff after the war commented 'Whatever was directed for carrying out the attack was wrong in almost every instance' and 'Action was taken without seeing the details.' *Ibid*, p.387.

87  *Ibid*, p.301. Pape intended to keep the Guard Fusilier regiment and Guard Jäger battalion as a reserve in the event of an unfavourable outcome of the battle.

88  Captain F. N. Maude, *Military Letters and Essays*, (Kansas City, Hudson Kimberly Publishing Co. 1895) pp.87–88.

89  3rd Guards fusiliers were commanded by Major von Notz, 1st Guards fusiliers by Major Count Finckenstein.

90  II/3rd Guards were commanded by Colonel von Holleben, II/1st Guards Colonel von Stülpnagel.

91  I/ 3rd Guards were commanded by Major von Seegenberg, I/1st Guards by Colonel von Oppell.

and girt with almost continuous wall, the town like village, the stone houses of which were occupied up to the roof storey.[92]

An officer in the 1st Foot Guards related how:

Between 3:30 p.m. and 4:00 p.m. the brigade to which we belonged stood 500 yards south of Sainte Marie aux Chênes, fronting north, the two regiments side by side with the fusilier battalion of each as first 'treffen' (or line), their flank companies in advance; the second battalion formed a second 'treffen' in half battalion columns (500 men) at deploying intervals and the remaining two battalions, the first of each regiment, stood in the same formation as third 'treffen'. For nearly two hours we lay, suffering constant losses from chassepot bullets and from shrapnel fire from the French batteries on our right flank about Saint Privat and the incessant strain, watching out for little white clouds of smoke which puffed out in the sky above us and then the few seconds of intense anxiety to know where the bullets thus released would strike, did not fail to have its effect. At last, about 5:30 p.m. came the long wished for order to advance and storm the village of Saint Privat. The task set us was about as follows; at the foot of a long glacis-like slope, which rose gently for some 3,000 paces and without a particle of cover to screen our movements, to change front half right and then to move to the left across the chausée, here enclosed by two deep side ditches and then to wheel into line again and advance to the assault.[93]

## The Killing Fields of Saint Privat

1st Brigade marched off at 5:45 p.m. making a quarter turn to the left so as to skirt Sainte Marie then, after crossing the highway, a quarter turn to the right so as to front their objective. After clearing the village, Kessel noted that 4th Brigade was much closer to the road than expected and to avoid any clash, ordered his men 'Half left! March!' As the brigade swung around Sainte Marie and then surged across the highway, the files on the outer flank again had to break into a run to keep position as the line wheeled to avoid the 4th. This correction soon developed into a full left turn and as the brigade continued to move in a north easterly direction, exposed its right flank to Saint Privat.

The fusilier battalions leading the advance, deployed skirmishers at the run as ordered but insufficient spacing had been left between the second and third lines and as they pressed forward to escape the chassepot fire, their closed up ranks presented a solid mass to the French. Deployed to the northwest of Saint Privat the 93rd and the 3/91st poured volley after volley into this inviting target and when the batteries deployed north and south of the village opened fire, the French positions became enveloped in rolling clouds of smoke.

As Kessel recalled: 'The first wheel was executed in good order, but immediately after passing the chausée, the columns came under so heavy a fire, both of artillery and chassepots, that

92    Clarke, *Franco-German War II*, pp.131–132.
93    Maude, *Military Letters*, pp.86–87.

the advance was seriously impeded.'[94] Observing the confusion, Pape and August both sent messengers to the supports instructing them to pause to give the skirmishers chance to deploy. Kessel also despatched three orderlies to the base company[95] ordering them to mark time but it was all to no avail as the rear ranks continued to push forward in a futile attempt to escape the French fire. An account from the officer in the Garde Regiment zu Fuß noted:

> The two fusilier battalions, having moved northwards across the chausée, wheeled to the right and advanced, that of the third Garde Regiment zu Fuß next to the road, ours next on its left. The second battalions followed across the road and also wheeled to the right, joining the fighting line then on the left of their respective fusilier battalions. The battalions of the third 'treffen' followed in a similar manner; but as soon as they crossed the road, the necessity of supporting at once the troops in the fighting line caused them to be broken up by companies and sent to join the fighting line wherever their aid was most required.[96]

Within the French lines, an officer of the 10th Chasseurs à Cheval described how:

> Towards 5:00 p.m. we could clearly see the columns forming up in front of Saint Marie aux Chênes and Saint Ail, which took position in front of their respective objectives. They were protected by their artillery situated to the south of St Ail. After a manoeuvre which is hard to explain – a sort of chassé-croisé[97] – they began to move forward in dense masses. However, before they'd travelled half the distance which separated us, they suffered such enormous losses that the slope was covered with their wounded. When their lines reached a small crest, they suddenly seemed to have disappeared; the men had lain down, tired, exhausted, unable to advance.[98]

Seeking to escape the murderous fire, the supports in the second and third lines advanced a considerable distance north of the road before halting at the base of two shallow valleys which led off to the right in the direction of Saint Privat. As they dashed forward to gain cover in the northernmost depression, the press of the rear formations again threw all the battalions together in a confused mass, a situation not helped by the loss of several senior officers in the front line.[99] In 1st Foot Guards, Lieutenant Colonel von Holleben was severely wounded and after the majority of his field officers were rendered *hors de combat*, command devolved to Lieutenant von Kracht. The intense enemy fire[100] served to further compress the supports and with losses increasing rapidly, only the front line formations had space in which to manoeuvre. As the fusiliers wheeled to the right to front Saint Privat, the second line battalions, after a

---

94   *Ibid*, pp.88.
95   12th Company 3rd Guard Regiment.
96   Maude, *Military Letters*, pp.86–87.
97   'A mix-up where people miss each other in turn.'
98   L'État-Major, *18 Août, Documents*, p.443.
99   Captain von Herwarth accompanying the Colour party was mortally wounded and the III/3rd Guards commander, Major von Notz was killed by shellfire.
100  From elements of the 91st and 93rd Ligne, they were later reinforced by men from the 10th.

half-hearted attempt to follow their lead, continued straight ahead, as though they were shying away from the deadly fire with Captain von Holleben[101] recalling: 'It was like a movement like that of a single man who, breasting a heavy rain and wind, involuntary stops and tries to get ahead by a movement to the side.'[102]

As Kessel's skirmishers pushed north across the Sainte Marie-Saint Privat road, the tirailleurs[103] in front of Hautmécourt ravine, hurriedly fell back on their supports, fearful that the advancing guardsmen would get in behind them. Of the troops tasked to defend Roncourt, just a single company remained within the village with two battalions[104] forming a semi-circle around its western edge. As the 2/10th fell back, they occupied the ground between these men and the units further to the south[105] with 1/91st taking position on the ground between them and the troops deployed in front of Saint Privat.[106] On their left flank, the 3/93rd extended across either side of the Sainte Marie-Saint Privat highway, their ranks being swelled by two companies from the 1st Battalion who had fallen back in front of the advancing Kaiser Franz regiment.

Kessel was out in front of his brigade, riding between the two leading fusilier battalions, [107] trusting his presence would steady the men and drive their attack forward despite the losses amongst the senior officers. He later recalled:

> About 100 paces in front of Saint Privat dense lines of French skirmishers lay skilfully concealed and their fire, which began by bugle sound, cost us dear. I saw at once that all the columns, irrespective of distances, caught it equally. The bullets, still effective after several ricochets, made all calculation, based on the principle of 'distances', illusory. The French shot without aiming and left it to the flat trajectory of the bullets to find their own billet. The nature of the ground compelled us to run forward by groups and then to throw ourselves down to take breath. With severe effort and leaving men behind us at every step, we managed to reach a slight fold some 600 yards in front of the village and our resolute advance had the effect of making the French skirmishers abandon their position and take shelter behind the walls of the village; their fire from this new position was fortunately less effective.[108]

Following Kessel's example, the regimental commanders[109] also rode at the head of their troops and after the brigade finally completed its wheel towards Saint Privat, the right wing of 3rd Foot Guards lead battalion was some 3–400 metres north of the highway, with the 1st Foot Guards being a similar distance to their left. After closing to within 5–600 metres of the outlying enemy positions, their skirmishers opened fire whilst the supports pushed into the fighting line. The II/3rd Guards moved into the gap between the two fusilier battalions, whilst the II/1st

---

101  General Staff Officer, 1st Guard Infantry Division.
102  Bell, *St Privat*, p.304.
103  From the 2/10th and 1/91st.
104  1/9th and 1/75th.
105  2nd and 3/75th and half the 3/10th.
106  2nd and 3/91st, half battalion 3/10th and 1/10th.
107  III/3rd Guards on the right, III/1st Guards on the left.
108  Maude, *Military Letters*, p.88.
109  Colonel von Röder of the 1st Foot Guards and Colonel von Linsingen from the 3rd Foot Guards

edged further to the north and took ground on the left of the III/1st, seeking to close on the French positions by a series of short rushes, the men advancing 'body bent down and face turned away as if seeking protection from a hailstorm.'[110] With chassepot fire ripping holes in their ranks, the guardsmen 'became panicky and huddled together in lines behind each other as if the rear line wanted to seek cover behind the one in front.'[111] Kessel observed:

> I'd sent the fusilier battalions which first crossed the road direct against the village and had allowed the following ones to continue the movement towards the north because I hoped they would find better cover further on. Also, I knew I could rely on my regimental commanders to join in as circumstances required. For myself, I remained near the chausée, as I felt my personal presence was most required there, for losses in officers was already great. From that moment I did nothing but drive the columns forward so as to get to closer quarters from which our shorter-range weapons might be used with effect. The noise of the bursting shells and heavy infantry fire rendered it almost impossible to make oneself heard; both skirmishers and columns had to throw themselves down to get breath although I must confess that they always rose to my call and resumed the advance. Whenever for a moment we offered a favourable target, we heard a bugle-call in the French lines and the next moment came such a hail of lead that all were compelled to throw themselves on their faces. The losses in the fighting line caused fresh troops to be sent up, the columns rapidly diminished, gaps began to appear in the front and the loss of officers became very sensible. Individuals went forward, mostly stooping low and with averted faces, with hands raised in front of them, as men instinctively do in a hailstorm, their features distorted by terror. The terrible moral effect could not remain unrecognised. I ordered all buglers and drummers to sound and beat the 'advance' and for myself kept reiterating the command, 'Forward, Forward!' By this time at least fifty officers in the brigade must have fallen. One must have commanded in such a crisis to know what this means. It struck me as I looked round that if things went on at this rate for long, the whole brigade would be down before we reached Saint Privat.[112]

Another officer, First Lieutenant Count von der Schulenberg, left this graphic account of the fusilier's advance:

> Already before crossing the chausée they'd come under heavy chassepot fire. They executed their change of front, quarter right, satisfactorily, in spite of a couple of shells which burst amongst them and went forward in the direction of Saint Privat. Suddenly, on the rising ground above the village, a line of smoke rose clear in the air and the next moment we were overwhelmed with a storm of projectiles and the men fell in heaps. General Kessel gave the order to two or three section leaders to extend their men and in a few moments almost the entire flank companies were dissolved – only Lieutenant von Alvenslaben II kept his men in hand about one hundred yards behind the skirmishers.

110  Bell, *St Privat*, p.305
111  *Ibid.*
112  Maude, *Military Letters*, pp.88–89.

Here, as everywhere, the advance was continued by alternative rushes. Though the distance was still far beyond the range of our weapons, the men were allowed to fire. Under the appalling rain of the enemy's projectiles, one seemed so powerless that any means of keeping up the men's spirits was resorted to. After a few moments to get breath, a fresh rush was attempted. The only drummer still standing had both arms torn off by a shell; Lieutenant von Halkewitz was hit in the side and fell; Lieutenant von Maltzahn was shot through the right foot and could not go on. The battalion adjutant, Lieutenant von Wartensleben, had his horse shot from under him, but joined a company and was himself disabled a few moments after by two bullets. The company rose again and raced forward some fifty paces. Captain Graf von Finckenstein was hit in the foot and gave over his command to his subaltern. When we got within 600 paces of the village, we saw the French falling back out of their advanced trenches on the village. The II battalion came up on our left. The losses increased from minute to minute and the noise of the bursting shells and the breach loaders was so deafening that no commands could be heard and only the whistle asserted its power. The right wing division of von Alvesleben's 'zug' was struck by a shell and at the same moment the left wing of the command was simply swept away by a round of mitrailleur, which struck the ground like a charge of shot.[113]

## The Attack Against Roncourt

As both fusilier battalions continued to edge their way towards Saint Privat, on the left of the firing line, 12th Company 1st Foot Guards came under fire from Roncourt, some 600 metres to their left front. Unable to respond, the company angled to the left so as to front this fire which resulted in a gap opening up between them and the 9th Company to their right. Seeking to avoid the worst of the fire, II and I battalions, following in the wake of the fusiliers, advanced some distance to the north of the main road where their massed ranks also drew fire from this direction. The regiment's commanding officer approached Kessel seeking permission to divert his advance towards Roncourt, so as to deal with this threat:

About this time Colonel von Röder came up to me and described the position of the left wing; half a battalion of his regiment was moving on Roncourt and a few of his skirmishers of his first battalion had also gone off in the same direction. The columns of the centre had directed themselves on a small height, which broke the level of the ground and were suffering less. I fully agreed to what he said, all the more as I could do nothing to alter things and gave him, as he was on foot, his horse having been killed, the horse of my adjutant, Lieutenant von Kessel who'd just been knocked clean out of his saddle by the blow of a chassepot bullet in the right shoulder. My second galloper, whom I'd sent to ride down the front and order the drums to beat the 'advance' received a bullet through his hand and did not return to me. Of my two orderlies, both had lost

---

113  *Ibid*, pp.91–92.

their horses and one was mortally wounded. The bullets now came in harder and faster than ever and through fear my horse had become almost unmanageable.[114]

Given the confusion, some of Röder's companies understandably failed to react to these new instructions and continued to follow in the wake of the fusilier battalion; as a result, the regiment became even more splintered as the greater part of I and II battalions veered off to the left, towards Roncourt, whilst the fusiliers continued to advance against Saint Privat.

The 5th and 6th companies[115] were the first to react to the new orders; Lieutenant von Brause at the head of two and a half companies, advanced by short rushes across the shallow depression that lay between them and Roncourt from where, at last, they could bring an effective fire against the tirailleurs who lined the northern rim of the basin. Brause was supported on his right by other platoons from the two companies – some in skirmish order, some closed up – led by Lieutenant Arnim, and their combined efforts succeeded in driving off the French. Arnim then moved his small command up alongside the left wing of the 12th Company 1st Foot Guards who were attempting to drive the French away from their positions alongside the road between Roncourt and Saint Privat. As the 12th continued to advance by short rushes, Arnim held his men back so as to create a reserve for the fusiliers in the event they had need of support.

From the other half battalion, the 7th Company, led by Lieutenant Colonel von Stülpnagel,[116] attempted to follow Arnim but the heavy fire they attracted caused them to deviate to the right, where they found themselves in the rear of the fusilier battalion. This manoeuvre, carried out under a 'hot sweeping fire' cost them half their strength, including Stülpnagel. Formed into a loose line, the remnants continued to push forward into the space between the two fusilier battalions where, given their losses, the company more or less dissolved. The 8th, deploying into skirmish formation, advanced across the basin and taking position some 150–200 metres to the left of Brause, supported the ongoing fire fight against Roncourt.

In an effort to reduce casualties, Major von Seegenberg instructed his battalion[117] to cross the highway a company at a time and in the general confusion, his men found themselves pushed up in the rear of Lieutenant Colonel von Oppell's I/1st Foot Guards, rather than alongside them as originally intended. Hurrying to close up with II Battalion, Oppell was then ordered to 'Take the extreme left wing of the battle front with the view to enveloping Saint Privat.'[118] Given the widespread disorder, this was no easy task; the individual companies had first to disentangle themselves from the confused mass and then make their way into the firing line.

To add to their problems, Kessel then directed the 1st and 2nd companies to reinforce the fusilier battalion, whilst Oppell, his command now reduced to just the 3rd and 4th companies, advanced in the direction of Roncourt in two half platoon columns, supported by the 1st Guard Pioneer Company. He soon caught up with the 8th Company and as his half battalion wheeled to the right to face the enemy deployed alongside the Roncourt-Saint Privat road, the leading two half platoons moved into the space on their left.

114 *Ibid*, pp.89–90.
115 They formed one of the II's half battalions originally deployed in the second line of the brigade.
116 The other battalion commander.
117 I/3rd Foot Guards.
118 Bell, *St Privat*, p.310.

In the face of this determined advance, the French withdrew into Roncourt, allowing the remnants of several companies[119] to inch their way towards the northwest of Saint Privat. As Oppell led his men off to the north, the I/3rd Foot Guards, having finally reorganised their ranks, were unable to find space in front of Saint Privat in which to deploy so followed I/1st Foot Guards and took up took position on the left wing of the brigade, along the northern edge of the basin.

## Prussian Disbelief

As Guard Corps staff watched the unfolding disaster from the eastern edge of Sainte Marie, August was stunned by the ferocity of the French response. There was no sign of XII Corps expected attack and during the brief time the Saxon artillery were in action, they had done little to supress the French defences. With even this limited artillery support for 1st Guards Division being abruptly withdrawn, August was anxious to secure reinforcements for his floundering attack. Just then, Captain Lignitz[120] arrived with an urgent request from Manstein for him to hasten his attack on Saint Privat, so as to relieve the pressure on IX Corps. August inquired if 3rd Guards Brigade were free to support him, but was informed they had already been committed to the action in the Bois de la Cusse.[121] Having launched his assault on Saint Privat without having adequately prepared the ground the realisation began to sink in that with no available reserves he would, after all, need the support of the Saxons if his corps were to escape complete destruction.

Meanwhile, as August looked on in horror, III/3rd Foot Guard, with drummers and trumpeters sounding the advance, made towards the northwest corner of Saint Privat by way of repeated short rushes. The wing companies[122] deployed into skirmish formation, with the remaining half battalions following in close order but their advance faltered in the face of the heavy fire and increasing losses. Colonel von Linsingen ordered up the supports and the fresh impetus they imparted took the fusiliers to within 500 metres of the foremost line of tirailleurs. Unable to continue their advance, the battalion gathered around its colours, spread out on the ground and opened a futile fire with their Dreyse rifles; two subsequent rushes at last brought them to within effective range – 250 metres – of the French positions, although by this time, the fusiliers been reduced in strength to just three officers and 250 men.

To their right, there was still a gap of some 400 metres to where the survivors of 4th Guards Brigade were clinging onto the exposed hillside to the south of the highway. With the French positions wreathed in white smoke from the chassepot fire, Kessel's guardsmen were unable to make any effective response as for the most part, they were still outside the range of their weapons. To the north of the highway, another opening had formed to the left of the fusiliers which was filled by the II/3rd Guards.

Originally in the second line, after wheeling to front Saint Privat, the battalion deployed into skirmish formation so as to reduce casualties. After repeated short rushes, the two leading

---

119  1st and 2nd, supported by the 9th and part of the 12th.
120  From IX Corps headquarters.
121  This did not prevent August from issuing orders to 3rd Brigade to support his attack on Saint Privat but by the time his despatch arrived, Manstein had already committed them to the attack on Amanvillers.
122  9th and 12th companies.

companies[123] pushed into the space to the left of the fusiliers and led by their only remaining unwounded officer,[124] engaged the tirailleurs defending Saint Privat's churchyard. However, having lost all their commanders, the other half battalion simply disintegrated,[125] the survivors falling back to Sainte Marie with just a few resolute and foolhardy individuals making their way into the firing line.

Within 1st Foot Guards, the first line wing fusilier companies [126] each deployed a platoon as skirmishers, with supports following as half battalions in company columns and staggering forward in the face of the relentless fire, found themselves opposite the northern exit of Saint Privat. A gap opened between their two leading companies as the 12th veered off to the left to face the fire coming from Roncourt, leaving the 9th, urged on by Kessel's repeated calls of 'Forward! Forward!' to advance towards the southern sector of the Saint Privat-Roncourt road.

The space between the lead companies increased as the 12th fronted towards Roncourt so the second line half battalion[127] closed up to the 9th and after deploying a platoon on either flank of their firing line, edged to within 300 metres of the enemy positions. Confronted by this threat and having fired off most of their ammunition, the tirailleurs holding the outlying rifle pits in front of Saint Privat, fell back on their main positions, as did those in front of Roncourt. After being reinforced by their third platoon, the 12th continued their push towards the village which in turn, helped relieve pressure on the battalions further to the south, enabling their supports who were sheltering further down the slope, to push into the firing line.

## The Struggle Intensifies

Pape followed 1st Brigade's progress with the detached eye of a professional soldier and although less surprised than August by the French response, was equally concerned at the direction and manner of their attack. Although their intended objective was the southwest corner of Saint Privat,[128] following their initial dash across the highway, the bulk of Kessel's men had veered left towards Roncourt in an instinctive attempt to escape the chassepot fire. As a consequence, the gap between Berger's brigade to south of the chaussée and Kessel's brigade to the north, continued to widen, making the prospect of any coordinated action increasingly doubtful, as well as leaving both open to being defeated in detail by an aggressive enemy.

Anxious to address this, Pape decided to commit additional troops to bridge the space between the diverging brigades. The only men available were 2nd Foot Guards Regiment whose commander, Colonel von Kanitz, riding alongside him, promptly volunteered for this task. Pape consented, urging him to get his men 'to follow 1st Brigade ... echeloned to the left rear'[129] as soon as possible. At 5:50 p.m., accompanied by Major General von Medem,[130] he began his

---

123  7th and 5th companies.
124  Lieutenant von Kratch.
125  8th and 6th.
126  12th and 9th.
127  10th and 11th companies.
128  So as to support 4th Brigades attack against Jérusalem.
129  Bell, *St Privat*, p.318.
130  Commander of the 2nd Guards Brigade.

advance but as the regiment[131] skirted the southern edge of Sainte Marie, he received new orders to deploy on the right flank of 1st Brigade.

Emerging from the cover afforded by the village, they were hit by the enemy artillery which caused the divisional cavalry[132] accompanying their advance, to face about and seek cover to the rear of Sainte Marie. Kanitz directed that II Battalion should place itself on the right of the I, with the fusiliers echeloned on their right rear. The leading battalion formed a single line to the south of the highway, with one platoon from each company deployed as skirmishers and advanced toward the Sainte Marie-Saint Privat highway in the face of intense enemy fire.

It did not take long for the desperate plight of the stalled Guards attack to become apparent to Kanitz; the remnants of 4th Brigade were spread out to his right, 1st Brigade to his left, the two forming a weak skirmish line ranged in an arc to the west and north-west of Saint Privat. His I Battalion crossed the highway at the run, about 400 metres east of Sainte Marie and then wheeled to face their objective, all the time taking heavy losses. After each short dash, the men knelt down whilst they recovered their breath; their officers remained standing and suffered accordingly for their foolhardiness.[133] Within a few minutes Medem, Kanitz and Lieutenant Colonel von Puttkamer[134] were all hit and by the time this preliminary manoeuvre was completed, I Battalion had lost eight officers and 276 men.

At the head of II Battalion, Major von Görne pushed forward two half battalions, his left wing[135] deploying into half platoon columns and some 400 metres north of the highway, they wheeled to face Saint Privat where their commander Captain von Collas, instructed: 'As skirmishers! To the attack! Rifles right! Drummers beat!'[136] No sooner had these words passed his lips when Collas fell, mortally wounded; the horse carrying the other company commander then fell and the column was suddenly left leaderless. Given the resultant confusion, with some men failing to heed the order, it took several minutes before the battalion deployed into skirmish order, all the while losing men to the French fire.

Nevertheless, they continued to advance despite the casualties being such that even with both battalions deployed, they formed little more than a thick skirmish line. Coming up alongside the I Battalion, the impetus they imparted carried both forward until, some 700 metres west of Saint Privat, they drew level with the II and Fusilier battalions 3rd Foot Guards. Spurred on by these reinforcements, the fusiliers rose to their feet and staggered forward once again, heads bowed down against the fire. The troops deployed by Canrobert in front of Saint Privat[137] withdrew step by step into the village, where they received support from reinforcements called up from reserve.[138] From their new firing positions concealed behind the garden walls, they brought down a fresh storm of chassepot fire against Pape's men which once again, stopped his advance in its tracks.

131  According to the Great General Staff monologue *The 18th of August*, it was formed in three lines; in two lines according to the German official history.
132  2nd Guard Lancers.
133  So many in fact that the majority were killed or wounded before they even entered the firing line.
134  Commanding I Battalion.
135  7th and 8th companies.
136  Bell, *St Privat*, p.319.
137  From the 1st and 3/93rd, 1st and 3/10th and 3rd and 2/91st.
138  12th, 4th, 5th and 6th companies, 1/94th, 9th Chasseurs and few men from the 4th Division.

## Prince August Calls a Halt

It was now around 6:45 p.m. and Kessel, given the losses incurred, concluded that to continue the advance against the still strongly defended village could only result in the destruction of his brigade and he issued orders for his brigade to halt and take cover. As the Great General Staff history relates, these orders were 'superfluous,'[139] general exhaustion and the enemy fire having already stalled his advance. Kessel instructed his remaining aide[140] and 1st Lieutenant von Falkenhausen[141] to inform the corps and divisional headquarters that in view of his casualties:

> As matters stood, we were too weak to advance further, but that under cover of our fire, columns might still be brought up in rear of the centre. My impression was that I'd certainly lost far the larger half of my officers and at least half of my men, without having yet inflicted any appreciable loss on the enemy. Still, as I watched I could plainly see that our opponent was no longer unshaken; detachments began to break back and were driven to the front again.[142]

Pfeil found Prince August and his staff to the west of Sainte Marie and briefed him on the situation. When questioned about losses he said that probably half the brigade were either dead or wounded and the remainder were unable to advance. The shattered debris of some 62 companies were deployed along a front of about 2,900 metres in front of Saint Privat and it was clear to August they had little prospect of capturing their objective. If he wished to salvage the debris of his corps, he had no alternative other than to call off the attack pending the arrival of XII Corps. He told Pfeil to inform Kessel that he would send reinforcements and then rode off to Sainte Marie seeking fresh troops with which to make good on his promise.

Pape had also headed into the village seeking additional support for his beleaguered brigade. He tried, unsuccessfully, to rally the shell shocked 4th Guard Grenadiers who had fled the fight but 'the men acting as though blind and insane'[143] simply ignored his pleas, preferring the shelter of Sainte Marie to the bullet swept slopes of Saint Privat. Frustrated, Pape followed in their wake and ordered 4th Foot Guards, posted in the centre of the village, to support the left wing of Kessel's brigade.

In fact, their commander Colonel von Neumann had already received instructions from the wounded Medem 'To follow up as second line the 2nd Guard Regiment advancing to the attack south of the road to Saint Privat'[144] so his men were able to move off without further delay. Medem suggested that they take the northern route out of Sainte Marie so as to avoid the worst of the chassepot fire but as the colonel rode back to implement these instructions, Pape, concerned that his advance would be delayed because of this detour, ordered I Battalion to use the eastern exit, enjoining their commander to reinforce the left wing of Kessel's brigade.

---

139  Bell, *St Privat*, p.321
140  2nd Lieutenant Count von Pfeil.
141  1st Guards regimental adjutant.
142  Maude, *Military Letters*, p.90
143  Bell, *St Privat*, p.307.
144  *Ibid*, p.321.

When Pfeil galloped up to Pape with Kessel's request for support, he was told that the I/4th was already en-route and the other battalions would follow shortly. Pape then crossed to the eastern exit of Sainte Marie where the Guard Fusilier regiment was positioned and warned their commander[145] to ready his troops for action and the Guard Rifle battalion were instructed to defend the village to the last man in the event of any reverse.

As I/4th Foot Guards traversed the gardens to the east of the village, Pape returned to post in front of Saint Privat, while Neumann led the other two battalions to Sainte Marie's northern exit where he met First Lieutenant von Falkenhausen[146] who after briefing him on the dire situation, requested his support for their stalled attack against Saint Privat.

With III Battalion leading the advance, 4th Foot Guards headed north along the road to Montois la Montagne and after passing through the Hautmécourt ravine, reached a shallow gulley that led up to the plateau between Saint Privat and Roncourt which provided a covered approach for their assault. The II, deployed in half battalions, were initially in the rear, although as the fusiliers struggled to deploy their companies into line in the confines of the gulley, soon found themselves out in front. Meanwhile, I Battalion, who were marking time to the east of Sainte Marie pending the arrival of the fusiliers out on their left flank, now began their advance, all four companies deployed in line.

By the time 4th Foot Guards ascended the shallow ravine leading up to the plateau, the French artillery fire had almost ceased and their infantry, which until recently had been deployed in advance of Saint Privat had, for the most part withdrawn into the village. Nonetheless, Neumann was only too aware of the losses suffered by 1st Brigade and sought to reduce his casualties by skilful use of the ground and the early deployment of companies into single platoons or even skirmish formation. Initially, he found it difficult to grasp the tactical situation; both 1st Brigade and the French positions were hidden by clouds of smoke which enveloped the battlefield and even within the regiment itself, only indistinct silhouettes could be made out.

As he pushed forward, the situation became slightly less confusing; dark lines of prone figures could be made out in front of Saint Privat and when the swirling clouds lifted, determined individuals and small groups could be seen engaging the French positions. More alarming were the large numbers of men, wounded and unwounded, streaming back down the main highway into Sainte Marie. As the smoke thinned, Neumann directed I Battalion to march on Saint Privat's church steeple so as to link up with Kessel's brigade.

With drill book precision the battalion advanced towards their objective[147] and ignoring the loss of their colonel, moved alongside 1st Brigade before continuing their advance, pushing their firing line ever closer to the French positions. Out on the left, 4th Company came to a halt to the north of the group commanded by Arnim[148] as the remainder of the battalion, sweeping up the remnants of the III/1st Foot Guards in their advance, took position to his right before opening fire, at a range of 500 metres, on the northeast corner of Saint Privat. After regaining their breath, the battalion endeavoured to get within effective rifle range by a series of short dashes.

---

145  Major Feldmann.
146  Adjutant, 1st Foot Guards.
147  Skirmishers in front, followed by supports in half platoons.
148  Two platoons from the 5th and 6th companies II/1st Foot Guards.

Following in their rear, the commander of II Battalion gained his first view of the battle. The enemy artillery were still in action to the north of Saint Privat and on the slopes to the north and west of the village, hidden in scrapes and firing pits, there were several lines of French infantry, one behind the other. Opposing them, spread out across the slopes between Roncourt and Saint Privat, the shattered battalions of Kessel's brigade.

Taking advantage of the cover afforded by the depression, he deployed his two half battalions into a single line, the companies out left [149] advancing by a series of short rushes; those on the right[150] followed their example as they sought to reinforce the Kessel's skirmish line, who could be glimpsed some metres to the front through the swirling clouds of smoke. Just as they were preparing to make the final dash into the firing line, the regimental adjutant Lieutenant von Daum galloped up with orders from the Corps commander, calling repeatedly: 'Halt! Halt! Don't advance, wait for the Saxons!'[151]

Both half battalions threw themselves to the ground amongst Kessel's skirmishers but as the smoke cleared, discovered they were still some distance from the north-western corner of Saint Privat and the French positions. To their right, formed in a broken arc in front of Saint Privat, the remnants of 1st Brigade. August's order to halt had yet to reach all the troops and to the north, III/1st Foot Guards continued their advance with all four companies deployed into line looking to sever the Roncourt-Saint Privat road about halfway between the two villages.[152] Coming under fire from both strongpoints, the fusiliers deployed a screen of skirmishers, under cover of which they pushed forward in a series of short rushes, although both centre companies[153] retained two platoons in close formation in the second line to guard against any flank attack from Roncourt.

## Stalemate in Front of Saint Privat

Following the withdrawal of Canrobert's outlying skirmishers, his main firing line was now positioned about 5–600 metres in advance of the road that ran from Saint Privat to Roncourt, from where a truly murderous fire was delivered against the advancing guardsmen. There was little attempt to coordinate their actions; individual companies and battalions simply blasted away at the nearest target until they ran out of cartridges. The troops in reserve, deployed higher up the slope, also joined in the fusillade, firing over the heads of the units in front. This uncontrolled fire soon exhausted their ammunition, with men dropping out of line, making their way to the rear.

Although the attackers had suffered heavy casualties, Canrobert was aware of the Saxon manoeuvring around his open flank and his sense of unease was increased as the dogged determination of the surviving guardsmen brought them ever nearer to Saint Privat. By 7:00 p.m., 1st Guards Division were ranged in an arc from the southwest of Roncourt across to the

149  6th and 5th companies.
150  8th and 7th companies.
151  Bell, *St Privat*, p.324.
152  Given the time they had taken to deploy, they reached the firing line considerably later than the other two battalions.
153  10th and 11th.

main Saint Privat-Sainte Marie highway from where their skirmishers could at last bring an effective fire against the outlying French positions.

Even though Kessel recognised that any assault against the strongly held western side of the village had little chance of success, the support provided by the introduction of the 2nd and 4th Foot Guards led him to conclude he had sufficient strength to launch an attack against the northwest corner. From his viewpoint out on the left wing, the defence in this area seemed somewhat shaken; individuals were falling out of the enemy firing line and columns of infantry could be seen moving about in the interior of village which he interpreted as signs that Canrobert was looking to evacuate Saint Privat, even though there was still no sign of the Saxon attack.

Pape's prognosis was considerably more pessimistic; after he led 4th Foot Guard Regiment into place on the left wing of the 2nd Foot Guards, it seemed to him that Kessel's extended brigade was so depleted that there was no way they could be expected to storm Saint Privat. The numbers of wounded and unwounded men making their way to the rear, coupled with the heavy loss in officers, only served to reinforce this view. Colonel Röder then approached to brief him on 1st Foot Guard's progress; although their advance had stalled, he remained confident that his I Battalion still had the strength to force its way into the northwest corner of Saint Privat. Pape pointed to 4th Foot Guards who were moving to support him and urged that he delay any assault until they arrived. He then decided to call up the Guard Fusilier regiment from Sainte Marie, looking to make a simultaneous attack against both the southwest and northwest corners of the village.

As he issued orders to his staff officer,[154] Röder pointed out that three regiments were already committed to the attack and a fourth partially engaged; to launch yet another against the same objective would be no guarantee of success; perhaps, he suggested, 'other means' should be employed to bring about the desired result? Pape was under no illusions as to what he meant and immediately despatched his orderly[155] across to the left wing to see if he could induce some of the Saxon batteries to open fire on Saint Privat; at the same time, he was ordered to bring Seegenberg's I/3rd Foot Guards into the firing line. If possible, Esbeck was to locate XII Corps infantry and find out what they were doing.

Pape's divisional adjutant[156] was sent across to the Guard artillery deployed south of the highway to request they deploy a few batteries to set the buildings within Saint Privat ablaze. Despite Röder's reservations about throwing yet more men into the fight, Holleben was instructed to order up the Guard Fusilier regiment from Sainte Marie and to remind the Rifles that in the event of any reverse, they were to defend the village to the last man. With his last orderly officer at his side[157] Pape took position alongside the highway, awaiting the execution of his instructions.

Despite August's order for the Guards to go to ground pending the arrival of XII Corps, out on the right wing of 1st Guards Brigade, III/3rd Foot Guards had moved to within 250 metres of the enemy's outer defensive line from where they could see the caps and heads of the tirailleurs sheltering behind the piled knapsacks and ammunition boxes which lined their rifle pits. The fusilier's skirmish line was reinforced by the remnants of II Battalion and the resultant

---

154  Captain von Holleben.
155  Lieutenant von Esbeck of the Guard Hussar Regiment.
156  Major Count von Ysenburg.
157  The orderly was on foot, his horse having been shot.

increase in their firepower, persuaded even more of the defenders to abandon their positions. Encouraged by this success, the surviving officers urged the fusiliers to their feet and with loud cheers, they charged towards the line of rifle pits, the 2nd Foot Guards joining in the advance on their left. This created a panic amongst the men occupying the outer defences who flooded back to Saint Privat, but the fire from the main French positions halted the attack some 6–700 yards short of the village. As this was still outside the effective range of the needle gun, they were unable to suppress the French fire and although additional reinforcements[158] joined the firing line, their advance ground to a halt.

Further to the north, the firing line of the III/1st Foot Guard Regiment, reinforced by two companies[159] from I Battalion made a similar charge which also succeeded in driving the tirailleurs from the outlying rifle pits back into Saint Privat. As a result of this latest effort, some three and a half battalions of guardsmen managed to establish positions within 600 metres of the Saint Privat-Roncourt road and the churchyard located in the north-eastern corner of the village. Unable to continue their advance due to the volume of fire coming from the northern part of the village, the guardsmen found whatever cover they could behind the piled cases of hardtack and cartridge boxes. Their only reserves consisted of the small force assembled by Lieutenant von Arnim a few hundred yards to their rear and the men gathered together by Brause who, at that time, were still engaged in a firefight with the French deployed along the Saint Privat-Roncourt road and the open country to the southwest.

As 8th Company 1st Foot Guards moved into position alongside Brause's group, the regiment's commanding officer rode along the front of the firing line, calling out 'Hurry! Forward Grenadiers.'[160] This desperate charge forced the tirailleurs to withdraw to the cover of dead ground between the two villages and brought the guardsmen 200 metres closer to the French positions, although the hot reception they received from the men still lining the garden walls of Saint Privat, prevented any further advance. Further to the north, around 6:45 p.m., two companies[161] from I/1st Foot Guard Regiment attempted to push into the space on the left of the I/3rd Foot Guards, seeking to strengthen their firing line. As they did so, the cry went up from Brause's men: 'Cavalry is coming! Form squares!'[162]

## Barail's Cavalry Charge

The horsemen were from General du Barail's division, who were deployed to the rear right flank of Saint Privat when Canrobert ordered him to 'attempt a charge in order to buy him breathing space time to fall back.'[163] Barail delegated the task to Bruchard's brigade,[164] intending to support their attack with the 2nd Chasseurs d'Afrique. Bruchard led his brigade forward, halting on the crest of the ridge running between Roncourt and Saint Privat, as two squadrons from the 3rd Chasseurs deployed into skirmish formation and rode at the gallop towards the Guards

---

158  From the 2/3rd and 7th Company 1st Guard Regiment.
159  1st and 2nd companies.
160  Bell, *St Privat*, p.315.
161  3rd and 4th.
162  Bell, *St Privat*, p.316.
163  L'État-Major, *St Privat*, p.466.
164  2nd and 3rd Chasseurs.

firing line. One troop headed directly towards Brause's men lining the Saint Privat-Roncourt road and their warning call, swiftly repeated along the line, had an electrifying effect on the guardsmen whose morale had been severely tested by the losses suffered and their exposure to the murderous chassepot fire. The impact of the cavalry attack was felt as far south as the main chausée between Sainte Marie and Saint Privat where the Kaiser Franz regiment, in accordance with their training, formed thick knots of guardsmen for protection, although this did little other than to provide a better target for the French infantry.

The skirmishers of the 2nd Foot Guard Regiment, who had just entered the firing line to the right of the 2nd Guard Grenadiers, showed more resolve and held their ground. To their north, the reaction of 1st Guard Brigade was, at best, mixed giving Kessel considerable cause for concern. The surviving fusiliers[165] from 3rd Foot Guards, were pulled back a few hundred yards to the rear and although they withdrew at walking pace, it proved difficult for their remaining officers to get them to halt until Pape rode up and ordered them to face front. Further north, the II/3rd Foot Guards, who lacked any officers, fell back in confusion and again it took the intervention of Pape, this time with harsher words of reprimand, to halt their retreat. The remainder of the brigade lay prone on the ground as Kessel, galloping from group to group, urged his men to hold their positions and await developments. He recalled:

> To the northeast of the village, I saw a regiment of cavalry on grey horses advancing, apparently with the intention of riding down our fighting line. Infantry which on open ground has already experienced considerable loss never quite likes it when it sees cavalry advancing to the charge. There is a considerable feeling of uncertainty as to how the matter will turn out. Just at this moment my horse was shot under me. Clearing myself from his body, I took my revolver out of the holster and walking up to the skirmishers, told them what to expect and gave the order to reserve their fire till the enemy were within fifty paces and if that did not stop them, to let themselves be ridden over. The men of the first 'Garde Regiment zu Fuß' were noticeably cool and collected, adjusted their sights and my adjutant stayed with them to give them the word of command. So as to give the same orders further down the line, I doubled across a small hollow, but was so blown and fatigued in my long boots and owing to the great heat, that I was almost speechless when I reached the next body of troops and here there was no single officer standing to receive my orders and all my staff had been left behind. The appearance of the cavalry had its effect along the whole line. Some prepared to receive them in rallying squares, others in groups and in the centre the men mostly remained lying down.[166]

Von Schulenberg, with the fusiliers of the 1st Foot Guards, described how: 'At this moment the cry 'Down! The cavalry is coming' was heard and to our left we saw the grey horses and white cloaks of the horsemen; but fortunately, the charge did not come off, for on all sides the want of ammunition was beginning to be felt.'[167] Within von Brause's group, the intended objective of the charge, his men attempted to form squares but were told to maintain skirmish formation

---

165  About 150 men.
166  Maude, *Military Letters*, p.91.
167  *Ibid*, p.92.

with the lieutenant instructing: 'Everyone will wait my command to fire; we will then fire carefully, aiming at the horses breasts.'[168] To either side of his group, shooting erupted from the guards skirmish line but Brause held his fire until the leading troopers approached to within 250 metres when he gave the word for independent fire. The ranks of the leading squadron were thrown into confusion and, wheeling about, galloped off to the rear followed by their supports.

After seeing off the cavalry, the indefatigable Brause, supported by the I/3rd Foot Guard, moved up alongside the 3rd and 4th companies' 1st Foot Guard who were struggling to hold their ground in face of the fierce fire from French skirmishers sheltering amongst some stone enclosures north of Saint Privat. Despite heavy losses, Brause's men continued to advance by short rushes, until the left of their line enveloped the French positions. Fearful of being outflanked, the majority of the defenders withdrew, some to Roncourt, others to the forêt de Jaumont but one foolhardy officer and two men continued to hold their ground until they were shot by the advancing guardsmen. Reinforced by the 1st Guard Pioneer Company, Brause then consolidated his hold on the strongpoint as precaution against any counter attack.

## August Feels the Pressure

When Bruchard's cavalry launched their attack, six companies from 2nd Foot Guards[169] had worked their way forward to the abandoned fighting positions opposite Saint Privat churchyard which finally brought them to within effective rifle range of Canrobert's main defensive position. The piles of abandoned knapsacks and boxes of hardtack afforded some slight protection from the enemy fire, which allowed them to engage the flank of the attacking cavalry and following their repulse, they opened 'an enormous rapid fire'[170] against the French within Saint Privat. The other half battalion moved up to support them, but within a few minutes most of their officers were disabled and half the men struck down. The remnants of 8th Company managed to close up into the firing line where they threw themselves to the ground although the 5th, finding its way blocked, came to a halt about 200 metres to their rear and took cover in the ditch alongside the highway amongst the remnants of the Kaiser Franz regiment.

Following this latest push, there was still a 200 metre gap between 2nd Foot Guards and the highway. Moving up from the rear, three fusilier companies[171] sought to fill this space, taking their place in the line alongside the 8th; the 11th and 10th in particular, taking heavy losses as they dashed forward. The 5th then moved up into the line alongside the 12th whilst the 9th remained south of the road where it deployed alongside with the survivors of the advanced elements of the Kaiser Franz regiment.

Although Barail's attack had been easily driven off, it did serve to add to the anxiety felt by the Guard's commanders as to just how long their men could continue to hold on to their exposed positions without Saxon support. Prince August, watching the battle unfold from his position alongside the eastern exit out of Sainte Marie, became increasingly despondent; all he could see were the dead and dying who covered the ground leading to Saint Privat and streams of walking wounded making for the dressing stations. The longer he viewed the scene, the more

168  Bell, *St Privat*, p.317.
169  I and 6th and 7th companies, II Battalion.
170  Bell, *St Privat* P.319.
171  11th, 10th and 12th 2nd Foot Grenadiers.

certain he was that even the introduction of 4th Foot Guards would not bring success and he took little comfort from Kessel's upbeat despatch. Disillusioned by the scene confronting him and having earlier dismissed Pape's entreaty to wait for the Saxons, August was persuaded that only their arrival would bring success.

Orders were issued for the Guards to stay their attack until XII Corps made their presence felt, although these were to a large degree irrelevant as the fighting line had been stationary for some time; the only troops to benefit being II/4th Foot Guards. As it transpired, August's instructions were overtaken by events as the Saxons finally began their long-awaited advance on Roncourt.

## The Resumption of Fighting Around Amanvillers

Following the repulse of IX Corps initial attack, Ladmirault could feel reasonably satisfied with the situation and in the ensuing pause, spent some time reorganising his troops. His front line battalions[172] deployed partly along and partly in front of the road running from la Folie to Habonville, their positions extending for some 2,000 metres. In reserve, another six battalions[173] were echeloned between Amanvillers and Montigny la Grange. Moreover, around 4:00 p.m., General Berger[174] reported that although 6 Corps and Cissey's division had been forced to retreat, shortly after, he witnessed them launching a counter attack which recaptured the ground previously abandoned.[175]

A little before 5:00 p.m., cheering erupted from the French troops all along the front of 4 and 6 corps and although the reason for this was unclear, taken in conjunction with Berger's earlier report, Ladmirault took this as further evidence that the Prussian attack had stalled. Just as well, for although his infantry were generally in good heart, the position regarding artillery within 4 Corps was a different picture altogether being, as noted by the French official history, almost 'reduite à rien'.[176]

Following the withdrawal of the 10/4th from Le Boeuf's 3 Corps, only two out of Ladmirault's 15 batteries were still in position and short of ammunition, were unlikely to be able to offer much resistance.[177] He was relieved therefore, to receive a note from General Bourbaki, commander of the Imperial Guard, advising of the arrival at Gros-Chênes, of a division of grenadiers which was making their way towards Amanvillers, news of which was immediately passed onto generals Berger and Lorencez to help bolster their troop's morale. Meanwhile 13th Line, which suffered considerably during the fighting,[178] was ordered to the rear, alongside the 43rd who had previously pulled out of the line after exhausting their ammunition. To fill the resultant gap in his line, 1st and 2/15th and subsequently 3/54th were redeployed. One of the few remaining

---

172 3/73rd, 1/54th, 5th Chasseurs, 2nd Chasseurs,1st, 2nd and 3/13th, 1st and 2/15th, 3/54th, 1st and 2/65th, 3rd and 1/64th and 2nd, 1st and 3/98th.
173 2/54th, 2/64th, 3/65th, 1st, 2nd and 3/33rd; of these the 2/64th had yet to be engaged.
174 Commander 2nd Brigade, 3rd Division, 4 Corps stationed on the heights near Amanvillers.
175 The French official history is at a loss to explain what Berger claimed to have seen.
176 L'État-Major, St Privat, p.473.
177 The 12-pdrs of Commandant Ladrange, the 11th and 12/1st.
178 Killed; five officers, 33 men, wounded 13 officers, 230 men; missing, 110 men.

12-pdr batteries[179] then withdrew after firing off their last rounds and finally, around 5:30 p.m., the 3/65th were deployed to reinforce the centre of the 98th. As a consequence, when Manstein renewed his attack, 4 Corps' fighting line, extending along a front of some 2,000 metres, 'formed but a thin line of contiguous battalions.'[180]

## 3rd Guard Brigade attack Amanvillers

Impatient to launch his IX Corps in a fresh assault against Amanvillers, Manstein kept a close eye on developments around Saint Privat from his command post at the northern edge of the Bois de la Cusse. Having sent his staff officer to request an update from August, Manstein noted Berger's brigade manoeuvring into position around Sainte Marie and without further delay, decided to renew his attack, instructing 3rd Guards Brigade to begin their advance on Amanvillers. All other available troops were ordered to redouble their efforts to close with the French lines, the only exceptions being 4th Hessian Brigade and the remnants of 18th Division[181] who were retained as a general reserve.

Just as Manstein issued his orders to the Guards Brigade, General von Wittich[182] arrived with confirmation that August intended to commence his attack against Saint Privat at 5:00 p.m. Shortly after, I Battalion Kaiser Alexander Regiment at Habonville and 4th Guard Brigade at St Ail were seen making their preparations for the assault.

Despite the fact that Frederick placed 3rd Guards Brigade at Manstein's disposal, August ordered them to 'support the advance of the 4th Guard Infantry Brigade on Saint Privat by advancing on the right wing.'[183] On receipt of these instructions, Colonel Knappe von Knappestädt[184] directed the battalion of Guard Sharpshooters 'to occupy the section of woods located east of Habonville and from their support the general attack of the division.' Just as these orders were being implemented, Manstein rode up with his conflicting instructions for the Sharpshooters 'to advance on the right wing of the Hessian division' so as to support his attack on Amanvillers. By this time, around 5:15 p.m., the battalion had already begun to traverse the Bois de la Cusse in support of August and so they were allowed to continue their march, although the remainder of the brigade were directed further south, so as to comply with Manstein's directive. Knappestädt subsequently directed two battalions of the Kaiser Alexander's regiment 'to advance to the attack with its left wing at the southern edge of the woods.'[185] In the second line, 10 companies from 3rd Guard Grenadier Regiment[186] moved into the wood at hill 316.

As the Guard Sharpshooter battalion worked their way in single file through the dense undergrowth of the Bois de la Cusse, they stumbled across the 3rd Hessian Regiment and

179 The 11/12th.
180 L'État-Major, *St Privat*, p.475. His remaining reserves comprised the 2/54th, 2/64th and 1st, 2nd and 3/33rd.
181 I and III/84th, II and III/36th and the remnants of the III/85th had pulled back into the Bois de la Cusse to reorganise.
182 Commander 49th Infantry Brigade.
183 Bell, *St Privat*, p.328.
184 Commander, 3rd Guard Infantry Brigade.
185 This and preceding quotes taken from Bell, *St Privat*, p.329.
186 The Königen Elizabeth; they were supported by 2nd and 3rd Field Pioneer companies.

swerving further south so as to avoid clashing, their lead companies paused at hill 316, waiting for the remainder of the battalion to come forward. Although there was little sign of the French within the Bois de la Cusse, their long-range fire harassing was still inflicting casualties, so Major von Fabeck[187] decided to press on with his attack rather than wait for the other two companies to come forward.

After briefing Knappestädt of his intentions, he deployed his leading formations[188] into skirmish order and led them forward at the double. His left wing was anchored on a ditch which ran in an easterly direction from the Bois de la Cusse into Amanvillers and after gaining 120 metres, the skirmishers threw themselves to the ground and opened fire on the enemy positions at a range of between 5–600 metres. Fabeck's advance did not go unnoticed and he came under intense fire from the 73rd and the 1/54th. Noting their plight, Major Trenk took his three fusilier companies[189] along the southern edge of the Bois de la Cusse to a position in the rear of the 3rd Hessian Regiment, before advancing onto the open ground to their left, hoping to sustain the firefight until the remainder of the Guards Brigade moved up alongside in support of the Sharpshooters line.

Meanwhile, two battalions from 1st Guard Grenadiers[190] pushed their way through the wood to the southwest corner of hill 316 from where the lead battalion of fusiliers made a left turn toward Amanvillers and then, under fire from the French lines, deployed two companies in open formation.[191] Their skirmish line advanced by short 50 metre rushes until they came alongside the Sharpshooters; initially the 10th and 11th companies remained in reserve, sheltered in the wood but as the firefight intensified, they were brought forward, extending the fusiliers firing line to the right.

On the right flank of Ladmirault's line, the 5th Chasseurs, who had recently replenished their ammunition, greeted this latest advance with a torrent of fire, forcing all bar a single platoon to deploy into skirmish formation. In view of the heavy French fire, especially from the 3/54th, who were to the south of the Chasseurs, the supporting companies of Guard Sharpshooters[192] were brought forward to extend the firing line to the north but their efforts met with little success and the few survivors pushed into the main firing line fronting Amanvillers.

## The Guards Attack Stalls in Front of Amanvillers

The section most threatened by the Guards attack was held by the 15th Ligne and although the brigade commander General Pajol was confident his men could hold the line, Ladmirault, observing additional troops advancing through the Bois de la Cusse, brought up the 1/33rd to reinforce his firing line.[193] As they were moved forward, the 2nd Chasseurs, holding the

---

187 Commander of the Guard Sharpshooters.
188 1st on the left, 2nd on the right in the front line, the 3rd and 4th subsequently formed a second support line.
189 The 9th Company became separated from the remainder of the battalion when they first entered the wood.
190 The Kaiser Alexander's.
191 12th and 9th.
192 3rd and 4th
193 The 33rd took position between the 1st and 2/ 15th and the 3/ 54th.

crossroads west of Amanvillers, began to give way. The battalion had been under heavy enfilade fire from the Guard batteries to the north of the railway for some time and as related within the unit history, 'their position was no longer tenable because the fire of the enemy artillery had redoubled and their blows hit home with frightful precision.'[194] Under this 'rain of iron' the sight of the Alexander's fusilier battalion resolute advance towards their position proved too much and the chasseurs began to give ground. Commandant Le Tanneur, assisted by his officers, successfully rallied his men and led them forward again in a bayonet charge against the Guards.[195]

The Alexander's were ordered to hold fire so as to conserve ammunition until the chasseurs were within effective range and several anxious minutes passed as the enemy column, preceded by thick chains of skirmishers, steadily advanced until only three hundred paces separated the two sides. As firing burst out all along the guardsmen's line some chasseurs, urged on by their officers, attempted to close with the Guards although the majority collected together in small groups, which only served to provide better targets for the Alexander's who were given timely support by the batteries of IX Corps horse artillery from the north of Champenois.

Unable to withstand this concerted rifle and cannon fire, the Chasseurs fell back with heavy losses and despite the efforts of their officers the battalion simply melted away, carrying away both 1st and 2/15th in their flight to the rear.[196] Assuming command of the 15th, Captaine adjutant major Bonnet uncased the regimental colours and after rallying the remnants of both battalions, led them back into the line, his efforts no doubt assisted by the timely arrival of the 1/33rd.

The Chasseurs rout coincided with the arrival in the enemy firing line of the III/3rd Guard Grenadiers whereupon troops from 35th Brigade who were sheltering in the eastern part of the bois de la Cusse[197] made a perfunctory attempt to support the Guard's attack. Although a few men from the 84th made their way into the grenadier's firing line, the majority quickly fell back to their original positions within the wood, their half-hearted attempt no doubt indicative of the shaken moral of these troops.

Meanwhile II/1st Guard Grenadiers[198] were ordered to 'Advance on the right of the Fusiliers and, at the same time, take over protection of IX Corps gun line from the 1st Hessian Rifle battalion'[199] and moved into position southeast of hill 316 on the left wing of the artillery positioned north of Champenois. Even in this relatively sheltered position, they came under increasingly heavy fire so that all bar a single platoon were deployed in extended order. With the Brigade's advance stalled, Major von Schmelling[200] was called forward to replace the Hessians who by now had exhausted their ammunition. His battalion advanced at the run and following

---

194  L'État-Major, *18 Août, Documents*, p.287.
195  The failure of the 5th Chasseurs to support the attack by 2nd Chasseurs left their flank open to a counter attack by the II/1st Guard Grenadiers; however, the chasseurs had sustained considerable losses during the day and perhaps they were concerned that they could be assaulted and cut off, their right flank being completely exposed to a counter attack by the 2/64th.
196  The 15th had lost their lieutenant colonel and two chefs de bataillon to the artillery fire.
197  They were in the second line.
198  They were in the second line.
199  Bell, *St Privat*, p.331.The Hessians were to the right of the guns but were low on ammunition.
200  Commander of II Battalion.

several short rushes deployed on the right of the brigade's line, the ground left littered with their dead and wounded.

This support came just in time, as a number of Hessians were already falling back into cover, their morale shattered by their exposure to the murderous French fire. After regaining their breath, the Grenadiers again rose to their feet and dashed forward, the 5th and 6th companies fronting towards Montigny, as some 300 metres to their left, the 3rd and 4th companies attempted to link up with the right flank of the fusilier battalion.

This last advance, which brought the brigade to within 400 metres of the French positions, came at heavy cost especially to the officers, but there still remained a 300-metre gap between Schmelling and III/1st Guard Grenadiers. Shortly after 6:00 p.m., Zeuner ordered up the 2nd and 3rd companies 1st Guard Grenadiers and III/3rd Guard Grenadiers from the wood north of hill 316 to fill this void, their advance being directed towards the church spire in Amanvillers.[201] As the steeple was hidden from view by the undulating terrain, the Elizabeth's commanding officer[202] instead designated a tall poplar tree, south of the village as their objective. This feature was soon obscured by dense clouds of smoke, and blindly stumbling forward III Battalion somehow found itself in the rear of the II/1st, facing Montigny, whilst two companies from the 1st Grenadiers inched their way along edge of the bois de la Cusse towards Amanvillers. However, in the face of heavy French fire, this advance also ground to a halt, their fighting line comprising dispersed groups of skirmishers rather than formed bodies of men.

Fortunately for the Guards, around 7:00 p.m., Colonel von Zeuner[203] was informed by IX Corps chief of staff that a brigade from III Corps would be arriving shortly to support Manstein's enveloping attack so there was no need for his men to continue their offensive. On receipt of this news, Zeuner ordered his men to cease their attack and assume a defensive stance along the positions won at such heavy cost; in reality his units were already so weak and short of ammunition that any further advance against strongly defended enemy positions was beyond them.

## IX Corps support for the Guards attack

To support the Guards attack on Amanvillers, Manstein set in motion IX Corps reserves which he had retained for this decisive moment. Major General von Wittich led the 49th Brigade forward, the axis of their advance being along railway line which ran at right angles across the battlefield. To the south of the track II/1st Hessian Regiment[204] under Major Hahn moved forward to occupy the ground on the left flank of the Guards; six companies[205] were already positioned north of the line following their earlier abortive attack and the 1st and 4th under Captain von Röder pushed forward into a grassy hollow to the north east.

201 This left the just the brigades final reserves, II/3rd Guard Grenadiers and two Guard Pioneer companies, in the southwest corner of the bois de la Cusse.
202 Colonel von Zaluskowski.
203 The commander of the 1st Guard Grenadier Regiment had assumed command of 3rd Brigade when von Knappstaedt's hand was shattered by a bullet and he had to relinquish command.
204 7th, 5th and 6th companies in the front line, 8th company in reserve. The 3rd and 4th companies from the 3rd Hessian Regiment posted in the bois de la Cusse followed in their wake.
205 From north to south; 5/2nd, 1st and 4/1st, 8/2nd and 6th and 7/2nd.

Meanwhile the 2nd and 3rd companies' 1st Hessian Regiment, under Major Anschütz, attempted to enter the line on their right but the heavy fire from their front and flank[206] caused them veer off to the left. The 5th company 2nd Hessian joined its sister companies under von Major Hoffman on Anschütz's right and as Wittich recalled in his post combat report:

> As the enormous losses had stopped the attack of the Guard, the companies which had penetrated into the sunken road were obliged to fall back on the battalions around the signal box. Major Hoffman[207] quickly gathered a half battalion from the 2nd Regiment; I assembled a myself column of about 150 scattered skirmishers from both regiments, and led it forward to attempt a new attack against Amanvillers … the force was insufficient, too isolated and not having any fresh troops, I was obliged to organise a new defensive position, near the level crossing.[208]

Spurred on by the determination shown by their infantry, two batteries[209] moved up from the Hessian gun line and took up position on the flank of the guns deployed by Ingelfingen to counter Cissey's attack against 4th Guard Infantry Brigade. To the south of the railway, Major Röder, who had assumed command after Hahn was killed, directed the II/1st against the same objective. Lieutenant Colonel Stamm, at the head of the 3rd Hessians, then pushed forward from the bois de la Cusse, crossed the track and attempted to occupy the space that had opened up between Anshütz and Hoffman.

However, as the German official history records 'these enterprises although carried out with commendable self-sacrifice, entirely failed before the adversary's heavy fire which swept in a truly annihilating manner over the open hillside.'[210] Following this setback, 49th Brigade withdrew to their starting positions whilst the 3rd Hessians retreated once again to the shelter of the wood, Stamm being one of the many casualties suffered in the abortive attack against the signal box.

To the south of the bois de la Cusse, the horse artillery batteries [211]echeloned along the ridge north of Champenois farm, provided suppressive fire for 3rd Guards Brigade's attack by shelling Amanvillers and when this target was masked by their advance, they shifted their fire towards Montigny. They received support from four batteries[212] under Captain von Eynatten positioned a few hundred yards to the rear on the southern flank of the ridge although their fire had limited impact as the ground to the west of Amanvillers was concealed by the rising ground.[213]

206  From the 3/73rd.
207  Commander, II/2nd.
208  Bell, *St Privat*, p.87.
209  Jourdan's 1st Light, von Eynatten's 2nd Light, Puttkamer's 1st Heavy from 1st Field Division IX Corps and Mente's 4th Light from 2nd Field Division IX Corps.
210  Clarke, *Franco German War*, p.124.
211  Franck's 1st Horse artillery and Von Gizyck's 3rd Horse artillery from III Corps and Königs 2nd Horse artillery from IX Corps.
212  Jourdan's 1st Light, v Eynatten's 2nd Light, Puttkamer's 1st Heavy from 1st Field Division IX Corps and Mente's 4th Light from 2nd Field Division IX Corps.
213  One of his batteries, commanded by Lieutenant Jourdan, suffered particularly heavy losses to the chassepot fire as it manoeuvred into a better firing position.

The remaining batteries[214] deployed around Champenois, targeted Ladmirault's defences in and around Montigny and General Bülow ordered Stöphasius[215] to support them from l'Envie. Due to the losses suffered in the fighting on 16 August, their teams only had four horses and made but slow progress through the thick clay so it was well past 6:45 p.m. before they came into action.

Even later, as darkness was falling, 3rd Field Division[216] moved up from Verneville into position alongside them which enabled the two remaining Hessian guns to withdraw to replenish their ammunition.[217] 2nd Field Division[218] were then brought forward to support their infantry[219] who lacked the strength to wrest control of Charmoise wood from the enemy. A little later, due to the losses suffered in the earlier fighting, 1st Company, 9th Rifles were withdrawn to Chantrenne alongside the III/36th, their senior officer, Major von Minckwitz, refusing to relinquish his command despite being wounded several times.

An ad hoc force[220] was assembled from the troops gathered around the farm and made repeated attempts to close with the French lines, the last shortly after 6:00 p.m. when 3rd Rifle company went over to the attack. Two companies[221] from the 85th, led by Lieutenant Colonel Köppen, attempted to support this assault but with losses mounting at every step and short of ammunition, the offensive stalled and the troops withdrew to the shelter of the bois de Genivaux.

Despite all their efforts, IX Corps had little to show in return for their heavy losses; by 7:00 p.m. the positions occupied by Manstein ran due south from the eastern corner of the bois de la Cusse south through Champenoise and l'Envie to the eastern corner of Genivaux wood, still well short of his objectives, Amanvillers and Montigny.

## The Situation Within 4 Corps

4 Corps had suffered equally heavy casualties and still without any orders or directions from Bazaine, as far as Ladmirault was concerned, Zeuner's decision to halt his brigade's attack gave his troops a welcome respite. His position had held, just, although nearly all his ready reserves had been fed into the firing line with only 2/54th being held back in Amanvillers. Although

---

214  Brandt's Hessian Horse artillery and von Unruhe's 5th Light Guard.

215  Commander, 1st Field Division: 1st Heavy, Captain Nöldecke and 2nd Heavy, Lieutenant Châles de Beaulieu.

216  5th Heavy, Captain Eunicke and 6th Heavy, Captain Meinecke; the Division was commanded by Lieutenant Colonel Beck.

217  On re-joining the firing line, they discovered their breech blocks had become so fouled the guns could no longer fire, and were withdrawn to the north of Verneville.

218  3rd Light, Lieutenant Beck; 3rd Heavy, Captain Vosz, 4th Heavy, Captain Fromme, 4th Light, Captain Fromme.

219  Two battalions from the 36th, Is and II/85th and 1st, 2nd and 4th companies' 9th Rifles. These troops had been reinforced by the II/84th.

220  From north to south on the open ground west of Charmoise wood: 4th Company 85th, 5th Company 84th, 2nd Company 9th Rifles, 3rd Company 85th, II/36th, 6th Company 67th, I/85th and then within Genivaux wood, 2nd Company 85th, 3rd Company 9th Rifles, 8th Company 84th, II/85th and 8th Company 69th.

221  2nd and 3rd.

Pradier's troops[222] to the south west of Montigny around hill 343 had not come under direct attack, they had been subjected to constant bombardment from the guns around Champenois which resulted in a number of casualties[223] and around 5:00 p.m. were reinforced by the 3/65th.

Towards 6:00 p.m., the 2nd and 3/33rd were sent forward to relieve the 98th and when these arrived, Pradier ordered the retreat to be sounded, followed by the call sign of his brigade. Unfortunately, the 33rd misheard the bugle call, and also went about. The colonel of the 98th, seeing the reinforcements dissolve into confusion, ordered his regiment to about face and led them back into the rifle pits they had just vacated. Recognising their mistake, the 33rd again turned about and managed to squeeze into the earthworks alongside Pradier's brigade. Fortunately, the enemy occupying the nearby farms of l'Envie and Chantrenne made no attempt to take advantage of this mix-up and remained entrenched within their positions, although if truth be told, they lacked both the strength and willpower to take any offensive action.

Around 7:00 p.m., the Prussian artillery opened a violent fire against hill 343 near Montigny. Pradier anticipated a new offensive against his lines and sent to Ladmirault for reinforcements; none were available, as all his reserves had been committed to fend off 3rd Guards Brigade's assault but to Pradier's considerable relief, no attack materialised. With both sides pausing for breath and short of ammunition, the firing died away and for the time being 'une passivité complete' descended over this sector of the battlefield.

## The Continuing Struggle Within the Mance Ravine

Around 5:00 p.m. General Wartesleben[224] rode up to the Royal entourage assembled on the heights west of Mogador farm to brief the assembled dignitaries as to the state of affairs confronting I Army[225] and shortly after, Lieutenant Colonel von Brandenstein delivered an update on II Army's progress.

His arrival coincided with a sudden increase in the noise of battle emanating from somewhere to the north of the bois de Génivaux and the headquarters staff took this as confirmation that, somewhat belatedly, the long-awaited envelopment of the French position around Saint Privat and Amanvillers was underway.

Thirty minutes later, General von Fransecky approached the group and was told by the king to hold II Corps ready at Steinmetz's disposal. For the last 90 minutes, he had been assembling his men around Rezonville, anxious for his corps to take some part in the battle after his long and exhausting 20-mile march from Pont à Mousson.[226] His advance guard was to the south of the village, 3rd Infantry Division to the west, the artillery to the north, whilst 4th Division were approaching from the direction of Onville.

---

222  The 2nd and 1/64th, 2nd, 1st and 3/98th.

223  The 98th lost 19 officers and 284 men.

224  I Army's Quartermaster in Chief.

225  His report was somewhat more objective than that previously given to the King by Steinmetz in as much as he confirmed that although the French fire had reduced, this was reflective of their fatigue rather than their forces being defeated.

226  Notwithstanding his men's considerable exertions, Fransecky was reproached by Moltke for arriving so late on the battlefield.

Following his earlier reprimand, Steinmetz had returned in a sulk to his field headquarters. Although he still thought it possible to seize the opposing heights, he was loath, especially after his public dressing down, to commit his last reserves[227] to the struggle until support was to hand. With the arrival of II Corps, he felt justified in ordering 32nd Brigade into action although Goeben had already pre-empted his instructions and told Colonel Rex[228] to push the 72nd and II/40th into the Mance ravine.[229] Verdy du Vernois recorded his impression of this latest attack:

> Suddenly the opposing slopes were lit up as if by a grand illumination; innumerable small flames shot forth from all the tiers of trenches and light blue clouds of vapour rose above them; near the crest, down below in the valley, in fact everywhere, the din of battle broke out again. Along the poplar avenue strong lines of infantry stood deployed, whose incessant independent firing produced a grand effect. And now, as if springing from the earth, the French batteries suddenly came into action again; shrapnel, common-shell, mitrailleuse bullets, came sweeping down into the valley. Even on the spot where we stood, the whizzing of the bullets became frequent, as well as the bursting of shrapnel high above our heads, the fragments of which cleft the air with a shrill sound. Altogether it was one of the most animated and splendid battle scenes that could possibly be imagined.[230]

Seeking a closer view of the fighting, the irrepressible Seton made his way across the ravine to Saint Hubert farm, where:

> Craning over one of the walls to try and make out if the French were issuing from their holes, I heard an unpleasant singing all round me like a discharge of grape and felt Gustavus sink gradually under me, till he sprawled on his side. Continuing mitrailleuse fire urged me after disengaging myself, to be content with tearing off my great coat and saddle bags and get sharp under cover of the wall, where I sat a little while with some of the 72nd. None of what may be called the garrison of Saint Hubert had, I believe, flinched during this temporary panic on the road and what troops had got cover on either side, were also free from it. I did not myself see any cause for the men in front giving way and was at the time inclined to think that the row made by the ammunition wagon had taken effect on men nervous from standing some time under the fire of an unseen enemy, without being able to return it.[231]

Goeben galloped across to Saint Hubert to review the situation on the far side of the valley and after praising Gnügge for his bravery in maintaining his guns in position after the other

---

227  Four battalions 32nd Brigade from VIII Corps and 10½ battalions from 25th, 27th and 28th Brigade from VII Corps who were around Gravelotte.
228  Commander 32nd Brigade.
229  The I/40th had been sent to Malmaison to cover the left flank, the III, to the valley in the bois de Génivaux.
230  Vernois, *Royal Headquarters*, pp.86–87.
231  Seton, *Notes*, pp.157–158.

batteries had withdrawn, was pleased to note that the farm and the immediate area appeared secure against counter attack. However, the confused situation on the valley floor was more of a cause for concern and he ordered the few surviving officers to rally their men and bring them back into the firing line. His instructions had little practical impact; the road across the ravine was almost blocked with abandoned wagons and broken limbers; dead and wounded littered the slopes and the officers were as shell shocked and confused as their men.

## II Corps Committed to the Struggle

Goeben's introduction of fresh troops into such a confused situation could only exacerbate matters and unsurprisingly, the reinforcements failed to make any impression on the tactical situation, their advance once more bogging down in the crowded ravine, with the men at the front of the crush calling out: 'Back!' whilst those at the rear cried: 'Forward!' Vernois recalled 'It quickly became evident that the enemy was too strong; indeed, we saw large bodies of our men coming down the slope again,'[232] whilst one of the king's aides, Lieutenant Colonel von Waldersee noted: 'After a short while Steinmetz came up and reported that the troops were not advancing any further. "Why are they not advancing?" asked the king in excited terms, "They no longer have any leaders, your Majesty, the officers are dead or wounded." '[233] The king, clearly exasperated at the failure of his troops to take the heights, exclaimed to those about him that, 'as the heights had once been carried and then lost, everything must be done to get possession of them again.'[234]

Looking around, William noticed that 3rd Division from Fransecky's corps had just reached Gravelotte[235] and against all military logic, placed them under Steinmetz's command, instructing him 'To attack the Point du Jour with all available forces'[236] As far as Moltke was concerned, not only was the direction of attack unsuitable, but given the difficulties experienced by Goeben's men as they attempted to push their way through the congestion within the ravine, he questioned the desirability of launching yet another offensive at such a late hour. His objections were curtly dismissed by the king, who insisted that his orders be carried out, as one onlooker observed:

> After some time, the King was again indignant and expressed himself to Moltke complaining of the troops and their not gaining ground. Moltke replied with equal heat 'They are fighting for your Majesty like heroes!' 'I am the best judge of that!' retorted the King whereupon Moltke gave spur to his horse and dashed forward down the incline towards Gravelotte where the head of the Third Division was now to assembling.[237]

---

232  Vernois, *Royal Headquarters*, p.87.
233  Alfred, Count von Waldersee, *A Field Marshal's Memoir*, (London, Hutchinson & Co. 1924) p.65.
234  Vernois, *Royal Headquarters*, p.85.
235  It was around 6:30 p.m.
236  Hoenig, *Twenty-Four Hours*, p.145.
237  Waldersee, *Field Marshal's Memoir*, p.65. In his memoirs, written sometime after the event, Moltke set out this carefully crafted criticism of the king's actions 'It would have been more proper if the Chief of the General Staff of the Army, who was personally on the spot at that time, had not permitted this

As II Corps marched to their fate, Verdy du Vernois described the scene:

> It was now about 8 o'clock and owing to the smoke which had settled down in the
> low-lying parts, it had become almost dark when we rode into Gravelotte. Before us
> 3rd Division was advancing, behind us the 4th Division was close in the rear with the
> 21st Regiment at its head. It was only the burning houses that allowed us to make out
> the route ... Now, in spite of hundreds of wounded streaming back from the front,
> in spite of the panic they had just witnessed, in the midst of shells striking in every
> direction, they marched through the village in well locked ranks with gallant bearing
> and loud cheers at the prospect of taking part in the action.[238]

## Frossard and Le Boeuf Make Ready

On the opposite side of the ravine, given the absence of any direction from Bazaine, Le Boeuf
and Frossard spent their time seeking to reorganise their battle-weary battalions; the artillery
made ready to resume their positions in the firing line; firing rifle pits were reoccupied, wounded
removed to the rear, ammunition redistributed and reserves told off for each brigade. From
their vantage point on the Point du Jour heights, it was clear to both corps commanders that
the enemy were preparing to launch another attack as the ground between Rezonville and
Gravelotte was covered with massed formations of infantry and artillery with 'the setting sun
glinting on a sea of helmets'[239] as they advanced towards the French positions.

Given the undulating terrain and poor light, it was difficult to accurately estimate their
number, although they believed it to be a reserve army, under the king of Prussia, amounting to
at least two corps. It did not take long for the two commanders to come to the conclusion that
there was no chance 'of winning a battle' and at best, they could only hope to get out of 'the
affair with honour.'[240]

Within 3 Corps sector, to the north of Moscou, 10 battalions[241] were deployed amongst the
earthworks, rifles pits and fortified farmyard building and held a front of some 1,700 metres.[242]
Between Leipzig and the Point du Jour, there were another 17 battalions from 3 Corps which
had yet to see action,[243] and although his defences had yet to be seriously threatened, Le
Boeuf instructed Aymard to reinforce his first line with the reserve battalions, as described by
Tissonnière:

movement at so late an hour of the evening. A body of troops which still completely intact, might have
been of great value the next day, but it could hardly be expected on this evening to effect a decisive
reversal of the situation.' See Moltke, *Franco-German War*, p.58.

238  Vernois, *Royal Headquarters*, pp.89–90.
239  Bonnal, *St Privat III*, p.187.
240  Hoenig, *Twenty-Four Hours*, p.138.
241  2/69th, 1st and 2/19th, 1/7th, 1/29th, 1st, 2nd and 3/59th, 2/60th and 3/44th.
242  They had lost less than 10 percent of their effective strength.
243  1st and 2/69th, 13th Chasseurs, 3/19th, 1st, 2nd and 3/41st, 2nd and 3/7th, 1st, 2nd and 3/71st, 3/2nd,
     1/60th 2/44th, 11th Chasseurs and 2/85th.

Six o'clock! A rain of shells but none hit us. Ah! There's a formation in line of battle,[244] very well dressed, coming to our support. The commandant, Maréchal in the centre, the colonel[245] on the right, Sourdille[246] to the left; it's the 3rd battalion. From my position I can see gaps in their line and as they approach us, they want to share the rifle pits that are barely sufficient for my men. We formed two ranks out of three. The men in the rifle pits didn't want to give up the cover they'd spent several hours working hard to improve. The officers went back and forth reorganising the firing line. The enemy fire intensified.[247]

Within 2 Corps, Frossard could be equally satisfied with his corps performance. The line between Moscou and the Point du Jour was held by eight battalions[248] and generally, had yet to suffer significant casualties; the 3rd Chasseurs for example had lost only 32 men. South of Point du Jour nine battalions,[249] for the most part hidden in the ditches lining the main road, held a front of some 1,200 metres. To their rear, hidden behind the crest, stood both corps' Reserves who were, for the most part, still at full strength. Even ignoring Lapassat's brigade which had been sent off to the left wing, Frossard still had some 13 fresh battalions[250] to hand with the account given by one of the commanders of those units, Colonel Ameller of the 66th, serving to illustrate of the abundance of troops in this sector.

A little before 6:30 p.m., Ameller was directed by his brigade commander Fauvart Bastoul, to relieve the 8th, who had only just taken up their positions, because they had lost all their superior officers. He recalled how he

> … led his regiment forward in line of battle and then executed a half turn to the left which brought him to a thicket which stretched between the old roman road and the new highway. After having placed my men behind an embankment along the roman road, I sent both the 1st and 2nd battalions towards the Point du Jour where General Sanglé-Ferrière,[251] who commanded the troops in this area, told me he had more than enough troops to defend the position. 'Would I please stop sending him men and go and speak with him?' I halted the 2nd Battalion, who'd just been sent forward, at once. Sanglé-Ferrière told me that there was no need for reinforcements, there were already too many men in the area and he begged me to take mine away. I told him I was only carrying out the orders of my brigade commander, but nonetheless I would withdraw my regiment and hold it as his disposal a little way to the rear by the bend in the road.[252]

244  80th Ligne.
245  Janin.
246  He died that evening from wounds received during the afternoon.
247  Bonnal, *St Privat III*, pp.189–190.
248  1/44th, 1/85th, 1/80th, 1st and 2/32nd, 3/23rd, 3rd Chasseurs and 3/80th.
249  12th Chasseurs, 1/55th, 2/76th, 2/55th, 3/76th, 1/76th and 1st, 2nd and 3/77th.
250  1st, 2nd and 3/8th, 1st and 2/23rd, 1st, 2nd and 3/66th, 1st, 2nd and 3/67th, 3/32nd and 3/55th.
251  Commander 2nd Brigade, 4th Division, 3 Corps.
252  L'État-Major, *18 Août, Documents*, p.115.

His three battalions were then withdrawn to the rear to act as supports for the firing line which, in the words of the French official history 'at this moment had no need of relief.'[253] The 67th was then sent to replace the 55th who had been engaged since the morning but again, their commander refused to withdraw.[254] Fauvart Bastoul ordered Colonel Haca of the 8th to relieve the 3/23rd, even though their losses were negligible. It was a little before 6:00 p.m. when Haca led his regiment forward along the old Roman road in column of platoons and cresting the plateau at hill 349, they were hit by enemy gunfire. Haca was amongst the first casualties as a bullet smashed his right hand[255] and given the losses amongst the superior officers during the fighting on the 16th, Captain Francot assumed command.[256] He then attempted to deploy part of the regiment along the Roman road, part behind the bend in the main road; the 1st Battalion to the north, the 2nd and 3rd to the south.

With the French positions again coming under heavy artillery bombardment, the units occupying this sector[257] were reluctant to leave the cover afforded by the ditches and rifle pits and there was understandable confusion as their reliefs moved into position. The 23rd broke and fled to the rear, fearing that the artillery bombardment presaged a new attack by the Prussians, whilst other battalions[258] simply refused to budge. To add to the difficulties, it seems that some of Haca's men accidently opened fire on their own men, as Tissonnière related:

Suddenly there was a noise to my rear. What was that? Are we turned? Some 200 metres to our rear, a battalion had appeared behind us, took cover and opened fire; they thought we were the enemy. We sounded the 'cease fire' and made signals to them; it had no effect. My sous-lieutenant Tournebize asked me permission to go over to them. He set off under a hail of bullets and made his way to the rear, where he reached some of their officers amongst whom were a number of doubters who asked 'If it were true that they were French?' The firing ceased shortly, the battalion from the 8th got to its feet and made its way towards us, but where to put them? Everyone lies down on the road, behind the rifle pits, anywhere and they all opened fire again. As they were deployed in ten ranks, the men in the front lines were shot at by those behind and threatened to return fire. I tapped a few of the men closest to me with my stick and sat on the front slope of gun pit 'The Prussian side' I said, 'It's less dangerous.'[259]

---

253  L'État-Major, St Privat, p.617.
254  Colonel Waldner told General Vergé's officier d'ordonnance 'Please, I beg you to inform the general that it's true that I have been engaged since this morning, but I've lost very few men and my position is excellent; I could hold it until 10:00 p.m. tonight and then retire under cover of darkness. If you want me to pull back during the day, across that open ground, I'll lose more men than I have so far today.' See l'État-Major St Privat, pp.614–615.
255  His forearm was later amputated.
256  Captain Adjutant Major Lacapelle commanded the 1st Battalion, Captain Turc the 2nd and Captain Loubeyre the 3rd.
257  From the 80th, 32nd and 23rd regiments.
258  1/80th, 1st and 2/32nd and 3/80th.
259  Bonnal, St Privat III, p.128. The post combat report of the 80th confirmed that a battalion from the 8th opened fire on them from the rear.

consequently over us. For some reason they did not advance farther, but we never knew what moment they might.[275]

General Sheridan also witnessed Barnekow's advance and noted how the attacking troops:

> … laboured up the glacis at the most exposed places; now crawling on their bellies, now creeping on hands and knees, but, in the main, moving with erect and steady bearing. As they approached within short range, they suddenly found that the French artillery and machine guns had by no means silenced – about two hundred pieces opening on them with deadly effect, while at the same time the whole crest blazed with a deadly fire from the chassepot rifles. Resistance like this was so unexpected by the Germans that it dismayed them and first wavering for a moment, then becoming panic stricken, they broke and fled back, infantry, cavalry and artillery coming down the slope without any pretence of formation, the French hotly following and pouring in a heavy and constant fire as the fugitives fled back across the ravine toward Gravelotte.[276]

## The Royal Entourage Withdraw from Gravelotte

With the French artillery lobbing shells into their midst, the staff of both Royal headquarters and I Army watched in horror as the mass of horsemen dashed wildly into the midst of the 60th and 33rd, whose officers were attempting to rally them on the highway after their earlier repulse. Assorted baggage wagons and caissons had been assembled to the right of the road leading into the ravine so as to leave the left hand lane free for the passage of troops but their teams, startled by the cavalry, broke free from their handlers and dashed into the confused mêlée.

As related by Hoenig, 'Hussars, infantry of various units, led horses and orderlies with baggage and other vehicles were all jumbled up together and rushed tumultuously along the road to the rear. The confusion was indescribable.'[277]

After dragging his wounded comrade to a field hospital in Gravelotte, Allanson Winn decided to check on the situation and made his way to the north of the village:

> Scarcely had I reached a point from which I could command pretty well the French position and was preparing my field glass, when I heard the hurtling of a shell apparently spinning through the air straight towards me. Two soldiers were running past me at the time, barely fifteen yards to my left, calling to me that the French were coming. I threw myself flat on the ground, motioning to them to do the same. I noticed that they only couched on their knees. The shell came down with a fearful whirlwind about it and burst with a crash somewhere close to me. What a ghastly sight! I looked towards the spot that had been occupied by the two soldiers. There was a hole similar to one caused by the digging out of a large wasp's nest and ominously blue smoke was curling

275 Allanson Winn, *What I saw*, p.106–107.
276 Sheridan, *Memoirs*, 374–375.
277 Hoenig, *Twenty-Four Hours*, p,144.

from it and from the rifts about it. Close to it lay a shapeless heap of blue cloth. It was formed by the corpses of the two Prussians. I went up to them. The one had his legs cut off and the top of his head sliced away as if by an axe, so that the brain cavity was completely empty; the other was torn from fork to shoulder. At this moment I heard, faintly in the distance to the rear, the national Anthem and I knew that the King in person was rallying his troops.[278]

Verdy du Vernois, attached to the Royal headquarters, described the confusion as the shaken troops fell back across the ravine:

At first only stragglers, then whole groups of men were seen in hasty retreat; faster and faster the crowd came rolling along, at last in full career; here and there galloped a few horsemen and vehicles of various kinds; then it seemed as if the artillery was also in full retreat and the whole movement spreading in our direction, the six cavalry regiments posted north of Gravelotte also faced about and fell back. We saw before us complete panic and many a face well have looked grave at that moment. The first thing to be done was to get the King out of it and to stop the fugitives. We all mounted our horses, some of the staff hurried towards the village to look after the latter; whilst others closed round the General to be at hand if need be. After the direction had been fixed upon in which the King was to ride back, Moltke turned with us and we rode once more towards Gravelotte, where the engagement had again become very severe.[279]

Sheridan accompanied Bismark as the Royal party made their way to Rezonville noting:

We set out to re-join the King and before going far, overtook his Majesty, who had stopped on the Châlons road and was surrounded by a throng of fugitives, whom he was berating in German so energetic as to remind me forcibly of the 'Dutch' swearing that I used to hear in my boyhood in Ohio. The dressing down finished to his satisfaction, the King resumed his course towards Rezonville, halting, however, to rebuke in the same emphatic style every group of runaways he overtook.[280]

Officers with drawn swords sought to arrest the rout but to no avail as the flood of men and horses pushed their way past the startled troops of II Corps, their cries of 'We're beaten'[281] spreading confusion along their path as their flight carried them all the way to Vionville. Such was the disorder that instructions were sent to the bridge commanders at the Moselle crossings to rid them of traffic so as to clear a way in the event that the Prussians were obliged to fall back to the far bank of the river.[282]

278  Allanson Winn, *What I saw*, p.109.
279  Vernois, *Royal Headquarters*, pp.87–88.
280  Sheridan, *Memoirs*, p.377
281  Hoenig, *Twenty-Four Hours*, p.144.
282  Unsurprisingly, there is no record of this in the official German accounts, but the French captured a trooper from the 7th Hussars near Moulins who told his captors that 'arrangements had been made

In stark contrast to the behaviour of the reservists whose panic triggered the rout, the remaining squadrons from the 9th Hussars held their ground along the road until Barnekow, seeking to salvage something from the desperate situation, ordered one of their officers, Captain von Isthlenfeld, to charge the French positions. He led a squadron forward which wheeled to the right but peering into the smoke and gloom could 'see nothing to charge, but only our infantry retiring, followed by hostile skirmishers.'[283] As such, he turned his troopers about so as to make room for the retreating infantry and retreated to a new position south of the road, about 150 metres in front of the trees lining the Mance ravine. Half an hour later, he withdrew his troopers to the rear of the 39th, so not to mask their fire, holding this position until 10:00 p.m.

Despite this latest panic, Steinmetz was determined to salvage something from the wreckage of the failed attack and keen to implement the king's orders,[284] instructed Zastrow and Fransecky[285] to renew the assault against the enemy positions.

Even though both corps were to be involved in the operation to seize the heights, Steinmetz, apparently still fuming at his earlier dressing down, made little attempt to coordinate his subordinate's actions, an omission made worse given the limited daylight available in which to undertake any attack. With Fransecky being allocated the main highway, Zastrow, by default, was forced to utilise the unmade track running east from the Mance mill towards Point du Jour, as the axis of his attack. He therefore directed the I/77th to move out of the valley towards the quarries, from where they were to launch their assault against the Pont du Jour. The three battalions from the 73rd holding the Mance mills were likewise ordered forward and during their advance were joined by the 1st and 13th companies from the 13th.

Although ordered to commit all his reserves to this effort, Zastrow held back a number of troops[286] who he judged to be too distant to take any effective part in the assault. To his right, five battalions[287] worked their way through the Bois de Vaux and moving out of the cover of the wood, made their way towards the highway about 150 yards away. A number of half-hearted attempts were made to reinforce the troops who had seized the quarries but they made little progress and when Zastrow subsequently ordered the 77th to withdraw into the Mance, these men, after repulsing a number of French counter attacks, withdrew into the wood.[288]

---

for the retreat and he had been one of those responsible for stopping all movement of passage on the Moselle and for clearing the roads to keep them free.' See L'État-Major, *St Privat*, p.630.

283 Hoenig, *Twenty-Four Hours*, p.144.

284 'To set in movement all available strength against the heights of the Point du Jour.' See Hoenig, Twenty-Four Hours, p.150.

285 To the former 'To lead those battalions of VII Corps which were still on the west side of the wood across the valley of the Mance.' To II Corps commander 'To advance against the front of Point du Jour and in conjunction with those troops of the VII Corps which were on his right, to capture the enemy's positions at all cost.' See Hoenig, *Twenty-Four Hours*, p.150.

286 The 74th, III/53rd, II/77th and III/77th.

287 7th Rifles, II and III/13th and I and II/52nd.

288 The sole exception being the 2/13th, under Lieutenant Colonel von der Busche, who remained within 100 yards of the French positions throughout the night.

## II Corps Attack

Whilst waiting for his men to complete their deployment, Fransecky took the opportunity to appraise the situation within the Mance. Having witnessed the earlier rout, he soon formed the view that yet another frontal assault held little prospect of success. At the same time, he knew that Steinmetz was not going to be persuaded to call off the attack and as a seasoned professional, was determined to make the best of the situation confronting him. He was not given any briefing on the tactical situation so was unclear as to which side held Saint Hubert farm. In fact, both the king and I Army's commander were similarly ignorant of the position, as no attempt had been made to establish communications with their front line commanders around the farm and the Rozerieulles quarries.

Whilst the general consensus at headquarters held that the farm was still in friendly hands, in the confusion, it seems that none of the commanders were aware that part of the quarry had in fact, also been captured and potentially provided a new avenue of attack around the enemy left wing. This occurred after elements of the 30th and subsequently the 40th, pushed forward to seize the ground vacated by Frossard, after he pulled most of his infantry out of their advanced positions to reinforce his main fighting line. These troops were supported by elements[289] of the 33rd Fusiliers and 39th who occupied part of sandpits and were subsequently reinforced by another four by platoons from the 33rd,[290] whose previous attempt to seize the quarry had been bloodily repulsed.

Later, when Frossard sought to reoccupy the ground, his efforts were greeted by a fierce fire that sent his men reeling back in panic to their lines. Following this repulse, it seems that one or more of the French brigade commanders in the area launched several section and company counter attacks which got to within 50 paces of the Prussians' positions but failed to recapture the quarries. Neither Steinmetz, nor II Corps' advance guard,[291] were aware of this development as they assembled at the western edge of the Mance wood waiting for the order to attack, where they were shortly joined by both Moltke and Fransecky.

With the rifle battalion leading the way, their buglers struck up the advance; this was taken up by the drummers of the 54th in their rear which, although attracting the hearty acclamation of the accompanying generals, also served to warn the French that a fresh attack was underway.[292] As they marched off into the gloom, Fransecky directed the rifles towards the 'Point du Jour, with the object of carrying out the main attack by way of Saint Hubert.'[293] Shortly after crossing the ravine, Major von Netzer shook his battalion out in attack formation to the south of the road, establishing links with the 39th to their left, before pushing to within 200 yards of the French positions at Point du Jour. Verdy du Vernois rode forward to observe this attack recalling:

289  2nd and 3rd companies 39th; 5th and 8th companies and two squads from the 1st Company of the 33rd.
290  2nd Company and 1st platoon, 1st Company.
291  2nd Rifles and 54th Regiment.
292  As Hoenig remarked 'Why did the troops advance with clanging bands over this road? No tactician can understand why. If it was desired to make the enemy's work easier and to draw his attention to the moment when he ought to open the gates of hell, the Germans could have thought of no better way of so doing.' See *Twenty-Four Hours*, p.155.
293  *Ibid*, p.155.

Everywhere we came upon bodies of men who'd been under fire and were re-forming. Before us marched the 14th and 54th Regiments. When the musketry fire increased on all sides, we rode off to the right, into the open, in order to get some idea of the battle, as far as was possible from the flashes of the rifles. Echoed back by the long walls of some extensive stables near us, it gave one the impression that we were ourselves in the midst of the engagement, although it was some distance off, on the other side of the valley ... But here too, we could see no more than a few hundred yards before us. The darkness became too great, only the burning buildings on the hills stood out like spectres from it. Suddenly the drums of the advancing Pomeranian battalions were heard and again the unceasing roll of the French fusillade resounded. In between rang out from one place our long-drawn call, the 'whole will advance.' From all sides, it was repeated; from every direction came thundering the hurrah of our gallant troops and distinctly we heard the crackling of our needle guns. Soon after, the fire from the shelter trenches died away, which we interpreted to mean that our men had got into them. But on and on the bugles sounded and again and again the Prussian hurrahs were borne back to us on the wind.[294]

Following in the rear of the rifles, the 54th closed in on Saint Hubert farm; Colonels von Decken[295] and von Busse[296] led the way at the head of the fusiliers and as they deployed into lines of company columns, the other two battalions formed closed up columns. In the gathering gloom and under the mistaken impression that the enemy retained control of the farm, the fusiliers approached Saint Hubert at the double, the rapidity of their advance denying their officers the opportunity to ascertain who lay to their front; friend or foe?

Approaching to within 400 metres of their objective, the fusiliers halted and formed line; a shot rang out and they opened a rapid fire at close range on the shadowy mass of figures to their front, unaware that the farm was still held by their fellow countrymen.[297] To the thousands of already shaken and frightened troops sheltering under the farmstead walls, this was the last straw;[298] after several hours under enemy fire their morale was shattered and 'a flood of fugitives from every unit poured out upon the 54th.' The fusiliers vainly sought to let the fleeing masses pass their ranks, calling out 'Through! Through!'[299] as their demoralised compatriots poured down into the ravine. I and II Battalions attempted to clear the road to give them passage but in the darkness, all order was lost and there was complete and utter confusion as the 54th attempted to rally their men.

294  Vernois, *Royal Headquarters* pp.90–91.
295  Commanding II Corps' advance guard.
296  Commander of the 54th.
297  As Seton remarked 'for in the little light that remained, a fresh arriving Commanding Officer could hardly have been much blamed, even if he had directed a volley into the crowd in front.' See *Notes*, p.159
298  There could have been men from as many as 59 companies gathered about the farm, predominantly from the 39th, 40th, 69th and 72nd.
299  Hoenig, *Twenty-Four Hours*, pp.156–157.

Eventually, with the help of both Fransecky and Hartmann[300] some semblance of order was restored and they resumed the advance was resumed in two assorted groups; the first[301] pushed their way alongside the line formed by 2nd Rifles, which brought them close to Rozerieulles. Similarly ignorant of the fact that the quarries were now in friendly hands, they opened fire on the shadowy figures to their front, just as the French launched a fresh counter attack. Assailed from front and rear, the men caught in this deadly crossfire repeatedly called out 'Prussians! Prussians!'[302] in an effort to make their presence known, but failed to make themselves heard above the noise of battle and the shooting continued unabated until a messenger managed to crawl back to advise the rifles of their mistake.

To add to the confusion, the sound of firing and drums was also heard coming from the area to the south of the quarries so officers were despatched to identify the source which turned out to be the 73rd advancing from Mance mill. In the gathering darkness they had failed to locate any of Zastrow's men[303] but searching further north, they stumbled across the 2nd Company 2nd Rifles and three companies from the 54th.[304] After being briefed on the situation, around 8:30 p.m., three companies[305] were sent forward to reinforce those troops holding the quarry.[306]

The second group[307] assembled by Fransecky and Hartmann, moved towards Saint Hubert where, implausibly, they launched yet another assault against the farm before realising it was occupied by friendly troops. After once again being rallied following this aborted attack, they blindly stumbled off in the dark in the general direction of Moscou farm. This latest effort fared no better than the previous attacks and they were driven off by the fierce French fire, the exhausted men dropping to the ground, seeking cover amongst the corpses of their comrades.[308]

Following on the heels of the advance guard, Major General von Koblinski[309] brought the main body[310] of the 3rd Division forward from Gravelotte; as the road past Saint Hubert was still blocked, he directed the 14th and then the 2nd to take position on the open ground to the south of the highway; the 42nd being held in reserve. The introduction of these additional troops simply added to the confusion; the 14th was drawn into the mass of men gathered around Saint Hubert, their commanding officer, Colonel von Voss was wounded and Major von Dantzen of the fusilier battalion killed. The I/2nd became embroiled in the combat around Point du Jour, whilst II Battalion, under Lieutenant Colonel von Massow, took position on their left flank facing the highway. Although, as it was impossible to see more than a few yards in the gloom, orders were given for the troops to close up on one another. Finally, around 8:30 p.m., the 42nd

---

300  Major General von Hartmann, Commander 3rd Division.
301  11th, 5th, 2nd, 4th and 12th companies.
302  Hoenig, *Twenty-Four Hours*, p.161.
303  General von Glümer had in fact halted the advance of the 73rd when he heard firing to his front and wisely withdrew his men into the woods.
304  4th, 5th and 11th.
305  The 2nd Company and part of the 4th Company 2nd Rifles and 11th Company 54th.
306  Intermittent firing continued around Rozerieulles until 9:30–10:00 p.m. when the order 'Cease fire!' was given; bugles repeated the call along the line and gradually the fighting died away, the French being just as exhausted as the Prussians.
307  9th, 10th, 8th, 7th, 6th, 3rd and 1st companies.
308  Casualties included von Busse and Major Prescher commander of the fusilier battalion.
309  Commander 5th Infantry Brigade.
310  II and III/14th, I and II/2nd and 42nd.

was brought across the ravine by Colonel von Wichmann[311] where they deployed alongside the shambolic mob sheltering on the hillside west of Pont du Jour.[312]

Despite the introduction of these fresh troops, there was no escaping the fact that 3rd Division's efforts had come to nothing; they had failed to seize the French position although their appearance apparently provoked a minor panic in their lines, with General Mangin reporting that several of his companies withdrew without orders and Colonel Haca of the 8th Ligne stated that between 3–4,000 men fell back towards his regiment. Describing it as a 'everyman for themselves'[313] moment, he only managed to restore order by getting his men to fix bayonets and his buglers to sound the charge; even so, parts of his 2nd and 3rd battalions were thrown into confusion by the retreat. Mangin claimed that part of the 66th was swept away by this rout but unsurprisingly, there is no mention of this in their post combat report.

## Steinmetz Calls a Halt

Around 9:00 p.m., the senior commanders from II Corps, Fransecky, Barnekow, Hartmann, Hann von Weyhern[314] along with the majority of brigade and regimental commanders, gathered for an impromptu council of war at Saint Hubert. Incredibly, given the confusion and numbers of troops already committed to the struggle, 4th Division was also ordered across the ravine. 8th Brigade led the way, even though no-one could see more than a few feet and given the crush of men milling around, there was simply no room to deploy.

As they reached the bottom of the defile, Moltke, concerned that far too many troops had already been committed to the battle, instructed them to halt. However, their brigadier, Major General von Kettler, anxious to see some action after his 20 mile march, simply ignored the order and led his men into the ravine. By 9:00 p.m., the 21st, with the divisional commander at their head, reached Saint Hubert, although progress understandably, was very slow. A few companies[315] pushed into the firing line where they were drawn into the ongoing firefight between Saint Hubert and Moscou farm whilst the remainder, formed in line of columns and cheering wildly, made their way further to the east. The 61st followed in their wake and took position on the open ground to the south of the highway and later, were joined by 7th Brigade[316] with the result that by 10:30 p.m., another 24 fresh battalions had squeezed into this already

---

311  II Corps' chief of staff.
312  About this time there were some five companies deployed in front of the farm at Point du Jour (1st, 3rd and part of the 4th Company, 2nd Rifles; 1st, 10th and part of the 2nd Company 2nd Regiment) who were engaged in a close range fire fight with the French lining the road. Further south, around 10 companies (2nd and 4th Rifles, 11th Company 54th, II and III/14th Regiment) were scattered around the quarries at Point du Jour. Another 20 companies (1st, 2nd, 3rd,5th, 6th, 7th, 8th, 9th and 10/54th, 5th, 6th, 7th, 9th, 11th and 12/2nd and the 4/73rd) were jumbled together around the farm at Saint Hubert and mixed up with the debris of Steinmetz's regiments, whilst another four (3rd, 4th, 8th and part of the 2/2nd), were amongst the many fugitives sheltering from the fighting at the base of the ravine.
313  L'État-Major, St Privat, p.663.
314  Commander, 4th Division.
315  4th Company at Moscou, 8th at Saint Hubert.
316  The 9th and 49th.

congested space.[317] Finally, recognising the futility of seeking any decisive result at this late hour, orders were issued to cease fire and the 61st made an about turn and retreated to Gravelotte.[318]

In a tacit admission that the attack had failed, VII and VIII corps were instructed to withdraw, leaving II Corps to secure a toehold on the plateau and consolidate their gains around Saint Hubert. 4th Division stumbled its way into the front line around 11:00 p.m. whilst to the north and south of the farm house, nine battalions from the 8th Brigade and the 42nd, were deployed across the plateau. 7th Brigade was concentrated around the farmstead with 3rd Division about 400 yards to their rear.

Given the confusion within the German ranks, there were numerous instances of the units opening fire on one another which resulted in a 'fratricidal struggle that caused an almost uninterrupted series of panics.'[319] Sometime later, when another disturbance broke out in the trenches between Moscou and Point du Jour, firing erupted along the line which caused a further alarm amongst the 21st where two companies had been sent out to scout the enemy positions; the 8th towards Point du Jour, the 4th, together with a company from the 54th, towards Moscou farm. Exhausted, the dog-tired soldiers[320] stumbled into the French positions where they were greeted with a 'feu terrible' from the 85th. Shaken from their stupor, they fled pell-mell to the rear, a number of them suffering injuries as they fell into the quarries in the dark.

Although they were eventually rallied, Fransecky sent the regiment to the rear and around 11.00 p.m., they arrived at Rezonville to recover their packs which had been discarded prior to going into action. VII and VIII corps were withdrawn in dribs and drabs throughout the night, such being the confusion that stragglers were still to be seen making their way across the ravine the following morning.[321]

As the survivors made their way into Gravelotte, they were greeted by the various regimental bands who struck up the traditional Prussian battle hymns, 'Nun danket alle Gott' and somewhat ironically in the circumstances, 'Heil dir im Siegerkranz.'[322] Allanson Winn's companion, Randal Roberts, was one of the many casualties receiving treatment in the village, having been wounded during the French counter attack and recalled:

I lay just below the farm of Saint Hubert until about 11.00pm when I was carried back into Gravelotte and fortunately found a heap of straw in a room with six officers, where a doctor kindly dressed my side for me. Imagine a room 15ft by 12, the floor spread with straw and blankets, mostly covered with blood. I am in a corner which was vacated for me by an officer of the 67th who was shot through the foot. To my right was a captain in the same regiment with the bones of his leg shattered to pieces below the

---

317   Altogether with the existing troops there were some 48 battalions crammed together in a space about a mile wide by 1,100 yards deep.
318   Although the fighting had died away, the wounded continued to fire off their rifles throughout the night, in an effort to attract the attention of the medical assistants who had been sent out to collect the casualties.
319   L'État-Major, St Privat, p.656.
320   They had been on the march since 1:00 a.m. that morning.
321   The notable exception to this were the troops who had captured the Point du Jour, the 67th and 8th Rifles and the 39th who all withdrew in good order.
322   The traditional Prussian victory anthem, "Hail to thee in Victors Crown.'

knee; to his right was a lieutenant, shot through the knee; whilst on my left lay three others, more or less dangerously wounded.[323]

## The Situation Within 3 Corps

As the assaults on Moscou and Saint Hubert subsided, Metman and Aymard withdrew the battered front line formations who had borne the brunt of the fighting, behind the crest of the plateau. Those who had seen less action kept watch from the ditches and trenches that ran along the fighting line, swiftly despatching any attempts to probe their lines with a hail of rifle fire. As the fighting died away along this sector, Le Boeuf was still unaware of Bazaine's intention to withdraw to a new defensive line closer to Metz and lacking orders, simply instructed his men to hold the positions they had occupied during the day, the exception being his two cavalry brigades which at 7:00 p.m., set off for Metz. The route they took, through Châtel and Longeville, was so encumbered with wagons and other debris that in places, the troopers were forced into single file and only reached their destination, the Porte de Thionville, at 11:00 p.m.

Instructions finally reached 3 Corps around 1:30 a.m. on the morning of 19 August; Le Boeuf was to undertake an immediate retreat to positions closer to Metz withdrawing along the two roads that led through Châtel St Germain, before occupying the plateau at Plappeville. He was to anchor his left on the villages of Scy and Lessy, with his right embedded in the village of Lorry. Given the exhausted state of his troops, it was 3.00 a.m. before the corps artillery and Montuadon's 1st Division began their march, followed by the 2nd and 3rd. In the confusion not everyone received the order to pull back; within 4th Division Tissonnière related how:

> To our rear, they sounded the retreat; all was black. Shouts rang out, the 8th! the 80th! 3rd battalion! 4th of the 1st! We were all called and counted off. Soon after I'd gathered around me the quartermaster, two sergeants and fourteen men from my company. The sergeant major had been killed during the last bayonet charge. I searched his effects for any personal papers but I couldn't find anything. In complete darkness, my seventeen men and I made my way north, towards the crest. We passed close by the commander's trench near Saint Hubert. This side of Rozerieulles and Jussy rifle fire from the skirmisher's outpost line cut through the night. The arm of my old sergeant, Barbaz, was broken. I looked for the old Roman road. We could make out the whispers of men to our left and right; a little later, in the cutting by Châtel we heard the noise of wagons. A shadow made its way towards us; it's the Adjutant, Sertorius. 'My captain; I've been sent after you. Captain Renouard, who's over there, is asking for orders.' 'Orders?' I replied 'What about his commander?' 'He's dead.' 'What about Captain Apchié?' 'He fell carrying the colours. You're commanding the battalion now'. 'Comrades' I said to my seventeen men 'Our place is over there, in the trench' The seventeen men spoke as one: 'We'll follow you.' Guided by the adjutant we passed through the lines of several battalions, all crouching down and crossing over the crest we finally reached the trench. Renouard addressed me 'Ah well, what

323  Roberts, *Modern War*, p.62.

are your orders?' 'Nothing' I replied, 'Now it's my turn to ask you, what should we do? I heard the retreat being sounded, but the 85th have not left their positions on my right and I'm reluctant to do so without orders'. 'You're right; let's stay put for now' Suddenly, from the trenches held by the 85th, a fusillade of shots rang out, cutting off my words. The firing spread to my trench as quick as lightning; the enemy in Saint Hubert responded. But then, to our rear, the bugles kept on repeating the call 'Cease fire!' Cease fire!' The shooting soon died away; I discovered that an enemy patrol had attempted to approach the trench held by the 85th. Our vedettes were sent out, two by two, with shielded lanterns, to search for the wounded. I continued my discussion with Renouard 'What's been happening? How did you fare during the day? Have you suffered many losses?' He replied 'The same shell which killed Commandant Bertrand did for Captain Grangie; come and take a look' Seated, one next to the other at the rear of the trench, they were struck whilst observing the movements of the enemy as they chatted. The commandant's eyes and mouth were wide open, the hands clenched and reaching forwards. He saw death coming and wanted to scream but it was all over in an instant. All his left side was torn open and the bag he carried had split open and his gold coins had spilled out, shiny and bright. The captain was laid out under a coat and guarded by his dog who growled when anyone approached. As I made my way back down the trench I was told about the losses, the munitions and the food. The dead were all laid out to the rear of the trench; the wounded were all along the bottom, moaning and groaning. Ammunition was in short supply, hardly one packet per man[324] and during the fighting the troops had nibbled at their bread and sipped their flasks, so they had neither food nor drink. The worst hardship however was the lack of sleep, which meant that the outposts had to be relieved at frequent intervals. This was the scene that greeted our eyes, awe inspiring, unforgettable: in front, Gravelotte, its flames lighting up the valley in a sinister light. To our left, the roof of the Point du Jour farmhouse had ceased burning and the beams collapsed, one after the other, throwing sparks into the night sky. Behind us, to our right, at Moscou, the flames had died down but the embers formed a huge brazier, from which arose the squeals of the pigs penned up in the under-croft. All of a sudden, from behind Saint Hubert a cheer arose! Another voice called out, another cheer, then a hymn followed by a word of command and then silence. Even the pigs had stopped squealing. It was midnight. A staff officer approached from out of the shadows. 'Who's in command here?' 'Me' I replied. 'And you are?' 'A captain, the commandant is dead' 'Ah well, my dear captain, don't move from here; your position is excellent. Can you give me that assurance? You have the 85th to your left.' 'That's correct. Further up the crest, there's the 8th and, at Point du Jour, there's the 66th.' 'I don't think so' he answered, 'When I carried out my inspection, the Prussians were there.' 'That's not correct,' I replied 'come with me.' and we made our way forwards where a battalion of the 66th had slipped into place at Point du Jour without making a sound.[325] We returned towards the trench; a

---

324  Nine rounds.
325  The 66th were part of Fauvert Bastoul's 2nd Brigade, 2nd Division, 2 Corps Their commanding officer, Colonel Ameller, detailed how General Mangin had sent him to reinforce a weak point in the line 'placing the 1st Battalion on the right and the 2nd Battalion on the left of the burning farmhouse, with

group had left the position at the Pointe du Jour and were making their way towards the north. 'Hey you there!' called the general 'Halt!' The command stopped us in our tracks. 'Halt' I said. 'At the double' came the response and they disappeared into the night! The general let out a curse. 'Ah well, my dear captain, it's alright. You remain here'. 'My general' I replied 'I don't have any ammunition, we're burdened with all the wounded, we haven't eaten anything since last night' 'You needn't worry about that; I will send you ammunition, bread and stretcher's. Tomorrow, I'll reinforce the troops on the plateau; I'm General Mangin.'[326] He left and I never saw him again. I woke up Renouard who'd fallen asleep on the grass and explained the situation to him and prayed that he let me get a few minutes sleep. How long was I out for? I don't know. It was a deep sleep and it was with much sorrow that the adjutant shook me awake. Dawn was approaching. 'Captain' he said 'the 85th has gone.' The trench to our left was empty and all we could make out was a something like a long black snake winding its way towards Moscou farm. 'Go and ask the 66th for orders, you'll find them behind us by the 8th' The adjutant returned; there was no sign of the 66th nor the 8th; we were alone. I called together the officers of the battalion. 'Gentlemen, what would you wish to do?' They were all quiet then, then a voice called out 'It's you who are in command' I was clear in what I wanted to do: 'This is what we are going to do. Two men from each squad will remain in the trench, the others will leave without making a sound, carrying the wounded over to the earthworks behind the crest and wait for orders. It was a miracle how the move was carried out. Not a shot was fired from Saint Hubert, which was filled with troops, against the skirmishers who then, upon my orders, left the trench and made their way slowly back towards the crest. I went back, for the last time, to salute the dead and then re-joined my men. On the heights by the Bois de Châtel, I first saluted general Aymard who, mounted on his horse, was keeping watch over his retreating division and then briefed him on the situation. 'That's good' he replied and I made my way back to my regiment near Lessy. I arrived, completely worn out, hungry and tired. That's how I saw the great battle on the 18th August 1870.' [327]

Besides Valabrègue's cavalry who left Longville at 5:00 a.m. for Ban Saint Martin, 2 Corps still held the positions so valiantly defended throughout the day. Around 1:30 a.m. in the morning, Frossard's received instructions to retreat to the rear of Longeville and establish a new position, with his right anchored on St Quentin and with a strong outpost pushed out beyond Longeville. In front, on his right, around Scy, he would find 3 Corps and to his rear, Forton's cavalry division. Frossard gave instructions for the withdrawal to commence at '4 heures très précises du matin par la droite.'[328] To the minute, 2nd Division pulled out of the line, followed by the 1st with Lapassat's brigade acting as rearguard.

---

the 1st Battalion being held 200 yards to the rear, in reserve.' See l'État-Major, *18 Août, Documents*, p.115 After spending the night in these positions, towards 4:00 a.m., Ameller received orders to retreat towards Longeville, expressing his regret how he was forced to leave behind a number of his men who were too seriously wounded to move.

326  Mangin commanded 1st Brigade, 2nd Division, 2 Corps.
327  Bonnal, *St Privat III*, pp.215–219. The 80th lost 23 officers and 390 men killed, wounded or missing.
328  *Ibid*.

For the most part, the retreat went off smoothly although around 6:00 a.m. as Jolivet's brigade withdrew from their positions to the east of the quarries at Point du Jour, firing erupted in front of the 76th; their vigorous response quickly silenced Fransecky outposts[329] and he was able to resume his retreat. Jolivet was followed by Lapassat, whose rearguard from the 84th abandoned their outposts around 7:00 a.m. Within an hour, Frossard and Le Boeuf had successfully completed the evacuation of their former positions between Leipzig and Point du Jour and withdrew unmolested to the relative safety of the high ground to the east of the Châtel ravine.

## Recriminations in Rezonville

As night fell, a decidedly downcast Royal entourage arrived in Rezonville; initially, the orderly officers were unable to find shelter for the king as the dwellings were full to overflowing with the wounded. Sheridan related how the weary group:

> … halted just beyond the village; there was a fire built and the King, his brother, Prince Frederick Charles and von Roon were provided with rather uncomfortable seats about it, made by resting the ends of a short ladder on a couple of boxes. With much anxiety and not a little depression of spirits, news from the battlefield was awaited.[330]

A similar air of uncertainty pervaded those officers of the general staff accompanying Moltke; Verdy du Vernois recalled 'When we had convinced ourselves that everything was going as well as we could wish, there was no sense in General von Moltke exposing himself to personal danger without doing any good thereby. When we put this to him, he still remained on the road for some time and only returned later on.'[331] Recognising that no more could be accomplished that evening from the depths of the Mance ravine, the chief of staff turned his horse around and rode back to find his quarters for the evening.

It was clear to everyone that the Prussian forces had suffered a considerable set back during the days fighting; losses had been heavy, morale was low and the troops were close to breaking point. As they rode back, Verdy du Vernois related how:

> The King's aide-de-camp Count Lehndorff, met us and informed the General that his Majesty was at Rezonville and was anxious to hear his report on the progress of the battle. So, we proceeded at a trot. But scarcely had we left Gravelotte, when I thought it proper to advise the General to ride slowly, as the rapid motion rearwards of so numerous a body of riders had already begun to impress the wounded and stragglers on both sides of the road and it was to be feared that another panic might arise like that of an hour ago.[332]

Moltke reached Rezonville around 11:00 p.m., he spoke little on the way, partly through exhaustion, partly no doubt in silent contemplation of the apparent failure of his plans. Despite

---

329  From the 9th and II/61st.
330  *Memoirs*, p.377. Sheridan was mistaken; Frederick Charles and II Army's staff bivouacked at Doncourt.
331  Vernois, *Royal Headquarters*, p.91.
332  *Ibid*.

all the setbacks, he resolved to continue the battle on the morrow with the objective of defeating the Imperial Army and so, on finding the Royal party standing warming themselves next to a fire at the end of the village, he dismounted and approached the monarch. Verdy du Vernois recalled:

> Just then I heard an officer saying to the King 'Now it is my humble opinion, sire, that we, considering our heavy losses today, should not continue the attack tomorrow, but await the attack of the French' This idea seemed to me so monstrous that I could not help blurting out 'Then I don't know why we attacked at all today!' Of course, I got my answer, which was not exactly spoken in a gracious tone; 'What do you want here Lieutenant Colonel?' But at this moment Moltke stepped forward between us two towards the King and said in his decided manner; 'Your Majesty only has to give the order for the continuation of the attack in case the enemy should make a further stand outside Metz tomorrow.' The orders were drawn up at once and then it was resolved to remain the night at Rezonville.[333]

As the dejected staff attempted to get some rest after the exertion of the past few days, a little after midnight a courier arrived with news from Frederick Charles; the Saxons and Guard Corps had seized Saint Privat; the French right wing had been turned and their troops were falling back on Metz! Victory had been seized from the jaws of disaster!

---

333 *Ibid*, p.92.

# 5

# The Battle of Gravelotte, 18 August 1870 – Victory

## The Saxons Flanking Manoeuvre

A little after 5:00 p.m., Prince Albert was overseeing the deployment of XII Corps from a hill to the west of Sainte Marie aux Chênes and watched in shocked disbelief as the Prussian Guard began to deploy for their attack on the French positions in Saint Privat.[1] It had always been Moltke's intention that if the French were found to have taken up a position before Metz, II Army would envelop their right flank; originally Prince Frederick had nominated the Guard Corps for this important task, the Saxons being allocated the secondary role of securing Sainte Marie aux Chênes and covering the Guards open flank. However, when the French were found to have taken possession of the village, Prince Albert decided to extend his march to the north, informing both Army HQ and Guard Corps of this decision.[2]

Later, when Albert decided to include Roncourt within his outflanking manoeuvre, he again briefed them on his plans[3] so neither Frederick Charles nor August could claim ignorance as to his intentions. The route he proposed to follow was between 14–15,000 paces in length which

---

1    Albert was only too aware of the casualties that would result from an unprepared attack on Saint Privat but given the dominant role of Prussia in the establishment of the German Empire and the aura of martial infallibility which surrounded the Großer Generalstab in the decades following the war, political expediency led to Prince August's gross tactical error being glossed over in public. According to this version of events, the Guard were given the credit for securing the victory in spite of the loss of so many blue-blooded Prussian officers with the Saxons role in the final assault being downplayed. XII Corps were also criticised for their tardy advance which exposed the Guard to the full weight of the defender's fire. These accusations resulted in decades of acrimony and debate within professional military circles before, somewhat belatedly, this misapprehension was finally acknowledged and responsibility for the pointless bloodletting correctly apportioned.

2    Earlier that day in an effort to speed communications, Albert and August exchanged staff officers (Captain von Ramm for the Guards and Captain von Minckwitz for the Saxons) who were mounted on thoroughbreds that could cover the 2,000 metres between their respective headquarters 'in exceedingly short time;' See Bell, *St Privat*, p.192.

3    His report read 'The Saxon Corps is advancing on Sainte Marie with the 24th Division while the 23rd is marching by Coinville and the wood between that place and Roncourt to turn the French right wing. See Clarke, *Franco-German War II*, p.49.

and it withdrew to the rear of Marengo where Montluisant was looking to assemble an artillery reserve to cover 6 Corps retreat. Exposed by the retreat of the infantry, their commander, Lieutenant Colonel Jamet, felt he had no option but to follow suit and withdrew the remaining batteries to Marengo.[34]

As the 45th pushed out of from the Bois d'Aboué, they deployed into attack formation[35] and approaching their objective, drew level with elements of Kessel's brigade.[36] Meanwhile, 48th Brigade continued their advance from Montois, neither formation encountering any significant resistance which, given the Saxon force amounted to some 15 battalions, is unsurprising.[37]

48th Brigade won the race into Roncourt with von Bosze storming the village at the head of the III/107th, seizing a few stragglers left behind as the units tasked with its defence withdrew towards Saint Privat. They were closely followed by scores of men from the Prussian Guard[38] who, half mad with thirst, crowded around the water pumps, blocking the streets and hindering the progress of the I/101st who entered the village from the west.

As the 108th Rifle Regiment took up defensive positions along the western edge of the village, to the north-east, several companies from 48th Brigade[39] fended off a counter attack by 1/9th de Ligne, before forming defensive clusters against the troopers sent out by the 2nd Regiment of Chasseurs d'Afrique who suddenly appeared on the horizon. Three companies of fusiliers[40] attempted to drive off a detachment of the 100th Ligne who were sheltering in a hollow to the southeast corner of Roncourt, but were themselves, driven back by the heavy chassepot fire from Saint Privat and the forêt de Jaumont. Even though supported by the 12th Company, the fusiliers were incapable of supressing the French fire and unable to advance, the 107th took up defensive positions around the south-eastern edge of the village.

## Saxon Preparations for the Assault on Saint Privat

To the east of Roncourt, the 9th, 10th and 11th companies from the 106th occupied the small hamlet Malancourt – deserted apart from three lone stragglers – and after filling their canteens at the well, took up defensive positions before receiving the call to move against Saint Privat. Meanwhile, five companies[41] from the 106th, under Colonel von Abendroth, had struck out in a south-easterly direction from the road running between Montois and Malancourt, intent on pursuing the retreating French into the forêt de Jaumont. They were supported by two regiments

---

34    5th, 6th and 7/14th. The 5th lost one horse; the 6th, six horses; the 7th, one man and four horses and the 9/13th, nine men and one horse.

35    From left to right: first line; I/101st, the 108th, the 100th Body Guard Regiment; second line: II and III/101st.

36    1st Guard Pioneer Company, 3rd and 4th companies, 1st Foot Guard Regiment and I/3rd Foot Guard Regiment.

37    Reckoning from the left wing; in the First Line: 1¼ battalions 106th, 3 batts 107th, 1 batt 101st, 3 batts 108th, 1½ batts 100th, 1¾ batts Prussian Guard; Second Line: 1½ batts 100th, Third Line, behind the 100th: 2 batts 101st.

38    The survivors of the 2nd and 3rd companies' 3rd Foot Guards, 1st Guard Pioneer Company and several platoons from the 1st Foot Guards.

39    I/106th, 12th Company 106th and 3/107th.

40    9th, 10th and 11th companies, 107th.

41    I Battalion and 12th Company, III Battalion.

of Heavy cavalry, under General von Senfft and their accompanying battery of horse artillery who swept around the east of village looking to charge the enemy infantry.

However, as the squadrons crested a rise, they were hit by heavy fire from the troops lining the edge of the wood[42] and unable to reply, wheeled about seeking cover on the reverse slope of the hill. The 106th were also ordered by the brigade commander to support the assault against Saint Privat but moving around the northeast corner of Roncourt, they came under heavy fire from the forêt de Jaumont as Abendroth recalled:

> Whilst experiencing a hot enfilading fire, which caused some losses, Captain von Treitschke of the general staff arrived and advised me to make a rapid charge against the forest of Jaumont on our left flank, which would materially help the corps artillery, which was about to take a decisive position. He stated that it would hardly be able to hold its position unless the hostile fire was silenced somehow. 'I surely will' replied I 'but in that case you must at once ride to Colonel von Schulz and report to him that I am a taking a course contrary to his orders and ask him to support me, as I have but five companies here and that force will hardly be sufficient for the purpose.[43]

Treitschke did as requested and subsequently, 13th Rifle battalion were sent to support Abendroth who, reinforced by von Bosze with the III/107th, led his men off to the flank seeking to clear the enemy skirmishers from the undergrowth and the raised road embankment skirting the forêt de Jaumont.[44] The tirailleurs, sheltering behind the solid stone walls and supported by batteries located in the rear of Saint Privat, greeted this attack 'with a hot fire at long range.'[45] Abendroth and Major von Decken were amongst the early casualties to this fire, as was the standard bearer of the I/106th, Sergeant Albert, who received a fatal wound in his stomach.

Despite these losses, the Saxons continued to edge forward and in the face of this growing pressure, the outnumbered defenders finally gave way.[46] Some fell back to Saint Privat, the majority making their way to the south-east seeking cover in the woods and from where their fire threatened to overwhelm the 106th. The 1st Horse and 2nd Heavy batteries provided the Saxons with additional support from alongside the Roncourt-Pierrevillers road and III/107th were sent to help them contain this threat.

Later, around 7.30p.m. when reinforced by 9th Company 107th, both regiments rose to their feet and charged the French deployed along the edge of the wood and within the Jaumont quarries. Confronted by superior numbers, the tirailleurs retreated into the depth of the forest where the struggle continued for some time, swinging first one way and then the other, until at last the French were driven away. Three companies of the III/106th, under Major Brinkmann, chased them into the depths of the wood until fighting ceased around 8.30pm and by the

---

42   They were from the 1/9th, supported by the Chasseurs d'Afrique.
43   Bell, *St Privat*, p.198.
44   The skirmishers were from the 75th and 100th Ligne.
45   Bell, *St Privat*, p.199.
46   From the 1/9th and 100th Ligne.

time Captain Schreiber called a halt to the pursuit, several platoons had advanced as far as Bronvaux.[47]

## 6 Corps Begin to Withdraw

Around 6:30 p.m., with his right crumbling in the face of the enveloping attack by the Saxons from the north and west and the Guards pushing forward from the direction of Sainte Marie, Canrobert decided that he could no longer delay his retreat and informed both Ladmirault and Bourbaki of his intention to withdraw.[48] As the French official history concedes 'It cannot be denied that from this moment the battle was lost, for the commanders and the troops were both convinced that the struggle could no longer have any other objective than to protect the retreat.'[49] In fact, a number of units to the north of Saint Privat had already fallen back, the 1/75th to replenish their ammunition, the 1st and 2/9th into the forêt de Jaumont and 2/10th to Bronvaux.

Canrobert was anxious to delay the capture of Saint Privat as long as possible so as to afford time to organise his retreat, the route of which ran along a single road through heavily wooded terrain; a difficult task at the best of times but one made doubly difficult by the onset of night and an aggressive enemy snapping at his heels. General Tixier was told to push the 4th and 3/100th into Saint Privat to bolster the defences whilst the 1st and 2/100th were left near Jérusalem, with orders to front towards Roncourt.

The 4th made their way into the burning village, led by brigade commander, General Péchot and took up defensive positions behind the garden walls. The 3/100th, led by Poilloue de Saint Mars, held the northern perimeter of the village and subsequently were reinforced by the remainder of the regiment moving up from Jérusalem; 1st Battalion under Major Née-Devaux, on the right of the line opposite Roncourt, the 2nd a little in front of the village, on a slight elevation which overlooked the terrain and from where they could give fire support to both battalions.

The 9th Chasseurs were in the centre of Saint Privat, with the churchyard and its immediate surroundings being defended by three companies of the 94th. The 93rd and the 3/9th were to the north, the 4th to the west, with the 1st and 2/12th watching over the road to Sainte Marie. Canrobert then placed the 73rd and 91st on his right flank, formed in squares, so as precaution against any attack by the Saxon cavalry from the direction of Roncourt.

It was around this time when Canrobert instructed General Barail 'to attempt a charge so as to give him a little breathing space, to protect his retreat and allow him to execute a change of front on his left wing.'[50] In his memoirs, Barail stated that he thought the order 'useless and impractical because he would have had to traverse 600 metres to reach the infantry and

---

47   Schreiber was subsequently joined by reinforcements from the 13th Rifle battalion and the three companies from the III/103rd from Melancourt who had been ordered forward by Colonel Schultz.

48   The despatch to Ladmirault stated that 'Canrobert was forced to evacuate Saint Privat which he couldn't hold any longer and was going to retreat through Saulny.' The staff officer sent to Bourbaki was told to warn him of the situation and request that he provide cover for his retreat but failed to locate him. See l'État-Major, St Privat, p.464–471.

49   L'État-Major, St Privat, p.471.

50   Ibid, p.466.

two kilometres before he reached the artillery;'[51] Evidently unaware of the desperate plight of Pape's guardsmen in front of Saint Privat – shaken and exhausted troops who could have been swept away by a determined charge launched from close range – and seemingly having little confidence that his squadrons would have any impact, he reluctantly gave the order to attack.[52]

General Bruchard[53] was instructed to: 'Execute a charge 'en fourrageurs', by squadrons, against the enemy infantry who are closing with the infantry of 6 Corps in front of Saint Privat.'[54] Five squadrons of the 3rd Chasseurs, formed in close column moved off and followed by the 2nd Chasseurs, advanced towards the ridge from their sheltered position at the rear of Saint Privat. Approaching the crest they could see, off to their right, midway between Roncourt and Saint Privat, the advancing Saxon and Prussian Guards.

The two lead squadrons, under the direct command of their colonel, sent successive waves of 'fourrageurs' out towards the enemy lines, as the remainder[55] were withdrawn behind the crest. Forming two weak lines and deployed in a loose open order, they charged towards II/1st Foot Guards but failed to press home their attack and halted and wheeled about. Despite the intense enemy fire, the chasseurs escaped with relatively few casualties and made their way back towards their start point, the troopers being rallied to the east of Saint Privat.[56]

Despite the brevity of the engagement and small number of troopers involved – only two squadrons from three regiments available were committed – both Bruchard and Barail claimed that this attack stopped the Prussian advance. As the French official history remarked, 'whatever the true result of this timid effort, the enemy advance had, nonetheless, come to a halt and Bruchard and perhaps even Barail thought there was no point in launching fresh squadrons into the attack.'[57] Both regiments withdrew to the rear, to the east of Saint Privat, fronting Roncourt which, by now, had fallen into the hands of the Saxons.

Meanwhile, 2nd Chasseurs d'Afrique, who were positioned alongside Bruchard's brigade, were preparing to attack when Canrobert approached their commander, informing him 'The time for a charge is already lost.'[58] The chasseurs wheeled about and when the Saxons pushed out from Roncourt, deployed 'fourrageurs' who formed a skirmish line running from the forêt de Jaumont to the right of the 100th Ligne. As the troopers exchanged shots with the Saxons, Becquet de Sonnay ordered the 1/91st and 2nd and 3/75th –who had suffered heavy losses to the enemy artillery – to assemble alongside the 94th to the rear of Saint Privat where they formed a large square, each regiment occupying one face, with the fourth kept open to collect

51    *Ibid.* This was probably because from his position to the rear right of Saint Privat the only enemy formations visible to him was the Saxon artillery deployed between Montois and Roncourt and the unshaken 4th Regiment of Foot Guards which had yet to come under fire

52    It would seem that the order to charge was given just as the guardsmen had, in response to Prince August's order, halted their attack on Saint Privat pending the arrival of the Saxons.

53    Commander, 1st Brigade; 2nd and 3rd chasseurs à cheval.

54    L'État-Major, *St Privat*, p.467.

55    3rd, 5th and 6th squadrons.

56    3rd Chasseurs; four officers, 28 men, 2nd Chasseurs: three men; 2nd Chasseurs d'Afrique; three men.

57    Bruchard said 'The attack by the Prussian infantry had been halted by this demonstration.' Barail claimed that the charge 'had obtained the desired effect' whilst the 3rd Chasseurs post combat report claimed the attack had 'halted the enemy and allowed our infantry to rally' See l'État-Major, *St Privat*, pp.468–469.

58    L'État-Major, *St Privat*, p.469.

the stragglers from 3rd Division. After restoring some semblance of order, Becquet de Sonnay utilised some of these troops to reinforce Saint Privat whilst the remainder, mainly from the 94th, took up a blocking position along the edge of the forêt de Jaumont, the infantry being supported by a battery, although due to the continuing shortage of ammunition, each gun was limited to just five rounds.

## The Saxon and Guard artillery Bombard Saint Privat

As Albert's long-anticipated attack got underway, the Guard and Saxon artillery began an intensive bombardment of Saint Privat, the village having previously only been subjected to an occasional harassing fire. At 7:00 p.m., Pape's adjutant, Major Count zu Ysenburg, ordered the Guard Corps Reserve artillery to target the village as General von Budritzky[59] issued similar instructions to his divisional batteries positioned along the Sainte Marie-Saint Privat road.[60] As a result, nine batteries[61] on the left wing of the Guards gun line, targeted the village whilst five on the right[62] continued to engage 4 Corps to prevent them supporting Canrobert. Fourteen Saxon batteries[63] repositioned from alongside the Bois d'Auboué to the south-west of Roncourt, adding their considerable weight to the ensuing bombardment, although the advance of the Prussian Guard masked the fire of a number of the guns.

If this formidable assembly of firepower was not enough, X Corps' artillery began to deploy amongst the batteries of the Guards and Saxons. Their commanding officer, General Voights Rhetz, had ridden ahead of his men to reconnoitre the scene from a hill to the southeast of St Ail and immediately ordered Colonel Baron von der Becke[64] to bring Colonel von der Goltz's Reserve artillery forward into action. As the foot batteries of the corps' Reserve[65] navigated their way through the difficult defile between Batilly and St Ail, Captain Saalmüller led the horse artillery[66] forward at a gallop taking ground between the divisions of von Buddenbrock[67] and von Rheinbaben.[68] Meanwhile, from 5th Cavalry Division, two horse artillery batteries[69] deployed alongside the Guard artillery and engaged 4 Corps.

The introduction of so many fresh batteries into the firing line prevented some from deploying all their guns but nonetheless, the effect of the combined artillery from three corps was overwhelming.[70] Subjected to an intense bombardment at ranges of between 800 to 1,600

---

59 Commander, 2nd Guard Infantry Division.
60 2nd Field Division commanded by Major von Krieger.
61 6th Heavy, 5th Heavy, 6th Light, 4th Light, 1st Horse, 3rd Horse, 2nd Horse, 3rd Heavy and 4th Heavy.
62 3rd Light, 2nd Heavy, 1st Heavy, 1st Light and 2nd Light. They were deployed south of the ridge running between the heights 328–321.
63 From north to South: 1st Light, 4th Heavy, 8th Heavy, 7th Heavy, 2nd Light, 5th Heavy, 5th Light, 6th Light, 2nd Horse, 6th Heavy, 1st Heavy, 4th Light, 3rd Light, 3rd Heavy.
64 X Corps artillery commander.
65 5th and 6th Light, 5th and 6th Heavy.
66 1st (Captain Frisch) and 3rd (Lieutenant Marcard).
67 1st, 3rd and 2nd Guards Horse artillery.
68 6th Heavy, 5th Heavy and 6th Light.
69 1st Horse artillery, 4th Field Artillery Regiment, 2nd Horse artillery, 10th Field Artillery Regiment.
70 It is difficult to reconcile the differing accounts but in addition, the 14 Saxon batteries deployed to the north of the Sainte Marie-Saint Privat highway as detailed in earlier footnote 390, the batteries

metres, the buildings within Saint Privat and Jérusalem were set ablaze, flames rising high into the night sky. Several of the larger structures were wrecked and the few remaining French batteries in Marengo withdrew behind the forêt de Jaumont to escape their murderous fire. As Kessel recalled, this bombardment buoyed the spirits of his hard-pressed men: 'In Saint Privat I saw columns advancing, but a pillar of smoke rose up from one of the farms by the road and stood out black against the sky, which was already touched with the sunset colours. The fire at least was a help to us and its appearance was greeted by our men with loud cheers.'[71]

In addition to sending his artillery forward, Voights Rhetz also ordered General Kraatz-Kochlau[72] to march on Saint Privat to lend additional support to the Guards assault. 40th Brigade,[73] accompanied by 10th Rifle battalion, headed their advance with skirmishers deployed and regimental colours flying; they were supported on their right by Major General von Woyna's 39th Brigade,[74] whilst 16th Dragoons out on their left flank, served as escorts to both the corps artillery and the infantry.

As Kraatz-Kochlau advanced from St Ail across the open ground towards the Sainte Marie-Saint Privat highway, it was swept by both rifle and cannon fire, evidence, if any were needed, that the French were still firmly ensconced in their positions. The noise from the Prussian and Saxon artillery was deafening, their incessant fire concealing his objective in rolling clouds of powder smoke; peering through the gloom it seemed to von Diringshofen that Roncourt was still occupied by the French so he detached 10th Rifles to mask this threat whilst directing the remainder of his division against Saint Privat. The 17th and 92nd were in the front line,[75] whilst the divisional batteries[76] pushed across the chausée and unlimbered on the right of XII Corps gun line, their deployment masking the fire of some Saxon's batteries.[77]

shelling Saint Privat from the south of the highway were, from north to south, as follows; From the Guard, 6th Heavy; from X Corps 3rd Horse artillery; from the Guard 5th Heavy and 6th Light; from X Corps 3rd and 1st Horse Artillery; from the Guard 1st, 3rd and 2nd Horse Artillery, 3rd Heavy; from X Corps 6th and 5th Heavy, 6th and 5th Light; from the Guard, 4th Heavy. The batteries firing on 4 Corps were, from north to south; from X Corps, 1st and 2nd Heavy, from 5th Cavalry Division, 1st and 2nd Horse artillery; from the Guard, 2nd Heavy, 1st Light and from the Hessian Division, 2nd Heavy and 2nd Light.

71   Maude, *Military Letters*, p.90.
72   Commander 20th Infantry Division, X Corps.
73   17th and 92nd Regiments, commanded by Major General von Diringshofen.
74   56th and 79th Regiments.
75   The two fusilier battalions and the 2/92nd in the front line, followed by the 1/92nd and six musketeer companies from the 17th; the 5th and 6th having been tasked with escorting the guns in action to the south of Saint Privat.
76   3rd and 4th Heavy, 3rd and 4th Light.
77   The 20th Division arrived too late to take part in the assault of Saint Privat, but the 2nd and fusilier battalions of the 17th advanced through the village to the northern side where they were employed to act as support for some of XII Corps and 20th Division's artillery, where they took prisoner 430 unwounded French soldiers. A battalion of the 92nd remained in the village, whilst another marched across to the eastern side, whilst their fusilier battalion advanced to the south of Saint Privat and pushed forward to forêt de Jaumont, where they joined forces with the 10th Rifles and 51st Fusiliers.

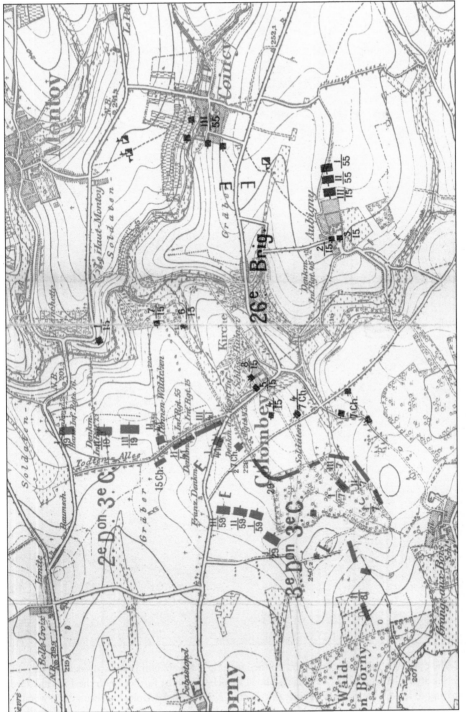

The Battle of Borny; The situation around 5:00 p.m. on August 14. 26th Brigade is just about to engage 3 Corps outpost line around Colombey as the Bazaine pulls his forces back through Metz across the Moselle. (B)

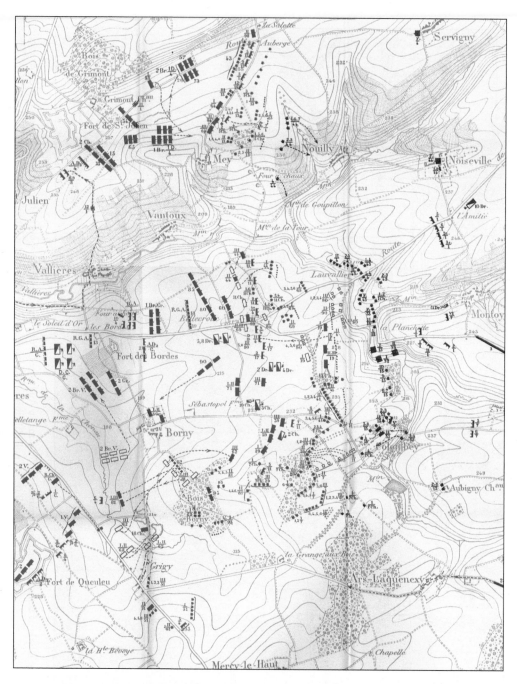

2　　　　The position a little after 6:00 p.m. To the north the 44th are falling back towards Nouilly. In the centre the attack has stalled at Lauvallières and la Planchette whilst further south the 15th and 73rd are preparing to launch their assault against the 'Todten Allée.' Von der Goltz has secured the woods around Château de Colombey but is unable to make further headway against the French defensive line, Further south, Woyna's 28th Brigade hastens to the sound of the guns with a view to work their way around the enemy right flank. The French outnumber the attackers but Bazaine has expressly forbidden any attack. (SH)

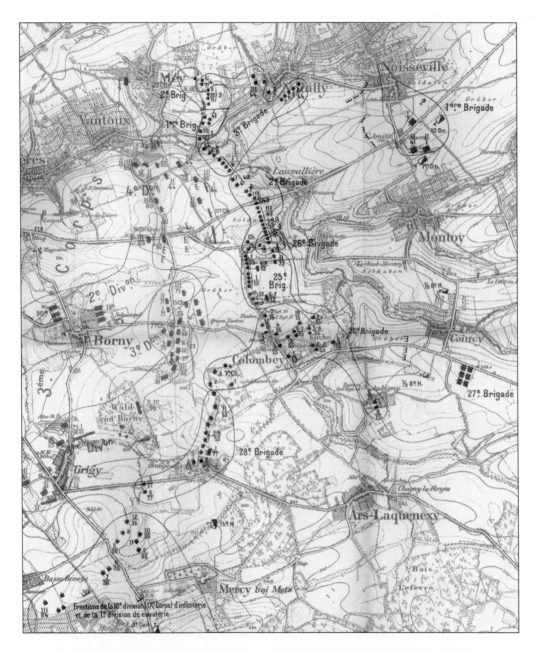

3        The situation around 7:30 p.m. In the centre although 'Todten Allée' has finally been taken, there is stalemate around Lauvallières and la Planchette. Further south the 53rd and 77th move forward from Grange aux Bois towards Borny wood but are too few in number to trouble the French. (B)

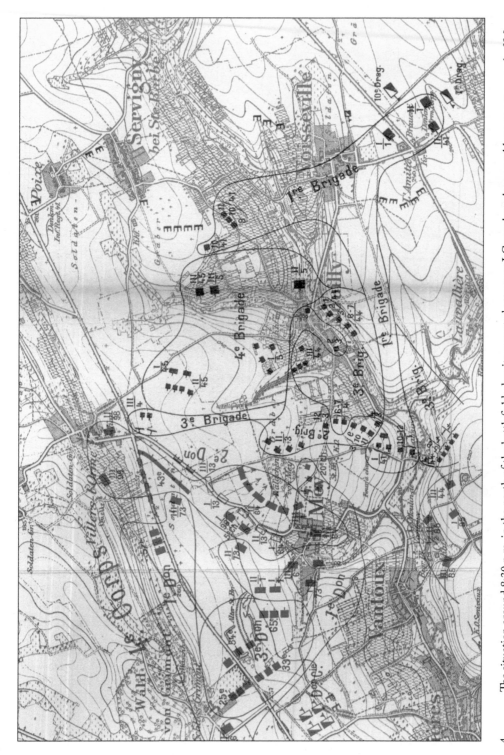

4    The situation around 8:30 p.m. in the north of the battlefield; despite repeated attempts I Corps have been unable to wrest control of Mey and with increasing numbers of French troops to the north, Manteuffel believes, erroneously, that they are seeking to outflank his right wing; (B)

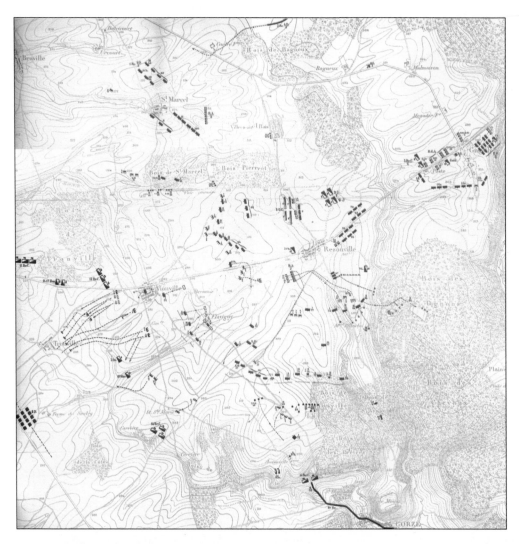

5      The Battle of Vionville, 14 August 1870; the situation around 10:15 a.m. After being surprised in their bivouacs by Barby's horse artillery, the French Reserve cavalry have rallied to the north of Rezonville whilst Frossard's 2 Corps have begun their advance against Rheinbarben's isolated batteries. Meanwhile a desperate General Bülow urges forward the reinforcements from the divisional and corps' Artillery reserve. (SH)

6    The situation around 12:30 p.m.

Having secured Vionville, Alvesleben has established a secure base of operations along the track running south from the Bois de St Marcel to the Metz–Verdun highway and Flavigny. III Corps artillery located on the plateau between Flavigny and Gorze have driven off 2 Corps attacks and they have fallen back in disorder. To their right, assisted by the firepower of the guns, 9th Brigade have pushed forward to line the edge of the Bois de Vionville and Bois de St Arnould. In response, Bazaine orders 3rd Lancers and the Guard Cuirassiers to charge to buy time to reorganise his defence. Elsewhere, the Guard infantry are deployed around Gravelotte with 4 Corps still to put in an appearance. Le Boeuf's 3 Corps, having finally received instructions from Bazaine, edge forward from St Marcel towards the Bois de St Marcel, seeking to extend the French right flank. (SH)

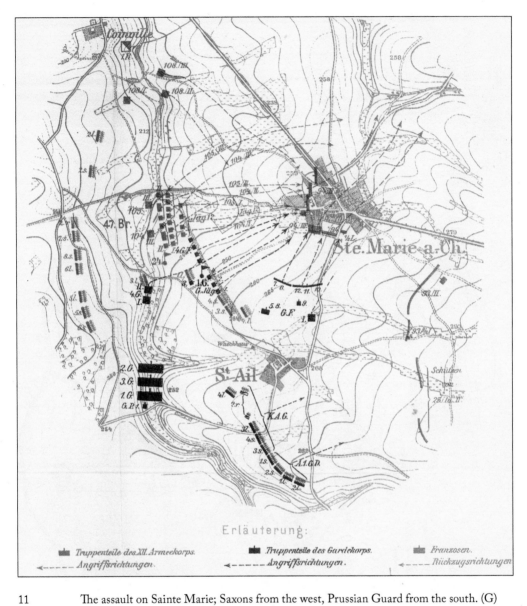

11     The assault on Sainte Marie; Saxons from the west, Prussian Guard from the south. (G)

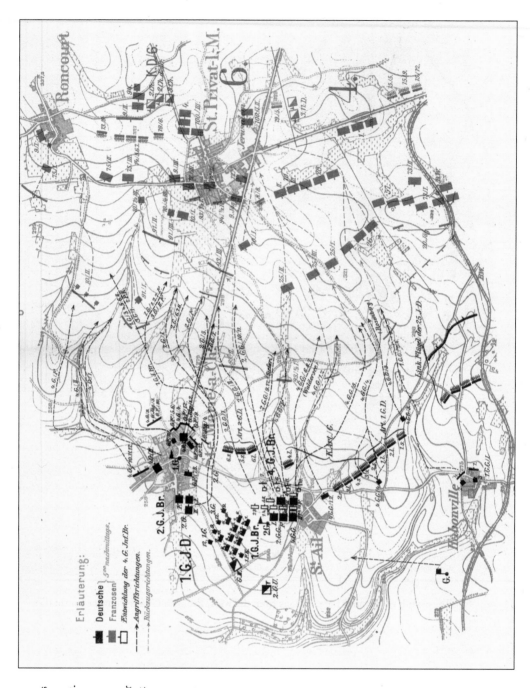

12 The Guards assault on Saint Privat. This plan shows the position shortly after their attack began. (G)

13    The situation around 6:30 p.m. in front of Saint Privat. In the south the Guard artillery has beaten back Cissey's counter attack. 4th Guards Brigade are inching their way towards the lane held by the French as the defenders successively pull back to replenish their ammunition. To the north of the road, 1st Guards Brigade are still pinned down before Saint Privat, unable to advance despite the introduction of 2nd Foot Guards. Further north the Saxons are massing to the west of Roncort waiting for 48th Brigade to launch their flanking attack from Montois. Canrobert is still holding his ground in Saint Privat although his outlying skirmishers have been forced to pull back towards the village perimeter and as successive battalions pull out of the line to replenish ammunition, his remaining reserves are drawn into the struggle. (G)

14    Salvation is at hand! Some 90 minutes after the Prussian Guard commenced their attack against Saint Privat the long-awaited flank attack by the Saxons gets underway with 48th and 45th brigades advancing on Roncourt. In front of Saint Privat, Pape's 1st Guards Division are still pinned down, unable to advance whilst to the south of the Sainte Marie – Saint Privat road, 4th Guards Brigade are inching forward, the French having abandoned their defensive positions along the lane that ran south from the village. Whilst Canrobert is still holding on in Saint Privat, many of his men and all his artillery have pulled back to Marengo to replenish their ammunition and, understandably, are reluctant to enter the maelstrom again. (G)

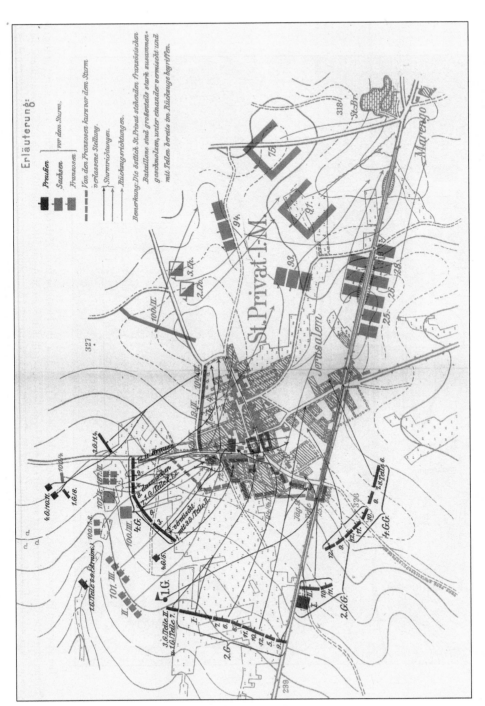

15    The final assault. The Prussian Guard and Saxons close in on Saint Privat; to the north 4th Foot Guards and 45th Brigade; from the west 1st and 2nd Foot Guards, from the south, 4th Guards Brigade with the 4th Grenadiers making for Jérusalem so as to cut off any retreat by the French still defending Saint Privat. Those defenders who can escape the inferno head for Marengo. (G)

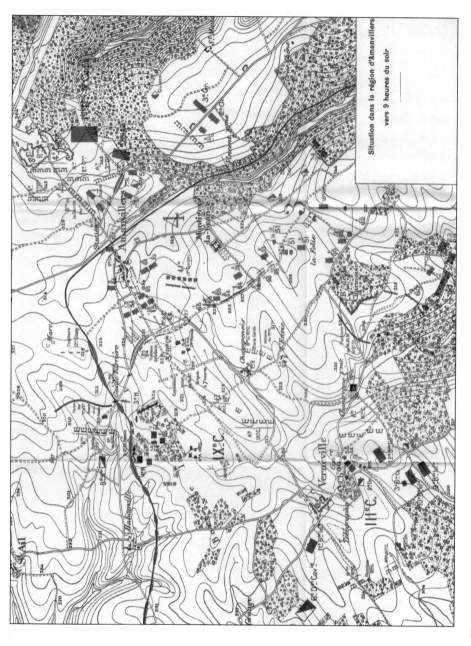

Situation dans la région d'Amanvillers

vers 9 heures du soir

16    The situation in front of Amanvillers towards the close of the battle; the Hessians from 25th Division attacking to the north of the railway line. To the south the Gardeschützen, 1st and 3rd Guard Grenadiers are stalled in front of Amanvillers. Further south IX Corps artillery maintain the pressure against the defenders of Montigny la Grange. Despite repeated attempts Manstein is unable to make any progress into the Bois de la Charmoise, with both 3 and 4 corps putting up a determined defence. (R)

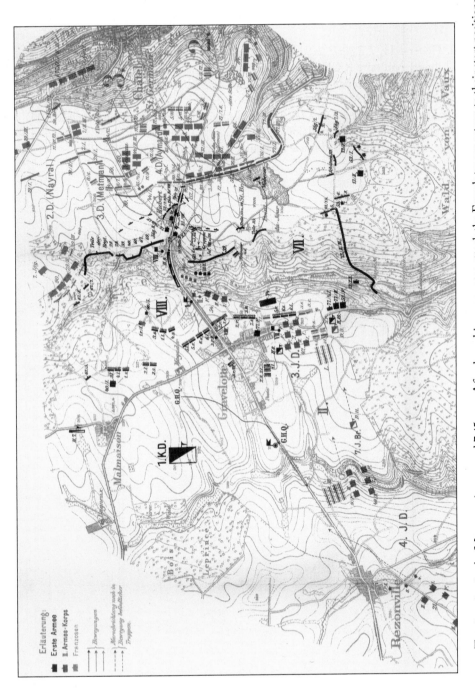

17    The situation in the Mance ravine around 7:45 p.m. After launching a counter attack the French troops return to their start positions without seeking to exploit their success. Fransecky's II Corps are committed to the fighting, serving little purpose other than to add to the confusion and already high casualty list. What the plan fails to convey is the utter confusion which existed in the rear areas of I Army at this time as the advancing troops attempted to force their way through the exhausted and demoralised masses that had fallen back in disarray. (G)

## Key to Map Sources

(B) Bonnal, General H, *L'Espirit de la Guerre Moderne, La Manoeuvre de Saint Privat Atlas* (Paris: Libraire Militaire R Chapelot et Cie. 1904)

(G) Großen Generalstabe *Studien zur Kriegesgeschichte und Taktik V Der 18 August 1870 Karten* (Berlin: Ernst Siegfried Mittler und Sohn, 1906)

(R) Captaine Roy *Études sur le 18 Aout 1870* (Paris: Libraire Militaire Bergier Levrault 1911)

(SH) Section Historique de l'État-Major de l'Armée, *La Guerre de 1870–71 Les Opérations Autour De Metz Atlas* (Paris: Librairie Militaire, R Chapelot et Cie, 1903–05)

## The Saxons Assault Roncourt

As X Corps moved to support the stalled Guards attack from the southwest, further north, Prince George was finally in position to launch his assault; Schulz's 48th Brigade from the direction of Montois la Montagne, Craushaar and the 45th from the Bois d'Auboué. The prince rode at the head of the 45th and when Schubert urged caution, replied, 'In the first battle I belong at the head of my Division.'[78]

As soon as Schulz cleared Montois, Craushaar ordered the I/101st Grenadier Regiment to march on Roncourt. As they moved up alongside the 100th, the Body Guard Grenadiers rose to their feet and advanced in support of the assault.[79] Two battalions[80] from the 101st echeloned to their right, provided additional weight to the attack with the 108th being held back on the edge of the wood as reserve. As the 45th pushed forward, their left wing made contact with 46th Brigade who emerged to the west of the woods between Montois la Montagne and Roncourt. With their belated appearance, the Saxon forces presented an almost unbroken line which ran in a shallow arc from the west to the north of their objective.

The three assault brigades were closing fast on Roncourt when a scarlet clad rider on a grey horse was seen galloping towards them from the south; it transpired the mysterious horseman was Pape's orderly, Lieutenant Esbeck, who had been tasked with locating the whereabouts of the Saxon infantry. After pausing his mission to request the commander of the I/3rd Foot Guards to bring his men into the firing line, he then galloped across to some infantry who had appeared west of the small wood between Montois and Roncourt. The unknown troops turned out to be from 48th Brigade and the officers of the leading battalions[81] directed him towards their commanding officer, Lieutenant Colonel von Schweinitz. Esbeck explained the situation confronting the Guards and asked when he was due to attack Roncourt which, as he understood, the Saxons intended to secure before launching any assault on Saint Privat. After a brief discussion, Schweinitz agreed that Saint Privat was the key to the French position and ordered I and II Battalions to divert to the south.[82]

As the Saxons wheeled to the right, Esbeck made his way back to inform Pape where, en-route, he stumbled across the II and III/101st Grenadiers from 45th Brigade at the southeast corner of the Bois d'Auboué. After being updated on the situation, Craushaar also agreed to abandon his attack on Roncourt and offered to support the Guard's stalled assault with the units under his command.[83] Meanwhile Albert, observing the fighting from his vantage point on the left of his corps, had independently come to the same conclusion and instructed 46th Brigade to

---

78   Bell, *St Privat*, p.414.
79   The regiment was deployed in two lines; III and I battalions in the front line, II, in two half battalions in the second alongside one another.
80   II and III.
81   I and II/107th.
82   In any event, Roncourt seemed not to be occupied by the enemy; he was unaware that it had been captured by von Bosze at the head of the III/107th.
83   Unfortunately, the adjutant carrying these orders to the Body Grenadiers had his horse shot from under him and as a consequence some formations – the I/100th and 5th and 6th companies from II Battalion – failed to receive this message and continued towards Roncourt. Their commander, Lieutenant Colonel von Schimpff, subsequently noted it had been abandoned by the French and wheeled his men to the south in support of 3rd and 4th companies' 1st Foot Guards under Lieutenant Colonel von Oppell.

abandon its march on Roncourt and instead make directly for Saint Privat; the 47th being held back as Corps' Reserve.

Esbeck galloped back to brief Pape on the news and as he rode along the embattled Guards firing line, proclaimed to resounding cheers, the imminent arrival of XII Corps. Encountering Kessel to the south of the large basin where the remnants of 1st Guard Brigade were sheltering from the French fire, Esbeck declared: 'Victory is ours! The Saxons are coming!'[84]

## Preparations for the Assault on Saint Privat

On the left flank of 1st Guard Brigade, the companies assembled by Oppell[85] seized the stone enclosure southwest of Roncourt and opened fire on the French skirmishers as they withdrew into Saint Privat. Röder ordered Oppell to continue his advance to clear away troops who continued to oppose the Saxon advance, instructing the 1st Guard Pioneer Company to support his assault. Confronted by this show of force, the remaining tirailleurs withdrew towards the forêt de Jaumont so Oppell swung his command south, so as to front Saint Privat, the left of his line brushing up against Roncourt. A heavy cross fire erupted from Saint Privat and the woods, forcing his men back to the shelter of the enclosure, from where they attempted to return fire. Just then, amidst the clouds of swirling powder smoke, Oppell noticed troops approaching from the west and galloped across to bring them up into the firing line; they were Seegenberg's 1/3rd Foot Guards[86] and the 100th Body Guard Regiment.[87]

The former, deployed in two half battalions and echeloned to the left, had served as flank guard for Kessel's brigade during his march on Saint Privat and were marking time in the shelter afforded by a slight depression to the southwest of Roncourt. As the attack on Saint Privat stalled, Pape's orderly officer ordered them to move into the firing line and as 1/3rd deployed, three companies of Saxons from the Body Guard Regiment[88] pushed into the space between their two half battalions; the 1st, 2nd and 3rd companies then appeared on Seegenberg's left rear whilst further to the south, the I/101st Grenadier Regiment could be seen, marching towards Roncourt. Then, the Saxons units diverted by Schweinitz and Craushaar[89] to support

---

Here, on the left flank of the assaulting line, they defeated several attempted counter attacks by the 2/100th, 94th and 10th Ligne.

84    Bell, *St Privat*, p.351. In the post war blame game about the role played by XII Corps in the capture of Saint Privat, some Saxon commentators claimed that the Guards had taken so many losses that Esbeck 'almost imploring begged' Craushaar for assistance. Esbeck later commented 'It is true that I urgently, if you want to call it so, requested General von Craushaar for flank support of the Guard but not for support in the attack on Saint Privat; what I actually said was 'General, for the past hour the Guard has been lying in front of Saint Privat in the hottest kind of battle; it will hold its place but cannot advance unless it receives flank support'. I was certainly in a hurry and it is quite natural that I was excited considering the importance of the situation; but I did not 'For God's sake' pray to bring help to the Guard bleeding to death in front of Saint Privat and I did not execute my mission 'imploringly' See Bell *St Privat*, p.470.

85    3rd, 4th and 8th companies' 1st Foot Guards and 1st Guards Pioneer Company.

86    From 1st Guard Brigade.

87    From the Saxon 45th Brigade.

88    4th, 6th and 5th companies.

89    7th and 8th companies and 3rd Battalion 101st Body Guard regiment and I and II Battalions 107th.

the Guards attack, appeared in the gap between these formations, marching almost due south towards Saint Privat.

This forced the companies on the right wing of 1/3rd Foot Guards,[90] to turn to the south, fronting Saint Privat and with the gap between the two half battalions increasing, Seel's men found themselves in the midst of several Guard units[91] who were sheltering within the stone enclosure at the junction to the southwest of Roncourt. To add to the confusion, the 4th Company of the Saxon Body Guard Regiment pushed into the firing line alongside Seel's men, with Oppell directing another two companies[92] to support the group holding the stone enclosure.

Further north, Altrock's half battalion,[93] followed by three companies of Body Guards,[94] advanced towards Roncourt where, just short of their objective, they stumbled into the I/101st Saxon Grenadiers who had just exited the village. As a result, the greater part of both regiments became jumbled together[95] and unsurprisingly, this inviting target came under a heavy fire from the tirailleurs[96] covering the retreat of their comrades from the village.

Given the apparent confusion, Seegenberg led Altenrock's half battalion towards Roncourt, which at that time was still under intermittent fire from the Saxon batteries, anxious to secure it against any sudden counter attack. Scouting the way ahead, his adjutant[97] discovered it was occupied by a platoon from the 101st Guard Grenadiers and elements of 1st Foot Guards[98] who had already secured the western exits.

As Altenrock moved into the village, his men came under chassepot fire from the direction of Saint Privat, so Seegenberg ordered the 3rd Company to occupy the southern perimeter, whilst 2nd Company and 1st Foot Guards moved into the centre, where sheltered from the French fire, they could rally and tend to their numerous wounded.[99] With their initial objective secured, the I/101st attempted to push onto Saint Privat but came under the same heavy fire that had driven Seegenberg to seek cover, as well as taking over shots from the Saxon batteries at Auboué and rounds fired by the French artillery to the southeast of Saint Privat.

Seeking to reduce the number of casualties, their officers attempted to deploy their men into skirmish formation, but exhausted by their rapid approach march and taking losses to the rifle and shell fire, Lieutenant Colonel von Leonhardi withdrew them into the shelter of Roncourt, from where they engaged in an intermittent long-range fire fight with the skirmishers along the

90   1st and 4th companies' 3rd Foot Guards under Captain von Seel.
91   Seel found himself between the 8th Company 3rd Foot Guards and Oppell's 3rd and 4th companies 1st Foot Guards who were supported by 1st Guard Pioneer Company.
92   5th and 6th companies Saxon Body Guard Regiment.
93   2nd and 3rd companies, I/3rd Foot Guards.
94   1st, 2nd and 3rd.
95   They included the 3rd and 4th companies' 1st Guard Regiment, the 1st Guard Pioneer Company; the 1st, 2nd, 3rd, 5th and 6th companies' 100th Body Guard Regiment. To their right were the 1st and 4th companies' 3rd Guard Regiment and 4th Company 100th Body Guard Regiment.
96   From the 9th Ligne.
97   Second Lieutenant Beneckendorf von Hindenburg.
98   3rd and 4th companies.
99   This influx of troops caused serious delays to the Saxons attack on Saint Privat as the Prussian guardsmen, 'tortured by thirst' after their long march crowded around the wells and water pumps causing 'an indescribable confusion' in the village streets; order was not restored until almost 8:00 p.m. See Bell, *St Privat*, p.354.

edge of the forêt de Jaumont, the I/101st occupying the southeast perimeter of the village until nightfall.

From 45th Brigade, the III/107th arrived in the northern part of the Roncourt at the same time as the 108th took up position to the west; content that the Saxons had secured the village against counter attack, Seegenberg ordered Altrock's half battalion of 3rd Foot Guards to form up prior to moving off in support of the attack against Saint Privat. Unfortunately, they had dispersed to fill their canteens from the well and the Saxon water carriers and given the resultant disorder, it was 8:00 p.m. before the half battalion, which by then were reinforced by parts of 1st Foot Guards, were ready to move out. As the assault on Saint Privat was already underway, given the continued fighting in the forêt de Jaumont, they were held back alongside Roncourt so as to confront any new threat from this direction.

Schubert was amongst the foremost troops who entered Roncourt and described the scene greeting the Saxons:

> It was 6:30p.m. when the whole horror of a large decisive battle spread out. Our staff halted in front of the entrance to Roncourt, which village was under a perfect hail of projectiles from Saint Privat, 1,000 paces distant. The terrain as far as Saint Privat proved here to be also a naked, gradually ascending slope on which several field walls, in parallel lines and rising one above the other like terraces, formed just so many defensive lines strongly occupied by French infantry. A few batteries in position in front of Saint Privat and the forest poured a very heavy fire on our advancing columns. One shell exploded in our immediate rear in a dense mass of men without, however, doing any damage. I well remember the droll incident of the Prince's servant, Liebsch, who rode behind the Prince and suddenly called out loud to him. When we turned around, he held his left hand up and showed us that he held only the ends of the four bridle reins, a shell having cut them clean through.[100]

Moving up from Auboué, 4th Company 100th Body Guards pushed into the crowded firing line alongside Seel and Oppell[101] and assisted by the advance of I/101st, which drew the enemy's fire, 3rd Foot Guards edged forward towards road running between Roncourt and Saint Privat. Coupled with the seizure of Roncourt, this served to relieve the immediate pressure against the disparate groups of guardsmen[102] who were clinging on to their exposed positions on the open ground north of Saint Privat. Adding to their pressure, 4th Foot Guards were brought forward to add their weight to the attack. Their I Battalion, having deployed all companies in line, advanced by rushes, to the south of the shallow depression which led up to the north-west of the village, their attack being supported by remnants of the 1st Foot Guards.[103]

Advancing along the northern side of the hollow, the fusilier battalion angled their march towards the open ground between Roncourt and Saint Privat where a number of French

---

100  *Ibid*, pp.414–415.
101  Seel:1st and 4th companies' 3rd Foot Guards; Oppell, 3rd and 4th companies' 1st Foot Guards.
102  Brause's group of men alongside other elements of II/1st Foot Guards and 8th Company, 3rd Foot Guards.
103  1st and 2nd companies and fusilier battalion who were commanded by their sole surviving officer. Arnim's two companies of 1st Foot Guards were held back as a last formed reserve.

skirmishers[104] were putting up a determined defence, sheltered behind a number of stone walls and enclosures. Sweeping up Brause's group of men in their advance, two companies of fusiliers[105] were dropped off as reserve alongside the 8th Company 1st Foot Guards, whilst the remainder pushed into the firing line between the 4th Company, 4th Foot Guards and Oppell's half battalion of 3rd Foot Guards.

From the behind cover of the field walls, the defenders responded to this threat in their usual manner; their rapid chassepot fire tore holes in the ranks of I/4th Foot Guards and their commanding officer[106] called his supports forward to reinforce the firing line. II Battalion rose up from their position to the rear of Arnim, with three companies charging forward along the southern edge of the basin into a gap between the 3rd and 4th, their attack taking them to within 250 metres of the French positions.

Meanwhile, the 5th Company, under Captain Esebeck, followed the right wing of I Battalion towards the enemy positions to the north of Saint Privat. In the face of this imminent threat, the last tirailleurs finally quit their positions and withdrew into the village. The II/4th Foot Guards set off in pursuit and almost seized the abandoned enclosures but the renewed fire from the village brought their advance to a halt along the road running between Saint Privat and Roncourt.

This movement of troops within Saint Privat, coupled with the sudden intensification of fire all along the French positions, gave rise to the belief that Canrobert was planning a counter attack. This did not materialise but the renewed chassepot fire resulted in even more losses to the already depleted Guard regiments. To add to the general confusion, the heavy supporting bombardment provided by the Saxon's and Prussian's, enveloped Saint Privat in clouds of smoke. As a result, the gunners had difficulty in estimating their range and many shells fell short of their intended target, exploding amidst the Guards shaken ranks.

## 6 Corps Strength Ebbs Away

After being driven from Roncourt and the outlying defences to the north of Saint Privat, the 2/9th took up new defensive positions in the village whilst 1/9th withdrew to the shelter of the forêt de Jaumont. 1st and 2/100th extended the defensive line taking up positions alongside the track that ran east from Saint Privat to the Jaumont quarries, with the 2nd Chasseurs d'Afrique covering their open flank. To the rear in support, Bruchard's brigade of Chasseurs and the 94th were placed on a small rise to the east of Saint Privat. Further south Levassor-Sorval rallied his division either side of the main road running into Metz; the 25th, 26th and 28th a few hundred metres east of Jérusalem farm, the 70th closer to Marengo farm.

The bulk of Becquet de Sonnay's brigade assembled east of Saint Privat and around 7:00 p.m., were united with all three battalions from the 93rd to the rear of Jérusalem. However, as noted by the French official history, it is impossible to be certain of the order in which the formations fell back, any reckoning being complicated by the large number of individuals who had already

---

104  From the 2/9th Ligne.
105  10th and 11th companies.
106  Lieutenant Colonel von Wolffradt.

fallen out of line.[107] What was beyond dispute was that Canrobert's fighting strength was fast ebbing away and the withdrawal of nearly all his artillery to the rising ground by the quarries at the Carrieres de la Croix, did little to bolster the morale of those remaining in the firing line.[108] Again, as the French official history notes, although Canrobert's troops were putting up a determined defence, the battle was nonetheless lost, as everyone from the corps commander to the lowest private had been 'overwhelmed by a feeling of helplessness in the face of such superior numbers.'[109]

Although the 10th Ligne pulled back to replenish their ammunition, the French official history estimates that Canrobert still had some 12 and half battalions under his command[110] although given the confusion that existed within the village at that time with buildings ablaze and under intense bombardment from the Prussian and Saxon artillery, it is difficult to be certain about which positions they held. To the southwest, 9th Chasseurs occupied a large fortified dwelling; they were reinforced by a few men from the 25th, assembled by Colonel Gibon, who held a trench which connected this building with the stone walls enclosing the western side of the village. Men from the 12th manned the dwellings in their rear, lining the windows, attics and hastily prepared loopholes. To their right, three companies from the 1/9th and skirmishers from the 12th defended the western perimeter, with formed companies being held back in the centre of the village.[111]

The northern side of Saint Privat was held by the 3rd and 2/9th and further to the east, lining the stone field walls along the road that led to Jaumont, the 3/100th lay in ambush. The 4th Ligne, who were pushed into the village sometime later, were distributed along both the western and northern flanks forming a second line of resistance.[112] The sector facing towards Roncourt was well suited to defence; the graveyard being enclosed by a high stone wall, which in turn was flanked by a partly constructed two storey farmhouse; to the northwest, the church was surrounded by stone walls and hastily dug trenches.

Despite these precautions, as noted by the French official history: 'Before the assault proper commenced, the German artillery had fired on the village for 20 minutes. All cover had been destroyed, numerous houses were in flames, roofs and walls were falling. It may be assumed therefore, that within a quarter of an hour the defenders left their positions, which had been made untenable by the hostile shells.'[113] This was confirmed by Captain Canonier:

107 These were predominately from the divisions of La Font de Villiers and Levassor-Sorval who had been exposed to the Prussian artillery fire for several hours.
108 The defender of Saint Privat received belated support from two batteries of the general reserve, the 6th and 7/13th and a few batteries from 4 Corps.
109 L'État-Major, St Privat, p.507.
110 9th Chasseurs, 1st, 2nd and 3/4th, 1st, 2nd and 3/12th, 3/9th, 1st, 2nd and 3/93rd, 3/100th and the 4th, 5th and 6th companies from the 1/94th.
111 Canrobert's engineers created openings in walls of the buildings to facilitate the easy movement of men from one section of the village to another.
112 The French official history places the 3/9th, 4th, 5th and 6th companies' 1/9th, the 12th and parts of the 4th along the western side of Saint Privat; the 3/9th, 3/100th and part of the 4th along the northern edge. The 93rd appears to have occupied, at least for a short while part of the western edge of the village, although around 7:00 p.m., it fell back to replenish its ammunition and took up position to the rear of Becquet Sonnay's brigade.
113 L'État-Major, St Privat, p.519.

The growing flames had a terrible effect upon the men in the village and just then, in the midst of all this confusion, the men of the 12th opened fire on the companies of the 94th,[114] who at that time, stood ready, with a plentiful supply of ammunition, to open a decisive fire against the enemy. This unfortunate accident caused an explosion of shouting and gunshots that led to a general retreat.[115]

As the Guards and Saxons closed on their objective, their artillery bombardment intensified, shells striking the village from the northwest and south at ranges of between 800 to 1,600 metres. Just prior to the infantry assault, the fire of 31 batteries from three corps were concentrated on the village; the effect was decisive with much of Saint Privat and Jérusalem now ablaze, flames shooting high into the darkening sky. In the confusion, some of X Corps guns opened fire on some batteries of Guard horse artillery who they mistook for the enemy, their error being corrected by Captain von Holleben who guided the Guard Fusiliers from Sainte Marie towards Saint Privat. This was not the only instance of friendly fire; many of the batteries participating in the bombardment inadvertently fired on the Saxon and Guardsmen as they closed on their objective, the darkness and clouds of gunpowder smoke making accurate observation impossible.

## The Assault on Saint Privat

Esbeck's announcement of the imminent arrival of XII Corps spread like wildfire throughout the Guard Corps where the divisional commander stood beside the main road, monitoring developments. With the artillery bombardment having done its deadly work and the foremost columns of Saxons making their way from Auboué and Roncourt, Pape felt that the balance had turned in favour of the attackers who could now launch their long-delayed assault on the village. At this time, from 1st Guards Division, the 1st and 4th Foot Guards were assembled around the north-west corner of Saint Privat; on their right, still some distance from village perimeter, stood, or rather crouched, the remnants of 2nd and 3rd Foot Guards.[116]

The traumatised remnants of 4th Guards Brigade were gathered opposite the south-west corner of the village, around the main road and hill 328.

To the north of the Guard Corps, Prince George's Saxons were closing in on Saint Privat; the first group, advancing in column of battalions, comprised III/100th Body Guard Regiment, II and III/107th and 7th and 8th companies from the 100th Body Guard. The second group consisted of II and III/101st Grenadiers, were formed in company columns, with General Craushaar at their head. From the west, 40th Brigade under Kraatz-Kochlau were marching towards Saint Privat. The Guard Fusilier regiment, advancing along either side of the main

---

114  3rd, 4th and 5th 1/94th.
115  L'État-Major, *18 Août, Documents*, p.393.
116  Their only reserves as such, were the group commanded by Lieutenant von Arnim, the 8th Company 1st Foot Guards, the 10th and 11th companies' 4th Foot Guards and along the Saint Privat-Roncourt road, the 1st and 4th companies, 3rd Foot Guards.

chausée,[117] moved forward from Sainte Marie looking to support the assault but Pape halted their advance and ordered them to take up a receiving position alongside the highway.[118]

Within 4th Guards Brigade, the grenadiers and fusiliers of the Königen Augusta and Kaiser Franz regiments, cautiously rose to their feet and with drums beating and bugles playing, closed in on the southern side of Saint Privat. Outnumbered, the defenders manning the perimeter defences melted away in the face of this attack, the foolhardy and brave few who continued to resist were bayonetted. The 7th and 8th Königen companies advanced towards Jérusalem, as their fusilier battalion and the 9th and 12th companies of the Kaiser Franz stormed into Saint Privat and more importantly, seized the main crossroads south of the village from where the guardsmen poured a heavy fire into the French fleeing to the rear.[119]

The remnants of the Franz regiment [120] sheltering in the ditches along the road, were swept along by this advance and after capturing the dwellings on the south-west corner of Saint Privat, quickly pushed through to the eastern side, occupying the exit that led towards Marengo. The 4th Ligne formed part of the second line of defence within Saint Privat and their post combat report described how the enemy troops swept into the burning village:

> The regiment hastened up on the run and dispersed throughout the village ... the fire was annihilating ... the enemy, advancing anew, retreated again to 300 metres from the village, throwing himself to the ground, his artillery redoubling its fire ... Shells came from all directions, the walls of the village tumbled down but our men held their ground. The bursting of the shells, the horrible noise made by the roofs and walls, the cries of the dying, the rattle of the infantry fire and the shrieking of the shells and shot made an absolute inferno out of the streets ... We have to admire the valour and self-sacrifice displayed by our men who remained in position facing certain destruction, rifles aimed, fingers on the trigger. The Prussian officers attempted to get their men to charge by calls and signs. Incendiary shells struck the roofs from all sides, a hospital was soon afire as well as other buildings and very soon the entire village was enveloped in flames.[121]

As 4th Guards Brigade launched their assault, Pape rode across to the northwest corner of the village where the left wing of the 2nd Foot Guards lay between remnants of the 3rd and 1st Foot Guards, behind the right wing of 4th Foot Guards, still some 600 metres short of the village. Whilst the 4th attempted to close the gap by way of repeated short rushes, Pape gathered the remnants of the three other regiments[122] together, ordering a trumpeter to sound the 'Rasch avanciren.' Men staggered to their feet 'from the piles of dead' and with 'one carrying forward the next'[123] rushed the stone walls at the western edge of the village.

117  The fusiliers deployed in column of companies, I Battalion to the south of the chausée, II and Fusiliers to the north.

118  This was to provide a bulwark behind which the division could reform if their assault was repulsed.

119  This loss of this junction had an important psychological impact on the defenders still holding out in Saint Privat as it severed their main line of retreat to Metz.

120  Equivalent to little more than two companies.

121  L'État-Major, *18 Août, Documents*, p.357.

122  1st, 2nd and 3rd Foot Guards.

123  Bell, *St Privat*, p.364.

A mixed force of Saxons and Guards[143] pressed into a quadrangle at the northwest of Saint Privat but greeted with a murderous fire from the defenders occupying the churchyard and surrounding houses, they were unable to make any further progress.

Further to the east, on the left wing of 1st Guards Division, the 12th, 9th and 4th companies' 4th Foot Guards edged into the Saxon's firing line and following their assault against the village, the Guards established a foothold amongst the enclosures and gardens opposite the northern entrance. Protected from the enemy fire, they massed their forces until they felt strong enough to launch an assault against the church in the centre of the village. Repeated attempts were made to storm this building, each time being driven off with heavy losses, but following one such one assault, several men secured a toehold in a dead angle of the churchyard wall. A shell then pierced the wall, the opening being enlarged by hand, whereupon the attackers shoved their rifles through the hole and opened fire, killing all 25 defenders. The continued resistance from the defenders occupying the neighbouring house, prevented the attackers from exploiting this small victory and unable to progress, around 300 men from the 4th Foot Guards under captains von Kunowski and von Krosigk, moved further south, linking up with Esebeck and the 5th Company and instead, stormed several of the fortified buildings lining the Roncourt road.

As the unrelenting struggle around the church continued, further south most defenders had fled the village, the only prolonged resistance coming from the schoolhouse, a new building adjacent to the church and a few dwellings to the east of the village square. Several buildings on the eastern outskirts remained in French hands but their occupants held their fire, seemingly reluctant to attract the enemy's attention. The school was eventually taken by a group of the 4th Foot Guards, under Captain von Kunowski, whilst the remaining strongholds in the village square were simply overwhelmed by sheer weight of numbers. With the fall of this strongpoint, a disorderly mass of soldiers pushed on south through the village, capturing the troops whose retreat had been cut off by the advance of 4th Guards Brigade.

## The Fall of Saint Privat

The final push to clear the French from Saint Privat began as the last rays of the sun disappeared below the horizon and the western sky was filled with a blood red glow. In the streets and gardens, the equally bloody struggle continued unabated as the defenders, especially those on the northern side of the village, continued to resist. Here, part of the 4th Ligne fought alongside the 2nd and 3/9th disputing every inch and offering, in the words of their official history, 'une résistance héroique' with ground only being conceded to the Saxons when the advance by 4th Guards Brigade threatened their rear. The 2/39th fell back through the ranks of their 3rd Battalion who had established a secondary blocking position a little way to their rear and then formed a new line on their flank, so as to give cover to the last few defenders as they finally evacuated the village. The post combat report by the 4th Ligne recalled how the fire from one particular enemy battery raked the main road through the village as they withdrew:

> The shells cleared everything away in that street and still our men only fell back step by step. Now the colonel ordered everyone to retreat, the men leave the village in all

---

143  1st, 2nd and 3rd companies, 4th Foot Guards and II and III/101st Grenadiers.

directions, pursued by the fire of the enemy, who does not dare attack us with the bayonet. At the quarries our officers assembled a portion of the regiment, whereupon it is marched to Woippy.[144]

The 3/100th occupied extreme north-eastern edge of Saint Privat and their commander,[145] his flank uncovered by the withdrawal of the 9th, had no option other than to fall back on his 2nd Battalion positioned to his rear, with his men conducting a fighting retreat to cover the escape of the remaining defenders as they fled the burning village. As so eloquently noted by the French official history: 'As the winds of defeat blew through the battalions of the corps and slowly continued its work of disintegration, a handful of heroes continued to fight on at Saint Privat, under the command of their valiant Marshal, so as to save the honour of their arms.'[146]

After the launch of the main assault around 7:30 p.m., fighting continued for at least an hour and in some places until as late as 9:00 p.m., although the majority of the combatants who avoided capture – including Canrobert who was one of the last to leave – left between 8–8:30 p.m. Those who continued the struggle were either shot or captured.[147] In the desperate last minutes of the struggle it seems that some units even contemplated a counter attack. A little before 8:00 p.m., the men of the 25th were rallied around their colours to the west of Marengo and to the strains of the 'Marseillaise' they were led by Colonel Gibon towards Jérusalem but by then, darkness had fallen and with the village now in the hands of the Prussians, Canrobert ordered them to withdraw.

Within Saint Privat, the bursting shells and the crush of Saxons and Guards made it impossible to bring any order to the confused mass of troops crammed within the village and still fearful of a French counter attack, Pape ordered up the Guard Fusiliers from their receiving position 600 yards west of Saint Privat. As they entered the village, their commanding officer Major Schmelling was killed whilst offering his horse to Pape, who had just lost his second mount of the day, so it fell to Major Feldmann to lead his three battalions to the high ground on the southern outskirts of the village from where he could make out a number of French batteries around the quarries to the rear of Marengo.

Looking to capture the guns, the 1st Battalion advanced as far as Jérusalem before one of Pape's orderlies caught up with them and directed Feldmann to occupy the southwest corner of Saint Privat, with just two platoons being left south of Jérusalem. Following close on the fusiliers' heels, the ever-present Pape sought to establish some semblance of order amongst the victorious troops, his priority being to ensure that Saint Privat, won at such cost, was secured against counter attack.[148]

---

144 L'État-Major, *18 Août, Documents*, pp 357–358. The 4th lost 14 officers and 574 men.
145 Pouilloue de Saint Mars.
146 L'État-Major, *St Privat*, p.472.
147 German sources claim about 2,100 men were captured in Saint Privat.
148 He feared that an enemy brigade forming up in front of the forêt de Jaumont was preparing to launch an assault.

## 6 Corps Withdraw Towards Metz

Canrobert was one of the last to quit the village after skilfully withdrawing most of his men from the death trap and rode back to the holding position established by Péchot to the rear of Marengo at the mouth of the defile running through the woods to Saulny. Initially, this force comprised just 9th Chasseurs with elements of the 4th and 12th Line but was later reinforced the 94th and 100th with General Baron Gondrecourt's dragoons[149] and the 2nd and 3rd chasseurs à cheval nearby at Marengo. Canrobert them arrived and as related by Colonel de Geslin,[150] the marshal appeared:

> Happy to find a small troop still showing some semblance of order and spoke a few words which went to my heart 'Ah well, colonel; Marshal Bazaine has informed me that he's finally sending me some artillery' and looking in the direction, he added 'These batteries are positioned on our right, on the edge of the wood, by the side of Amanvillers.' As to the 94th he placed them on the left of the road, behind the artillery, which he ordered to remain in position until they'd fired their last shell, so as to stop the enemy and prevent them from pushing out of Saint Privat. 'You will not resume your march until the last caisson has left'. I obeyed this order to the letter.[151]

When Canrobert recognised the impossibility of defending Saint Privat against such overwhelming odds, he took the precaution of sending his aide, Commandant Caffarel, to Plappeville to warn Bazaine of his intention to fall back on Woippy. As he stated to the post war Inquiry: 'I withdrew very slowly, stopping every ten minutes; always hoping to receive reinforcements. Finally, seeing that I was going to get nothing, I sent an officer of my staff to report to Bazaine, that I'd been obliged to retreat and to request orders.'[152] Shortly after, the cavalry on Péchot's flank began to pull back; 2nd Chasseurs d'Afrique were first to depart, being followed by Bruchard's brigade.[153] A little later, the 100th slipped away and finally, the 9th set off for Woippy. The regiments deployed by La Font de Villers, formed in square between Saint Privat and the Bois de Féves,[154] still held firm and three regiments[155] rallied by Levassor-Sorval

---

149  3rd and 11th Dragoons from 4 Corps.

150  CO of the 94th who assumed command of 2nd Brigade after General Colin was wounded.

151  L'État-Major, *18 Août, Documents*, pp.403–404.

152  The officer in question, Cafferal later reported how 'Canrobert told me to advise Bazaine that after 6 Corps had run out of ammunition, he'd been forced to evacuate Saint Privat and that he'd given the order to retire along the road to Saulny to Woippy. He begged me to inform him at the same time that he had taken all precautions to defend the entrance of the gorge of Saulny to the last man.' After being introduced to the commander in chief, Cafferal noted how Bazaine appeared unperturbed by the news of 6 Corps set back and after he had asked him to relate the various stages of the battle, said 'You don't have to worry about this retreat; the movement underway at present was going to be done tomorrow morning anyway; we're simply doing it twenty-two hours earlier and the Prussians won't have too much to boast about of having made us retreat. Tell Canrobert to take up tomorrow the positions that the chief of staff will distribute to all the chiefs of staff of the various corps.' See Anon, *Procés Bazaine*, p.225 and p.283.

153  2nd and 3rd Chasseurs à Cheval.

154  75th, 91st and 93rd.

155  The 25th, 26th and 28th.

alongside the main road between Jérusalem and Marengo, held their ground until night fell, a little after 8:00 p.m.

The ground to the rear of the blocking force rose steeply up towards the de la Croix quarries and here, on the thickly planted terraced slope which afforded excellent firing positions, Montluisant skilfully deployed 12 batteries from 6 Corps and the army Reserve.[156] After replenishing their ammunition[157] from the caissons sent by Bazaine, they opened a rapid fire on Saint Privat and Jérusalem, the flash of their guns, the white clouds of shrapnel and the flare of their bursting shells, being clearly visible to the Germans against the night sky.

They shifted their attention to the Prussian and Saxon artillery when they moved to new positions following the assault on Saint Privat and a little later, their fire was augmented by four batteries from the Imperial Guard, deployed to the north of Amanvillers.[158] The 12-pdrs of the reserve[159] engaged the enemy artillery at ranges of between 1,700 and 2,000 metres with some success, blowing up several caissons, the enemy guns being illuminated by flames from Saint Privat.

However, the continuing shortage of ammunition, particularly amongst Tixier's batteries, forced several to fall out of the firing line although a few resumed their position after replenishing their ammunition, their fire helping to cover Canrobert's retreat.[160] The 9th and 10/13th joined in the counter battery fire taking up position alongside the 6/19th, although the former soon expended its ammunition and withdrew.[161] Jamet's batteries[162] opened up with 'un fue violent' around 8:00 p.m. against the Prussian Guard artillery and the 6/17th, from 4 Corps, also joined the firing line but only got off a few rounds before Canrobert ordered them to retire.

As noted by the French official history, it would seem that out of the 30 batteries positioned between Amanvillers and the forêt de Jaumont, possibly 10 or 12 participated in this counter battery fight but given the range and the difficult conditions, they had negligible impact on the German artillery. A little to the south, 11 batteries from 4 Corps[163] took up firing positions west and south of the quarries at de la Croix, overlooking the heights at Amanvillers but saw no action.

---

156  5th, 7th, 8th and 12/8th; 5th, 6th and 7/14th and from the reserve, 9th and 10/13th.
157  6 Corps guns had only a little over 100 rounds per gun at the start of the battle. As they began to run short, they were obliged to reduce the rate of fire, the guns only firing one round every quarter of an hour until they only had 10 or 15 rounds left, which were kept for emergency use.
158  3rd and 4th Field artillery and 3rd and 4th Horse artillery.
159  6th and 7/13th.
160  5th, 8th and 12/8th.
161  6 Corps artillery were down to their last few rounds. 4 Corps sent them a few caissons and Commandant Abraham led forward a convoy from the reserve which consisted of eight caissons for the 4-pdrs, four for the 12-pdrs and eight with ammunition for the infantry. It arrived in the rear of Amanvillers sometime after 6:00 p.m. just as the infantry were beginning to fall back from Saint Privat. Leaving the caissons behind, Abraham went into Saint Privat to check out which batteries were low on munitions; unfortunately, as a result of some misunderstanding only the 4-pdr caissons were sent forward as Abraham failed to tell anyone about the 12-pdrs. The chassepot cartridges were distributed amongst 4 Corps infantry.
162  5th, 6th and 7/14th.
163  11th and 12/1st, 6th and 9/8th, 5/17th, 5th, 6th and 7/1st, 8th, 9th and 10/11th.

## The Redeployment of the Saxon and Guard artillery

As Guards and Saxons launched their final assault on Saint Privat, the fire from their artillery was masked by the advancing infantry and the guns fell silent. When it became clear that the village had finally fallen, the batteries quickly limbered up and moved to new positions so as to help secure the gains won at such high cost. To the south, Lieutenant Colonel Bychelberg moved three batteries[164] forward under heavy rifle and cannon fire to engage Amanvillers; to his left Captain Reinsdorff deployed 3rd Field Division from X Corps.[165]

On hill 328, as Esbeck was announcing the imminent arrival of the Saxons to a group of skirmishers, he was approached by an NCO from the Königen regiment, who drew his attention to the casualties being inflicted on them by the Guard artillery to their rear. Esbeck was just about to gallop off to tell the guns to cease fire, when he noticed the French defenders flooding back down the road to Marengo and realised that if the artillery moved further up the heights, they could bring their guns to bear on this inviting target. He rode over to the gun line and persuaded Major von Buddenbrock to move his three Guard horse artillery batteries[166] forward, their redeployment being undertaken under fire from the French guns at la Croix. Encouraged by their example, several batteries followed suit, forming a new line which ran from the southwest corner of Saint Privat to the Hessian batteries west of knoll 322.

From Rheinhaben's division of Guard artillery,[167] Captain Ising's 6th Light and Captain von Roon's 5th Heavy found space to deploy alongside two guns from von Oppell's 6th Heavy. To the north, seven Saxon batteries and Major Krause's 2nd Field Division formed a new gun line which ran in an arc from the north-east corner of Saint Privat towards the forêt de Jaumont, which enabled them to sweep the open ground to the east of the village with their fire. From X Corps, Captain Saalmüller's 3rd Horse pushed into the line whilst Frisch's 1st Horse deployed further to the north amidst Krause's guns. Voights Rhetz ordered Major Körber to move forward with 5th Cavalry Division's horse artillery[168] deploying between the guns of Prittwitz[169] and Bychelberg's division, all the while under fire from Montluisant's gun.

It was during this period that Captain Ising of the 6th Light lost his arm and Captain Roon was injured. Another shell passed between Captain von Grävenitz's legs 'the rush of air rolling him over and over and so severely bruised was he, that he had to be lifted on his horse.'[170] Lieutenant Dudy had a similar narrow escape; a shell passing between his legs as he dismounted; it destroyed the saddle injuring his mount, but he escaped with just slight bruising.

Twilight was falling as Lieutenant Colonel Stumpf with the Hessian guns and Lieutenant Colonel Schumann with 1st Field Division from X Corps, moved into line and given the confined space, several batteries were unable to find space in which to deploy; a number remained in their

---

164  1st Heavy, 1st and 2nd Light, 1st Guard Field Division.
165  5th and 6th Light followed by 5th and 6th Heavy.
166  1st, 2nd and 3rd.
167  3rd Guard Field Division.
168  Bodes 1st and Schirmer's 2nd.
169  2nd Heavy, 1st Guard Field Division.
170  Hoffbauer, *German Artillery*, p.298

previous positions, whilst others simply got lost in the increasing gloom.[171] The repositioned batteries initially shelled the French rearguard at ranges of between 800 and 2,000 paces but as night fell, they targeted the flashes of the enemy guns whose fire forced two batteries from X Corps[172] to change face so as to confront this menace. The ensuing counter battery struggle only ceased around 8:15 p.m., although intermittent shelling continued until after 10:00 p.m. when the guns finally fell silent.

## The Guards and Saxons in Saint Privat

As the artillery continued their struggle, Pape's main priority was to secure his hard-won gains in Saint Privat. The feared counter attack failed to materialise so when he met with Kessel, they agreed their efforts should be directed towards reorganising the regiments that had participated in the final assault, it being impossible to do this within the confines of the burning village. A number of assembly points were designated along the chausée running to Sainte Marie, although given the general state of confusion and the number of wounded, little was accomplished before night fell.

From XII Corps, I/92nd and 10th Rifles formed a picquet line to the east of Saint Privat, two battalions from 46th Brigade[173] and 13th Rifles extending the line to the north. Montois was occupied by 24th Division as Crown Prince Albert found accommodation in a small dwelling in Roncourt, with Prince George spending the night in a tavern across the street. Schubert recalled:

Here, at the fall of dusk we met the Crown Prince and his staff and congratulated him ... There could be no thought of bringing order into the masses which filled the dark terrain. Every one remained lying where he had fought and we also sought in the nearby Roncourt for a sleeping place which we finally found in a saloon after I

---

171  It is difficult to reconcile the differing accounts as to how just many batteries took part in this final engagement and exactly where they deployed but Hoffbauer identifies 39 batteries that participated in the final engagement and details them as follows: From north to south:- from XII Corps: Leonhardi's 2nd Heavy, Zenker's 1st Horse artillery, Groh's 4th Heavy, Portius's 8th Heavy; from X Corps: Ribbentrop's 4th Heavy; from XII: Corps: von Götz's (for Hammer) 5th Heavy, Müllers 2nd Horse artillery; from X Corps: Burbach's 3rd Light, Mittelstädt's 4th Light, Heyn's 3rd Heavy; from the Guard: von Oppell's (under Poncet) 6th Heavy; from X Corps: Saalmüller's 2nd Horse artillery; from the Guard: von Roon's 5th Heavy, Ising's 6th Light, von d Planitz's 1st Horse artillery, von Anker's 3rd Horse artillery; from X Corps: Baumbach's 2nd Light; from the Guard: Grävenitz's 2nd Horse artillery; from X Corps: Schede's 6th Heavy, von Scheven's 5th Heavy, Richard's 6th Light, Brendt's 5th Light; from the Guard: (at an earlier hour von Friederici-Steinmann's 3rd Light), Seeger's 4th Heavy, Prittwitz's 2nd Heavy; from X Corps: Bode's 1st Horse artillery , Schirmer's 2nd Horse artillery; from the Guard: von Sametzki's 1st Heavy, von Voights Rhetz's (for von Dewitz) 1st Light, Karbe's (for von Niederstetter) 2nd Light; from the Hessian's: Hoffman's 2nd Heavy, Leydhecker's (for Weygand) 2nd Light. It is probable that the following Hessian batteries also deployed and participated in the final engagement: Kehrer's (for Ronstadt) 3rd Light, Frank's 1st Light, Reh's 1st Heavy; from IX Corps: Hesler's (for Bastineller) 3rd Light; from X Corps: Knauer's 1st Light, Lancelle's 2nd Heavy and Kleine's 1st Heavy.

172  5th and 6th Light.

173  III/102nd and III/103rd.

in part to re-establish order.'[202] Around 9:00 p.m. Colonel v Zalukowski issued orders for the 3rd Guard Grenadiers to close up, but given the prevailing disorder it took some time for them to rally, their officers efforts being interrupted as lost and disorganised hostile detachments stumbled into their position.[203] By this time, the gathering gloom made it increasingly difficult to distinguish friend from foe and night brought the fighting around Amanvillers to a close.

## Ladmirault and Bourbaki

Earlier that afternoon, Ladmirault was handed a note announcing Bourbaki's division of grenadiers had arrived at Gros-Chêne and naturally assuming they had been sent to reinforce his position, despatched his premier aide-de-camp[204] to guide them into Amanvillers. When Tour du Pin located Bourbaki around ten minutes later, he 'explained to the general what he thought were intentions of his commander, although he hadn't been given all the details.'[205] During their discussion the ADC got the distinct impression that Bourbaki was reluctant to commit his grenadiers in support of Ladmirault. The sight of large numbers of men from the adjoining 6 Corps falling out of line, seemingly unsettled the Guards' commander and anxious to reassure him, Tour du Pin explained that although 4 Corps had suffered heavy losses, 'the fire on both sides was slackening, that the enemy appeared to be exhausted and that consequently fresh troops would win the victory.'[206]

According to the ADC's testimony, Bourbaki, 'who had a good telescope, said several times "You have to be blind to not see these troops" and refused to move from his position. He continued: "The location I currently occupy is of the greatest importance; I can't move from it without receiving an order." ' In his evidence to the post war inquiry, Tour du Pin stated 'I had the honour to serve under Bourbaki's command and knowing him as I did, I allowed myself to be very insistent in expressing the opinion of my commander, who was confident as to the outcome of the battle. The general, never the less, decided not to intervene.'[207] Around 6:20

202  Bell, *St Privat*, p.339
203  One such detachment, approaching in the dark mistook the 7th company for the enemy and called upon them to surrender; a request which they greeted with a volley of shots.
204  Captain Charles Hubert Réné de La Tour du Pin Chambly de la Charce.
205  Anon, *Procés Bazaine*, p.282. Tour de la Pin told the Inquiry that whilst he knew that the Guards' commander had briefed Ladmirault about the arrival of the Guards at Gros-Chêne, Bourbaki had not confirmed that he would send the division to assist him at Amanvillers. On the other hand, General Berger gave evidence that Ladmirault sent him a note informing of Bourbaki's arrival at Gros-Chêne and that the division of Grenadiers would be coming forward to support them. Notwithstanding the evident confusion as to whether the division were going to remain at Gros-Chêne or advance to Amanvillers, the fact that Ladmirault sent his to guide Picard's grenadiers into the village, does seem indicate that he thought the reinforcements were heading for Amanvillers.
206  Anon, *Procés Bazaine*, p.282.
207  *Ibid*, p.282. In his typical ambiguous command style, Bazaine had earlier informed Bourbaki that he would be free to utilise his reserves 'As and when he deemed it appropriate.' In equally typical fashion, seeking to excuse his own indecision, Bourbaki claimed that his he felt his hands tied by Bazaine's instructions, telling the post war Inquiry 'I repeat that I did not consider myself completely free, as long as Marshal Bazaine was there. These were his last reserves and if I'd been instructed to utilise these troops, I should have first asked the marshal to tell me exactly the position of all his corps d'armee and to inform me of their needs. That's how I understood my position and my task when, in the morning,

p.m., Commandant Pesme[208] galloped up to the party and insisted, in the name of General Ladmirault, that the grenadiers march to Amanvillers without delay. Bourbaki still hesitated; his men occupied a commanding position blocking the road that ran from Amanvillers to Fort Plappeville and French corps commanders were not accustomed to displaying such initiative. He had received no clear instructions from Bazaine and through his telescope could clearly see the heavy fighting raging around Saint Privat. Large numbers of stragglers seemed to be falling back through the woods and if Canrobert's position was in peril, his was the only force available to hold back the Prussians. Bourbaki later claimed:

> I said to the two officers that I only had this one Grenadier division under my control and that it would be imprudent of me not to be on my guard against a turning manoeuvre which might throw everything into confusion and jeopardise the results of the day. They insisted so much I understood that success needed to be complete if it were to achieve anything. At 6:25 p.m. I started off with my division of grenadiers, guided by Commandant Pesme who assured me that the enemy was still far off and I sent a messenger off in all haste to bring up the reserve batteries from the guard.[209]

Tour du Pin galloped off to Amanvillers where he briefed an expectant Ladmirault on the imminent arrival of the long-expected reinforcements before returning to seek out the Guard's commander. In the meantime – it was now between 6:30 and 6:45p.m. – Bourbaki, followed by Jeanningros's brigade and the batteries from the 2nd Division,[210] had emerged from the copse that ran between the Bois de Rappes and Saulny where, mounting a small rise, the confusion around Saint Privat, as well as evident congestion and disarray in the rear echelons of 4 Corps, was clear to see. For the already vacillating commander this was the last straw and he quickly concluded that 'the extreme right wing of the army had given way' and that 'it was no longer a matter of helping 4 Corps to secure victory but of protecting the retreat that was already underway.'[211]

As Tour du Pin rode up, Bourbaki, clearly agitated, rebuked the aide 'That's not good, captain, what you did! You promised me a victory. Now you've got me involved in a rout. You had no right to do that! There was no need to make me leave my magnificent positions for this.' Tour du Pin could not contain himself and responded: 'Well General, in that case, take them back to your 'positions magnifique.'[212] Bourbaki, answered: 'That's what I'm going to do' ordering his men: 'Halt! About turn!' As the French official history comments, 'these words can only be explained by the disappointment and bad humour that took possession of the commander when he realised that instead of the anticipated laurels of victory, his role was going to be saving the

---

M. de Mornay told me that I was free to use my judgement; first of all, I had to inquire, because I couldn't know how all the different part of the battle being fought by the troops that were in contact with me was progressing.' See Anon. *Procès Bazaine*, p.234.

208  Chef d'escadron au corps d'état-major 4e Corps.
209  L'État Major, *St Privat*, p.497.
210  Despite Bourbaki's statement that he was bringing forward the whole division, it would seem that he left half, General of Brigade le Poitevin de la Croix Vaubois' 2nd Brigade, at Gros-Chêne.
211  L'État Major, *St Privat*, p.496.
212  Anon. *Procès Bazaine*, p.282. In his testimony to the Inquiry, he said 'I was wrong, I admit, to answer him back.'

army from a situation he felt to be very compromised.' The history concludes that 'at best this outburst betrayed a naïve state of mind and an understanding of the conduct of war that was sadly lacking.'[213]

Meanwhile, his brigade had left the road which was blocked by the wounded and were making their way in column of battalion divisions through the copse. When the order to retire reached them, they immediately turned about and marched off towards Gros-Chêne. The wounded and malingers who were sheltering in the wood assumed the Guard had given way under pressure from the enemy, prompting an immediate rout as the men ran to the rear uttering cries of terror and 'sauve qui peut.'[214] The sight of this uncontrollable rabble triggered confusion and panic amongst the baggage wagons of the train and a torrent of carts, limbers and men swept along the track towards Lorry.

As the fugitives emerged through the woods, Lieutenant Colonel Delatte[215] ordered two batteries of horse artillery forward from their position at St Vincent farm, their teams deploying at right angles across the road about 600 metres from where the terrified men had left the woods, so as to form a physical barrier to hold back the troops. The sight of these guns restored some order amongst the men, who were also no doubt, reassured by the nearby presence of the 2nd and 3rd Grenadiers. However, the air of desperation soon began to infect the guardsmen who then started breaking ranks.

Bourbaki, alarmed by this precipitate retreat tried to rally the brigade; he succeeded in stopping the Zouaves, but the grenadiers and artillery simply ignored his calls and only halted when they reached the emplacements at Gros-Chêne vacated half an hour earlier. This retreat was witnessed by George Boyland:

> The right wing, where we were stationed, had fallen back, leaving several large caissons of ammunition together in the open field. By some chance or intention, a shell struck this and there was a fearful detonation that shook the very ground on which we stood, as bodies of caissons, wheels, limbers, etc. flew into the air in a thick black cloud. About this time, we saw the whole country alive with soldiers turning to flee. A battalion of the guard came up and formed a line to prevent this; but the retreating soldiers paid no more attention than if they had not been there and rushed through them as if they had been made of paper. The guard battalion had been commanded by their officers to fire. They had refused to do so saying 'We will not shoot our brothers.'[216]

---

213  Tour du Pin's account, as that of Bourbaki's, is taken from the transcript of the post war Inquiry into the causes of the French defeat and the French official history. See l'État-Major, *St Privat*, pp.298–299, *Procès Bazaine*, p.233 and p.282. Bourbaki told the Inquiry that he 'arrived in the middle of a wood near a rise formed by a plateau which ended with a fairly steep slope. To get into position, I had to deploy all my division without artillery support, believing that I'd be covered by the victorious troops on my left. I went down to the head of the column. but when I arrived, I saw at first glance what was going on. I couldn't stop myself from reproaching the aide 'Instead of telling me about success' I exclaimed. 'You should have told me the truth.' You had, in the woods on the right, our wing in full retreat on Saulny. I didn't have a single piece of artillery to support the deployment of my column. If I'd continued, I would have murdered my grenadiers and so, in the grip of a bad temper, I ordered 'half turn.'

214  L'État-Major, *St Privat*, p.300.

215  Commander of the four batteries horse artillery of the 17th, from 3 Corps' Reserve.

216  Boyland, *Six Months*, p.71.

## 4 Corps Retreat

Around 7:00 p.m. Cissy's guns had finally run out of ammunition and were no longer able to support the infantry he had pushed forward to cover Canrobert's left flank. The fire from the Guard and Hessian batteries continued unabated and as his artillery withdrew to the relative safety of the quarries at la Croix, the 12/15th abandoned three caissons in their haste to escape the enemy fire; according to their post combat 'It was the worst moment of the whole day.'[217] When the 5/12th pulled out of line, one of their limbers was struck by an enemy shell and as they retreated along the main road:

> The reserve caissons, the administrative train, the intendance, food wagons, were all seized by a violent panic and engaged in a mad race towards Metz, crashing, falling over one another in the sharp turns and fast descents; it was complete disorder. The drivers cut the traces of their horses and left them behind so as to make a faster escape and we saw these crazy horsemen executing a furious charge through the wagons, at the risk of spilling everything in their path.[218]

The officer who wrote this report was amazed at this panic and noted the inevitable outcome: 'This mad dash was only halted when a few wagons fell off Saulny bridge and formed, in this narrow passage, a kind of dam. However, the road is still blocked with wagons and limbers as the various batteries fell back from their positions, which left us all exposed to the fire of the Prussian artillery.'[219]

Boyland's ambulance was also swept up in the flight to safety:

> Now ensued a complete rout. Cavalry, infantry, artillery, rushed pell-mell down the road leading back behind the forts of the city. It was a grand mixing up of everything: officers riding about without men – men running down the hill without officers; fourgons had their wheels knocked off, caissons were upset, horses bruised, riders thrown – all intermingled with shouts, yells and curses. All the while wounded men were trying to keep up and crying for surgeons. Such a sight it rarely falls to the lot of man to witness. The soldiers were throwing their guns and side arms, in order to flee more rapidly; all seemed panic stricken. The same being enacted on other roads leading to Metz. I was in the midst of this and now tore along at a mad pace – to stop would have been certain death.[220]

On the northern flank of Ladmirault's position, Cissey, observing how the Prussian 4th Guard Grenadiers had pushed into the space vacated by Levassor-Sorval, felt he had no choice but to withdraw. Lacking artillery support and threatened by the grenadiers on their flank he recounted:

217 L'État-Major, *18 Août, Documents*, p.259.
218 *Ibid*, p.257.
219 *Ibid*.
220 Boyland, *Six Months*, pp.71–72.

We'd been under fire since five o'clock; General de Goldberg had been hit on his shoulder by a shell fragment; Colonel Supervielle[221] had been carried from the field with his legs smashed; Colonel Frémont[222] was also wounded; all my staff officers had had their horses shot; my escort broken and dispersed; the whole field strewn with the most frightful debris.[223]

Meanwhile, Tour du Pin had broken the news to Ladmirault that the expected reinforcements were not going to materialise; upon hearing this, the stunned general 'dropped his bâton onto the neck of his horse.'[224] Worse was to come; Commandant Lonclas then arrived with news that 6 Corps was in full retreat. 4 Corps' commander was hit hard by this double blow; the news regarding Canrobert was confirmed by Cissey whose position on the right wing to the north of the railroad was being 'crushed by cannon' and believing a withdrawal to be inevitable, 'demanded orders from General Ladmirault.'[225]

If Cissey pulled back, 4 Corps right wing would be exposed and the Prussians could then outflank his position at Amanvillers; a fact that did not escape him. Bourbaki's abrupt turnabout had only increased his sense of anxiety; it was time for 4 Corps to retreat and Ladmirault's immediate priority was to prepare a receiving position to north-east of Amanvillers, through which his troops could fall back. He turned to his aide-de-camp and instructed: 'Go to General Bourbaki and tell him that I think I will be obliged to do the same to avoid being outflanked.'[226] He then ordered Cissey to withdraw Goldberg's brigade[227] and any men he could spare from his 1st Brigade and take up a new position along the western edge of the Bois de Saulny.

Lorencez was ordered to hold his position along the heights west of Amanvillers to Montigny la Grange for as long as possible in order to buy time for the withdrawal. He also briefed Le Boeuf on 6 Corps retreat and asked if he could send a few battalions from his reserve at la Folie to Amanvillers. After issuing these instructions, he rode back to the quarries in the rear of the village where his artillery had assembled after running low on ammunition. As Cissey recalled, his division began their retreat around 7:00 p.m.

We crossed the ground where we'd bivouacked, but it wasn't possible to collect our haversacks on the way; the enemy shells were still falling amongst us, so I reckoned, on reaching the edge of the wood, to send the men back in small packets to collect their effects with minimal danger, but once we reached the woods there was no way to restrain them.[228]

To counter the threatened envelopment, the 1st Ligne had been called up from reserve and pushed forward in a north westerly direction facing hill 321 but suffered heavy casualties to

221  From the 73rd.
222  From the 1st.
223  L'État-Major, *18 Août, Documents*, p.245.
224  Anon. *Procés Bazaine*, p.282.
225  L'État-Major, *18 Août, Documents*, p.245.
226  L'État-Major, *St Privat*, p.504.
227  57th and 73rd.
228  L'État-Major, *18 Août, Documents*, p.250.

the flanking fire of both the Hessian and Guard artillery. Knoll 322 and the railway cutting to the east of the crossing house, were still held by a few tirailleurs and at least their fire kept the Hessians infantry at bay. Under cover of this screen, the 57th and 73rd began to fall back towards the quarries, as did the 3rd, 4th and 5th companies of the 20th Chasseurs who, as they withdrew through the burning village of Amanvillers, noted 'numerous wounded men were stretched out in front of every house, where a few doctors were attempting to treat them amidst the flames.'[229] According to the official history their retreat was initially undertaken 'in good order under a crushing fire'[230] and on reaching shelter behind the crest of the slope, the officers rallied their men, formed a new line and again resumed fire against the enemy lines. They were followed by the remainder of the infantry although these formations, under constant shell fire, quickly lost their cohesion and the division more or less fell apart.

Cissey managed to rally a few troops within the shelter of quarries and then led them back to Metz between 8:00 and 9:00 p.m. conceding in his post combat report 'Many men were completely exhausted and that hunger drove them to sneak off in the dark through the woods in small groups towards Metz.'[231] Lieutenant Patry, whose regiment had previously withdrawn to the rear of Amanvillers confirms this, recalling how, as darkness fell:

> Finally, around nine o'clock, everyone took the road which descended through the woods towards Metz. Rousset and I, having been unable to find a single man of the company, followed. Like everyone else, no doubt, we were starving. At the start of the descent, we came across provision wagon full of fresh bread. Some men who'd climbed aboard passed out loaves to the fortunate souls who passed by. Rousset caught one and we had a delicious supper. We spent the whole night tramping along this road and at daybreak, we had still to reach Metz. It wasn't until ten o'clock that we arrived at Le Sansonnet where we were halted.[232]

Captain Delherbe from the 20th Chasseurs left a similar account, noting how:

> At 11 o'clock the brigade headed for Metz by the Lorry road. The men were exhausted; they hadn't eaten since the morning and having lost their packs, were now destitute. The route was covered with wagons, most of which had been abandoned and overturned on the side of the road. It was the convoy which had left that morning and was returning from Metz with provisions for the army. It was too late now; the road to France had been cut. Around half past midnight we arrived at Lorry.[233]

Another Chasseur officer, Lieutenant Palle echoed these sentiments, noting:

> The road was horribly congested; the officers tried to rally their men in the clearings by the side of the road, but can only gather in a few souls; the others were busily engaged

229  *Ibid*, p.248.
230  L'État-Major, *St Privat*, p.555.
231  L'État-Major, 18 *Août, Documents*, p.248.
232  Patry, *La Guerre*, pp.113–114.
233  L'État-Major, *18 Août, Documents*, p.248.

in looting the provision wagons which are parked or tangled together to the left and right of the road. A few shots go off in the wood; it's said that they are from people paid by the Prussians to increase the panic and disorder which the gendarmes had tried to stop.[234]

The troops in front of Amanvillers had been equally exposed to the murderous gun fire and were showing unmistakable signs of weariness. The 5th Chasseurs, who had fallen back closer to Amanvillers, were now being pressed by the advance of the grenadiers to their front and in the gathering gloom, were increasingly jumpy; especially as the retreat of Cissey's division had exposed their right flank and they were coming under effective fire from the Prussian and Hessian artillery to the north of the railway line. As their post combat report details:

All of a sudden, a shell burst on the road throwing the ranks of soldiers one against the other; then a second and a third, each in quick succession. It was if the Prussian batteries were trying to sweep us from the road. The fire from these guns was very rapid and to make our situation even more perilous the Prussian infantry were closing in on our right. We made a fighting retreat towards Amanvillers, where several houses were already on fire. Saint Privat was burning in the background. Our bivouac, close by Amanvillers was being ploughed up by shells; several of the camp guards were killed at their post. An hour earlier we could have retired in good order, by section, towards the wooded heights of the quarries which dominated Amanvillers. But now, it was too late; the three chefs du corps[235] realised that there was only one course of action open to them; that of retreating towards the heights, at a run, so as to get there before the enemy. As soon as the order was given, the whole line beat a retreat – at the pas de gymnastique – under a hail of shot, towards Amanvillers where several of our ambulances had just been shot up and burst into flames without being able to remove all the wounded.[236]

The Chasseurs withdrew through the burning houses of Amanvillers and rallied to the rear of the village. The 5th was then sent by Ladmirault to cover the edge of the Bois de Saulny, which Bourbaki had failed to secure, whilst the 1/54th fell back to the heights in the rear where it was subsequently reinforced by their 3rd Battalion. Following this withdrawal, the ground to the south of the railway line was more or less void of French troops which, as a consequence, left the flank of the fighting line between Amanvillers and Montigny la Grange, held by Lorencez and Grenier, open to being turned.

## 3 Corps Cover Ladmirault's Retreat

4 Corps positions around Montigny la Grange still held firm but as Cissey and then Lorencez fell back, single companies followed by complete battalions were seen to fall out of line and head

234 L'État-Major, *St Privat*, p.549.
235 The colonel of the 54th and the commanders of the 2nd and 5th chasseur battalions.
236 L'État-Major, *18 Août, Documents*, p.268.

off to the rear. Around 7:00 p.m. General Pajol[237] received instructions from Ladmirault to pull back to the bois de Châtel but given the disarray amongst his command it took some time to execute this order with the 2nd and 3/33rd only quitting their position to the rear of Pradier's brigade sometime after 8:00 p.m. After collecting their 1st Battalion along the way, they headed off towards Amanvillers where they stumbled into the troops that were being rallied in this area; the 3rd and 1st battalions halted but the 2nd, together with their colonel and Pajol, pushed their way through the milling mass of men and disappeared into the gloom. Following the withdrawal of the 33rd, the 1st and 2/15th were rallied around their colours and marched off accompanied by the 3/64th just as 2nd Chasseurs were vacating Amanvillers. By 9:00 p.m. the bulk of Pajol's brigade had made its way to the plateau of Saint Vincent, and passed the night in their old bivouac.

Too late to avert Ladmirault's retreat, the reinforcements[238] sent by Le Boeuf, carefully made their way towards Amanvillers. The 1st and 3/71st halted at the edge of the Châtel woods east of la Folie and took up a covering position whilst the 41st, formed in two lines and 'with drums beating and bugles sounding' advanced in a north westerly direction into the gloom, with only the burning villages and farm buildings to light their way. Somehow avoiding contact with the enemy forces, they moved forward at the double and found their way into Ladmirault's fall-back position close to la Folie farm, where their commanding officer, Colonel Saussier, deployed them alongside the 15th. He placed two battalions in the front line, the 3rd in support with double spacing between their companies and, 'as instructed by their colonel his men all shouted 'Vive la France! Vive l'Empereur' and kept up a continuous tremendous cheering.'

Saussier recalled:

> It was around 8:00 p.m. when the regiment reached Montigny la Grange. Darkness had fallen across the horizon and there were only the flames of the vast fires which consumed the villages of Vernéville, Amanvillers and the surrounding farms. At last, we could make out the 15th, fighting fiercely around their colours. It's time to act. I went over to the attack. After having all the officer's dismount, I alone remaining on horseback in order to better direct the operation and watch over events, I gave the order to charge. Drums beating and bayonets fixed, the regiment launched their attack![239]

At about the same time, cheering suddenly erupted out all along the front of 3rd Guards Brigade as the guardsmen staggered to their feet for one final push. It seems that those on the right seized the high ground at point 331 whilst the left wing were content with a nominal

---

237  Commander 1st Brigade within Lorencez's division.

238  41st and 71st Ligne and 1st and 2nd batteries à cheval du 17th. En-route, the artillery received orders from General Berckheim, commander of 3 Corps' Reserve and Parc, to return to their original positions at Leipzig as he was under the mistaken impression that the Prussians had withdrawn.

239  L'État-Major, *18 Août, Documents*, p.173. Saussier claimed that his charge pushed the Guards back into the Bois de la Cusse but there is no record of any counter attack at this time in their regimental accounts. His casualties, just nine men, suggest some degree of exaggeration by the erstwhile colonel, whilst the French official history concluded that he was either inventing events or simply deluded! Although neither German nor French official histories were able to identify the target of Saussier's bayonet attack, his presence undoubtedly buoyed the spirits of Lorencez's division who were rallying in the area and in particular the 54th, whose morale was in poor shape following their earlier withdrawal.

Bazaine's communications with the emperor. The Saxons were therefore ordered to push a division forward to Woippy, so as to block the road to Thionville whilst the Guards and IX Corps were to undertake a gradual right wheel towards Metz. III Corps were to act as reserve for the centre, X Corps for the left wing.

As these orders were being issued, reports arrived confirming the withdrawal of the French into Metz; 2nd Hessian Cavalry had found no trace of the enemy at Saulny, 1st Hessian Cavalry had discovered that they had abandoned Montigny la Grange. In front of 18th Division, the French outposts at la Folie and Leipzig gradually withdrew and subsequently, a squadron of the 6th Dragoons, under Major von Tresckow, found the ridge to the north of Châtel St Germain devoid of enemy troops. On receipt of this information, Frederick instructed the Guard to occupy Amanvillers and Montigny la Grange before riding over to the Royal headquarters at Rezonville.

## I Army Following the Battle

Early on the 19th, Steinmetz's chief engineer, General Biehler, issued instructions for the troops to construct earthworks on the plateau at Point du Jour to help secure their positions against any French counter attack. The troops undertaking this work came under intermittent fire from the guns in the fort of St Quentin, so were supported by 4th Division from II Corps; 3rd Division being withdrawn across the Mance ravine to the east of Gravelotte alongside their corps artillery. 26th Brigade was at Jussy whilst the remainder of VII Corps, VIII Corps and 1st Cavalry Division were in their bivouacs around Gravelotte and Rezonville.

Steinmetz was informed by his patrols that the French had evacuated the positions occupied the previous day and in accordance with Moltke's instructions, brought his supply trains and ambulances across from the east bank of the Moselle to replenish ammunition and assist in the evacuation of the wounded. On the far side of the river, Manteuffel's I Corps secured the road leading south from Metz, to guard against any attempt to break through to Strasbourg; 3rd Cavalry Division was at Coin les Curvy. These forces were supplemented by the 3rd Reserve Division under Lieutenant General von Kummer who occupied Retonfay. The noose drawn around Metz by Moltke, was gradually tightening.

## The Day After

The Royal entourage spent the night at Rezonville, although due to the number of wounded, most had to find shelter as best they could as related by Verdy du Vernois:

> Blume, Holleben, Alten, Kruse, Clear and myself lay down in some large stables in which our horses had already found shelter, but where there was an abominable draft owing to the broken windows and doors. We did not examine long the composition of our beds but fell asleep pretty soon, in spite of the groans and cries of the wounded near

von Caprivi and from XII Corps Lieutenant Colonel von Zezschwitz.

us. During the night we were wakened continually by our men who were in search of shelter and by the stamping of our horses, who got restless from time to time.[257]

On the morning of 19 August, Vernois was ordered to Metz with a flag of truce to arrange for the removal of the thousands of French dead and wounded abandoned on the battlefield:

> Near the end of the village, we bought a napkin from an old woman who chanced to be in possession of one, in order to equip ourselves for our business. After crossing the defile of Gravelotte we came across a dragoon regiment of II Army Corps, who were asked for a trumpeter and here we fixed the napkin to a long pole to represent the flag of truce. The ride across this part of the battlefield presented a sad sight, on account of the large numbers of bodies of our men, which only too plainly proved what heavy losses we had suffered, while we only saw very few corpses on the ground which had been held by the French. Only in some of the shelter trenches there were still a considerable number of dead; they lay there still as if in the ranks, their rifles pushed forward over the parapet as if ready to fire; they startled us from a distance, they looked so much like a deployed line of French skirmishers. On approaching nearer it seemed as if these trenches had been suddenly taken in the flank by our artillery, which accounted for the enemy's losses. As we continued our ride, we suddenly saw rifle barrels flash out of some bushes on the top of a steep embankment of the road. But these belonged to men of our VII Corps, whose foremost detachment had been pushed forward to this point … Several cavalry patrols of two or three men each galloped in succession back in the direction of Metz and as they came on a level with us, at a distance of about a hundred yards, they were so obliging as to fire their carbines at us, the bullets whistling about our ears. This was not a promising beginning, but worse was yet to come. As we came round a fresh bend in the road and approached a building which lay some 80 yards ahead, we noticed a double sentry near it. I ordered a halt; the trumpet was sounded and the improvised flag of truce waived. By way of answer the two men fired at us. We again sounded the trumpet and tried, without stirring from the spot, to make ourselves understood by shouting. Immediately a small detachment of French infantry deployed along the garden wall and poured a rapid fire into us, which came, to judge from the sound of the bullets which whistled past us, from the so-called Tabatière rifles. These men seemed to be gardes mobiles, but it did not matter who they were and seeing no hopes of stopping the firing, we could not remain there any longer, so we turned about and made off at a gallop. After having gone a few yards, we noticed that the bay horse of the trumpeter was rider less. Fortunately, we managed, thanks to the windings of the road, to get out of the way of the bullets sent after us. Here we found that the bay horse was slightly wounded on the foreleg; the trumpeter we saw coming after us on foot, a shot through the bridge of the nose had thrown him from his horse. We waited for him round a corner and then went back. The incident afterwards gave rise to various diplomatic representations. When I made my report to the King on the result of my mission, his majesty was still visibly affected by the great sacrifices which the previous

257 Vernois, *Royal Headquarters*, p.93.

day had demanded. No further attempt was made to enter into communication with the French Commander in Chief.[258]

Moltke was only too aware of the heavy losses incurred on the 18th and the danger they posed to the health of his forces; at 8:45 a.m. instructed:

> Burial of the dead and of dead horses will be carried out by the troops within their billet areas; the southern road from Metz to Verdun forming the dividing line between the First and Second Army. The villages situated along the road are assigned to First Army, including the II Army Corps. This division of billet areas will hold good also for requisitions.[259]

As Vernois commented, the losses were such that 'I have given up asking after friends, as I get to each question no other answer than 'dead' or 'wounded'.'[260] It was not only casualties from the previous days fighting that had to be cleared away; large numbers of dead from the battle on the 16th still lay where they fell as Allanson Winn found to his cost as he returned to his lodgings at Gorze during the night of the 18th:

> Occasionally a French shell, pitched further over Gravelotte than intended, would light up a small bit of it. During one of these temporary illuminations, caused by a shrapnel bursting about thirty yards from me and eight or nine yards from the ground, I saw, as if by magic, a dead French artilleryman and his horse, scarcely having time to see the colour of his uniform when with the returning darkness the picture vanished from my sight. I hastened on, holding my breath as often as I could to avoid inhaling the noisome odours that rose from the many corpses which lay unburied. At points where I knew they lay thickly, I would run, to get past the fever breeding smell as quickly as possible. It was on one of the occasions, while hastening past a spot where in the morning both myself and my companion had remarked seven or eight French bodies in a heap that I suddenly stumbled against a mound and fell completely over. I put down my hand to raise myself and a creeping sensation came over me as I felt it press against something like a hard cushion covered with rough cloth. I then noticed that in the dark I had mistaken my way, falling over the very danger I had tried to avoid and to lift myself had placed my hand on the still chest of one of the bodies. I hurried forward with more care than before and soon came to the road, having in parts of the ground traversed, literally to thread my way through corpses ... I arrived at Gorze about midnight ... I went into the shop and thence to the little room ... In the shop lay three wounded men (a Frenchman and two Prussians) brought to Gorze since the morning from Gravelotte. The Frenchman woke up and asked me for some water. I then asked him how he came to be made prisoner. 'Oh,' he said 'I was lying on the ground firing over my knapsack and was about to retire, when a side shot broke my ankle. I could not go away then, so I lay firing until the Prussians advancing took me

258  *Ibid*, pp.94–95.
259  Lanza, *Franco-German War*, p.262.
260  Vernois, *Royal Headquarters*, p.103.

prisoner. I expected, of course, that they would pin me to the ground where I lay with a bayonet; but indeed, I find them kind enough.'[261]

In fact, the countryside between Gravelotte in the south to Roncourt in the north was strewn with the debris of the conflict; dead and dying stretched as far as the eye could see. One of the many war correspondents who accompanied the Prussian Army left this description of the Mance ravine on the morning after the battle:

As I rode up the hill leading to the French position, I wondered not at the frightful files of corpses all around me, but that such a position could be taken at all. On the further side of the road the French had thrown up twelve small épaulements about breast high; in eight of them they had placed mitrailleuses, for the empty cases were scattered all about. In one épaulement alone I counted forty-three cartridge holders. Now, as each one of these boxes contains twenty-five cartridges, 1,075 shots are fired by one during the day. Doubtless many more had actually been fired, for nearly everyone did as I did and carried off an empty case as a relic. The slope immediately beneath the French position, on the Verdun road, was a frightful spectacle. Hundreds of Prussian corpses were strewed in quite a small place on the flat slope. Where the Prussian battery had been placed there were thirty horses lying almost touching on another, many with the drivers beside them, still grasping their whips. Most of the corpses were on their backs, with their hands clenched. This position was explained by the fact that most of the men had been shot grasping their muskets and their hands clenched as they dropped their weapons and fell. Many corpses of Prussian officers lay by those of their men, with their white glove on their left hand, the right being bare, in order better to grasp the sword. In the hollow road itself, the bodies of men and horses also lay thick; the corpses all along the sides of the road, for nearly 1,000 yards, made one continually unbroken row. A little lower down I found the tirailleur corpses. Many of these men had still their muskets in their hands, many forefingers being stiff on the trigger. On the left of the French position were two small cottages which had been a mark for the Prussian cannon and their shells had made a complete ruin of the buildings. One roof was completely gone and the whole front wall of the upper story of the other had been blown in. On the plateau behind the French earthworks all the ground was ploughed and torn by the Prussian shells, which, when they got the range, were admirably aimed. One third of its horses lay dead beside it. A shell had burst beneath one of the horses and had blown him, the limber and one of the gunners, all to pieces. All the French prisoners with whom I have spoken agree in asserting that it was the terrible accuracy of the Prussian artillery which forced them to yield their position.[262]

The same scene was repeated in front of Saint Privat; Schubert, who had spent the night at Roncourt, wished to attend the burial of General Craushaar and left this description of the ground over which the Guard Corps had advanced:

261  Winn, *What I Saw*, pp.120–121.
262  L. P. Brocket, *The Great War of 1870 between France and* Germany (New York: Gaylord Watson, 1871) pp.163–164.

The Prince had heard that he would be buried at 9 o'clock in Sainte Marie and therefore rode with me to that place, our path leading across the field over which the Guards had attacked. It was a sorrowful ride. The entire space between Saint Privat and Sainte Marie was covered with corpses of the brave, strong men who had known no falling back. It was especially painful to hear the calls of a number of dying and wounded lying there unattended – and we could not help them. The sanitary soldiers had stuck each man's rifle bayonet in the ground beside the wounded, so as to find them easily and such marks numbered into hundreds as far as we could see. At the church in Sainte Marie we met Lieutenant Schmalz, von Craushaar's adjutant and a number of Saxon soldiers who'd constructed a coffin out of rough boards. Deeply moved we buried the brave general. A handful of earth was the last sign of honour we could give him. All the houses in Sainte Marie were filled to overflowing with wounded and we had great difficulty in locating the house in which Major Moritz Allmer of the Rifle Regiment lay. He'd received a bullet through the left shoulder into the breast and appeared to be beyond hope. The return over the battlefield was as sorrowful as the going. With the consent of the Prince I killed the wounded horse of a Guard officer with my revolver. It was a fine English mare, whose nose had been shot off by a shell and was standing with a hanging head, slowly bleeding to death. It took five or six shots in the head to bring it to the ground.[263]

## Recriminations and Reflections

The huge losses suffered by Guard Corps, especially the officers, all of whom came from amongst the highest strata of Prussian society, was the cause of much argument and accusation, although for political reasons in the immediate aftermath of the war, the belated appearance of XII Corps was held responsible for the inflated casualty list. However, in private, the senior commanders of the Guard were held to be at fault; one of Bismarck's colleagues reported the Chancellor believed that August's chief of staff, Dannenberg, had 'without waiting for the Saxons, intended to finish the matter alone and whose method of throwing the best and picked troops, the Guard Rifles and Jägers, against the trenches of Saint Privat not in skirmish order, but in column, he condemned as criminal.'[264] As Blumenthal noted, William was much troubled by the appalling casualty list:

> The King had become strained by the fatigues of the campaign and had become quite nervous. What affected him most were the terrible losses amongst the officers in the battle on the 18th. He complained bitterly that the officers of the higher grades appeared to have forgotten all that had been taught them so carefully in manoeuvres and had apparently all lost their heads. Battles like that we could not stand for long.

263  Lanza, *Franco-German War*, p.417.
264  Bell, *St Privat*, p.462

Moltke was cold and calm, as always and was not troubled with cares, a state of mind I cannot share with him.[265]

One of III Corps staff officers wrote to his wife 'The poor Guard! An insane leadership caused it to suffer losses which can never be made good; there are no depot battalions for the officer corps.'[266] Many of the line officers were equally distraught as Allanson Winn noted following a visit to friends in Wedell's 29th Brigade which had been caught up in the blood bath of the Mance ravine:

From afar we recognised the familiar shape of the colonel's tent and wended our way thither. A cursory glance told us that their ranks had been terribly thinned. As we approached, we saw that the colonel was safe. He was sitting outside at a rickety table with two adjutants, who were also our great and much-loved friends, Lieutenants Homburg and Gatung. They were drawing up the official report of their losses and welcomed us with their usual cordiality. The pressure of the colonel's hand was as much from the heart as ever; but when he tried to speak, he failed in the attempt and resumed his seat with the air of a man struggling with deep emotion. Presently he came to us and began the doleful story. He said 'To-day I command 650 fewer soldiers than two days ago. Amongst these I do not include twenty-four brave and intelligent officers' 'Ah' he said with a sigh 'there is joy in the glory of commanding a regiment like this; but only the father who has just buried two or three of his dearest children can know the bitterness of a colonel's lot who lives to bring his regiment out of a severe engagement. Several of my companies are without officers at all and each battalion has lost its major.'[267] ... We now determined to walk up to the point that had formed the French position and on our way pass through the bivouac of the 60th Regiment and make inquiries for our friends. There a still sadder bulletin awaited us. A major of the second battalion informed us that the regiment had lost 930 men *hors de combat*, besides 38 officers.[268] We went on and presently came to the valley ... Discarded boots, helmets, bits of rag, strewed the way plenteously. But the bodies here had nearly all been buried; for the Prussian generals had decided that the regiments which were going to do outpost duty on this side of Metz should push forward their bivouacs to the battlefield of the 18th. As we neared Saint Hubert we met a gang of at least 200 peasants under escort. At first, we supposed they had been turned out to commence the earthworks; but on inquiring of one of them, we found that it was the unwelcome duty of burying the dead that had been forced on them. At the French position about Moscou we found no dead or wounded and did not see many signs of either. In fact, everything tended to show that this point was wrested from the French at a fearful sacrifice to the victors ...What was the farm Saint Hubert has been left with scarcely one stone upon another. In one side of the farm house of Moscou I counted thirty-six

---

265 Albrecht von Blumenthal, *Journals of Field Marshal Count Von Blumenthal for 1866 and 1870–71*, (London: Edward Arnold, 1903) pp.98–99.
266 Bell, *St Privat*, p.163.
267 The 33rd lost 24 officers and 631 men.
268 The official history gives the losses at 35 officers and 685 men.

separate shell holes. It formed one end of the house and was about 30 feet high and 24 broad and presented something of the appearance of an immense sieve. Everything in the shape of a wall or bank had been utilised to the utmost by the French tirailleurs.[269]

Another sightseer out and about on the 20th, Archibald Forbes, described how:

Within a space of about six miles in length by four in depth there was not a space so large as Piccadilly Circus that did not bear some token that one or more men had fallen upon it. Now the tokens were dead bodies, sometimes straggling so that several yards intervened, sometimes so close that you could hardly step without treading on the dead; again, they consisted of bloody coats, pieces of linen, helmets, cuirasses with the tell-tale holes in them, knapsacks riddled by bullets, dead horses all but blown into fragments by the busting of shells. The lines of demarcation between the German and French dead were in places drawn with almost mathematical accuracy. On one of the roads leading up the steep slope out of Gorze I came on an outlying part of the table-land where the Germans lay very thickly ... Then I came to the place where the column had struggled into deployment and had got within 200 yards distance of the Frenchmen. The latter lay far thicker than the Germans had lain in the first space. Burial parties were working at this place, but seem bewildered to decide where to make a beginning. I advised one of the officers to double trench the ground all over, laying the dead along the hollow of each successive trench, something like a celery bed; so many were they that this market gardening style of grave would have been, I am convinced, the best plan for getting them out of sight; saving transport to isolated grave pits and lessening the temptation to bury to near to the surface, which is always strong with burial parties who have excavated a large pit into which they are anxious to crowd all the corpses in the neighbourhood, regardless of the fact that the uppermost are so near the surface that the plough of the next spring must uncover their remains. The surface of the little churchyard at Gravelotte had been raised three feet all over in one day. The church had been crowded with the most severely wounded in the Thursday's battle and as the poor fellow died they had been carried out into the churchyard. This with its loop holed wall had been the scene of a desperate stand on the part of the French and already had more than its own share of corpses; so that, when I had seen it on Friday, the bodies, chiefly of Frenchmen, were lying two deep all over its edge. The interior of the church was a sight I can never forget ... The white alter cloth was splashed with blood, the floor was bedded over with the wounded and the atmosphere had become tainted and malaria-laden.[270]

Later that afternoon Moltke returned to Pont à Mousson in his carriage, accompanied by Winterfield and Vernois:

269 Winn, *What I saw*, pp.137–138.
270 Forbes, *My Experiences*, pp.208–209.

We drove on in silence; nor did the chief break his train of thought except for three short remarks. The first time was when we crossed, on the way from Rezonville to Gorze, a part of the battlefield of the 16th August and came across heaps of still unburied French Voltigeurs of the Guard, in whose foremost ranks lay a young non-commissioned officer of our 11th Regiment still grasping in his hands his rifle with fixed bayonet. Seeing him the General said 'This was the bravest of the brave.'[271] Later on, he remarked 'I have learned once more that one cannot be too strong on the field of battle.' The last remark of the General was made as we approached Pont à Mousson and saw before us the church towers and outlines of the houses picturesquely lit up by the evening sun. Then he exclaimed 'What would be our feelings now, if we had been beaten?'[272]

In the days immediately following the battle, the Prussian forces spent their time burying the dead, tending to the wounded, resting and reorganising their forces, prior to beginning the next, decisive phase of the campaign. The king remained at Pont à Mousson, Frederick Charles established his headquarters at Doncort whilst Steinmetz relocated to Ars, on the far bank of the Moselle. The newly formed Army of the Meuse, under the Crown Prince of Saxony, was headquartered at Jarny, with Major General von Schlotheim being appointed chief of staff.

## Bazaine Prevaricates

What of Bazaine? He had spent most of the 18th between Plappeville and fort St Quentin, seemingly impervious to the bloody struggle underway just a few kilometres to the west. After returning to his headquarters around 7:00 p.m., as the fighting around Saint Privat was at its height, officers of his general staff, the Deputy of Moselle, M de Boueiller and even the telegraphist in the bell tower at Metz cathedral, all attempted to draw his attention to the gravity of the situation on his right flank; their efforts were in vain with Bazaine responding: 'It's nothing! I know it's nothing!'[273] Seemingly oblivious to the disaster that was shortly to befall 6 Corps, he was later to claim that these reports 'were nothing to give him concern.'[274] According to his chief of staff, Jarras, Bazaine continued to 'display the same optimism that he'd shown throughout the afternoon.'[275] The French official history remarks that 'It's surprising that neither Captain Chalus's report at 3:00 p.m. nor the 'urgent notice' he received at 5:30 from Canrobert setting out the gravity of his situation and his lack of ammunition, gave rise to any concern.' The official history continues:

> Moreover, it's quite incomprehensible that the reports which he'd received since the commencement of the battle, warning of an envelopment of the right wing, didn't

271 In a telling contrast, during the later stages of the battle, Bazaine, observing the panic which spread through a column of wounded soldiers in the rear of Saint Privat, turned to his staff officers and said 'What can you do with such troops?' See Guedalla, *Two Marshals*, p.192.
272 Vernois, *Royal Headquarters*, pp.100–101.
273 Lanza, *Source Book*, p.728.
274 Bazaine, *Épisodes*, p.72.
275 L'État–Major, *St Privat*, p.684.

cause serious concern, because he'd foreseen such a danger himself and he'd insisted on the need to hold onto Saint Privat at all costs[276] so as to allow the whole army to execute, without any undue pressure from the enemy, what he euphemistically termed 'a change of front to occupy the positions in the rear'.

It continues in the same dismissive vein 'It is absolutely unbelievable that there could have been any uncertainty about the importance of the battle, given that the violent cannonade he'd heard must have left him in no doubt that a general action was being fought all along the army's front' before concluding with this scathing summary:

> Quite characteristic of Bazaine and showing just how much, he deliberately engaged in a maze of deceptions and lies, when he gave an account of the fierce struggle which had been going on all afternoon to his sovereign, he summed it up with the following few words ' … I reached the plateau. Just then, about 7:00 p.m. the firing ceased … Our troops are holding their positions. One regiment, the 60th suffered heavy casualties in the defence of the farm at Saint Hubert.' The painful truth is that when the commander in chief did consent to leave his quarters at Plappeville for a few hours, he was still some 4 kilometres to the rear of the field of battle. The fighting didn't stop at 7:00 p.m. – on the contrary it continued violently all along the front and the French troops had yet to abandon their positions and it wasn't only one regiment that had suffered great losses, but four army corps who'd fought with admirable bravery for almost seven hours and left some 13,000 men on the ground.[277]

Seeking to throw some light on Bazaines' actions, the authors of the official history conclude that as early as the battle at Rezonville, his single preoccupation was to secure his communications with Metz and in particular, in view of the protection he thought it afforded his army, the route that ran past the fort at Mont St Quentin into the city. From the evidence given by Tour du Pin at the post war Courts Martial, it seems that this was still his intention on the 18th, regardless of the actions of the Prussians, the instructions of the emperor or indeed, the outcome of the days fighting. According to his testimony it appears the commander in chief had already decided to withdraw, regardless of the outcome of the battle, exclaiming: 'That's what it's all about! We were going to leave tomorrow morning. Now we'll go tonight, that's all!'[278]

Fixated by the apparent security afforded by Metz, Bazaine had failed to take advantage of the opportunities provided by Frossard and Le Boeuf when they repulsed successive attacks across the Mance ravine; neither had he provided effective support to Ladmirault or Canrobert,

---

276 This was the letter sent by Bazaine to Canrobert at 10:00 a.m. that morning.
277 L'État–Major, *St Privat*, pp.684–687.
278 Anon, *Procés Bazaine*, p.282–283. When confronted with this testimony at the post war Inquiry, Bazaine gave the not too convincing explanation: 'I would like to make an observation about my conversation with M de La Tour du Pin. At that time, I'd just become aware of new information concerning the enemy, which was growing in strength and said to amount to 250,000 men or more on the plateau. To lift the morale of these gentlemen, or rather to support them as they were not demoralised, I said to them, without telling them the news, 'You'd have to do this movement tomorrow morning. We would have been forced to because of the enemy reinforcements; well, we'll do it tonight' My remarks had no other meaning.'

where possibly, a division of the Guard could have turned tide in favour of the French. The bravery and determination shown by his troops and the 13,000 casualties incurred during the days fighting were, it seems, all in vain. Even if Moltke had left the French to their own devices, it seems likely that Bazaine would have still withdrawn into Metz.

As Tour du Pin and Ladmirault's ADC left his headquarters, Jarras handed them a copy of the movement order that Colonel Lewal had supposedly given to their respective commanders earlier that morning. It was probably drafted sometime during the late morning, before the fighting got underway, but it made no reference whatsoever to the nearby presence of the enemy forces, or the measures to be adopted if the planned withdrawal was threatened. Moreover, neither Bazaine nor Jarras saw fit to make any amendments to its contents following the Prussian attack. Although the order was in line with the commander in chief's intentions, it was clearly not drafted by him, the French official history remarking that 'this order contrasts sharply in many respects with those which had been dictated since the new commander took over on August 14' such that it 'appears almost like a novelty in the history of the sad days marked by the leadership of Marshal Bazaine.'[279]

## Bazaine's Fatal Decision

Whatever the reasons for his inertia and inactivity following Napoleon's departure, the decision to withdraw into Metz placed the Army of the Rhine at a severe strategic and tactical disadvantage; it would have required a commander of considerable competence and talent to salvage the situation, something that was certainly beyond Bazaine's capabilities. Whilst he claimed at his subsequent trial that his actions had delayed the advance of the two Prussian armies, so affording the emperor time to assemble new forces around Châlons, this excuse conveniently ignored the fact that he had disobeyed a direct order from his sovereign to put his army 'on the road to Verdun as soon as you can.'

Even with the benefit of hindsight, it is difficult to comprehend just what Bazaine intended to do; remain in Metz or attempt a break out? During the morning of the 18th, he received a dispatch from MacMahon briefing him on the situation of the forces being assembled around Châlons: 'Tomorrow morning, all the troops under my command will have been reorganised. Failly is at Virty le Francois, Margueritte with a cavalry division is at Sainte Menehould. If the Crown Prince attempts anything, I'll take up a position between Épernay and Rheims, so that I can join you, or march on Paris if circumstances force me to do so.'[280]

Bazaine, unsure as to what to do with his own army, had no intention of assuming responsibility for McMahon's and at noon sent this typically evasive response: 'I have only just received your dispatch from this morning. I presume the Ministry will have given you orders, your operations being outside of my area of action for the moment and I'd be afraid to point you in the wrong direction.'[281] At 2:00 p.m. in the afternoon when the battle was still undecided, it seems as if he may have harboured some fleeting thoughts of withdrawing to the north. He requested the

---

279  L'État-Major, St Privat, p.696. For example, in sharp contrast to the vague instructions usually issued by Bazaine, the order included departure times, each corps were given their own itinerary and a specific area for their bivouac.
280  Bazaine, l'Armée du Rhin, p.77.
281  Bazaine, Épisodes p.111.

authorities in Thionville to report if the Ardennes railway line was still open and ordered the Compagnie de l'Est in Metz to place all their rolling stock at his disposal. A few hours later, with the battle raging to his front still unresolved, it would appear he had decided to remain in Metz, informing MacMahon at Châlons:

> As a consequence of the successive battles fought on the 14th and 16th, my march on Verdun has been arrested and I've been obliged to remain in the northern part of Metz so as to replenish my ammunition and food. Since this morning the enemy has assembled strong forces, who seem to be marching towards Briey and who may be looking to attack Marshal Canrobert, who occupies Saint Privat la Montagne, with his left resting on 4 Corps at Amanvillers. So, we are again on the defensive, until I know where the troops opposing us are located, especially the army of the reserve, that is said to be in Pange on the right bank of the Moselle, under the command of the King, who's headquartered at the Château of Aubigny. Please pass this message on to the Emperor and the Ministry of War.'[282]

As if to confirm he had abandoned all thoughts of breaking out to the north, he added the comment: 'I'm worried about the Ardennes Railway.'[283] Later that evening, from his quarters at Plappeville, he finally responded to Napoleon's query as to what should be done with the supply dump at Verdun and it would seem from his reply – 'I'm not sure about the importance of the Verdun depot. I think it's only necessary to leave what I would need if I managed to force my way through to the place' – he still held out some hope of forcing his way through to Châlons, although possibly this was said simply to placate the emperor.[284] He then provided a brief account of the day's events; the message, which attracted so much opprobrium from the authors of the French official history, reads in full: 'I arrived on the plateau. The attack was very lively. At that moment, 7 o'clock, the fire ceased. Our troops remain in their positions. A regiment, the 60th has suffered greatly in defending the farm at Saint Hubert.'

On 19 August, the French Army passed the day reorganising their formations with the exhausted troops at last having the chance of some rest and the opportunity to replenish stocks of food and ammunition. Safely ensconced in his new headquarters at Ban Saint Martin, Bazaine sent another despatch to the emperor which although lengthier, provided but scant detail about the battle which had such an impact on the outcome of the campaign:

> The army fought yesterday between the Saint Privat and Rozerieulles and they held these positions. It was only towards 9:00 p.m. that the 4th and 6th corps made a change of front and threw back their right wing in order to check a movement which the enemy were attempting to carry out under cover of the dark. This morning I withdrew the 2nd and 3rd corps and the army is now in new positions on the left bank of the Moselle,

282  Bazaine, F. A. Marshal *Armée du Rhin* (Paris, Henri Plon, 1872) pp.77–78.
283  *Ibid*, p.78.
284  L'État-Major, *St Privat*, p.84. He had previously sent a despatch to Napoleon at 4:35 p.m. which stated 'At this moment, 4 o'clock, an attack, led by the king of Prussia in person, with considerable strength, has begun all along our line. The troops have held out until now, although the batteries have been forced to cease their fire.'

from Longeville to Sansonnet, forming a curved line passing through the heights of Ban Saint Martin, behind the forts of Saint Quentin and Plappeville. The troops are tired with these endless battles which don't allow them time to recover; they must be given two- or three-days' rest. The king of Prussia is, this morning, in Rezonville with Moltke and all indications are that the Prussian army intends to blockade Metz.[285]

He then made a throw away remark which, many were to allege resulted in the destruction of the Imperial Army, the overthrow of the Napoleonic dynasty and subsequent defeat of France: 'I still reckon to move northwards and fight my way out via Montmédy on the Ste Ménéhould-Châlons road, if it's not too strongly occupied; if it is, I will march as far north as Sedan or even Mézières to reach Châlons.'[286] In its consideration of Bazaine's actions, the French official history posed this question:

What were the real intentions of the commander in chief at this time? Was not this idea which he referred to simply presented to his sovereign as something to mask the apathy which gripped him? It can be said that by suggesting this course of action to Marshal MacMahon, it was the cause of the disaster which struck the last standing French army at Sedan.[287]

285  Bazaine, *l'Armée du Rhin*, pp.74–75.
286  *Ibid*, p.75.
287  L'État-Major, *St Privat*, p.714.

| | | | | |
|---|---|---|---|---|
| **3 Corps:** Commander: General Decaen. Chief of General Staff: General of Brigade Maneque. Commander of Artillery: General of Division Grimaudet de Rochebouet. Chief of Staff : General Maneque. | | | | |
| **1st Division:** Commander: General of Division Montaudon. Chief of Staff: Colonel Folloppe. Staff Officers: Farey, Mercier, Lahalle. | | | | |
| **1st Brigade:** | | | | |
| 18th Chasseur Battalion: Commandant Rigault | | | | |
| 51st Line Infantry Regiment: Colonel Delebecque | | | | |
| 62nd Line Infantry Regiment: Colonel Dauphin | | | | |
| **2nd Brigade:** General of Brigade Clinchant | | | | |
| 81st Line Infantry Regiment: Colonel d'Albici | | | | |
| 95th Line Infantry Regiment: Colonel Davout d'Auerstadt | | | | |
| **Divisional Artillery:** Lieut. Colonel Fourgous | | | | |
| No 5 Battery 4th Field Artillery Regiment | | | | 6 |
| No 6 Battery 4th Field Artillery Regiment | | | | 6 |
| No 8 Battery 4th Field Artillery Regiment | | | | 6 |
| Engineers : 1 Company of 1st Engineer Regiment | | | | |
| **Total 1st Division** | | 9,875 | 578 | 18 |
| **2nd Division:** Commander: General of Division de Castigny. Chief of Staff: Colonel Bonneau du Martray. Staff Officers: Ruyneau de Saint-Georges, Graff, Contesse. | | | | |
| **1st Brigade:** General of Brigade Nayral | | | | |
| 15th Chasseur Battalion: Commandant Lafouge | | | | |
| 19th Line Infantry Regiment: Colonel de Launay | | | | |
| 41st Line Infantry Regiment: Colonel Saussier | | | | |
| **2nd Brigade:** General of Division Duplessis | | | | |
| 69th Line Infantry Regiment: Colonel le Tourneur | | | | |
| 90th Line Infantry Regiment: Colonel de Courcy | | | | |
| **Divisional Artillery:** Lieut. Colonel Delange | | | | |
| No 11 Battery 4th Field Artillery Regiment | | | | 6 |
| No 12 Battery 4th Field Artillery Regiment | | | | 6 |
| No 9 Battery 4th Field Artillery Regiment | | | | 6 |
| Engineers : 1 Company of 1st Engineer Regiment | | | | |
| **Total 2nd Division** | | 10,201 | 788 | 18 |

| | | | | |
|---|---|---|---|---|
| **3rd Division:** Commander: General of Division Metman. Chief of Staff: Lieutenant Colonel D'Orleans. Staff Officers: Schassere, Dumas, De Champflour. | | | | |
| **1st Brigade:** General of Brigade de Potier | | | | |
| 7th Chasseur Battalion: Commandant Rigaud | | | | |
| 7th Line Infantry Regiment: Colonel Cotteret | | | | |
| 29th Line Infantry Regiment: Colonel Lalanne | | | | |
| **2nd Brigade:** General of Brigade Arnaudeau | | | | |
| 59th Line Infantry Regiment: Colonel Duez | | | | |
| 71st Line Infantry Regiment: Colonel de Ferussac | | | | |
| **Divisional Artillery:** Lieut. Colonel Sempe | | | | 6 |
| No 6 Battery 11th Field Artillery Regiment | | | | 6 |
| No 7 Battery 11th Field Artillery Regiment | | | | 6 |
| No 5 Battery 11th Field Artillery Regiment | | | | |
| Engineers : 1 Company of 1st Engineer Regiment | | | | |
| **Total 3rd Division** | | 10,272 | 628 | 18 |
| **4th Division:** Commander: General of Division Amyard. Chief of Staff: Lieutenant Colonel De La Soujeole. Staff Officers: Versigny, Parison, Bertrand. | | | | |
| **1st Brigade:** General of Brigade de Brauer | | | | |
| 11th Chasseur Battalion: Commandant de Pillot | | | | |
| 44th Line Infantry Regiment: Colonel Fournier | | | | |
| 60th Line Infantry Regiment: Colonel Boissie | | | | |
| **2nd Brigade:** General of Brigade Sangle-Ferriere | | | | |
| 80th Line Infantry Regiment: Colonel Janin | | | | |
| 85th Line Infantry Regiment: Colonel Planchut | | | | |
| **Divisional Artillery:** Lieut. Colonel Maucourant | | | | |
| No 9 Battery 11th Field Artillery Regiment | | | | 6 |
| No 10 Battery 11th Field Artillery Regiment | | | | 6 |
| No 8 Battery 11th Field Artillery Regiment | | | | 6 |
| Engineers : 1 Company of 1st Engineer Regiment | | | | |
| **Total 4th Division** | | 10,024 | 747 | 18 |
| **Cavalry Division:** Commander: General of Division Clerembault. Chief of Staff: Lieutenant Colonel De Jouffroy D'Abbas. Staff Officers: Scellier de Lample, Dutheil de la Rochere, Vincent. | | | | |
| **1st Brigade:** General of Brigade Bruchard | | | | |
| 2nd Chasseurs a Cheval: Colonel Pelletier | | | | |
| 3rd Chasseurs a Cheval: Colonel Sanson de Sansal | | | | |

| | | | | | |
|---|---|---|---|---|---|
| 10th Chasseurs a Cheval: Colonel Nerin | | | | | |
| **2nd Brigade:** General of Brigade Gayrault de Maubranches | | | | | |
| 2nd Dragoon Regiment: Colonel du Paty de Clam | | | | | |
| 4th Dragoon Regiment: Colonel Cornat | | | | | |
| **3rd Brigade:** General of Brigade Begougne de Juiniac | | | | | |
| 5th Dragoon Regiment: Colonel Lachene | | | | | |
| 8th Dragoon Regiment: Colonel Boyer de Fonscolombe | | | | | |
| **Total Cavalry Division** | | | 4,624 | 4,112 | |
| **Artillery Reserve:** Commander: Colonel de Lajaille. | | | | | |
| No 7 Battery 4th Field Artillery Regiment | | | | | 6 |
| No 10 Battery 4th Field Artillery Regiment | | | | | 6 |
| No 11 Battery 11th Field Artillery Regiment | | | | | 6 |
| No 12 Battery 11th Field Artillery Regiment | | | | | 6 |
| No 1 Battery 17th Horse Artillery Regiment | | | | | 6 |
| No 2 Battery 17th Horse Artillery Regiment | | | | | 6 |
| No 3 Battery 17th Horse Artillery Regiment | | | | | 6 |
| No 4 Battery 17th Horse Artillery Regiment | | | | | 6 |
| **Total** | | | | | 48 |
| **Engineer Reserve** | | | | | |
| 1½ companies 2nd Engineer Regiment | | | | | |
| Detachment of sappers of 2nd Engineer Regiment | | | | | |
| **Total Engineers & Artillery** | | | 2,603 | 2,706 | |
| **Support Services** | | | | | |
| **Total Support Services** | | | 660 | 761 | |
| **Total 3 Corps** | | | 48,259 | 10,320 | 120 |
| *As at 12th August | | | | | |
| **4 Corps:** General Commanding: General of Division de Ladmirault. Chief of General Staff: General of Brigade Osmont.Commander of Artillery: General of Brigade Lafaille. Commander of Engineers, General of Brigade Prudon. | | | | | |
| Etat Major | 51 | 82 | 133 | 145 | |
| **1st Division:** Commander: General of Division Courtot de Cissey. Chief of Staff: Colonel De Place. Staff Officers: Debize, Gargin, De La Boulaye. | | | | | |
| Etat | 10 | | 10 | 35 | |
| **1st Brigade:** General of Brigade Brayer | | | | | |

| | | | | | |
|---|---|---|---|---|---|
| 20th Chasseur Battalion: Commandant de Labarriere | 23 | 875 | 898 | 9 | |
| 1st Line Infantry Regiment: Colonel Fremont | 66 | 2,028 | 2,094 | 29 | |
| 6th Line Infantry Regiment: Colonel Labarthe | 67 | 1,735 | 1,802 | 34 | |
| 2nd Brigade: General of Brigade de Goldberg | | | | | |
| 57th Line Infantry Regiment: Colonel Giraud | 68 | 2,065 | 2,133 | 26 | |
| 73rd Line Infantry Regiment: Colonel Supervielle | 63 | 2,226 | 2,289 | 29 | |
| **Divisional Artillery:** Lieut. Colonel de Narp | | | | | |
| No 5 Battery 15th Field Artillery Regiment | 7 | 132 | 139 | 121 | 6 |
| No 9 Battery 15th Field Artillery Regiment | 4 | 145 | 149 | 127 | 6 |
| No 12 Battery 15th Field Artillery Regiment | 4 | 147 | 151 | 124 | 6 |
| | | | | | |
| Train des equipage | 1 | 43 | 44 | 51 | |
| Services Administratifs | 12 | 110 | 122 | 10 | |
| Engineers : 1 Company of 2nd Engineer Regiment | 5 | 78 | 83 | 20 | |
| **Total 1st Division** | **334** | **9,629** | **9,960** | **691** | **18** |
| **2nd Division:** Commander: General Grenier. Chief of Staff Lieutenant Colonel: De Rambault. Staff Officers: Goumenault des Plantes, Bassot, Guerin-Precourt | | | | | |
| Etat Major | 15 | | 15 | 45 | |
| **1st Brigade:** General of Brigade Veron-dit-Bellecourt | | | | | |
| 5th Chasseur Battalion: Commandant Carre | 23 | 773 | 796 | 11 | |
| 13th Line Infantry Regiment: Colonel Lion | 65 | 2,299 | 2,364 | 34 | |
| 43rd Line Infantry Regiment: Colonel de Viville | 65 | 1,970 | 2,035 | 34 | |
| **2nd Brigade:** General of Brigade Pradier | | | | | |
| 64th Line Infantry Regiment: Colonel Leger | 66 | 2,074 | 2,140 | 29 | |
| 98th Line Infantry Regiment: Colonel Lechesne | 60 | 2,347 | 2,407 | 31 | |
| **Divisional Artillery:** Lieut. Colonel de Larminat | | | | | |
| No 6 Battery 1st Field Artillery Regiment | 5 | 149 | 154 | 127 | 6 |
| No 7 Battery 1st Field Artillery Regiment | 4 | 155 | 159 | 123 | 6 |
| No 5 Battery 1st Field Artillery Regiment | 4 | 151 | 155 | 120 | 6 |
| Reserve | | 48 | 48 | 74 | |
| Train des equipage | 1 | 42 | 43 | 50 | |
| Services Administratifs | 13 | 66 | 79 | 13 | |
| Engineers : 1 Company of 2nd Engineer Regiment | 4 | 81 | 85 | 18 | |
| **Total 2nd Division** | **325** | **10,155** | **10,480** | **711** | **18** |

| | | | | | |
|---|---|---|---|---|---|
| **3rd Division:** Commander: General of Division Latrille, Count de Lorencez. Chief of Staff: Lieutenant Colonel Villette. Chief of Staff Beillet, Acaries, Duquesnay. | | | | | |
| Etat Major | 12 | | 12 | 45 | |
| **1st Brigade:** General of Brigade Count Pajol | | | | | |
| 2nd Chasseur Battalion: Commandant Le Tanneur | 22 | 841 | 863 | 10 | |
| 15th Line Infantry Regiment: Colonel Fraboulet de Kerleadec | 67 | 2,266 | 2,333 | 33 | |
| 33rd Line Infantry Regiment: Colonel Bounetou | 67 | 1,952 | 2,019 | 43 | |
| **2nd Brigade:** General of Brigade Berger | | | | | |
| 54th Line Infantry Regiment: Colonel Caillot | 64 | 1,946 | 2,010 | 36 | |
| 65th Line Infantry Regiment: Colonel See | 60 | 2,143 | 2,203 | 40 | |
| **Divisional Artillery:** Lieut. Colonel Legardeur | | | | | |
| No 9 Battery 1st Field Artillery Regiment | 7 | 155 | 162 | 128 | 6 |
| No 10 Battery 1st Field Artillery Regiment | 4 | 148 | 152 | 120 | 6 |
| No 8 Battery 1st Field Artillery Regiment | 4 | 148 | 152 | 126 | 6 |
| Reserve | 1 | 46 | 47 | 76 | |
| Train des equipage | | 42 | 42 | 48 | |
| Services Administratifs | 11 | 57 | 68 | 13 | |
| Engineers : 1 Company of 2nd Engineer Regiment | 5 | 102 | 107 | 20 | |
| **Total 3rd Division** | **324** | **9,845** | **10,169** | **738** | **18** |
| **Cavalry Division:** Commander: General of Division Legrand. Chief of Staff: Colonel Campeon. Staff Officers: Cretin, Rispaud, Bach. | | | | | |
| Etat Major | 10 | | 10 | 41 | |
| **1st Brigade:** General of Brigade Montaigu | | | | | |
| 2nd Hussar Regiment: Colonel Carrelet | 46 | 616 | 662 | 612 | |
| 7th Hussar Regiment: Colonel Chausee | 48 | 649 | 697 | 663 | |
| **2nd Brigade:** General of Brigade Baron Gondrecourt | | | | | |
| 3rd Dragoon Regiment: Colonel Bilhau | 41 | 490 | 531 | 549 | |
| 11th Dragoon Regiment: Colonel Huyn de Verneville | 40 | 540 | 580 | 536 | |
| Train & Services Administratifs | 8 | 55 | 63 | 15 | |
| **Total Cavalry Division** | **193** | **2,350** | **2,543** | **2,426** | |
| **Artillery Reserve:** Commander: General Lafaille. | | | | | |
| Etat Major | 5 | | 5 | 21 | |
| No 11 Battery 1st Field Artillery Regiment | 4 | 196 | 200 | 169 | 6 |
| No 12 Battery 1stField Artillery Regiment | 3 | 193 | 196 | 170 | 6 |

| | | | | | |
|---|---|---|---|---|---|
| No 6 Battery 8th Field Artillery Regiment | 4 | 142 | 146 | 120 | 6 |
| No 9 Battery 8th Field Artillery Regiment | 4 | 139 | 143 | 120 | 6 |
| No 5 Battery 17th Horse Artillery Regiment | 4 | 157 | 161 | 182 | 6 |
| No 6 Battery 17th Horse Artillery Regiment | 4 | 155 | 159 | 177 | 6 |
| Parc du corps d'armee | 8 | 517 | 525 | 597 | |
| **Total Artillery Reserve** | **36** | **1,499** | **1,535** | **1,556** | **36** |
| **Engineer Reserve** | | | | | |
| 1 company 2nd Engineer Regiment | 4 | 97 | 101 | 16 | |
| Parc du genie | | 39 | 39 | 61 | |
| **Total Engineer Reserve** | **4** | **136** | **140** | **77** | |
| **Train des equipages** | | | | | |
| 1st Regt 2nd Co | 2 | 78 | 80 | 78 | |
| 3rd Regt 3rd Co | 2 | 188 | 190 | 204 | |
| 3rd Regt 10th Co | 3 | 197 | 200 | 260 | |
| **Force publique** | 5 | 85 | 90 | 65 | |
| **Service de substances** | 2 | 80 | 82 | 2 | |
| **Service des hospitaux** | 9 | 113 | 122 | 3 | |
| **Services du campement** | 1 | | 1 | | |
| **Tresor et Postes** | 17 | 31 | 48 | 31 | |
| **Total** | **41** | **772** | **813** | **643** | |
| **4 Corps Total** | **1,305** | **34,468** | **35,773** | **6,987** | **90** |
| *As at 14th August | | | | | |
| **5 Corps** | | | | | |
| **1st Brigade:*** General of Brigade Lapasset | | | | | |
| **Total 1st Brigade** | | | **2,700** | **40** | |
| **Cavalry** | | | | | |
| 12th Chasseurs a Cheval | | | 120 | 100 | |
| 3rd Lancer Regiment: | | | 500 | 100 | |
| **Total Cavalry** | | | **620** | **200** | |
| **Artillery** | | | | | |
| No 7 Battery 2nd Field Artillery Regiment | | | | | |
| **Total Artillery Reserve** | | | **150** | **100** | **6** |
| **Approximate Total** | | | **3,470** | **680** | **6** |

| | | | | |
|---|---|---|---|---|
| * General Lapasset rallied several detachments of men destined for 5 Corps during the retreat from Froeschwiller which were attached to 2 Corps and commanded by a Lieutenant Colonel from the 84th Regiment, and included men from the 14th Chasseurs, 46th, 49th, 68th and 88th Line. It also included detachments from two cavalry regiments and a battery of artillery. | | | | |
| **Summary French Forces available at Borny on 14th August** | | | | |
| Total Imperial Guard | | 19,210 | 5,265 | 72 |
| Approximate Total 2 Corps | | 25,000 | 5,000 | 90 |
| Total 3 Corps | | 48,259 | 10,320 | 120 |
| Total 4 Corps | | 35,773 | 6,987 | 90 |
| Approximate Total 5 Corps | | 3,470 | 680 | 6 |
| **Grand Total** | | **131,712** | **28,252** | **378** |

| Lehautcourt in La Retraite sur la Moselle, Borny, gives the total effectives within the French army around Metz on the 13th August as follows: | Men | Horses |
|---|---|---|
| **2 Corps** | | |
| 1st Division | | |
| 2nd Division | | |
| 3rd Division | 10,768 | 868 |
| Brigade Lapassat | 3,470 | 680 |
| Cavalry Division | | |
| Reserve artillery & Engineers | | |
| **Total** | **31,936** | **5,911** |
| **3 Corps** | | |
| Various | 660 | 761 |
| 1st Division | 9,875 | 578 |
| 2nd Division | 10,201 | 788 |
| 3rd Division | 10,272 | 628 |
| 4th Division | 10,024 | 747 |
| Cavalry Division | 4,624 | 4,112 |
| Reserve artillery & Engineers | 2,603 | 2,706 |
| **Total** | **48,259** | **10,320** |
| **4 Corps** | | |
| Divers | 834 | 713 |
| 1st Division | 9,960 | 691 |
| 2nd Division | 10,017 | 708 |

| | | | |
|---|---|---|---|
| 3rd Division | | 10,034 | 731 |
| Cavalry Division | | 2,543 | 2,426 |
| Reserve artillery & Engineers | | 1,675 | 1,633 |
| **Total** | | **35,063** | **6,902** |
| **Imperial Guard** | | | |
| Divers | | 449 | 648 |
| 1st Division | | 8,013 | 173 |
| 2nd Division | | 6,219 | 156 |
| Cavalry Division | | 4,236 | 3,825 |
| Reserve artillery & Engineers | | 2,548 | 2,327 |
| **Total** | | **21,465** | **7,129** |
| **Grand Total** | | **136,723** | **30,262** |

| Heft 11 of the Kriegsgeschichtliche Einzelschriften, published in 1899 before the French Official History was released gives the numbers of French troops that actually participated in the fighting, as opposed to those being avaialable in the vicinity, as follows:- | Battalions | Squadrons | Artillery | Mitrailleuses |
|---|---|---|---|---|
| **Imperial Guard** | 24 | 29 | 12 | 2 |
| **2 Corps** | 8 | | 3 | 1 |
| **3 Corps** | 52 | 31 | 20 | 4 |
| **4 Corps** | 39 | | 13 | 3 |
| **Bazaine's Duty Squadron** | | 1 | | |
| **Totals** | **123** | **61** | **48** | **10** |
| It takes the average battalion and squadron strength as follows:- | Battalions | Squadrons | | |
| **Imperial Guard** | | | | |
| **2 Corps** | 540 | | | |
| **3 Corps** | 650 | 115 | | |
| **4 Corps** | 650 | | | |
| **Bazaine's Duty Squadron** | | 115 | | |
| It gives the following totals for the numbers engaged as follows:- | Men | Cavalry | Guns | Mitrailleuses |
| **Imperial Guard** | 13,440 | 3,625 | 72 | 12 |
| **2 Corps** | 4,320 | | 18 | 6 |
| **3 Corps** | 33,800 | 3,565 | 120 | 24 |
| **4 Corps** | 25,350 | | 78 | 18 |
| **Bazaine's Duty Squadron** | | 115 | | |
| **Totals** | **76,910** | **7,305** | **288** | **60** |

# Appendix II

## German Order of Battle, Borny

| | Battalions | Squadrons | Guns |
|---|---|---|---|
| **German forces engaged in the Battle of Borny.** The units engaged are as recorded within the German Official History. These differ somewhat from the information given within the Kriegsgeschlichtliche Einzelschriften published in 1899 which list additional forces from both X Corps and 6th Cavalry Division as being present, although these forces are not mentioned within the Official account | | | |
| **I Army:** General Steinmetz | | | |
| **I Corps: General Commanding: General of Cavalry Baron v Manteuffel. Chief of General Staff: Lt Colonel v d Burg. Commander of Artillery: Maj General v Bergmann. Commander of Engineers and Pioneers: Major Fahland. Staff Officers; Stieler v Amelunxen, v d Hude, Lignitz.** | | | |
| **1st Infantry Division: Commander: Lt General v Bentheim. Officer of General Staff: Major v Schrotter. Staff Officers: Michaelis, v Tresckow.** | | | |
| 1st Infantry Brigade: Maj General v Gayl | | | |
| 1st (Crown Prince) Grenadiers: Colonel v Massow | 3 | | |
| 41st Regiment: Lt ColonelBaron v Meerscheidt-Hullessem | 3 | | |
| **2nd Infantry Brigade:** Maj General v Falkenstein | | | |
| 3rd Grenadiers: Colonel v Legat | 3 | | |
| 43rd Regiment: Colonel v Busse | 3 | | |
| 1st Rifle Battalion: Lt Colonel v Ploetz | 1 | | |
| 1st Dragoons(Prince Albrect of Prussia): Lt Colonel v Massow | | 4 | |
| 1st Field Division, 1st FA Regiment; | | | |
| 1&2 heavy, 1&2 light batteries: Major Munk | | | 24 |
| 2nd Field Pioneer Company 1st Corps with entrenching | | | |
| Tool column: Captain Neumann | | | |
| No 1 Sanitary Detachment | | | |
| **Total 1st Infantry Division** | **13** | **4** | **24** |
| **2nd Infantry Division: Commander: Maj General v Pritzelwitz.Officer of General Staff: Captain v Jarotzki. Staff Officers: Piepersberg, v Saucken** | | | |
| 3rd Infantry Brigade: Maj General v Memerty | | | |
| 4th Grenadiers: Colonel v Tietzen and Hennig | 3 | | |
| 44th Regiment: Colonel v Boecking | 3 | | |
| **4th Infantry Brigade:** Maj General v Zglinitzki | | | |

| | | | |
|---|---|---|---|
| 5th Grenadiers: Colonel v Einem | 2 | | |
| 10th Dragoons:Colonel Baron v d Goltz | | 4 | |
| 3rd Field Division, 1st Field Artillery Regiment; | | | |
| 5&6 heavy, 5&6 light batteries: Major Muller | | | 24 |
| 1st Field Pioneer Company 1st Corps with light field bridge train: Captain Ritter | | | |
| No 2 Sanitary Detachment | | | |
| **Total 2nd Infantry Division** | **8** | **4** | **24** |
| **Corps Artillery: Colonel Junge Commander 1st Field Artillery Regiment** | | | |
| Horse Artillery Division, 1st Field Artillery Regiment, | | | |
| 2 & 3 horse artillery batteries: Major Gerhards | | | 12 |
| 2nd Field Artillery Division, 1st Field Artillery Regiment | | | |
| 3 & 4 heavy, 3 & 4 light batteries: Lt Colonel Gregorovius | | | 24 |
| 3rd Sanitary Detachment | | | |
| **Total Corps Artillery** | | | **36** |
| **Total I Corps** | **21** | **8** | **84** |
| **VII Corps: General Commanding: General of Infantry v Zastrow. Chief of General Staff: Col v Anger. Commander of Artillery: Maj General v Zimmermann. Commander of Engineers and Pioneers: Major Treumann. Staff Officers; v Kaltenborn- Stachau, v Westerhagen, v Mikusch-Buchberg. Present at HQ Hereditary Prince of Schaumburg-Lippe.** | | | |
| **13th Infantry Division: Commander: Lt General v Glumer. Officer of General Staff: Major v Werder. Staff Officers: v Loeper, v Boch, Polach.** | | | |
| 25th Infantry Brigade: Maj General Baron v d Osten Sacken | | | |
| 13th Regiment: Colonel v Frankenberg-Ludwigsdorff | 3 | | |
| 73rd Fusiliers: Lt Colonel v Loeball | 2 | | |
| **26th Infantry Brigade:** Maj General Baron v d Goltz | | | |
| 15th Regiment: Colonel v Delitz | 3 | | |
| 55th Regiment: Colonel v Barby | 3 | | |
| 7th Rifle Battalion: Lt Colonel Reinike | 1 | | |
| 8th Hussars: Lt Colonel Arent | | 4 | |
| 3rd Field Division, 7th FA Regiment; | | | |
| 5 & 6 heavy, 5 & 6 light batteries: Major Wilhemi | | | 24 |
| 2nd Field Pioneer Company VIIth Corps with entrenching tool column: Captain Gotze | | | |
| 3rd Field Pioneer Company VIIth Corps: Captain Cleinow | | | |
| No 1 Sanitary Detachment | | | |

| | | | |
|---|---|---|---|
| **Total 13th Division** | **12** | **4** | **24** |
| **14th Infantry Division: Commander: Lt General v Kameke. Officer of General Staff: Major Baron v Hilgers. Staff Officers: v Borcke, Meese.** | | | |
| 27th Infantry Brigade: | | | |
| 74th Regiment: Colonel v Panneitz | 3 | | |
| 39th Fusiliers: Colonel v Eskens | 3 | | |
| **28th Infantry Brigade:** Maj General v Woyna | | | |
| 53rd Regiment: Colonel v Gerstein-Hohenstein | 2 | | |
| 77th Regiment: Colonel v Conrady | 2 | | |
| 15th Hussars: Colonel v Cosel | | 4 | |
| 1st Field Division, 7th FA Regiment; | | | |
| 1 & 2 heavy, 1 & 2 light batteries: Major Baron v Eynatten | | | 24 |
| 1st Field Pioneer Company VIIth Corps with light field bridge train: Captain Junker: | | | |
| No 2 Sanitary Detachment | | | |
| **Total 14th Division** | **10** | **4** | **24** |
| **Corps Artillery:** Colonel v Helden Sarnowski Commander 7th Field Artillery Regiment. | | | |
| Horse Artillery Division, 7th Field Artillery Regiment, | | | |
| 2 & 3 horse artillery batteries: Major Coester | | | 12 |
| 2nd Field Artillery Division, 7th Field Artillery Regiment | | | |
| 3 & 4 heavy,3 & 4 light batteries: Lt Colonel v Wellman | | | 24 |
| 3rd Sanitary Detachment | | | |
| **Total Corps Artillery** | | | **36** |
| **Total VII Corps** | **22** | **8** | **84** |
| **From IX Corps** | | | |
| **18th Infantry Division: Commander: Lt General Baron v Wrangel. Officer of General Staff: Major Lust. Staff Officers: v Bulow, v Marklowski.** | | | |
| 35th Infantry Brigade: Maj General v Blumenthal | | | |
| 36th Fusiliers: Colonel v Brandenstein | 2 | | |
| 84th Regiment: Colonel v Winkler | 1 | | |
| 1st Field Division, 9th FA Regiment; | | | |
| 2 heavy & 2 light batteries: Major v Gayl | | | 12 |
| 6th Dragoons: Colonel Baron von Houwald | | 4 | |
| **Total 18th Division** | **3** | **4** | **12** |
| **1st Cavalry Division: Commander: Lt General v Hartmann. Officer of General Staff: Major v Saldern. Staff Officers: v Eichstedt-Peterswaldt, z Eulenburg.** | | | |

| | | | |
|---|---|---|---|
| **1st Cavalry Brigade:** Maj General v Luderitz | | | |
| 2nd Cuirassiers (Queens):Colonel v Pfuhl | | 4 | |
| 4th Lancers: Lt Colonel v Radecke | | 4 | |
| **2nd Cavalry Brigade:** Maj General Baumgarth | | | |
| 3rd Cuirassiers (Count Wrangel):Colonel v Winterfield | | 4 | |
| 1st Horse Artillery Battery 1st Field Artillery Regiment: Captain v Selle | | | 6 |
| **Total 1st Cavalry Division** | | **12** | **6** |
| **3rd Cavalry Division: Commander Lt General Count v d Groben. Officer of General Staff: Captain Count v Wedel. Staff Officers V Rosenberg, V Kluber.** | | | |
| **6th Cavalry Brigade:** Maj General v Mirus | | | |
| 8th Cuirassiers: Colonel Count v Roedern | | 4 | |
| 7th Lancers: Lt Colonel v Pestel | | 4 | |
| **7th Cavalry Brigade:** Maj General Count zu Dohna | | | |
| 5th Lancers: Lt Colonel Baron v Reitzenstein | | 4 | |
| 14th Lancers: Colonel v Luderitz | | 4 | |
| 1st Horse Artillery Battery 7th Field Artillery Regiment: Captain Schrader | | | 6 |
| **Total 3rd Cavalry Division** | | **16** | **6** |
| Heft 11 of the Kriegsgeschlichtliche Einzelschriften states that the average strength of an infantry battalion in the 1st Division was 920 men and squadrons averaged 140 troopers. The average strength of a battalion in the 2nd Division was 910 men with the squadrons averaging 140 troopers. In 13th Division the battalions averaged 870 men, the squadrons 140 troopers. In 14th Division the battalions averaged 710 men and the squadrons averaged 140 troopers. In 18th Division the battalions averaged 910 men, the squadrons 140. 1st Cavalry Division's squadrons averaged 130 sabres, 3rd Cavalry Division 140 sabres and 6th Cavalry Division 130 sabres. The total number of battalions, squadrons, guns and engineer companies engaged are as follows:- | | | |
| I Corps | 21 | 8 | 84 |
| II Corps | 22 | 8 | 84 |
| 18th Division | 3 | 4 | 12 |
| 1st Cavalry Division | | 12 | 6 |
| 3rd Cavalry Division | | 16 | 6 |
| Total | 46 | 48 | 192 |
| This provided the following:- | | | |
| I Corps | 19,240 | 1,120 | 84 |
| VII Corps | 17,540 | 1,120 | 84 |

| | | | |
|---|---|---|---|
| IX Corps | 2,370 | 560 | 24 |
| 1st Cav Div | | 1,560 | 6 |
| 3rd Cav Div | | 2,240 | 6 |
| **Total** | **39,150** | **6,600** | **192** |
| With batteries averaging about 140 men, and including the pioneer companies this would give a total of about 51,000 men. | | | |

| Heft 11 of the Kriegsgeschlichtliche Einzelschriften published in 1899 puts the numbers involved as follows:- | **Battalions** | **Squadrons** | **Guns** |
|---|---|---|---|
| I Corps | 24½ | 8 | 84 |
| II Corps | 23 | 8 | 84 |
| 18th Division | 10¼ | 4 | 16 |
| 1st Cavalry Division | | 12 | 6 |
| 3rd Cavalry Division | | 16 | 6 |
| 6th Cavalry Division | | 5 | |
| **Total** | **57¾** | **53** | **196** |

| This provided the following:- | **Infantry** | **Cavalry** | **Guns** |
|---|---|---|---|
| I Corps | 22,420 | 1,120 | 84 |
| VII Corps | 18,410 | 1,120 | 84 |
| IX Corps | 9,327 | 560 | 16 |
| 1st Cav Div | | 1,560 | 6 |
| 3rd Cav Div | | 2,240 | 6 |
| 6th Cav Div | | 650 | |
| **Total** | **50,157** | **7,250** | **196** |
| With batteries averaging about 140 men, and including the pioneer companies this would give a total of about 62,500 men. | | | |

| | **Men** | **Batteries** | |
|---|---|---|---|
| I Corps | 29,700 | 14 | |
| VII Corps | 29,700 | 14 | |
| 18th Division | 2,450 | 2 | |
| 1st & 3rd Cavalry Divisions | 6,300 | 2 | |
| **Total** | **68,150** | **32** | |

| From this figure the losses at Spicheren are deducted along with those incurred on the march, so the estimate of the likely totals are between 62,000-64,000 men with 32 batteries/192 guns. Somewhat surprisingly the German Official History puts the troops available at over 67,000 with 204 guns. | **Infantry (incl pioneers)** | **Cavalry** | **Guns** |
|---|---|---|---|
| **I Corps** | | | |
| 1st Division | 13,408 | 618 | 24 |

| | | | |
|---|---|---|---|
| 2nd Division | 11,782 | 601 | 24 |
| Corps Artillery | | | 36 |
| **Total** | **24,830** | **1,219** | **84** |
| **VII Corps** | | | |
| 13th Division | 12,407 | 615 | 24 |
| 14th Division | 8,565 | 618 | 24 |
| Corps Artillery | | | 36 |
| **Total** | **20,972** | **1,228** | **84** |
| 18th Division | 12,857 | 615 | 24 |
| 1st Cav Div | | 3,307 | 6 |
| 3rd Cav Div | | 2,365 | 6 |
| **Grand Total**** | **58,659** | **8,734** | **204** |
| * The figures exclude officers and train soldiers. | | | |

# Appendix III

## French losses, Borny

| French losses at battle of Borny | officers killed | officers wounded | men killed | men wounded | men missing | horses killed | horses missing | munitions expended |
|---|---|---|---|---|---|---|---|---|
| **3 Corps** | | | | | | | | |
| **General Staff** | 1 | 1 | | | | | | |
| | | | | | | | | |
| **1st Division** | | | | | | | | |
| **1st Brigade** | | | | | | | | |
| 18th Chasseurs | | | | | | | | |
| 51st | | | | 1 | | | | |
| 62nd | | | | | | | | |
| **2nd Brigade** | | | | | | | | |
| Staff | | | | | | | | |
| 81st | | | 1 | 2 | | | | |
| 95th | | | 1 | | | | | |
| **Artillery** | | | | | | | | |
| 5th/4 | 1 | 1 | 4 | 5 | | 6 | 4 | |
| 5th/4 | | | | | | | 1 | }312 |
| 8th/4 | | | | | | | | 60 |
| Engineers 6th Co/1st Regt | | | | | | | | |
| **2nd Division** | | | | | | | | |
| Staff | | 1 | | | | | | |
| **1st Brigade** | | | | | | | | |
| 15th Chasseurs | 2 | 3 | 5 | 133 | 45 | | | |
| 19th | 2 | 9 | 31 | 250 | 81 | | | |
| 41st | 5 | 16 | 15 | 243 | 90 | | | |
| **2nd Brigade** | | | | | | | | |
| Staff | | 2 | | | | | | |
| 69th | 2 | 11 | 21 | 152 | 15 | | | |
| 90th | 4 | 7 | 17 | 225 | 39 | | | |
| Artillery | | | | | | | | |
| 9th/4 | | | | | | | | 384 |

| | | | | | | | | |
|---|---|---|---|---|---|---|---|---|
| 11th/4 | | 1 | 1 | 3 | | 4 | 1 | 518 |
| 12th/4 | | | | | | | | |
| Engineers 10th Co/1st Regt | | | | | | | | |
| **3rd Division** | | | | | | | | |
| **1st Brigade** | | | | | | | | |
| Staff | | | | | | | | |
| 7th Chasseurs | 1 | 2 | | 19 | 2 | | | |
| 7th | 1 | 6 | 7 | 80 | 83 | | | |
| 29th | 7 | 6 | 13 | 94 | 92 | | | |
| **2nd Brigade** | | | | | | | | |
| Staff | | | | | | | | |
| 59th | 3 | 16 | 25 | 166 | 35 | | | |
| 71st | 4 | 8 | 73 | 210 | 24 | | | |
| Artillery | | | | 3 | | | | 96 |
| 5th/11 | | | | 4 | | 3 | | 266 |
| 6th/11 | | | | 2 | | 2 | 3 | 330 |
| 7th/11 | | | | | | | | |
| Engineers 11th Co/1st Regt | | | | | | | | |
| **4th Division** | | | | | | | | |
| Staff | | | | | | | | |
| **1st Brigade** | | | | | | | | |
| 11th Chasseurs | 1 | 2 | 18 | 58 | | | | |
| 44th | 1 | 7 | 27 | 96 | 3 | | | |
| 60th | 1 | 6 | 7 | 72 | 1 | | | |
| **2nd Brigade** | | | | | | | | |
| 80th | 1 | 5 | 1 | 21 | | | | |
| 85th | | 2 | 1 | 27 | 4 | | | |
| Artillery | | | | | | | | |
| 8th/11 | | 1 | | 4 | | | | 243 |
| 9th/11 | | | | 5 | | }6 | }7 | 607 |
| 10th/11 | | | | 1 | | | | |
| Engineers 12th Co/1st Regt | | | | | | | | |
| **Cavalry Division** | | | | | | | | |
| **1st Brigade** | | | | | | | | |
| 2nd Chasseurs | | 1 | | | | | | |
| 3rd Chasseurs | | | | | | | | |
| 10th Chasseurs | | | | | | | | |
| **2nd Brigade** | | | | | | | | |

| | | | | | | | | |
|---|---|---|---|---|---|---|---|---|
| 2nd Dragoons | | | | 7 | | | | |
| 4th Dragoons | | | | 5 | | | | |
| 3rd Brigade | | | | | | | | |
| 5th Dragoons | | 1 | | 6 | | | | |
| 8th Dragoons | | 1 | | 1 | | | | |
| **Reserve Artillery** | | | | | | | | |
| 7th/4 | | | | | | | | |
| 10th/4 | | | | | | | | |
| 11th/11 | | | | | | | | |
| 12th/11 | | | | | | | | }195 |
| 1st/17 | | | | 1 | | | 6 | 25 |
| 2nd/17 | | | | 1 | | | | 90 |
| 3rd/17 | | | | | | | | |
| 4th/17 | | | | | | 1 | | 98 |
| **Engineer Reserve** | | | | | | | | |
| Part 1st Co & 4th Co/1st Regt | | | | | | | | |
| **Total 3rd Corps: 2,840 men** | | | | | | | | |
| **4 Corps** | | | | | | | | |
| General Staff | | 2 | | | | | | |
| **1st Division** | | | | | | | | |
| **1st Brigade** | | | | | | | | |
| 20th Chasseurs | 2 | | 4 | 19 | | | | |
| 1st | | | 2 | 21 | | | | |
| 6th | | | | 5 | | | | |
| **2nd Brigade** | | | | | | | | |
| 57th | | | 1 | 3 | 3 | | | |
| Artillery | | 1 | 1 | 21 | 5 | | | |
| 5th/15 | | | 1 | 7 | | 5 | | 720 |
| 9th/15 | | | 1 | 3 | | 2 | 1 | 320 |
| 12th/15 | | | 1 | 3 | | 2 | 5 | 240 |
| Engineers 9th Co/2nd Regt | | | | 1 | 1 | | | |
| **2nd Division** | | | | | | | | |
| **1st Brigade** | | | | | | | | |
| staff | | 1 | | | | | | |
| 5th Chasseurs | 4 | 3 | 12 | 88 | 12 | | | |
| 13th | 8 | 5 | 25 | 121 | 25 | | | |
| 43rd | | 2 | 3 | 14 | | | | |
| **2nd Brigade** | | | | | | | | |

| | | | | | | | | |
|---|---|---|---|---|---|---|---|---|
| 64th | 7 | 9 | 22 | 118 | 109 | | | |
| 98th | | 1 | 1 | 11 | 5 | | | |
| Artllery | | | | | | | | |
| 5th/1 | | | 1 | 7 | | 5 | | 720 |
| 6th/1 | | 1 | | | | 2 | 1 | 320 |
| 7th/1 | | | 1 | 6 | 2 | 7 | | 330 |
| Engineers 10th Co/2nd Regt | | | | | | | | |
| **3rd Division** | | | | | | | | |
| staff | | 1 | | | | | | |
| **1st Brigade** | | | | | | | | |
| 2nd Chasseurs | | | | | | | | |
| 15th | | | | 1 | | | | |
| 33rd | | | | | | | | |
| **2nd Brigade** | | | | | | | | |
| 54th | | | | | | | | |
| 65th | | 1 | 1 | 14 | | | | |
| Artllery | | | | | | | | |
| 8th/1 | | | 1 | 1 | | 1 | 1 | |
| 9th/1 | | | | 1 | | 5 | 3 | 74 |
| 10th/1 | | | | 3 | | | 6 | 111 |
| Engineers 13th Co/2nd Regt | | | | | | | | |
| **Cavalry Division** | | | | | | | | |
| **1st Brigade** | | | | | | | | |
| 2nd Hussars | | | | | | | | |
| 7th Hussars | | | | 2 | | | | |
| **2nd Brigade** | | | | | | | | |
| 3rd Dragoons | | | | 1 | | | | |
| 11th Dragoons | | | | | | | | |
| **Reserve Artillery** | | | | | | | | |
| 11th/1 | | | | 2 | | | 2 | 106 |
| 12th/1 | | | | 1 | | | | 38 |
| 6th/8 | | | | | | | | |
| 9th/8 | | | | 1 | | | | 5 |
| 5th/17 | | | | | | | | |
| 6th/17 | | | | 1 | 1 | | | |
| Engineer Reserves | | | | | | | | |
| 2nd Co/2 Regt | | | | | | | | |
| **Total 4 Corps: 768 men** | | | | | | | | |

| | | | | | | | | |
|---|---|---|---|---|---|---|---|---|
| **Imperial Garde** | | | | | | | | |
| **1st Division** | | | | | | | | |
| Artillery | | | | | | | | |
| 1st | | | | | | | | |
| 2nd | | | | | | | | 10 |
| 5th | | | | | | | | 15 |
| **Total Imperial Garde: 25 men** | | | | | | | | |
| **2 Corps** | | | | | | | | |
| **3rd Division** | | | | | | | | |
| Artillery | | | | | | | | |
| 7th/15 | | | | 1 | | | | 29 |
| 8th/15 | | | | | | | | 1 |
| 11th/15 | | | | 1 | | | | 130 |
| **Total 2 Corps: 162 men** | | | | | | | | |
| **Reserve Artillery** | | | | | | | | |
| 1st/18 | | | | | | 1 | | |
| 2nd/18 | | | | | | 1 | | |
| 3rd/18 | | | | 2 | | | | 15 |
| 4th/18 | | | | | | | | |
| 5th/18 | | | | 1 | | 5 | 3 | 31 |
| 6th/18 | | | | 1 | | 1 | | |
| 7th/18 | | | | | | | | |
| 8th/18 | | | | | | | | |
| **Total Reserve Artillery: 4 men** | | | | | | | | |
| **Fort de Queuleu** | | | | | | | | 68 de 24 |
| | | | | | | | | 10 de 12 |
| **Summary** | | | | | | | | |
| 3 Corps | 37 | 116 | 268 | 1,903 | 546 | 22 | 22 | 3,224 |
| 4 Corps | 22 | 30 | 78 | 475 | 163 | 22 | 20 | 2,466 |
| Garde | | | | | | | | 25 |
| 2 Corps | | | | 2 | | | | 160 |
| Res Art | | | | 4 | | 8 | 3 | 46 |
| Ft de Queuleu | | | | | | | | 78 |
| **Sub Totals** | 59 | 146 | 346 | 2,384 | 709 | 52 | 45 | 5,999 |
| **Grand Total: 3,614** | | | | | | | | |

# Appendix IV

# German losses, Borny

| German casualties at Borny | Killed | | | Wounded | | | Missing | | | Total | | | Rounds Fired | |
|---|---|---|---|---|---|---|---|---|---|---|---|---|---|---|
| | Officers | Men | Horses | Officers | Men | Horses | Officers | Men | Horses | Officers | Men | Horses | Shell | Case |
| **I Corps** | | | | | | | | | | | | | | |
| **1st Infantry Division** | | | | | | | | | | | | | | |
| Staff | | | | 1 | | | | | | 1 | | | | |
| **1st Infantry Brigade** | | | | | | | | | | | | | | |
| staff | | | 1 | | | | | | | | | 1 | | |
| 1st (Crown Prince) Grenadiers | | | | | 6 | | | | | | 6 | | | |
| 41st Regiment | | 7 | 2 | 1 | 46 | | | 2 | | 1 | 55 | 2 | | |
| **2nd Infantry Brigade** | | | | | | | | | | | | | | |
| 3rd Grenadiers | 6 | 137 | 6 | 17 | 418 | 2 | | 27 | | 23 | 582 | 8 | | |
| 43rd Regiment | 11 | 202 | 3 | 21 | 519 | | | 14 | 1 | 32 | 735 | 4 | | |
| 1st Rifle Battalion | 3 | 80 | | 8 | 209 | | | | | 11 | 289 | | | |
| 1st Dragoons(Prince Albrect of Prussia) | | 1 | 3 | | 3 | 2 | | | | | 4 | 5 | | |
| 1st Field Division, 1st FA Regiment | | 5 | 34 | 7 | 40 | 23 | | | | 7 | 45 | 57 | | |
| 1st heavy | | | | | | | | | | | | | 163 | |
| 2nd heavy | | | | | | | | | | | | | 124 | |
| 1st light | | | | | | | | | | | | | 302 | 6 |
| 2nd heavy | | | | | | | | | | | | | 280 | |
| **Total of 1st Infantry Division** | 20 | 432 | 49 | 55 | 1,241 | 27 | | 43 | 1 | 75 | 1,716 | 77 | 869 | 6 |
| **2nd Infantry Division** | | | | | | | | | | | | | | |
| **3rd Infantry Brigade** | | | | | | | | | | | | | | |
| staff | | | 2 | | | | | | | | | 2 | | |
| 4th Grenadiers | 9 | 76 | 7 | 10 | 380 | 3 | | 27 | 2 | 19 | 483 | 12 | | |
| 44th Regiment | 8 | 126 | | 15 | 324 | 3 | | 12 | | 23 | 462 | 3 | | |
| **4th Infantry Brigade** | | | | | | | | | | | | | | |
| 5th Grenadiers | | | | | 10 | | | | | | 10 | | | |

| | | | | | | | | | | | | | | |
|---|---|---|---|---|---|---|---|---|---|---|---|---|---|---|
| 10th Dragoons | | 3 | 3 | | 8 | 12 | | | | | 11 | 15 | | |
| 3rd Field Division, 1st Field Artillery Regiment | | 1 | 2 | | 7 | 6 | | | | | 8 | 8 | | |
| 5th heavy | | | | | | | | | | | | | 100 | |
| 6th heavy | | | | | | | | | | | | | 46 | |
| 5th light | | | | | | | | | | | | | 57 | |
| 6th light | | | | | | | | | | | | | 315 | |
| 1st Field Pioneer Company 1 Corps | | 1 | | | 3 | | | | | | 4 | | | |
| No 2 Sanitary Detachment | | | | | 1 | | | | | | 1 | | | |
| **Total of 2nd Infantry Division** | 17 | 207 | 14 | 25 | 733 | 24 | | 39 | 2 | 42 | 979 | 40 | 518 | |
| **Corps Artillery** | | | | | | | | | | | | | | |
| Horse Artillery & 2nd Field Division, 1st Field Artillery Regiment | | 1 | 15 | | 7 | 11 | | | | | 8 | 26 | | |
| 2nd HA | | | | | | | | | | | | | 168 | |
| 3rd HA | | | | | | | | | | | | | 175 | |
| 3rd heavy | | | | | | | | | | | | | 35 | |
| 4th heavy | | | | | | | | | | | | | 75 | |
| 3rd light | | | | | | | | | | | | | 1 | |
| 4th light | | | | | | | | | | | | | 1 | |
| 3rd Sanitary Detachment | | | 1 | 1 | | 1 | | | | | | | | |
| **Total Corps Artillery** | | 1 | 16 | 1 | 7 | 12 | | | | | 8 | 26 | 455 | |
| **Total I Corps** | 37 | 640 | 79 | 81 | 1,981 | 63 | | 82 | 3 | 118 | 2,703 | 145 | 1,842 | 6 |
| **VII Corps** | | | | | | | | | | | | | | |
| Staff | | | | | 1 | 1 | | | | | 1 | 1 | | |
| **13th Infantry Division** | | | | | | | | | | | | | | |
| Staff | | | 1 | | | 1 | | | | | | 2 | | |
| **25th Infantry Brigade** | | | | | | | | | | | | | | |
| Staff | | | | 2 | | 1 | | | | 2 | | 1 | | |
| 13th Regiment | 6 | 72 | 3 | 7 | 190 | 2 | | 2 | | 13 | 264 | 5 | | |
| 73rd Fusiliers | 8 | 96 | 3 | 12 | 343 | | | 31 | | 20 | 470 | 3 | | |
| **26th Infantry Brigade** | | | | | | | | | | | | | | |
| 15th Regiment | 7 | 123 | 6 | 22 | 334 | 1 | | 6 | | 29 | 463 | 7 | | |
| 55th Regiment | 5 | 136 | | 16 | 389 | | | | | 21 | 525 | | | |
| 7th Rifle Battalion | 1 | 12 | | 2 | 28 | 34 | | 1 | | 6 | 40 | 54 | | |
| 8th Hussars | | | 3 | | 4 | 7 | | | | | 4 | 10 | | |
| 3rd Field Division, 7th FA Regiment | 4 | 11 | 20 | 2 | 28 | 34 | | 1 | | 6 | 40 | 54 | | |
| 5th heavy | | | | | | | | | | | | | 28 | |

| | | | | | | | | | | | | | | |
|---|---|---|---|---|---|---|---|---|---|---|---|---|---|---|
| 6th heavy | | | | | | | | | | | | | 182 | |
| 5th light | | | | | | | | | | | | | 134 | |
| 6th light | | | | | | | | | | | | | 134 | |
| 2nd Field Pioneer Company VII Corps | | 1 | | | 1 | 2 | | | | | 2 | 2 | | |
| No 1 Sanitary Detachment | | 1 | | | | | | | | | 1 | | | |
| **Total 13th Division** | 31 | 452 | 36 | 63 | 1,317 | 82 | | 41 | | 97 | 1,809 | 138 | 478 | |
| **14th Infantry Division** | | | | | | | | | | | | | | |
| **27th Infantry Brigade** | | | | | | | | | | | | | | |
| 74th Regiment | | | | | | | | | | | | | | |
| 39th Fusiliers | | | | | 2 | | | | | | 2 | | | |
| **28th Infantry Brigade** | | | | | | | | | | | | | | |
| 53rd Regiment | 2 | 9 | | 5 | 56 | | | | | 7 | 65 | | | |
| 77th Regiment | | 4 | | 3 | 47 | | | 2 | | 3 | 53 | | | |
| 15th Hussars | | | | | | | | | | | | | | |
| 1st Field Division, 7th FA Regiment | | | 1 | | | | | | | | | 1 | | |
| 2nd heavy | | | | | | | | | | | | | | |
| 1st light | | | | | | | | | | | | | 7 | |
| 2nd light | | | | | | | | | | | | | | |
| **Total 14th Division** | | | | | | | | | | | | | | |
| **Corps Artillery** | | | | | | | | | | | | | | |
| Horse Artillery, and 2nd Field Artillery Division, 7th Field Artillery Regiment | | 1 | | | 3 | 5 | | | | | 4 | 5 | | |
| 2nd horse artillery | | | | | | | | | | | | | 58 | |
| 3rd horse artillery | | | | | | | | | | | | | 68 | |
| 4th heavy | | | | | | | | | | | | | 1 | |
| **Total Corps Artillery** | | 1 | | | 3 | 5 | | | | | 4 | 5 | 127 | |
| **IX Corps** | | | | | | | | | | | | | | |
| **18th Infantry Division** | | | | | | | | | | | | | | |
| **35th Infantry Brigade** | | | | | | | | | | | | | | |
| 36th Fusiliers | | 12 | | | 19 | | | | | | 31 | | | |
| 84th Regiment | | | | | 1 | | | 3 | | | 4 | | | |
| 1st Field Division, 9th FA Regiment | | | | | | | | | | | | | | |
| 2nd heavy | | | | | | | | | | | | | 26 | |
| 2nd light | | | | | | | | | | | | | 76 | |
| **Total 18th Division** | | 12 | | | 20 | | | 3 | | | 35 | | 102 | |
| **1st Cavalry Division** | | | | | | | | | | | | | | |

| | | | | | | | | | | | | | | |
|---|---|---|---|---|---|---|---|---|---|---|---|---|---|---|
| **1st Cavalry Brigade** | | | | | | | | | | | | | | |
| 2nd Cuirassiers | | | 1 | | | | | | | | | 1 | | |
| **2nd Cavalry Brigade** | | | | | | | | | | | | | | |
| 3rd Cuirassiers | | | 2 | | 1 | 1 | | | | | 1 | 3 | | |
| 1st Horse Artillery Battery 1st Field Artillery Regiment | | | | | 3 | 3 | | | | | 3 | 3 | 227 | |
| **Total of 1st Cavalry Division** | | | 3 | | 4 | 4 | | | | | 4 | 7 | 227 | |
| **3rd Cavalry Division** | | | | | | | | | | | | | | |
| **6th Cavalry Brigade** | | | | | | | | | | | | | | |
| 7th Lancers | | | 2 | | 1 | 1 | | | | | 1 | 3 | | |
| **7th Cavalry Brigade** | | | | | | | | | | | | | | |
| 5th Lancers | | | | | | 1 | | | | | | 1 | | |
| 1st Horse Artillery Battery 7th Field Artillery Regiment | | 1 | | | | | | | | | 1 | | 66 | |
| **Total 3rd Cavalry Division** | | 1 | 2 | | 1 | 2 | | | | | 2 | 4 | 520 | |
| I Corps | 37 | 640 | 79 | 81 | 1,981 | 63 | | 82 | 3 | 118 | 2,703 | 145 | 1,842 | 6 |
| VII Corps | 33 | 466 | 37 | 71 | 1,432 | 55 | | 42 | | 104 | 1,940 | 92 | 732 | |
| IX Corps | | 12 | | | 20 | | | 3 | | | 35 | | 102 | |
| 1st Cav Div | | | 3 | | 4 | 4 | | | | | 4 | 7 | 297 | |
| 3rd Cav Div | | 1 | 2 | | 1 | 2 | | | | | 2 | 4 | 293 | |
| Total | 70 | 1,119 | 121 | 152 | 3,438 | 124 | | 127 | 3 | 222 | 4,684 | 248 | 3,266 | 6 |

# Appendix V

## Note on forces engaged and casualties, 16 August 1870

---

### Vionville: Orders of Battle and Casualty Returns

It is difficult to establish with any degree of accuracy just how many men participated in many of the engagements covered in this and the previous volume; Rezonville is no exception. The respective official histories contain little detail – that of the French makes no mention of the total involved whilst the German account merely comments that their opponents had 'more than twofold' their number. The numerous post war studies written about the battle give wildly conflicting figures and reflect understandable national bias; each side seeking to inflate the number of their opponents whilst downplaying their own strength. To illustrate this disparity, in his account of the battle, Bonnal estimates the two armies at 72,000 French and 58,000 Prussian. Le Faure states that the French army totalled between 110–115,000 men, the Prussians 90,000 whilst Von der Goltz has 125,000 French opposed by 60,000 Prussians. Bonnet has 85,000 Prussians against 96,000 French, Fay 120,000 French and 90/95,000 Prussians. Rousset puts the forces engaged at 136,000 French equipped with 364 guns and 66 mitrailleuses taking the field against 91,000 Prussians with 222 guns. Hoffbauer is probably closer to the mark with 138,000 French with 476 guns opposed by 67,000 Prussians with 222 guns. Somewhat surprisingly given the usual tendency of the authors to downplay the number of German forces engaged, the figure given in the appendices of their official history total some 93,000 men with 246 guns. To make any approximation of forces engaged even more problematic, both sides continued to receive reinforcements during the day and although not all those present took part in the fighting, undoubtedly the French had the advantage of superior numbers.

In compiling the German Order of Battle I have used *Heft 11* of the *Kriegsgeschichtliche Einzelschriften* published in 1899 which took advantage of the detailed research into regimental records undertaken in the years after the war and which estimates the numbers of Prussians engaged at 52,075 infantry, 10,920 cavalry and 228 guns, although the forces detailed in this work differ somewhat with the returns listed in the German official history.

The *Kriegsgeschichtliche* adds a further level of complication by seeking to differentiate between those units present but who took no part in the fighting and those actually engaged and again, cross referencing this information against the casualty returns given in the official history, it is difficult to reconcile both accounts. With regard to Bazaine's army, I have used the numerous returns prepared pre and post the battle as detailed within the French official history and then subtracted or added back the losses suffered on the 16th as appropriate. Unsurprisingly, the figures derived from this exercise do not precisely tally but are within a few percent of one another and so provide a reasonable basis on which to estimate the force Bazaine had at his disposal.

To further complicate matters, the manner in which the French numbers are collated are far from consistent and vary greatly between corps and divisions. Some returns simply provide totals for 'hommes' and 'cheveaux'; others go into minute detail, listing staff, fighting troops, ancillaries, non-combatants and train and even going so far as to differentiate between the number of horses and mules present in a particular unit. The relevant volume of the French official history published in 1904, *Les Opérations autour de Metz*, III, *Documents Annexes*, includes a table giving the total number of battalions, squadrons and batteries present on 17 August which gives the average number of men available per battalion, squadron and battery but, as it makes clear, 'the average manpower available doesn't only include the men actually present in the ranks (the precise number of men present being impossible to determine from the available documents) but also all those who were detached for the conduct and escort of regimental trains or battery reserves'. It is noted that the battalions of chasseurs have, in general, a much greater strength than those of the battalions of the line, the average size of these is thus considerably increased. The same remark applies to the 'batteries de 12' and some horse artillery batteries, which also include the average of the 'batteries montées de 4' from the artillery reserve. The table does not take into account the two escort squadrons of Marshal Bazaine nor that of Marshal Canrobert; the other escort squadrons are included among the cavalry divisions of which they formed part. The figures taken from this work produces a total of 119,427 infantry, 13,200 cavalry with 498 guns, subject to all the various caveats as set out in the official history. It is difficult to reconcile the various accounts especially given the lack of any uniform basis on which the figures were compiled, but the best estimate would indicate that the French had around 118–120,000 infantry, 13–14,000 cavalry, 408 guns and 54 mitrailleuses to hand, but the dearth of orders from Bazaine and the lack of initiative displayed by the subordinate corps commanders, meant many of the troops present took little or no part in the fighting.

Similar problems exist with casualty returns; both French and German official histories provide detailed breakdowns, listing numbers of officers and men killed, wounded or missing, together with numbers of horses lost and ammunition expended. However, no differentiation is made between those slightly wounded who remained with their regiments or re-joined the ranks after a short absence and those more seriously injured who were sent to the rear for treatment. Similar difficulties arise with those listed as missing; many were no doubt dead, captured or otherwise incapacitated but others returned to their regiments at a later date. To illustrate how these factors can impact on numbers, the French official history refers to the returns compiled immediately after the battle listing losses of 837 officers and 16,117 men and those prepared in September, by which time regimental rolls had been checked and amended, which show revised total casualties of 13,761. For example, 2 Corps losses were recorded as 5,081 immediately after the battle; in September the figure was corrected to only 4,190. Indicative of the problems faced by staff officers compiling such returns, close scrutiny of the French post combat reports reveals differing numbers of casualties recorded at regimental, brigade and divisional level for the same formation.

The French casualty figures reproduced in this volume are taken from the relevant volume of their official history dealing with *Les Opérations autour de Metz* which relied in turn, on Martinien's *Archives historiques* for losses amongst officers and the information furnished by the various corps d'armee for other ranks. As the official history cautions, the information furnished by the individual corps was often erroneous, as illustrated by the example cited and given the confusion which existed during the period of the three great battles around Metz, this is perhaps not surprising. Therefore, during September when the army had settled into their new bivouacs around Metz, the various units undertook an exercise to revise and double check the information provided in the immediate aftermath of each battle. Sometime around 25 September, the general staff produced new tables of losses, which after checking and verification with the relevant unit, resulted in the figures which are given in the official history.

As the authors of this work counsel, the distribution of casualties between the various categories of tués, blessés et disparus does need to treated with some caution; given the retreats which followed these engagements, it was often impossible to determine who had been killed, wounded or simply captured and evidence from those who had been present at the battle was, for understandable reasons, not always reliable. Usually, it was only after a death had been seen by three witnesses was it recorded as such and even then, errors still arose. For this reason, the numbers of men recorded as missing are often inflated (the parent unit still being able to draw down rations for men listed as disparus) but as far as the overall unit casualties are concerned, the sum of the three categories of killed, wounded and missing can be taken as a realistic representation of their loss.

The Prussians casualty returns are not immune from such mistakes; Hoffbauer records in great detail the discrepancies in the casualties suffered by Wedell's 38th Brigade as listed in the regimental history with those given in the German official history. Such confusion is understandable in the immediate aftermath of any battle, especially for the losing side when commanders had more pressing concerns, but it does serve to emphasise that all Orders of Battle and casualty returns should always be treated with caution; they offer no more than an approximate snapshot of the strength or losses incurred by any particular body during a particular engagement. Subject to this important caveat, they do serve to put the forces available and the casualties suffered in some context and if nothing else, demonstrate the ferocity of the fighting.

# Appendix VI

## German Order of Battle, Rezonville

| German forces at Vionville | Officers | Men | Battalions | Men | Squadrons | Guns | Engineer Co's |
|---|---|---|---|---|---|---|---|
| **II Army: Commander in Chief: HRH General of Cavalry Prince Friedrick Charles of Prussia. Chief of General Staff: Maj General v Stiehle. Staff Officers: Schmidt, v Haeseler, Steffen, Richthoffen, Hugo, v d Goltz.** | | | | | | | |
| **11th Cavalry Brigade:** Maj General v Barby | | | | | | | |
| 4th Cuirassiers: Colonel v Arnim | | | | 560 | 4 | | |
| 13th Lancers: Colonel v Schack | | | | 560˙ | 4 | | |
| 19th Dragoons: Colonel v Trotha | | | | 560 | 4 | | |
| **12th Cavalry Brigade:** Maj General v Bredow | | | | | | | |
| 7th Cuirassiers: Lt Colonel v Larisch | | | | 525 | 3¾ | | |
| 16th Lancers: Major v d Dollen | | | | 560 | 4 | | |
| 13th Dragoons: Colonel v Brauchitsch | | | | 560 | 4 | | |
| **13th Cavalry Brigade:** Maj General v Redern | | | | | | | |
| 10th Hussars:Colonel v Weise | | | | 420 | 3 | | |
| 11th Hussars: Lt Colonel Baron v Eller Eberstein | | | | 560 | 4 | | |
| 17th Hussars: Lt Colonel v Rauch | | | | 560 | 4 | | |
| 1st Horse Artillery Battery 4th Field Artillery Regiment: Captain Bode | | | | | | 6 | |
| 2nd Horse Artillery Battery 4th Field Artillery Regiment: Captain Schirmer | | | | | | 6 | |
| **Total 5th Cavalry Division** | | | | **4,865** | **34¾** | **12** | |

| | | | | | | |
|---|---|---|---|---|---|---|
| **6th Cavalry Division:** Commander: HH Duke William of Mecklenburg-Schwerin. Officer of General Staff: Major v Schonfels. Staff Officers: v Treskow, v Usedom. | | | | | | |
| **14th Cavalry Brigade:** Maj General Baron v Diepenbroick-Gruter | | | | | | |
| 6th Cuirassiers (Emperor Nicholas I of Russia): Lt Colonel Count z Lynar | | | 560 | 4 | | |
| 3rd Lancers (Emperor of Russia): Colonel Count v d Groben | | | 280 | 2 | | |
| 15th Lancers: Colonel v Avensleben | | | 560 | 4 | | |
| 15th Cavalry Brigade: Maj General v Rauch | | | | | | |
| 3rd Hussars: Colonel v Ziethan | | | 560 | 4 | | |
| 16th Hussars: Colonel v Schmidt | | | 560 | 4 | | |
| 2nd Horse Artillery Battery 3rd Field Artillery Regiment: Captain Wittstock | | | | | 6 | |
| **Total 6th Cavalry Division** | | | **2,520** | **18** | **6** | |
| **III Corps: General Commanding: Lt General v Alvensleben II. Chief of General Staff: Col v Voigts-Rhetz. Commander of Artillery: Maj General v Bulow. Commander of Engineers and Pioneers: Major Sabarth. Staff Officers; v Kretschman, v Stuckradt, v Twardowski.** | | | | | | |
| **5th Infantry Division: Commander: Lt General v Stulpnagel. Officer of General Staff: Major v Lewinski II. Staff Officers: Wodtke, v Bernstorff.** | | | | | | |
| 9th Infantry Brigade: Maj General v Doring | | | | | | |
| 8th Body Guard Grenadiers: Lt Colonel v L'Estoeq | 67 | 2,480 | 2 | | | |
| 48th Regiment: Lt Colonel v Garrelts | 58 | 2,040 | 3 | | | |
| **10th Infantry Brigade:** Maj General V Schwerin | | | | | | |
| 12th Grenadiers: Colonel v Reuter | 44 | 2,040 | 3 | | | |
| 52nd Regiment: Colonel v Wulffen | 76 | 2,630 | 3 | | | |
| 3rd Rifle Battalion: Major v Jena | 23 | 890 | 1 | | | |

| | | | | | | |
|---|---|---|---|---|---|---|
| 12th Dragoons: Major Pfeffer v Salomon | | | | 420 | 3 | |
| 1st Field Division, 3rd FA Regiment; | | | | | | |
| 1 & 2 heavy, 1 & 2 light batteries: Major Gallus | | | | | | 24 |
| No 1 Sanitary Detachment | | | | | | |
| **Total 5th Division** | 268 | 10,080 | 12 | 420 | 3 | 24 |
| **6th Infantry Division: Commander: Lt General Baron v Buddenbrock. Officer of General Staff:Major v Geissler. Staff Officers: Pohl, V Krocher.** | | | | | | |
| 11th Infantry Brigade: Maj General v Rothmaler | | | | | | |
| 20th Regiment: Colonel v Flatow | | | 3 | | | |
| 35th Fusiliers: Colonel du Plessis | | | 3 | | | |
| **12th Infantry Brigade:** Colonel v Bismarck | | | | | | |
| 24th Regiment: Colonel Count zu Dohna | | | 3 | | | |
| 64th Regiment: Colonel Baron Treusch v Buttlar-Brandenfels | | | 3 | | | |
| 2nd Dragoons: Colonel v Drigalski | | | | 560 | 4 | |
| 3rd Field Division, 3rd FA Regiment; | | | | | | |
| 5 & 6 heavy, 5 & 6 light batteries: Major Beck | | | | | | 24 |
| No 2 Sanitary Detachment | | | | | | |
| **Total 6th Division** | | | 12 | | 4 | 24 |
| **Corps Artillery:** Colonel v Dresky Commander 3rd Field Artillery Regiment. | | | | | | |
| Horse Artillery Division, 3rd Field Artillery Regiment, | | | | | | |
| 1 & 3 horse artillery batteries: Major Lentz | | | | | | 12 |
| 2nd Field Artillery Division, 3rd Field Artillery Regiment | | | | | | |
| 3 & 4 heavy,3 & 4 light batteries: Major v Lyncker | | | | | | 24 |
| No 3 Sanitary Detachment | | | | | | |
| **Total Corps Artillery:** | | | | | | 36 |
| **Total Corps** | | | 24 | | 7 | 84 |

| | | | | | | | |
|---|---|---|---|---|---|---|---|
| **X Corps: General Commanding: General of Infantry v Voigts-Rhetz. Chief of General Staff: Lt Colonel v Caprivi. Commander of Artillery: Colonel Baron v de Becke. Commander of Engineers and Pioneers: Lt Colonel v Cramer. Staff Officers; Seebeck, Baron v Hoiningen or Huene, Podbielski.** | | | | | | | |
| **19th Infantry Division: Commander: Lt General v Schwarzkoppen. Officer of General Staff: Major v Scherff. Staff Officers: Eggeling, v Bernuth.** | | | | | | | |
| 37th Infantry Brigade: Colonel Lehmann | | | | | | | |
| 78th Regiment: Colonel Baron v Lyncker | | | 2 | | | | |
| 91st Regiment: Colonel v Kameke | | | 2½ | | | | |
| **38th Infantry Brigade:** Maj General v Wedell | | | | | | | |
| 16th Regiment: Colonel v Brixen | 62 | 2,721 | 3 | | | | |
| 57th Regiment: Colonel v Cranach | 33 | 1,855 | 2 | | | | |
| 9th Dragoons: Lt Colonel Count v Hardenberg | | | | 560 | 4 | | |
| 1st Field Division, 10th FA Regiment; | | | | | | | |
| 1 & 2 heavy, 1& 2 light batteries: Lt Colonel Schaumann | | | | | | 24 | |
| 2nd Field Pioneer Company Xth Corps with entrenching tool column: Captain Meyer | | | | | | | 1 |
| 3rd Field Pioneer Company Xth Corps: Captain Lindow | | | | | | | 1 |
| No 1 Sanitary Detachment | | | | | | | |
| **Total 19th Division** | | | 9½ | | 4 | 24 | 2 |
| **20th Infantry Division: Commander: Maj General v Kraatz-Koschlau. Officer of General Staff: Captain Baron v Willisen. Staff Officers: v Schenckendorf, Baron v Elverfeldt.** | | | | | | | |
| 39th Infantry Brigade: Maj General v Woyna | | | | | | | |
| 56th Regiment: Colonel v Block | | | 2 | | | | |
| 79th Regiment: Colonel v Valentini | | | 2 | | | | |

| | | | | | | | |
|---|---|---|---|---|---|---|---|
| **40th Infantry Brigade:** Maj General v Diringshofen | | | | | | | |
| 17th Regiment: Colonel v Ehrenberg | | | 3 | | | | |
| 92nd Regiment: Colonel Haberland | | | 2 | | | | |
| 10th Rifle Battalion: Major Dunin v Przychowsky | | | 1 | | | | |
| 16th Dragoons: Lt Colonel v Waldow | | | | 560 | 4 | | |
| 2rd Field Division, 10th FA Regiment; | | | | | | | |
| 3 & 4 heavy, 3 & 4 light batteries: Major Krause | | | | | | 24 | |
| No 2 Sanitary Detachment | | | | | | | |
| **Total 20th Division** | | | **10** | | **4** | **24** | |
| **Corps Artillery:** Colonel Baron v d Goltz Commander 10th Field Artillery Regiment | | | | | | | |
| Horse Artillery Division, 10th Field Artillery Regiment, | | | | | | | |
| 1 & 3 horse artillery batteries: Major Korber | | | | | | 12 | |
| 3rd Field Artillery Division, 10th Field Artillery Regiment | | | | | | | |
| 5 & 6 heavy, 5 & 6 light batteries: Lt Colonel Cotta | | | | | | 24 | |
| No 3 Sanitary Detachment | | | | | | | |
| **Total Corps Artillery** | | | | | | 36 | |
| **Total X Corps** | | | **19½** | | **8** | **84** | **2** |
| **Attached to X Army Corps** | | | | | | | |
| **3rd Brigade of Dragoons of the Guard** | | | | | | | |
| 1st Dragoons of the Guard: Colonel v Auerswald | | | | 560 | 4 | | |
| 2nd Dragoons of the Guard: Colonel Count v Finckenstein | | | | 560 | 4 | | |
| 1st Horse Artillery battery Guard Field Artillery Regiment | | | | | | 6 | |
| **Total Guards Brigade** | | | | | **8** | **6** | |
| **I Army** | | | | | | | |
| **VIII Corps:** General Commanding: General of Infantry v Goeben. | | | | | | | |
| **16th Infantry Division:** Commander: Lt General v Barnekow | | | | | | | |

| | | | | | | | |
|---|---|---|---|---|---|---|---|
| **32nd Infantry Brigade:** Colonel v Rex | | | | | | | |
| 40th Fusiliers: Colonel Baron v Eberstein | 38 | 2,055 | 3 | | | | |
| 72nd Regiment: Colonel v Helldorf | | 2,798 | 3 | | | | |
| 9th Hussars: Colonel v Wittich or Hinzmann-Hallman | | | | | 3 | | |
| 3rd Field Division, 8th FA Regiment; | | | | | | | |
| 5 & 6 heavy, 5 light batteries: Lt Colonel Hildebrandt | | | | | | 18 | |
| **Total 16th Division** | | **4,891** | **6** | | **3** | **18** | |
| **IX Army Corps:** General Commanding: General of Infantry v Manstein | | | | | | | |
| **18th Infantry Division (Placed under Orders of VIII Army Corps): Commander: Lt General Baron v Wrangel. Officer of General Staff: Major Lust.** | | | | | | | |
| 11th Grenadiers: Colonel v Schoning | 75 | 2,710 | 3 | | | | |
| **Total 18th Division** | **75** | **2,710** | **3** | | | | |
| **25th Grand Ducal Hesse Infantry Division: Commander:** Lt General HRH Prince Louis of Hesse. Commander of Field Artillery: Lt Colonel Stumpff. | | | | | | | |
| **49th Infantry Brigade: Maj General v Wittich** | | | | | | | |
| 1st Body Guard Regiment: Lt Colonel Coulmann | | | 2 | | | | |
| 2nd (Grand Duke) Regiment:Colonel Kraus | | | 2 | | | | |
| 1st Cavalry (Guard Chevaux Legers) Lt Colonel v Grolmann | | | | | 4 | | |
| Field Division, 1st & 2nd heavy and 1st light batteries: | | | | | | 18 | |
| **Total Hessian Division** | | | **4** | | **4** | **18** | |
| **Total Forces engaged** | | | **57** | | **78** | **228** | **2** |

| | | | | | | | | | | | | | | |
|---|---|---|---|---|---|---|---|---|---|---|---|---|---|---|
| 3rd Guard Voltigeur Regiment: Colonel Lian | | | | 3 | | | | | | | | | | |
| 4th Guard Voltigeur Regiment: Colonel Ponsard | | | | 3 | | | | | | | | | | |
| Divisional Artillery: Lieut. Colonel Gerbaut | | | | | | | | | | | | | | |
| No 1 Battery Field Artillery Regiment of the Guard | | | | | | | | | | 6 | | | | |
| No 2 Battery Field Artillery Regiment of the Guard | | | | | | | | | | 6 | | | | |
| No 5 Battery Field Artillery Regiment of the Guard | | | | | | | | | | | 6 | | | |
| Total Artillery | | | | | | | | 17 | 418 | | | | | |
| Engineers : 8th Company of 3rd Engineer Regiment | | | | | | | | | | | | 4 | 109 | 1 |
| **1st Division Total** | | | 8,108 | 13 | | | | 17 | 418 | 12 | 6 | 4 | 109 | 1 |
| **2nd Division: Commander: General of Division Picard** | | | | | | | | | | | | | | |
| **1st Brigade:** General of Brigade Jeanningros** | | | | | | | | | | | | | | |
| Guard Zouave Regiment: Colonel Giraud | 49 | 1,266 | | 2 | | | | | | | | | | |
| 1st Guard Grenadier Regiment: Colonel Theologue | 82 | 1,956 | | 3 | | | | | | | | | | |
| **2nd Brigade:** General of Brigade le Poitevin de la Croix Vaubois** | | | | | | | | | | | | | | |
| 2nd Guard Grenadier Regiment: Colonel Lecointe | 94 | 2,395 | | 3 | | | | | | | | | | |

| | | | | | | | | | | | | | | |
|---|---|---|---|---|---|---|---|---|---|---|---|---|---|---|
| 3rd Guard Grenadier Regiment: Colonel Cousin | 73 | 1,642 | | 2* | | | | | | | | | | |
| **Divisional Artillery:** Lieut. Colonel Denecey de Cervilly | | | | | | | | | | | | | | |
| No 3 Battery Field Artillery Regiment of the Guard | | | | | | | | | | 6 | | | | |
| No 4 Battery Field Artillery Regiment of the Guard | | | | | | | | | | 6 | | | | |
| No 6 Battery Field Artillery Regiment of the Guard | | | | | | | | | | | 6 | | | |
| **Total Artillery** | | | | | | | | 19 | 540 | | | | | |
| Engineers : 10th Company of 3rd Engineer Regiment | | | | | | | | | | | | 2 | 59 | 1 |
| **2nd Division Total** | 298 | 7,259 | 7,557 | 10 | | | | 19 | 540 | 12 | 6 | 2 | 59 | 1 |
| **Cavalry Division:*** Commander: General of Division Desvaux | | | | | | | | | | | | | | |
| **1st Brigade:** General of Brigade Halna du Fretay | | | | | | | | | | | | | | |
| Guides Regiment: Colonel de Percin-Northumberland | | | | | 40 | 530 | 4* | | | | | | | |
| Chasseurs a Cheval: Colonel de Montarby | | | | | 48 | 664 | 5 | | | | | | | |
| **2nd Brigade:** General of Division de France | | | | | | | | | | | | | | |
| Lancers of the Guard: Colonel Latheulade | | | | | 39 | 537 | 5 | | | | | | | |
| Dragoons of the Guard: Colonel Sautereau Dupart | | | | | 46 | 655 | 4* | | | | | | | |

| | | | | | | | | | | | | |
|---|---|---|---|---|---|---|---|---|---|---|---|---|
| **3rd Brigade:** General of Brigade du Preuil | | | | | | | | | | | | |
| Guard Cuirassier Regiment: Colonel Dupressoir | | | 48 | 655 | 5 | | | | | | | |
| Guard Carabinier Regiment: Colonel Petit | | | 47 | 638 | 5 | | | | | | | |
| **Divisional Artillery** | | | | | | | | | | | | |
| No 1 Battery Horse Artillery of the Guard | | | | | | 5 | 142 | 6 | | | | |
| No 2 Battery Horse Artillery of the Guard | | | | | | 6 | 142 | 6 | | | | |
| **Cavalry Division Total** | | | 268* | 3679* | 20 | 11 | 284 | 12 | | | | |
| **Artillery Reserve** | | | | | | | | | | | | |
| Commander: Colonel Clappier | | | | | | | | | | | | |
| No 3 Battery Horse Artillery of the Guard | | | | | | | | 6 | | | | |
| No 4 Battery Horse Artillery of the Guard | | | | | | | | 6 | | | | |
| No 5 Battery Horse Artillery of the Guard | | | | | | | | 6 | | | | |
| No 6 Battery Horse Artillery of the Guard | | | | | | | | 6 | | | | |
| **Total Artillery Reserve** | | | | | | 25 | 587 | 24 | | | | |
| **Total Guard** | | 15,665 | 23 | 268 | 3,679 | | 72 | 1,829 | 60 | 12 | 4 | 168 | 2 |
| * Strength of Guard taken from returns of 13th/14th August | | | | | | | | | | | | |
| **Figures reflect effectives on 17th + losses incurred on 16th | | | | | | | | | | | | |
| *** Battalion/ Squadron strength reduced to reflect detachments on escort duties | | | | | | | | | | | | |

| | | | | | | | | | | | | | |
|---|---|---|---|---|---|---|---|---|---|---|---|---|---|
| **2 Corps:*** General Commanding: General of Division Frossard | 13 | | | | | | | | | | | | |
| **1st Division:** Commander: General of Division Verge | 12 | | | | | | | | | | | | |
| **1st Brigade:** General of Brigade Letellier-Valaze | | | | | | | | | | | | | |
| 3rd Chasseur Battalion: Commandant Thoina | 18 | 594 | | 1 | | | | | | | | | |
| 32nd Line Infantry Regiment: Colonel Merle | 50 | 1,718 | | 3 | | | | | | | | | |
| 55th Line Infantry Regiment: Colonel de Waldner de Freudenstein | 63 | 1,895 | | 3 | | | | | | | | | |
| **2nd Brigade:** General of Brigade Jolivet | | | | | | | | | | | | | |
| 76th Line Infantry Regiment: Colonel Brice | 54 | 1,750 | | 3 | | | | | | | | | |
| 77th Line Infantry Regiment: Colonel Fevrier | 63 | 1,709 | | 3 | | | | | | | | | |
| **Divisional Artillery:** Lieut. Colonel Chavaudret | | | | | | | | | | | | | |
| No 5 Battery 5th Field Artillery Regiment | | | | | | | | | | 6 | | | |
| No 12 Battery 5th Field Artillery Regiment | | | | | | | | | | 6 | | | |
| No 6 Battery 5th Field Artillery Regiment | | | | | | | | | | | 6 | | |
| **Artillery Total** | | | | | | | | 18 | 447 | | | | |
| Engineers : 9th Company of 3rd Engineer Regiment | | | | | | | | | | | | 5 | 151 | 1 |

| | | | | | | | | | | | | | | |
|---|---|---|---|---|---|---|---|---|---|---|---|---|---|---|
| 15th Chasseur Battalion: Commandant Lafouge | | | | 1 | | | | | | | | | | |
| 19th Line Infantry Regiment: Colonel de Launay | | | | 3 | | | | | | | | | | |
| 41st Line Infantry Regiment: Colonel Saussier | | | | 3 | | | | | | | | | | |
| **2nd Brigade:** General of Division Duplessis | | | | | | | | | | | | | | |
| 69th Line Infantry Regiment: Colonel le Tourneur | | | | 3 | | | | | | | | | | |
| 90th Line Infantry Regiment: Colonel de Courcy | | | | 3 | | | | | | | | | | |
| **Divisional Artillery:** Lieut. Colonel Delange | | | | | | | | | | | | | | |
| No 11 Battery 4th Field Artillery Regiment | | | | | | | | | | 6 | | | | |
| No 12 Battery 4th Field Artillery Regiment | | | | | | | | | | 6 | | | | |
| No 9 Battery 4th Field Artillery Regiment | | | | | | | | | | | 6 | | | |
| Engineers : 1 Company of 1st Engineer Regiment | | | | | | | | | | | | | | 1 |
| **2nd Division Total** | 281 | 8,907 | 9,188 | 13 | | | | | | 12 | 6 | | | 1 |
| **4th Division:** Commander: General Aymard | | | | | | | | | | | | | | |
| **1st Brigade:** General of Brigade de Brauer | | | | | | | | | | | | | | |
| 11th Chasseur Battalion: Commandant de Pillot | | | | 1 | | | | | | | | | | |

| | | | | | | | | | | | | |
|---|---|---|---|---|---|---|---|---|---|---|---|---|
| 44th Line Infantry Regiment: Colonel Fournier | | | 3 | | | | | | | | | |
| 60th Line Infantry Regiment: Colonel Boissie | | | 3 | | | | | | | | | |
| **2nd Brigade:** General of Brigade Sangle-Ferriere | | | | | | | | | | | | |
| 80th Line Infantry Regiment: Colonel Janin | | | 3 | | | | | | | | | |
| 85th Line Infantry Regiment: Colonel Planchut | | | 3 | | | | | | | | | |
| **Divisional Artillery:** Lieut. Colonel Maucourant | | | | | | | | | | | | |
| No 9 Battery 11th Field Artillery Regiment | | | | | | | | | 6 | | | |
| No 10 Battery 11th Field Artillery Regiment | | | | | | | | | 6 | | | |
| No 8 Battery 11th Field Artillery Regiment | | | | | | | | | | 6 | | |
| Engineers : 1 Company of 1st Engineer Regiment | | | | | | | | | | | | 1 |
| **4th Division Total** | 309 | 9,709 | 10,018 | 13 | | | | | | 12 | 6 | | 1 |
| **Cavalry Division:** Commander: General of Division Clerembault | | | | | | | | | | | | |
| **1st Brigade:** General of Brigade Bruchard | | | | | | | | | | | | |
| 2nd Chasseurs a Cheval: Colonel Pelletier | | | | | | 5 | | | | | | |
| 3rd Chasseurs a Cheval: Colonel Sanson de Sansal | | | | | | 5 | | | | | | |

| | | | | | | | | | | | | | |
|---|---|---|---|---|---|---|---|---|---|---|---|---|---|
| 10th Chasseurs a Cheval: Colonel Nerin | | | | | | 5 | | | | | | | |
| **2nd Brigade:** General of Brigade Gayrault de Maubranches | | | | | | | | | | | | | |
| 2nd Dragoon Regiment: Colonel du Paty de Clam | | | | | | 4 | | | | | | | |
| 4th Dragoon Regiment: Colonel Cornat | | | | | | 4 | | | | | | | |
| **3rd Brigade:** General of Brigade Begougne de Juiniac | | | | | | | | | | | | | |
| 5th Dragoon Regiment: Colonel Lachene | | | | | | 4 | | | | | | | |
| 8th Dragoon Regiment: Colonel Boyer de Fonscolombe | | | | | | 4 | | | | | | | |
| **Cavalry Division Total** | | | | 322 | 4,078 | 31 | | | | | | | |
| **Artillery Reserve:** Commander: Colonel de Lajaille | | | | | | | | | | | | | |
| No 7 Battery 4th Field Artillery Regiment | | | | | | | | 6 | | | | | |
| No 10 Battery 4th Field Artillery Regiment | | | | | | | | 6 | | | | | |
| No 11 Battery 11th Field Artillery Regiment | | | | | | | | 6 | | | | | |
| No 12 Battery 11th Field Artillery Regiment | | | | | | | | 6 | | | | | |
| No 1 Battery 17th Horse Artillery Regiment | | | | | | | | 6 | | | | | |
| No 2 Battery 17th Horse Artillery Regiment | | | | | | | | 6 | | | | | |

| | | | | | | | | | | | | | | |
|---|---|---|---|---|---|---|---|---|---|---|---|---|---|---|
| No 3 Battery 17th Horse Artillery Regiment | | | | | | | | | | 6 | | | | |
| No 4 Battery 17th Horse Artillery Regiment | | | | | | | | | | 6 | | | | |
| **Total Artillery Reserve** | | | | | | | | 43 | 1,345 | | | | | |
| **Engineer Reserve** | | | | | | | | | | | | 15 | 215 | 1½ |
| **Total 3 Corps** | 1,004 | 29,053 | 30,057 | 39 | 322 | 4,078 | 31 | 43 | 1,345 | 84 | 18 | 15 | 215 | 4½ |
| * Strength of 3 Corps taken from Jounal de Marche of 17th August to which have been added losses incurred on 16th | | | | | | | | | | | | | | |
| **4 Corps:**\* General Commanding: General of Division de Ladmirault | 54 | 82 | | | | | | | | | | | | |
| **1st Division:** Commander: General of Division Courtot de Cissey | 10 | | | | | | | | | | | | | |
| **1st Brigade:** General of Brigade Brayer | | | | | | | | | | | | | | |
| 20th Chasseur Battalion: Commandant de Labarriere | 23 | 875 | | 1 | | | | | | | | | | |
| 1st Line Infantry Regiment: Colonel Fremont | 66 | 2,028 | | 3 | | | | | | | | | | |
| 6th Line Infantry Regiment: Colonel Labarthe | 67 | 1,735 | | 3 | | | | | | | | | | |
| 2nd Brigade: General of Brigade de Goldberg | | | | | | | | | | | | | | |
| 57th Line Infantry Regiment: Colonel Giraud | 68 | 2,065 | | 3 | | | | | | | | | | |
| 73rd Line Infantry Regiment: Colonel Supervielle | 63 | 2,226 | | | | | | | | | | | | |

| | | | | | | | | | | | |
|---|---|---|---|---|---|---|---|---|---|---|---|
| **2nd Brigade:** General of Brigade Colin | | | | | | | | | | | |
| 93rd Line Infantry Regiment: Colonel Guazin | 72 | 2,197 | 3 | | | | | | | | |
| 94th Line Infantry Regiment: Colonel de Geslin | 66 | 2,278 | 3 | | | | | | | | |
| **Divisional Artillery:** Lieut. Colonel Jamet | | | | | | | | | | | |
| No 5 Battery 14th Field Artillery Regiment | | | | | | | | 6 | | | |
| No 6 Battery 14th Field Artillery Regiment | | | | | | | | 6 | | | |
| No 7 Battery 14th Field Artillery Regiment | | | | | | | | 6 | | | |
| Engineers: 7th Company of 3rd Engineer Regiment | | | | | | | | | | | 1 |
| **3rd Division Total** | | 9,290 | 12 | | | | | 18 | | | 1 |
| **4th Division:** Commander: General of Division Levassor-Sorval | | | | | | | | | | | |
| **1st Brigade:** General of Brigade de Marguenat | | | | | | | | | | | |
| 25th Line Infantry Regiment: Colonel Gibon | | | 3 | | | | | | | | |
| 26th Line Infantry Regiment: Colonel Hanrion | | | 3 | | | | | | | | |
| **2nd Brigade:** General of Brigade Count De Chanaleilles | | | | | | | | | | | |
| 28th Line Infantry Regiment: Colonel Lamothe | | | 3 | | | | | | | | |
| 70th Line Infantry Regiment: Colonel Bertier | | | 3 | | | | | | | | |

| | | | | | | | | | | | | | |
|---|---|---|---|---|---|---|---|---|---|---|---|---|---|
| From Artillery Reserve: Chef d'escadron Kesner | | | | | | | | | | | | | |
| No 7 Battery 18th Horse Artillery Regiment | | | | | | | | | 6 | | | | |
| No 8 Battery 18th Horse Artillery Regiment | | | | | | | | | 6 | | | | |
| **4th Division Total** | | 9,484 | 12 | | | | | | 12 | | | | |
| **Cavalry Division** | | | | | | | | | | | | | |
| 2nd Chasseurs a Cheval | | | | | | 5 | | | | | | | |
| **Total 6 Corps** | | 31,721 | 40 | | 440 | 5 | | 2,179 | 66 | | | | 2 |
| *Strength of 6 Corps taken from returns of 17th to which have been added losses incurred on 16th | | | | | | | | | | | | | |
| **Cavalry Reserve** | | | | | | | | | | | | | |
| **1st Division:** * Commander: General of Division du Barail | | | | | | | | | | | | | |
| **2nd Brigade:** General of Brigade de Lajaille | | | | | | | | | | | | | |
| 2nd Regiment Chasseurs d'Afrique: Colonel de la Martiniere | | | | 40 | 584 | 5 | | | | | | | |
| * Strength on 13th | | | | | | | | | | | | | |
| **Divisional Artillery:** Chef d'Escadron Loyer | | | | | | | | | | | | | |
| No 5 Battery 19th Horse Artillery Regiment | | | | | | | | | 6 | | | | |
| No 6 Battery 19th Horse Artillery Regiment | | | | | | | | | 6 | | | | |
| **Artillery Total** | | | | | | | 13 | 307 | | | | | |
| **3rd Division:*** Commander: General of Division de Forton | | | | | | | | | | | | | |

| | | | | | | | | | | | | | |
|---|---|---|---|---|---|---|---|---|---|---|---|---|---|
| 1st Brigade: General of Brigade Prince Murat | | | | | | | | | | | | | |
| 1st Dragoon Regiment: Colonel de Forceville | | | | 48 | 470 | 4 | | | | | | | |
| 9th Dragoon Regiment: Colonel Reboul | | | | 45 | 504 | 4 | | | | | | | |
| **2nd Brigade:** General of Brigade de Gramont Duke of Esparre | | | | | | | | | | | | | |
| 7th Cuirassier Regiment: Colonel Nitot | | | | 41 | 526 | 4 | | | | | | | |
| 10th Cuirassier Regiment: Colonel Yuncker | | | | 42 | 473 | 4 | | | | | | | |
| **Divisional Artillery:** Chef d'Escadron Clerc | | | | | | | | | | | | | |
| No 7 Battery 20th Horse Artillery Regiment | | | | | | | | 6 | | | | | |
| No 8 Battery 20th Horse Artillery Regiment | | | | | | | | 6 | | | | | |
| **Artillery Total** | | | | | | | 23 | 409 | | | | | |
| **3rd Division Total** | | | | 176 | 1,973 | 16 | 23 | 409 | 12 | | | | |
| * Strength on 17th to which have been added losses incurred on 16th | | | | | | | | | | | | | |
| **Total Reserve Cavalry** | | | | 216 | 2,557 | 21 | 36 | 718 | 24 | | | | |
| **Artillery Reserve:** Commander: General Canu | | | | | | | | | | | | | |
| **13th Artillery Regiment:** Commander: Colonel Salvador | | | | | | | | | | | | | |
| No 11 Battery | | | | | | | | 6 | | | | | |
| No 12 Battery | | | | | | | | 6 | | | | | |
| **Total 13th Regiment** | | | | | | | | 12 | | | | | |

| | | | | | | | | | | | |
|---|---|---|---|---|---|---|---|---|---|---|---|
| **18th Horse Artillery Regiment:** Commander Colonel Toussaint | | | | | | | | | | | |
| No 1 Battery | | | | | | | 6 | | | | |
| No 2 Battery | | | | | | | 6 | | | | |
| No 3 Battery | | | | | | | 6 | | | | |
| No 4 Battery | | | | | | | 6 | | | | |
| No 5 Battery | | | | | | | 6 | | | | |
| No 6 Battery | | | | | | | 6 | | | | |
| **Total 18th Regiment** | | | | | | | 36 | | | | |
| **Total Reserve Artillery** | | | | | | 1,265 | 48 | | | | |
| **Main Engineer Reserve** | | | | | | | | | | | 3 |
| **Total** | 117,684 | 160 | 15,747 | 96 | | 11,680 | 408 | 54 | 37 | | 15½ |
| Total Guard | 15,665 | | 3,947 | | | 1,901 | 60 | | | 172 | 2 |
| Total 2 Corps | 21,688 | | 2,469 | | | 2,142 | 66 | | | 317 | 2 |
| Total 3 Corps | 30,057 | | 4,078 | | | 1,388 | 84 | | | 230 | 4½ |
| Total 4 Corps | 18,983 | | 2,480 | | | 2,081 | 60 | | | 167 | 2 |
| Total 6 Corps | 31,721 | | 440 | | | 2,179 | 66 | | | | 2 |
| Total Reserve Cavalry | | | 2,773 | | | 754 | 24 | | | | |
| Total Reserve Artillery | | | | | | 1,265 | 48 | | | | |
| Main Engineer Reserve | | | | | | | | | | | 3 |
| **Total** | 118,114* | | 16,187* | | | 11,710* | 408 | | | 886 | 15½ |
| *Includes officers where recorded | | | | | | | | | | | |

Totals: 160¼ battalions (118,114 infantry), 96 squadrons (16,187 cavalry), 408 guns and 54 mitrailleuses (11,710 gunners) and 15½ engineer companies (886 sappers) giving a grand total available on the battlefield of 146,897. 3rd Division 3 Corps had a strength of 10,536 men as at the 17th August and 3rd Division 4 Corps had a strength of 10,169 as at the 13th August which gives a total number of men available in the vicinty of the battlefield of some 167,602 men with 462 guns and mitrailleuses.

| The following table is taken from the French Official history and provides details of the average strength of the battalions, squadrons and batteries present on August 16th. | | | | | | | | |
|---|---|---|---|---|---|---|---|---|
| | No of Battalions | Average Strength | Total | No of Sqadronss | Average Strength | Total | No of batteries | Average Strength | Total |
| **2 Corps** | | | | | | | | | |
| 1st Div | 13 | 580 | 7,540 | | | | 3 | 150 | 450 |
| 2nd Div | 13 | 670 | 8,710 | | | | 3 | 150 | 450 |
| Brigade Lapasset | 6.25 | 630 | 3,937 | 4 | 100 | 400 | 1 | 135 | 135 |
| Divisional Cavalry | | | | 18 | 110 | 1,980 | | | |
| Artillery Reserve | | | | | | | 6 | 160 | 960 |
| Total | 32.25 | | 20,187 | 22 | | 2,380 | 13 | | 1,995 |
| **3 Corps** | | | | | | | | | |
| 1st Div | 13 | 670 | 8,710 | | | | 3 | 150 | 450 |
| 2nd Div | 13 | 580 | 7,540 | | | | 3 | 140 | 420 |
| 3rd Div | 13 | 640 | 8,320 | | | | 3 | 150 | 450 |
| 4th Div | 13 | 630 | 8,190 | | | | 3 | 150 | 450 |
| Divisional Cavalry* | | | | 26 | 110 | 2,860 | | | |
| Artillery Reserve | | | | | | | 8 | 160 | 1,280 |
| Total | 52 | | 32,760 | 26 | | 2,860 | 20 | | 3,050 |
| *This reflects the 4 squadrons from 2nd Chasseurs attached to 6 Corps | | | | | | | | | |
| **4 Corps** | | | | | | | | | |
| 1st Div | 13 | 680 | 8,840 | | | | 3 | 140 | 420 |
| 2nd Div | 13 | 650 | 8,450 | | | | 3 | 150 | 450 |
| 3rd Div | 13 | 690 | 8,970 | | | | 3 | 145 | 435 |
| Divisional Cavalry | | | | 16 | 110 | 1,760 | | | |
| Artillery Reserve | | | | | | | 6 | 160 | 960 |

| | | | | | | | | |
|---|---|---|---|---|---|---|---|---|
| **Total** | **39** | | **26,260** | **16** | | **1,760** | **15** | | **2,265** |
| **6 Corps** | | | | | | | | | |
| 1st Div | 13 | 710 | 9,230 | | | | 4 | 130 | 520 |
| 2nd Div | 3 | 530 | 1,590 | | | | 2 | 180 | 360 |
| 3rd Div | 12 | 670 | 8,040 | | | | 3 | 150 | 450 |
| 4th Div | 12 | 660 | 7,920 | | | | 2 | 135 | 270 |
| 2nd Chasseurs | | | | 4 | 110 | 440 | | | |
| **Total** | **40** | | **26,780** | **4** | | **440** | **11** | | **1,600** |
| **Imperial Guard** | | | | | | | | | |
| 1st Div | 13 | 580 | 7,540 | | | | 3 | 140 | 420 |
| 2nd Div | 10 | 590 | 5,900 | | | | 3 | 140 | 420 |
| Divisional Cavalry | | | | 29 | 110 | 3,190 | | | |
| Artillery Reserve | | | | | | | 6 | 145 | 870 |
| **Total** | **23** | | **13,440** | **29** | | **3,190** | **12** | | **1,710** |
| **Reserve Cavalry** | | | | | | | | | |
| 1st Div | | | | 4 | 120 | 480 | 2 | 155 | 310 |
| 2nd Div | | | | 16 | 110 | 1,760 | 2 | 155 | 310 |
| **Total** | | | | **20** | | **2,240** | **4** | | **620** |
| **Reserve Artillery** | | | | | | | | | |
| 13th Regt | | | | | | | 2 | 170 | 340 |
| 18th Regt | | | | | | | 6 | 135 | 810 |
| **Total** | | | | | | | **8** | | **1,150** |
| **Summary** | | | | | | | | | |
| 2 Corps | 32.5 | | 20,187 | 22 | | 2,380 | 13 | | 1,995 |
| 3 Corps | 52 | | 32,760 | 26 | | 2,860 | 20 | | 3,050 |
| 4 Corps | 39 | | 26,260 | 16 | | 1,760 | 15 | | 2,265 |
| 6 Corps | 40 | | 26,780 | 4 | | 440 | 11 | | 1,600 |
| Imperial Guard | 23 | | 13,440 | 29 | | 3,190 | 12 | | 1,710 |
| Reserve Cavalry | | | | 20 | | 2,240 | 4 | | 620 |

| | | | | | | | | | |
|---|---|---|---|---|---|---|---|---|---|
| Reserve Artillery | | | | | | | 8 | | 1,150 |
| H Q Escorts** | | | | 3 | 110 | 330 | | | |
| **Grand Total** | **186.5** | | **119,427** | **120** | | **13,200** | **83** | | **12,390** |
| **At Bazaine's HQ, 5th sq 5th Hussars & 1st Sq 2nd Chasseurs, at Canrobert's HQ, 6th Sq 6th Chasseurs. | | | | | | | | | |

# Appendix VIII

## Bazaine's Report on the Battle of Rezonville

---

### Bazaine's Report on the Battle of Vionville to the Emperor Napoleon

Pappeville, 17 août

Sire,

I have the honour to confirm to Your Majesty my earlier telegram of today's date, and enclose with this letter a copy of my letter addressed to the Emperor sent at 11:00 p.m. I do not know the exact number of our losses. As soon as these are available, I will forward with all haste a roll call to the Minister of War. General Bataille was wounded but the remainder of his staff escaped without incident. It is reported that the King of Prussia, at the head of an army of 100,000 men, is now at Pange or at Château d'Aubigny, and that, moreover, large masses of troops have been observed on the Verdun road and at Mont sous les Côtes. I am induced to attach a certain amount of credence to this report of the arrival of the king of Prussia from the fact that at the time I now have the honour of addressing Your Majesty the Prussians are making a serious attack on Fort Queuleu. They have established batteries at Magny, at Mercy le Haut and at the Bois de Puilyy, and their fire, is, at this moment, tolerably lively. On our side the troops are but poorly supplied with provisions. I shall endeavour to obtain supplies by the Ardennes road which is still clear. General Soleille, whom I have sent into Metz, reports that place is badly provided with ammunition and cannot supply us with more than 800,000 cartridges, which, with our soldiers, would not last more than one day. Also, that there are but a limited number of rounds for the 4-pounder field guns. Finally, that the plant necessary to finish the cartridges does not exist in the arsenal. General Soleille has been compelled to demand the necessary equipment from Paris; but it is questionable whether it will arrive in time. The regiments of general Frossard's corps are without camp equipage and unable to cook their rations. We shall make every attempt to complete our supplies in two days' time. I propose taking the Briey road. No time will be lost provided that my plans are not defeated by a fresh call to arms. I enclose for Your Majesty a translation of an order found on a Prussian colonel killed in the battle on the 16th. It will show Your Majesty the movements carried out by the enemy that day. I also attach a copy of General Soleille commandant of the armies' artillery which show the lack of supplies available in Metz to replenish the artillery's and infantry's stocks of ammunition.

l'État-Major, *Journées des 17 et 18 Août, Documents Annexes*, pp.12–13.

| | | | | | | | | | |
|---|---|---|---|---|---|---|---|---|---|
| 97th Line Infantry Regiment: | 12 | 9 | 24 | 49 | 286 | 101 | 436 | | | |
| Detachment 46th Line Infantry Regiment: | 1 | 1 | 2 | | 3 | 6 | 9 | | | |
| 7th Battery of Artillery 2nd Field Artillery Regiment | | 1 | 1 | 2 | 7 | 8 | 15 | 9 | 14 | 1,800 |
| 3rd Lancer Regiment: | | 3 | 3 | | 15 | 20 | 35 | | | |
| **Total** | **18** | **32** | **50** | **95** | **482** | **168** | **745** | **9** | **14** | **1,800** |
| **Cavalry Division** | | | | | | | | | | |
| **1st Brigade:** | | | | | | | | | | |
| 4th Chasseurs a Cheval: | | 1 | 1 | 2 | 2 | 4 | 3 | | | |
| 5th Chasseurs a Cheval: | 2 | 10 | 12 | 2 | 44 | 1 | 47 | | | |
| **2nd Brigade:** | | | | | | | | | | |
| 7th Dragoon Regiment: | | 3 | 3 | 1 | 8 | | 9 | | | |
| 12th Dragoon Regiment: | | 1 | 1 | | 3 | 3 | 6 | | | |
| **Total** | **2** | **15** | **17** | **5** | **57** | **4** | **66** | | | |
| **Artillery Reserve** | | | | | | | | | | |
| No 10 Battery 5th Field Artillery Regiment | 1 | 1 | 2 | | 10 | | 10 | 6 | | 840 |
| No 11 Battery 5th Field Artillery Regiment | | 1 | 1 | | 12 | | 12 | 8 | | 550 |
| Staff | 1 | | 1 | | | | | | | |
| No 6 Battery 15th Field Artillery Regiment | | 2 | 2 | 3 | 5 | | 8 | 16 | 15 | 200 |
| No 10 Battery 15th Field Artillery Regiment | | 1 | 1 | | 10 | | 10 | 13 | | 230 |
| Staff | | 1 | 1 | | | | | | | |
| No 7 Battery 17th Horse Artillery Regiment | | | | 1 | 1 | | 2 | 20 | | 900 |
| No 8 Battery 17th Horse Artillery Regiment | | 1 | 1 | 2 | 14 | | 16 | 9 | 13 | 600 |

| | | | | | | | | | | |
|---|---|---|---|---|---|---|---|---|---|---|
| **Total** | 2 | 7 | 9 | 6 | 52 | | 58 | 72 | 28 | 4,020 |
| **Service Administration** | 2 | | 2 | | | 4 | | | | |
| **Total 2 Corps** | 69 | 145 | 214 | 243 | 2,178 | 1,883 | 4,304 | 155 | 47 | 10,966 |
| **3 Corps** | | | | | | | | | | |
| **1st Division** | | 1 | 1 | | | | | | | |
| Staff | | | | | | | | | | |
| **1st Brigade:** | | | | | | | | | | |
| Staff | | 1 | 1 | | | | | | | |
| 18th Chasseur Battalion: | | | | | 1 | | 1 | | | |
| 51st Line Infantry Regiment: | 11 | 14 | 25 | 40 | 257 | 79 | 376 | | | |
| 62nd Line Infantry Regiment: | 5 | 7 | 12 | 9 | 150 | 38 | 197 | | | |
| **2nd Brigade:** | | | | | | | | | | |
| 81st Line Infantry Regiment: | | 2 | 2 | 3 | 3 | | 6 | | | |
| 95th Line Infantry Regiment: | | | | | 16 | | 16 | | | |
| Divisional Artillery: | | | | | | | | | | |
| No 5 Battery 4th Field Artillery Regiment | | 1 | 1 | | 5 | | 5 | 3 | 4 | |
| No 6 Battery 4th Field Artillery Regiment | | | | | | | | | | 840 |
| No 8 Battery 4th Field Artillery Regiment | | | | | | | | | | 1,020 |
| **Total** | 16 | 26 | 42 | 52 | 432 | 117 | 601 | 3 | 4 | 1,860 |
| **2nd Division** | | | | | | | | | | |
| Staff: | | 1 | 1 | | | | | | | |
| **1st Brigade:** | | | | | | | | | | |
| 41st Line Infantry Regiment: | | | | | 1 | 1 | 2 | | | |
| **2nd Brigade:** | | | | 1 | 2 | 1 | 4 | | | |
| 69th Line Infantry Regiment: | | | | 1 | 10 | 3 | 14 | | | |
| 90th Line Infantry Regiment: | | | | | | | | | | |
| Divisional Artillery: | | | | | | | | | | |

| | | | | | | | | | |
|---|---|---|---|---|---|---|---|---|---|
| No 11 Battery 4th Field Artillery Regiment | | | | | | | | | 56 |
| No 12 Battery 4th Field Artillery Regiment | | | | | | | | | |
| No 9 Battery 4th Field Artillery Regiment | | | | | | | | | 85 |
| **Total** | **1** | **1** | **2** | **13** | **5** | **20** | | | **141** |
| **4th Division** | | | | | | | | | |
| Staff: | 1 | 1 | | | | | | | |
| **1st Brigade:** | | | | | | | | | |
| 11th Chasseur Battalion: | | | 2 | 5 | | 7 | | | |
| 44th Line Infantry Regiment: | | | 3 | 13 | 2 | 18 | | | |
| 60th Line Infantry Regiment: | 1 | 1 | 2 | 3 | 1 | 8 | | | |
| **2nd Brigade:** | | | | | | | | | |
| 80th Line Infantry Regiment: | 2 | 2 | 5 | 36 | 1 | 42 | | | |
| 85th Line Infantry Regiment: | 1 | 1 | 2 | 20 | 1 | 23 | | | |
| **Divisional Artillery:** | | | | | | | | | |
| No 8 Battery 11th Field Artillery Regiment | | | 1 | 2 | | 3 | 2 | | 244 |
| No 9 Battery 11th Field Artillery Regiment | | | | | | | | | |
| No 10 Battery 11th Field Artillery Regiment | | | | 2 | | 2 | 2 | 3 | 694 |
| **Total** | **5** | **5** | **15** | **83** | **5** | **103** | **4** | **3** | **938** |
| **Cavalry Division** | | | | | | | | | |
| **1st Brigade:** | | | | | | | | | |
| 2nd Chasseurs a Cheval: | 1 | 1 | 2 | | 1 | | 1 | | |
| 3rd Chasseurs a Cheval: | | | | | 1 | | 1 | | |
| 10th Chasseurs a Cheval: | | | | | 1 | | 1 | | |

| | | | | | | | | | | |
|---|---|---|---|---|---|---|---|---|---|---|
| **2nd Brigade:** | 2 | | 2 | | | | | | | |
| 2nd Dragoon Regiment: | | | | 1 | 4 | 3 | 8 | | | |
| 4th Dragoon Regiment: | | | | | | | | | | |
| **3rd Brigade:** | | | | | | | | | | |
| 5th Dragoon Regiment: | | | | | 1 | | 1 | | | |
| **Total** | 3 | 1 | 4 | 1 | 8 | 3 | 12 | | | |
| **Artillery Reserve** | | | | | | | | | | |
| No 7 Battery 4th Field Artillery Regiment | | 2 | 2 | 1 | 5 | | 6 | 10 | | 900 |
| No 10 Battery 4th Field Artillery Regiment | | | | 1 | 5 | | 6 | 3 | | 900 |
| No 11 Battery 11th Field Artillery Regiment | | | | | 1 | | 1 | | | 400 |
| No 12 Battery 11th Field Artillery Regiment | | | | | 4 | | 4 | | | 530 |
| No 1 Battery 17th Horse Artillery Regiment | | | | | | | | | | 150 |
| No 2 Battery 17th Horse Artillery Regiment | | | | | | | | | | 30 |
| No 3 Battery 17th Horse Artillery Regiment | | | | | 7 | | 8 | 2 | 8 | 151 |
| No 4 Battery 17th Horse Artillery Regiment | | | | | 3 | | 3 | 2 | 6 | 159 |
| **Total** | | 2 | 2 | 3 | 25 | | 28 | 17 | 14 | 6,159 |
| **Service Administration** | | | | | | 1 | 1 | | | |
| **Total 3 Corps** | 19 | 35 | 54 | 73 | 561 | 131 | 765 | 24 | 21 | 6,159 |
| **4 Corps** | | | | | | | | | | |
| Staff | | 1 | 1 | | | | | | | |
| **1st Division** | | | | | | | | | | |
| Staff | | 2 | 2 | | | | | | | |
| **1st Brigade:** | | | | | | | | | | |
| Staff | 2 | | 2 | | | | | | | |

| | | | | | | | | | |
|---|---|---|---|---|---|---|---|---|---|
| No 7 Battery 10th Field Artillery Regiment | | | | | 5 | | 5 | 5 | 3 | 120 |
| No 8 Battery 10th Field Artillery Regiment | | 1 | 1 | 1 | 8 | | 9 | 12 | 4 | 360 |
| **Total** | **19** | **44** | **63** | **104** | **634** | **300** | **1,038** | **17** | **7** | **480** |
| **Total 6 Corps** | **67** | **152** | **219** | **340** | **2,237** | **1,273** | **3,850** | **105** | **15** | **4,568** |
| **Cavalry Reserve** | | | | | | | | | | |
| **1st Division** | | | | | | | | | | |
| **2nd Brigade:** | | | | | | | | | | |
| 2nd Regiment Chasseurs d'Afrique: | 1 | 4 | 5 | 1 | 30 | 20 | 51 | | | |
| **Divisional Artillery:** | | | | | | | | | | 12 |
| No 5 Battery 19th Horse Artillery Regiment | | | | | | | | | | 24 |
| No 6 Battery 19th Horse Artillery Regiment | | | | | | | | | | |
| **Total** | **1** | **4** | **5** | **1** | **30** | **20** | **51** | | | **36** |
| **3rd Division** | | | | | | | | | | |
| Staff | | 1 | 1 | | 1 | | 1 | | | |
| **1st Brigade:** | | | | | | | | | | |
| 1st Dragoon Regiment: | | 7 | 7 | 3 | 13 | 4 | 24 | | | |
| 9th Dragoon Regiment: | | 6 | 6 | | 13 | 30 | 43 | | | |
| **2nd Brigade:** | | | | | | | | | | |
| Staff | | 1 | 2 | | | | | | | |
| 7th Cuirassier Regiment: | | 4 | 4 | 1 | 16 | 2 | 19 | | | |
| 10th Cuirassier Regiment: | | 1 | 1 | 1 | 7 | 2 | 10 | | | |
| **Divisional Artillery:** | | | | | | | | | | |
| No 7 Battery 20th Horse Artillery Regiment | 1 | 3 | 4 | | 22 | 3 | 25 | 36 | 7 | 760 |
| No 8 Battery 20th Horse Artillery Regiment | | 2 | 2 | | 22 | 4 | 26 | 25 | 1 | 400 |

| | | | | | | | | | | |
|---|---|---|---|---|---|---|---|---|---|---|
| **Total** | 1 | 25 | 26 | 7 | 96 | 45 | 148 | 61 | 8 | 1,160 |
| **Total Reserve Cavalry** | **2** | **29** | **31** | **8** | **126** | **65** | **199** | **61** | **8** | **1,196** |
| **Artillery Reserve** | | | | | | | | | | |
| **13th Artillery Regiment** | | | | | | | | | | |
| No 11 Battery | | | | | 9 | 1 | 13 | 14 | | 378 |
| No 12 Battery | | | | | 9 | 1 | 12 | 23 | | 147 |
| **18th Horse Artillery Regiment** | | | | | | | | | | |
| No 1 Battery | | | | | 6 | | 6 | 2 | 5 | |
| No 2 Battery | | | | 2 | 19 | | 21 | 29 | | |
| No 3 Battery | 1 | 1 | 2 | 3 | 9 | | 12 | 28 | | 2,363 |
| No 4 Battery | 1 | 1 | 2 | 13 | 7 | | 20 | 41 | | |
| No 5 Battery | | | | | 15 | | 15 | 11 | 9 | |
| No 6 Battery | 1 | | 1 | 1 | 10 | | 11 | 10 | 9 | |
| **Total Reserve Artillery** | **3** | **2** | **5** | **21** | **81** | **2** | **110** | **178** | **23** | **2,888** |
| **Totals** | **251** | **583** | **834** | **945** | **7,734** | **4,218** | **1,297** | **613** | **172** | **34,972** |
| **Total losses at Rezonville 16th August 1870: 13,761** | | | | | | | | | | |

# Appendix X

# German losses, Rezonville

| German Casualties Battle of Rezonville | Killed | | | Wounded | | | Missing | | | Total | | |
|---|---|---|---|---|---|---|---|---|---|---|---|---|
| | Officers | Men | Horses | Officers | Men | Horses | Officers | Men | Horses | Officers | Men | Horses |
| **II Army** | | | | | | | | | | | | |
| **Guard Cavalry Division** | | | | | | | | | | | | |
| 3rd Guard Cavalry Brigade | | | | | | | | | | | | |
| 1st Dragoons of the Guard | 9 | 17 | 204 | 4 | 60 | | 1 | 5 | | 14 | 82 | 204 |
| 2nd Dragoons of the Guard | 3 | 12 | 105 | 3 | 92 | 45 | | 11 | | 6 | 115 | 150 |
| 1st Horse Artillery battery Guard Field Artillery Regiment | | | 3 | | 3 | 4 | | | | | 3 | 7 |
| TOTAL | 12 | 29 | 312 | 7 | 155 | 49 | 1 | 16 | | 20 | 200 | 361 |
| **III Army Corps** | | | | | | | | | | | | |
| Headquarters Staff | 1 | | | 1 | | | | | | 2 | | |
| **5th Infantry Division** | | | | | | | | | | 1 | | |
| **9th Infantry Brigade** | | | | | | | | | | | | |
| Brigade Staff | 1 | | | | | | | | | | | |
| 8th Body Guard Grenadiers | 10 | 121 | | 17 | 391 | | | 11 | | 27 | 523 | |
| 48th Regiment | 8 | 171 | | 16 | 421 | | | 4 | | 24 | 596 | |
| **10th Infantry Brigade** | | | | | | | | | | | | |
| Brigade Staff | 1 | | 1 | | | 1 | | | | 1 | | 2 |
| 12th Grenadiers | 4 | 106 | | 12 | 297 | | | 19 | | 16 | 422 | |
| 52nd Regiment | 18 | 345 | 2 | 32 | 806 | 3 | | 51 | | 50 | 1,202 | 5 |
| 3rd Rifle Battalion | 1 | 62 | | 7 | 121 | 1 | | 1 | | 8 | 184 | 1 |
| 12th Dragoons | | 3 | 28 | | 10 | 4 | | | | | 13 | 32 |
| 1st Field Division, 3rd FA Regiment | 4 | 36 | 165 | 9 | 125 | 44 | | 1 | | 13 | 162 | 209 |
| No 1 Sanitary Detachment | | 1 | | | 4 | | | | | | 5 | |
| TOTAL | 47 | 845 | 196 | 93 | 2,175 | 53 | | 87 | | 140 | 3,107 | 249 |
| **6th Infantry Division** | | | | | | | | | | | | |
| Division Staff | | | | 1 | | | | | | 1 | | |

| | | | | | | | | | | | | |
|---|---|---|---|---|---|---|---|---|---|---|---|---|
| **11th Infantry Brigade** | | | | | | | | | | | | |
| Brigade Staff | | | 2 | | | | | | | | | 2 |
| 20th Regiment | 8 | 154 | 4 | 35 | 533 | 1 | | 13 | | 43 | 700 | 5 |
| 35th Fusiliers | | 250 | 11 | 18 | 584 | 3 | | 17 | | 25 | 851 | 14 |
| **12th Infantry Brigade** | | | | | | | | | | | | |
| Brigade Staff | | | | 1 | | | | | | 1 | | |
| 24th Regiment | 15 | 294 | 6 | 33 | 719 | 3 | | 86 | | 48 | 1,099 | 9 |
| 64th Regiment | 14 | 187 | 2 | 28 | 496 | 1 | | | 2 | 42 | 683 | 5 |
| 2nd Dragoons | | 2 | 16 | 1 | 11 | 10 | | | | 1 | 13 | 26 |
| 3rd Field Division, 3rd FA Regiment | | 13 | 61 | 2 | 52 | 36 | | | | 2 | 65 | 97 |
| No 2 Sanitary Detachment | | | | | 1 | 1 | | | | 1 | | 1 |
| **TOTAL** | 44 | 900 | 102 | 119 | 2,396 | 55 | | 116 | 2 | 164 | 3,412 | 159 |
| **Corps Artillery** | | | | | | | | | | | | |
| Horse Artillery Division, 3rd Field Artillery Regiment | 1 | 8 | 92 | 7 | 44 | 47 | | | | 8 | 52 | 139 |
| 2nd Field Artillery Division, 3rd Field Artillery Regiment | | 16 | 59 | 2 | 51 | 50 | | | | 2 | 67 | 109 |
| No 3 Sanitary Detachment | | | | | | 1 | | | | | | 1 |
| **TOTAL** | 1 | 24 | 151 | 9 | 95 | 98 | | | | 10 | 119 | 249 |
| **Columns Division 3rd Field Artillery Regiment 3rd Artillery Column:** | | 1 | 12 | | 2 | 5 | | | 3 | | 3 | 20 |
| **Total III Corps** | 93 | 1,770 | 461 | 222 | 4,668 | 211 | | 203 | 5 | 315 | 6,641 | 677 |
| **IX Army Corps** | | | | | | | | | | | | |
| **18th Infantry Division** | | | | | | | | | | | | |
| 35th Infantry Brigade | | | | | | | | | | | | |
| 36th Fusiliers | 17 | 339 | | 24 | 750 | | | 30 | 1 | 41 | 1,119 | 1 |
| **TOTAL** | 17 | 339 | | 24 | 750 | | | 30 | 1 | 41 | 1,119 | 1 |
| **25th Grand Ducal Hesse Infantry Division** | | | | | | | | | | | | |
| **49th Infantry Brigade** | | | | | | | | | | | | |
| 1st Body Guard Regiment | | 13 | 1 | | 34 | | | | | | 47 | 1 |
| 2nd (Grand Duke) Regiment | | 7 | | 1 | 18 | | | 2 | | 1 | 27 | |
| Field Division, 2 heavy, 1 | | | 1 | | 1 | | | | | | 1 | 1 |
| Pioneer Company with light field bridge train: Captain Brentano | | | | | | | | | | | | |
| Sanitary Detachment | | | | | | | | | | | | |
| **TOTAL** | | 20 | 2 | 1 | 53 | | | 2 | | 1 | 75 | 2 |

| | | | | | | | | | | | |
|---|---|---|---|---|---|---|---|---|---|---|---|
| **Total IX Corps** | 17 | 359 | 2 | 25 | 803 | | | 32 | 1 | 42 | 1,194 | 3 |
| **X Army Corps** | | | | | | | | | | | | |
| Headquarters Staff | | | | | | | 1 | | | | | 1 |
| **19th Infantry Division** | | | | | | | | | | | | |
| 37th Infantry Brigade | | | | | | | | | | | | |
| 78th Regiment | 4 | 199 | 5 | 29 | 394 | 1 | | 32 | 1 | 33 | 625 | 7 |
| 91st Regiment | 13 | 126 | 1 | 13 | 264 | 2 | | 13 | 1 | 26 | 403 | 4 |
| **38th Infantry Brigade** | | | | | | | | | | | | |
| Brigade Staff | | | 1 | 1 | | 2 | | | | 1 | | 3 |
| 16th Regiment | 27 | 526 | 15 | 21 | 787 | 1 | 1 | 423 | | 49 | 1,736 | 16 |
| 57th Regiment | 6 | 366 | 5 | 18 | 422 | | | 18 | | 24 | 806 | 5 |
| 9th Dragoons | | | 6 | 1 | 10 | 6 | | | 2 | 1 | 10 | 14 |
| 1st Field Division, 10th FA Regiment | | 13 | 31 | | 31 | 9 | | | | | 44 | 40 |
| 2nd Field Pioneer Company X Corps | 1 | | | | 5 | 1 | | | | 1 | 5 | 1 |
| 3rd Field Pioneer Company X Corps | | | | | | 3 | | | | | 3 | |
| No 1 Sanitary Detachment | | | | 1 | 2 | | | | | 1 | 2 | |
| TOTAL | 51 | 1,230 | 64 | 84 | 1,918 | 22 | 1 | 486 | 4 | 136 | 3,634 | 91 |
| **20th Infantry Division** | | | | | | | | | | | | |
| **39th Infantry Brigade** | | | | | | | | | | | | |
| 56th Regiment | 14 | 187 | 11 | 14 | 495 | 2 | | 35 | | 28 | 717 | 13 |
| 79th Regiment | 2 | 65 | 1 | 16 | 233 | 2 | | 16 | | 18 | 314 | 3 |
| **40th Infantry Brigade:** | | | | | | | | | | | | |
| 17th Regiment | 2 | 7 | 3 | 4 | 46 | | | | | 6 | 53 | 3 |
| 92nd Regiment | | 3 | | 1 | 8 | | | 2 | | 1 | 13 | |
| 10th Rifle Battalion | | 3 | | 1 | 7 | | | | | 1 | 10 | |
| 16th Dragoons | 1 | 3 | 17 | 3 | 16 | 6 | | 3 | 20 | 4 | 22 | 43 |
| 2nd Field Division, 10th FA Regiment | | 13 | 32 | 5 | 26 | 11 | | | | 5 | 39 | 43 |
| TOTAL | 2 | 31 | 118 | 5 | 112 | 51 | | | | 7 | 143 | 169 |
| **Total X Corps** | 72 | 1,542 | 246 | 133 | 2,861 | 95 | 1 | 542 | 24 | 206 | 4,945 | 365 |
| **5th Cavalry Division** | | | | | | | | | | | | |
| **11th Cavalry Brigade** | | | | | | | | | | | | |
| Brigade Staff | | | | 2 | | | | | | 2 | | |
| 4th Cuirassiers | 1 | 11 | 50 | 5 | 28 | | | 3 | 6 | 6 | 42 | 56 |
| 13th Lancers: | 1 | 9 | 24 | 5 | 35 | 19 | | 6 | 18 | 8 | 50 | 61 |
| 19th Dragoons | 4 | 10 | | 8 | 94 | | | 9 | 95 | 12 | 113 | 95 |
| **12th Cavalry Brigade** | | | | | | | | | | | | |
| Brigade Staff | | | 1 | 1 | | | | | | 1 | | 1 |

| | | | | | | | | | | | | |
|---|---|---|---|---|---|---|---|---|---|---|---|---|
| 7th Cuirassiers | 3 | 55 | | 4 | 121 | 25 | | 13 | 184 | 7 | 189 | 209 |
| 16th Lancers | 2 | 51 | 172 | 6 | 104 | 28 | 2 | 19 | | 10 | 174 | 200 |
| 13th Dragoons | 1 | 4 | 12 | 6 | 74 | 35 | | 8 | 18 | 7 | 86 | 65 |
| **13th Cavalry Brigade** | | | | | | | | | | | | |
| Brigade Staff | | | 1 | 1 | | | | | | 1 | | 1 |
| 10th Hussars | 1 | 2 | 10 | 4 | 22 | 13 | | 4 | 15 | 5 | 28 | 38 |
| 11th Hussars | | 6 | 18 | 1 | 15 | | | | | 1 | 21 | 18 |
| 17th Hussars | | 7 | 74 | 2 | 68 | | | 14 | | 2 | 89 | 74 |
| 1st Horse Artillery Battery 4th Field Artillery Regiment: | 1 | 5 | 21 | 1 | 12 | 15 | | | | 2 | 17 | 36 |
| 2nd Horse Artillery Battery 10th Field Artillery Regiment: | | 6 | 47 | | 15 | | | | | | 21 | 47 |
| **Total 5th Cavalry** | **14** | **166** | **429** | **46** | **588** | **137** | **2** | **76** | **336** | **62** | **830** | **902** |
| **6th Cavalry Division** | | | | | | | | | | | | |
| **14th Cavalry Brigade:** | | | | | | | | | | | | |
| Brigade Staff | 1 | | | | | | | | | 1 | | |
| 6th Cuirassiers | | | 4 | 1 | 6 | 5 | | | | 1 | 6 | 9 |
| 3rd Lancers | 1 | 8 | 24 | 1 | 14 | 20 | | | 24 | 2 | 22 | 68 |
| 15th Lancers | | 5 | 18 | 3 | 24 | 12 | | 5 | | 3 | 34 | 30 |
| **15th Cavalry Brigade** | | | | | | | | | | | | |
| Brigade Staff | | | 1 | 1 | | | | | | 1 | | 1 |
| 3rd Hussars | 3 | 51 | 133 | 5 | 88 | | 1 | 21 | | 9 | 160 | 133 |
| 16th Hussars | 1 | 6 | 11 | 2 | 27 | 61 | | | | 3 | 33 | 72 |
| 2nd Horse Artillery Battery 3rd Field Artillery Regiment: | | 5 | 23 | | 14 | 18 | | | | | 19 | 41 |
| **Total 6th Cavalry** | **6** | **75** | **214** | **13** | **173** | **116** | **1** | **26** | **24** | **20** | **274** | **354** |
| **I Army** | | | | | | | | | | | | |
| **VIII Army Corps** | | | | | | | | | | | | |
| **16th Infantry Division** | | | | | | | | | | | | |
| Division Staff | | | 1 | | | | | | | | | 1 |
| **32nd Infantry Brigade** | | | | | | | | | | | | |
| 40th Fusiliers | 5 | 17 | 1 | 12 | 73 | | | 4 | | 17 | 94 | 1 |
| 72nd Regiment | 16 | 220 | 3 | 20 | 569 | | | 63 | | 36 | 852 | 3 |
| 9th Hussars: | | | 2 | | 1 | 3 | | | | | 1 | 6 |
| 3rd Field Division, 8th FA Regiment | 1 | 7 | 27 | 1 | 41 | 37 | | | | 2 | 48 | 64 |
| **Total VIII Corps** | **22** | **244** | **34** | **33** | **684** | **40** | | **67** | | **55** | **995** | **74** |
| **Grand Total** | **236** | **4,185** | **1,698** | **479** | **9,932** | **648** | **5** | **962** | **390** | **720** | **15,079** | **2,736** |

# Appendix XI

# Note on forces engaged and casualties, 18 August 1870

## Gravelotte–Saint Privat: Forces engaged and casualties suffered

Gravelotte-Saint Privat was one of the largest post Napoleonic battles fought on European soil during the 19th Century. Typically, as this snapshot of the various histories illustrates, different authors provide widely contradictory numbers for troops involved; Howard: 188,332 Germans with 732 guns against 112,800 French with 520 guns; Rich: 110,000 French opposed by 240,000 Germans; Bonnet: 150,000 French against 260,000 Germans. De Lonlay puts the French at 147,780, Rousset: 125,000 French versus 284,000 Germans. Hoffbauer reckons 150,600 French and 210-225,000 Germans whilst Boulanger has 136,363 infantry, 18,831 cavalry supported by 546 guns for Bazaine, with Moltke fielding 178,818 infantry, 24,584 cavalry with 726 guns. Bazaine, in his L'Armée du Rhin, claimed the Germans fielded 250,000 men with 650 cannon against his 100,000 men with 450 guns.

These disparities are perhaps, to be expected given the way the various strengths were recorded and it is challenging to offer anything more than an approximate number of troops present on 18 August. It is also necessary to differentiate between the number of forces available to a commander and the number actually engaged; on the French side the Imperial Guard had little if any involvement and Bazaine also had considerable forces at his disposal in Metz. On the German side, II Corps took little part in the days fighting and neither commander made any significant use of the large numbers of cavalry available to them.

With regard to the German forces involved, their official history gives a total of 178,818 infantry, 24,584 cavalry with 726 guns whilst a later work, *Heft 11* of the *Kriegsgeschichtliche Einzelschriften* estimates the available German forces at 164,000 infantry, 21,200 cavalry and 732 guns, of which 109,200 infantry and 638 guns were engaged,[1] with the artillery firing off some 34,680 rounds. For the French, *Les Opérations autour de Metz III~Documents Annexes* provides considerable, although sometimes contradictory, detail. The Tableau d'effectif des troupes de l'armée du Rhin for 18 August lists the number present under arms following the battle as 154,481 men and if the recorded casualties are added back onto this figure, it gives Bazaine's army an overall strength at the commencement of the battle of around 165,259 men. However, whilst this figure includes a number of supernumeraries which inflates the number of troops, it does not account for those men absent from their regiment, nor those in hospitals

---

1　The Kriegsgeschichtliche does not always tally with the casualty returns given in the Official History which list, albeit minor, losses amongst certain of the cavalry regiments which were present on the 18th which seems to indicate they were, in some way, 'engaged' in the fighting on the 18th. The same can be said about certain French formations.

or dressing stations. For example, within the total quoted above it is recorded that 2nd Division from Frossard's 2 Corps had 7,565 men and officers present and under arms. However, the more detailed Situation d'effectif prepared by the divisional commander on the same date refers to additional support staff such as the Prévôté, sapeurs conducteurs, officiers supérieurs et médecins, services administratifs and the train des équipages and it is far from clear which, if any, of these were included within the total as submitted by the corps commander.[2] This document also differentiates between those men present with their unit and those who are absent, for whatever reason from the parent formation. It lists 7,684 men and officers as 'available' (i.e., 119 more than stated within the corps report) and a further 1,016 listed as 'unavailable'. Another 1,017 men and officers are noted as being in hospital with 1,599 in aid stations. This would equate to a total strength for 2nd Division of 11,316 officers and men and illustrates some of the difficulties in establishing the true strength of the Imperial army at Gravelotte, or indeed at any other engagement during the campaign.

As to the effective fighting strength at Bazaine's disposal, the *Kriegsgeschichtliche* published in 1889 calculates his available strength at 99,500 infantry, 13,300 cavalry with 520 guns and mitrailleuses, of which it estimates 83,500 infantry, 550 and 398 guns and mitrailleuses were actually engaged in the fighting. However, in arriving at this total, the average battalion strength adopted for the various formations are somewhat lower than the figures provided within the French official history. On the reasonable assumption that the authors of the relevant volume, *Les Opérations autour de Metz*, published in 1905, had better access to the French official returns than the *Kriegsgeschichtliche*, this would indicate that Bazaine had at his disposal some 109,745 infantry with 12,200 cavalry supported by 456 guns and 66 mitrailleuses manned by 12,485 gunners. Of this total, it would seem that the total number of French troops engaged numbered around 97,000 infantry and 550 cavalry supported by 398 guns which fired some 35,459 rounds.

Victory for the German forces came at heavy cost, their official history detailing total losses amounting to 909 officers, 19,254 men and 1,877 horses or about 18 percent of the troops 'engaged'. The Guard in particular suffered heavily as a result of their incompetent handling losing 308 officers, 7,922 men and 420 horses. Overall, this represented a casualty rate of almost 30 percent within this elite formation, losses amongst the officer corps being disproportionally high, with 30 holding the rank of captain or above being killed and a further 51 wounded.[3] As for French casualties I have used the data provided within the relevant volumes of their official history, which were compiled in September after a thorough review of regimental records. They record losses of 619 officers and 12,599 men or about 13 percent of the forces 'engaged'. Indicative of their inactivity during the battle, the combined casualties for the Imperial Guard, Reserve cavalry and Reserve artillery amounted to just 3 officers and 85 men. Given their role in defeating Steinmetz's assault against the Saint Hubert-Point du Jour heights, 2 and 3 corps losses are remarkably low; just 146 officers and 2,578 men. Canroberts' corps, unsurprisingly, suffered heavily with casualties amounting to 195 officers and 4,616 men, of which 3,106 were listed as missing.

---

2    Where any doubt existed the understandable inclination for any commander was to inflate the numbers present as this figure determined the allocation of rations and ammunition to a particular unit from the Commissariat.

3    The losses in field and company officers were such that captains of the Rifle and Pioneer battalions of the Guard were used to fill the position of battalion commanders until such time as suitable replacements could be brought forward from the depots in Prussia..

| | | | | | | | | | | | |
|---|---|---|---|---|---|---|---|---|---|---|---|
| 4th Thuringian Infantry Regiment No 72: | | | 3 | 760 | 2,280 | | | | | | |
| 2nd Rhine Hussar Regiment No 9: Colonel v Wittich or Hinzmann-Hallman | | | | | | 4 | 140 | 560 | | | |
| 3rd Field Division, 8th FA Regiment; | | | | | | | | | | | |
| 5 & 6 heavy, 5 & 6 light batteries: Lt Colonel Hildebrandt | | | | | | | | | 4 | 24 | |
| 1st Field Pioneer Company VIII Corps : Captain Richter II | | | | | | | | | | | 1 |
| No 2 Sanitary Detachment | | | | | | | | | | | |
| **Total 16th Division** | 10,138 | 599 | 12 | | 9,120 | 4 | | 560 | 4 | 24 | 1 |
| Corps Artillery: Colonel v Broeckeri Commander 8th Field Artillery Regiment | | | | | | | | | | | |
| Horse Artillery Division, 8th Field Artillery Regiment, | | | | | | | | | | | |
| 1, 2 & 3 horse artillery batteries: Lt Colonel Borkenhagen | | | | | | | | | 3 | | |
| 2nd Field Artillery Division, 8th Field Artillery Regiment | | | | | | | | | | | |
| 3 & 4 heavy, 3 & 4 light batteries: Major Zwinnemann | | | | | | | | | 4 | | |
| 3rd Sanitary Detachment | | | | | | | | | | | |
| **Total Corps Artillery** | | | | | | | | | 7 | | |
| **Total VIII Army Corps** | 23,378 | 1,242 | | | 21,340 | | | 1,120 | 15 | 90 | |
| **1st Cavalry Division:** Commander: Lt General v Hartmann. Officer of General Staff: Major v Saldern. | | | | | | | | | | | |
| **1st Cavalry Brigade:** Maj General v Luderitz | | | | | | | | | | | |
| Queen's Cuirassier Regiment (Pomeranian) No 2: Colonel v Pfuhl | | | | | | 4 | 125 | 500 | | | |
| 1st Pomeranian Lancer Regiment No 4: Lt Colonel v Radecke | | | | | | 4 | 125 | 500 | | | |
| 2nd Pomeranian Lancer Regiment No 9: Lt Colonel v Kleist | | | | | | 4 | 125 | 500 | | | |
| **2nd Cavalry Brigade:** Maj General Baumgarth | | | | | | | | | | | |

| | | | | | | | | | | | | |
|---|---|---|---|---|---|---|---|---|---|---|---|---|
| East Prussian Cuirassier Regiment No 3 (Count Wrangel): Colonel v Winterfield | | | | | | 4 | 125 | 500 | | | | |
| East Prussian Lancer Regiment No 8: Colonel v Below | | | | | | 4 | 125 | 500 | | | | |
| Lithuanian Lancer Regiment No 12: Lt Colonel v Rosenberg | | | | | | 4 | 125 | 500 | | | | |
| 1st Horse Artillery Battery 1st East Prussian Field Artillery Regiment: Captain Preinitzer | | | | | | | | | 1 | | | |
| **Total of 1st Cavalry Division** | | 3,301 | | | | 24 | | 3,000 | 1 | | | |
| **Total I Army** | 42,455 | 5,753 | | | | | | | | | | |
| **II Army:** Commander in Chief: HRH General of Cavalry Prince Frederick Charles of Prussia. Chief of General Staff: Maj General v Stiehle. Quartermaster in Chief: Colonel v Hertzberg. Commander of Artillery: Lt General v Colomier. | | | | | | | | | | | | |
| **Guard Corps:** General Commanding: HRH General of Cavalry Prince Augustus of Wurttemberg. Chief of General Staff: Maj General v Dannenberg. Commander of Artillery: Maj General Prince Kraft zu Hohenlohe-Ingelfingen. | | | | | | | | | | | | |
| **1st Guard Infantry Division:** Commander: Maj General v Pape. Officer of General Staff: Captain v Holleben. | | | | | | | | | | | | |
| 1st Guard Infantry Brigade: Maj General v Kessel | | | | | | | | | | | | |
| 1st Regiment of Foot Guards: Colonel v Roeder | | | 3 | 900 | 2,700 | | | | | | | |
| 3rd Regiment of Foot Guards: Colonel v Linsingen | | | 3 | 900 | 2,700 | | | | | | | |
| **2nd Guard Infantry Brigade:** Maj General Baron v Medem | | | | | | | | | | | | |
| 2nd Regiment of Foot Guards: Colonel v Kanitz | | | 3 | 900 | 2,700 | | | | | | | |
| Guard Fusilier Regiment: Colonel Count v Erckert | | | 3 | 900 | 2,700 | | | | | | | |
| 4th Regiment of Foot Guards: Colonel v Neumann | | | 3 | 900 | 2,700 | | | | | | | |
| Guard Rifle Battalion: Major v Arnim | | | 1 | 900 | 900 | | | | | | | |

| | | | | | | | | | | | |
|---|---|---|---|---|---|---|---|---|---|---|---|
| Hussars of the Guard: Lt Colonel v Hymmen | | | | | | 4 | 135 | 540 | | | |
| 1st Field Division, Guard FA Regiment; | | | | | | | | | | | |
| 1 & 2 heavy, 1 & 2 light batteries: Lt Colonel Bychelberg | | | | | | | | | 4 | 24 | |
| 1st Field Pioneer Company of the Guard Corps with light field bridge: Captain v Bock | | | | | | | | | | | 1 |
| No 1 Sanitary Detachment | | | | | | | | | | | |
| **Total 1st Guard Infantry Division** | **15,432** | **588** | **16** | | **14,400** | **4** | | **540** | **4** | **24** | **1** |
| **2nd Guard Infantry Division:** Commander: Lt General v Budritzki. Officer of General Staff: Major v Ostau. | | | | | | | | | | | |
| 3rd Guard Infantry Brigade: Colonel Knappe von Knappstadt | | | | | | | | | | | |
| 1st Guard Grenadier Regiment (Emperor Alexander): Colonel v Zeuner | | | 3 | 895 | 2,685 | | | | | | |
| 3rd Guard Grenadier Regiment (Queen Elizabeth):* Colonel v Zaluskowski | | | 3 | 895 | 2,239 | | | | | | |
| **4th Guard Infantry Brigade:** Maj General v Berger | | | | | | | | | | | |
| 2nd Guard Grenadier Regiment (Emperor Francis): Lt Colonel v Boehn | | | 3 | 895 | 2,685 | | | | | | |
| 4th Guard Grenadier Regiment (Queen Augusta's): Colonel Count v Waldersee | | | 3 | 895 | 2,685 | | | | | | |
| Guard Sharpsooters Battalion: Major v Fabeck | | | 1 | 895 | 895 | | | | | | |
| 2nd Lancers of the Guard: HH Prince Henry of Hesse | | | | | | 4 | 140 | 560 | | | |
| 3rd Field Division, Guard FA Regiment; | | | | | | | | | | | |
| 5 & 6 heavy, 5 & 6 light batteries: Lt Colonel v Rheinbaben | | | | | | | | | 4 | 24 | |
| 3rd Field Pioneer Company of the Guard Corps: Captain Spankeren with entrenching tool column. | | | | | | | | | | | 1 |
| No 2 Sanitary Detachment | | | | | | | | | | | |
| **Total 2nd Guard Infantry Division** | **12,728** | **602** | **13** | | **11,189** | **4** | | **560** | **4** | **24** | **1** |

| | | | | | | | | | | |
|---|---|---|---|---|---|---|---|---|---|---|
| *The 1st and 4th companies were absent. | | | | | | | | | | |
| **Guard Cavalry Division:** Commander: Lt General Count v Goltz. Officer of General Staff: Captain v Weiher. | | | | | | | | | | |
| 1st Guard Cavalry Brigade: Maj General Count v Brandenburg I | | | | | | | | | | |
| Gardes du Corps: Colonel v Krosigk | | | | | | 4 | 140 | 560 | | |
| Guard Cuirassier Regiment: Colonel Baron v Brandenstein | | | | | | 4 | 140 | 560 | | |
| **3rd Guard Cavalry Brigade:** Lt General Count v Brandenburg II | | | | | | | | | | |
| 1st Guard Dragoon Regiment: | | | | | | 4 | 90 | 560 | | |
| 2nd Guard Dragoon Regiment: | | | | | | 4 | 90 | 560 | | |
| **Total Guard Cavalry Division** | | 1,991 | | | | 16 | | 2,240 | | |
| **Corps Artillery:** Colonel v Scherbening, Commander Guard Field Artillery Regiment | | | | | | | | | | |
| Horse Artillery Division, Guard Field Artillery Regiment | | | | | | | | | | |
| 1, 2 & 3 horse artllery batteries: Major Baron v Buddenbrock | | | | | | | | | 3 | 18 |
| 2nd Field Artillery Division, Guard Field Artillery Regiment | | | | | | | | | | |
| 3 & 4 heavy,3 & 4 light batteries: Major v Krieger | | | | | | | | | 4 | 24 |
| 3rd Sanitary Detachment | | | | | | | | | | |
| **Total Corps Artillery** | | | | | | | | | 7 | 42 |
| **Total Guards Corps** | 28,160 | 3,181 | | 25,987** | | | | 2940*** | | 90 |
| ** Includes 400 men from Guard Pioneer companies | | | | | | | | | | |
| ***Although the total of the individual units amounts to 3,340 sabres, the Kriegsgeschichtliche Einzelschriften gives a total for the Guard cavalry of 2,940 | | | | | | | | | | |
| **II Army Corps:** General Commanding:General of Infantry v Fransecky. Chief of General Staff: Colonel v Wichmann. Commander of Artillery: Maj General v Kleist. | | | | | | | | | | |

| | | | | | | | | | | | |
|---|---|---|---|---|---|---|---|---|---|---|---|
| **3rd Infantry Division:** Commander: Maj General v Hartmann. Officer of General Staff:Major v Gottberg | | | | | | | | | | | |
| 5th Infantry Brigade: Maj General v Koblinski | | | | | | | | | | | |
| Grenadier Regiment King Frederick William IV (1st Pomeranian) No 2: Colonel v Ziemietzki | | 3 | 920 | 2,760 | | | | | | | |
| 5th Pomeranian Infantry Regiment No 42:Colonel v d Knesebeck | | 3 | 920 | 2,760 | | | | | | | |
| **6th Infantry Brigade:** Colonel v d Decken | | | | | | | | | | | |
| 3rd Pomeranian Infantry Regiment No 14:**** Colonel v Voss | | 2 | 920 | 1,840 | | | | | | | |
| 7th Pomeranian Infantry Regiment No 54: Colonel v Busse | | 3 | 920 | 2,760 | | | | | | | |
| Pomeranian Rifle Battalion No 2: Major v Netzer | | 1 | 920 | 920 | | | | | | | |
| Neumark Dragoon Regiment No 3: Colonel Baron v Willisen | | | | | 4 | 140 | 560 | | | | |
| 1st Field Division, 2nd Pomeranian Field Artillery Regiment; | | | | | | | | | | | |
| 1 &2 heavy, 1 & 2 light batteries: Major Baron v Eynatten | | | | | | | | 4 | 24 | | |
| 1st Field Pioneer Company II Corps with light field bridge train: Captain v Wissmann | | | | | | | | | | 1 | |
| No 1 Sanitary Detachment | | | | | | | | | | | |
| **Total of 3rd Infantry Division** | 12,822 | 611 | 12 | | 11,040 | 4 | | 560 | 4 | 24 | 1 |
| **** The 1st battalion was at Pont a Mousson as guard for the HQ | | | | | | | | | | | |
| **4th Infantry Division:** Commander: Lt General v Hann v Weihern. Officer of General Staff: Captain Boie. | | | | | | | | | | | |
| 7th Infantry Brigade: Maj General du Trossel | | | | | | | | | | | |
| Colberg Grenadier Regiment (2nd Pomeranian) No 9: Colonel v Ferentheil and Gruppenberg | | 3 | 890 | 2,670 | | | | | | | |

| | | | | | | | | | | | | |
|---|---|---|---|---|---|---|---|---|---|---|---|---|
| 6th Pomeranian Infantry Regiment No 49: Lt Colonel Laurin | | | 3 | 890 | 2,670 | | | | | | | |
| **8th Infantry Brigade:** Maj General v Kettler | | | | | | | | | | | | |
| 4th Pomeranian Infantry Regiment No 21: Lt Colonel v Lobenthal | | | 3 | 890 | 2,670 | | | | | | | |
| 8th Pomeranian Infantry Regiment No 61: Colonel v Wedell | | | 3 | 890 | 2,670 | | | | | | | |
| Pomeranian Dragoon Regiment No 11: Lt Colonel v Guretzki-Cornitz | | | | | | 4 | 140 | 560 | | | | |
| 3rd Field Division, 2nd Pomeranian Field Artillery Regiment; | | | | | | | | | | | | |
| 5 & 6 heavy, 5 & 6 light batteries: Lt Colonel Bauer | | | | | | | | | 4 | 24 | | |
| 2nd Field Pioneer Company II Corps with entrenching tool column: Captain Grethen | | | | | | | | | | | | 1 |
| 3rd Field Pioneer Company II Corps: Captain Balcke | | | | | | | | | | | | 1 |
| No 2 Sanitary Detachment | | | | | | | | | | | | |
| **Total 4th Infantry Division** | 11,702 | 607 | 12 | | 10,680 | 4 | | 560 | 4 | 24 | 2 | |
| Corps Artillery: Colonel Petzel Commander of the 2nd Pomeranian Field Artillery Regiment | | | | | | | | | | | | |
| Horse Artillery Division, 2nd Pomeranian Field Artillery Regiment, | | | | | | | | | | | | |
| 2 & 3 horse artillery batteries: Lt Colonel Maschke | | | | | | | | | 2 | 12 | | |
| 2nd Field Artillery Division, 2nd Pomeranian Field Artillery Regiment | | | | | | | | | | | | |
| 3 & 4 heavy, 3 & 4 light batteries: Major Hubner | | | | | | | | | 4 | 24 | | |
| 3rd Sanitary Detachment | | | | | | | | | | | | |
| **Total Corps Artillery** | | | | | | | | | 6 | 36 | | |
| **Total II Army Corps** | 24,524 | 1,218 | | | 21,720 | | | 1,120 | 14 | 84 | | |

| | | | | | | | | | | | |
|---|---|---|---|---|---|---|---|---|---|---|---|
| **III Army Corps:** General Commanding: Lt General v Alvensleben II. Chief of General Staff: Col v Voigts-Rhetz. Commander of Artillery: Maj General v Bulow. | | | | | | | | | | | |
| 5th Infantry Division: Commander: Lt General v Stulpnagel. Officer of General Staff: Major v Lewinski II. | | | | | | | | | | | |
| 9th Infantry Brigade: Maj General v Doring | | | | | | | | | | | |
| Lieb Grenadier Regiment (1st Brandenburg) No 8: Lt Colonel v L'Estocq | | | 3 | 545 | 1,635 | | | | | | |
| 5th Brandenburg Infantry Regiment No 48: | | | 3 | 545 | 1,635 | | | | | | |
| **10th Infantry Brigade:** Maj General V Schwerin | | | | | | | | | | | |
| 2nd Brandenburg Grenadier Regiment No12: Colonel v Reuter | | | 3 | 545 | 1,635 | | | | | | |
| 6th Brandenburg Infantry Regiment No 52: Colonel v Wulffen | | | 3 | 545 | 1,635 | | | | | | |
| Brandenburg Rifle Battalion No 3: Major v Jena | | | 1 | 545 | 545 | | | | | | |
| 2nd Brandenburg Dragoon Regiment No 12: Major Pfeffer v Salomon | | | | | | 4 | 135 | 540 | | | |
| 1st Field Division, Brandenburg FA Regiment No 3 | | | | | | | | | | | |
| 1 & 2 heavy, 1 & 2 light batteries: Major Gallus | | | | | | | | | 4 | 24 | |
| 3rd Field Pioneer Company III Corps: Captain Thelemann | | | | | | | | | | | 1 |
| No 1 Sanitary Detachment | | | | | | | | | | | |
| **Total 5th Division** | 8,056 | 584 | 13 | | 7,085 | 4 | | 540 | 4 | 24 | 1 |
| 6th Infantry Division: Commander: Lt General Baron v Buddenbrock. Officer of General Staff: Major v Geissler | | | | | | | | | | | |
| 11th Infantry Brigade: Maj General v Rothmaler | | | | | | | | | | | |
| 3rd Brandenburg Infantry Regiment No 20: Colonel v Flatow | | | 3 | 610 | 1,830 | | | | | | |

| | | | | | | | | | | | |
|---|---|---|---|---|---|---|---|---|---|---|---|
| Brandenburg Fusilier Regiment No 35: Colonel du Plessis | | | 3 | 610 | 1,830 | | | | | | |
| **12th Infantry Brigade:** Colonel v Bismarck | | | | | | | | | | | |
| 4th Brandenburg Infantry Regimen No24: Colonel Count zu Dohna | | | 3 | 610 | 1,830 | | | | | | |
| 8th Brandenburg Infantry Regiment No 64: Colonel Baron Treusch v Buttlar-Brandenfels | | | 3 | 610 | 1,830 | | | | | | |
| 1st Brandenburg Dragoon Regiment No 2: Colonel v Drigalski | | | | | | 4 | 135 | 540 | | | |
| 3rd Field Division, Brandenburg FA Regiment No 3 | | | | | | | | | | | |
| 5 & 6 heavy, 5 & 6 light batteries: Major Beck | | | | | | | | | 4 | 24 | |
| 2nd Field Pioneer Company III Corps with entrenching tool column: Captain Bredan | | | | | | | | | | | 1 |
| No 2 Sanitary Detachment | | | | | | | | | | | |
| **Total 6th Division** | **8,057** | **590** | **12** | | **7,320** | **4** | | **540** | **4** | **24** | **1** |
| Corps Artillery: Colonel v Dresky Commander Brandenburg FA Regiment No 3 | | | | | | | | | | | |
| Horse Artillery Division, Brandenburg FA Regiment No 3 | | | | | | | | | | | |
| 1 & 3 horse artillery batteries: Major Lentz | | | | | | | | | 2 | 12 | |
| 2nd Field Artillery Division, Brandenburg FA Regiment No 3 | | | | | | | | | | | |
| 3 & 4 heavy, 3 & 4 light batteries: Major v Lyncker | | | | | | | | | 4 | 24 | |
| 1st Field Pioneer Company III Corps with light field bridge train: Captain Kuntze | | | | | | | | | | | 1 |
| No 3 Sanitary Detachment | | | | | | | | | | | |
| **Total Corps Artillery** | | | | | | | | | **6** | **36** | **1** |
| **Total III Army Corps** | **16,113** | **1,174** | | | **14,405** | | | **1,080** | **14** | **84** | |
| **IX Army Corps:** General Commanding:General of Infantry v Manstein. Chief of General Staff: Major Bronsart v Schellendorf. Commander of Artillery: Maj General Baron v Puttkammer. | | | | | | | | | | | |

| | | | | | | | | | | |
|---|---|---|---|---|---|---|---|---|---|---|
| 1st Brigade No 45: Maj General von Craushaar | | | | | | | | | | |
| 1st Body Guard Grenadier Regiment No100: Colonel Garten | | 3 | 855 | 2,565 | | | | | | |
| 2nd (King William of Prussia) Grenadier Regiment No 101: Colonel Count v Seydlitz-Gerstenberg | | 3 | 855 | 2,565 | | | | | | |
| Skirmishers (Fusiliers) Regiment No 108: Colonel Baron v Hausen | | 3 | 855 | 2,565 | | | | | | |
| **2nd Brigade No 46:** Colonel v Montbe | | | | | | | | | | |
| 3rd Infantry Regiment (Crown Prince's) No102: Colonel Rudorff | | 3 | 855 | 2,565 | | | | | | |
| 4th Infantry Regiment No 103: Lt Colonel Dietrich | | 3 | 855 | 2,565 | | | | | | |
| 1st Reiter Regiment (Crown Prince) Lt Colonel v Sahr | | | | | 4 | 140 | 560 | | | |
| 1st Field Division, 12th FA Regiment; | | | | | | | | | | |
| 1 & 2 heavy, 1 & 2 light batteries: Lt Colonel v Watzdorff | | | | | | | | 4 | 24 | |
| 2nd Company 12th Pioneer Battalion with entrenching tool column: Captain Richter | | | | | | | | | | 1 |
| No 1 Sanitary Detachment | | | | | | | | | | |
| **Total 23rd Division** | **13,999** | **616** | **15** | | **12,825** | **4** | | **560** | **4** | **24** | **1** |
| **2nd Infantry Division No 24: Commander: Maj General Nehrhoff v Holderberg. Officer of General Staff: Major v Tschirschky. Staff Officers: v Bulow, v Carlowitz.** | | | | | | | | | | |
| 3rd Brigade No 47: Maj General v Leonhardi | | | | | | | | | | |
| 5th Infantry Regiment (Prince Frederick Augustus) No104: Colonel v Elterlein | | 3 | 875 | 2,625 | | | | | | |
| 6th Infantry Regiment No 105: Colonel v Tettau | | 3 | 875 | 2,625 | | | | | | |
| 1st Rifle Battalion (Crown Prince's) No 12: Major Count Holtzedorff | | 1 | 875 | 875 | | | | | | |
| **4th Infantry Brigade No 48:** Colonel v Schulz | | | | | | | | | | |

| | | | | | | | | | | | |
|---|---|---|---|---|---|---|---|---|---|---|---|
| 7th Infantry Regiment (Prince George) No106******: Colonel v Abendroth | | | 2 | 875 | 1,750 | | | | | | |
| 8th Infantry Regimen No 107: Lt Colonel v Schweinitz | | | 3 | 875 | 2,625 | | | | | | |
| 2nd Rifle Battalion No 13: Colonel v Gotzf | | | 1 | 875 | 875 | | | | | | |
| 2nd Reiter Regiment: Major Genthe | | | | | | 4 | 140 | 560 | | | |
| 2nd Field Division, 12th FA Regiment; | | | | | | | | | | | |
| 3 & 4 heavy, 3 & 4 light batteries: Major Richter | | | | | | | | | 4 | 24 | |
| 3rd Company 12th Pioneer Battalion with light field bridge train: Captain Schubert | | | | | | | | | | | 1 |
| No 2 Sanitary Detachment | | | | | | | | | | | |
| **Total 24th Division** | **13,189** | **638** | **13** | | **11,375** | **4** | | **560** | **4** | **24** | **1** |
| ****** The 2nd battalion was in Pont a Mousson | | | | | | | | | | | |
| **12th Cavalry Division:** Commander: Maj General Count v Lippe.Officer of General Staff: Captain Reyher. Staff Officers: v Kirchbach, v Konneritz. | | | | | | | | | | | |
| 1st Cavalry Brigade No 23: Maj General Krug v Nidda | | | | | | | | | | | |
| Guard Reiter Regiment: Colonel v Carlowitz | | | | | | 4 | 130 | 520 | | | |
| **2nd Cavalry Brigade No 24:** Maj General Senfft v Pilsach | | | | | | | | | | | |
| 3rd Reiter Regiment: Colonel v Standfest | | | | | | 4 | 130 | 520 | | | |
| 1st Horse Artillery Battery 12th Field Artillery Regiment: Captain Zenker | | | | | | | | | 1 | 6 | |
| **Total 12th Cavalry Division** | | **2,287** | | | | **8** | | **1,040** | **1** | **6** | |
| **Corps Artillery:** Colonel Funcke, Commander 12th Field Artillery Regiment | | | | | | | | | | | |
| 3rd Field Division, 12th FA Regiment; | | | | | | | | | | | |
| 5 & 6 heavy, 5 light batteries: Major Hoch | | | | | | | | | 3 | 18 | |
| 4th Field Artillery Division, 12th Field Artillery Regiment | | | | | | | | | | | |

| | | | | | | | | | | |
|---|---|---|---|---|---|---|---|---|---|---|
| 7 & 8 heavy & 6 light batteries and 2nd HA Battery 12th FA Regiment: Lt Col Oertel | | | | | | | | 4 | 24 | |
| **Total Corps Artillery** | | | | | | | | 7 | 42 | |
| **Total XII Army Corps** | 27,188 | 3,541 | | | 24,200 | | | 2,160 | 16 | 96 | |
| 5th Cavalry Division: Commander: Lt General v Rheinbaben. Officer of General Staff: Captain v Heister. | | | | | | | | | | |
| **11th Cavalry Brigade:** Maj General v Barby | | | | | | | | | | |
| Westphalian Cuirassier Regiment No 4: Colonel v Arnim | | | | | 4 | 100 | 400 | | | |
| 1st Hanovarian Lancer Regiment No 13: Colonel v Schack | | | | | 4 | 100 | 400 | | | |
| Oldenburg Dragoon Regiment No 19: Colonel v Trotha | | | | | 4 | 100 | 400 | | | |
| **12th Cavalry Brigade:** Maj General v Bredow | | | | | | | | | | |
| Magdeburg Cuirassier Regiment No 7: Lt Colonel v Larisch | | | | | 4 | 100 | 400 | | | |
| Altmark Lancer Regiment No16: Major v d Dollen | | | | | 4 | 100 | 400 | | | |
| Schleswig Holstein Dragoon Regiment No 13; Colonel v Brauchitsch | | | | | 4 | 100 | 400 | | | |
| **13th Cavalry Brigade:** Maj General v Redern | | | | | | | | | | |
| Magdeburg Hussar Regiment No 10: Colonel v Weise | | | | | 4 | 100 | 400 | | | |
| 2nd Westphalian Hussar Regiment No11: Lt Colonel Baron v Eller Eberstein | | | | | 4 | 100 | 400 | | | |
| Brunswick Hussar Regiment No 17: Lt Colonel v Rauch | | | | | 4 | 100 | 400 | | | |
| 1st Horse Artillery Battery 4th Field Artillery Regiment: Captain Bode | | | | | | | | | 1 | 6 | |
| 2nd Horse Artillery Battery 10th Field Artillery Regiment: Captain Schirmer | | | | | | | | | 1 | 6 | |
| **Total 5th Cavalry Division** | | 4,210 | | | | 36 | | 3,600 | 2 | 12 | |

| | | | | | | | | | | | | |
|---|---|---|---|---|---|---|---|---|---|---|---|---|
| **6th Cavalry Division:** Commander: HH Duke William of Mecklenburg-Schwerin. Officer of General Staff: Major v Schonfels. | | | | | | | | | | | | |
| **14th Cavalry Brigade:** Maj General Baron v Diepenbroick-Gruter | | | | | | | | | | | | |
| Brandenburg Cuirassier Regiment (Emperor Nicholas I of Russia) No 6: Lt Colonel Count z Lynar | | | | | | 4 | 115 | 460 | | | | |
| 1st Brandenburg Lancer Regiment (Emperor of Russia) No 3: Colonel Count v d Groben | | | | | | 4 | 115 | 460 | | | | |
| Schleswig Holstein Lancer Regiment No 15: Colonel v Avensleben | | | | | | 4 | 115 | 460 | | | | |
| **15th Cavalry Brigade:** Maj General v Rauch | | | | | | | | | | | | |
| Brandenburg Hussar Regiment No 3 (Zeiten's Hussars): Colonel v Ziethen | | | | | | 4 | 115 | 460 | | | | |
| Schleswig Holstein Hussar Regiment 16: Colonel v Schmidt | | | | | | 4 | 115 | 460 | | | | |
| 2nd Horse Artillery Battery 3rd Field Artillery Regiment: Captain Wittstock | | | | | | | | | | 1 | 6 | |
| **Total 6th Cavalry Division** | | 2,570 | | | | 20 | | 2,300 | 1 | 6 | | |

| Summary | OH Infantry | OH Cavalry | KE Infantry | KE Cavalry | OH/KE Guns |
|---|---|---|---|---|---|
| **I Army** | | | | | |
| 1 Corps, 4th Infantry Brigade | | | 5,220 | 135 | 6 |
| VII Corps | 19,077 | 1,210 | 17,365 | 1,120 | 84 |
| VIII Corps | 23,378 | 1,242 | 21,340 | 1,120 | 90 |

| | | | | | |
|---|---|---|---|---|---|
| 1st Cavalry Division | | 3,301 | | 3,000 | 6 |
| **Total I Army** | **42,455** | **5,753** | **43,925** | **5,375** | **186** |
| **II Army** | | | | | |
| Guard Corps | 28,160 | 3,181 | 25,987 | 2,940 | 90 |
| II Corps | 24,524 | 1,218 | 21,720 | 1,120 | 84 |
| III Corps | 16,113 | 1,174 | 14,405 | 1,080 | 84 |
| IX Corps | 21,827 | 1,809 | 19,400 | 1,640 | 90 |
| X Corps | 18,551 | 1,128 | 16,785 | 1,020 | 90 |
| XII Corps | 27,188 | 3,541 | 24,200 | 2,160 | 96 |
| 5th Cavalry Division | | 4,210 | | 3,600 | 12 |
| 6th Cavalry Division | | 2,570 | | 2,300 | 6 |
| **Total II Army** | **136,363** | **18,831** | **122,497** | **15,860** | **552** |
| **Combined totals for I and II Armies** | **178,818** | **24,584** | **166,422** | **21,235** | **738** |

The Kriegsgeschichtliche Einzelschriften regards a number of units that were held back as being a 'tactical reserve', and only some of which should be included within the total number of troops actually 'engaged' in the fighting; these are detailed below. The casualties/ammunition expended gives an idea as to the extent of their involvement in the actual fighting.

| | |
|---|---|
| **I Army** | |
| VII Corps: | 5th & 9th companies, 3th Infantry Regiment |
| | Fusilier battalion, 15th Infantry Regiment |
| | 74th Infantry Regiment (The 74th lost 13 men and 2 horses on the 18th) |
| | Fusilier battalion, 53rd Infantry Regiment |
| | 1st company 2nd battalion & Fusilier battalion 77th Infantry Regiment |
| | 8th and 15th Hussar regiments (*15th Hussars lost 7 men and 14 horses*) |
| VIII Corps: | 1st battalion , 40th Fusilier Regiment |
| | 7th and 9th Hussar regiments (*7th lost 1 man and 7 horses, 9th lost 14 men and 32 horses*) |
| | 1st Cavalry Division, except their attached horse artillery (*the divisional cavalry lost 73 men and 145 horses*) |
| **2 Army** | |
| Guard Corps | 1st & 3rd companies 1st Guard Grenadier Regiment |
| | The whole of the cavalry (*the Guard Hussars lost 4 men and 9 horses, the 2nd Guard Lancers, 6 men and 11 horses*) |
| II Corps | 8th company, 2nd Grenadier Regiment |
| | 1st battalion, 42nd Infantry Regiment |
| | 3rd Dragoon Regiment (*3rd Draggons lost 1 man and 2 horses*) |

| | |
|---|---|
| | 1st & 2nd Heavy batteries,2nd Field Artillery Regiment (the 1st lost 7 horses killed & wounded and fired 1 shell; the 2nd lost 1 man and 2 horses, killed and wounded) |
| | The 4th Infantry Division, except the 4th and 8th companies, 21st Infantry Regiment ( 4th Division lost 323 men killed and wounded, the 5th Light fired 1 round) |
| | The Corps artillery (*the Corps artillery lost 1 man and 2 horses; 3rd Heavy fired 1 round as did the 3rd Horse artillery*) |
| III Corps | The Corps artillery and the 1st, 2nd, 5th & 6th Heavy batteries 3rd Field Artillery Regiment(the artilery lost 95 horses, 59 men and fired off 3 rounds. |
| IX Corps | The 6th, 7th and 9th companies 84th infantry Regiment |
| | 2nd & Fusilier battalion 11th Grenadier Regiment |
| | 3rd company 4th Hessian Infantry Regiment |
| | 3rd Cavalry Regiment (The OOB lists the cavalry belonging to this corps as being the 1st and2nd Regiments; there is no mention of the 3rd) |
| X Corps | The entire artillery (*The artillery lost 21 men and 62 horses, killed and wounded and fired off 1,582 rounds*) |
| | The 2nd & Fusilier battalions 17th Infantry Regiment (*The regiment lost 34 men killed and wounded*) |
| | The 2nd & Fusilier battalions 92nd Infantry Regiment (*The regiment lost 40 men killed and wounded*) |
| | 10th Rifles (*The battalion lost 3 men*) |
| XII Corps | 46th Infantry Brigade (*The brigade lost 5 men*) |
| | 1st and 2nd Reiter Regiments (*The regiments lost 15 men and 29 horses*) |
| | The Guard Reiter Regiment , excepting the 1st squadron |
| | The 3rd Reiter Regiment (*The regiment lost 1 man and 4 horses*) |
| 5th Cavalry Div | All except their horse artillery |
| 6th Cavalry Div | All |
| The Kriegsgeschichtliche Einzelschriften identifies a number that were 'detached to the battlefield' that should be included within the total number of troops 'engaged' as follows:- | |
| **1 Army** | |
| 1st Corps 4th Brigade: | 9th company, 45th Infantry Regiment and the battery of guns |
| VII Corps: | 6th company, 55th Infantry Regiment |
| VIII Corps: | 7th company, 60th Infantry Regiment |
| **2 Army** | |
| XII Corps | 1st squadron Guard Reiter & 2nd squadron 3rd Reiter regiments |

| After the above allowances are reflected within the OOB the Kriegsgeschichtliche Einzelschriften estimates the number of forces actually 'engaged' in the fighting as follows:- | Battns | Men | Sqdrns | Troopers | Batts | Guns | Pioneers |
|---|---|---|---|---|---|---|---|
| **I Army** | | | | | | | |
| 1 Corps, 4th Infantry Brigade | ¼ | 217 | | | 1 | 60 | |
| VII Corps | 17 | 13,800 | | | 14 | 82 | |
| VIII Corps | 23¾ | 20,445 | | | 15 | 90 | |
| 1st Cavalry Division* | | | | | 1 . | 6 | |
| **II Army** | | | | | | | |
| Guard Corps | 28 | 25,540 | | | 15 | 90 | 2 |
| II Corps | 11¼ | 10,335 | | | 2 | 12 | |
| III Corps | | | | | 10 | 60 | |
| IX Corps | 17½ | 16,039 | | | 15 | 90 | |
| X Corps | 5 | 3,825 | | | 14 | 84 | |
| XII Corps | 22 | 19,070 | | | 16 | 96 | |
| 5th Cavalry Division | | | | | 2 | 12 | |
| 6th Cavalry Division | | | | | | | |
| **Combined totals for I and II Army** | **124¾** | **109,271** | **0** | **0** | **105** | **682** | **2** |
| Or, in round terms 109,200 infantry supported by 628 guns. | | | | | | | |
| * The omission of the troopers of 1st Cavalry Division from the troops 'engaged' is hard to explain given that they were comitted to the attack across the Mance Ravine, even though their advance ended in chaos. | | | | | | | |

# Appendix XIII

## French Order of Battle, Gravelotte

French Army of the Rhine at the battle of Gravelotte-Saint Privat. The figures detailed below are taken from Les Opérations autour de Metz Journées des 17 et 18 Août Documents Annexes and whilst comprehensive, the way the individual units completed their returns helps to illustrate why various authors provide such widely differing numbers for troops involved. For example on the 17th the Grenadier Division within the Imperial Guard reported an effective strength of 343 officers and 7,290 men. However included within this total were 261 men in hospital and 1,183 men who were absent, which meant that only 6,012 were actually present, under arms. Some units provide returns pre and post battle and where these are given, the pre battle strength is listed. Where no such information is available the strengths have been calculated by adding the rolls taken after the battle to the losses reported by each unit to give a pre battle strength for each unit. Where additional information is availble for individual unit strength, this has also been included.

| Commander in Chief Marshal Francois Achille Bazaine. Chief of Staff General de division Jarras. Commandant de l'artillerie General de division Soleille | Composite totals | Infantry Officers | Men | Horses |
|---|---|---|---|---|
| **Imperial Guard**\* General Commanding: General of Division Bourbaki. | | | | |
| **1st Division:** Commander: General of Division Deligny | | | | |
| **1st Brigade:** General of Brigade Brincourt | | | | |
| Guard Chasseur Battalion:Commandant Dufaure du Bessol | | | | |
| 1st Guard Voltigeur Regiment: Colonel Dumont | | | | |
| 2nd Guard Voltigeur Regiment: Colonel Peychaud | | | | |
| **2nd Brigade:** General of Brigade Garnier | | | | |
| 3rd Guard Voltigeur Regiment: Colonel Lian | | | | |
| 4th Guard Voltigeur Regiment: Colonel Ponsard | | | | |
| **Divisional Artillery:** Lieut. Colonel Gerbaut | | | | |
| No 1 Battery Field Artillery Regiment of the Guard | | | | |
| No 2 Battery Field Artillery Regiment of the Guard | | | | |
| No 5 Battery Field Artillery Regiment of the Guard | | | | |
| Engineers : 8th Company of 3rd Engineer Regiment | | | | |

| | | | |
|---|---|---|---|
| **1st Division Total** | **8,033** | | |
| **2nd Division:** Commander: General of Division Picard (1) | | | |
| État Major | | 10 | | 38 |
| Services administratifs | | 8 | 1 | 8 |
| Trésor | | 3 | | 2 |
| **1st Brigade:** General of Brigade Jeanningros | | | | |
| Guard Zouave Regiment:Colonel Giraud | | 42 | 1,104 | 28 |
| 1st Guard Grenadier Regiment: Colonel Theologue | | 57 | 1,572 | 28 |
| **2nd Brigade:** General of Brigade le Poitevin de la Croix Vaubois* | | | | |
| 2nd Guard Grenadier Regiment: Colonel Lecointe | | 49 | 1,232 | 30 |
| 3rd Guard Grenadier Regiment: Colonel Cousin | | 25 | 720 | 23 |
| **Divisional Artillery:** Lieut. Colonel Denecey de Cervilly | | | | |
| No 3 Battery Field Artillery Regiment of the Guard | | | | |
| No 4 Battery Field Artillery Regiment of the Guard | | | | |
| No 6 Battery Field Artillery Regiment of the Guard | | | | |
| **Total Artillery** | | 17 | 463 | |
| Engineers : 10th Company of 3rd Engineer Regiment | | 2 | 58 | 7 |
| Gendarmerie | | 1 | 16 | 11 |
| Train | | 1 | 50 | 69 |
| Infirmiers | | | 15 | |
| Ouvriers | | | 11 | |
| Guides | | 41 | 522 | |
| **2nd Division Total** | **6,160** | **256** | **5,764** | **244** |
| **Cavalry Division:** Commander: General of Division Desvaux | | | | |
| **1st Brigade:** General of Brigade Halna du Fretay | | | | |
| Guides Regiment: Colonel de Percin-Northumberland | | | | |
| Chasseurs a Cheval: Colonel de Montarby | | | | |
| **2nd Brigade:** General of Division de France | | | | |
| Lancers of the Guard: Colonel Latheulade | | | | |

| | | | | |
|---|---|---|---|---|
| Dragoons of the Guard: Colonel Sautereau Dupart | | | | |
| **3rd Brigade:** General of Brigade du Preuil | | | | |
| Guard Cuirassier Regiment: Colonel Dupressoir | | | | |
| Guard Carabinier Regiment: Colonel Petit | | | | |
| **Divisional Artillery** | | | | |
| No 1 Battery Horse Artillery of the Guard | | | | |
| No 2 Battery Horse Artillery of the Guard | | | | |
| **Cavalry Division Total** | 3,998 | | | |
| **Artillery Reserve** | | | | |
| **Artillery Reserve:** Commander: Colonel Clappier | | | | |
| No 3 Battery Horse Artillery of the Guard | | | | |
| No 4 Battery Horse Artillery of the Guard | | | | |
| No 5 Battery Horse Artillery of the Guard | | | | |
| No 6 Battery Horse Artillery of the Guard | | | | |
| **Total Artillery Reserve** | 2,125 | | | |
| **Divers** | 456 | | | |
| **Total Imperial Guard** | 20,772 | | | |
| *Figures from recorded casualties added to those present after battle | | | | |
| Including sick men and livestock and those detached on other duties the 2nd Guard Division had a total strength of 7,603 men and 1,301 horses | | | | |
| **2 Corps* General Commanding: General of Division Frossard.** | | | | |
| General Staff | | 12 | | |
| **1st Division:** Commander: General of Division Verge | | | | |
| General Staff | | 10 | | 30 |
| 1st Brigade: General of Brigade Letellier-Valaze | | | | |
| 3rd Chasseur Battalion:Commandant Thoina | | 10 | 454 | 10 |
| 32nd Line Infantry Regiment: Colonel Merle | | 32 | 1,328 | 32 |
| 55th Line Infantry Regiment: Colonel de Waldner de Freudenstein | | 52 | 1,763 | 30 |
| **2nd Brigade: General of Brigade Jolivet** | | | | |
| 76th Line Infantry Regiment: Colonel Brice | | 34 | 1,225 | 28 |

| | | | |
|---|---|---|---|
| 77th Line Infantry Regiment: Colonel Fevrier | | 56 | 1,483 | 30 |
| **Divisional Artillery:** Lieut. Colonel Chavaudret | | | | |
| No 5 Battery 5th Field Artillery Regiment | | | | |
| No 12 Battery 5th Field Artillery Regiment | | | | |
| No 6 Battery 5th Field Artillery Regiment | | | | |
| **Artillery Total** | | 16 | 422 | 357 |
| Engineers : 9th Company of 3rd Engineer Regiment | | 5 | 151 | 21 |
| Servces administratifs | | 5 | 47 | 14 |
| Train des equipages | | 1 | 45 | 72 |
| **1st Division Total** | 7,139 | 221 | 6,198 | 624 |
| **2nd Division:** Commander: General of Division Fauvart-Bastoul | | | | |
| Etat-major general | | 2 | | 6 |
| Etat-major general et officiers d'ordonnance | | 10 | | 16 |
| **1st Brigade:** General of Brigade Pouget | | | | |
| 12th Chasseur Battalion:Commandant Jeanne-Beaulieu | | 12 | 599 | 10 |
| 8th Line Infantry Regiment: Colonel Haca | | 41 | 1,569 | 23 |
| 23rd Line Infantry Regiment: Colonel Roland | | 44 | 1,666 | 27 |
| **2nd Brigade:** General of Division Fauvart-Bastoul | | | | |
| 66th Line Infantry Regiment: Colonel Ameller | | 36 | 1,523 | 23 |
| 67th Line Infantry Regiment: Colonel Mangin | | 39 | 1,276 | 22 |
| 5th squadron 5th Chasseurs a Cheval | | 6 | 98 | 114 |
| Engineers : 12th Company of 3rd Engineer Regiment | | 4 | 148 | |
| Sapeurs Conducteurs | | | 8 | 16 |
| Divisional Artillery:Lieut. Colonel de Maintenant | | | | |
| Officiers superieurs et medecins | | 3 | | |
| No 7 Battery 5th Field Artillery Regiment | | 4 | 148 | 114 |
| No 8 Battery 5th Field Artillery Regiment | | 4 | 143 | 112 |
| No 9 Battery 5th Field Artillery Regiment | | 6 | 149 | 119 |
| Detachment 4th company 2nd Regiment | | | 49 | 66 |
| Services administratifs | | 10 | 43 | 7 |

| | | | | |
|---|---|---|---|---|
| Train des equipages | | | 29 | 46 |
| Prevote | | 1 | 14 | 12 |
| **2nd Division Total** | **7,684** | **222** | **7,462** | **733** |
| **Cavalry Division:** Commander: General of Brigade De Valabregue | | | | |
| **1st Brigade:** General of Brigade de Valabregue | | | | |
| 4th Chasseurs a Cheval: Colonel du Ferron | | 47 | 585 | 589 |
| 5th Chasseurs a Cheval: Colonel de Sereville | | 41 | 611 | 572 |
| 2nd Brigade: General of Brigade Bachelier | | | | |
| 7th Dragoon Regiment: Colonel de Gressot | | 34 | 489 | 470 |
| 12th Dragoon Regiment: Colonel D'Avocourt | | 36 | 523 | 448 |
| **Cavalry Division Total** | **2,366** | **158** | **2,208** | **2,079** |
| **Artillery Reserve:** Commander: Colonel Beaudouin | | | | |
| No 10 Battery 5th Field Artillery Regiment | | | | |
| No 11 Battery 5th Field Artillery Regiment | | | | |
| **Artillery Total 1st Division** | | 4 | 265 | 218 |
| No 6 Battery 15th Field Artillery Regiment | | | | |
| No 10 Battery 15th Field Artillery Regiment | | | | |
| **Artillery Total 2nd Division** | | 7 | 359 | 308 |
| No 7 Battery 17th Horse Artillery Regiment | | | | |
| No 8 Battery 17th Horse Artillery Regiment | | | | |
| Artillery Total 3rd Division | | 8 | 264 | 257 |
| **Reserve Artillery Total** | **907** | **19** | **888** | **783** |
| **Engineer Reserve** | **192** | | | |
| **Total 2 Corps** | **18,288** | **620** | **17,476** | **4,219** |
| **Brigade Lapasset:** General of Brigade Lapasset | | | | |
| General staff | | 3 | 9 | 17 |
| 2nd Co 14th Chasseur Battalion: Captain de Garros | | 2 | 103 | |
| 84th Line Infantry Regiment: Colonel Benoit | | 41 | 1,575 | 36 |
| 97th Line Infantry Regiment: Colonel Copmartin | | 48 | 1,682 | 26 |
| Part of 11th Line Infantry Regiment | | 2 | 67 | |
| Part of 46th Line Infantry Regiment | | 3 | 91 | |
| Part of 86th Line Infantry Regiment | | 3 | 98 | |

| | | | |
|---|---|---|---|
| No 7 Battery 2nd Field Artillery Regiment | | 4 | 125 | 116 |
| 3rd Lancers | | 26 | 374 | 401 |
| Train des equipages | | 3 | 180 | 212 |
| **Total Brigade Lapassat** | **4,436** | **135** | **4,304** | **808** |
| * Figures from pre battle roll call | | | | |
| **3 Corps:** Marshal Le Boeuf | | | | |
| État Major Général | | 17 | 22 | 58 |
| Services du quartier général | | 33 | 438 | 378 |
| **1st Division:** Commander: General of Division Montaudon | | | | |
| **1st Brigade:** General Plombin | | | | |
| 18th Chasseur Battalion: Commandant Rigault | | | | |
| 51st Line Infantry Regiment: Colonel Delebecque | | | | |
| 62nd Line Infantry Regiment: Colonel Dauphin | | | | |
| **2nd Brigade:** General of Brigade Clinchant | | | | |
| 81st Line Infantry Regiment: Colonel d'Albici | | | | |
| 95th Line Infantry Regiment: Colonel Davout d'Auerstadt | | | | |
| **Divisional Artillery:** Lieut. Colonel Fourgous | | | | |
| No 5 Battery 4th Field Artillery Regiment | | | | |
| No 6 Battery 4th Field Artillery Regiment | | | | |
| No 8 Battery 4th Field Artillery Regiment | | | | |
| Engineers : 1 Company of 1st Engineer Regiment | | | | |
| **1st Division Total** | **10,138** | **324** | **9,814** | **723** |
| **2nd Division:** Commander: General Nayral | | | | |
| **1st Brigade:** | | | | |
| 15th Chasseur Battalion: Commandant Lafouge | | | | |
| 19th Line Infantry Regiment: Colonel de Launay | | | | |
| 41st Line Infantry Regiment: Colonel Saussier | | | | |
| **2nd Brigade:** General of Division Duplessis | | | | |
| 69th Line Infantry Regiment: Colonel le Tourneur | | | | |

| | | | | |
|---|---|---|---|---|
| 90th Line Infantry Regiment: Colonel de Courcy | | | | |
| **Divisional Artillery:** Lieut. Colonel Delange | | | | |
| No 11 Battery 4th Field Artillery Regiment | | | | |
| No 12 Battery 4th Field Artillery Regiment | | | | |
| No 9 Battery 4th Field Artillery Regiment | | | | |
| Engineers : 1 Company of 1st Engineer Regiment | | | | |
| **2nd Division Total** | **9,242** | **280** | **8,887** | **886** |
| **3rd Division:** Commander: General of Division Metman | | | | |
| **1st Brigade:** General of Brigade de Potier (2) | | | | |
| 7th Chasseur Battalion:Commandant Rigaud | | | | |
| 7th Line Infantry Regiment: Colonel Cotteret | | 54 | 1,736 | 27 |
| 29th Line Infantry Regiment: Colonel Lalanne | | 56 | 2,157 | 30 |
| (2) Including sick and those detached on other duties 1st Brigade had a total strength of 111 officers, 4,178 men and 57 horses. | | | | |
| **2nd Brigade:** General of Brigade Arnaudeau (3) | | | | |
| État Major | | 2 | | 9 |
| 59th Line Infantry Regiment: Colonel Duez | | 55 | 2,009 | 31 |
| 71st Line Infantry Regiment: Colonel de Ferussac | | 49 | 1,862 | 25 |
| (3) Including sick and those detached on other duties 2nd Brigade had a total strength of 116 officers, 4,291 men and 65 horses. | | | | |
| **Divisional Artillery:** Lieut. Colonel Sempe (4) | | | | |
| État Major | | 3 | | |
| No 6 Battery 11th Field Artillery Regiment | | 4 | 143 | |
| No 7 Battery 11th Field Artillery Regiment | | 4 | 149 | |
| No 5 Battery 11th Field Artillery Regiment | | 5 | 153 | |
| 7 company 1st Regiment du Train | | 1 | 45 | |
| (4) Including sick and those detached on other duties the divisional artillery had a total strength of 17 officers, 490 men and 426 horses. | | | | |
| Engineers : 1 Company of 1st Engineer Regiment | | | | |

| | | | | |
|---|---|---|---|---|
| **3rd Division Total** | 10,536 | 312 | 10,224 | 122 |
| **4th Division:** Commander: General Aymard | | | | |
| **1st Brigade:** General of Brigade de Brauer | | | | |
| 11th Chasseur Battalion: Commandant de Pillot | | | | |
| 44th Line Infantry Regiment: Colonel Fournier | | | | |
| 60th Line Infantry Regiment: Colonel Boissie | | | | |
| **2nd Brigade:** General of Brigade Sangle-Ferriere | | | | |
| 80th Line Infantry Regiment: Colonel Janin | | | | |
| 85th Line Infantry Regiment: Colonel Planchut | | | | |
| **Divisional Artillery:** Lieut. Colonel Maucourant | | | | |
| No 9 Battery 11th Field Artillery Regiment | | | | |
| No 10 Battery 11th Field Artillery Regiment | | | | |
| No 8 Battery 11th Field Artillery Regiment | | | | |
| Engineers : 1 Company of 1st Engineer Regiment | | | | |
| **4th Division Total** | 9,910 | 304 | 9,606 | 849 |
| **Cavalry Division** | | | | |
| **Cavalry Division:** Commander: General of Division Clerembault | | | | |
| **1st Brigade:** General of Brigade Bruchard (sent to support 6 Corps) | | | | |
| 2nd Chasseurs a Cheval: Colonel Pelletier (sent to support 6 Corps) | | | | |
| 3rd Chasseurs a Cheval: Colonel Sanson de Sansal ( sent to support 6 Corps around 2.00pm) | | | | |
| 10th Chasseurs a Cheval: Colonel Nerin (acted as escort for LeBoeuf) | | | | |
| **2nd Brigade:** General of Brigade Gayrault de Maubranches | | | | |
| 2nd Dragoon Regiment: Colonel du Paty de Clam | | | | |
| 4th Dragoon Regiment: Colonel Cornat | | | | |
| **3rd Brigade:** General of Brigade Begougne de Juiniac | | | | |
| 5th Dragoon Regiment: Colonel Lachene | | | | |

| | | | | |
|---|---|---|---|---|
| 8th Dragoon Regiment: Colonel Boyer de Fonscolombe | | | | |
| **Cavalry Division Total** | **4,385** | **318** | **4,066** | **4,018** |
| **Artillery Reserve:** Commander: Colonel de Lajaille | | | | |
| No 7 Battery 4th Field Artillery Regiment | | | | |
| No 10 Battery 4th Field Artillery Regiment | | | | |
| No 11 Battery 11th Field Artillery Regiment | | | | |
| No 12 Battery 11th Field Artillery Regiment | | | | |
| No 1 Battery 17th Horse Artillery Regiment | | | | |
| No 2 Battery 17th Horse Artillery Regiment | | | | |
| No 3 Battery 17th Horse Artillery Regiment | | | | |
| No 4 Battery 17th Horse Artillery Regiment | | | | |
| **Total Artillery Reserve** | **2,419** | **44** | **1,317** | **1,278** |
| Parc d'artillerie | 778 | 19 | 759 | 1,076 |
| Engineer Reserve | 230 | 15 | 215 | 149 |
| Gendarmerie du quartier général | 13 | 1 | 12 | 12 |
| **Total 3 Corps** | **47,024** | **1,664** | **45,360** | **10,488** |
| *Figures from roll call on 17th | | | | |
| **4 Corps:*** General Commanding: General of Division de Ladmirault | | | | |
| **1st Division:** Commander: General of Division Courtot de Cissey | | | | |
| **1st Brigade:** General of Brigade Brayer | | | | |
| 20th Chasseur Battalion: Commandant de Labarriere | | | | |
| 1st Line Infantry Regiment: Colonel Fremont | | | | |
| 6th Line Infantry Regiment: Colonel Labarthe | | | | |
| **2nd Brigade:** General of Brigade de Goldberg | | | | |
| 57th Line Infantry Regiment: Colonel Giraud | | | | |
| 73rd Line Infantry Regiment: Colonel Supervielle | | | | |
| **Divisional Artillery:** Lieut. Colonel de Narp | | | | |
| No 5 Battery 15th Field Artillery Regiment | | | | |
| No 9 Battery 15th Field Artillery Regiment | | | | |
| No 12 Battery 15th Field Artillery Regiment | | | | |

| | | | | |
|---|---|---|---|---|
| Engineers : 1 Company of 2nd Engineer Regiment | | | | |
| **1st Division Total** | 8,679 | | | |
| **2nd Division:** Commander: General Grenier | | | | |
| **1st Brigade:** General of Brigade Veron-dit-Bellecourt | | | | |
| 5th Chasseur Battalion: Commandant Carre | | | | |
| 13th Line Infantry Regiment: Colonel Lion | | | | |
| 43rd Line Infantry Regiment: Colonel de Viville | | | | |
| **2nd Brigade:** General of Brigade Pradier | | | | |
| 64th Line Infantry Regiment: Colonel Leger | | | | |
| 98th Line Infantry Regiment: Colonel Lechesne | | | | |
| **Divisional Artillery:** Lieut. Colonel de Larminat | | | | |
| No 6 Battery 1st Field Artillery Regiment | | | | |
| No 7 Battery 1st Field Artillery Regiment | | | | |
| No 5 Battery 1st Field Artillery Regiment | | | | |
| Engineers : 1 Company of 2nd Engineer Regiment | | | | |
| **2nd Division Total** | 9,234 | | | |
| **3rd Division:** Commander: General of Division Latrille, Count de Lorencez | | | | |
| **1st Brigade:** General of Brigade Count Pajol | | | | |
| 2nd Chasseur Battalion: Commandant Le Tanneur | | | | |
| 15th Line Infantry Regiment: Colonel Fraboulet de Kerleadec | | | | |
| 33rd Line Infantry Regiment: Colonel Bounetou | | | | |
| **2nd Brigade:** General of Brigade Berger | | | | |
| 54th Line Infantry Regiment: Colonel Caillot | | | | |
| 65th Line Infantry Regiment: Colonel See | | | | |
| **Divisional Artillery:** Lieut. Colonel Legardeur | | | | |
| No 9 Battery 1st Field Artillery Regiment | | | | |
| No 10 Battery 1st Field Artillery Regiment | | | | |
| No 8 Battery 1st Field Artillery Regiment | | | | |
| Engineers : 1 Company of 2nd Engineer Regiment | | | | |

| | | | | |
|---|---|---|---|---|
| **3rd Division Total** | 10,472 | | | |
| **Cavalry Division:** Commander: General of Gondrecourt | | | | |
| **1st Brigade:** General of Brigade Montaigu | | | | |
| 2nd Hussar Regiment: Colonel Carrelet | | | | |
| 7th Hussar Regiment: Colonel Chausee | | | | |
| 2nd Brigade: General of Brigade Baron Gondrecourt | | | | |
| 3rd Dragoon Regiment: Colonel Bilhau | | | | |
| 11th Dragoon Regiment: Colonel Huyn de Verneville | | | | |
| **Cavalry Division Total** | 2,291 | | | |
| **Artillery Reserve:** Commander: General Lafaille | | | | |
| No 11 Battery 1st Field Artillery Regiment | | | | |
| No 12 Battery 1stField Artillery Regiment | | | | |
| No 6 Battery 8th Field Artillery Regiment | | | | |
| No 9 Battery 8th Field Artillery Regiment | | | | |
| No 5 Battery 17th Horse Artillery Regiment | | | | |
| No 6 Battery 17th Horse Artillery Regiment | | | | |
| 1 Co 2nd Engineer Regiment & detachment of sappers of 2nd Engineer Regiment | | | | |
| **Total Artillery Reserve** | 1,801 | | | |
| **Divers Total** | 823 | | | |
| **Total 4 Corps** | 33,300 | | | |
| *Figures from recorded casualties added to those present after battle | | | | |
| **6 Corps:*** General Commanding: Marshal Canrobet | | | | |
| **1st Division:** Commander: General of Division Tixier | | | | |
| **1st Brigade:** General of Brigade Pechot | | | | |
| 9th Chasseur Battalion: Commandant Mathelin | | | | |
| 4th Line Infantry Regiment: Colonel Vincendon | | | | |
| 10th Line Infantry Regiment: Colonel Ardant du Picq | | | | |
| **2nd Brigade:** General of Brigade Leroy de Dais | | | | |
| 12th Line Infantry Regiment: Colonel Lebrun | | | | |

| | | | |
|---|---|---|---|
| 100th Line Infantry Regiment: Colonel Gremion | | | |
| **Divisional Artillery:** Lieut. Colonel Montluisant | | | |
| No 5 Battery 8th Field Artillery Regiment | | | |
| No 7 Battery 8th Field Artillery Regiment | | | |
| No 8 Battery 8th Field Artillery Regiment | | | |
| No12 Battery 8th Field Artillery Regiment | | | |
| Engineers: 3rd Company of 3rd Engineer Regiment | | | |
| **1st Division Total** | **10,672** | | |
| **2nd Division:** Commander: General of Division Bisson | | | |
| **1st Brigade:** General of Brigade Noel | | | |
| 9th Line Infantry Regiment: Colonel Roux | | | |
| **From Artillery Reserve** | | | |
| No 9 Battery 13th Field Artillery Regiment | | | |
| No10 Battery 13th Field Artillery Regiment | | | |
| **2nd Division Total** | **2,098** | | |
| **3rd Division:** Commander: General of Division Lafont de Villiers | | | |
| **1st Brigade:** General of Brigade Becquet de Sonnay | | | |
| 75th Line Infantry Regiment: Colonel Amadieu | | | |
| 91st Line Infantry Regiment: Colonel Daguerre | | | |
| **2nd Brigade:** General of Brigade Colin (5) | | | |
| État Major | | 2 | | 5 |
| 93rd Line Infantry Regiment: Colonel Guazin | | 43 | 1,553 | |
| 94th Line Infantry Regiment: Colonel de Geslin | | 42 | 1,792 | |
| (5) Including sick and those detached on other duties 2nd Brigade had a total strength of 131 officers, 4,734 men and 57 horses. | | | |
| **Divisional Artillery:** Lieut. Colonel Jamet | | | |
| No 5 Battery 14th Field Artillery Regiment | | | |
| No 6 Battery 14th Field Artillery Regiment | | | |
| No 7 Battery 14th Field Artillery Regiment | | | |
| Engineers: 7th Company of 3rd Engineer Regiment | | | |

| | | | | |
|---|---|---|---|---|
| **3rd Division Total** | 10,873 | | | |
| **4th Division:** Commander: General of Division Levassor-Sorval | | | | |
| **1st Brigade:** General of Brigade de Marguenat | | | | |
| 25th Line Infantry Regiment: Colonel Gibon | | | | |
| 26th Line Infantry Regiment: Colonel Hanrion | | | | |
| **2nd Brigade:** General of Brigade Count De Chanaleilles | | | | |
| 28th Line Infantry Regiment: Colonel Lamothe | | | | |
| 70th Line Infantry Regiment: Colonel Bertier | | | | |
| **From Artillery Reserve:** Chef d'escadron Kesner | | | | |
| No 7 Battery 18th Horse Artillery Regiment | | | | |
| No 8 Battery 18th Horse Artillery Regiment | | | | |
| **4th Division Total** | 10,239 | | | |
| **Attached from Cavalry Reserve** | | | | |
| **1st Division:** Commander: General of Division du Barail (6) | | | | |
| **2nd Brigade:** General of Brigade de Lajaille | | | | |
| 2nd Regiment Chasseurs d'Afrique: Colonel de la Martiniere | | 35 | 501 | |
| (6) Including sick men and livestock and those detached on other duties the 2nd Chasseurs d'Afrique had a total strength of 643 men and 572 horses. | | | | |
| **Attached from 3rd Corps** | | | | |
| **1st Brigade:** General of Brigade Bruchard | | | | |
| 2nd Chasseurs a Cheval: Colonel Pelletier (7) | | 34 | 492 | |
| 3rd Chasseurs a Cheval: Colonel Sanson de Sansal (arrived around 2.00pm) | | | | |
| (7) Including sick men and livestock and those detached on other duties the 2nd Chasseurs a Cheval had a total strength of 561 men and 538 horses. | | | | |
| **Divisional Artillery:** Chef d'Escadron Loyer | | | | |
| No 5 Battery 19th Horse Artillery Regiment (8) | | 7 | 157 | |
| No 6 Battery 19th Horse Artillery Regiment (9) | | 6 | 155 | |

| | | | |
|---|---|---|---|
| (8) Including sick men and livestock and those detached on other duties the 5th Battery had a total strength of 168 men and 190 horses. | | | |
| (9) Including sick men and livestock and those detached on other duties the 6th Battery had a total strength of 164 men and 179 horses. | | | |
| **Cavalry Division & attached 1st Division Total** | 2,941 | | |
| **Total 6th Corps** | 36,823 | | |
| *Figures from recorded casualties added to those present after battle | | | |
| **Cavalry Reserve*** | | | |
| **3rd Division:** Commander: General of Division de Forton | | | |
| **1st Brigade:** General of Brigade Prince Murat | | | |
| 1st Dragoon Regiment: Colonel de Forceville | | 38 | 586 | 526 |
| 9th Dragoon Regiment: Colonel Reboul | | 37 | 500 | 492 |
| **2nd Brigade:** General of Brigade de Gramont Duke of Esparre | | | |
| 7th Cuirassier Regiment: Colonel Nitot | | 37 | 509 | 492 |
| 10th Cuirassier Regiment: Colonel Yuncker | | 41 | 463 | 467 |
| **Divisional Artillery:** Chef d'Escadron Clerc | | | |
| No 7 Battery 20th Horse Artillery Regiment | | | |
| No 8 Battery 20th Horse Artillery Regiment | | | |
| **Artillery Total** | | 7 | 269 | 304 |
| Gendarmerie | | 1 | 20 | |
| Train | | | 8 | 2,281 |
| **3rd Division Total** | **2,516** | **161** | **2,355** | **2,281** |
| * Figures from recorded casualties added to those present after battle | | | |
| **Artillery Reserve:*** Commander: General Canu | | | |
| **13th Artillery Regiment:** Commander: Colonel Salvador | | | |
| No 5 Battery | | | |
| No 6 Battery | | | |
| No 7 Battery | | | |
| No 8 Battery | | | |
| No 11 Battery | | | |

| | | | | | |
|---|---|---|---|---|---|
| No 12 Battery | | | | | |
| **18th Horse Artillery Regiment: Commander Colonel Toussaint** | | | | | |
| No 1 Battery | | | | | |
| No 2 Battery | | | | | |
| No 3 Battery | | | | | |
| No 4 Battery | | | | | |
| No 5 Battery | | | | | |
| No 6 Battery | | | | | |
| **Total Reserve Artillery** | 2,100 | | | | |
| *Figures from recorded casualties added to those present after battle | | | | | |
| **Summary** | | | | | |
| Total Guard | 20,772 | | | | |
| Total 2 Corps( including Lapasset) | 22,724 | | | | |
| Total 3 Corps | 47,024 | | | | |
| Total 4 Corps | 33,300 | | | | |
| Total 6 Corps | 36,823 | | | | |
| Total Reserve Cavalry | 2,516 | | | | |
| Total Reserve Artillery | 2,100 | | | | |
| **Total** | 165,259 | | | | |

| The following table is taken from the French official history and provides details of the average strength of the battalions, squadrons and batteries present on the 18th. Information regarding the number and composition of the French artillery is taken from Rouquerol's 'L'Artillerie dans la Bataille du 18 Aout' | No of Battalions | Average Strength | Total | No of Sqadronss | Average Strength | Total | No of batteries | Batterie de 4 | Batterie de 12 | Batterie a cheval | Mitrailleuses |
|---|---|---|---|---|---|---|---|---|---|---|---|
| **2 Corps** | | | | | | | | | | | |
| 1st Div | 13 | 565 | 7,345 | | | | 3 | 2 | | | 1 |
| 2nd Div* | 13 | 500 | 6,500* | | | | 3 | 2 | | | 1 |
| Brigade Lapasset | 6 | 520 | 3,250 | 4 | 90 | 360 | 1 | 1 | | | |
| Divisional Cavalry | | | | 18 | 100 | 1,800 | | | | | |
| Artillery Reserve | | | | | | | 6 | 2 | 2 | 2 | |
| **Total** | **32** | | **17,095** | **22** | | **2,160** | **13** | **7** | **2** | **2** | **2** |
| **3 Corps** | | | | | | | | | | | |
| 1st Div | 13 | 635 | 8,255 | | | | 3 | 2 | | | 1 |

| | | | | | | | | | | |
|---|---|---|---|---|---|---|---|---|---|---|
| 2nd Div | 13 | 580 | 7,540 | | | | 3 | 2 | | | 1 |
| 3rd Div | 13 | 640 | 8,320 | | | | 3 | 2 | | | 1 |
| 4th Div | 13 | 625 | 8,125 | | | | 3 | 2 | | | 1 |
| Divisional Cavalry | | | | 21 | 110 | 2,310 | | | | | |
| Artillery Reserve | | | | | | | 8 | 2 | 2 | 4 | |
| **Total** | **52** | | **32,240** | **21** | | **2,310** | **20** | **10** | **2** | **4** | **4** |
| **4 Corps** | | | | | | | | | | | |
| 1st Div | 13 | 665 | 8,645 | | | | 3 | 2 | | | 1 |
| 2nd Div | 13 | 630 | 8,190 | | | | 3 | 2 | | | 1 |
| 3rd Div | 13 | 690 | 8,970 | | | | 3 | 2 | | | 1 |
| Divisional Cavalry | | | | 16 | 100 | 1,600 | | | | | |
| Artillery Reserve | | | | | | | 6 | 2 | 2 | 2 | |
| **Total** | **39** | | **25,805** | **16** | | **1,600** | **15** | **8** | **2** | **2** | **3** |
| **6 Corps** | | | | | | | | | | | |
| 1st Div | 13 | 660 | 8,580 | | | | 6 | 4 | 2 | | |
| 2nd Div | 3 | 465 | 1,395 | | | | | | | | |
| 3rd Div | 12 | 505 | 6,060 | | | | 3 | 3 | | | |
| 4th Div | 12 | 575 | 6,900 | | | | 2 | | | 2 | |
| Divisional Cavalry | | | | 13 | 105 | 1,365 | 2 | | | 2 | |
| **Total** | **40** | | **22,935** | **13** | | **1,365** | **13** | **7** | **2** | **4** | |
| **Imperial Guard** | | | | | | | | | | | |
| 1st Div | 13 | 540 | 7,020 | | | | 3 | 2 | | | 1 |
| 2nd Div | 10 | 465 | 4,650 | | | | 3 | 2 | | | 1 |
| Divisional Cavalry | | | | 29 | 95 | 2,755 | 2 | | | 2 | |
| Artillery Reserve | | | | | | | 4 | | | 4 | |
| **Total** | **23** | | **11,670** | **29** | | **2,755** | **12** | **4** | | **6** | **2** |
| **Reserve Cavalry** | | | | | | | | | | | |
| 3rd Div | | | | 16 | 105 | 1,680 | 2 | | | 2 | |
| **Total** | | | | **16** | | **1,680** | **2** | | | **2** | |
| **Reserve Artillery** | | | | | | | | | | | |
| 13th Regt | | | | | | | 6 | | 6 | | |
| 18th Regt | | | | | | | 6 | | | 6 | |
| **Total** | | | | | | | **12** | | **6** | **6** | |
| **Batteries de 4** | | | | | | | | 36 | | | |
| **Batteries de 12** | | | | | | | | | 14 | | |
| **Batteries à Cheval** | | | | | | | | | | 26 | |

| Mitrailleuses | | | | | | | | | | 11 |
|---|---|---|---|---|---|---|---|---|---|---|

| Summary | No of Battalions | Avg Strength | Total | No of Sqadronss | Avg Strength | Total | No of batteries | No of guns | of which Mitrailleuses batteries | No of Mitrailleuses |
|---|---|---|---|---|---|---|---|---|---|---|
| Imperial Guard | 23 | | 11,670 | 29 | | 2,755 | | | | 12 |
| 2 Corps | 33 | | 17,095 | 22 | | 2,160 | | | | 13 |
| 3 Corps | 52 | | 32,240 | 21 | | 2,310 | | | | 20 |
| 4 Corps | 39 | | 25,805 | 16 | | 1,600 | | | | 15 |
| 6 Corps | 40 | | 22,935 | 13 | | 1,365 | | | | 13 |
| Reserve Cavalry | | | | 16 | | 1,680 | | | | 2 |
| Reserve Artillery | | | | | | | | | | 12 |
| H Q Escorts** | | | | 3 | 110 | 330 | | | | |
| **Grand Total** | 187 | | 109,745 | 120 | 110 | 12,200 | | | | 87 |

\* Note; by way of comparison the total number of men as detailed within the 2nd Division Situation d'effectif is 6,628 plus 172 officers. The strength of the individual regiments ranges from 1,276 to 1,666.

\*\* Bazaine, 5th sq 5th Hussars & 1st sq 2nd Chasseurs, Canrobert, 6th sq 6th Chasseurs.

| The information detailed below is taken from Heft 11 of the Kriegsgeschichtliche Einzelschriften which does not accord in every respect with the information detailed within the French official history | No of Battalions | Average Strength | Total | No of Sqadronss | Average Strength | Total | No of batteries | No of guns | of which Mitrailleuses batteries | No of Mitrailleuses |
|---|---|---|---|---|---|---|---|---|---|---|
| **Imperial Guard** | 23 | 475 | 10,925 | 29 | 110 | 3,190 | 12 | 72 | 2 | 12 |
| **2 Corps** | 26 | 470 | 12,220 | 18 | 110 | 1,980 | 12 | 72 | 2 | 12 |
| **Brigade Lapasset** | 6 | 540 | 3,330 | 4 | 80 | 320 | 1 | 6 | | |
| **3 Corps** | 52 | | 30,290 | 16 | 115 | 1,840 | 20 | 120 | 4 | 24 |
| (1st, 2nd & 4th Inf Divs) | | 595 | | | | | | | | |
| (3rd Inf Div) | | 545 | | | | | | | | |
| **4 Corps** | 39 | | 22,230 | 16 | 110 | 1,800 | 15 | 90 | 3 | 18 |
| (1st & 2nd Divs) | | 535 | | | | | | | | |
| (3rd Div) | | 640 | | | | | | | | |
| **6 Corps** | 40 | 515 | 20,600 | 21 | 110 | 2,310 | 13 | 76 | | |
| **Reserve Cavalry** | | | | 16 | 110 | 1,760 | 2 | 12 | | |

| | | | | | | | | | | | | |
|---|---|---|---|---|---|---|---|---|---|---|---|---|
| 4th Grenadiers | 14 | 270 | 8 | 13 | 620 | 3 | | 12 | | 27 | 902 | 11 |
| Guard Sharpshooter Battalion | 10* | 147 | 4 | 9 | 269 | 3 | | 15 | | 19* | 431 | 7 |
| 2nd Lancers of the Guard | | | 5 | | 6 | 6 | | | | | 6 | 11 |
| 3rd Field Division Guard FAR | 2 | 4 | 24 | 5 | 53 | 41 | | 4 | | 7 | 61 | 65 |
| **Total** | **61*** | **1,090** | **69** | **80*** | **2,492** | **67** | | **90** | | **141*** | **3,672** | **136** |
| *Plus 1 Assistant/Staff Surgeon | | | | | | | | | | | | |
| **Corps Artillery** | | | | | | | | | | | | |
| Horse artillery & 2nd Field Division Guard FAR | 1 | 4 | 65 | 4 | 54 | 39 | | 2 | | 5 | 60 | 104 |
| Guard Pioneer Battalion | | 4 | | 1 | 9 | | | | | 1 | 13 | |
| **Total Guard Corps** | **128*** | **2,312** | **252** | **180*** | **5,431** | **168** | | **179** | | **308*** | **7,922** | **420** |
| *Plus 1 Assistant/Staff Surgeon | | | | | | | | | | | | |
| **II Corps** | | | | | | | | | | | | |
| HQ Staff | | | 3 | | | | | | | 3 | | |
| **3rd Infantry Division** | | | | | | | | | | | | |
| **5th Infantry Brigade** | | | | | | | | | | | | |
| 2nd Grenadiers | 4 | 54 | 2 | 6 | 205 | 1 | | 4 | | 10 | 2,632 | 3 |
| 42nd Regiment | 2 | 54 | 2 | 2 | 95 | 2 | | | | 4 | 103 | 2 |
| **6th Infantry Brigade** | | | | | | | | | | | | |
| 14th Regiment | 1 | 20 | 2 | 5 | 120 | | | | | 6 | 140 | 2 |
| 54th Regiment | 6 | 45 | 4 | 10 | 239 | 3 | | 4 | | 16 | 288 | 7 |
| 2nd Rifle Battalion | | 18 | | 1 | 62 | | | | | 1 | 80 | |
| 3rd Dragoons | | 1 | 2 | 1 | | | | | | 1 | 1 | 2 |
| 1st Field Division 2nd FAR | | | 8 | 1 | 2 | 6 | | | | 1 | 2 | 14 |
| **Total** | **13** | **146** | **18** | **29** | **723** | **12** | | **8** | | **42** | **877** | **30** |
| **4th Infantry Division** | | | | | | | | | | | | |
| Divisional Staff | | | | | | | | | 1 | | | 1 |
| 7th Infantry Brigade | | | | | | | | | | | | |
| 9th Grenadiers | | 3 | | 2 | 37 | | | | 1 | 2 | 40 | 1 |
| 49th Regiment | 1 | 11 | 1 | 5 | 85 | 1 | | | | 6 | 96 | 2 |
| 8th Infantry Brigade | | | | | | | | | | | | |
| 21st Regiment | | 14 | | 2 | 146 | | | | | 2 | 160 | |
| 61st regiment | | 1 | | 2 | 14 | | | | | 2 | 15 | |
| 3rd Field Division 2nd FAR | | | 1 | | | 5 | | | | | | 6 |
| **Total** | **1** | **20** | **2** | **11** | **282** | **6** | | **2** | | **12** | **311** | **10** |
| Corps Artillery | | | | | | | | | | | | |

| | | | | | | | | | | | | |
|---|---|---|---|---|---|---|---|---|---|---|---|---|
| 2nd Field Division 2nd FAR | | | | | 2 | 1 | | | | | 21 | |
| Sanitary Detachments | | | | * | 2 | | | 1 | | * | 3 | |
| **Total II Corps** | **14** | **175** | **20** | **40\*** | **1,009** | **19** | | **9** | **2** | **54\*** | **1,193** | **41** |
| \* Pus 1 Staff Surgeon | | | | | | | | | | | | |
| **III Corps** | | | | | | | | | | | | |
| 3rd FAR | | 4 | 57 | 2 | 45 | 2 | | 1 | | 2 | 50 | 59 |
| **Total III Corps** | | **4** | **57** | **2** | **45** | **2** | | **1** | | **2** | **50** | **59** |
| **IX Corps** | | | | | | | | | | | | |
| HQ Staff | 1 | | | | 2 | | | | | 3 | | |
| **18th Infantry Division** | | | | | | | | | | | | |
| **35th Infantry Brigade** | | | | | | | | | | | | |
| Brigade Staff | 1 | 1 | 2 | 1 | | 1 | | | | 2 | 1 | 3 |
| 36th Fusiliers | 8 | 143 | 3 | 21 | 410 | 2 | | 3 | 1 | 29 | 556 | 6 |
| 84th Regiment | 10 | 159 | 2 | 22 | 362 | 2 | | 4 | | 32 | 525 | 4 |
| **36th Infantry Brigade** | | | | | | | | | | | | |
| 11th Grenadiers | | | | | 1 | | | | | 1 | | |
| 85th Regiment | 11 | 253 | 6 | 11 | 499 | 2 | | 10 | | 22 | 762 | 8 |
| 9th Rifle Battalion | 2 | 45 | | 7 | 118 | 2 | | | | 9 | 163 | 2 |
| 6th Dragoons | | 3 | 7 | | 3 | 4 | | | | | 6 | 11 |
| 1st Field Division 9th FAR | 2 | 21 | 183 | 6 | 86 | 31 | | | | 8 | 107 | 214 |
| Sanitary Detachment | | | | 1 | 2 | | | | | 1 | 2 | |
| **Total** | **35** | **625** | **203** | **71** | **1,481** | **44** | | **17** | **1** | **106** | **2,123** | **248** |
| **Grand Ducal Hesse Division** | | | | | | | | | | | | |
| Divisional Staff | 1 | | 1 | | 1 | 2 | | | | 1 | 1 | 3 |
| **49th Infantry Brigade** | | | | | | | | | | | | |
| 1st Regiment | 6 | 88 | 3 | 10 | 219 | 1 | | 3 | | 16 | 310 | 4 |
| 2nd Regiment | 5 | 78 | | 11 | 226 | 2 | | 3 | | 16 | 307 | 2 |
| 1st Rifle Battalion | 7 | 67 | 1 | 3 | 217 | 1 | | 1 | | 10 | 285 | 2 |
| **50th Infantry Brigade** | | | | | | | | | | | | |
| Brigade Staff | | | 1 | 1 | 1 | 2 | | | | 1 | 1 | 3 |
| 3rd Regiment | 4 | 72 | 1 | 8 | 226 | 1 | | 6 | 1 | 12 | 304 | 3 |
| 4th Regiment | 3 | 24 | 1 | 2 | 77 | 1 | | 2 | 1 | 5 | 103 | 3 |
| 2nd Rifle Battalion | 4 | 33 | 2 | 5 | 126 | | | 4 | | 9 | 163 | 2 |
| 1st Cavalry | | 3 | 2 | 1 | 8 | 18 | | | | 1 | 11 | 20 |
| 2nd Cavalry | | 1 | 3 | | 2 | 2 | | | | | 3 | 5 |
| Grand Ducal Hesse Field Artillery Division | 3 | 26 | 35 | 6 | 82 | 16 | | | | 9 | 108 | 51 |
| **Total** | **33** | **392** | **50** | **47** | **1,185** | **46** | | **19** | **2** | **80** | **1,596** | **98** |

| | | | | | | | | | | | | |
|---|---|---|---|---|---|---|---|---|---|---|---|---|
| **Corps Artillery** | | | | | | | | | | | | |
| 2nd Field Division & 2nd Horse Artillery battery 9th AR | 4 | 39 | 259 | 12* | 128 | 42 | | 2 | | 16* | 169 | 301 |
| **Total IX Corps** | 72 | 1,056 | 512 | 130* | 2,794 | 132 | | 38 | 3 | 202* | 3,888 | 647 |
| *Plus 1 Staff Surgeon & 2 Assistant Staff Surgeons | | | | | | | | | | | | |
| **X Corps** | | | | | | | | | | | | |
| **19th Infantry Division** | | | | | | | | | | | | |
| 1st Field Division 10th FAR | | | | | 1 | 3 | | | | | 1 | 3 |
| **Total** | | | | | 1 | 3 | | | | | 1 | 3 |
| **20th Infantry Division** | | | | | | | | | | | | |
| **39th Infantry Brigade** | | | | | | | | | | | | |
| Brigade Staff | | | | | | | | | 1 | | | 1 |
| 79th Regiment | | 1 | | 1 | | | | | 1 | 1 | 1 | 1 |
| **40th Infantry Brigade** | | | | | | | | | | | | |
| 17th Regiment | | 9 | | | 18 | 1 | | 7 | | | 34 | 1 |
| 92nd Regiment | | 4 | | 1 | 35 | 2 | | | | 1 | 39 | 2 |
| 10th Rifle Battalion | | | | | 3 | | | | | | 3 | |
| 16th Dragoons | | | | | 1 | 1 | | | | | 1 | 1 |
| 2nd Field Division 10th FAR | | | 3 | | 2 | 4 | | | | | 2 | 7 |
| **Total** | 1 | 15 | 17 | 3 | 12 | 12 | | 1 | | 4 | 18 | 29 |
| **Total X Corps** | 1 | 19 | 20 | 5 | 72 | 23 | | 8 | 2 | 6 | 99 | 45 |
| **XII Corps** | | | | | | | | | | | | |
| **23rd Infantry Division** | | | | | | | | | | | | |
| **45th Infantry Brigade** | | | | | | | | | | | | |
| Brigade Staff | 1 | | 2 | | | 2 | | | | | 1 | 4 |
| 100th Grenadiers | 3 | 38 | 2 | 12 | 219 | 2 | | 25 | | 15 | 282 | 4 |
| 101st Grenadiers | 3 | 65 | 4 | 9* | 231 | 1 | | 25 | | 12* | 321 | 5 |
| 108th Rifles | 2 | 34 | 3 | 4 | 124 | 2 | | 6 | 1 | 6 | 164 | 6 |
| **46th Infantry Brigade** | | | | | | | | | | | | |
| 102nd Regiment | | | | | 1 | | | 2 | | | 3 | |
| 103rd Regiment | | | | | 2 | | | | | | 2 | |
| 1st Cavalry | | 2 | 13 | | 3 | 3 | | 1 | 4 | | 6 | 20 |
| 1st Field Division 12th FAR | | | | 1 | 3 | 3 | | | | 1 | 3 | 3 |
| **Total** | 9 | 139 | 24 | 26* | 583 | 13 | | 59 | 5 | 35* | 781 | 42 |
| *Plus 1 Assistant Surgeon | | | | | | | | | | | | |
| **24th Infantry Division** | | | | | | | | | | | | |

| | | | | | | | | | | | | |
|---|---|---|---|---|---|---|---|---|---|---|---|---|
| Divisional Staff | | | | | 1 | 1 | | | | | 1 | 1 |
| **47th Infantry Brigade** | | | | | | | | | | | | |
| Brigade Staff | | | 1 | 1 | | | | | | 1 | | 1 |
| 104th Regiment | 3 | 43 | 2 | 9 | 163 | 3 | | 37 | | 12 | 243 | 5 |
| 105th Regiment | 8 | 89 | 7 | 7 | 338 | | | 31 | | 15 | 458 | 7 |
| 12th Rifle Battalion | 1 | 33 | 1 | 3 | 50 | | | 4 | | 4 | 87 | 1 |
| **48th Infantry Brigade** | | | | | | | | | | | | |
| Brigade Staff | 1 | | | | | | | 1 | | | | |
| 106th Regiment | 5 | 21 | 2 | 2 | 40 | 1 | | 6 | | 7 | 67 | 3 |
| 107th Regiment | 13 | 85 | 3 | 11 | 292 | | | 52 | | 24 | 429 | 3 |
| 13th Rifle Battalion | | 1 | | | 1 | | | | | | 2 | |
| 2nd Cavalry | | 2 | 4 | | 6 | 5 | | 1 | | | 9 | 9 |
| 2nd Field Division 12th FAR | | 2 | | 2 | 7 | 5 | | | | 2 | 9 | 5 |
| 3rd Company 12th Pioneer battalion | | | | | 1 | | | | | | 1 | |
| **Total** | **31** | **276** | **20** | **35** | **899** | **15** | | **131** | | **66** | **1,306** | **35** |
| **12th Cavalry Division** | | | | | | | | | | | | |
| Guard Cavalry | | | 5 | 1 | 4 | | | | | 1 | 4 | 5 |
| 3rd Cavalry | | 1 | 2 | 1 | | 2 | | | | 1 | 1 | 4 |
| 1st Horse Artillery Battery | | 1 | 2 | | | 9 | | | | | 1 | 11 |
| **Total** | | **2** | **9** | **2** | **4** | **11** | | | | **1** | **6** | **20** |
| **Corps Artillery** | | | | | | | | | | | | |
| 3rd Field Division 12th FAR | | | | | | | | | | | | |
| 4th Field Division & 2nd Horse Artillery 12th FAR | | | | | | | | | | | | |
| 3rd Sanitary Detachment | | | | | 1 | | | | | | 1 | |
| **Total** | | **3** | **16** | **2** | **17** | **15** | | | | **2** | **20** | **31** |
| **Staff of ammunition Train Division** | | | | 1 | | | | | | 1 | | |
| **Total XII Corps** | **40** | **420** | **69** | **66\*** | **1,503** | **54** | | **190** | **5** | **106\*** | **2,113** | **128** |
| *Plus 1 Assistant Surgeon | | | | | | | | | | | | |
| **5th Cavalry Division** | | | | | | | | | | | | |
| 12th Hussars | | | | 1* | | | | | | 1* | | |
| **Total 5th Cavalry Divison** | | | | 1* | | | | | | 1* | | |
| *Staff Surgeon Major | | | | | | | | | | | | |

| Summary | Killed | | | Wounded | | | Missing | | | Total | | | Ammunition | | |
|---|---|---|---|---|---|---|---|---|---|---|---|---|---|---|---|
| | Officers | Men | Horses | Officers | Men | Horses | Officers | Men | Horses | Officers | Men | Horses | Common Shell | Shrapnel | Case |
| Total 1 Corps | | | | | | | | | | | | | 783 | | |
| Total VII Corps | 11 | 154 | 159 | 28* | 654 | 50 | | 13 | 4 | 39* | 821 | 213 | 3,221 | | 16 |
| *Plus 1 Assistant Surgeon | | | | | | | | | | | | | | | |
| Total VIII Corps | 67 | 758 | 72 | 117 | 2,267 | 72 | | | 3 | 184 | 3,089 | 147 | 5,919 | | |
| Total 1st Cavalry Division | | 7 | 47 | 7 | 81 | 106 | | | 24 | 7 | 88 | 177 | | | |
| Total Guard Corps | 128* | 2,312 | 252 | 180* | 5,431 | 168 | | 179 | | 308* | 7,922 | 420 | 8,429 | | |
| *Plus 1 Assistant/ Staff Surgeon | | | | | | | | | | | | | | | |
| Total II Corps | 14 | 175 | 20 | 40* | 1,009 | 19 | | 9 | 2 | 54* | 1,193 | 41 | 26 | | |
| * Plus 1 Staff Surgeon | | | | | | | | | | | | | | | |
| Total III Corps | | 4 | 57 | 2 | 45 | 2 | | 1 | | 2 | 50 | | 2,786 | | |
| Total IX Corps | 72 | 1,056 | 512 | 130* | 2,794 | 132 | | 38 | 3 | 202* | 3,888 | 647 | 9,679 | | 4 |
| *Plus 1 Staff & 2 Asst Surgeons | | | | | | | | | | | | | | | |
| Total X Corps | 1 | 19 | 20 | 5 | 72 | 23 | | 8 | 2 | 6 | 99 | 45 | 1,582 | | |
| Total XII Corps | 40 | 420 | 69 | 66* | 1,503 | 54 | | 190 | 5 | 106* | 2,113 | 128 | 2,056 | 179 | |
| *Plus 1 Assistant Surgeon | | | | | | | | | | | | | | | |
| Total 5th Cavalry Divison | | | | 1* | | | | | | 1* | | | | | |

| | | | | | | | | | | | | | | |
|---|---|---|---|---|---|---|---|---|---|---|---|---|---|---|
| *Staff Surgeon Major | | | | | | | | | | | | | | |
| Grand Total | 332 | 4,905 | 1,208 | 577 | 13,856 | 626 | | 493 | 43 | 909 | 19,254 | 1,877 | 34,481 | 179 | 20 |

Total losses 5,730 officers and men killed or missing, 14, 433 officers and men wounded. 1,251 horses were killed or missing, 626 wounded. The German artillery fired a total of 34,680 rounds.

# French losses, Gravelotte

| French losses at the battle of Gravelotte- Saint Privat | Officers | | | Men | | | | Horse | | |
|---|---|---|---|---|---|---|---|---|---|---|
| 2 Corps | Killed | Wounded | Total | Killed | Wounded | Missing | Total | Killed | Wounded | Rounds fired |
| **1st Division** | | | | | | | | | | |
| **1st Brigade:** | | | | | | | | | | |
| 3rd Chasseur Battalion: | | 2 | 2 | 2 | 8 | 22 | 32 | | | |
| 32nd Line Infantry Regiment: | | 3 | 3 | 6 | 58 | 23 | 87 | | | |
| 55th Line Infantry Regiment: | 1 | 2 | 3 | 8 | 24 | 5 | 37 | | | |
| **2nd Brigade:** | | | | | | | | | | |
| 76th Line Infantry Regiment: | | 5 | 5 | 2 | 26 | 13 | 41 | | | |
| 77th Line Infantry Regiment: | | 2 | 2 | 13 | 64 | 7 | 84 | | | |
| No 5 Battery 5th Field Artillery Regiment | | | | | 2 | | 2 | 2 | | 495 |
| No 12 Battery 5th Field Artillery Regiment | | | | 1 | 2 | | 3 | 7 | | 438 |
| No 6 Battery 5th Field Artillery Regiment | | | | 1 | 2 | | 3 | 3 | | 976 |
| Total | 1 | 14 | 15 | 33 | 186 | 70 | 289 | 12 | | 1,909 |
| **2nd Division** | | | | | | | | | | |
| **1st Brigade:** | | | | | | | | | | |
| 12th Chasseur Battalion: | | 2 | 2 | | 25 | 3 | 28 | | | |
| 8th Line Infantry Regiment: | 1 | 4 | 5 | 2 | 26 | 15 | 43 | | | |
| 23rd Line Infantry Regiment: | 1 | 2 | 3 | 1 | 39 | 19 | 59 | | | |
| **2nd Brigade:** | | | | | | | | | | |
| 66th Line Infantry Regiment: | 1 | 1 | 2 | | 19 | 8 | 27 | | | |
| 67th Line Infantry Regiment: | | | | | 9 | 1 | 10 | | | |
| No 7 Battery 5th Field Artillery Regiment | | | | | 1 | | 1 | 1 | 1 | 245 |
| No 8 Battery 5th Field Artillery Regiment | | | | | | | | | | 200 |

| | | | | | | | | | | |
|---|---|---|---|---|---|---|---|---|---|---|
| No 9 Battery 5th Field Artillery Regiment | | | | | 6 | | 6 | 24 | | 12 |
| **Genie** | | | | | 1 | | 1 | | | |
| **Total** | **3** | **9** | **12** | **3** | **126** | **46** | **175** | **25** | **1** | **457** |
| **Brigade Lapasset (from 5th Corps)** | | | | | | | | | | |
| 84th Line Infantry Regiment: | | | | 5 | 12 | 7 | 24 | | | |
| 97th Line Infantry Regiment: | 3 | 1 | 4 | 7 | 23 | 5 | 35 | | | |
| Detachment 46th Line Infantry Regiment: | | | | | | | | | | |
| 7th Battery of Artillery 2nd Field Artillery Regiment | | | | | 1 | | 1 | | 5 | 258 |
| **Total** | **3** | **1** | **4** | **12** | **36** | **12** | **60** | | **5** | **258** |
| **Cavalry Division** | | | | | | | | | | |
| **1st Brigade:** | | | | | | | | | | |
| 4th Chasseurs a Cheval: | | | | | 1 | | 1 | | | |
| **Total** | | | | | **1** | | **1** | | | |
| **Artillery Reserve** | | | | | | | | | | |
| No 10 Battery 5th Field Artillery Regiment | | | | 1 | 5 | | 6 | 7 | | 84 |
| No 11 Battery 5th Field Artillery Regiment | | | | 3 | 8 | | 11 | 5 | 2 | 720 |
| No 6 Battery 15th Field Artillery Regiment | | | | | 1 | | 1 | | | |
| No 10 Battery 15th Field Artillery Regiment | | | | | 2 | | 2 | | 1 | 60 |
| No 7 Battery 17th Horse Artillery Regiment | | | | | 1 | 1 | 2 | 2 | 4 | |
| No 8 Battery 17th Horse Artillery Regiment | | | | | 2 | | 2 | 1 | | |
| **Total** | | | | **4** | **19** | **1** | **24** | **15** | **7** | **864** |
| **Service Administration** | **2** | | **2** | | | **3** | **3** | | | |
| **Total 2 Corps** | **9** | **24** | **33** | **52** | **368** | **132** | **552** | **52** | **23** | **3,488** |
| **3 Corps** | | | | | | | | | | |
| Staff | | 3 | 3 | | | | | | | |
| **1st Division** | | | | | | | | | | |
| **1st Brigade:** | | | | | | | | | | |
| 18th Chasseur Battalion: | | | | 2 | 6 | 1 | 9 | | | |
| 51st Line Infantry Regiment: | 1 | 3 | 4 | 1 | 28 | 6 | 35 | | | |
| 62nd Line Infantry Regiment: | 1 | | 1 | 4 | 39 | 6 | 49 | | | |
| **2nd Brigade:** | | | | | | | | | | |
| 81st Line Infantry Regiment: | 3 | 3 | 6 | 35 | 199 | 24 | 258 | | | |
| 95th Line Infantry Regiment: | 2 | 9 | 11 | 17 | 115 | 12 | 144 | | | |

| | | | | | | | | | | |
|---|---|---|---|---|---|---|---|---|---|---|
| No 5 Battery 4th Field Artillery Regiment | | 1 | 1 | | | | | | | |
| No 6 Battery 4th Field Artillery Regiment | | | | 3 | 5 | 1 | 9 | 12 | | 257 |
| No 8 Battery 4th Field Artillery Regiment | | 1 | 1 | | 11 | | 11 | 9 | 4 | 650 |
| **Genie** | | | | | | | | | | |
| **Total** | 7 | 17 | 24 | 62 | 103 | 50 | 545 | 21 | 4 | 907 |
| **2nd Division** | | | | | | | | | | |
| **1st Brigade:** | | | | | | | | | | |
| 15th Chasseur Battalion | | | | | 2 | | 2 | | | |
| 19th Line Infantry Regiment | | 1 | 1 | 3 | 8 | | 11 | | | |
| 41st Line Infantry Regiment: | | | | | 6 | 3 | 9 | | | |
| **2nd Brigade:** | | | | | | | | | | |
| 69th Line Infantry Regiment: | | 1 | 1 | | 3 | 3 | 6 | | | |
| 90th Line Infantry Regiment: | 1 | | 1 | 3 | 30 | | 33 | | | |
| No 11 Battery 4th Field Artillery Regiment | | | | 1 | 5 | | 6 | 20 | | 493 |
| No 12 Battery 4th Field Artillery Regiment | | | | 1 | 3 | | 4 | 8 | | } |
| No 9 Battery 4th Field Artillery Regiment | | | | | 1 | | 1 | 2 | 3 | } 440 |
| **Total** | 1 | 2 | 3 | 8 | 58 | 6 | 72 | 30 | 3 | 933 |
| **3rd Division** | | | | | | | | | | |
| Staff | | 1 | 1 | | | | | | | |
| **1st Brigade:** | | | | | | | | | | |
| 7th Chasseur Battalion | 2 | 4 | 6 | 21 | 71 | 28 | 120 | | | |
| 7th Line Infantry Regiment | | 1 | 1 | 4 | 13 | 3 | 20 | | | |
| 29th Line Infantry Regiment: | 1 | 4 | 5 | 13 | 97 | 81 | 191 | | | |
| **2nd Brigade:** | | | | | | | | | | |
| 59th Line Infantry Regiment: | 3 | 11 | 14 | 20 | 119 | 38 | 177 | | | |
| 71st Line Infantry Regiment: | | 4 | 4 | 3 | 28 | 34 | 65 | | | |
| No 5 Battery 11th Field Artillery Regiment | | 1 | 1 | 2 | 7 | | 9 | 4 | 2 | 646 |
| No 6 Battery 11th Field Artillery Regiment | | | | 1 | 5 | | 6 | 5 | 4 | } |
| No 7 Battery 11th Field Artillery Regiment | 1 | | 1 | | 12 | | 12 | 6 | 6 | } 1,132 |
| **Total** | 7 | 26 | 33 | 64 | 352 | 184 | 600 | 15 | 12 | 1,778 |
| **4th Division** | | | | | | | | | | |
| **1st Brigade:** | | | | | | | | | | |
| 11th Chasseur Battalion: | | 1 | 1 | 4 | 18 | | 22 | | | |

| | | | | | | | | | | |
|---|---|---|---|---|---|---|---|---|---|---|
| 44th Line Infantry Regiment: | 3 | 5 | 8 | 6 | 63 | 1 | 70 | | | |
| 60th Line Infantry Regiment: | 4 | 7 | 11 | 18 | 113 | 41 | 172 | | | |
| **2nd Brigade:** | | | | | | | | | | |
| 80th Line Infantry Regiment: | 7 | 16 | 23 | 36 | 236 | 118 | 390 | | | |
| 85th Line Infantry Regiment: | | 4 | 4 | 11 | 89 | 13 | 113 | | | |
| No 8 Battery 11th Field Artillery Regiment | | | | | 1 | 1 | 2 | | | 611 |
| No 9 Battery 11th Field Artillery Regiment | | | | 1 | 6 | | 7 | 23 | 16 | } |
| No 10 Battery 11th Field Artillery Regiment | | | | 1 | 10 | 1 | 12 | | | } 857 |
| **Total** | **14** | **33** | **47** | **77** | **536** | **175** | **788** | **23** | **16** | **1,468** |
| **Cavalry Division** | | | | | | | | | | |
| **1st Brigade:** | | | | | | | | | | |
| Staff | 1 | | | | | | | | | |
| **Total** | **1** | | | | | | | | | |
| **Artillery Reserve** | | | | | | | | | | |
| No 7 Battery 4th Field Artillery Regiment | | | | 5 | 8 | | 13 | | | } |
| No 10 Battery 4th Field Artillery Regiment | | 1 | 1 | 1 | 6 | | 7 | 11 | | } 508 |
| No 11 Battery 11th Field Artillery Regiment | | | | | 8 | | 8 | | | 403 |
| No 12 Battery 11th Field Artillery Regiment | | | | | | | | | | |
| No 1 Battery 17th Horse Artillery Regiment | | 1 | 1 | 1 | 7 | | 8 | 3 | 2 | 240 |
| No 2 Battery 17th Horse Artillery Regiment | | | | | 1 | | 1 | 1 | | |
| No 3 Battery 17th Horse Artillery Regiment | | | | | 6 | | 6 | 1 | 9 | 1,324 |
| No 4 Battery 17th Horse Artillery Regiment | | | | | 8 | | 8 | 5 | 7 | 876 |
| **Total** | | **2** | **2** | **7** | **44** | | **51** | **21** | **18** | **3,353** |
| **Total 3 Corps** | **30** | **83** | **113** | **218** | **1,393** | **415** | **2,026** | **110** | **53** | **8,349** |
| **4 Corps** | | | | | | | | | | |
| Staff | | 2 | 2 | | | | | | | |
| **1st Division** | | | | | | | | | | |
| Staff | | 2 | 2 | | | | | | | |
| **1st Brigade:** | | | | | | | | | | |
| 20th Chasseur Battalion: | 2 | 3 | 5 | 9 | 83 | 7 | 99 | | | |
| 1st Line Infantry Regiment: | 4 | 19 | 23 | 45 | 344 | 71 | 460 | | | |

| | | | | | | | | | | |
|---|---|---|---|---|---|---|---|---|---|---|
| 6th Line Infantry Regiment: | 13 | 10 | 23 | 41 | 177 | 48 | 266 | | | |
| **2nd Brigade:** | | | | | | | | | | |
| Staff | | 1 | 1 | | | | | | | |
| 57th Line Infantry Regiment: | 4 | 11 | 15 | 28 | 224 | 216 | 468 | | | |
| 73rd Line Infantry Regiment: | 5 | 14 | 19 | 37 | 285 | 174 | 496 | | | |
| No 5 Battery 15th Field Artillery Regiment | 1 | 1 | 2 | 5 | 6 | 1 | 12 | 5 | 2 | 910 |
| No 9 Battery 15th Field Artillery Regiment | | | | 1 | 8 | 1 | 10 | 4 | | 577 |
| No 12 Battery 15th Field Artillery Regiment | | | | 1 | 10 | | 11 | 18 | 7 | 1,380 |
| Engineers : 9th Company of 2nd Engineer Regiment | | | | 2 | | 1 | 3 | | | |
| **Total** | 29 | 61 | 90 | 169 | 1,137 | 519 | 1,825 | 27 | 9 | 2,867 |
| **2nd Division** | | | | | | | | | | |
| Staff | | 1 | 1 | | | | | | | |
| **1st Brigade:** | | | | | | | | | | |
| Staff | | 1 | 1 | | | | | | | |
| 5th Chasseur Battalion: | | 2 | 2 | 8 | 85 | 18 | 111 | | | |
| 13th Line Infantry Regiment: | 5 | 13 | 18 | 33 | 230 | 110 | 373 | | | |
| 43rd Line Infantry Regiment: | 15 | 16 | 31 | 22 | 376 | 103 | 503 | | | |
| **2nd Brigade:** | | | | | | | | | | |
| Staff | | 1 | 1 | | | | | | | |
| 64th Line Infantry Regiment: | 4 | 8 | 12 | 26 | 197 | 83 | 306 | | | |
| 98th Line Infantry Regiment: | 6 | 13 | 19 | 36 | 225 | 23 | 284 | | | |
| Staff | 1 | | 1 | | | | | | | |
| No 5 Battery 1st Field Artillery Regiment | | 2 | 2 | 3 | 14 | | 17 | 20 | 5 | 1,020 |
| No 6 Battery 1st Field Artillery Regiment | | | | | 6 | | 6 | 7 | 8 | 647 |
| No 7 Battery 1st Field Artillery Regiment | 2 | 1 | 3 | | 16 | | 16 | 4 | 5 | 727 |
| Engineers : 10th Company of 2nd Engineer Regiment | | | | 1 | 2 | 2 | 5 | | | |
| **Total** | 33 | 58 | 94 | 129 | 1,151 | 341 | 1,621 | 31 | 18 | 2,394 |
| **3rd Division** | | | | | | | | | | |
| **1st Brigade:** | | | | | | | | | | |
| 2nd Chasseur Battalion: | 2 | 11 | 13 | 21 | 157 | 42 | 220 | | | |
| 15th Line Infantry Regiment: | 7 | 9 | 16 | 31 | 234 | 48 | 313 | | | |
| 33rd Line Infantry Regiment: | 2 | 4 | 6 | 7 | 113 | 5 | 125 | | | |
| **2nd Brigade:** | | | | | | | | | | |

| | | | | | | | | | | |
|---|---|---|---|---|---|---|---|---|---|---|
| 54th Line Infantry Regiment: | 10 | 15 | 25 | 66 | 360 | 107 | 533 | | | |
| 65th Line Infantry Regiment: | 8 | 13 | 21 | 34 | 315 | 137 | 486 | | | |
| Staff | | | | | | | | | | |
| No 8 Battery 1st Field Artillery Regiment | | | | | 2 | | 2 | | 1 | 660 |
| No 9 Battery 1st Field Artillery Regiment | | | | 5 | 19 | | 24 | 18 | | 647 |
| No 10 Battery 1st Field Artillery Regiment | | | | 1 | 5 | | 6 | 7 | 3 | 780 |
| Engineers : 13th Company of 2nd Engineer Regiment | | | | | 2 | | 2 | | | |
| **Total** | **29** | **52** | **81** | **165** | **1,207** | **339** | **1,711** | **25** | **4** | **2,087** |
| **Cavalry Division** | | | | | | | | | | |
| **1st Brigade:** | | | | | | | | | | |
| 2nd Hussar Regiment: | | 2 | 2 | | 8 | 2 | 10 | | | |
| 7th Hussar Regiment: | | | | | | | | | | |
| **2nd Brigade:** | | | | | | | | | | |
| 3rd Dragoon Regiment: | | | | | 6 | | 6 | | | |
| 11th Dragoon Regiment: | | 2 | 2 | 3 | 10 | 4 | 17 | | | |
| **Total** | | **4** | **4** | **3** | **25** | **6** | **34** | | | |
| **Artillery Reserve** | | | | | | | | | | |
| No 11 Battery 1st Field Artillery Regiment | | 1 | 1 | 3 | 19 | | 22 | 8 | 11 | 446 |
| No 12 Battery 1stField Artillery Regiment | | 2 | 2 | | 18 | | 18 | 7 | 1 | 548 |
| Staff | 1 | | 1 | | | | | | | |
| No 6  Battery 8th Field Artillery Regiment | 1 | | 1 | 3 | 10 | 3 | 16 | 17 | | 1,100 |
| No 9 Battery 8th Field Artillery Regiment | | 1 | 1 | 1 | 4 | | 5 | 4 | 3 | 1,000 |
| No 5 Battery 17th Horse Artillery Regiment | | | | 4 | 26 | 18 | 48 | 20 | 58 | 719 |
| No 6 Battery 17th Horse Artillery Regiment | | | | 1 | 6 | 4 | 11 | 1 | 4 | 1,036 |
| **Total** | **2** | **4** | **6** | **12** | **83** | **25** | **120** | **57** | **77** | **4,849** |
| **Services Administration** | | 1 | 1 | 3 | 4 | 2 | 9 | | | |
| **Total 4 Corps** | **93** | **182** | **275** | **481** | **3,607** | **1,232** | **5,320** | **140** | **108** | **12,497** |
| **6 Corps** | | | | | | | | | | |
| Staff | | 1 | 1 | | | | | | | |
| **1st Division** | | | | | | | | | | |
| **1st Brigade:** | | | | | | | | | | |
| 9th Chasseur Battalion: | 4 | 5 | 9 | 7 | 37 | 95 | 139 | | | |

| | | | | | | | | | |
|---|---|---|---|---|---|---|---|---|---|
| 4th Line Infantry Regiment: | 7 | 7 | 14 | 11 | 39 | 524 | 574 | | | |
| 10th Line Infantry Regiment: | 6 | 18 | 24 | 49 | 155 | 435 | 639 | | | |
| **2nd Brigade:** | | | | | | | | | | |
| 12th Line Infantry Regiment: | 5 | 18 | 23 | 49 | 155 | 435 | 639 | | | |
| 100th Line Infantry Regiment: | 1 | 5 | 6 | 5 | 58 | 45 | 108 | | | |
| No 5 Battery 8th Field Artillery Regiment | | | | | 1 | | 1 | | 700 | |
| No 7 Battery 8th Field Artillery Regiment | | | | | 11 | | 11 | | 2 | 600 |
| No 8 Battery 8th Field Artillery Regiment | | | | 2 | 13 | 3 | 18 | 5 | 4 | 660 |
| No12 Battery 8th Field Artillery Regiment | | | | | 7 | | 7 | 4 | | 600 |
| Engineers : 3rd Company of 3rd Engineer Regiment | 1 | | 1 | | 4 | 12 | 16 | | | |
| **Total** | **24** | **54** | **78** | **88** | **386** | **1,455** | **1,929** | **9** | **6** | **2,560** |
| **2nd Division** | | | | | | | | | | |
| Staff | | 1 | 1 | | | | | | | |
| **1st Brigade:** | | | | | | | | | | |
| Staff | | 1 | 1 | | | | | | | |
| 9th Line Infantry Regiment: | 1 | 9 | 10 | | 75 | 66 | 111 | | | |
| No 9 Battery 13th Field Artillery Regiment | | | | | 5 | 4 | 9 | 1 | | 533 |
| No 10 Battery 13th Field Artillery Regiment | | | | 1 | 7 | 2 | 10 | 9 | 2 | 434 |
| **Total** | **1** | **11** | **12** | **1** | **87** | **72** | **160** | **10** | **2** | **967** |
| **3rd Division** | | | | | | | | | | |
| **1st Brigade:** | | | | | | | | | | |
| 75th Line Infantry Regiment: | 1 | 4 | 5 | 9 | 41 | 49 | 99 | | | |
| 91st Line Infantry Regiment: | 5 | 6 | 11 | 1 | 80 | 33 | 114 | | | |
| **2nd Brigade:** | | | | | | | | | | |
| Staff | | 1 | 1 | | | | | | | |
| 93rd Line Infantry Regiment: | 2 | 7 | 9 | | 127 | 309 | 436 | | | |
| 94th Line Infantry Regiment: | 5 | 6 | 11 | 5 | 26 | 286 | 317 | | | |
| Staff | | 1 | 1 | | | | | | | |
| No 5 Battery 14th Field Artillery Regiment | | | | | | | | 1 | | 987 |
| No 6 Battery 14th Field Artillery Regiment | | | | | | | | 4 | 2 | 550 |
| No 7 Battery 14th Field Artillery Regiment | | | | | | | | 2 | 2 | 800 |

| | | | | | | | | | | |
|---|---|---|---|---|---|---|---|---|---|---|
| Engineers : 7th Company of 3rd Engineer Regiment | | | | | 1 | 4 | 5 | | | |
| **Total** | **13** | **25** | **38** | **15** | **276** | **684** | **972** | **7** | **4** | **2,337** |
| **4th Division** | | | | | | | | | | |
| **1st Brigade:** | | | | | | | | | | |
| 25th Line Infantry Regiment: | 2 | 8 | 10 | 21 | 80 | 146 | 247 | | | |
| 26th Line Infantry Regiment: | 2 | 6 | 8 | 9 | 134 | 87 | 230 | | | |
| **2nd Brigade:** | | | | | | | | | | |
| 28th Line Infantry Regiment: | 5 | 18 | 23 | 51 | 193 | 408 | 652 | | | |
| 70th Line Infantry Regiment: | 6 | 13 | 19 | 9 | 112 | 230 | 351 | | | |
| No 7 Battery 10th Field Artillery Regiment | | | | 1 | 8 | | 9 | 18 | 5 | 900 |
| No 8 Battery 10th Field Artillery Regiment | | | | | 1 | | 1 | 15 | | 630 |
| **Total** | **15** | **45** | **60** | **91** | **528** | **871** | **1,490** | **33** | **5** | **1,550** |
| **Cavalry Division** | | | | | | | | | | |
| **1st Brigade:** | | | | | | | | | | |
| 2nd Chasseurs a Cheval | | | | | 2 | 1 | 3 | | | |
| 3rd Chasseurs a Cheval | | 4 | 4 | 3 | 18 | 7 | 28 | | | |
| **2nd Brigade:** | | | | | | | | | | |
| 2nd Chasseurs d'Afrique | | | | | 3 | | 3 | | | |
| 11th Dragoon Regiment: | | | | | | | | | | |
| No 5 Battery 19th Horse Artillery Regiment | | 2 | 2 | 4 | 7 | 1 | 12 | 15 | 2 | 1,023 |
| No 6 Battery 19th Field Artillery Regiment | | | | | 1 | | 1 | 8 | | 875 |
| **Total** | | **6** | **6** | **7** | **31** | **9** | **47** | **23** | **2** | **1,898** |
| **Services Adminstratifs** | | | | | | 18 | 18 | | | |
| **Total 6 Corps** | **53** | **142** | **195** | **202** | **1,308** | **3,106** | **4,616** | **82** | **19** | **9,312** |
| **Imperial Guard** | | | | | | | | | | |
| Staff | | 1 | 1 | | | | | | | |
| **1st Division** | | | | | | | | | | |
| **1st Brigade:** | | | | | | | | | | |
| 1st Guard Voltigeur Regiment: | | | | | 11 | | 11 | | | |
| 2nd Guard Voltigeur Regiment: | | 1 | 1 | 2 | 34 | 1 | 37 | | | |
| 2nd Brigade: | | | | | | | | | | |
| 3rd Guard Voltigeur Regiment: | | | | | 3 | | 3 | | | |
| **Total** | | **1** | **1** | **2** | **48** | **1** | **51** | | | |
| **2nd Division** | | | | | | | | | | |
| 1st Brigade: | | | | | | | | | | |

| | | | | | | | | | | |
|---|---|---|---|---|---|---|---|---|---|---|
| Guard Zouave Regiment: | | 1 | 1 | | 4 | | 4 | | | |
| 1st Guard Grenadier Regiment: | | | | | 5 | 1 | 6 | | | |
| Artillery | | | | | | | | | | |
| 3rd Guard Field artllery regiment | | | | 1 | 5 | | 6 | 4 | 7 | 182 |
| 4th Guard Field artillery regiment | | | | | 2 | | 2 | | 2 | 182 |
| **Total** | | 1 | 1 | 1 | 16 | 1 | 18 | 4 | 9 | 364 |
| Reserve artillery | | | | | | | | | | |
| No 3 Battery Horse Artillery of the Guard | | | | | | | | | | } |
| No 4 Battery Horse Artillery of the Guard | | | | | | | | | | } 633 |
| **Total** | | | | | | | | | | 633 |
| **Total Guard Corps** | | 3 | 3 | 3 | 64 | 2 | 69 | 4 | 9 | 997 |
| **Cavalry Reserve** | | | | | | | | | | |
| **3rd Division** | | | | | | | | | | |
| 2nd Brigade: | | | | | | | | | | |
| 7th Cuirassier Regiment: | | | | | 2 | | 2 | | | |
| **Total Reserve Cavalry** | | | | | 2 | | 2 | | | |
| **Artillery Reserve** | | | | | | | | | | |
| **13th Artillery Regiment** | | | | | | | | | | |
| No 5 Battery | | | | | | | | | | } |
| No 6 Battery | | | | 2 | 3 | | 5 | 4 | | } 816 |
| No 7 Battery | | | | | 9 | | 9 | 13 | | } |
| No 8 Battery | | | | | | | | | | } |
| **Total Reserve Artillery** | | | | 2 | 12 | | 14 | 17 | | 816 |
| **Summary** | | | | | | | | | | |
| Total 2 Corps | 9 | 24 | 33 | 52 | 368 | 132 | 552 | 52 | 23 | 3,488 |
| Total 3 Corps | 30 | 83 | 113 | 218 | 1,393 | 415 | 2,026 | 110 | 53 | 8,349 |
| Total 4 Corps | 93 | 182 | 275 | 481 | 3,607 | 1,232 | 5,320 | 140 | 108 | 12,497 |
| Total 6 Corps | 53 | 142 | 195 | 202 | 1,308 | 3,106 | 4,616 | 82 | 19 | 9,312 |
| Total Guard Corps | | 3 | 3 | 3 | 64 | 2 | 69 | 4 | 9 | 997 |
| Total Reserve Cavalry | | | | | 2 | | 2 | | | |
| **Total Reserve Artillery** | | | | 2 | 12 | | 14 | 17 | | 816 |
| **Summary Total** | 185 | 434 | 619 | 958 | 6,754 | 4,887 | 12,599 | 405 | 212 | 35,459 |

Total losses as reported for the 18th amounted to 619 officers, 12,599 men and 617 horses, killed, wounded or missing. The artillery fired a total of 35, 459 shells. It should be noted that in the days following the battle a number of men listed as missing returned to the ranks.

# Bibliography

Anon, *Affaire de la Capitulation de Metz, Procés Bazaine* (Paris: Libraire du Moniteur Universal, 1873)

Anon, *The War Correspondence of the Daily News 1870*, (London: Macmillan And Co, 1871)

Allanson Winn, C. *What I saw of the War at the battles of Speichem Gorze & Gravelotte* (Edinburgh: William Blackwood, 1870)

Aronson, Theo, *The Fall of the Third Napoleon* (London: History Book Club,1970)

Ascoli, David, *A Day of Battle, Mars la Tour 16 August 1870* (London: Harrap Ltd 1987)

Bazaine, F. A. Marshal, *l'Armée du Rhin* (Paris: Henri Plon, 1872)

Bazaine, F. A. Marshal, *Épisodes de la Guerre de 1870 et le Blocus De Metz* (Madrid: Gaspar, Éditeurs, 1833)

Bell, Harry, *Saint Privat, German Sources*, (Kansas: Staff College Press, Fort Leavenworth, 1914)

Bonie, T. General, *La Cavalerie Française* (Paris: Amyot,1871)

Bonnal, H. General, *L'Espirit de la Guerre Moderne, La Manoeuvre de Saint Privat I* (Paris: Libraire Militaire R Chapelot et Cie. 1904)

Bonnal, H. General, *L'Espirit de la Guerre Moderne, La Manoeuvre de Saint Privat II* (Paris: Libraire Militaire R Chapelot et Cie. 1906)

Bonnal, H. General, *L'Espirit de la Guerre Moderne, La Manoeuvre de Saint Privat III* (Paris: Libraire Militaire R Chapelot et Cie. 1912)

Boyland, George Halstead, *Six Months Under the Red Cross with the French Army* (Cincinnati: Robert Clarke & Co. 1873)

Brockett, L. P., *The Year of Battles or the Franco German War of 1870–71* (New York, J. W. Goodspeed & Co, 1871)

Brocket, L. P., *The Great War of 1870 between France and Germany* (New York: Gaylord Watson, 1871)

Clarke, F. C. H. , *The Franco German War 1870–71 Vol. I* (London: Topographical and Statistical Department of the War Office,1874)

Clarke, F. C. H. , *The Franco German War 1870–71 Vol. II* (London: Topographical and Statistical Department of the War Office,1876)

d'Andlau, Baron, Metz: *Campagne et Négotiations par un Officier Supérieur de l'Armée du Rhin* (Paris: Libraire Militaire de J. Dumaine, 1871)

de Baillehache, Marcel, *Souvenirs Intimes d'un Lancier de la Garde Impériale* (Paris: 1894)

de la Chapelle, Count Alfred, *The War of 1870. Events and Incidents of the Battlefields* (London: Chapman & Hall 1870)

de Lancey Landon, Melville, *The Franco Prussian war in a nutshell* (New York: G W Carleton & Co. 1871) de Lonlay, Dick, *Francais & Allemandes Histoire Anecdotique de la Geurre de 1870–1871 Tome II*, (Paris: Garnier Frères, 1888)

de Montluisant, Lieutenant Colonel, *Armée du Rhin ses épreuves la chute de Metz* (Montélimar: Imprimerie et Lithographie Bourron,1871)

Fay, Charles, *Journal d'un Officier de l'Armée du Rhin* (Paris: J Dumaine, 1871)

Forbes, Archibald, *My Experiences of the War between France and Germany Vol. I*, (London: Hurst and Blackett, 1871)

Großen Generalstabe, *Kriegsgeschlichtliche Einzelschriften heft 11–14*, (Berlin: Ernst Siegfried Mittler und Sohn, 1889)

Großen Generalstabe, *Kriegsgeschichtliche Einzelschriften heft 25* (Berlin: Ernst Siegfried Mittler und Sohn, 1898)

Guedalla, Philip, *The Two Marshals, Bazaine Pétain* (London: Hodder and Stoughton, 1943)

Hale, Major Lonsdale A., *Tactical Studies of the Battles of Columbey–Nouilly and Vionville* (London: W. Clowes & Sons, 1877)

Hildyard A. A. G, Colonel H. T., 'Précis of the Regimental History of the 3rd Brandenburg Infantry Regiment (No 20) During the Campaign of 1870–71', *Royal United Services Institution. Journal.* 35:163, 972–1027, DOI: 10.1080/ 03071849109416687

Hoenig, Fritz, *Inquiries Concerning Tactics of the Future* (London: Longmans, Green and Co. 1899)

Hoenig, Fritz, *Twenty-Four Hours of Moltke's Strategy* (Woolwich: Royal Artillery Institution, 1895)

Hoffbauer, E., *The German Artillery in the battles Near Metz* (London: Henry S. King & Co, 1874)

Howard, Michael, *The Franco Prussian War* (London: Rupert Hart Davis 1962)

Kraft zu Hohenlohe Ingelfingen, Prince Karl August Eduard Friedrich, *Letters on Artillery* (London: Edward Stanford, 1890)

Kraft zu Hohenlohe Ingelfingen, Prince Karl August Eduard Friedrich, *Letters on Infantry*, (London: Edward Stanford, 1892)

Jarras, General, *Souvenirs du Général Jarras*, (Paris: Libraire Plon, 1892)

Lanza, Conrad H., *Franco German War of 1870 Source Book* (Fort Leavenworth: General Service Schools Press 1922)

Lecaillon, Jean-Francois, *Été 1870 La guerre racontéé par les soldats*, (Paris: Bernard Giovanangeli, 2020)

Lehautcourt, Pierre, *Histoire de la Guerre 1870–71 Tome IV La Retraite sur la Moselle. Borny* (Paris: Berger-Leverault & Cie. 1904)

Lehautcourt, Pierre *Histoire de la Guerre de 1870–1871 Tome Von Rezonville et Saint Privat* (Paris: Berger-Leverault et Cie, 1905)

Kelly, Alfred, *Carl Rückert's Memoirs of the Franco-Prussian War*, (Cham: Palgrave Macmillan, 2019)

Kirchof, George Heinrich, *Das 3 Brandenburgische Infanterie Regiment Nr 20 in den Feldzug 1866 und 1870–71* (Berlin: Mittler und Sohn, 1881)

M. A. *The War of 1870–71* (London: Edward Bumpus, 1873)

Martinien, A., *État Nominatiff par affaires et par corps des officiers tués ou blesses*, (Paris: Libraire Militaire R Chapelot et Cie, 1902)

Maude, Captain F. N., *Military Letters and Essays*, (Kansas City: Hudson Kimberly Publishing Co. 1895)

Maurice, Major General J. F. (trans), *The Franco-German War 1870–71 by Generals and Other Officers who took part in the campaign* (London: Swan Sonnenschein and Co Ltd, 1900)

Moltke, Count Helmuth von, *The Franco German War of 1870–71* (London: Harper Brothers, 1907)

Patry, Léonce, *La Guerre telle qu'elle est (Campagne de 1870–71)* (Paris: Montgredien et Cie, 1897.)

Rich, Elihu, *Germany and France a popular history of the Franco German War Vol. I* (London: James Hagger, 1884)

Roberts, Randal H., *Modern War, or The Campaigns of the First Prussian Army, 1870–71* (London: Chapman and Hall, 1871)

Robinson, G. T., *The Fall of Metz*, (London: Bradbury, Evans & Co. 1871)

Rouquerol, Gabriel, *L'Artillerie dans la Bataille du 18 Août* (Paris: Berger-Levrault et Cie, 1906)

Rousset, Lieutenant Colonel, *Le 4 Corps de L'Armée de Metz* (Paris: Henri Charles-Lavauzelle. 1900)

Seton, J. L., *Notes on the Operations of the North German Troops in Lorraine and Picardy, etc.* (London: W Mitchell and Co, 1872)

Section Historique de l'État-Major de l'Armée, *La Guerre de 1870–71 Les Opérations Autour De Metz Du 13 au 18 Août I Journées des 13 et 14 Août Bataille de Borny* (Paris: Librairie Militaire, R. Chapelot et Cie, 1903)

Section Historique de l'État-Major de l'Armée, *La Guerre de 1870–71 Les Opérations Autour De Metz Du 13 au 18 Août I Journées des 13 et 14 Août Bataille de Borny Documents Annexes* (Paris: Librairie Militaire, R. Chapelot et Cie, 1903)

Section Historique de l'État-Major de l'Armée, *La Guerre de 1870–71 Les Opérations Autour De Metz Du 13 au 18 Août II Journées des 15 et 16 Août Bataille de Rezonville* (Paris: Librairie Militaire, R. Chapelot et Cie, 1904)

Section Historique de l'État-Major de l'Armée, *La Guerre de 1870–71 Les Opérations Autour De Metz Du 13 au 18 Août II Journées des 15 et 16 Août Documents Annexes* (Paris: Librairie Militaire, R. Chapelot et Cie, 1905)

Section Historique de l'État-Major de l'Armée, *La Guerre de 1870–71 Les Opérations Autour De Metz Du 13 au 18 Août III Journées des 17 et 18 Août, Bataille de Saint Privat* (Paris: Librairie Militaire, R. Chapelot et Cie, 1905)

Section Historique de l'État-Major de l'Armée, *La Guerre de 1870–71 Les Opérations Autour De Metz Du 13 au 18 Août III Journées des 17 et 18 Août, Documents Annexes* (Paris: Librairie Militaire, R. Chapelot et Cie, 1905)

Sheridan, General P. H., *Personal Memoirs Volume II* (New York, Charles L. Webster & Co. 1888)

von Blumenthal, Albrecht, *Journals of Field Marshal Count von Blumenthal for 1866 and 1870–71*, (London: Edward Arnold, 1903)

von Moltke, Helmuth, *The Franco-German War of 1870–71*, (London: Harper and Brothers, 1907)

von Pelet-Narbonne, General, *Cavalry on Service* (London: Hugh Rees, Ltd, 1906)

von Schell, A., *The Operations of the First Army under General Steinmetz to the capitulation of Metz*, (London: Henry S. King & Co. 1873) von Verdy du Vernois, General Julius, *With The Royal Headquarters In 1870–71* (London: Kegan Paul, Trench, Trûbner & Co, 1897)

von Waldersee, Alfred, Count, *A Field Marshal's Memoir,* (London: Hutchinson & Co. 1924)

Wagner, Arthur L., *Cavalry Studies from Two Great Wars* (Kansas City: Hudson Kimberly Publishing Company, 1896)

Wawro, Geoffrey, *The Franco-Prussian War, The German Conquest of France in 1870–71,* (Cambridge: New York: Cambridge University Press)